D1832770

ENCYCLOPAEDIA OF BACKWARD CASTES: RESERVATION

ENCYCLOPAEDIA OF BACKWARD CASTES
(In 4 Volumes)

1. RESERVATION
2. COMMISSIONS
3. MANDAL, MEDIA AND AFTERMATH
4. JUDGEMENTS: BEFORE AND AFTER MANDAL JUDGEMENT

ENCYCLOPAEDIA
OF
BACKWARD CASTES
(In 4 Volumes)

RESERVATION
(Volume 1)

M.L. Mathur
Senior Research Officer
Ministry of Social Justice and Empowerment
Government of India, New Delhi.

PUBLICATIONS

KALPAZ PUBLICATIONS
DELHI - 110052

ENCYCLOPAEDIA OF BACKWARD CASTES: RESERVATION
[Scheduled Castes and OBCs]

Rs. 3600/- (Set)

ISBN: 81-7835-069-6 (Set)
ISBN: 81-7835-268-0 (Vol. 1)

©M.L. Mathur

This book may not be reproduced in any manner without written permission of the author and the publisher.

Published in 2004 in India by
Kalpaz Publications
C-30, Satyawati Nagar,
Delhi-110052
e-mail: kalpaz@hotmail.com

Laser Typeset at: Alphabet, Delhi
Printed at: Mehra Offset Press, Delhi

Contents

PREFACE

Hierarchy of castes into Brahmins, Kshatriyas, Vaishyas and Shudras exists in the Indian society. The first three castes are termed dwija castes and are forward castes as they are regarded as socially and educationally advanced by virtue of their origin and traditional occupation. The last category of castes is ranked low by virtue of their origin from feet and low status traditional occupation and they are regarded as backward. The category of backward broadly constitute Scheduled Castes, Scheduled Tribes and Other Backward Classes. Persons belonging to this category are generally engaged in occupation of 'service' as labour, involving physical work, etc. For example, Kumhars (potter), Lohars or Luhars (Blacksmith), and Nai or Hajjam (barber) are engaged in their traditional occupation of making earthen pitchers, casting iron utensils and cutting hairs, respectively. They are regarded as socially backward. The term 'Backward Class' is not found in the Constitution of India and is used to identify Scheduled Castes, Scheduled Tribes and Other backward Classes. Here I deliberately chose the term 'backward caste' in place of commonly use 'Other Backward Classes' for sociological reasoning.

Encyclopaedia of Backward Castes is a first systematic effort to critically analyse and present different issues in each volume. This is an attempt to present series of work under this title. To begin with, I chose the following four themes: Reservation (Volume 1), Commissions (Volume 2), Mandal, Media and Aftermath (Volume 3) and Judgements (Volume 4). On the issue of reservation some scholars have brought out their work more related to Scheduled Castes and Scheduled Tribes and less on Backward Castes as they got recognised only after the Supreme Court's judgement in a famous case *Indira Sawhney and Others* vs. *Union of India and Others*, on 16th November, 1992. The Volume 1 on Reservation focus on origin and rationale behind reservation, reservation policies for backward castes. History of reservation reveals that persons belonging to backward castes have been striving hard for over a century for getting the benefit of reservation in educational institutions and in employment in government service when their estimated population (based on Census of India 1931) is 52 per cent. They had their genuine and justified grudge as Scheduled Castes and Scheduled Tribes having only 16 per cent and 7.5 per cent population in 1991 are getting the benefit of reservation in educational institutions and employment. What were the reasons that they could not get the reservation benefit earlier? This work explored that leaders like B.R. Ambedkar and M.K. Gandhi took interest in welfare of Scheduled Castes as they were considered socially, educationally and economically backward as compared to backward castes. Among Scheduled Castes they were more concerned about 'Untouchables'. There were some leaders among backward castes such as Shri Naryan Guru Swamy and Shri Mahatma Jyotiba Phule who had their impact in limited geographical area of the country. Non-Brahmin movement was seen in Tamil Nadu and Madras Presidency was the first Presidencies in the Country, framed Grant-in-Aid Code in 1885 to regulate financial aid to educational institutions, providing special facilities for students of depressed classes. In 1927 the Presidency issued 'Communal Government Order' making reservation quota on caste basis.

Mysore State [a princely State] accepted the recommendations of first Backward Classes Commission headed by Sir L.C. Miller in 1918 extending special facilities to backward communities with regard to education and recruitment in state services. In 1928 Bombay Presidency appointed a committee under the chairmanship of Mr. O.H.B. Satre. The Committee gave its report in 1930 and identified backward classes and classified them into 'depressed classes', 'aboriginal and hill tribes' and 'other backward classes' and recommended for special facilities regarding reservation policy for backward castes in education and recruitment in government service to them. Pre-independence history shows only three states were concerned for welfare of backward castes. One of the reasons for this kind of development was higher literacy rate among backward castes in these Presidencies and a State as compared to other areas. At all India level first systematic attempt for the welfare of 'depressed classes' was made with the introduction of Montugue-Chelmsford's reform policy in 1919 for giving separate reservation to depressed classes on number of public bodies. In official parlance the omnibus term 'depressed classes' at that time included Scheduled Castes, Scheduled Tribes, and Other Backward Classes. To encourage them for pursuing education an order was issued in 1949 for granting scholarship to students belonging to Scheduled Castes, Scheduled Tribes and Other Backward Classes.

The Volume II examines recommendations of various Committees and Commissions in different States. After Independence of the Country Government of India appointed two national level Commissions to identify backward castes, study their conditions and recommend quantum of reservation for them in government service. Kaka Kalelkar was the Chairman of the first Commission on Backward Classes. He was appointed by Government of India on 29th January 1953. He submitted the report on backward classes on March 30, 1955. The first Commission identified 2399 castes backward out of which 837 castes were found most backward. The Commission gave many recommendations. Some of the important recommendations were reservation of 70 per cent seats in all technical and professional institutions; treating all women as a class as 'backward', i.e., minimum reservation of vacancies in all government services and local bodies for OBCs on the following scale 25 per cent in class I, 33.33 per cent in Class II and 40 per cent in class III and IV.

The report of the Commission was not unanimous. The Government of India laid a copy of the report of the Commission along with a Memorandum of action taken before each House of Parliament on September 3rd, 1956 in compliance with Article 340 (3) of the Constitution of India. The report was not discussed in the Parliament. As the Castes were not identified on any scientific criteria and lack objectivity, the Government of India did not act upon the recommendations of Kaka Kalelkar Commission. However, Government of India left it open to all the States to draw their own lists of backward classes. 10 States drew the lists of backward classes on the basis of recommendations of Committees/Commissions appointed by them in different periods. These States were Andhra Pradesh, Bihar, Gujarat, Jammu and Kashmir, Karnataka, Kerala, Maharashtra, Punjab, Tamil Nadu and Uttar Pradesh. Further 8 States and Union Territories have notified lists of OBCs for the grant of educational employment and other benefits. These are Assam, Delhi, Haryana, Himachal Pradesh, Meghalaya, Orissa, Pondicherry and Rajasthan. These State Governments and Union Territories mostly relied on the lists of OBCs maintained by them for grant of Post-Matric Scholarships, etc. under the Education Ministry's Scheme formulated in 1944 and another list prepared by the Commissioner for Scheduled Castes and Scheduled Tribes at the time of drafting the First Five Year Plan. When the first non-Congress (I) government, i.e., Janta Party came to power, it fulfilled its one of the promises made in the election manifesto by appointing second Backward Classes Commission on 20th December, 1978 for welfare of backward classes. This Commission was headed by Shri Bindhyeshwari Prasad Mandal. He submitted his report on 31st December, 1980. The Second Backward Classes Commission identified 3743 castes as backward castes, recommended 27 per cent reservation for OBCs in government service as well as technical and professional institutions both in the Centre and the States (Chapter XIII p. 64). Janta Party government in power could not act upon the report and was out of power. When Congress (I) government returned to power it laid the report before each House of the Parliament once in 1982 and again in the year 1983. The government faced difficulties in arriving at unanimous decision about implementation of recommendations of backward classes in the Parliament. Finally the report gathered the dust. Thus persons belonging to backward castes again lost the regained hope.

National Front Government came to power in 1989. They also made promises in their election manifesto to implement recommendations of second Backward Classes Commission. Shri V.P. Singh was the Prime Minister of the Country and leader of the Front. He announced on 7th August, 1990 in the Lok Sabha to implement recommendations of second Backward Classes

Commission thus granting benefit of 27 per cent reservation in government service and fulfilled the promises made by his party in the election manifesto. The Volume III Mandal, Media and Aftermath explores in detail compulsions, which led V.P. Singh to implement recommendations of Mandal Report. What was his political expediency? This was his haste decision and his political calculation went wrong. There was strong opposition from Congress (I) and CPI (M) Members of Parliament in both House of the Parliament. Bhartiya Janta Party, a partner in the National Front Government was disinclined to support the government move. What were the political compulsions of V.P. Singh to implement Mandal Commission Report? This book explored that he wanted to counter the effect of Devi Lal's Kisan rally and L.K. Advani's rath yatra from Somnath to Ayodhya. Outside the Parliament there was agitation all over the country against the government's decision. Peaceful States like Orissa, Rajasthan, Haryana, Himachal Pardesh, Delhi reported cases of arson, self-immolation, etc. Media played its role in communicating facts to the people. This volume also presented views of Cross Sections of Society published in various leading newspapers. Former Secretary in the Mandal Commission, S.S. Gill expressed his experiences gained during his field visit that caste was a passport to social status. Former Cabinet Secretary, Dharam Vir was of the view that reservation would politicize the civil services and Govind Narain held the view that caste could not be a sole criteria for determining backwardness of the Caste. Veteran politician, Madhu Limaye expressed that reservation for backward castes would create a new social order. Among social scientist, B.K. Roy Burman, M.N. Srinivas, A.M. Shah, A.M. Khusro, C.P. Bhambri, D.L. Sheth, Dipankar Gupta and Ghanshyam Shah also gave their pros and cons of reservation policy announced by Government of India. Arun Shourie said that reservation would be anti-meritarian because it would mar chances of meritorious students belonging to forward castes. People from different walks of life expressed their views in print-media and electronic media. Even three experts B.K. Roy Burman, M.N. Srinivas and Yogender Singh associated with the Mandal Commission disowned the report on the ground that they were not consulted. The others expressed that caste can't be a sole criteria for determining backwardness but social, educational and economic determinanants should also be taken into determining a caste backward. FIICI and Trade Unions opposed quota system.

It was not the first time in the Indian history that reservation order had been challenged in different courts. Many writs were filed in different High Courts and a Writ was filed in the Supreme Court. Judgments (Volume IV) presents selected summary of 26 cases decided by different High Courts and Supreme Court under Article 15(4) and 27 cases under Article 16(4) of Constitution of India. The Supreme Court of India in *Indira Sawhney and others* verses *Union of India and others* case in 1992 upheld the Government of India order of 1990 for providing 27 per cent reservation to other backward classes in government service with slight modification to exclude those who are socially and economically advanced. In pursuance of the directions given by the Supreme Court the Government of India set up a permanent body National Commission for Backward Classes to examine request of any class of Individuals for inclusion in the Central list of Backward Classes. As an affirmative action towards educational and economical development of Other Backward Classes, Government of India introduced schemes of Pre-Matric Scholarships, Post-Matric Scholarships and construction of Hostels for Boys and Girls belonging to other backward classes in 1998. National Backward Classes Finance and Development Corporation was set up in 1992. The Finance Corporation provides loan facilities to persons belonging to other Backward Classes under Micro-Credit and Term loan facilities. This volume presents number of persons benefited in different periods under these schemes.

Acknowledgement: In completion of this work I received encouragement and support from different sources. I would like to thank Professor J.S. Gandhi Centre for Study of Social System, School of Social Sciences, Jawahar Lal Nehru University, New Delhi and Professor B.K. Nagla Department of Sociology, M.D. University Rohtak for continuously encouraging me to bring out this work on different themes in a series. I am thankful to my colleague Smt. Meena Sharma, Under Secretary in Backward Classes Division of Ministry of Social Justice and Empowerment for providing me notified copies of Central list of Backward Classes and Dr. Shish Ram Sharma Research Officer in National Commission for Backward Classes for providing me notified copies of State Lists of Backward Classes. Central Secretariat Library was the main source of consulting reference material available there. I wish to express my thanks to staff of the Library for arranging books and other relevant materials available there to me. This Encyclopaedia is out in the published form for which entire credit goes to the Kalpaz Publications for accepting the manuscript and agreeing to bring out the Encyclopaedia in continuous series on different themes. Lastly I would like to express my gratitude to my parents and thank to my wife Basu, daughter Mahima and son Ashish. All have been very inquisitive and curious to see this work in the published form.

Delhi **M.L. Mathur**

Introduction

The question of reservation for backward castes (Other Backward Classes) became prominent only after Independence at National Level by appointing Kaka Kalelkar Commission in 1953 and then B.P. Mandal Commission in 1978. Before Independence some states like Tamil Nadu (Madras), Karnataka (Mysore) and Maharashtra (Bombay) were pioneering states in considering right of backward castes for the purpose of reservation in government service. Of course, orders issued by these governments were struck down and these had to be modified from time to time. The other states did some initiatives in this direction but only after independence.

Backward castes, though, numerically preponderant did not get their long cherished demand of reservation while sections of people under the category of 'depressed classes', 'scheduled castes' and 'scheduled tribes' got this sort of benefit quite early. Social distance between forward castes and backward castes (class) and among backward classes exist in Indian society in the form of social inequality.

Chapter 1 'The Origin and Rational Behind Reservations' focus on some of these very pertinent issues in context of historical social reality. There had been many anti-caste movements in India. Buddhism and Jainism were expressions of a rational and humanitarian social vision. During the British rule all the socio-religious reform movements like Brahmo Samaj, Satya Shodhak Samaj, Arya Samaj, the Rama Krishna Mission and the Prathna Samaj were all directed towards bringing social equality in the society. Gopal Krishna Gokhale and Justice Ranade were pioneering leaders during those days who championed for cause of downtrodden and untouchables. The origin of special representation to SCs can be traced back as early as decades of the

20th Century when British education and administration led to an introspection among many forward thinking individuals in the country.

During national movement it was Gandhi who took a lead and included depressed classes and Muslims into their fold alongwith others. He did so having suffered from indignities of apartheid in South Africa. He realised that depressed classes should not suffer from cruelty of upper castes. He also knew that there was no leader among depressed classes the fight for their cause. The emergence of such trend awakened British rulers during those days. Britishers realised that when Hindus and Muslims could unite together then forward and backward castes could also come together. This hidden psychology worked and depressed classes got their representatives in the Provincial Councils. It was in 1929 there was demand for reservation. Three years later 'The Poona Pact' came into being as a fallout of the report of the Franchise Committee which was set up to decide the means of enfranchising the Depressed Classes. McDonald's Communal Award of 1932 was intended to give separate electorates to the Muslims, Sikhs, Europeans and Christians and sought to strike an ideal balance for depressed class identity in the Hindu Community. Both Raja and Ambedkar had to overcome their mutual antipathy and criticized the communal award as they felt that the seats alloted to them in special constituencies was very less as compared to other communities and that the representation to depressed classes had been ruthlessly scaled down. Gandhiji fully supported their grievances and even he threatened a "Fast unto death" against the communal award. The award was altered to save his life. Ambedkar again reposed his faith in Gandhiji's movement and realization of sufferings of depressed classes. This chapter covered the issues related to depressed classes.

The history of reservation for backward classes can be traced back from 1856. It was in June 1856 that a Scheduled Caste boy applied for admission into a government school in Dhariwal, Bombay Presidency. This incident draw attention of the rulers and a education policy was framed. Chapter Two critically analyses and examines historical reality of reservation policies and programmes for backward classes. Madras Govt. introduced Grant-in-Aid Code in 1885 and Mysore Government issued circular for making provision of reservation of certain posts in favour of backward castes in 1895. The Government of India Act, 1919, for the first time in the Indian history gave recognition to the existence of depressed classes and recognized their claim for political representation. B.R. Ambedkar submitted a memorandum to Simon Commission for the safeguards and protection of the depressed classes. The Simon Commission did recognize the facts. In course of development controversy crept in between Ambedkar and Gandhi. Gandhi went on fast unto death against the McDonald Communal award. The Govt. of India Act, 1935 took care of the development arising from Round Table Conference as well as Poona Pact. In 1942, the Government of India first time decided to fix a certain percentage of jobs for the depressed classes in order to give them necessary stimulus to equip themselves with better qualification in order to become eligible for posts and services. The history of reservation clearly suggest that depressed classes were always under consideration and backward castes (OBCs) never came to the mind of the ruler.

Chapter 3 deals with legal position of caste in particular of backward castes. It has always been debated whether a caste should be a sole criteria for determining caste's status? The question is whether a caste is a socially and educationally backward class? In many cases it was decided that a caste can not be sole or dominant criteria for determining caste's status. The most famous case is *Balaji* vs *State of Mysore*. In this case it was decided that "though castes in relation to Hindus may be a relevant factor to consider in determining the social backwardness of groups or class of citizens it cannot be made the sole or the dominant test in that behalf". In other cases it was decided that caste cannot be ignored altogether in determining the caste's status. A comparative analysis was made on the level of backwardness between backward castes and SCs & STs. Backwardness of any caste depend upon social backwardness and educational backwardness. Article 16(4) of the Constitution of India speaks for social and educational backwardness of any backward class. *Janaki Prasad Parimoo* vs *State of J&K, K.C. Vasanth Kumar* vs *State of Karnataka* are few important court decisions related to this issue. The Mandal Judgement (1992) also examined the same issue.

Revolving round the issue of social and educational backwardness of any class is one point for discussion. How do we identify a caste backward? When the Drafting Committee was preparing draft of the Constitution the Committee confronted with the term "backward" to be included under Article 10(3) or now Article 16(4).

The Supreme Court in its Mandal judgement (1992) examined the issue of reservation of OBCs in Government service under Article 16(4). The Court recommended for a setting up of a permanent body to examine requests of any individual class for inclusion in the Central list of Backward Classes. This majority judgement also gave directions for categorization of backward classes into most backward and more backward. Some of the States like Karnataka, Tamil Nadu, A.P. and Bihar have already classified their state lists into various groups.

Prior to the Mandal judgement for reservation of OBCs (1992) backward castes strived hard to get this benefit parallel to Scheduled Castes and Scheduled Tribes. They did not get it for a long time even after Independence. This is well evidenced by the fact that Government of India did not accept the recommendations of two national level Commissions Kaka Kalelkar (1958) and B.P. Mandal (1980) for lack of objectivity and political will. When Government of India did not act upon the recommendations of the first commission on backward classes it decided to leave the matter to all states of preparing their own list of backward classes. This shows there was no line of conformity between Government of India and States on the issue of identification of castes in the list of backward castes as in case of Sscheduled Castes and Scheduled Tribes. Government of India notifies a list for all States. Then many States drew their own lists before the Second Backward Classes Commission was setup by Government of India in 1978. It is important to note that States particularly Southern states Tamil Nadu, Karnataka were leading states in recognizing rights of backward classes. Non-Brahmin movement was the leading socio-political force behind their goal.

What was the reason for non-implementation of recommendations of two backward classes? As stated in the preceding paragraph that political will was one of the attributing factor. If we look at the composition of Government at that time we find that representation of backward classes was almost none. That means there was absence of political force to further their cause. This was the situation in one of the biggest states of India Uttar Pradesh.

In the last chapter the reservation issue was examined in context of some of important court's decisions. The expression backward classes has not been defined anywhere in the Constitution. Backward classes includes SC, ST and OBCs. Article 15(4) use the words "Socially and educationally backward classes" and Article 16(4) uses "any backward class citizen". There was a good debate over this issue. The Constitution of India under various Articles and Directive Principles emphasise need for protection and welfare of people in general and weaker sections in particular. They have got right to secure social justice.

B.P. Mandal (1980, p. 21, Vol. 1) quotes Justice K. Subba Rao's views from his book on *Social Justice and Law* as follows:—

"In a limited sense, the right to social justice may be defined as the right of the weak, aged, destitute, poor, women, children and other underprivileged persons to the protection of the state against the ruthless competition of life. It seeks to give the necessary adventitious aids to the underprivileged so that they may have the equal opportunity with the more advanced in the race of life. It is a bundle of rights; in one sense it is carved of other rights; in another sense it is a preserver of other rights. It is the balancing wheel between haves and have-nots.

Justice Rao's view is very much relevant. How many persons belonging to backward castes (OBCs) got employment in Government service at different levels? This is an indicator their educational backwardness because of which they cannot get entry into government service. Social backwardness is inherent with their caste's traditional occupation.

This volume is presented into the following chapters:—

Chapter One The Origin and Rationale Behind Reservation.

Chapter Two	Reservation: Historical Backward.
Chapter Three	Reservational Justice to Backward Castes: Some Issues.
Chapter Four	Reservation Policy for Backward Castes: Problems.
Chapter Five	Reservational Justice: Problems and Solutions.
Chapter Six	Social Justice, Constitution and Law.

One

The Origin and Rationale Behind Reservation

Before Independence there was no policy of reservation for OBCs. Even after fifty years of Independence backward castes remained deprived for so long while Scheduled Castes and Scheduled Tribes got the benefit of reservation. When National Front government was in power it decided to implement one of its promises made in the election manifesto, that was implementation of recommendations given in the Mandal report giving benefit of reservation to OBCs in government services and other sectors. It was in late 1990. This decision of the National Front Government led wide spread agitation, especially in Bihar and UP, and to severe condemnation in most of the English Language press. During that time attention of all sections of society was drawn to debate over.

The policy of reservation is not only implemented in India but also in other countries (often known by other names, such as reverse discrimination or affirmative action), but in at least some of them the issues are openly and extensively discussed in striking contrast to India. Moreover, policy of reservation is instituted, it is practically impossible to reverse it. Then the question arises what would be the basis or criteria of reservation—caste based or class based? Dharam Kumar (1990)[1] outlined the problem in a special issue of seminar (1990, 375) on reservation.

In India, it is more relevant to talk of 'caste' than just class, as caste is intrinsically mixed up with class. Inspite of modern development the social disparities and disadvantages of castes and sub-castes have not disappeared. They have still to be contended with as facts of life though Jawahar Lal Nehru once said that caste and socialism cannot coexist. Social justice cannot close its eyes to the ugly reality of caste but has to cope with it by a wide spectrum of measures, including the expedient of reservations as long as they are necessary (Ghorpade 1990).[2]

Andre Beteille (1990)[3] raised a very pertinent question is job reservation a good policy? He raised this issue while emphasising need to distinctly make clear between matters of right and matters of policy. Caste quotas in public institutions are a matter of policy and not of right. He also put forth two important questions which have direct implications on reservation issue. Firstly, such a policy has to make some assessment of the burden of disability and disadvantage that it seeks to redress. Secondly, it has to make some assessment of the costs to institutions of different kinds that have to bear the burden of reservations.

The question then arises how long those social groups would continue to suffer from social inequality, educational inequality when they could not be brought at par with general population or say those who have advanced themselves, Reservation is, therefore one way to make benefits available to deprived sections of society so that their coming generation can cope up with such social disabilities. Let us go into historical background of root causes of the problem.

Steeped in an ancient culture dating back to thousands of years, frequently invaded by men of different races and religions, India and Indians presented a unique example of a multi-racial, multi-lingual and multi-religious society. In an effort to protect itself from frequent onslaughts on its culture and religion, Hinduism hardened into a rigid code of rites and rituals, purity and pollution and the division of itself into castes and sub-castes. Much ground had been traversed between the Aryan Varna and the mid-nineteenth century division of society into higher and lower castes, the low position of untouchables and the untenable status of women. Mahatma Gandhi faced the ugliness of apartheid in South Africa but what he experienced in his own country defied description. The hardening of the caste structure of Hindu society brought in its wake the outrage of untouchability.

For close to two thousand years, the practice of untouchability became an established norm of the socio-religious life of the country. From time to time, religious reformers strove to reform Hindu society but their impact was not significant enough to have any impact on the lives of the victims of the rigid codes of Hinduism—the untouchables, or the lowest of the low, the fifth order or Pancham, who were beyond the five orders of the Hindu social system. Social inequality is perhaps a universal feature of all societies. As P.A. Sorokin points out, there has not been and does not exist, any permanent social group which is flat and in which all members are equal. The traditional Hindu caste system which puts Brahmins at the top and untouchables at the bottom of the caste pyramid is one of the most obvious examples of inequality." Some have termed it a system of legalised inequality, a system in which one's role and status in society are determined by non-rational principles. Everything was determined based on birth and by heredity one's position in society, one's profession, norms of behaviour, rights and duties. Sachchidananda[4] points out that while it may have offered stability and continuity to a closed and organic social system, it also created the worst kind of inequality, negating the most cherished ideals of Hinduism world egalitarianism and brotherliness propounded by the classical Hindu scriptures. Westerners, apologetic under the attacks of materialism, so often directed at their style of life, were often puzzled at the apparent discrepancy between a society which extolled the dignity of man, but which also degraded one of every three of its people.

For more than three millennia a system of social inequality and social stratification was foisted on a large segment of the hapless population. Within the folds of Hinduism there existed an ever increasing fragmentation of higher or lower castes and even within the lower castes, a never-ending chain of castes and sub-castes, each with their own rites and rituals. The repeated onslaught of foreign invasions and foreign domination was faced by a hardening of the hierarchical and ritualistic caste formations. J.H. Hutton (1951)[5] in his book *Caste in India* states that the "Subcontinent of India has been likened to a deep net into which various races and peoples of Asia have drifted and been caught." Composed of many diverse races, with varying customs, languages and religions, Hutton believes that people were able to live together with a degree of stability in a multiple society because of the caste system which he says, "has proved capable of absorbing any intrusions on society, and no intruders have yet succeeded in revolutionising it, though it is not so rigid that a caste cannot rise in social scale."

Each caste became an individual social unit. Each caste started following its own rituals of eating, drinking, intermarrying etc. Of the approximate three thousand castes in India some are derived from tribal or racial elements, others were members of common guilds or crafts, while some were religious in origin. Such was the strongleho1d of the caste system in Indian society that even a change of religion did not mean total break from the system. Muslims, Jews and later Christians and Sikhs often formed castes or sects analogous to castes. In Goa, for example, Saraswat [Brahmin] Christians do not intermarry with other Christians and within the Sikh fold also there is a division between Sikhs and Mehzabi Sikhs who were converts from so called lower castes.

Caste System and its Origin

There are number of theories available about origin of caste system in India. Many scholars have given their view points ranging from functional aspect, occupational, varnacular, etc. The origins and reasons for the caste system have been written about and dealt with by eminent scholars from both India and abroad. However, one could briefly recall that the main features of caste were to be found in the Rig Veda, the earliest written Sanskrit document available. The division of society under the Rig Vedic people was mainly based on occupation with the emergence of four *varnas,* each with a specific task allotted to them. The terms Brahma, Rajanyha [Kshatriya], Vaisya and Sudra first appeared in the later part of the Rig veda [RV X 90.12). Being hierarchically structured, the Aryans placed themselves in the first three *varnas* and the occupational groups under Vaisyas and the non-wealthy, the conquered and hostile groups under the Sudras.

The Varna system had within its fold priests, kings and warriors, traders and merchants, peasants and servants or Brahmins, Kshatriyas, Vaisyas and Sudras. The Antyajas Avarnas were those who did not find place to any fold. The varna system served as a built-in caste multiplier as a result of which even today, each linguistic region has 2000-3000 castes and sub-castes which are not similar to the linguistic divisions of the country.

Whereas Brahmanical values were rationalised with appropriate myths, professions such as scavenging, leather workers, removing of dead bodies and those who were butchers or dealt with intoxicants and toddy were considered defiling. Blood sacrifice was made an integral part of the religion of lower castes, perhaps with the intention of hindering their upward social mobility. Religious awekening and impact of western education on society as a whole generated some kind of enthusiasm towards moving upward but at slow pace. Despite, sanskritisation it was difficult to overcome the barrier of untouchability which led them to embrace other faiths such as Islam, Christianity, Sikhism and Buddhism. These factors caused deep anguish among down trodden to accept other religions which gace them proper place.

Reform Movements

There had been many anti-caste movements in India. Buddhism and Jainism were expressions of a rational and humanitarian social vision. The Bhakti movement of the medieval period sought to create a world where all devotees were spiritually equals regardless of their caste affiliations. However, such movements were unable to change the existing economic system and hence could not ameliorate the condition of the downtrodden classes. During the British rule all the socio-religious reform movements made the removal of untouchability an integral part of their programme. The Brahmo Samaj, the Satya Shodhak Samaj, the Arya Samaj, the Ramakrishna Mission and the Prarthna Samaj were all moved by the spirit of social equality. At the turn of the last decade of the nineteenth century the freedom struggle united the largely middle class caste Hindus and imbued them with a new sense of national unity and racial pride. The Indian National Congress was formed in 1885 and the Indian Council Act of 1892 increased the representation of Indians on the Central and Provincial Legislative Councils and granted them permission to discuss the budget and ask questions.

This Act was important for two reasons. Firstly, it established that the British Government gave recognition to the principle of popular representation as the basis for the constitution of legislatures in India. Whereas the Act did not provide for the election of representatives to the legislatures, it permitted local bodies and other limited electorates to nominate persons to those bodies. The Government held the power to decide whether these persons were acceptable or not but their nominations were generally accepted. Secondly, the necessity of separate representation for Muslims was conceded in principle. Although the Depressed Classes were not directly affected, it nevertheless brought together active members of the lower castes who could combine for constitutional reform. It was this Act which showed the possibility of the formation of popular bodies on a communal basis.

With the publication of the *Census of India* in 1872,[6] a whole lot of information came to the fore. Sir Herbert Risley, the Census Commissioner became determined to obtain the exact rank of every caste but the institution of "caste precedence committees" aroused resentment as it was taken to be an instrument of creating caste distinction within the country.

News of the ill-treatment meted out to Indians in South Africa, along with granting of the concession of separate representation to Muslims, brought about some soul searching in the minds of progressive Indians over the treatment meted out to the lower castes within the country. Justice Ranade utilised the opportunities on which Gandhi narrated the tales of oppression towards Indians in South Africa to direct the national consciousness and turn the searchlight inwards. While it was significant to denounce foreigners and cry hoarse about the injustices in Natal Colony, what about the oppression, repression and degradation meted out to a huge segment of one's own countrymen? The Indian Social Conference, a sister organisation of the Indian National Congress which had held its first session in 1887, passed resolutions by 1895 for the amelioration of the Depressed Classes because of the chastisement of Justice Ranade. There was a rising consciousness of the numerical strength of the downtrodden and the need for political and social advancement which could never be made unless these glaring inequalities were removed from society.

Gopal Krishna Gokhale came forward with his anti-touchability campaign and carried the arguments of Justice Ranade further. He asked how Hindus could perpetrate arbitrary allocation of vocations on a huge segment of its people while professing indignation at the compulsory allotment of locations to certain classes in South Africa. With consciences being pricked all around, a determined effort was made to enlighten and educate the lower classes. The Maharashtra Village Education Society, the Mangalore Social Reform Association and the Depressed Classes Mission Society of India founded in 1906 by V.R. Shinde were pioneers in this effort.

With these environmental and attitudinal changes came a new awakening in the Depressed Classes and a desire to waken themselves from the stupor, bondage and inferiority of centuries. The Depressed Classes led by the Mahars of Western India set out on a mission of self-help towards improving their social and economic status. The Shanais of Madras sought to worship in temples and when they were prevented from doing so, riots and violence took place. The Thiyas of Malabar and the Vokkaligas of Mysore met at their own conference in an effort to improve their conditions.

Origin of Separate Representation

The genesis of the special status accorded to the Scheduled Castes under the Constitution of India in 1950, can be traced as far back as the early decades of the 20th century when British education and administration led to an introspection amongst many forward thinking individuals in the country. With the nomination of members of the Depressed Classes to Provincial Legislative Councils, educated members felt the inadequacy of mere social, moral or religious work in the emancipation of the community. They, therefore, plunged into active politics and soon realised that they could not forever go together with the non-Brahmin middle castes. In July 1922, M.C. Rajah accused the Justice Party for its reactionary role in the Legislative Council where it was functioning as a "non-Brahmin Hindu oligarchy."

Non-Brahmin parties in Bombay also were not successful in the role of creating equal feelings for the members of the Depressed Classes with the Marathas soon preaching their superiority vis-a-vis others, the irony being, that even in educational conferences of the non-Brahmins, the untouchables were seated at a distance to avoid the pollution. Like that of its counterpart in Madras the non-Brahmin movement in Bombay also failed to meet the legitimate aspirations of the Depressed Classes. Later, they used the movement for their sectarian motives and excluded Depressed Classes from its orbit.

The pulls and pressures of any caste-based movement and the induction of the British to help against the social pressures imposed by caste Hindus were effectively brought out by Mrs. Annie Besant, President of the Indian National Congress at its Calcutta Session in December 1917. In her speech she said: "The higher castes are finding that attempts are being made by official and non-official Europeans to stir this class into opposition to Home Rule. They play upon the contempt with which they had been treated and threaten them with a return of it, if Brahmin Rule as they call it, is gained. Twenty years ago and more, I ventured to urge the danger to Hindu society that was hidden within the neglect of the submerged, and the folly of making it profitable for them to embrace Islam or Christianity which offered them a higher social status. Much has been done since then, but it is only a drop in the ocean. It is the urgent duty of every lover of the motherland to draw these neglected children into common homes."

The compulsions of World War I forced the Government to step up the pace of industrialisation in India which helped all sections of society, including the artisan castes amongst the Depressed Classes. The Chamars or leather workers could secure higher wages for their produce which founded their way to international markets. The Noniyas of Bihar benefited from the government order for both the supply of bricks as well as for construction, thereby becoming richer than many caste Hindus. The war economy came to the rescue of the Depressed Classes who were able to strengthen their independence from caste Hindus. With better economic status and political aspirations, came a determination to take the initiative in improving their position rather than become pawns in the hands of political parties and their leaders. At many Depressed Class conferences in which there were eminent leaders such as G.A. Gavai, Chattar Singh Lalji of Gujarat and B.R. Ambedkar of Bombay, there was a clear trend towards self help, and the expression of resentment against the invasion of social and national rights denied to them as human beings. Although social in nature, such meetings had their political repercussions on society, on the British Government, and on such leaders as Mahatma Gandhi.

Gandhi, the Depressed Classes and the National Movement

Gandhi's emergence on the national scene completely changed the tenor of Indian politics, for under his leadership the Indian National Congress, from being a peaceful and law abiding body, came to be a militant and revolutionary organisation due to the means of protest propounded by him. The concept of "non-violence, non-cooperation, Satyagraha, courting arrest, the return to the village and the induction of both the Depressed Classes and the Muslims in this fold, characterised the most revolutionary though peaceful, freedom struggle in history. Having witnessed the indignities of apartheid in South Africa, Gandhi sought to break free the artificial and cruel restrictions of casteism and bring the Depressed Classes within the accepted fold of society. Vowing that he himself and all members of the Congress would become the protectors of the Antyajas, he advised the untouchables not to join hands with the British but to help him to win Swaraj. Moreover he wanted that the religious interests of every community be respected. The secular credentials of the Indian state rested on Gandhi's belief that religion is a matter of personal choice and should have no place in politics and that there should be no state religion even though the whole community might have one religion.

Seeing no capable leader within the Depressed Class community. Gandhi thought that he would personally led them and encourage them to join the freedom struggle. *The Census of India 1921* describes Gandhiji's contribution with the following words: "The special turn which his movement has given to the religious life of the people was to rescue it from antagonism towards Islam, and secondly to set men's minds towards the removal of the taint of untouchability and the upliftment of the Depressed Classes." Voicing this desire in the Bardoli Programme of February 1922, he exhorted Congressmen to organise the Depressed Classes for a better life, to improve their social, mental and moral condition, to encourage them to send their children to national schools and to make available for them the ordinary facilities which other citizens enjoy. These ideas of Gandhiji's did not find favour from all quarters immediately and many were unable to comprehend the connection between Swaraj and the removal of untouchability as an essential pre-requisite. Moreover, the political atmosphere was such that along with the Congress, other political affiliations also gave great importance to the emancipation of the Depressed Classes and championed of their rights of access to schools, temples and public wells.

The Depressed Classes Mission Society of India, at an All India Conference in 1925, announced that the representation of Depressed Classes by nomination was both unsatisfactory and often mischievous. They demanded their own elected representatives in all local and central bodies, whose numbers should be according to the proportion of their population in their respective jurisdictions. It also required that government should periodically fix the percentage of posts reserved for them.

The Depressed Classes and the British

With the growth of nationalist pressures and Gandhiji's influence, the British took keen interest in the affairs of Depressed Classes. Realising from the experience of the 1857 Mutiny that Hindus and Muslims could combine against a common foe, they sought to find other divisions within Indian society which could be used as a counterpoise against the growing Hindu-Muslim amity. The old British philosophy of 'divide and rule' into which net Indians fell time and again, was once again evolved. With each succeeding wave, as political movement grew more intense out of the conflict between the British government in India and the Gandhian Congress, interest came to be focussed on dissensions within the national community. A rapid deterioration set in as the British, aware of their weakness as a foreign government, tried to substitute the internal dissensions for direct challenge. In the category of "other divisions" the divide between the caste Hindus and Depressed Classes was wide and with increasing political awareness, the educated sections of this group were anti-Congress. In addition, the British noticed that while the question of Hindus and Muslims, Brahmin and non-Brahmin and the special position of Indian states could be surmounted by suitable constitutional provisions, the adjustment with the Depressed Classes was not all that easy. The British officers in India, therefore, were strongly motivated to the social upliftment of the Depressed Classes.

A significant outcome of these ameliorative measures on the part of the British was that the Depressed Classes were grateful and dependent of Englishmen in their quest for equality. In 1924, for example, leaders of the Depressed Classes in their written statements to the Reform Enquiry Committee protest against further Indianisation of services and wanted the presence of a predominantly European element, so that the voices of the dumb millions would reach the councils of the Empire, Rajah insisted that by "British" he referred to the elements of a sense of fairness, equal distribution of power, tolerance, sympathy for the weak and depressed classes which was lacking in the Indian officers. He went so far as to state that given the option to serve under a British or an Indian officer, most members of the Depressed Classes would unhesitatingly and overwhelmingly choose a European officer.

The Untouchables Conference of 1926 thanked the government for recognising their "political entity as a class" and in thanking them for giving them a position usurped by Hindus, wanted a complete separation in everything from the Hindus, Muslims and Christians who were either their oppressors or their competitors and from whom they could expect no gain in terms of political, social or economic justice. It is indeed a slur on the rigid dogma of Hinduism that a large section of its population felt so strongly against it that it sought refuge under the British umbrella so openly.

Simon Commission

The Simon Commission landed in India in February 1928 to re-analyse the Indian problem drawing widespread protests due to the all British membership of the team. Whereas most eminent Indian political leaders boycotted the proceedings, the Depressed Classes decided not to do so. Lord Birkenhead, Secretary of State for India, justified the exclusion of Indians on the grounds that the interests of the Depressed Classes had to be protected. In inquiring into the extent of changes in the position of the Depressed Classes, the Simon Commission appreciated the efforts of the Depressed Classes. The Mission Society and the Salvation Army, as well as the work of individual high caste Hindus in an effort to ameliorate the position of these victimised members of society. In this connection, nominations would not assist in helping them to secure political experience nor would be demand for a separate electorate be acceptable as it would create new and further impediments to their ultimate amalgamation with caste Hindus.

The Commission ultimately suggested that in all eight provinces there should be some reservation of seats for the Depressed Classes and the number of these seats, in relation to seats in general constituencies, should be three-quarters of the proportion of the Depressed Classes population to the total population of the electoral area of the province. The Commission stressed that some means would have to be evolved to ensure that the candidates for the reserved seats were genuine representatives of their community and not mere nominees of influential members of the higher castes. Undertaking a practical point of view the Central Committee accorded the following representation for the Depressed Classes on the basis of the existing strength of the Provincial Councils.

States	*Proposed No.*	*Existing No.*
Madras	14	10
Bombay	8	2
Bengal	8	1
Uttar Pradesh	10	1
Punjab	6	0
Bihar and Orissa	6	2
Central Province	8	4
Assam	9	0

In so far as the Legislative Assembly was concerned it was realised that reservation of 12 seats in a proposed Assembly of 300 members would meet the demands of justice vis-a-vis the Depressed Classes.

As far back as 1929, therefore, one can see that there was demand for reservation, special status and recruitment to the civil services as a means of gaining social acceptance and prestige. The reaction to the recommendations of the Simon Commission were mixed. The leaders of the Depressed Classes in Bombay, in a meeting of November 28, 1930 rejected the Simon Commission's recommendations (regarding certification, nomination, joint electorate and non-Depressed Classes) of men representing them. Here too there was a demand for "statutory safeguards" for recruitment of the Depressed Classes in the Army, Police and Civil Services in British India as well as the Indian states.

Although the demands of the Depressed Classes were not fully taken into consideration by the Simon Commission, with their plea for employment in the military and civil administration being disregarded, yet it may be concluded that the Commission was an attempt made by the British government to assess the problem of the Depressed Classes, giving them some political representation and a thrust as a major political force determined to assert itself.

Social Position of Depressed Classes

The socio-economic conditions of the Antyajas or Avarnas made them backward and depressed in all respects, hence they were known as Depressed Classes by the beginning of the 20th century. Montague Chelmsford as well as the Stuart Committee used the term Depressed Class in 1910, while Manekjio Dadabhai Naoroji used the term Depressed Classes in various legislatures to refer to untouchable castes, tribes and criminal. In 1922 and 1927 Government records this term which was also used in the Communal Award of 1933 to convey the meaning of socio-economic and cultural backwardness of the people. Mahatma Gandhi called them *panchamas* (fifth class) as they were excluded from the four varnas of Brahmin, Kshatriyas, Vaisyas and Sudras.

The Depressed Classes were the most miserable part of humanity, condemned to menial and degrading jobs. Even in the 1930's an untouchable was expected to maintain a distance ranging between 30 and 64 feet from the person he was addressing, depending on the caste hierarchy of the person to whom he was talking. He had to address the higher caste person in honorofic terms, bend his body, cover his mouth and refer to himself in disparaging terms. Both untouchable men and women were barred from wearing clothes above the waist and below the knees. They were also prohibited from wearing gold and silver ornaments and shoes. The untouchable was not allowed to enter the house of the upper caste except for work as labourer during construction, repair or putting grains inside the house. The house was subsequently "purified" by sprinkling cow urine or cowdung. Non-inflammable things touched by untouchables were purified by putting them on the fire. Food was given to untouchables only outside the house in leaves or broken vessels, which they had to clean themselves before and after use. It is against this background that Gandhi and Ambedkar came forward with their revolutionary ways to free large sections of the population from a life of hell on earth. Their efforts were all the more laudable as they not only had to tackle entrenched blind orthodoxy but also the inbuilt acceptance of the long suffering Depressed Classes to their fate.

The primary drive behind the removal of disabilities of the Depressed Classes came from nationalistic rather than religious or humanitarian considerations. Nationally-minded caste Hindus noticed the movement of many members of these classes into Christianity, Islam, Sikhism and Buddhism with alarm, especially as it came together with Government's decision to allot power to the "natives" on a communal grounds.

The British attitude towards the Depressed Classes was a combination of "paradoxical admixture of progression and retrogression". Whereas they barred any discrimination in Government-supported schools yet no action was taken against caste Hindus who terrorised and punished those untouchables who made efforts to send their children to schools. While there was no legal ban so far as public institutions and public services were concerned, yet untouchables were not admitted into the army and police. While British law formally rejected caste as the criterion for judgement in criminal, civil and commercial law yet equal access of the untouchables to law did not make the British interfere in the tradition of untouchability, which was not tampered with as part of the policy of non-interference in the social and religious life of the people. The British allowed economic and employment opportunities to the untouchables yet upheld the exclusion of the Depressed Classes from temples, even in the face of progressive native opinion as they maintained that such access would be offensive to the religious feelings of the people which government was duty-bound to protect.

Many amongst the Depressed Classes could see through the British policy of publicising their unfortunate situation not in order to improving their lot, but more with the motive of slowing down the political progress of India. The Depressed Class struggle was a movement within the freedom struggle, for while Indian on the whole was struggling to achieve equality with other nations, the Depressed Classes were striving for equal rights and social acceptance within the country. The Depressed Classes were more involved in struggle to their own freedom, which often made them pawns in the British policy of divide and rule. However, the caste Hindus could not absolve themselves of their failure to emotionally and psychologically integrated the Depressed Classes into the freedom struggle.

The Poona Pact

The Poona Pact came into being as a fall out of the report of the Franchise Committee which was set up to decide the means of enfranchising the Depressed Classes. The Communal Award (MacDonald's Award of 17 August, 1932) which gave separate electorates to the Muslims, Sikhs, Europeans and Christians, sought to strike an ideal balance for Depressed Class identity in the Hindu community. The award stated that all Depressed Class voters who were otherwise qualified could vote with caste Hindus in general constituencies. In addition they would also be entitled to an extra vote for the next twenty years in the special seventy-one Depressed Class constituencies (which were provided everywhere except in Sind, N.W. Frontier and Punjab).

Both Rajah and Ambedkar had to overcome their mutual antipathy and criticised the Communal Award as they felt that the seats allotted to them in special constituencies was very less as compared to other communities and that Depressed Class representation had been ruthlessly scaled down. However, their grievances were not justified as under the special provisions, there could be no fear of the Depressed Classes being eclipsed by caste Hindus as feared by Ambedkar. Rajah's apprehension that untouchability would be perpetuated under separate electorates were unfounded as the system of separate constituencies was to be in force for twenty years only. The announcement of the Communal Award threw caste Hindus into a state of consternation for having helplessly accepted the principle of separate electorates for Muslims. They however reacted strongly to the extension of the same principle to the Depressed Classes, even as a protective measure.

Rabindranath Tagore wrote against the "iniquious separatism" and Gandhiji threatened a "fast until death". Whereas it was agreed in principle that the Depressed Classes needed special treatment so as to be adequately represented in legislatures, the procedures to be adopted in securing adequate representation led to difficulties and discussions. Gandhiji's fast-unto-death led to a flurry of activity in which many steps were taken to immediately effect a merger between caste and non-caste Hindus in activities which had hitherto been considered impossible. Temples, wells and public places were thrown open to untouchables and at mass meetings many resolutions were passed eliminating invidious distinctions against the Depressed Classes. The orthodox Pandit Sabha of Patna issued a manifesto against untouchability and the Ram Mandir of Benaras and Kalighat Temple at Calcutta were thrown open to all. The Shankaracharya of Kolhapur arranged an anti-caste dinner at which Bhangis, Chamars, Mahars sat together. Sections of the Depressed Classes also responded, with Rajah describing Gandhi as the greatest benefactor of the Depressed Classes and issuing an appeal to all sections of society for a combined effort to save the Mahatma's life. He even offered to set aside his opposition to Ambedkar and give the leadership of the Depressed Classes to him if it solved the problem.

In order to save Gandhi's life the Communal Award had to be altered and the big question mark was whether Ambedkar would have enough courage to modify the privileges he had wrested for the Depressed Classes. As the man of the hour Ambedkar did not fully appreciate the onus which was thrust on him and said angrily, "I do not care for these political stunts. This threat of Mr. Gandhi to starve himself to death is not a moral fight but only a political move... I will never be moved by those methods... My decision stands. If Mr. Gandhi wants to fight with his life for the interests of the Hindu Community, the Depressed Classes will also be forced to fight with their lives to safeguard their interests. Gandhiji was a social reformer and idealist and a great champion of the cause of the Depressed Classes. Despite the differences which Ambedkar had and his frequent clashes with Gandhi, the pressure was now on him to go in for a compromise in order to save the Mahatma's life. There was a series of confabulations and efforts to reach a compromise which would be widely acceptable.

Ambedkar was finally convinced about Gandhiji's sincerity when he told him: "You are untouchable by birth, but I am now going to make what might appear as an astounding claim for a man in my position. I am untouchable by adoption and as such much more of an untouchable in mind than you. Any scheme that is really good should subserve the interest not of this group or of that, but of the Depressed Classes as a whole." Under the Poona Pact the quantum of seats was brought down to 148 as it was accepted that the number of seats to be fixed should be based upon the proportion of the Depressed Classes to the total Hindu population. The number of candidates to constitute to panel was ultimately fixed at four. In general legislature, 18 per cent of the general constituencies were to be reserved for Depressed Classes. The question remained of fixing the time at which the special provisions of primary elections and reservations of seats would no longer operate.

Ambedkar wanted a referendum after twenty-five years to settle the issue. Gandhi wanted that the question of retaining reserved seats should be taken up at the end of every five years and if there was a vote in favour of such reservation, another referendum should be held at the end of ten years and the process should then be repeated every ten years.

The Hindu leaders' conference held in Bombay in September ratified the Poona Pact and urged the British government to change the Communal Award by withdrawing the provision of separate electorates for the Depressed Classes so that Gandhiji could break his fast. They also pledged to discard all social disabilities placed on the untouchables by allowing them full access to public wells, public schools, public roads and public institutions including temples.

The British government endorsed the Poona Pact and it was a significant agreement in that for the first time there was a tripartite agreement between the British Cabinet, the leaders of the Depressed Classes and the leaders of the Caste Hindus. The most far reaching outcome of this was that caste Hindus formally agreed to withdraw the social discrimination placed on the Depressed Classes. Gandhiji devoted his life to prevent further fragmentation and alienation within the Hindu Community and made a positive bid for retaining the Depressed Classes within its fold. He emphasised need for time frame for the period of reservation. It must be objectively stated that despite the euphoria witnessed during and after the signing of the Poona Pact and the collective awakening of social conscience, the Depressed Classes always felt being cheated and used as pawns in a political game. The same feeling of being let down had earlier also come from the leaders of the non-Brahmin movement who had also used the Depressed Classes in their fight against the Brahmins, yet had oppressed separate representation for the Depressed Classes.

B.R. Ambedkar

It became important for the Depressed Classes, therefore, to have their own leader and an attitude of self-help in order to ameliorate their condition. The onus of this fell on educated members of the community and it was as a fall out of this that B.R. Ambedkar rose to the position of supreme leader and spokesman of the community. The majority of the Depressed Classes had neither education nor economic sustenance and it was Ambedkar's impatience to secure equal opportunities for them that led him to go in a twin measure, separate electorates and a separate religion for the community. However, his limited success was because of the fact that neither political separatism nor a change of faith were significant unless it was backed by economic upliftment of the masses of landless, homeless, agricultural workers and artisans who were economically dependent on caste Hindus. He made use of every occasion to emphasize that the Depressed Classes were quite apart from the Hindus and due to their social and economic backwardness, they needed special favours for their elevation. It was, in fact, due to

Ambedkar that the Depressed Classes secured between 1927 and 1937, a vast machinery of protective discrimination resulting in reserved seats in legislative bodies, reservation in government jobs and assistance to students from these sections.

However, being a city-based leader, Ambedkar did not adequately understand that political power, legislation against social disability or reservation of jobs in government would benefit only the microscopic minority of educated people. Many complained that his programme concentrated on providing opportunities to the urban, educated untouchable elite to compete with caste Hindus, while the vast masses of rural untouchables remained excluded in any significant socio-economic movement against exploitation by powerful landed elements. Although he diagnosed the problem of the Depressed Classes as a socio-economic and educational one, yet paradoxically, Ambedkar sought the solution to the problem in conversion of religion overlooking the fact that the problem was intrinsically created. A more significant social revolution would have resulted had he sought an economic solution to the age-old thraldom in which rural untouchables found themselves.

Being a Mahar, Ambedkar had felt the stigma of being an untouchable student right from an early age and the cruel disabilities left an indelible mark on his psyche. His political policies were developed not only in the light of the abnormal social and economic conditions of which he was a product but also due to his status as an untouchable, for he had unrivalled knowledge of the plight of an untouchable and the social prejudices and humiliations to which they were subjected. He was conscious of the fact that secular forces like education and urban industrial occupations would go a long way in equalising the status of untouchables with that of others.

Through *satyagrahas* for temple entry he tried to reform the orthodoxy of Hinduism but later embraced Buddhism believing that untouchability would vanish with conversion. Hence one could see that despite his modern, liberal reformist and legal side, Ambedkar nevertheless made his criterion for liberation from untouchability a religious one. In fact, despite the marginal differences in viewpoints, both Gandhi and Ambedkar linked untouchability to religion and neither fully understood that socio-economic factors were responsible for untouchability and that neither a change of religion amongst the Depressed Classes, nor a change of heart amongst caste Hindus, could bring about the emancipation of the untouchables. Only a change in their socio-economic condition could result in the liberation of the Depressed Classes from the yolk of the untouchability.

Ambedkar and Gandhi

Gandhi viewed the problem of untouchability in religious moral terms whereas Ambedkar tried to initially view it in historical terms but later sought the solution in the religious realm. Dismissing all the traditional theories regarding the origin of caste, he heavily drew upon the word "antaya" frequently found in Hindu scriptures. He asserted that Brahmins and untouchables belonged to the same race and untouchability came about because the Brokenmen, who lived inside the village, ate beef and were Buddhists suffered the scorn and contempt of the Brahmins. In their quest for one-upmanship over the Buddhists, the Brahmins not only gave up beef-eating but also declared the cow a sacred animal and beef-eating a sacrilege. The Brokenmen who continued eating beef became guilty of sacrilege and were considered unfit for association, hence they became untouchable. Ambedkar also attacked Gandhi's belief that caste and *varna* were two different things and that the latter was not bad as a social institution. According to him both were evil ideas since the idea of varna caused the birth of caste and if the idea of caste was pernicious, it was entirely because of the viciousness of the concept of *varna*. Secondly, both assigned tasks to individuals, not on the basis of any trained capacity, but on the social status of the parents. In order to build a new society in India it would have to get rid of the old concepts of pigeon holding the individual and consequently his economical exploitation him in a system which institutionalised uncontrolled economic exploitation, and which functioned due to the absence of condemnation either from public opinion or the administrative machinery.

Mahatma Gandhi's views on untouchability were a reflection of his dual role as a politician saint in Indian public life. He often repeated that as long as Hindus wilfully regarded untouchability as part of their religion and considered it a sin to touch a mass of their brethren, Swaraj could not be attained. Gandhi's perception of the plight of untouchables was symbolised in his mind by the image of Uka, a sweeper who used to remove night soil from his house. He also called himself a *bhangi* and stressed that they deserved the highest reverence for the sanitary service they rendered to society. He was angry with the British for professing to speak on behalf of the Depressed Classes and resisting the demand for Swaraj as they felt that the Depressed Classes needed protection from caste Hindus. He disapproved the idea of separate electorates for the Depressed Classes as he believed that it would create a division among Hindus leading to violence and bloodshed. Time and again Gandhiji linked the removal of untouchability to the attainment of Swaraj for as he wrote in *Young India* in October 1921, the Hindus were slave-holders themselves; they could not strive against the yolk of foreign domination if they did not unconditionally first ameliorate the plight of untouchables. In offering political concessions in return for their support to the National Movement, Gandhi emphases that there would be no untouchability under Swaraj and that the law would not tolerate any arrogation of superiority by individuals or classes in the name of custom or religion.

Gandhi reiterated that the perpetuation of untouchability in the name of religion was abhorrent and that the claim of untouchability being sanctioned by the Vedas was a misconception. Gandhi supported the theory of *Varnashrama* as he believed that it defined the duties of men belonging to different vocations. Although based on birth, the Varnashrama of Gandhi's perception entitled the labourer of Sudra and the Brahmin or thinker to the same measure of consideration.

Although strongly against untouchability, Gandhi adopted a policy of peaceful and patient pursuasion towards the caste Hindus in overcoming the prejudices and blind orthodoxy of centuries. At his Ashram, untouchables were treated on equal terms with other inmates and Gandhi adopted an untouchable girl as his daughter. Moreover, he stated that if he were reborn he would want to be born an untouchable. He also advised the untouchables to be patient and to give cooperation and credit to the social reformers.

He exhorted the untouchables to maintain cleanliness and hygiene, advising them to give up killing cows and eating carrion, and leftover rotten foods, give up drinking and gambling and urged them to educate their children.

Ambedkar and Gandhi had both at first sought to work for the integration of the untouchables within the Hindu fold. However, Ambedkar encouraged the Depressed Classes to build an army to fight for their rights in every village and force the Hindu upper castes into a change of attitude. After the Poona Pact, Ambedkar became a disillusioned man and felt that attitude of the caste Hindus and National leaders was not sufficiently radical and hence exhorted his followers that "religion is for man and not man for religion. If you want to organise, consolidate and be successful in this world, change this religion. The religion that does not recognise you as human beings, or give you water to drink or allow you to enter the temples is not worthy to be called a religion. He told them that they had nothing to lose and a lot to gain if they go for a change of religion.

Gandhiji, however, was irreconciliable to the alienation of untouchables from Hindus, whether religiously or politically, and could not countenance their conversion by Christians, Muslims or any other faith. Writing in the *Harijan* in September 1936 he declared that it would be good for the country if the leaders of different religions ceased to vie with each other in an attempt to entice untouchables into their fold. As a national opposed to untouchability, he wanted moral education, preaching and a peaceful struggle to be the instruments in fighting the problem. Militancy on the part of untouchables and antagonism between the castes were fraught with twin dangers of disunity and disaffection. Politically, he would provide for statutory co-option by elected members of the Depressed Classes and did though reluctantly, agree to the reservation of seats in general constituencies. However, he was convinced that the Communal Award which gave separate electorates to the untouchables would cause a division in differences. Hindu society and he staked his life to avoid this cleavage.

Although Gandhi and Ambedkar had differences, their roles were complementary in the task of abolishing untouchability.

Gandhi's greatest achievements were to integrate the removal of untouchability with the struggle for freedom and to convince the caste Hindus that untouchability was not the will of God but creation of man and hence had to be eradicated just as any other social maladjustment. While Ambedkar may have been too radical for Gandhi and Gandhi not reformist enough for Ambedkar, the contribution of these two great leaders assumes significance when viewed against the socio-cultural, economic and religious milieu in which they lived.

The concept of reservation and giving special status to the Depressed Classes are directly attributed to Ambedkar who had a vital role in formulating the constitution. He had said, "If all these communities are to be brought up to the level of equality, then the only remedy is to adopt the principle of inequality and to give favoured treatment to those who are below the level."

References

1. Kumar, Dharam, "The Problem", in Seminar (375), 1990, p. 12-13.
2. Ghorpade, M.Y., "The Rationale", in Seminar (375), 1990, p. 14.
3. Beteille, Andre, "Is Job Reservation a Good Policy", in Seminar (375), 1990, p. 41.
4. Sachidanand, *The Harijan Elite* (Haryana, Thomson Press, 1977), pp. 37-38.
5. Hutton, J.H., *Caste in India: Its Nature and Functions and Origins*, Oxford University Press, London: 1951 (Second edition).
6. Census of India, 1871.

Two

Reservation: Historical Background

The policy of reservation in India was quite firmly established during the times of the British rule itself but such a policy was aimed at minimising communal inequalities in the representation in public services rather than a social engineering device to eradicate the deep-rooted socio-economic inequalities of the disadvantaged section of the society owing to past social discrimination.[1] The British India government had introduced special provisions and concessions for the educational advancement of backward classes people which was later converted into caste based reservations for jobs. The people of these classes had obtained entry into the four walls of literate learning consequent to the social reform movements which were to certain extent supported by the liberal attitude of Englishmen during 19th century. The entry of a non-forward caste/shudra into an educational institution in the country was recorded in year 1856.[2] It was in June, 1856 that a scheduled caste boy applied for admission into a government school in Dharwal, Bombay Presidency. The incident had created furore in the administration which ultimately attracted the attention of the rulers. The board of directors were then forced to formulate an educational policy where it was stated that those schools run by government, would give admission to all students without any distinction of caste, religion and race. This policy was further strengthened with the enactment of the Caste Disability Act of 1872.[3] This Act was a severe blow to the social and legal inequalities suffered by weaker sections. This was how a small beginning was made in the field of educational development of weaker sections in India which was later supported by legislations. The demand for entry into educational institutions and for equality of opportunity was first started in the south. The Southern States including parts of Maharashtra witnessed movements of the weaker sections for equality because of the pioneering work done by Brahma Naidu, Narayana Guru, Jyothirao Phule among others.

Reservation policy for Backward classes (Scheduled Castes, Scheduled Tribes and Other Backward Classes) was introduced by two southern Provincial Governments Madras and Mysore and one in western India Bombay Presidency. All these developments took place before Independence.

Madras

It is for more than hundred years ago that Provincial governments in India have been implementing special programmes for the welfare of depressed or deprived sections of society. The first such step was taken by Madras Government with the framing of Grant-in-Aid code in 1885 to regulate financial aid to educational institutions providing special facilities for students of depressed classes.

Madras Presidency continued its efforts to ameliorate the conditions of depressed classes. After 36 years of implementation of Grant-in-Aid Code in 1885 the Government in 1921, acting on a resolution passed by the state legislative council, took steps for higher representation of non-brahmins in Government Services. The scheme was reviewed in 1927 and the scope of reservation was exchanged further, dividing all the communities in the state into five broad categories and earmarking separate quota for each category. These categories were:

Mysore

After ten years of introduction of Grant-in-Aid code in 1885 by Madras Government, Mysore Government issued circular making provision of reservation of certain posts in favour of backward castes in June 19-21, 1895.[4]

On the basis of representations received from the Depressed Communities in 1918, the Maharaja of Mysore appointed a Miller Committee to suggest measures for adequate representation of non-Brahmins in the service of the state.[5] The Government of Mysore, on the basis of the above committee report, extended special benefits to these classes, in education and recruitment in the state services.

Bombay

Bombay Presidency was third government which introduced reservation policy for backward classes after almost four decades of Madras and Mysore Governments. It was in 1928, that the Government of Bombay set up a committee under the Chairmanship of O.A.B. Starte to identify Backward Classes and recommend special provisions for their improvement. In its report submitted in 1930 this Committee divided backward classes into three categories, i.e. "Depressed Classes, Aboriginals and Hill Tribes and other Backward Classes."[6]

Reservation Policy: At National Level

Political representation as a means to emancipate the backward sections of Indian society from the age old bondage was not accorded due recognition during the nineteenth century. Thus the Government of India Act of 1858 and the Indian Council Acts of 1861 and 1892 did not recognise the special claims of the depressed classes.[7] The dawn of twentieth century also did not herald their recognition as a political entry. In the Government of India Act, 1909 certain privileges were provided to Muslims, but no representation for the depressed classes was provided.

The Montford Report (1918) recognised the claims only of Sikhs. However, the Franchise Committee (1918-19) while recognising the claims of depressed classes, favoured the system of nomination in place of election as more reliables and practical method of political representation for them. The committee recommended for each Provincial Council the nomination from depressed classes in the following way[8] :

Madras	:	2
Bombay	:	1
Bengal	:	1
United Province	:	1
Punjab	:	nil
Bihar and Orissa	:	1
Central Provinces and Berar	:	1
Assam	:	nil

The Government of India Act, 1919, for the first time in the Indian history gave recognition to the existence of depressed classes and recognised their claim for political representation. The Government of India Act, 1919 provided for communal representations for Muslims, Sikhs, Anglo-Indians, Indian Christians, Depressed Classes, Aborigines etc.[9] Among the 14 non-official members nominated by the Governor General to the Central Legislative Assembly, one representative was of the depressed classes. In the Provincial Legislature the depressed classes were represented through four nominations in the Central Provinces, two in Bombay, two in Bihar and one each in Bengal and the United Provinces. In Madras ten members got nomination as representatives of nine specified depressed classes.[10]

Ambedkar, Gandhi and Depressed Classes: Rights of Representation in Legislatives

The next constitutional advancement included the existence of the principle of responsible self-government in the provinces. B.R. Ambedkar submitted a classic memorandum to the Simon Commission for the safeguards and protection of the Depressed Classes. He did this on behalf of the Behishkrit Hitkarini Sabha. The memorandum stated that those in charge of nation's affairs always did injustice to the dumb millions and complained that under the Act of 1919 grave injustice was done to the depressed classes who constitute one-fifth of the population of British India. It demanded 22 out of 140 seats in Bombay Legislative Council, vehemently opposed the principal of nomination, and insisted upon the extension of the principle of election to the depressed classes. It said that they were in need of political education and as ministership was an important privilege, they must find a place in the Cabinet.[11]

The Simon Commission (1930) noted that "our object is to make a beginning which will bring the depressed classes within the circle of elected representation." It did not accept the system of separate electorate as it would mean "a precise definition of all who are covered by the team and the boundary would be in some cases difficult to draw. It means stigmatising each individual voter in the list and militated against the process which is already beginning, and which needs to be in every way encouraged that of helping those who are depressed to rise in the social and economic scale."[12] It recommended that there should be reservation of seats for depressed classes with a cap of three quarters of the depressed class population to the total population of the electorate area of the province. The convening of a Round Table Conference in London in 1930 was a very significant event in the history of India. It was for the first time in history that their claims were being considered along with other Indians including the right to be consulted in the framing of the constitution for India. It marked the beginning of the claims of the untouchables in the arena of the devoluation of the political power from the British rulers to the Indian natives.[13]

The Second Round Table Conference is indeed very historic as the Congress also agreed to take part in the conference and secondly there began a historic and long drawn controversy between Mahatma Gandhi and B.R. Ambedkar regarding the position of the depressed classes in India. Mahatma Gandhi wanted to change the society with the willing consent of the orthodox, but Ambedkar was not willing for any pretences. He was forthright in first demanding adequate share for the most dehumanised people, the untouchables, followed by fight for the backwards and other weaker sections of society. His priorities included breaking the shackles of social bondage of the untouchables from the Brahminical order followed by political independence. Mahatma Gandhi refused to consider both the separate electorates for the depressed classes as well as any form of special representation including reserved seats. He said in the committee, "I do not mind the untouchables being converted to Islam or Christianity. I should tolerate that, but I cannot possibly tolerate what is in store for Hinduism if there are these two divisions set up in every village. Those who speak of political rights of untouchables do not know India and do not know how Indian society is today constructed. Therefore, I want to say with all the emphasis that I cannot command that if I was the only person to resist this thing I will resist it with my life."[14]

After the Third Round Table Conference in 1932, the Communal Award of Ramsay Macdonald was declared. According to this award the Mohammedan, Sikh and depressed classes would elect their candidate by voting in separate communal electorates. The most important part of the Award namely the one relating to the depressed classes ran as follows : "Members of the depressed classes qualified to vote will vote in a general constituency. In view of the fact that for a considerable period these classes would be unlikely, by the means alone to secure adequate representation in the legislatures, a number of special seats will be assigned to them. These seats will be filled by election from special constituencies in which only members of the depressed classes, electorally qualified, will be entitled to vote. Any person voting in such a special constituency will, as stated above, be also entitled to vote in a general constituency. It is intended that those constituencies should be formed in selected areas where the depressed classes are most numerous, and that, except in Madras, they should not cover the whole area of the province."[15]

Gandhi's Fast

Thereafter Mahatma Gandhi undertook a fast unto death against the Communal Award. Ambedkar had to compromise to save Gandhiji's life and Poona Pact was thus born. The deprived got right to enter Parliament and occupy positions of authority. The five thousand years old rock like walls of Brahmanism were pierced. Fresh air went in equal place in political life, but in ultimate analysis Mahatma Gandhi succeeded in securing a promise from Ambedkar and a new lease of life for Hindus, at the same time making the caste Hindus realise that there shall be seats reserved for depressed classes out of the general electorate seats in the Provincial Legislatures as follows[16]: Madras 30; Bombay and Sind 15; Punjab 8; Bihar and Orissa 18; Central Provinces 20; Assam 7; Bengal 30; United Provinces 20; Total 148. Whereas there were only 71 seats in the Communal Award for these depressed classes. In the Central Legislative 18 per cent of the seats were to be reserved for the depressed classes. The voting was to be on the principle of joint electorate system. The Poona Pact had given birth to two principal concepts: 1. That depressed castes will remain within the Hindu fold. 2. That they will enjoy rights to rule themselves jointly with others.

The Government of India Act, 1935 took care of the development arising from Round Table Conference as well as the Poona Pact. The new chapter in our social and constitutional history bade good-bye to Manu and adopted the code of Modern Manu Ambedkar. The excluded became included. The expression Scheduled Caste, which was first coined by Simon Commission was used in the Government of India Act, 1935. Under it the Scheduled Castes replaced Depressed Classes and a separate list of Scheduled Castes was notified for various provinces in 1936. The First Scheduled Part I Section 26 of Government of India Act, 1935 defined the term Scheduled Caste. Scheduled Castes means such castes, races or tribes or parts of or groups within castes, races or tribes being castes, races, tribes, parts or groups which appear to His Majesty-in-Council to correspond the classes of persons formerly known as the "Depressed Class" as His Majesty-in-Council may specify.[17] Under the Government of India Act, 1935 the proportion of seats was given as:[18] Council of State, British India; Total membership—156 and Scheduled Castes—7; Central Assembly : Total membership—250 and Scheduled Castes—19. Ever since 1925 the scheme of reservation applied to Indian Civil Service, Class I, Class II and Subordinate Services under the administrative control of the Government of India with the exception of certain services for which high technical qualifications were essential.[19] The Government of India issued instructions on July 4, 1934 for reserving posts for depressed classes.[20] The Government, however, did not consider it necessary as that stage to reserve a fixed percentage of vacancies for the depressed classes in view of their educational backwardness.

In 1942, the Government of India for the first time decided to fix a certain percentage of jobs for the Depressed Classes in order to give them necessary stimulus to equip themselves with better qualification in order to become eligible for posts and services.[21] Several steps like age concessions, reduction in examination fee etc. were taken. In 1943, 8.5 per cent of job-reservation was provided for the Depressed Classes and it was decided to consider the question of raising this percentage as soon as sufficient number of qualified candidates were found available. However, the percentage of the Scheduled Castes population according to 1931 census was 12.75 per cent. This reservation was applicable only in case of recruitment and not for promotion. In 1946, however, the percentage of reservation was raised from 8.5 to 12.5 per cent corresponding to their population.[22]

Era of Emancipation

Therefore, however the era of emancipation of these depressed castes from the legacy of the past began with the advent of the British rule and leading of the stature of Ambedkar and Mahatma Gandhi took keen interest in their affairs. But the real constitutional provisions on it came after 1950, with special justice as the fundamental constitutional end. The Constitution-makers were fully aware of their fact and hence resolved to constitute India into a sovereign, socialist, secular,[23] Democratic and Republic and *inter-alia* secure justice, social, economic and political as enshrined in the preamble. The Constitution is an instrument for social, economic and political transformation of the nation. It has therefore, provided in Article 37(1)[24], under directive principles that "the state shall strive to promote the welfare of the people by effectively securing and protecting a social order in which justice, economic and political shall inform all the institutions of the national life". Article 37(2): The State shall in particular strive to minimise the inequalities in income, and endeavour to eliminate inequalities in status, facilities and opportunities not only among individuals but also amongst groups of people residing in different areas or engaged in different vocations." It has further been provided in Article 39[25], that the state shall direct its policy towards securing that (a) the citizens, men and women equally have the right to an adequate means of livelihood; (b) that the ownership and control of the material resources of the community are so distributed as to best subserve the common good; (c) that the operation of the economic system does not result in the concentration of wealth and means of production to the common detriment.

The area of employment, offices and appointments under the state is governed by Art. 16[26] alone and preferences within this area must be within the scope of Article 16(4). This includes judicial offices as well as administrative posts, but not elective offices.

Article 16(4) covers not only preferences in initial recruitment into government services but also preferences in promotions within the services.

The legal provisions are embodied in Part XVI of the Constitution of India, which is entitled : "Special provisions relating to certain classes.[27]" From these provisions it is clear that in 1950 the Constitution-makers visualised need to make special provisions only for the following classes: Scheduled Castes and Scheduled Tribes; Anglo-Indian Community; and Socially and Educationally backward classes.

For these special categories of persons, the Constitution-makers provided for several types of concessions. For the Scheduled Castes and Scheduled Tribes, under Articles 330 and 332[28] seats in Lok Sabha and Vidhan Sabhas were needed to be reserved on the basis of their population. It was visualised that these reservation of seats would be available for a period of 10 years only. But with later amendments to the Constitution, this period has been extended from time to time and these provisions still remain in force. However there was no reservation for socially and educationally backward classes in Part XVI.

The other category of special provision under Part XVI relates to appointment to services and posts in connection with the affairs of the Union or of a State for the Scheduled Castes and Scheduled Tribes and the Anglo-Indian communities. For the anglo-Indians Article 336[29] provides reservation in different organisation like Railways, Custom, Post and Telegraph services of the Union Government on the same basis as they were available to them immediately before August 15, 1947. These reservations, however, were to be decreased every two years by 10 per cent and it was also envisaged that there should be no reservation for them from year 1960 onward.

For the Scheduled Castes and Scheduled Tribes, however, Article 335[30] of the Constitution provides that consistent with the maintenance of efficiency of the administration the claims of the members of the Scheduled Castes and Scheduled Tribes shall be taken into account in the making of appointment to services and posts in connection with the affairs of the Union or of the States. No cut-off period of two years or ten years was fixed in the matter of recruitment of Scheduled Castes and Scheduled Tribes to the services and posts in the Constitution.

After independence, out of the posts filled directly on an All-India basis by open competitive examination, 12.5 per cent were reserved for Scheduled Castes and five per cent for Scheduled Tribes. These percentages were later raised to 15 per cent to Scheduled Castes and 7.5 per cent to Scheduled Tribes in 1970.[31]

At the State level there are similar reservations for Scheduled Castes and Scheduled Tribes. The scheme of reservation is applicable to Public Sector Undertakings also. Voluntary agencies which receive grant-in-aid from the government are also required to adopt certain specific features of the reservation scheme in their establishment. But they have not done so.

As regards the socially and educationally backward classes, popularly known as "OBCs" the only special provision for them is under Article 340[32] of Part XVI of the Constitution. In consonance with the provisions of Directive Principles of State Policy, under Article 340 of the Constitution, provision has been made for the appointment of a permanent body like The Government of India has implemented National Commission for Backward Classes Act, 1993 in pursuance of Supreme Court's Judgement in the Mandal Case (1992). Under this Act the Government of India appoints members of the Commission for a period of three years. The function of the Commission is to examine requests of Individual/Class to include the caste/sub-caste/communities in the CLBC Commission to investigate the conditions of Backward Classes and tender advice to the Central Government to include a caste in the Central list of Backward Classes. The provision under Article 340 is supplemented by clause (4) of Article 15 which says that nothing in this Article (Art. 15 relates to prohibition of discrimination on ground of religion, race, caste, sex and place of birth) or in clause (2) of Article 29 (Art. 29 relates to protection and interest of minorities) shall prevent the State from making any special provision for the advancement of any socially and educationally Backward Classes of citizens or for the Scheduled Castes and Scheduled Tribes.

The Mandate in the Constitution

In accordance with the mandate contained in the preamble of the Constitution and the Directive Principles of State Policy, the Government of India appointed the First Backward Classes Commission under Article 340 on January 29, 1953 with Kakasaheb Kalelkar as its Chairman. The Commission submitted its reports on March 30, 1955. On the basis of criteria evolved by it the Commission listed 2,399[33] castes as socially and educationally backward. It recommended various welfare measures for OBCs which included reservation in government services and educational institutions. The Central Government, however did not accept the recommendations of the Commission on the ground that it had not applied any objective tests for identifying backward classes.

While rejecting the main recommendations of this Commission the Central Government informed the State Governments that they were free to draw their respective lists of Backward Classes on the basis of criteria worked out by them and take whatever further action they deemed necessary in the matter.

Consequently, a number of State Governments set up their own Commissions or Committees for defining criteria for backwardness and recommending measures for its removal. Immediately ten state Governments setup fifteen Commissions and committees in this behalf. These states were: Andhra Pradesh, Bihar, Gujarat, Jammu & Kashmir, Karnataka, Kerala, Maharashtra, Punjab, Uttar Pradesh and Tamil Nadu. Further 8 other states and Union Territories had notified lists of other Backward classes for the grant of various educational, employment and other benefits. These are: Assam, Delhi, Haryana, Himachal Pradesh, Meghalaya, Orissa, Pondicherry and Rajasthan. These State Governments and UTs mostly relied on the lists of OBCs maintained by them for the grant of post-Matric scholarships, etc. under the Education Ministry's scheme formulated in 1944 and another list prepared by the Commission for SCs and STs at the time of drafting of First Five Year Plan.

More than two decades the Government of India did not take any action plan for giving reservation benefit to Other Backward Classes. With the change of government at the Centre in 1977, the backward classes problems received the attention of the Janata Party government, and subsequently the Second Backward Classes Commission was appointed in December 1978 under the Chairmanship of B.P. Mandal. The Commission presented its report to President on December 31, 1980. Various welfare measures for the castes listed as socially and educationally backward were recommended in this report.

The Janata Party Government did not implement the recommendations of the Second Backward Classes. As a result this report also met the same fate into cold storage as the first one for a decade. After the fall of Janata Party Government Congress Party Government did not act upon the report realising heart and pulse of people of the country. National Front Government came into power at the Centre in December 1989. The manifesto of National Front included the implementation of Mandal Commission recommendation[34] as one of its promises. Hence the government declared its decision on the implementation of some recommendations of Mandal Commission Report regarding reservations in employment. The Government of India issued a Office Memorandum dated 13th August, 1990 declaring 27 per cent reservation for Other Backward Classes in Government Services, etc. After declaration of the decision of the government there was a spate of reactions by people belonging to different walks of life. The decision of the government to implement some of its recommendations in a precipitated manner agitated the minds of the Indian public, particularly in the Hindi heartland. This led to unprecedented loss of young lives and valuable property which caused extreme distress, but the government showed unpardonable insensitivity towards the feelings of young people. After about a year the Government of India issued another office Memorandum dated 25th September, 1991 on this subject.

However, the new government of Congress (I) at the Centre gave a new twist to whole of the issue by providing ten per cent reservation to the poor among forward castes and also by introducing an economical criteria to the OBCs. This policy of the government was stated in the affidavit submitted to the Supreme Court. The court referred the case to nine judge bench and the Supreme Court in a majority judgement upheld job reservations for backward classes in the Central Government and declared valid the V.P. Singh government's order on 27 per cent job quotas but struck down the economic criteria that was later inducted by the Narasimha Rao government. To exclude economically well off persons belonging to OBCs the Government of India appointed an Expert Committee for specifying the criteria for identification of socially advanced persons among the socially and educationally backward classes under the Chairmanship of Justice Ram Nandan Prasad. The Expert submitted its report to the Government of India on the 10th March, 1993 which was accepted by the Government.

As per directions in the Mandal Judgement (1992) the Government of India setup a National Commission for Backward Classes under the National Commission for Backward Classes Act, 1993. Similar action was also taken by State Governments.

References

1. Parmanand Singh, Equality, Reservation and Discrimination in India, (New Delhi, Deep and Deep Publications, 1985), p. 80.
2. K.S. Chalam, "Caste Reservation and Equality of Opportunity in Education", Economic and Political Weekly, Vol. XXV, No. 41, Oct. 13, 1990.
3. *Ibid.*
4. Karnataka Backward Commission Report, Government of Karnataka, 1975, p. 100.
5. K.S. Padhy and Jayashree Mahapatra, Reservation Policy in India, (New Delhi, Ashish Publishing House, 1988), p. 17.
6. K.S. Padhy and Jayashree Mahapatra, *op. cit.* p. 19.
7. R.G. Mishra and Gurvinder Kaur, Reservation Policy and Personnel Selection, (New Delhi, Uppal Publishing House, 1990), p. 14.
8. J.R. Kamble, Rise and Awakening of Depressed Classes in India, (New Delhi, National, 1979), pp. 67-68.
9. Parmanand Singh, *op. cit.*, p. 82.
10. J.R. Kamble, *op. cit.* p. 69.
11. Dhananjay Keer, Dr. Ambedkar : Life and Mission, (Bombay, Popular, 1962), p. 115.
12. B.A.V. Sharma and Madhusudan Reddy, Reservation Policy in India (New Delhi, Light and Life, 1982), pp. 14-15.
13. Sandanshiv, *op. cit.*, p. 7.
14. *Ibid.*, p. 8.
15. Gwyer and Appadorai, Speeches and Documents on Indian Constitution, 1921, Vol. 1, Oxford, 1957, pp. 261-265.
16. Dr. B.R. Ambedkar, Pakistan or the Partition of India, (Bombay, Thackar and CO., 1945), pp. 462-63.

17. K.S. Padhy and Jayashree Mahapatra, *op. cit*. p. 20.
18. R.G. Mishra and Gurvinder Kaur, *op. cit*., p. 15.
19. Gwyer and Appadorai, *op. cit*., pp. 116-17.
20. *Ibid*., p. 117.
21. Scheduled Castes and Scheduled Tribes Commission Report, 1951, p. 23.
22. *Ibid*., p. 124.
23. The words 'socialist' and 'secular' were added by the 42nd Amendment Act, 1976.
24. The Constitution of India, (New Delhi, Delhi Controller of Publications, Ministry of law and Justice, 1986), p. 14.
25. *Ibid*. p. 14.
26. *Ibid*. p. 6.
27. *Ibid*. p. 113.
28. *Ibid*.
29. *Ibid*. p. 115.
30. *Ibid*.
31. R.G. Mishra and Gurvinder Kaur, *op. cit*., p. 39.
32. The Constitution of India, *op. cit*., p. 16.
33. Second backward Classes Commission, 1980, p. 2.
34. National Front: Lok Sabha Election Manifesto, 1989, p. 36.

Three

Reservational Justice to Backward Castes: Some Issues

Presently reservation benefits are available to backward classes that includes Scheduled Castes, Scheduled Tribes and Other Backward Classes (OBCs). The first two categories of people have been granted Constitutional benefits while Other Backward Classes have been granted benefits under executive order. The Constitution specifically mentions Scheduled Castes and Scheduled Tribes under Articles 15(4), 46, 334, 338, 341 and 342. Article 335 mentions their claims to services and posts. It reads, "the claims of the members of the Scheduled Castes and the Scheduled Tribes shall be taken into consideration, consistently with the maintenance of efficiency of administration, in making of appointments to services and posts in connection with the affairs of the Union and of a State." It is only they for whom reservation of seats is provided in the House of the People and in the Legislative Assemblies of the States.[1] They belong to weaker sections with special mention. Article 46 provides that "the State shall promote with special care the educational and economic interests of the weaker sections of the people, and, in particular, of the Scheduled Castes and the Scheduled Tribes, and shall protect them from social injustice and all kinds of exploitations." If any provision deals with backward class of citizens without specific mention of SCs and STs, their claim is first charged in respect of backwardness. To make it more specific `backward' used in Article 16(4) is wider than 'Socially and Educationally backward' used in Article 15(4) and 'weaker sections' used in Article 46. SCs/STs are covered in all the expressions.

The expression 'Backward Class' in Article 16(4) takes in Other Backward Classes, Scheduled Castes and Scheduled Tribes.

The accent in Article 16(4) is upon social backwardness. Social backwardness leads to educational backwardness and economic backwardness. They are mutually contributory to each other and are inter-twined with low occupations in the Indian society. The Constitution of India has commitment to ensure justice to all sections of the people. But it does not incorporate the use of expression Other Backward Classes (OBCs). The Constitution uses the expression Socially and Educationally Backward Classes (SEBCs).

Thus, the category of backward classes other than SCs/ STs belongs to SEBCs also. Article 15(4) speaks of making special provisions for advancement of SEBCs and Article 340 speaks of appointment of a Commission by the President to investigate into conditions of the SEBCs. Under this Article Kaka Kalelkar Commission in 1953 and Mandal Commission in 1978 were appointed for investigating conditions of backward classes. The Notification regarding implementation of Mandal Commission's recommendations has been upheld by the Supreme Court of India in Indira Sawhney and others *versus* Union of India and others on 16.11.1992.[2] Parliament enacted National Commission for Backward Classes Act, 1993 in order to constitute a permanent statutory body[3] National Commission for Backward Classes. The Commission shall examine requests of any individual of any backward caste in the Central List of Backward Classes. The present chapter examines what is/are criterion of backwardness of a caste from legal point of view. In many cases of High Courts and Supreme Court eminent jurists have given their decisions whether a caste is socially backward or educationally backward or both? Further, can backwardness of a caste be compared with Scheduled Castes and Scheduled Tribes. How should we identify a caste, 'backward' by applying 'means test'. Can we classify backward castes/class into backward and most backward. While we are certainly concerned about right of OBCs to reservation, we should also see other side of the coin whether reservation will be antimeritarian? Can we take any affirmative action? In the following paragraphs all these issues will be critically examined and analysed.

Caste as basis of backwardness: Legal position

The Constitution of India intends to wipe out discrimination on the ground of caste. But the real problem which the country is confronting within: can caste be eliminated from the criterion of identification of backward classes? In pre-Constitution period the expressions, 'class' and 'caste' were used interchangeably. As a matter of fact Ambedkar declared in his speech in the Parliament at the time of the First Amendment to the Constitution that "Backward Classes are nothing else but a collection of certain castes." A caste is an enclosed class. Issuing clarification of the use of the word class in Article 16(4) Kania, C.J. and Venkatachaliah, Ahmadi and Jeevan Reddy, JJ. pointed out in *Mandal Case* (1992), vol I, that the obvious reason of using the expression 'Class' in Article 16(4) was that otherwise non-Hindus would have got excluded from its purview as they do not use 'caste'. Therefore, from the use of the word 'class' in Article 16(4), it cannot be deducted either that 'class' is antithetical to "caste" or that a caste cannot be a class or that a caste as such can never be taken as a backward class of citizens.

Earlier it was thought that our Constitution is caste blind and the objective was to set up a casteless society. But different provisions of the Constitution do not speak in such language that one can draw conclusions to the effect of the abolition of caste. Mr Justice Wad in his one of non-judicial writings points out, "Our Constitution-makers did not take a bold decision of expressly abolishing the caste system by providing for it in the fundamental right and organic document for the governance of the Indian society. If abolition of caste system was a fundamental right a Constitutional remedy in the form of Article 32 would have been available to enforce the said provision."[4] He is of firm opinion that in India the root cause or arch villain of social inequality is the caste system based on hierarchy of birth.[5] There are provisions of Articles 15, 16 and 29 on the one hand equating discrimination to religious discrimination. On the other hand, there are provisions of Articles 25, 26 and 30 which are available even to smaller religious denominations. The conclusion of Mr Justice Wad is realistic when he says:

"There is no clear-cut definition of denomination. There are overlapping characteristics or features of a denomination and a caste. Both may have definite religious institutions, religious doctrines and rituals. As a common religious institution, caste may be able to consolidate themselves as religious denominations.[6] Caste is the only criterion for awarding benefits to SCs/STs. About OBCs 'class' is used and it has caused serious concern whether class should be equated to caste. Whether such Classes are castes? Absence of a categorical value measure of a casteless society has been strongly condemned by Ghurye, who says, "we are marching towards caste pluralism instead of a casteless society."[7] Many castes in India are bound together by common faith and organisation. The Gowda Saraswat Brahmins are a caste which was recognised as a denomination in Chinnamma versus D.P.I.[8] The question then arises can a caste be taken as basis for determining backwardness? Let us discuss the position analytically from legal point of view.

(a) Neither sole nor dominant criteria

During 1960s the Supreme Court of India attempted to dilute the domineering role of caste in identification of backwardness. In Balaji versus State of Mysore,[9] P.B. Gajendragadkar, J. speaking for the unanimous Constitution Bench conceding the harsh reality of caste factor among Hindus pointed out that, "though castes in relation to Hindus may be a relevant factor to consider in determining the social backwardness of groups or class of citizens it cannot be made the sole or the dominant test in that behalf."[10] Subba Rao, J, further secularised it in his majority decision in R. Chitralekha versus State of Mysore.[11] He stressed that under no circumstances a 'class' could be equated to a 'caste', though the caste of an individual or a group of individuals may be regarded along with other relevant factors in putting him in a particular class. He also stressed that if caste is excluded in ascertaining backwardness of a class in a particular situation it would not be bad. In his dissenting judgement Mudholkar, J. declared that taking into account the `caste' of a person to identify backwardness of a class would be against Article 15 or 29(2). In his view non-abstante clause of Article 15(4) does not justify the inference that "castes have any relevance in ascertaining what are socially and educationally backward communities."[12]

(b) Some shift started: caste not to be ignored altogether

A somewhat different tone started in judicial verdicts by the end of 1960s. In P. Rajendran versus State of Madras[13] Wanchoo, C.J. speaking for the Constitution Bench conceding that determination of backwardness based solely on caste without taking into consideration the social and educational backwardness would be violative of Article 15(1), clarified the point: "But it must not be forgotten that a caste is also a class of citizens and if the caste as a whole is socially and educationally backward, reservation can be made in favour of such a caste on the ground that it is a socially and educationally backward class of citizens within the meaning of Article 15(4).[14] In *State of* Andhra Pradesh versus P. Sagar[15] the Supreme Court spoke in similar tone avoiding caste as sole criterion but granting that "the expression 'class' means a homogeneous section of the people grouped together due to certain likeness or common traits and who are identifiable by some common attributes such as status, rank, occupation, residence in a locality, race, religion and the like. In determining whether a particular section forms a class, caste cannot be excluded altogether."[16] Shah J. speaking for the Constitution Bench of the Supreme Court in Triloki Nath *versus* State of J and K.[17] (II) took note of both *P. Sagar's case* and *P. Rajendran case*. As to *P. Sagar's* message he took the stand that test of backwardness should not base solely on caste and as to *P. Rajendran's* note he recognised the entire caste may form a class.

(c) Caste as a Class

Hegde J. asserted in A. Peeriakaruppan versus State of T.N.[18] that "a caste has always been recognised as a Class."[19] So was the tone of Vadialingam J. in State of A.P. versus U.S.V. Balaram[20] wherein various test of backwardness were pointed out but the list of backward classes was to be accepted even though the said list was "exclusively based on caste".[21]

(d) Extremism for a while

Chief Justice A.N. Ray said in K.S. Jayashree versus State of Kerala[22] that 'in determining social backwardness of a class of citizens it may not be irrelevant to consider the caste of the group of citizens, Caste cannot however be made only or dominant test.[23] This echoed *Balaji's* ruling. But the tone of Ray, C.J. appeared to be so what changed with emphasis on Article 15(1) in State of U.P. versus Pradip Tandon.[24] The learned Chief Justice elaborated.

> "It is true that Article 15(1) forbids discrimination only on the ground of religion, race, caste, but when a classification takes recourse to caste as one of the criteria in determining socially and educationally backward classes the expression classes is that case violates the rule of *expressio-unius est exclusio alterius*. The socially and educationally background classes of citizens are groups other than groups based on caste."[25]

(e) 1980s scenario: caste reality by birth

In K.C. Vasantha Kumar versus State of Karnataka[26] barring Chief Justice Chandrachud, all other four learned judges of the Constitution Bench thoroughly discussed the issue of caste backwardness relationship. After analysing the role of caste in the Indian social structure. O. Chinnappa Reddy, J. spoke: "Social hierarchy and economic position exhibit an indisputable mutuality. The lower the caste the poorer its members. The poorer the members of a caste, the lower the caste and economic situation, reflecting each other as they do are the *deus examchina* of the social status occupied and the economic poor wielded by an individual or class in the rural society". The obvious conclusion of Chinnappa Reddy, J. is that:

> "Social status and economic power are so woven and fused into the caste system in Indian rural society that one may without hesitation, say that if poverty be the cause, caste is the primary index of social backwardness, so that social backwardness is often readily identifiable with reference to a person's caste.[27]

D.A. Desai, J. also accepted the reality of the role of caste in the Indian Society, but in order to get rid of pernicious effect of caste-system he wanted economic and poverty criterion of the identification of backwardness. A.P. Sen J. wished poverty as criterion but acknowledged caste for identification of acute backwardness. Likewise[28] E.S. Venkataramiah, J. preferred means test. But he exposed the ill impact of ugly practices connected with castes. The learned judge pointed out, "An examination of the question in the background of the Indian social conditions shows that the expression 'backward classes' used in the Constitution referred only to those who are born in particular castes, or who belonged to particular races or tribes or religious minorities which were backward."[29] The learned judge ruled that 'the caste of a person is governed by his birth in a family.[30] Caste in India has primeval force and there is omnipresence of caste in Indian society. "So sadly and oppressively deep-rooted is caste in our country that it has cut across even the barriers of religion."[31]

One conclusion through judicial verdicts upto start of 1990s is that irrespective of stress on the extent of role, caste has always been a criteria to be taken into account by Courts while ascertaining backwardness of a class.

Indira Sawhney and others vs. Union of India and Others etc., etc. (1982)

These writ petitions were heard in the first instance by a Constitution Bench presided over by the then Chief Justice Shri Rangnath Misra. After hearing them for some time, the Constitution Bench referred them to a special bench of nine judges to finally settle the legal position relating to reservations.

Kania, C.J. and Venkatachaliah, Ahmadi and Jeevan Reddy, JJ. forming the leading majority verdict made it clear that a caste is nothing but a social class—a socially homogeneous class. It is also an occupational group with the difference that its membership is hereditary. One is born into it. Its membership is involuntary. Even if one stops to follow that occupation still he remains and continues to be a member of that group. Caste is a socially and occupationally homogeneous class. Endogomy is its main feature. The conclusion of leading majority verdict is that a caste can be and generally is a social class in India. If it is backward socially, it would be backward class for the purposes of Article 16(4). Class under Article 16(4)[32] is neither antithetical to caste nor can it be said that it cannot be a class or that caste as such can never be taken as a backward class of citizens.

Pandian, J. in his concurring judgment expressed the opinion that a caste is also a class of citizens and that if that caste satisfies the requisite tests of backwardness, the classification of that caste as a backward class is not opposed to Article 16(4).[33]

Sawant J. in his concurring judgement pointed out that casteism has been the bane of entire Indian society. Every individual is born in a particular caste which he cannot change.[34] A caste by itself may constitute a class. However, Sawant, J. observed that in order to constitute a backward class the caste concerned must be socially backward and its educational and economic backwardness must be due to its social backwardness.[35] In their dissent Thommen and Kuldip Singh, JJ ruled out caste as criteria for determination of backward classes. Thommen, J. expressed the opinion that the grounds prohibited in Article 15(1) including caste cannot be the only or dominant criterion. Instead along with them there should be criterion of illiteracy, poverty, demeaning occupation, malnutrition, etc. Kuldip Singh, J. expressed the opinion that 'class' under Article 16(4) cannot be read as 'Caste' and castes cannot be adopted as collectivities for the purpose of identifying backward class "under Article 16(4). In his view caste-collectivity is unconstitutional and as such not permitted.[36] Similar opinion was expressed by Sahai, J. in his dissent.[37] From the above analysis two view points emerge. First, caste by itself may constitute class and can be the basis of backwardness, Second, caste cannot be read as class and therefore as such be basis for determination of backwardness.

Backwardness of Other Backward Classes vis-a-vis Backwardness of Scheduled Castes/Scheduled Tribes

Scheduled Castes, Scheduled Tribes and Other Backward Castes (OBCs) are three different social class or groups having different level of social and educational backwardness. There is difference in degree of backwardness between the two and this attracts different treatment. But there have been some astray observations both judicial and extra judicial which have shown the similarity between the two. In Balaji versus State of Mysore[38] while dealing with the issue of division of backwards into backward and more backward, the Supreme Court made certain remarks which give the impression that the backwardness of the Backward Class under Article 16(4) being social and educational must be similar to the backwardness from which the Scheduled Castes and Scheduled Tribes suffer. The Supreme Court of India observed:

> "It seems fairly clear that the backward classes of citizens for whom special provision is authorised to be made are, by Article 15(4) itself, treated as being similar to the Scheduled Castes and Scheduled Tribes. Scheduled Castes and Scheduled Tribes which have been defined were known to be backward and the Constitution makers felt no doubt that special provision had to be made for their advancement. It was realised that in the Indian society there were other classes of citizens who were equally, or may be somewhat less backward than the Scheduled Castes and Tribes and it was thought that some special provision ought to be made even for them.[39]

After referring to Articles 338(3), 340(1) 341 and 342, the Court said:

> "It would be seen that this provision contemplates that some Backward Classes may by the Presidential order be included in Scheduled Castes and Tribes. That helps to bring out the point that the Backward Classes for whose improvement special provision is contemplated by Article 15(4) are in the matter of their backwardness comparable to Scheduled Castes and Scheduled Tribes.[40]

The Balaji test was elaborated by the Supreme Court in Janki Prasad Parimoo versus State of J and K.[41] to mean that backwardness for whose improvement special provision was contemplated by Article 15(4) must be comparable to Scheduled Castes and Scheduled Tribes who are standing examples of backwardness socially and educationally.[42] Similar opinion was expressed in K.S. Jayshree versus State of Kerala.[43] In K.C. Vasanth Kumar versus State of Gujarat.[44] Chief Justice Chandrachud in his separate judgement spoke of comparability of backwardness of Backward Classes to Scheduled Castes and Scheduled Tribes. These opinions represent one side of the coin which does not properly appreciate the use of alternate expressions and separate provisions in the Constitution.[45]

The other side of the issue attracting Constitutional dimension is represented in various set of opinions finally getting approval of majority opinions in Indira Sawhney and Others versus Union of India and Others.[46] In State of A.P. versus U.S.V. Balaram,[47] the earlier opinion was explained by pointing out that *Balaji* ruling does not lay down that backwardness of the other backward classes must be exactly in all respects to that of the Scheduled Castes and Scheduled Tribes. Referring to the above referred observations in *Balaji's case*. Mr Justice O. Chinnappa Reddy, J. expressed the opinions in K.C. Vasanth Kumar versus State of Karnataka[48] that:

> "We do not think that these observations were meant to lay down any proposition that the socially backward classes were those classes of people, whose conditions of life were very nearly the same as those of the Scheduled Castes and Tribes... There is no point in attempting to determine the social backwardness of other classes by applying the test of nearness to the conditions of existence of the Scheduled Castes. Such a test would practically nullify the provision for reservation for socially and educationally Backward Classes other than Scheduled Castes and Tribes.[49]

Similar explanation was attached by Mr Justice Sawant in his concurring opinion view in *Mandal Case*.[50] The learned judge ruled that the test of comparable backwardness laid down in Balaji[51] has not been and is not to be understood to mean that backwardness of the other backward classes has to be of the same degree as or similar in all respects to that of the Scheduled Castes and the Scheduled Tribes.[52] The learned judge placed main reliance upon the constitutional provisions and gave two convincing arguments for his conclusions.

1. That it is necessary that the social, educational and economic backwardness of the other backward classes should be exactly of the same kind and degree as that of the Scheduled Castes and the Scheduled Tribes is recognised by the different provisions of the Constitution itself since they make difference between the Scheduled Castes and the Scheduled Tribes on the one hand, and other "socially and educationally backward classes" or "backward classes of citizens" on the other.[53]

2. What is further, if the other backward classes are backward exactly in all respects as the Scheduled Castes and Scheduled Tribes, the President has power to notify them as Scheduled Castes and Scheduled Tribes, and then they would not remain the other backward classes.[54]

Similar and some additional arguments were given by B.P. Jeevan Reddy J. (speaking for M.H. Kania, C.J. and M.N. Venkatachaliah, A.M. Ahmadi, JJ. and himself). While delivering the majority decision in *Mandal Case*[55] the learned judge found no reason to qualify or limit the meaning of the expression "backward class of citizens" by saying that it meant those other backward classes who were situated identically to Scheduled Castes and/or Scheduled Tribes. Jeevan Reddy, J. clarified difference in language of Article 15(4) and Article 16(4). The latter does not refer to SCs or STs keeping in view this difference the learned judge said, "if so, there is no reason why we should consider their backwardness as the standard backwardness for all those claiming its protection",[56] said the learned judge:

> "As a matter of fact, neither the several castes/groups/tribes within the Scheduled Castes and Scheduled Tribes are similarly situated nor are the Scheduled Castes and Scheduled Tribes similarly situated. If any group or class is situated similarly to the Scheduled Castes, they may have a case for inclusion in that class but there seems to be no basis either in fact or in principle for holding that other classes or groups must be situated similarly to them for qualifying as backward classes. There is no warrant to import any such *a priori* notions into the concept of Other Backward Classes.[57]

Pandian, J. also expressed the opinion that it is not necessary for a class to be designated as a backward class that it should be situated similarly to the Scheduled Castes and Scheduled Tribes.[58] Thus in *Mandal case* Kania C.J. and Venkatachaliah, Ahmadi, Jeevan Reddy, Pandian and Sawant, JJ. expressed the view that OBCs, need not be identically situated to SCs and STs. Only Thommen, J. dissented[59] and stressed on the comparability of the backwardness of OBCs to SCs and STs.

Does the Backward Class of Citizens Mean both Socially and Educationally Backward Class?

One of the significant issues in relation to 'backward class of citizens' under Article 16(4) is whether backwardness under that clause is both social and educational. So far as clause (4) of 15 is concerned it was ruled in Balaji versus State of Mysore[60] that backwardness contemplated under that Article was both social and educational. It is not either only social or only educational but it is both social and educational. In Janki Prasad Parimoo versus State of J and K[61] the Court read expression, backward class of citizens used in Article 16(4) to mean "socially and educationally backward class of citizens". Mr Justice Palekar who pronounced the judgement proceeded to equate the two terms on assumption that "it was well settled that the expression `Backward Class' in Article 16(4) implies the same thing as the expression, any socially and educationally Backward Classes of citizens in Article 15(4). It is submitted that the conclusion was based on assumptions and none of the decisions had tried to equate the two terms.[62] Similarly in K.C. Vasanth Kumar versus State of Karnataka,[63] Mr Justice Chinnappa Reddy,[64] Justice D.A. Desai,[65] Justice Sen[66] and Justice Venkataramaiah[67] proceeded on the footing that Backward Class of citizens' was synonymous with the expression 'socially and educationally backward class. But the leading majority judgment in *Mandal Case* delivered by B.P. Jeevan Reddy, J. (for himself Kania, C.J. Venkatachaliah and Ahmadi, JJ) did not approve of the above logic. It found no basis of the assumption that the expression Backward Class of citizens in Article 16(4) implies the same thing as the expression, any socially and educationally 'Backward Class of citizens' in Article 15(4). It was made clear that clause (4) of Article 16 does not contain the qualifying words `socially and educationally' as does clause (4) of Article 15.[68] The majority decision pointed out the width of Article 16(4). It is wider than as contemplated by Articles 15(4) and Article 340. Thus, the expression 'Backward Class of citizens' in Article 16(4) includes SCs/STs and all Other Backward Classes of citizens including the socially and educationally backward classes. And, therefore, certain classes which may not qualify for Article 15(4) may qualify for Article 16(4) as backward class of citizens.[69] The backwardness contemplated under Article 16(4) is chiefly social backwardness and therefore it would not be right to say that the backwardness under Article 16(4) should be both social and educational.[70] Backwardness under Article 16(4) is much wider. The accent in Article 16(4) is more on social backwardness. Of course, social, educational and economic backwardness are closely interwined in the Indian context.[71] Likewise Pandian, J. in his concurring judgment made it clear that the primary consideration in identifying a class and in ascertaining the insufficient representation of that class in the services under the State under Article 16(4) is social backwardness which results in educational backwardness, both of which end up in economic backwardness. Said, Pandian, J.:

> "The degree of importance to be attached to the social backwardness is much more than the importance to be given to the educational backwardness and the economic backwardness, because in identifying and classifying a section of people as a backward class within the meaning of Article 16(4) for the reservation of appointments or posts, the social backwardness plays a predominant role.[72]

Mr Justice Sawant also put main stress on social backwardness.[73] He made it clear that the only 'backward class' for which reservations are provided and Article 16(4)[74] is the 'socially backward class' whose educational and economic backwardness is on account of the social backwardness. He stressed that 'a class which is not socially and educationally backward though economically or even educationally backward is not a backward class for the purposes of the said clause [Article 16(4)]. Sawant, J. very clearly pointed out the actual purpose behind Article 16(4): "the purpose of keeping reservations even in favour of socially and educationally backward classes under Clause (4), is not to alleviate poverty but to give it an adequate share in power."[75]

In their dissenting judgments Thommen, J. Kuldip Singh, J. and Sahai, J. expressed different opinions.Thommen, J. expressed the view that 'backward class' used in Article 16(4) is synonym for the classes mentioned in Article 15(4)[76] Kuldip Singh, J. did not agree with proposition that social backwardness is an essential feature of the 'backward class' under Article 16(4)[77] and R.M. Sahai J. considered both social and educational backwardness necessary for the purpose of Article 16(4).[78]

Identification of OBCs

Article 16(4) speaks of reservations in public employments for 'backward class of citizens'. This expression was not originally suggested by the *Ad hoc* Committee whose recommendation read: "Nothing herein contained shall prevent the State from making provision for reservation of appointments or posts in favour of any of citizens who in the opinion of the State are not adequately represented in the services under the State". 10(3)

It was the drafting committee under the chairmanship of Dr. B.R. Ambedkar that inserted the word "backward" in between the words "in favour of any" and "class of citizens". The discussion on draft Article 10 took place on November 30, 1948. Several members including S/Sri Damodar Swaroop Seth, Pt. Hirdya Nath Kunzru and R.M. Nalavade complained that the expressions 'backward' and 'backward classes' are quite vague and are likely to lead to complications in future. They suggested that the appointments in public services should be made purely on the basis of merit. Some others suggested that such reservations should be available only for a period of first ten years of the Constitution. To this criticism the Vice-President of the Assembly (Dr. H.C. Mookherjee) replied at length. Mookherjee also received support of Sri Chandrika Ram (Bihar-General) and Sri P. Kakkan (Madras-General) on expression 'backward classes'. It is mentioned that draft Article 10 corresponds to Article 16. The debate in the Constituent Assembly on draft Article 10 and particularly clause (3), thereof (corresponding to clause (4) of Article 16 helps us to appreciate the background and understand the objective underlying Article 16, and in particular, clause (4) thereof.

In *Mandal Case*, the leading majority decision for four learned judges made it clear that the Government of India and the State Governments have power to, and ought to, create a permanent mechanism in nature of Commission or Tribunal for examination of requests of inclusion and complaints of over-inclusion or non-inclusion in the list of OBCs and to advise the Government and in the case of the non-acceptance of the advice by the Government, it must record its reasons thereof.[79] Similar views were shared by Pandian, J[80] who favoured permanent Commission/Committee, Thommen, J. who wished periodic administrative review by a permanent expert body[81] and Sawant, J. who agreed in principle.[82] The Commission/Committee may be constituted either under clause (4) of Article 16 itself or under Article 16(4) read with Article 340.[83]

Parliament/Legistatures as Authorities for Reservation to OBCs

In Balaji versus State of Mysore[84] provision under clause (4) of Article 16 was allowed to be made by the executive wing of the government. The same was done by the Supreme Court in Comptroller and Auditor-General of India versus Mohan Lal Mehrotra.[85] An unsuccessful attempt was made in *Mandal Case*[86] to challenge the validity of Government Memorandum on the plea that since the provisions of Article 16(4) affect fundamental rights of other citizens such a provision can be made only by the Parliament/Legislature. It was pleaded that exercise of power by the executive was attune to misuse of power because of political and electoral conclusions. On the other hand, legislature will offer proper forum for deliberation and balanced decision. The leading majority decision delivered by Jeevan Reddy, J. ruled out the apprehension about misuse of powers by executive in the light of the objectivity stipulated in determination of backwardness.[87] The Court put emphasis on definition, of law given under Article 13(3)(a) which includes order, 'bye-law', 'rule' and 'regulation' and definition of 'State' under Article 12 of the Constitution. Keeping in view these provisions the Court ruled that:

> "it becomes clear that a measure of the nature contemplated by Article 16(4) can be provided not only by the Parliament/Legislature but also by the executive in respect of Central/State services and by local bodies and 'other authorities' contemplated by Article 12, in respect of their respective services."[88]

Thus in *Mandal case* Kania, C.J. and Venkatachaliah, Ahmadi, Jeevan Reddy,[89] Pandian,[90] Kuldip Singh[91] and Sawant,[92] JJ. upheld the Memorandum as it need not necessarily be made by the

Parliament. Sahai, J. pointed out that reservation by executive order may not be valid but since it was being made for the first time in services under the Union the propriety demanded that it should have been laid before Parliament because of two reasons: (i) to lay down a healthy convention, and (ii) to take into account the change in social, economic and political conditions of the country as nearly ten years had elapsed from the date of the submission of Mandal Commission Report which was a period considered sufficient for re-evaluation if the reservation may be continued or not.[93]

As to the efficacy of the Memorandum Kania, C.J. and Venkatachaliah, Ahmadi and Kuldip Singh, JJ. held the view that any provision made under Article 16(4) becomes effective and enforceable by itself. They fall under Article 73 read with Article 16(4).[94] Sawant, J. also took the similar view.[95] Kuldip Singh, J. expressed the opinion that executive instructions under Articles 16(4), 73 and 162 providing reservation contrary to rules under Article 309 shall not be operative so far as it is contrary to statutory provisions/rules[96] Sahai, J.thought it proper to be laid before Parliament.[97]

Division of OBCs into Backward and Most Backward Classes

It is not that the backwardness of all backward classes will be of the same magnitude. Whether backward classes may be divided into backward classes and most backward classes came to be decided in Balaji versus State of Mysore.[98] It had two main features: (i) it related to Article 15(4), and (ii) it was meant for giving reservations separately to the two classes and thereby raising percentage of reservation. This aspect was noted by Gajendragadkar, J. (as he then was) who delivered the judgment. The learned judge pointed out that the sub-classification made by the Order between Backward Classes and More Backward Classes and did not seem to be justified under Article 15(4) because that authorise special provision being made for the really backward classes. Said, Gajendragadkar, J.:

> "In introducing two categories of Backward Classes, what the impugned order, in substance, purports to do is to devise measures for benefit of all the classes of citizens

> who are less advanced compared to the most advanced classes in the State and that in our opinion is not the scope of Article 15(4)."[99]

Gajendragadkar, J. observed that the result of method adopted by impugned order was that nearly 90 per cent of the population of the State was considered as backward and that illustrated how the order in fact divided the population of the State into the most advanced and the rest and put latter into two categories of backward classes and most backward. In his view that was not warranted under Article 15(4). In K.C. Vasantah Kumar versus State of Karnataka[100] Chinnappa Reddy, J. conceded that the propriety of such a course may be open to question on the facts of each case, but he found no justification "Why on principle there cannot be classification into Backward Classes and More Backward Classes, if both classes are not merely a little behind, but far behind the most advanced classes". He expressed the opinion that:

> "In fact such a classification would be necessary to help the more Backward Classes: otherwise those of Backward Classes who might be a little more advanced than the more backward classes might walk away with all the seats, just as, if reservation was confined to the more Backward Classes and no reservation was made to the slightly more advanced backward away with all the seats available for the general category leaving none for the backward classes.[101]

Chinnappa Reddy, J. pointed out that "all that we can say is that sub-classification may be permissible if there are classes of people who are definitely far behind the advanced classes but ahead of the very backward classes." The difference between Articles 15(4) and 16(4) is that the former deals with the issue of the extent of the special provision to be made thereunder and latter is invoked with regard to so-called meritarian principle which argues that large reservation would inevitably affect efficiency. In his Report of Third Karnataka Backward Classes Commission Chinnappa Reddy, J. identified three factors interrelatively contributing towards backwardness. Such factors are Caste, Economic and Educational. Lack of economic development, educational unawareness and caste humiliation all contribute backwardness. Since caste is by birth therefore, to fight with this factors the other two evils need to be eradicated. Chinnappa Reddy, J. divided backward classes into three categories — for awarding reservation and not for denying it. It also allotted separate percentage for each categories.

Category	*No. of Communities*	*Basis*	*Perecentage of Population*	*Percentage of Reservation*
I	52	Caste/Community/size	80	5
II	14	-do-	33	28
III	Innumerable occupational groups	Occupation	Indefinite	5

Earlier Bihar Government appointed a Backward Classes Commmission under the chairmanship of Mungeri Lal in June 1971 and it submitted its report in February 1976. The Commission identified 128 communities as 'backward' and 94 of them as 'most backward'. It recommended 20 per cent reservation for them in all Government Departments, local bodies, and state Government Undertakings for the candidates of OBCs and 30 per cent each for women and economically weaker sections (only those candidates should be given this benefit whose family income was below the minimum income-tax limit) and 24 per cent seats in engineering, medical and other professional institutions for students of OBCs and grant of various other benefits like allotment of house sites, grant of scholarships, reimbursement of tution fees, etc. to OBCs. The State Government accepted the recommendations of Mungeri Lal Commission in October 1978 and this gave rise to a lot of agitation as both forward and backward communities were unsatisfied with Government's order. Based on that Report on Nov. 18, 1978 Karpoori Thakur Government issued a G.O. providing for reservation. The G.O. provoked widespread backlash on the part of the forward castes. The universities and colleges were closed. Trains and buses were attacked. The government property was damaged.

Subsequently, the Government of Bihar corrected this misconception in July, 1979 and clasified that the reservation quota indicated the minimum and not the maximum quota for backward class candidates. It was also clarified that the percentage of backward class candidates selected on merit should be adjusted against their reserved quota.

So far the identification of backward classes and most backward classes was done in an order to give separate percentage of reservations among them so as to ensure justice intra backward classes. Second point to be noted is that the issue of reservation to backward classes related to reservation in state services and not national services wherein no scheme of reservation was applicable for OBCs.

Mandal Commission was confronted with the issue of dividing backwards among backwards and most backwards on the plea of anti-reservationists that the benefit of reservation will be cornered by forwards among the backwards. Mandal clarified it on different counts.

1. Such arguments were given by the ruling elite which was keen on preserving its privileges. Thus reasoning was partisan one.
2. The objective of Mandal Report was not to provide job to BCs and convert them into forward, but to provide psychological 'spin off' and moral booster.[102]

Report reads:

> "It is not at all our contention that by offering a few thousand jobs to OBC candidates we shall be able to make 52 per cent of the Indian population as forward. But we must recognise that an essential part of the battle against social backwardness is to be fought in the minds of the backward people. In India, Government service has always been looked upon as a symbol of prestige and power. By increasing the representation of OBCs in Government services, we give them an immediate feeling of participation in the governance of this country.... (para 13.4, p. 57)"[103]

The Report narrates the effect of reservational services to OBCs "when a backward class candidate becomes a collector or a Superintendent of Police, the material benefits accruing from its position are restricted to the members of his family only. But the psychological spin off of this phenomenon is tremendous; the entire community of that backward class candidates feels socially uplifted. Even when no tangible benefits flow to the community at large, the feeling that now it has its "Own man" in the "Corridors of power" works as a moral booster (para 13.4, p. 57).[104]

The Mandal Commission's refusal to divide backward among backward and more backward depended on the class character of reservation intended under Article 16(4)—for the above described reason. Even in his Minute of dissent Mr L.R. Naik, Ex-M.P. divided backwards into two categories (i) the intermediate backward classes, and (ii) Depressed classes. Treating latter nearer to SC/STs, he suggested separate treatment for them. Mr Naik preferred division among backwards on ancient adage "if a big fish and a small fish are put together, the former will swallow the latter." His division of backward classes was for separate treatment and not for denial to any segment.

His recommendation may be put as under:

Category of B.Cs	*Population Percentage*	*Reservation Percentage*
Intermediate Backward class	26.44	12
Depressed Backward class	25.56	15
Total	52.00	27

The issue of division of backward classes again came up in the *Mandal Case*. The majority was of view that there is no constitutional bar to classify the backward classes of citizens into backward and more backward categories. It did not recommend that it needs to be done. It only said that if the Government chose to do that that would not be invalid. Such a divison was approved on two grounds:

1. On Mandal Criteria itself the division is approved, as any caste, group or class which scored eleven or more points was constituted as a backward class. It is not as if all the

many thousands of castes/groups/class scored identical points. There may have been some castes/groups/classes which have score points between 20 to 22 and there may have been some who have scored points between 11 to 13. It cannot reasonably be denied that there is no difference between these two sets of castes/groups/classes.[105]

2. Article 16(4) recognises only one class viz., "Backward Class of citizens" and does not speak of SCs/STs separately as does Article 15(4). Even then SCs/STs are included in "Backward Class of citizens" and separate reservation is made for them. The logic behind it is that if SCs/STs and OBCs are grouped together, OBCs will take away all the vacancies leaving SCs and STs high and dry. The same logic also warrants categorisation as between more backward and backward.[106]

The majority was not emphatic on it. It clarified: "we do not mean to say—we may reiterate—that should be done. We are only saying that if a state chooses to do it, it is not impermissible in law."[107]

Pandian, J. dealt extenso with OM dated 25th September, 1991 whose para 2(1) read: "Within the 27 per cent of the vacancies in civil posts and services under the Government of India reserved for SEBCs, preference shall be given to candidates belonging to the poorer sections of SEBCs. In case sufficient number of such candidates are not available, unfilled vacancies shall be filled by the other SEBC candidates."

The learned judge observed that if means test is adopted to divide SEBCs it may serve as an umbrella for many to get into this segregated section by adopting all sorts of illegal and unethical practices. The test may also be totally unworkable and impracticable in that determination of "getting some body in and getting some body out" from among same identified SEBCs. In his opinion if means test argument is accepted and put into action by scanning the identified SEBCs by applying a super imposition test, the very aim and purpose of reservation, intended for the socially backward class would reach only a cul-de-sac and the identified SEBCs would be left in a maz."[108] The learned judge ruled out division between and among SEBCs for the following various reasons.

(1) The expression 'poorer sections' mentioned in para 2(i) of the amended office memorandum of 1991 denotes a division among SEBCs on economic criteria. Therefore, no division or sub-classification as 'poorer section' and other backward classes (non poorer section) out of the identified SEBCs can be made by application of 'means test' based on economic criterion. Therefore, he struck down para 2(i) of the said O.M.

(2) If this apex Court puts its seal of approval to para 2(i) of the second OM whereunder a section of the people under the label of 'poorer sections' is carved out from among the SEBCs, it becomes a law declared by this Court for the entire nation under Article 141 of the Constitution and is binding on all the Courts within the territory of India and that the decision of this Court on a constitutional question cannot be over-ridden except by the constitutionally recognised norms. When such is the legal position, the law so declared should be capable of being effectively implemented in its full measure, in the generality of cases and not confined in its applicability to some rare or freakish cases. The law should not be susceptible of being abused or misused and leave scope for manipulation which can remain undetected. If the law so declared by this Court is indecisive and leaves perceivable loopholes, by the aid of which one can defeat or circumvent or nullify that law by adopting an insidious, tricky, fraudulent and strategic device to suit one's purpose then that law will become otiose and remain as a dead letter.

He gave various reasons in support of his opinion that this process of elimination or exclusion of a section of people from and out of the same category of SEBCs cannot be sustained leave apart the authority of the Government to take any decision and formulate its policy in its discretion or opinion provided that the policy is not violative of any constitutional or legal provisions or that discretion or opinion is not vitiated by non-application of mind, arbitrariness, formulation of collateral grounds or consideration of irrelevant and extraneous material, etc.

(a) If annual gross income of a government servant derived from all his sources during a financial year is taken as a test for identifying the 'poorer sections', that test could be defeated by reducing the income below the ceiling limit by a Government servant voluntarily going on leave on loss of pay for the few months during that financial year so that he could bring his annual income within the ceiling limit and claim the benefit of reservation meant for 'poorer sections'. Similarly, a person owning extensive land also may lay a portion of his land fellow in any particular year or dispose of a portion of his land so as to bring his agricultural income below the ceiling limit so that he may fall within the category of 'poorer sections'.

(b) The fluctuating fortunes or misfortunes also will play an important role in determining whether one gets within the area of 'poorer sections' or gets out of it.

(c) Take a case wherein there are two brothers belonging to the same family of 'backward class' of whom one is employed in Government service and another is privately employed or has chosen some other profession. The annual income of the Government employee if slightly exceeds the ceiling limit, his children will not fall within the category of 'poorer sections' whereas the other brothers can deceitfully show his income within the ceiling limit so that his children can enjoy that benefit.

(d) Among the pensioners also, the above anomaly will prevail as pointed out in *Janki Prasad*.[109]

(e) Any member of SEBCs who is in Government job and is on the verge of his superannuation and whose income exceeds the ceiling limit, will go out of the purview of 'poorer sections' but in the next financial year, he may get into the 'poorer sections' if his total pensionary benefits fall within the ceiling limit.

(f) A person who is within the definition of 'poorer sections' may suddenly go out of its purview by any intervening fortuitous circumstances such as getting a marital alliance in a rich family or by obtaining any wind-fall wealth.

(g) If poverty test is made applicabale for identifying the 'poorer sections' then in a given case wherein a person is socially oppressed and educationally backward but economically slightly advanced in a particular year, he will be deprived of getting the preferential treatment.

The above are only by way of illustrations, though this type can be multiplied, for the purpose of showing that a person can voluntarily reduce his income and thereby circumvent the declared law of this Court. In all the above illustrations, enumerated as (a) to (g), the chance of 'getting into or getting out of' the definition of 'poorer sections' will be like a see-saw depending upon the fluctuating fortunes or misfortunes.

(3) The income test for ascertaining poverty may severally suffer from the vice of corruption and also encourage patronage and nepotism.

(4) When the Government has accepted and approved the list of SEBCs, identified by the test of social backwardness, educational backwardness and economic backwardness, there is no justification by dividing the SEBCs into two groups, thereby allowing one section to fully enjoy the benefits and another on a condition only if there are unfilled vacancies.

(5) The elimination of a section of SEBCs by putting an arbitrary and unnecessary barrier on the basis of economic criterion is absolutely unjustified. This process of elimination or exclusion of a section of SEBCs will be tantamount to pushing those persons into the arena of open competition along with the forward class if there are no unfilled vacancies out of the total 27 per cent meant for SEBCs. This will cause an irretrievable injustice to all the non-poorer sections though they are also theoretically declared as SEBCs.

(6) The second OM providing a scanning test is neither feasible nor practicable, it will be perceptible and effectual only if the entire identified backward class enjoys the benefit of reservation.

(7) The proposed means test is highly impressionistic test, the result of which is likely to be influenced by many uncertain and imponderable facts.

(8) It may theoretically sound well but in practice attempts may be made in an underhanded way to get round the problem."

Pandian, J. did not think that the above explanation was

exhaustive and pointed out that it is "only the tip of iceberg and more of it is likely to surface at the time when any scanning process and superimposition tests are put into practice."[110]

Thommen, J. pointed out that among the backward classes of citizens correctly identified based on poverty, illiteracy, disease unhygienic living conditions, low caste and consequential isolation, preference may be legitimately extended to the comparatively poorer or more disadvantaged sections.[111]

Sawant J. also ruled that there may be a great diference in backwardness among the backwards themselves therefore it is not only advisable but also imperative to make the sub-classification if all backward classes are to achieve equitable benefit for the special provisions under the Constitution. However, the learned judge said that for each of them a special quota has to be prescribed. This was recommended because of obvious reason that "if it is not done, as in the present case, and the reserved posts are first offered to the more backward and only the remaining to the backward or less backward, the more backward may take away all the posts leaving the backward with no posts.[112] And, as a result "the backward will neither get his post in the reserved quota nor in the general category for want of capacity to compete with the forward."[113]

Therefore, Sawant, J. was of the view that Article 16(4) permits classification of backward classes into backward and most backward classes but such classification is permitted only on the basis of degree of social backwardness and not based on the economic consideration alone.[114] Anyway, if backward classes are classified into backward and more or most backward classes, separate quotas of reservations will have to be alloted for each of such classes. Accordingly, Sawant, J. expressed the opinion that in the absence of such separate quotas, the reservations will be illegal.[115]

Kuldip Singh, J. favoured classification of backward classes in categories and sub-categories for identification. Sahai, J took an entirely different view and ruled out any further classification of backward classes under Article 16(4). The following picture emerges as to point of classification of backward classes into backward and most backward or poorer section different from others.

Broadly speaking seven judges agreed to classification of backward classes and two judges did not allow any sub-classification. The purpose of division may be served better if it is taken in a spirit in which Karpoori Thakur formula adopted it or which was devised by Chinnappa Reddy Commission in Karnataka. Likewise Cheddi Lal Sathi Commission on Most Backward Classes in UP categorised backward classes into three groups and prescribed separate reservation percentage for them in services as follow:

	Name of Category	*Percentage of Reservation*
1.	List 'A' comprising those who are landless labourers, unskilled workers, non-artisans and domestic servants	17
2.	List 'B' comprising marginal and small cultivator	10
C.	List 'C' Muslim Backward Classes	2.5
	Total	29.5

The main aim must be to give representation to all sections of backward classes and not to isolate some by giving preference to most backward or poorer section as Thommen, J. desired in *Mandal Case* or the OM dated 25.9.91 spoke. The Memo spoke that "within the 27 per cent of the vacancies in civil posts and services under the Government of India reserved for SEBCs, preference shall be given to candidates belonging to the poorer sections of SEBCs. In case sufficient number of such candidates are not available, unfilled vacancies shall be filled by the other SEBC candidates." Though majority approved of it when the government identified them but it is conceded that isolation of some backwards may be the cause of injustice to them. Sawant, J. has very well pointed out that "for each of them a special quota has to be prescribed. If it is not done, as in the present case (OM No. 2) and the reserved posts are first offered to the more backward and only the remaining to backward or less backward, the more backward may take away all the posts leaving the backward with no posts. The backward will neither get his post in the reserved quota nor in the general category for lack of capacity to compete with the forward.[116] It is submitted that there is another danger towards which the attention of the Hon'ble Court was not drawn, i.e., dangers to backwards falling prey of unwritten reservations where minimum qualifications are laid down and worth is left to be assessed by the selection committee consisting mainly of upper caste members and even if selection committee does justice, the backward teachers may fell victim of Executive Council, as illustrated by the examples of withholding promotions of backward classes teachers in Gorakhpur university despite the unanimous recommendation of Selection Committees in the Department of Law and Geography. Reservation will atleast ensure merit among backwards otherwise worst of forward having minimum or in some cases even without that will win the run of open competitions for Lecturers/Readers/Professors and best talented backward may loose because of unwritten reservation.

The whole thing depends upon priority and objective of Article 16(4). Since the aim of Article 16(4) is not to provide jobs to few individuals but to ensure share in power of the governance of the country, the division among deprived sections should be applied only after the quotas have been fully filled.[117]

Backward Caste's Right to Reservation

The nature of reservational right as fundamental right or otherwise is very much linked to the nature of the provision of Article 16(4). During the first two decades of the functioning of the Constitution there had been some controversy on the point. Dealing with clause (4) of Article 15 in Balaji versus State of Mysore,[118] Gajandragadkar, J. ruled that "there is no doubt that Article 15(4) has to be read as a proviso or an exception to Articles 15(1) and 29(2). Following Balaji ruling the majority in T. Devadasan versus Union of India[119] said that "clause (4) of Article 16 is by way of a proviso or an exception to clause (1)." However, Subba Rao, J. expressed the opinion in his dissent that Article 16(4) is not an exception to Article 16(1). The dissenting opinion of Subba Rao, J. took some time to take the shape of rule. In meanwhile in a series of cases Article 16(4) was conceded as an exception to the general rule of equality enshrined in clause (1).[120] The dissent of Subba Rao, J. in Devadasan case received majority support in State of Kerala versus N.M. Thomas[121] wherein Ray, C.J. and

Mathew, Krishna Iyer and Fuzl Ali, JJ. expressed the opinion that Article 16(4) is not an exception to Article 16(1). It is an emphatic way of stating a principle implicit in Article 16(1). *Thomas* ruling held that Article 16(1) being a facet of equality enshrined in Article 14 permits reasonable classification just as Article 14 does. This view of *Thomas case* was considered as correct one by Chief Justice Kania and Venkatachaliah, Ahmadi and Jeevan Reddy, JJ. in Indira Sawhney versus Union of India.[122] It was explained:

> "...Article 16(1) does permit reasonable classification for ensuring attainment of the equality of opportunity assured by it. For assuring equality of opportunity it may well be necessary in certain situations to treat unequally situated persons unequally. Not doing so, would perpetuate and accentuate inequality."[123]

It was further made clear that:

> "Article 16(4) is an instance of such classification, put into place the matter beyond controversy. The "backward class of citizens are classified as a separate category deserving a special treatment in the nature of reservation of appointments/posts in the services of the State . . . It is an instance of classification implict and permitted by clause (1)."[124]

Mandal case ruling further clarified situational differences and changing judicial outlook since *Balaji* and *Devadasan*. It elaborated, "it must be remembered that at that time it was not yet recognised by this court that Article 16(1) being a facet of Article 14 does implicitly permit classification. Once this characteristic was recognised the theory of clause (4) being an exception to clause (1) became untenable. It had to be accepted that clause (4) is an instance of classification inherent in clause (1)."[125]

Pandian, J. agreed with majority that Article 16(4) is neither an exception nor a proviso to Article 16(1).[126] Sawant, J in his concurring view clarified that clause (4) of Article 16 is merely an emphatic way of stating what is implicit in clause (1).[127] He explained what was otherwise clear in clause (1) where the expression "equality of opportunity" is not used in a formal but in a positive sense, was made explicit in clause (4) so that there was no mistake in understanding either the real import of the "right to equality" enshrined in the Constitution or the intention of the

Constitution Framers in that behalf. In this way Article 16(4) carves out from different classes for whom reservation can be made, a specific class, viz. the backward class of citizens, for emphasis and to put things beyond doubt.[128]

Kuldip Singh and R.M. Sahai, JJ agreed on the point that Article 16(1) and Article 16(4) operate in the same field. Article 16(4) is another fact of Article 16(1). It exclusively provides for reservation which is one of the forms of classification. Article 16(4) being a special provision regarding reservation it completely takes away such classification from the purview of Article 16(1).[129] Sahai, J. made it clear that Articles 16(1) and 16(4) both are directed towards achieving equality of opportunity under the State.[130]

As a matter of fact out of nine Hon'ble judges in *Mandal case* Thommen, J. was alone on the point who regarded clause (4) of Article 16 as an exception or a a proviso to the general rule of equality enshrined in Article 16(1).[131]

The general trend and overwhelming opinion on the point is that Article 16(4) is the very part of equalitarian justice. Article 16(1) and (4) operate in the same field. The crucial question that comes up: can the right envisaged under Article 16(4) be claimed as a fundamental right by backward castes?

The leading majority judgement is silent on the point. Pandian, J. in his concurring judgement considers clause (4) of Article 16 as an enabling provisions and permissive in character.[132] Thommen, J. in his dissenting view also considered Article 16(4) is an enabling provision conferring a discretionary power on the State.[133] Sahai, J. dealt most extensively with the issue. According to him, Article 16(1) is broader in sweep and expansive in reach and Article 16(4) is restricted in approach and narrow in applicability. Former applies to all citizens whereas latter is available to 'any' class of backward citizens. Use of word "all" in Article 16(1) and 'any' in Article 16(4) read together suggest that they are part of the same scheme. But Sahai, J. elaborated the difference in nature of the two provisions:

> "The one is substantive equality and the other is protective equality. Article 16(1) is a fundamental right of a citizen whereas Article 16(4) is an obligation of the State. The former is enforceable in a court of law, whereas the latter

is "not constitutional compulsion" but an enabling provision . . . One is mandatory and operates automatically whereas the other comes into play on identification of backward class of citizens and their inadequate represenation."[134]

Pandian, J. as referred, earlier considered Article 16(4) as enabling and permissive power. But the learned judge clarified that "the power conferred on the State under Article 16(4) is one coupled with a duty and, therefore, the State has to exercise that power for the benefit of all those, namely, backward class for whom it is intended.[135]

The issue of the reservational right as fundamental right has become a debatable issue. Professor M.P. Singh (1994) comments that "due to this variety of provisions, doubt persists whether Articles 15(4) and 16(4) confer fundamental rights." He gives following justifications for his conclusions :

(1) Judicial pronouncements like Thomas, Akhil Bharatiya Soshit Karamchari Sangh (Rly) versus Union of India[136] and *Mandal case* establish that Article 16(4) is not an exception to Article 16(1). It is rather an effective method of realising and implementing it. He points out, "Clause (4) does not derogate from anything in clauses (1) and (2) of Article 16 but rather gives them positive support and content. It serves the same function, i.e., securing of equality of opportunity, as do clauses (1) and (2). Obviously, therefore, it is as much a fundamental right as clauses (1) and (2) or any other provision of that Article."[137]

(2) The proper understanding of equality, i.e., right to be treated equally among equals and unequal treatment of equals is equally a violation of that right as equal treatment of unequals. In relation to positive equality or affirmative action he refers to Prof. Ronald M. Dworkin who says comprehensive and satisfactory test by keeping separate the right to equal treatment and the right to treatment as equal. Acording to him the latter is the fundamental right while the former is only a derivative right. The right to treatment as an equal consists in equal respect and concern while the right to equal treatment consists in identical

treatment.[138] Identical treatment is neither possible nor consistent with right to equality.[139] Singh argues that every difference in treatment is not *per se* inconsistent to equality. It becomes so if it lacks equal concern. He concludes that 15(4) promotes equality as do Articles 15(1) and 29(2). Therefore, it is as much a fundamental right as Article 15(1) and 29(2) are. This logic also applies to Article 16(4) which is as much a fundamental rights as Articles 16(1) and 16(2) are.

(3) Constitutional practice of allowing State action under Articles 15(4) and 16(4) through executive orders without legislation and declaring that no fundamental right or for that matter any right can be denied without the authority of law also prove that Articles 15(4) and 16(4) are fundamental rights. The obvious reason is that the two propositions consistently adhered by Courts cannot stand together if Article 15(4) is considered an exception to Articles 15(1) and 29(2) or Article 16(4) is treated as exception to rest of the provisions of that Article. They can stand together if the two clauses are treated as aspect of the fundamental rights.

(4) It is also warranted by the fundamental right's harmonisation with the Directive Principles of State Policy and giving effect to the Directive Principles in association with fundamental rights.[140] The Court's view is that directive principles are not justiciable *per se* but become so after a legislation is passed in pursuance of them.[141] Irrespective of proclaimed non-justiciability of directive principles, the Supreme Court has recognised a fundamental right to education exactly in terms of the Directive Principles in Articles 41, 45 and 46 read with the Fundamental Right to life and personal liberty in Article 21.[142] And therefore, Article 15(4) and 16(4) are to be considered as a fundamental right in view of Article 46 read with Article 21.

(5) Article 335 may also support the opinion that Article 16(4) is a fundamental right. As pointed out by Kania, C.J. and Venkatachaliah, Ahmadi and Jeevan Reddy, JJ. in *Mandal*

Case the mandate of Article 335 is not maintenance of efficiency of administration but to take claims of SCs/STs consistent with a maintenance of efficiency of administration. Admonition in Article 335 is to be respected equally while considering claims of Other Backward Classes and Other Weaker Sections.[143] Now after *Mandal case* and read into formula of the Supreme Court Article 335 is also applicable to OBCs. That Article speaks of claims — one of the forms of right and when it is read with Article 16 (4) it makes the latter fundamental right.

(6) The rule of *Ubijus ibi remedium* also justifies that Articles 15(4) and 16(4) are fundamental rights. So far, state actions have been challenged and inaction has not been brought before the Court but it is likely to be brought at appropriate time. Quoting *Mandal case* and direction of Mr Justice Pandian, Singh points out, "Atleast one of the majority judges did infact issue directions in *Mandal case* for the immediate implementation of the government notification even though the petition was against the State action."[144]

Another view point was given by Parmanand Singh.[145] He finds it illogical, unsound as well as unbalanced and even undesirable in the light of D.M.K. leadership's claim of 69 per cent reservation in Tamil Nadu despite *Mandal case* and Kerala's unwillingness to implement creamy layer. His main stress is on the following grounds:

1. Articles 15(4) and 16(4) are subject to many limitations like: (a) firm evidence of clear and legitimate identification of backward classes; (b) impermissibility of reservation in promotions; (c) no reservation in specialities and super specialities like Medicine and Engineering, University Professorship, Defence, Space Science and Nuclear Research.
2. If they are recognised as guaranteed right each individual claim to secure enforcement of such right will be subject to judicial determination.
3. Even until *Mandal case* courts are not responsive to such claims as a matter of enforceable right. Even *Mandal case* has recognised Articles 15(4) and 16(4) as enabling provision.

4. A distinction has to be made between equality as a matter of policy and equality as a matter of right. Articles 15(4) and 16(4) present the matter of policy. According to him a policy stipulates a collective goal which a community seeks to achieve. A right is an individual claim which seeks to protect individual interest. Thus, Articles 15(4) and 16(4) may be considered as authorising norms in Kelsenian sense, justifying encroachment of the individual's right to equality for achieving real equality for the members of the disadvantaged groups.[146]
5. Professor Dworkin's thesis of right as 'trump' advanced for the defence of affirmative action may help M.P. Singh's claim of preferential discrimination but not for justifying a fundamental right to reservation.[147] In the opinion of Parmanand Singh, the justification of debate that takes place in America is of little relevance in India in view of a clear Constitutional policy of compensatory discrimination as mentioned in Articles 15(4) and 16(4).[148]
6. Main thesis of fundamental right of reservation based on judicial verdicts as to the nature of Articles 15(4) and 16(4) not as an exception to 15(1) and 16(1) and (2) but as a separate provision as part of equality also looses force in view of: (i) non-abstante clause attached with Article 15(4) which is wider and Article 16(4) is restricted to reservation and exceptional nature is not disturbed even by *Mandal case*. Even *Thomas* supports extent of reservation and does not acknowledge a fundamental right to affirmative action.[149]
7. Article 16(4) exhausts all power of backward class preferences and in this sense is recognised as an exception to clause (1) of Article 16 in relation to backward classes.
8. The analogy of right to education in view of directive principles and Articles 21 is also disputable. Such positive claims can only be promoted and are not capable of being 'enforced' by affirmative litigation. It can be further justified in light of reluctance of court to recognise right to work and means of livelihood as enforceable right[150] and restricting of right to education upto primary education in *Unnikrishnan's case*.

Accepting the weakening thread of Hohfeldian right-duty correlativity, Parmanand Singh arrived at conclusion that "the claims advanced in guise of right to reservation should be accepted as a social or collective goals or as a matter of policy rather than acknowledged as fundamental rights."

Articles 15(4) and 16(4) as Fundamental Rights

The move towards recognition of Article 16(4) as fundamental right gained strength after *Thomas case* though the seeds were sown by Justice Subba Rao in *Devadasan* through his dissent that Article 16(4) has not really carved out an exception, but has preserved a power untrammeled by the other provisions of the Article.[151] Thomas began a new constitutional vista and a foreigner eminent scholar[152] on competing equalities in India foresaw a number of contingencies during the starting year of 1980s.

"*First*, do the litigants and their lawyers have the legal imagination to devise these claims;

Second, do they have the capacity to organise to sustain such litigation and press for the implementation of favourable rulings? (Of Course, the capacity for organisation might be enhanced by creative deployment of legal services.)

Third, are the judges like to be responsive to such claims, claims that ask them to depart from deeply held notions about judicial role? They would not only have to innovate original standards of what is appropriate movement towards equality, they would have to undertake a sustained activist monitoring of government that they may find both ideologically uncongenial and institutionally discomfiling.

Fourth, even if claimants come forward and courts are responsive, do the realities of litigation in India, the delay and maneuver and cost, make it possible for groups to improve their position through litigation against powerful adversaries?

Fifth, are the real barriers to improvement of the conditions of these groups reachable by even most well disposed and capable juiciary ?"[153]

Some illusion and dilemma is observed in judicial outlook. In Kumari Usha Rani versus M.D. University, Rohtak,[154] the power of the University to reduce seats for admission, to the Medical

College from 150 to 115 and reservation for backward classes from ten per cent to two per cent was challenged. Taking unconsciously recourse to Hohfeldian concept of right *strict sensu* M.M. Punchi, J. ruled that "Article 16(4) does not confer any right to a citizen to have created reservations in favour of any backward class of citizens. Correspondingly, there is no constitutional duty imposed on the Government to make reservations in favour of Scheduled Castes/Scheduled Tribes and Backward Classes.[155] Treating Articles 16(4) and 15(4) as enabling provisions giving only discretionary power on State, the learned judge ruled that "no one can claim reservation as a matter of right".[156] More surprising was the decision of Bombay High Court in Anil versus The Dean, Government Medical College, Nagpur,[157] wherein a backward class student challenged Rule 5A(d) which provided ten per cent reservation for backward classes. The clarification issued to the Rule provided that "10 per cent is not an overall ceiling for the OBC candidates. It is open to the OBC candidates to secure more than 10 per cent seats on the basis of merit. However, if the admissions they secure on merit are less than 10 per cent there should be reservation for them to the extent of the shortfall below 10 per cent." The contention of backward classes was 10 per cent seats must be reserved in addition merit seats irrespective of those seats occupied by BCs too. And this was the right content. But it did not appeal to the High Court. Rejecting the argument Ginwala, J. ruled that 'provision made in Clause (4) of Article 15 is only by way of exception to the fundamental right guaranteed under Clause (1) of Article 15, and Clause (2) of Article 29 and that it is only enabling provision."[158] Ginwala, J. emphatically ruled that "Clause (4) of Article 15 of Constitution does not confer any right, much less a fundamental right in the classes, castes or tribes specified in that clause to have seats reserved for them in services or educational institutions."[159] It need not be described here that logic in both the cases was misplaced and so unconvincing and against the basic philosophy of reservational justice that it has lost its force in light of later decisions of the Supreme Court and specific rules made by the government explaining application of the reservation rule.

In P. and T. SC/ST Employees Welfare Association versus Union of India,[160] the Supreme Court directed the Government of

India to pursue the same policy of reservation for SCs and STs in the Post and Telegraph department as it pursued in other departments. Thus, if the government does something to discriminate among the various departments of the government services, the Supreme Court has chosen to interfere. In the above referred case by an agreement in 1983 between the Ministry of Communication and certain Associations a consistent policy of promotion to higher cadre was fixed after 16 years irrespective of being SC/ST general category members. Earlier SC/ST candidates were getting promotion after completion of 12 to 13 years. Delivering the judgment of the Court Venkataramiah, J. made it clear that:

"Deprivation violated the equality clause of the Constitution. Similar advantage was being enjoyed by persons belonging to the Scheduled Castes and Scheduled Tribes in other Departments and only the employees of P and T Department had been deprived of it. While it may be true that no writ can be issued ordinarily compelling the Government to make reservation under Article 16(4) which is only an enabling clause, the circumstances in which the members belonging to the Scheduled Castes and Scheduled Tribes in the Posts and Telegraphs Department are deprived of indirectly the advantage of such reservation which they were enjoing earlier while others who are similarly situated in the other departments are allowed to enjoy it make the action of Government discriminatory and invite intervention by the Court."[161] In this case the court did not take recourse to Article 16(4) but granted relief under equality clause. It could have very well said that once the government creates right in favour of certain classes it could not deprive them of that benefit and to do so would violate Article 16(4). In Joy Kanta Hira versus State of Assam[162] the High Court did the same thing. It granted relief to a member of SC which he was entitled under a government notification but was denied by administration. The High Court supported its decision by reference to Articles 39 and 46 of the Constitution. The same analogy would apply to OBCs.

Is Reservation to OBCs Anti-Meritarian?

Reservation as such is argued to be anti-meritarian. This blunt conclusion is drawn in view of lowering down of admission marks in favour of those for whom reservation is intended.

Furthermore, most of the objections against reservation refer to the period when reservation had not consolidated itself into fruitful exercise and it was meant only for SCs/STs. OBCs were not given such benefits in Central services. So far as it is concerned upto first quarter century since the commencement of the Constitution, it was assumed that reservations were necessarily anti-meritarian. The views of Gajendragadkar, J. in Balaji versus State of Mysore,[163] dealing with admissions in University education, was that the inevitable consequence of reservation is lowering of merit.[164] The learned judge was not agreeable to concede the argument of Attorney General that reservation of a large number of seats for the weaker section of society would not affect either the depth of or efficiency of scholarship at all. The learned A.G. supposed his argument with the Report of the Backward Classes Commission that had found no complaint in the State of Madras, Andhra, Travancore-Cochin and Mysore where the system of recruiting candidates from OBCs to reserve quota had been in vogue for many decades.[165] This impressionistic note as to anti-meritarianism of reservation was again expressed in Janaki Prasad Parimoo versus State of J and K[166] wherein it was noted that "it is implicit in the idea of reservation that a less meritorious person be preferred to another who is more meritorious." In minority view Khanna, J. echoed same voice in State of Kerala versus N.M. Thomas.[167] Even Subba Rao, J. who did not agree with the above view, had conceded in his dissent in T. Devadasan versus Union of India[168] that 'it is inevitable in the nature of reservation that there will be a lowering of standards to some extent." But he allowed it in view of prescribed minimum qualifications.

A change in judicial outlook is discernible since the middle of 1970s. By this period some practical outlook stated as to determination of merit. Mr Justice V.R. Krishna Iyer more explictly decried the impression that reservation was anti-meritarian. In State of Kerala versus N.M. Thomas,[169] Krishna Iyer, J. said:

> "Efficiency means, in terms of good government not marks in examinations only, but responsible and responsive service to the people. A chaotic genius is a grave danger in public administration. The inputs of efficiency include a sense of belonging and of accountability which springs

> in the bosom of the bureacuracy (not pejoratively used) if its composition takes in also the weaker segments of "we the people of India". No other understanding can reconcile the claim of the radical present and the hangover of the unjust past."[170]

Krishna Iyer, J. again questioned the concept of merit in Akhil Bharatiya Soshit Karamchari Sangh (Rly) versus Union of India.[171] The learned judge asked the fundamental question: what is merit and suitability? And he himself gave the answer: "Elites whose sympathies with the masses have dried up are, from the standard of the Indian people, least suitable to run government and least meritorious to handle state business, if we envision a Service State in which the millions are the consumers. A sensitized heart and a vibrant head, turned to the tears of the people, will speedily quicken the developmental needs of the country, including its rural stretches and slum squalor."[172]

The learned Judge ruled that—

> "Sincere dedication and intellectual integrity—these are some of the major components of 'merit' and 'suitability'—not the degrees from Oxford or Cambridge, Harvard or Stanford or Simian—though, Indian Institutions."[173]

The learned judge also pointed out the shortcoming of examination system, said Krishna Iyer, J. "our examination system makes memory the master of merit" and banishes creativity in exile.[174] Echoing with arguments of Krishna Iyer, J., Chinnappa Reddy, J. touched the more real problem of Indian Society in K.C. Vasanth Kumar versus State of Karnataka.[175]

The learned judge said:

> "The mere securing of marks at an examination may not necessarily markout a good administrator. An efficient administrator, one takes it must be one who possesses among other qualities the capacity to understand with sympathy and, therefore, to tackle bravely the problems of a large segment of population constituting the weaker sections of the people. And, who better than the ones belonging to those very sections?"[176]

Chinnappa Reddy, J. put forth some very serious and realist questions:

> Why not ask ourselves why 35 (now 57) years after Independence, the position of the Scheduled Castes, etc. has not greatly improved? Is it not a legitimate question to ask whether things might have been different had the District Administrators and the State and Central bureaucrats been drawn in larger numbers from these classes?[177]

Reddy, J. wished that one need not make a fastidious fetish of it (meritarian plea).

The issue was again brought up with new vigour in Indira Sawhney versus Union of India.[178] The learned counsel for petitioners argued that reservation necessarily means appointment of less meritorious persons, which in turn leads to lowering of efficiency in administration. Kania, C.J. and Venkataramiah, Ahmadi, Jeevan Reddy,[179] Pandian[180] and Thommen, JJ[181] were of the opinion that in light of the requirement of Article 335, which speaks about SCs/STs is equally applicable to reservation to OBCs as such cannot be considered to be anti-meritarian. But they did not discuss in detail on merit and illustration. Kania, C.J. and Venkataramiah, Ahmadi, Jeevan Reddy and Pandian, JJ. accepted exception to the rule of reservation to certain services and posts. Since Sawant, J. alone discussed the issue at length with examples it would be better to discuss his observations in continuity. One may very well agree with O. Chinnapa Reddy, J. that "efficiency is very much on the lips of the privileged whenever reservation is mentioned."[182] Sawant, J. gave befitting answer to merit-mongers. He tried to attack at the denial of participation opportunity to backward classes. In his words "the consequences of the *status quo* are startling and ruinous to the country. One of the major causes of the backwardness of the country in all walks of life is the denial of more than 75 per cent of the population of an opportunity to take part in the running of the affairs of the country."[183] He issued a note of caution "where a majority of the population is denied its share in actual power, there exists no real democracy."[184] In his opinion, "if all sections of the society had such opportunity, this country's achievements in all fields and walk of life would have been many times more. That this is a realistic estimate and not a mere rhetoric is proved by history."[185] Citing the example of Dr B.R. Ambedkar, Sawant, J. made it clear—

> "If what is handed down to us as history is to be believed, then the epic of `Mahabharata' was penned by Vyasa, who was born of a fisher woman; Ramayana was authored by Valmiki, who belonged to a tribe forced to live by depredations. The immortal poet Kalidasa's ancestry is not known. These few instances demonstrate that intelligence, perception, character, scholarship, and talent are not a monopoly of any section of the society. Given opportunity, those who are condemned to the lowest stations in life can rise to the loftiest status in society. One can only guess how much this country has lost for want of opportunities to the vast majority all these centuries."[186]

How to judge the merit? Those who advance merit contention unfortunately neglect the basic fact that "the traditional method of evaluating merit is neither scientific nor realistic. Marks in one time oral or written test do not necessarily prove the worth or suitability of an individual to a particular post, much less do they indicate his comparative calibre. What is more, for various posts, different tests have to be applied to judge the suitability."[187] Sawant, J repudiated the charge of anti-meritarian and ruled that the assumption that the reservations lead to the appointment or admission of non-meritorious candidates is factually not correct.

1. In the first instance, there are minimum qualifying marks prescribed for appointment/admission.[188]
2. Secondly, there is a tough competition among the backward class candidates for the seats in reserved quota. This has resulted in the cut-off marks for the seats in the reserved quota, reaching very near to cut-off line for seats in the general quota as some surveys made on the subject show.[189]

The learned judge reproduced a sample of such surveys made for the State of Tamil Nadu admissions in professional courses by Era Sezhian and published in the issue of *The Hindu* dated October 8, 1990.

SELECTION TO PROFESSIONAL COURSES: CUT-OFF LEVEL

(Percentage)

Course of study	*Open Competition*	*Backward*	*Most Backward*	*Scheduled Caste*
Engineering Course (Anna University)				
Computer Science	97.98	96.58	93.25	84.38
Electronics	97.74	96.08	92.16	82.22
Electrical	95.84	95.42	91.48	81.98
Mechanical Engg.	95.78	94.10	90.66	79.21
Medical Course (University of Madras)				
M.B.B.S.	95.22	93.18	89.62	83.98
Agricultural Course (Agricultural University Coimbatore)				
B.Sc. Agri	90.90	90.08	86.10	78.04
B.E. Agri	92.66	91.96	87.46	76.14
Veterinary (Tamil Nadu Veterinary and Animal Sciences University)				
B.V.Sc.	94.90	93.48	91.18	85.24
B.F. Sc.	96.96	95.58	95.02	93.02

The above study reveals that differences are very meagre. And pertinent question of Sawant, J. was: by what logic can it be said that the above marks secured by the candidates from the backward classes are not meritorious?[190]

On the other hand leading majority decision of Jeevan Reddy, J. for himself and three other brethren judges and concurring decision of Pandian, J. did not go at length with the issue. Referring to conflicting opinions reservation means appointment of less meritorious and that marks obtained at the examination/test/ interview at the stage of entry into service is not an indicium of the inherent merit of a candidate, Jeevan Reddy, J. did not think it necessary to express at any length the correctness of such opinions.[191] He took a middle course. Conceding that efficiency, competence and merit may not be synonymous even then the relevance and importance of merit at the stage of initial recruitment cannot be ignored. The leading majority judgment pointed out that "it cannot also be neglected that the very idea of reservation implies selection of a less meritorious person".[192] However, it was conceded that "this much cost has to be paid, if the constitutional promise of social justice is to be redeemed." Again, the majority had firm believe that:

> "Given an opportunity, members of these classes are bound to overcome their initial disadvantages and would compete with—and may, in some cases, excell — members of open competition. It is undeniable that nature has endowed merit upon members of backward classes as much as it had endowed upon members of other classes and that what is required is an opportunity to prove it. It may not, therefore, be said that reservations are anti-meritarian. Merit there is even among the reserved candidates and the small difference, that may be allowed at the stage of initial recruitment is bound to disappear in course of time. These members too will compete with and improve their efficiency along with others."[193]

The Court observed that in some cases removal of minimum qualifying marks in cases of SCs/STs in admissions to medical course as demonstrated in State of M.P. versus Nivedita Jain[194] should not be treated as trend setter due to its falling under Article 15. In that case Article 335 was not attracted. The Court ruled that "in case of Article 16, Article 335 would be relevant and any order on the lines of the order of the Government of Madhya Pradesh (in *Nivedita Jain*) would not be permissible, being inconsistent with the efficiency of administration."[195]

The majority, though dismissed the charge of anti-meritarianism against reservation, it formed the opinion that the very idea of reservation implies selection of a less meritorious persons. And this led it to declare certain services and position unreservable—either due to the nature of duties attached to them or level (hierarchy) at which they obtain and need merit alone to be counted.[196] Without being exhaustive the following list was given by majority with likelihood of more additions by the Government of India to declare services to which the rule of reservation would not apply.

1. Defence services including all technical posts therein but excluding civil posts.
2. All technical posts in establishments engaged in Research and Development including those linked with atomic energy and space and establishments engaged in production of defence equipment.
3. Teaching posts of Professors—and above, if any.
4. Posts in super specialities in Medicine, Engineering and other similar scientific and technical subjects, and
5. Posts of pilots (and co-pilots) in Indian Airlines and Air India.[197]

Such posts due to their nature and duties attached were treated to be such that call for highest level of intelligent skill and duties attached. They were considered to form a category apart — and therefore reservation therein may not be consistent with 'efficiency of administration' contemplated by Article 335. Pandian, J. agreed with exclusion of certain services mentioned in majority decisions to keep outside the rule of reservation.[198] Thommen, J. also ruled that reservation too has to be consistent with the need of efficiency in context of Article 335.[199]

It is to be noted that the above exceptions recorded by majority are based on two assumptions. *First*, reservation is inherently less meritorious, and *Second*, the open posts are filled strictly on merit without any extraneous considerations. It is submitted with respect that the majority failed to appreciate the real societal interest embedded in representation of all sections of the society in administration. The interpretation of *Mandal Case* observation on the point in Ajay Kumar Singh versus State of Bihar[200] is a welcome move. The Court did not rule out reservation in all cases narrated therein; it rather left to government to evolve a consistent policy on the issue. This aspect of the issue was very well narrated by Sawant, J. in his concurring judgement. Said Sawant, J.:

> "What should further not be forgotten is that hither to for centuries, there have been cent per cent reservations in practice in all fields, in favour of the high castes and classes, to the total exclusion of others. It was purely caste and caste-based reservation."

He further observed:

> "Administration in the States where reservations are in vogue for about three quarter of century now, further cannot be said to be inferior to others in any manner. The reservations are aided at securing proper representation in administration to all sections of the society, intelligence and administrative capacity being not monopoly of any one class, caste or community."[201]

There is flood of personal promotees and double personal promotees.[202] How are they promoted can be best seen in the article of Dr Armrik Singh, himself a noted scholar. In his article, 'Merit versus Mass Promotion'[203], he points out 'over the years decision-making in higher education has become less and less academic and more and more a matter of political expediency. Nothing illustrates this state of affairs more tellingly than the decision to institute the Merit Promotion Scheme (MPS) in the early 1980s. The experience since then has been highly disenchanting from the academic point of view. Out of over 350 Professors in Delhi University, about 300 are what is decisively called 'promotees'; it is only the remaining ones who are there in their own right. If this is true of Delhi, what about other Universities?[204] Lamenting on Merit Promotion Scheme being converted into Mass Promotion Scheme and commenting on the result of Dr Rashmi Srivastava versus Vikram University,[205] Dr Amrik Singh says: "can there be two types of professors"? In other words can there be a genuine type and a false?[206] How promotions are materialised? Singh says: "There is Delhi scandal of 10–20 lecturers being promoted to Readership within half an hour. The modality for that was a mass interview. Individual teachers were not interviewed. Instead, teachers were interviewed in mass. Even if experts in various subjects were present, there was no occasion for them to ask any question or receive any answer."[207] This is the state of affair about University Professorship.

Examples are there, showing the appointment of dominant caste teachers with lesser qualifications to the neglected academically far superior backward class teachers and arbitrarily withholding the appointment of backward class teachers even after the clear recommendation of the Selection Committee are clear pointer that open posts, how so high they may be, are not always filled in by meritorious persons. In such cases unwritten reservations prevail of which Justice Sawant had given some indications.

This all is not due to merit. And, therefore, reservation in most of cases is essential to recognise the merit of OBCs against the mighty hands of unwritten reservation.

(i) It is not anti-meritarian as merit does not rest only with intelligent persons but also with diligent persons.

(ii) The criterion of determining merit is never fool proof and scientific.

(iii) In light of Article 335 which has been interpreted to be applied to OBCs in addition to SCs/STs, the efficiency has to be ensured in reservations.

As a matter of fact reservation itself has significant objectives and merit. Justice Sawant rightly cited a bunch of celebrated cases[208] decided by the American Supreme Court pointing out reservation or affirmative action to be undertaken to rectify the "persisting or present and continuing effects of past discrimination"; to lift the "limitation to access to equal opportunities", to grant "opportunity for full participation in the governance" of the society; to recognise and discharge, "special obligations" towards the disadvantaged and "discriminated social groups", "to overcome the substantial chronic under representation of a social group" or "to serve significant governmental objectives". And, he found similarity between U.S.A. and India so far as national objective is concerned. Said the learned judge, "What applies to American society, applies *ex proprio vigore* to our society."[209] But Sawant, J observed that "the discrimination in our society is more chronic and its continuing effects more discernible and disastrous. Unlike in America, the all pervasive discrimination here is against vast majority."[210] The greatest merit of well thought policy of reservation is that it is means to serve the significant objectives of State policy spelled out in the Constitution. To quote Justice Sawant:

> "There cannot be a more compelling goal than to achieve the unity of the country by integration of various social groups. Social integration cannot be achieved without giving equal status to all. The administration of the country

cannot also be carried out impartially and efficiently without the representation in it of all the social groups and interests, and without the aid and assistance of all the opinions and social experiences. Neither democracy nor unity will become real, unless all sections of the society have an equal and effective voice in the affairs and the governance of the country."[211]

Article 16(4) and The Concept of Reservation in Favour of OBCs

The question of providing reservation to OBCs under Article 16(4) has been debated at length in various cases. The Mandal Judgement also threw light on it and decided the case.

Kania C.J. and Venkatachaliah, Ahmadi and Jeevan Reddy, JJ took the view in *Mandal case* that clause (4) of Article 16 is exhaustive of the provisions that can be made in favour of the backward classes in the matter of employment.[212] Pandian, J. in his concurring view made it clear that Article 16(4) is exhaustive of all the reservations that can be made in favour of any backward classes of citizens. He further made it clear that no reservation can be made under Article 16(4) for classes other than backward classes.[213] Sawant, J. in his concurring judgment made it clear that so far as 'backward classes are concerned, the reservation for them can only be made under clause (4) as they have been taken out from classes intended under Article 16(1). The implicit message of Article 16(4) is that it is exhaustive for backward classes and therefore no reservation can be made under Article 16(4) for any class other than "backward classes". That is to say it would not be open to make provision for reservation in services in favour of physically handicapped, army personnel and freedom fighters and their dependents, project affected persons, etc. under Article 16(4). Thommen, J. too considered Article 16(4) as exhaustive for backward classes.[214] Kuldip Singh, J. allowed its exhaustiveness in light of permissible classification of the equality of opportunity. Clause (4) of Article 16 was treated as another facet of Article 16(1) and it exclusively provides for reservation which is one of the forms of the classification[215] Sahai, J. too expressed the similar opinion.[216]

(2) Kania, C.J. and Venkatachaliah, Ahmadi and Jeevan Reddy, JJ. in their judgement made it clear that:

> "Clause (4) is not, and cannot be held to be, exhaustive of the concept of reservations: it is exhaustive of reservations in favour of backward classes alone. Merely because one form of classification is stated as a specific clause, it does not follow that the very concept and power of classification implicit in clause (1) is exhausted thereby. To say so would not be correct in principle.[217]

And, a note of caution was issued:

> "But at the same time, one thing is clear. It is in very exceptional situation — and not for all and sundry reasons — that any further reservations, of whatever kind, should be provided under clause (1). In such cases, the State has to satisfy, if called upon that making such a provision was necessary (in public interest) to redress a specific situation. The very presence of clause (4) should act as a damper upon the propensity to create further classes deserving special treatment. For, if reservations are made both under clause (4) as well as clause (1), the vacancies available for the free competition as well as reserved categories would be correspondingly whittled down and that is not a reasonable thing to do.[218]

Pandian, J. in his concurring judgment expressed the opinion that clause (4) of Article 16 is exhaustive for backward classes. For other classes Article 16(1) is to be invoked. Pandian, J. ruled that under clause (1) of Article 16 reservation for appointments or posts can be made to other sections of the society such as physically handicapped, etc.[219]

Sawant, J. in his concuring view expressed the opinion that classification can be made in favour of physically handicapped, army personnel and freedom fighters and their dependents, project affected persons. Such classification would not be hit by Article 16(2). Sawant, J. clarified it, "Apart from the fact that they cut across all classes, the reservations in their favour are made on considerations other than that of backwardness within the meaning of clause (4)."[220]

Kuldip Singh, J. and R.M. Sahai, J. ruled out the possibility of any reservation in addition to reservation of backward classes under Article 16(4). R.M. Sahai, J. ruled that Article 16(4) being part of the scheme of equality doctrine is exhaustive of reservation, therefore, no reservation can be made under Article 16(1). The learned judge gave many reasons for his conclusion.

First, extension of reservation to new categories under Articles 15(4) and 16(4) beyond the 50 per cent rule laid down in *Balaji* and *Devadasan*, as such to government nominees, political sufferers, defence personnel, sportsmen, children of MISA and DISIR detenus, etc. under the cover of reasonable classification is a constitutional distortion and therefore cannot be legitimately and legally accepted as valid.[221]

Second, reservation cannot be linked with population. On plain construction inadequacy of representation cannot be the measure of reservation. Proportionate representation cannot be read into Article 16(4).[222]

Third, since the Constitution considers all citizens equal for purposes of employment except those who fall under Article 16(4) any further classification or grouping for reservation would be constitutionally invalid.[223]

On the above reasons, the conclusion of Sahai, J. is that no reservation can be made for any class other than backward class either under Article 16(1) or 16(4).[224] Kuldip Singh, J. fully endorsed it.[225]

Unlike Kania, C.J. and Venkatachaliah, Ahmadi, Jeevan Reddy, Pandian and Sawant, JJ. Thommen, Kuldip Singh and Sahai, JJ. were not agreeable to give reservation to classes other than backward classes under Article 16(1). Thommen, J. was willing to grant preferences without reservation like prescribing longer period for passing a test or by awarding additional marks or granting other advantages such as relaxation of age or other minimum requirements to all disadvantaged classes of citizens. Thus he observed that disadvantaged citizens like blind, deaf, dumb and maimed and like may be beneficiaries of preferences short of reservation.[226] Kuldip Singh, J. held that protective discrimination, short of reservations, which satisfy the test of reasonableness, is permitted under Article 16(1).[227] R.M. Sahai, J. at length discussed the preferential treatment which can be allowed under Article 16. He maintained distinction between the reservation and preferential treatment: "in one a group of class or collectivity is separately provided for and the competition is amongst them only. Whereas in preferential treatment, the collectivity is part of the same group but it is permitted with some weightage due to social, economic or any justifiable reason."[228]

R.M. Sahai, J. elaborate it:

> "For purposes of achieving equality by result Article 16 creates two compartments, one general and the other reserved and then both are paired together. But preference is available in the same compartment. Validity of one depends on constitutional sanction whereas the second has to stand on test of reasonableness. For instance, the reservation of backward class cannot be assailed as being violative of constitutional guarantee whereas preferential treatment can be upheld only if it is reasonable with the nexus it seeks to achieve."[229]

So long as only preferential treatment is allowed to disadvantaged sections other than backwards, as conceded by Thommen, Kuldip Singh and Sahai, JJ. there is no problem of adjustment. But if reservation is conceded to them as recognised by majority the problem of adjustment may come up. In cases of reservations made under Article 16(1) it has to be so adjusted and implemented as not to exceed the level of representation fixed for the backward classes of citizens. The adjustment is to be done within 50 per cent limit and the case of handicapped, political sufferer's dependents, etc. is adjusted in quota meant for his castes' other men, i.e., if he belongs to upper caste his case would be adjusted against open posts, if OBCs, then within 27 per cent and SCs/STs then within 23 per cent.

(3) In the case of State of Kerala versus N.M. Thomas.[230] Instead of reservation for SCs/STs candidates in matters of promotion to the category of Upper Division Clerk from Lower Division Clerk, the facility of passing test was provided by providing additional chances. The facility or exemption was a lesser form of special treatment than reservation. In *Thomas*, Ray, C.J. justified the classification of employees belonging to those groups to afford them an extended period to the test for promotion as "a just and reasonable classification having rational nexus to the object of promoting equal opportunity—relating to public

employment.[231] This innovative doctrinal approach was based on reason that just as rational classification is permissible under the general equal protection provision of Article 14 so it is permissible to treat unequals unequally under Article 16.[232] This rule may be considered as "implementation of a policy of qualified or partial or conditional reservation" which could be justified under Article 16(4).[233] Mathew, J. adopted the concept of "equality of result."[234] The constitutional equality of opportunity was wide enough to include compensatory measures and therefore implies, differential treatment of persons who are unequal.[235] Krishna Iyer, J. took the plea of 'real, not formal', equality[236] and ruled that in addition to reservations provided by Article 16(4), the state was also competent to confer 'lesser orders of advantages' on the principle of classification under Article 16(4).[237] Krishna Iyer, J restricted such preferential treatment to SCs/STs. But Mathew, J. was of the view that compensatory measures authorised by Article 16(1) might be extended to "all members of the backward classes."[238] Likewise in Akhil Bharatiya Soshit Karmachari Sangh (Rly.) versus Union of India[239], many concessions, exemptions and other measures issued by Railway administration were instances of supplementary, incidental and ancillary provisions made in order to make the main provision of reservation effective, i.e., to ensure that the members of the reserved class fully avail of provision of reservation in their favour.

As to the exhaustiveness of reservation under Article 16(4) Kania, C.J. and Venkatachaliah, Ahmadi and Jeevan Reddy, JJ. interpreted reservation in view of its use. The words "any provision for the reservation of appointments or posts," were taken into consideration and the question to be put was whether the said words contemplate only one form of provision namely reservation simpliciter, or do they take in other forms of special provisions such as preferences, concessions and exemptions. The conclusion drawn was:

> "...reservation is the highest form of special provision, while preference, concession and exemption are lesser forms. The constitutional scheme and context of Article 16(4) induces us to take the view that larger concept of reservations take within its sweep all supplemental and ancillary provisions

> as also lesser types of special provisions like exemptions, concessions and relaxations, consistent no doubt with the requirement of maintenance of efficiency of administration — the admonition of Article 335."[240]

Sawant, J. in his concurring judgment too recognised different forms of reservations including preferences, concessions, exemptions, extra facilities, etc. or often exclusive quota in appointments. Sawant, J. made clear, "when measures other than an exclusive quota for appointments are adopted, they form part of the reservation measures or are ancillary to or necessary for availing of the reservations. Whatever the form of reservation, the backward classes have to look for them to Article 16(4) and the other classes to Article 16(1)".[241]

Real Aims of Affirmative Actions and Protective Discrimination for OBCs

By now it is well accepted principle of equalitarian justice that it has to be made effective by equalising measures. Article 15(4) speaks of making special provisions and Article 16(4) speaks of 'reservation'. One invites positive action programmes and the other positive discrimination programmes. Does it makes any difference?

In *Mandal Case*, the leading majority decision of Kania, C.J. Venkatachaliah, Ahmadi and Jeevan Reddy, JJ. discounted the possibility of compartmentalisation of the constitutional scheme into positive action and positive discrimination. It was elaborated:

> "By now, it is well settled that reservation in educational institutions and other walks of life can be provided under Article 15(4) just as reservations can be provided in services under Article 16(4). If so, it would not be correct to confine Article 15(4) to programmes of positive action alone. Article 15(4) is wider than Article 16(4) in as much as several kinds of positive action programmes can also be evolved and implemented thereunder (in addition to reservation) to improve the conditions of SEBCs. Scheduled Castes and Scheduled Tribes, whereas Article 16(4) speaks of only one type of remedial measure, namely, reservation of appointment/posts."[242]

Minority clarified that "it may not be entirely right to say that Article 15(4) is a provision envisaging programmes of positive action. Indeed, even programmes of positive action may sometimes involve a degree of discrimination."[243]

Thommen, J. spoke in different tone, conceding that Articles 15(4) and 16(4) refer to the same classes of backward citizens and both are enabling provision allowing state to adopt affirmative actions, the learned judge was of the opinion that they do not refer to identical remedies. (i) The former speaks of special provisions for uplift of backward classes whereas the latter speaks in terms of reservations in appointments; (ii) Unlike Article 16(4) Article 15(4) is not so worded as to suggest that it is exclusionary in character; (iii) though reservation may be included in special provisions under Article 15(4), reservation quota falling under Article 16(4) must be subjected to even greater scrutiny than cases falling under Article 15(4).[244]

Sahai, J. too maintained a distinction between reservation and preferential treatment. According to him, (i) in reservation under Article 16(4) a group or class or collectivity is separate provided for and the competition is among them only, whereas in preferential treatment, the collectivity is a part of the same group but it is with permitted some weighage because of social, economic or any justiciable reasons; (ii) for purposes of acquiring equality by result Article 16 creates two compartments, one general and the other reserved and then both are paired together. But preference is available in the same compartment; (iii) validity of reservation depends on constitutional sanction whereas the validity of preferential treatment stands on the test of reasonableness.[245]

Article 15(4) and 16(4) present two sides of the same coin. Some differences shown between the two are not very convincing. For instance, Thommen, J. pointed out in *Mandal Case* that "reservation is a remedy for historical discrimination and its continuing ill-effects, other affirmative action programmes are intended to redress discrimination of all kinds, whether current or historical."[246] With due respect it is submitted that conceptualisation and generalisation on the basis of theoretical formulations do not reveal the clear picture. The cases narrated in the beginning may indicate that everything is not right with non-reserved posts. The less meritorious may get job through unwritten reservations and meritorious OBCs may be ousted. Thus, in some cases reservation may be necessary for protection of merit,[247] and resisting and eradicating the ill-effect of current-hostile discrimination.

The real difference between the positive action under Article 15(4) and positive discrimination under Article 16(4), what one may prefer to say, is that the chief aim behind the positive action in the form of preferential treatment through special provisions is the amelioration of the status of backward classes for the purpose of the redressal of backwardness. It may be part of compensatory justice appropriately compensating the victims of past discrimination. It may be needed to qualify the test of distributive justice seeking to ensure that community resources are more equitably and justly shared among all classes of citizens, as Thommen, J. observed in *Mandal case*.[248] On the other hand, "the provision for reservation in appointments under Article 16(4) is not aimed at economic upliftment or alleviation of poverty. Article 16(4) is specifically designed "to give a due share in the State power to those who have remained out of it mainly on account of their social and, therefore, educational and economic backwardness."[249] Thus, the main objective of Article 16(4) is to give to backward classes their fair share in power. This debate throw a question "whether power structure in Indian Society is static or dynamic in nature? In caste based society where apparatus is like water tight compartment Caste status and position remain at the same level what has been ascribed, and goes on from generation to generation. This answers static nature of society. Educational and Economic advancement of an individual person belonging to SC, ST and Backward Caste is an individual achievement and not of a caste as a whole. In that sense this can be case of dynamic nature of Indian society.

References

1. Article, 334.
2. A.I.R. 1992.
3. The National Commission of Backward Classes Act, 1993.
4. Justice S.B. Wad, Caste and the Law in India (1984) p. 19.
5. *Ibid.*

6. *Ibid.*, p. 21.
7. G.S. Ghurye, Caste and Class in India (3rd ed.) 1957, Bombay, Popular Book Depot.
8. A.I.R. 1964 A.P. 277.
9. A.I.R. 1963 S.C. 649 (1963) Supp. I.S.C.R. 439.
10. *Ibid.*, p. 460 (of S.C.R.)
11. (1964) 6 S.C.R. 368 AIR 1964 S.C. 1823.
12. (1964) 6 S.C.R. 368 at pp. 410 - 411.
13. (1968) 2 S.C.R. 786.
14. *Ibid.*, at 790.
15. (1968) 3 S.C.R. 595 A.I.R. 1968 S.C. 1379.
16. *Ibid.*, p. 600.
17. (1969) 1 S.C.R. 103, A.I.R. 1969 S.C.I.
18. (1971) 1 S.C.C. 38.
19. *Ibid.*, p. 48 (para 25).
20. (1972) 1 S.C.C.660.
21. *Ibid.*, p. 689.
22. (1976) 3 S.C.C. 730.
23. *Ibid.*, p. 735.
24. (1975) 1 SCC 267.
25. *Ibid.*, p. 274.
26. 1985 Supp. S.C.C. 714, A.I.R. 1985 S.C. 1485.
27. *Ibid.*, p. 742 (para 440).
28. *Ibid.*, p. 770.
29. *Ibid.*, p. 787.
30. *Ibid.*, p. 786.
31. *Ibid.*, p. 742 (para 40) (Chinnappa Reddy, J.)
32. *Ibid.*, p. 470 (para 859).
33. *Ibid.*, p. 96 (para 115).
34. *Ibid.*, p. 206 (para 399).
35. *Ibid.*, p. 272 (para 552).
36. *Ibid.*, p. 180 (para 351).
37. *Ibid.*, pp. 315 - 318 (para 604 - 608).
38. 1963 Supp. 1 S.C.R. 439, A.I.R. 1963 S.C. 649.
39. *Ibid.*, 458.
40. *Ibid.*
41. (1973) 1 S.C.C. 420.
42. *Ibid.*, pp. 434 - 35 (para 25)
43. (1976) 3 S.C.C. 730 at p. 733.
44. A.I.R. 1985 S.C. 1495, 1985 Supp. S.C.C. 714.
45. For Critical study, see, Marc Galanter, Competing Equalities, Oxf. Univ. Press, 1984, pp. 246 -249.
46. 1992 S.C.C. (L and S) Supp. 1.
47. (1992) 1 S.C.C. 660.
48. (1985) Supp. S.C.C. 714.
49. *Ibid.*, pp. 747 - 748 (para 51).
50. 1992 S.C.C. (L and S.) Supp. 1.

51. A.I.R. 1963 S.C. 649.
52. 1992 S.C.C. (L and S) Supp. 1 at p. 226 (para 446).
53. *Ibid.*, p. 227 (para 447).
54. *Ibid.*, pp. 227 - 228 (para 447).
55. *Ibid.*, p. 430 (para 794).
56. *Ibid.*, p. 430 (para 795).
57. *Ibid.*
58. *Ibid.*, p. 100 (para 126).
59. *Ibid.*, p. 142 (264).
60. A.I.R. 1963 S.C. 649.
61. (1973) 1 S.C.C. 420.
62. Mandal Case p. 223 (para 437).
63. 1985 Supp. S.C.C. 714.
64. *Ibid.*, 745 - 46 (para 49).
65. *Ibid.*
66. *Ibid.*
67. *Ibid.*
68. Mandal Case pp. 423 - 424 (para 786 - 787).
69. *Ibid.*, p. 424 (para 787).
70. *Ibid.*, p. 424 - 426.
71. *Ibid.*, pp. 423 - 426 (paras 786 - 789).
72. *Ibid.*, pp. 97 - 98 (para 117).
73. *Ibid.*, p. 245 (para 492).
74. *Ibid.*
75. *Ibid.*
76. *Ibid.*, pp. 144 - 145 (para 267).
77. *Ibid.*, pp. 180 - 190 (paras 352 - 371).
78. *Ibid.*, pp. 317 - 318 (para 607).
79. Mandal Case pp. 460-561 (para 847).
80. *Ibid.*, p.133
81. *Ibid.*, p. 155 (para 287).
82. *Ibid.*, p. 217 (para 422).
83. *Ibid.*, p. 461 (para 847).
84. A.I.R. 1963 S.C. 649
85. (1992) 1 S.C.C. 20
86. 1992 S.C.C. (L & S.) Supp. 1.
87. *Ibid.*, pp.392-393 (para 737).
88. *Ibid.*, pp.392 (para 736).
89. *Ibid.*, pp.391-393 (para 735-736).
90. *Ibid.*, pp.111-112. (paras 170 to 172).
91. *Ibid.*, p. 199 (para 392).
92. *Ibid.*, p. 261 (para 526).
93. *Ibid.*, pp.334 - 335 (para 636).
94. *Ibid.*, pp.393-394 (para 739).
95. *Ibid.*, pp.261-262 (para 527).
96. *Ibid.*, 199 (para 392).
97. *Ibid.*, pp.334-335 (para 636).

98. (1963) Supp. I.S.C.R. 439.
99. *Ibid.*, pp. 465-466.
100. A.I.R. 1985 S.C. 1495.
101. *Ibid.*, p. 1517 (paras 55).
102. II. B.C.C. 1980 Chapter XIII.
103. *Ibid.*
104. *Ibid.*
105. Mandal Case, p. 434 (para 802)
106. *Ibid.*, (para 803)
107. *Ibid.*, p.435 (para 803).
108. *Ibid.*, p.121 (para 207).
109. Janki Prasad Parimoo v. State of J & K. (1973) I SCC 420.
110. Mandal case, p. 123 (para 208)
111. *Ibid.*, p.166 [para 324(a)].
112. *Ibid.*, p.260 (para 524).
113. *Ibid.*, p.261.
114. *Ibid.*, p.273 (para 552).
115. *Ibid.*
116. *Ibid.*, pp. 260-261 (para 524).
117. Speech of V.P. Singh at America's Harvard University Pioneer 13.2.96, p.12.
118. A.I.R. 1963 S.C. 649.
119. (1964) 4 S.C.R. 680, A.I.R. 1964 S.C. 179.
120. General Manager, Southern Rly. v. Rangachari (1962) 2 S.C>R. 586; Balaji v. State of Mysore, A.I.R. 1963 S.C. 649; State of A.P. v. P. Sagar (1968) 3 S.C.R. 595; Triloki Nath v. State of J and K. (1I) (1969) 1 S.C.R. 103; C.A. Rajendra v. Union of India (1968) 1 S.C.R. 721; State of Punjab v. Hiralal (1970) 3 S.C.R. 567. For critical appraisal see, Marc Galanter, Competing Equalities (1984) p.p. 377-382.
121. A.I.R. 1976 S.C. 490, (1976) 2 S.C.C>310. For critical study see, Marc Galanter, Competing Equalities (1984) pp. 382-395.
122. 1992 S.C.C. (L and S.) Supp, 1.
123. *Ibid.*, p. 395 (para 741).
124. *Ibid.*, p. 395-396 (para 741).
125. *Ibid.*, p. 396 (para 742).
126. *Ibid.*, p. 111 (para 168).
127. *Ibid.*, (para 428).
128. *Ibid.*, p. 220 (para 430).
129. *Ibid.*, p. 195 (para 382).
130. *Ibid.*, p. 284(para 563).
131. *Ibid.*, p. 152 (para 284).
132. *Ibid.*, p. 111 (para 168).
133. *Ibid.*, p. 153 (para 284).
134. *Ibid.*, p. 284-285 (para 563).
135. *Ibid.*, p. 395 [para 243 (6)].
136. (1981) 1 S.C.C. 246.
137. M.P. Singh, 'Are Articles 15(4) and 16(4) Fundamental Rights' (1994) 3 SCC (Jour. Sect) 33 at p.34.

138. R, Dwirkin, Taking Rights Seriously (1977) 227.
139. M.P. Singh, supra p.35.
140. M.H. Hoskot v. State of Maharashtra, (1978) 3 S.C.C. 544, PUDR v. Union of India, (1982) 3 S.C.C. 235; Bandhua Mukti Morcha v. Union of India (1984) 3. S.C.C. 161; Mohini Jain v. State of Karnataka, (1992) 3 S.C.C. 666: Unnikrishnan v. State of A.P., (1993) 1 S.C.C. 645.
141. Bandhua Mukti Morcha v. Union of India, (1984) 3 S.C.C. 161.
142. Unnikrishnan v. State of A.P., (1993) 1 S.C.C. 645.
143. Mandal case, p. 342 (para 655) per majority.
144. Mandal case, para 633 (Pandian, J.)
145. Parmanand Singh, Fundamental Right to Reservation: A Rejoinder (1995) 3 S.C.C. 6.
146. *Ibid.*, p.8.
147. *Ibid.*, p.9.
148. Dworkin himself concedes, "The fairness and constitutionality of any admission program is justified if it served a proper policy that respects the rights of all members of the community to be treated as equals." Ronald Dworkin, Taking Rights Seriously (1977) p. 239.
149. Parmanand Singh, supra p. 10.
150. D.D. Horticulture Employees Union v. Delhi Administration, (1992) 4 S.C.C. 99.
151. A.I.R. 1964 S.C. 179 at p. 190 (Subba Rao, J.).
152. Marc Galanter, Competing Equalities (1984) pp. 394-395.
153. *Ibid.*, p. 395.
154. A.I.R. 1984 P and H. 297.
155. *Ibid.*, p. 299.
156. *Ibid.*
157. A.I.R. 1985 Bomb. 153.
158. *Ibid.*, p. 159.
159. *Ibid.*, See also SBI SC/ST Employees' Welfare Assn. V. State Bank of India, (1996) 4 SCC 119.
160. A.I.R. 1989 S.C. 139.
161. *Ibid.*, p. 142.
162. A.I.R. 1988 Gau. 24.
163. (1963) 1 S.C.R. 439.
164. *Ibid.*, p. 469.
165. *Ibid.*
166. (1973) 1 S.C.C. 420.
167. A.I.R. 1976 S.C. 490, at p. 512.
168. (1964) 4 S.C.R. 680: A.I.R. 1964 S.C. 179.
169. A.I.R. 1976 S.C. 490, (1976) 2 S.C.C. 310.
170. *Ibid.*, p. 534 (157).
171. (1981) 1 S.C.C. 246.
172. *Ibid.*, p. 299.
173. *Ibid.*
174. *Ibid.*
175. 1985 Supp. S.C.C. 714, A.I.R. 1985 S.C. 1485.

176. *Ibid.*, p. 1509 (para 36).
177. *Ibid.*
178. 1992 S.C.C. (L and S) 1.
179. *Ibid.*, pp. 454-455 (para 836).
180. *Ibid.*, p. 105. (para 144.
181. *Ibid.*, pp. 159-160 (para 298).
182. K.C. Vasanth Kumar v. State of Karnataka, A.I.R. 1985 S.C. 1485 at p. 1509.
183. Indra Sawhney v. Union of India, 1992 S.C.C. (L & S.) I at 209 para 403.
184. *Ibid.*
185. *Ibid.*
186. *Ibid.*
187. *Ibid.*, pp. 210-211 (para 406).
188. *Ibid.*, (para 408). In S. Vinod Kumar v. Union of India, (1996) 6 S.C.C. 580 the Supreme Court disallowed any relaxation in qualifying marks and evaluation.
189. *Ibid.*
190. *Ibid.*, p. 142212 (para 408).
191. *Ibid.*, p. 454 (para 836).
192. *Ibid.*, p. 455 ([para 836).
193. *Ibid.*
194. (1981) S.C.C. 296.
195. *Ibid.*, p. 455 (para 837).
196. *Ibid.*, (para 838).
197. *Ibid.*, p. 456 (para 839).
198. *Ibid.*, p. 133 [para 243(11)].
199. *Ibid.*, p. 159-160 (para 298).
200. (1994) 4 S.C.C 401 (decided on 17.3.1994). This case is discussed in detail in connection with the issue of no reservation in certain jobs.
201. Mandal case, p. 211 (para 407).
202. Anirudh Prasad, Recent S.C. Decisions and Determination of Seniority of Direct recruit vis-à-vis promottees. Legal Education, News letter, Nov. 1995.
203. Amrik Singh, 'Merit v. Mass Promotion', The Hindustan Times, 28.5.95.
204. *Ibid.*
205. (1995) S.C.C.
206. Merit v. Mass Promotion, Supra f.n. 210.
207. *Ibid.*
208. Oliver Brown v. Board of Education, 347 U.S. 483 1954; Spott Wood, Thoms Bolling v. C. Melvin Sharpe, 347 U.S. 497: Marco De Funis v. Charles Udegaard, 416 U.S. 312 (1974); Regents of the University of Clifornia v. Allan Bakke, 438 U.S. 265 (1978); H. Earl Fullilove v. Phillip M. Klutznick, 448 U.S. 1980; Metro Broadcasting Inc. v. Federal Communication Commission, 581 W. 503 (decided on June 27, 1990).
209. Mandal case, p. 216 (para 419).
210. *Ibid.*
211. *Ibid.*
212. Mandal case (1992) S.C.C. (L & S) Supp. 1 at p. 396-397 (para 743).

213. *Ibid.*, p. 132 [para 243(2)].
214. *Ibid.*, p. 166 [para 323(3)].
215. *Ibid.*, p. 195 (para 382).
216. *Ibid.*, p. 287 (para 566).
217. *Ibid.*, p. 399 (para 744).
218. *Ibid.*, p. 399 (para 744).
219. *Ibid.*, p. 111 (para 168).
220. *Ibid.*, p. 220 (para 430).
221. *Ibid.*, p. 321 (para 612).
222. *Ibid.*, pp. 322-323 (para 613).
223. *Ibid.*, pp. 323-324 (para 615).
224. *Ibid.*, p. 326 (para 619).
225. *Ibid.*, p. 195 (para 382).
226. *Ibid.*, pp. 157-158 (para 293).
227. *Ibid.*, p. 195 (para 382).
228. *Ibid.*, p. 325 (para 617).
229. *Ibid.*
230. A.I.R. 1976 S.C. 490.
231. *Ibid.*, at p.500.
232. *Ibid.*, at p.502
233. *Ibid.*, p.524.
234. *Ibid.*, p.518.
235. *Ibid.*, p. 516.
236. *Ibid.*, p. 529.
237. *Ibid.*, p. 536.
238. *Ibid.*, p. 519.
239. (1981) 1 S.C.C. 246.
240. Mandal case, p. 397 (para 743).
241. *Ibid.*, 221 (para 432).
242. (1992) S.C.C. (L. and S.) Suppl 1 at pp. 459-460 (para 846).
243. *Ibid.*
244. *Ibid.*, p. 156 (para 289).
245. *Ibid.*, p. 325 (para 617).
246. *Ibid.*, p. 168 [323(14)].
247. See Dr. Anirudh Prasad, "Arakshana Yogyata Rakshana Ke Liye Avasyak Hai" Vidhika, 1993 (3-4) pp. 173-180.
248. (1992) S.C.C. (L, d S.) Supp. 1 at p. 165 (para 321).
249. *Ibid.*

Four

Reservation Policy for Backward Castes: Problems

The question of need of reservation policy for backward castes (OBCs) was taken up as early as in 1950s by appointing first National Commission Kaka Kalelkar Commission. It was Congress government in power having two-third majority in the Parliament. Then again second Backward Classes Commission was appointed by Janta Party Government in 1978 which was headed by Shri B.P. Mandal. Both the governments did not accept recommendations of both these commissions for lack of objectivity as well as lack of political will.

The call for evolving a national concensus on the issue of reservations policy for the Other Backward Classes (OBCs) was given by several leaders of various political parties. A significant cross-section of active political leaders holding important official positions recognized the need for a set of guidelines which can regulate the future evolution of OBC reservations policy. During Congress (I) rule Prime Minister Shri Rajiv Gandhi gave a call to all on 20th July, 1985 to build a national consensus on the reservation policy for OBCs when Gujarat Government was seriously considering increase in reservation quota in educational institutions for OBCs following the report of Rane Commission. Later similar statements were made by atleast three Chief Ministers—those of Karnataka, Andhra Pradesh and Gujarat. Take instance of Gujarat where anti reservation agitation occured in 1981, 1985 and 1990. The first was against SCs/STs, second and third wasagainst the OBCs. Gujarat is also one of the states unlike Tamil Nadu, Maharashtra, Bihar and U.P., where backward classes movement was there. (Shah, 1990)[1]. This provides the basis for discussion and analysis of the problem in this chapter.

At the outset of this examination it is necessary to explain why the subject of reservations for the category widely known as OBCs—mentioned in the Constitution of India as "socially and educationally backward classes" (Articles 15(4); 16 (4)—needs to be treated separately from the issue of reservations for the Scheduled Castes (SCs) and the Scheduled Tribes (STs). In brief, the explanation lies as much in the history, sociology and politics of reservation policy as it does in the objective of efficient and egalitarian economic development. However, it would be wrong to identify SCs/STs and OBCs as being members of followers of particular political parties. No one can doubt the fact that it was the Congress party and its leaders who won over Dr. B.R. Ambedkar, the leader of the Depressed Classes, from a position of relative hostility to one of cooperation and leadership of the Constituent Assembly. In the post-1947 period too the Congress governments were active in promoting several welfare and participatory schemes for the Scheduled Castes, Scheduled Tribes and Other Backward Classes. In the case of the "socially and educationally backward" classes being involved in the scheme of preferential policies, the Congress and its leaders again played an important role. The Objectives Resolution of the Constituent Assembly was moved by Jawaharlal Nehru on December 13, 1946 and it resolved to provide sufficient safeguards for minorities, backward tribal areas, depressed and other backward classes." So also, the famous clause 4 of Article 15 in which it is said "that nothing in this article shall prevent the state from making any special provision for the advancement of any socially and educationally backward classes citizens or for the Scheduled Castes and the Scheduled Tribes," was also moved for adoption by Prime Minister Nehru. It was again the cabinet, led by Jawaharlal Nehru which decided in August, 1961 that since no agreement could be reached on the implementation of the report of the Kaka Kalelkar Commission, which had given prominence to caste and not to economic criteria, the states could frame their own OBC lists under Article 15(4) and 16(4).

At the time of the framing of the Indian Constitution most political leaders were linked with the Congress party in one way or another. Later on when some of them parted company with their parent organisation, they tried to project the scheduled caste and the OBC issues in their own fashion. Dr. B.R. Ambedkar founded the Republican Party of India to represent the interests of the Depressed Classes, but it did not perform well in the elections except in a few districts of Maharashtra. Ram Manohar Lohia outlined his opinions on the position of backward castes in Indian society and make that the basis of one aspect of politics of the Socialist Party. He assumed that his division of Hindu society into the dominant "twice born" and other castes actually conformed to political or potential political groups in the all-India national or electoral arena. A closer analysis of the regional variations and changes in social structure within the country would belie the kind of expectations likely to follow from Ram Manohar Lohia's views. Subsequent to the decision of the central government that the states were free to formulate their own lists of backward classes, several leading political figures like Devraj Urs from the Congress party in Karnataka again took the initiative in furthering the evolution of a reservations policy for the backward classes. Indeed, starting from the latter half of the 1960s, between 1965 to 1987 Backward Classes Commissions reported twice in Kerala, Karnataka, and Gujarat and once in Tamil Nadu, Bihar, Jammu and Kashmir, in addition to the second National Backward Classes Commission or the Mandal Commission in 1980. It is interesting to note that these commissions were appointed both by Congress and non-Congress governments and generally as a result of initiatives coming from above or in pursuance of a strategy for promoting social justice towards the backward classes. However, on this particular issue generally a non-Congress government (as in the case of the Venkataswamy Commission in Karnataka or the Mandal Commission at the Centre) took up the issue after coming into power. In the case of the Mandal Commission again, it was initiated by the Janata government.

It has not only been the various governments which have agreed on this method of appointing a Public Commission for drawing up OBC lists. A comprehensive survey of the views of political leaders in 1978 in the Karimnagar district of Andhra Pradesh showed how views about reservation policy cut across party lines. Of the leaders interviewed, 72 per cent were from the

Congress (I), 11 per cent to the Janata Party, another 11 per cent to the CPI and the rest had no party affiliations. Of these, 74 per cent said that reservations in general should be time-bound and hence renewable after the expiry of the stipulated deadline while 18 per cent opined they should be time-barred and hence not renewable (N. Ramchander, 1983)[3].

It is therefore clear that on the issue of reservations, the lines between various political parties were and are blurred and when it comes to actual policy formulation and implementation mostly there is a considerable overlap between the policies followed by various governments. One fact which stands out, both in the evolution of policy and in terms of agitational or protest politics intended to shape reservation policy, is that much greater controversy and differences surround OBC reservations than those meant for the scheduled castes and tribes. This also means that there are many aspects of the criteria used for classifying OBCs which remain under continuing discussion as also the extent of jobs/college seats reserved for them. By contrast, the quotas sanctioned for SC/ST as well as the scheduled lists naming the SC/ST enjoy greater acceptance among several national parties. One reason for looking at the possible reasons explaining the greater social consensus about SC/ST reservations and the more numerous differences relating to OBC reservations is to find out whether at the policy level the factors leading to the first result cannot be helpful in promoting a similar effort relating to the OBC issue. In this context, it might be noticed that in recent years the consensus relating to SC/ST reservations was under some strain in a few regions due to inter-caste conflicts. What possible consequences such conflicts may have, if at all, for the scheme of SC/ST reservation remains a separate matter for study. In this chapter, the focus is strictly on the backward classes and compare with reservations for analysis purpose.

A vigorous intellectual and reformist opinion against the presence of untouchability within Hindu society was first highlighted by the social reform movements which started in the 19th century. Both the *Brahmo Samaj*, in Bengal and the *Arya Samaj* in Punjab believed in promoting a dual process of reform when it concerned the issue of untouchability. As the *Arya Samaj* did through the *Shudhi* movement, the untouchables were to become caste Hindus either by formally adopting ritual ceremonies of the latter or through possible inter-caste marriages as promoted by the *Brahmo Samaj*. The fact that a struggle against untouchability needed a change of perception and practice on the part of the upper castes was best brought out in the philosophy and actions of Mahatma Gandhi. Temple entry movements for Dalits were to be accompanied by an effort at changing the traditional dislike of manual labour by the upper castes. In retrospects, it was the sort of thinking which underpinned the policy of reservations for the Depressed Classes. Job reservations would also ensure that upper caste employees would work in the company of the former untouchables. By this it was hoped to better the conditions of SC/ST who provided the most *visible* examples of social and regional backwardness in contemporary Indian society. Such a policy was supposed to be an illustration of social justice. Facts too supported the view that untouchability in itself constituted a key element of enforcing hierarchy within the caste system and that attempts to undermine it, when successful would alter that system. Although the law of occupational specialization in regard to untouchable castes had already been weakened considerably by the time of the 1931 census, that of rigid residential segregation and marital exclusion in rural India was and is applicable. As per the 1931 census, e.g. of the Bombay Presidency, several known untouchable castes had shifted from their traditional occupations to others within the rural economy and society. Amongst the *bhangis* or the scavengers almost 572 out of every 1000 persons had stopped pursuing their traditional occupations. Similarly, 547 out of every 1000 *chamars/mochis* or shoemakers were no longer engaged in their traditional operations.

Among the mahars or the village watchmen in the Bombay Presidency only 179 out of every 1000 were said to be following their traditional occupation. If occupational specialization or diversification is to be regarded as a yardstick for modernization, the above mentioned untouchable castes were clearly ahead of others. Among the sutars or carpenters, for example, 776 out of every 1000 persons were following their traditional occupations in 1931. Among the lohars or blacksmiths in Bombay Presidency this ratio was 731 out of every 1000 (*Census of India*, 1931)[4].

In the pre-1947 days occupational diversification however did not remove the social disabilities linked with the stigma of untouchability, a fact which is true even today when the Indian Constitution has abolished and outlawed untouchability and social practices based on it. Discrimination on grounds of being an untouchable was not necessarily associated to being more or less well-off or poor. The mere fact that one belonged to a caste locally considered as untouchable might exclude him/her from using the village well, temple or the village *chaupal* and the right to use such facilities is a subject of *many* unknown informal personal struggles even today. G.S. Sharma has documented for us several such situations in which barbers refused to serve *chamars* even when the latter were willing to pay for the former's service (G.S. Sharma, 1975)[5]. Such cases are known only when a formal complaint is lodged or a commission of inquiry appointed.

A Commission of inquiry was appointed by the Rajasthan High Court to enquire into reports on the continuing practice of untouchability in the town of Bari Sadri and has found that not only is it prevalent there but is sometimes seen in its crudest form. It has been observed that such discrimination prevails in government offices, the municipal council and in the lower *munsif* courts. Affidavits have been submitted to the Commission by the scheduled caste employees in the primary health centre testifying that they were not allowed to drink the stored water nor did the night chowkidar of the municipal council allow them to use the office supplies, and the *munsif* court denied minimum wages to its scheduled caste employees for three years. An all-India survey by a team of experts discovered many regional variations in the extent of participation by scheduled castes in the educational system. However, one common factor they observed was the communing belief in caste endogamy. Another was the invisible rule that scheduled caste students could make friends only among the scheduled castes and that they continued to have a poor image of their own status due to the treatment they received from other caste students. Consequently, they lacked the confidence to compete openly for employment and were diffident about venturing into the private sector. Another study of college students found that many from urban and rural areas were prejudiced against the Dalits.

The need for protective discrimination or for job and political reservations was first voiced by those among the untouchables who had performed well in relative economic terms. The *mahars* in the Bombay Presidency, for example, had been among the first to shift from their traditional occupation as village watchmen and took up jobs in the army and the railways. This headstart made them motivated for reform and the growth of political awareness among them. The movement for political representation for the Depressed Classes was led by a successful mahar barrister, B.R. Ambedkar. Similarly in the case of chamars in the United Provinces, their consolidation into a recognizable constituency followed the growth amongst them of a fairly affluent section because a sudden rise in the demand for leather goods during the Second World War. These better off sections provided the leadership to the scheduled castes/tribes.

The untouchable castes found advocates and leaders not only from among the ranks of their own better off section but also from among the several illustrious thinkers and social activists involved in the growth of Indian nationalism—Swami Vivekananda, Jyotiba Phule, Narain Guruswami, Ramaswami Naicker, Lokhitwadi, Gokhale, Agarker, Munshi Premchand, B. Pantulu, R. Venkatraman, etc. By the 1920s the country was dotted with movement for giving an equal status to untouchables within Hindu society. By 1924 the *mahars* in the Bombay Presidency had launched a "self respect" movement under the leadership of Dr Ambedkar. In Punjab the Adi-Dharm movement began in 1926. In Bengal there was the Nama Sudra Andolan, in the Madras Presidency the Adi-Dravida, and in Kerala the Adi Karnataka Andolan. The Charuman, Palaya, etc. *harijan* groups started movement against untouchability. In Andhra there was an Adi Andhra movements and in Kanpur an Adi Hindu movement. Later Mahatma Gandhi published the newspaper *Harijan*. He also renamed the Akhil Bharatiya Anti-Untouchability League, started by Amritlal V. Thakkar, the Servants of Untouchables Society and this later became the now famous *Harijan Sevak Sangh*. There was thus an all-India scope and dimension to the movement for helping the scheduled castes to fight untouchability through economic, political, cultural and educational means. It was easy to achieve a consensus on this issue.

It is to be stressed that whereas untouchability in its different dimensions provided an easy all-India demarcating line within which the scheduled castes could be identified and about the removal of which a number of social and political leaders were in agreement with each other, the same was not true of the factors which led to the rise of the non-Brahmin movement, the progenitor of the social category later to be mentioned as the *Other Backward Classes* (OBCs) in South India and particularly in Tamil Nadu and Bombay Presidency. This analysis suggests that purely political factors and responses had a much greater role to play in shaping the OBCs as a constitutional, legal and social beneficiary. Hence political action has a much greater relevance in determining the legal and political time frame within which such a category can be socially beneficial, than is the case with the SC/ST groups, who constitute a collectivity in a more fundamental cultural, economic and geographical sense.

The origins of the social category called the OBCs dates back to the non-Brahmin movement and the decisions made by the ruler of Mysore to give preference to the backward classes. In re analysing this piece of history one has to ask a question which is of great contemporary relevance for policymakers today. Was the classification of the OBCs, which emerged during this period, a natural outcome of a social movement or a policy decision of the existing government? This distinction has a vital relevance since the degree to which the state has fashioned its own criteria and imposed its own interpretation on social events is more easily changeable than a policy framework that is the direct outcome of social conditions not acceptable to large groups of people. Thus untouchability creates a deprived social constituency which is unique in its own right and for whose abolition many special social devices are required. Is this equally true of the OBCs? In order to answer this question one needs to reconsider some history.

M.S.A. Rao's (1987)[6] work on social movements and social transformation was a pioneer work in the field of sociological researches. He studied two backward classes movements— the Shri Narayana Dharma Paripalana Movement (Movement for the propagation of the philosophy of Shri Narayana Guru Swamy) in Kerala and the All-India Yadava movements. He found that these movements had brought about social transformation representing middle level structural change between reform on the one hand and revolution on the other. We discuss now non-brahmin movements, a beginning made by backward castes towards their recognition of rights for reservation.

The Non-Brahmin Movement: Regional Phenomenon

One of the factors that distinguished the social structure in Tamil Nadu from various other parts of India during the late 19th century was the interlinkage between large landholding educational, professional and political leadership within several Brahmin families, which set them apart from families belonging to other castes and gave the Brahmins as a whole a well-knit appearance as a social and a political group. It is significant to note that even at the start of the 20th century Tamil Nadu—then a part of the Madras Presidency—was not a region dominated by extensive commercial agriculture. It could boast of few merchant princes and even fewer captains of industry. Unlike the Permanent Settlement in Bengal, the *Ryotwari* Settlement in the Madras Presidency did not lead to a large scale transfer of land, basically because the extent of the revenue burden imposed on agriculture had over the years been more closely linked to the costs of production. The large scale "sunset" auctioning of land in Bengal initiated certain changes in the social composition of the landed elites. It created an avenue for upward mobility for persons who had gained wealth in trade as agents or carriers for the East India Company, which had been active in that region of India for more than three centuries. Such a social process also widened the caste base of the Bengal landed and urban elites, a phenomenon that led to the coining of a new phrase, the *Bhadralok*, to describe the Bengal elite—a term which spanned families from at least three castes, Brahmanas, Vaidyas or Vaishyas and Kayasthas. This to a certain extent foreclosed the efforts to mobilize sections of the affluent upper castes to head a non-Brahmin movement. It is to be observed that the caste associations formed in Bengal in the 19th century have disappeared after Independence. There has also not been any real pressure from below for instituting OBC reservations which do not exist in Bengal. Such social mobility was typical of areas where landed property showed a quick turnover as in Bengal, or where clan systems were more prevalent than sub-castes. Government sponsored new land settlements in western UP, where peasants of different origins predominate over older land settlements is another such example. In the Jat-based villages, as in Punjab, Haryana, or in regions of intensive commercial agriculture as in Gujarat, many Kanbis could rise to become Patidars or Patels along with a related increase in their affluence during intervals of price rise, as during the cotton boom in the 1860s or the First World War. Also, in Bengal, western UP, Punjab and Gujarat no effort was made at mobilizing a political movement for demanding caste-based privileges, except for the untouchables, who were there everywhere in Hindu society.

In contrast to other regions of India, in Tamil Nadu and Mysore, both parts of the Madras Presidency at that time, many of the Brahmin families wielded economic and social power quite out of proportion to their numbers. In Madras Presidency as a whole the Brahmins constituted 3.3 per cent of the Hindu population. In Tamil Nadu their share of the total population ranged from one per cent in the Nilgiris to 3.7 per cent in Tinnevelli, Chingleput and Trichinnapally. This contrasted for example with Gujarat where Brahmins constituted five per cent of the population in Baroda state, in central Gujarat and north Gujarat, four per cent in south Gujarat and nearly seven per cent in Kathiawad. (*Census of India*, 1931, Madras Presidency and Baroda State).[7,8] In Tamil Nadu the Brahmins constituted a high proportion among the large landowners. In Gujarat this position was occupied by Rajput or Patidar (Patel). In the Madras Presidency mostly, the Brahmins had long been the literate and hence occupied the position of clerks, administrators and officials, whether the rulers were Tamil kings, Vijaynagar viceroys or the East India Company. Once again, the comparison with Gujarat or Bengal is an interesting one because in these two regions the leterates came not only from among the Brahmins but also from the other castes like the Kayasthas or the

Vaishyas, who as traders in Gujarat looked after personal or public accounts, etc. There were once the famous Nagar Sheths of Gujarat who ran their businesses on their own. In Tamil Nadu the Brahmins invariably held the position of the village *Karnam* or the village accountant and in appreciation of their religious and secular services they had been given land rights as *Mirasdars* and *Inamdars*. In the case of the Tamil and to a certain extent Telugu Brahmins, traditional status, access to landed wealth, generations of involvement in the administration and aloofness from cultivation were responsible for the Brahmin domination of the western-educated, professional middle class from the middle of the 19th century onwards. Male literacy rates in English were 28.2 per cent for the Tamil Brahmins as against 17.4 per cent for the Vellalas, the leading non-Brahmin caste group in Tamil Nadu. Also, because of their greater involvement with English education the Brahmins could not be closely identified with the renaissance of the Tamil language and literature, a task performed mostly by members of the non-Brahmin intelligentsia. This again meant that the issue of developing a Tamil culture could become an added element in the opposition to Brahmin dominance as such.

One of the consequences of the explicit Brahmin dominance at the regional level in several parts of the Madras Presidency was the attempt by the educated and professional sections of other castes to mobilize their caste associations. Between 1905 and 1930 a great number of caste associations were established with the objectives of strengthening caste identity, improving caste status and fostering mutual assistance. This provided the backdrop to the formation of the Justice Party and the demand for reserved seats for the non-Brahmins in the legislature.

Just the existence of caste associations or even a non-Brahmin movement was not sufficient to get the principle of political reservations for the non-Brahmins accepted. It was also a fact that at this time the British government, sensing the growing support for the nationalist movement, was looking for new allies who would support it within the framework of a limited constitutional government. The criteria for choosing such allies was that unlike the earlier ones (*zamindars*, for example) who were chosen mainly for their loyalty, the new allies should enjoy proven mass support. The ability of the non-Brahmin movement to institutionalize itself into the Justice Party and win support from caste associations was a good reason why in March 1920 the British appointed arbitrator Lord Meston decided in his judgement on the implementation of the Montague-Chelmsford Reforms to reserve 28 of the 65 non-Muhammedan general seats. It was of course the political factor which weighed with the Justice Party when they got the issue of reservations in the legislature settled in their favour. For the British government this was an act of expediency but in the special social situation of Tamil Nadu it signified the entry of a new social strata into political life and activity. It required the special sanction and support of the British state at that time to convert the heterogenous social groupings constituting the non-Brahmin movement into a reserved political constituency within Tamil Nadu. Once the Congress-led Constituent Assembly had decided to introduce adult suffrage in 1949 the need for continuing with the political reservations for the backward classes was no more required. In this regard, it must be noted that the principle of reservations in employment or educational institutions for the backward classes in the Indian Constitution was based on the concept of according welfare and equality to the backward sections of society and not on the principle of political expediency. In this sense there was a difference in the nature of the political principles that were behind the question of reservation for backward classes in the pre-1947 period and the way this issue was defined in the Indian Constitution.

This distinction in the case of political reservations for the backward classes, which were discontinued after 1947, also extends to the reservation of government jobs. In connection with this issue the term "backward classes" first received a technical meaning in the princely state of Mysore. In 1918, the Mysore government appointed a committee to look into the question of encouraging members of the "backward communities" in public service. Marc Galanter has narrated the details of this process (Marc Galanter, 1984)[9]. What he has not emphasized is that during the British period the official communities, by and large, either included the untouchables and the tribes within the rubric of the "backward classes" or when they excluded them they often went by the opinion generated by the non-Brahmin movement that everyone except the Brahmins were backward. At least in South India this opinion became so widespread that the Miller Committee, appointed by the Mysore government in 1918 under the chairmanship of Sir Lesley Miller, was prepared to neglect the facts that a few castes had the same literacy rate as the Brahmins. The Miller Committee classified the Mudaliars and Pillais as backward when they had a 10 per cent literacy rate, almost the same as Brahmins. By this method the Mysore government hoped to keep all the non-Brahmin castes as their own supporters as they wrongly identified the leadership of the freedom movement with the presence of power hungry Brahmin leaders. Thus, purely political considerations were always crucial in the pre-1947 period in the classification of the backward classes. The need to turn a policy of granting concessions to the backward classes into an instrument for securing some sort of broad support against the nationalist movement meant that no strict criteria could be formulated for classifying the OBCs. Many committees used wide definitions to net as large a cross section as possible and there was no agreement on an all-India basis on who constituted the backward classes.

After the issue of the Non-Brahmin Manifesto in 1916 and the formation of the government in Madras by the Justice Party, the latter provided a definitive push to job reservations for the non-Brahmins in the government. The First Communal Government Order on September 16, 1921 extended job reservations for non-Brahmins from revenue to all departments. A staff selection board and then a public services commission was set up to implement these reservation quotas. However, the attempt to raise the non-Brahmin movement to an all-India level on a social plane was a failure. The first all-India non-Brahmin congress was convened in Bombay by Ramaswamy Mudaliar. He openly called the non-Brahmin movement as "jobocracy: the securing of jobs of the men of our communities and I am not ashamed of calling myself a job hunter." No other words could show better the fact that at root it was the educated section of the landed non-Brahmin castes who were in the forefront of the demand for job reservations. The second and last effort to convene an all-India non-Brahmin congress was at Amaraoti in 1925. This occasion was marked only by a speech from the Raja of Panagal who recommended some Constitutional reforms and inclusion of items like handspinning from the programme of the Indian National Congress. It was not only the case that the backward classes movement remained restricted to the local and regional levels. Even when organisations like the BAMCEF were formed during the 1970s, these were associations mostly of persons already having government jobs and striving for better or faster promotions. In this sense the non-Brahmin movement was the largest one of its kind and created the ground in South India for the formation of many caste-based associations that continue to sustain the demand for and practice of reservations there till today. The special conditions which led to the non-Brahmin movement in the South did not exist elsewhere in India to the same extent. The Non-brahmin movement was not the beginning to its end goal but thinking on this issue got birth in the dabate of the Constituent Assembly.

The Constituent Assembly and the Constitutional Provisions

The perspective in terms of which the issue of reservations for the scheduled castes/tribes/other backward classes (SCs/STs/OBCs) was to be viewed, was to change with the dawn of freedom. The British administration had provided a number of ad hoc responses and estimates of population of the Depressed Classes, in order to gain their political support to oppose the Congress by granting a few concessions. Neither the objective nor the criteria of an implicit preferential policy were ever stated clearly. They could not be, since in the minds of the British rulers most of these concessions were only a short-term political device to try and split the nationalist movement. The debates in the Constituent Assembly on the other hand, and the measures or principles this distinguished gathering embodied in the Indian Constitution, set out the approach towards a reservations policy with the objectives of promoting national integration and providing social justice to the deprived sections of the population. The exact meaning of the ideas and formulations of the Constituent Assembly need to be restated today, when opposite arguments are being given either for entirely doing away with a policy of reservations or for indiscriminately extending it on a grand scale. The middle course proposed by the Constituent Assembly, even if it was not laid down in the Constitution explicitly, needs to be elucidated in order to devise a practical programme of action for trying to build a national consensus on the reservations policy issue.

The first characteristic to note in relation to the principle of preferential treatment in the Indian Constitution for SC/ST/OBCs is that the word caste is used only in relation to the *Scheduled Castes*. Both in Article 15(4) (which is a part of the broader article prohibiting discrimination on grounds of religion, race, caste, sex or place of birth) and in Article 16(4) which is included within Article 16 promising equality of opportunity in matters of public employment, the reference to those deserving special treatment is to "any socially and educationally backward classes of citizens or the Scheduled Castes and the Scheduled Tribes" and to "any backward class of citizens which in the opinion of the State is not adequately represented in the services under the State." It is well known that both Article 15(4) and Article 16(4) were introduced by Pandit Jawaharlal Nehru after two judgements by the Supreme Court questioning the validity of the system of 'communal' reservations of government jobs for the non-Brahmins in the Madras Presidency. In a significant intervention during the debate, Jawaharlal Nehru explained why the word "economically" had not been used exclusively in phrasing Article 15(4). According to Jawaharlal Nehru, this was because those who drafted Article 15(4) thought of backwardness as cumulative. The word 'Socially' in the Article, he said, covered a number of things and most certainly included 'economically'. (Parliamentary Debates, Vol. XII-XIII (Part II), Col. 9830).[10]

Those number of things that cumulative would constitute backwardness were not spelt out by the Constituent Assembly nor listed in the Constitution as such. It was supposed that this task would be performed by the Commission which may, according to Article 340, be appointed by the President "to investigate the conditions of the socially and educationally backward classes within the territory of India and the difficulties under which they labour and to make recommendations as to the steps that should be taken by the Union or any state to remove such difficulties and to improve their condition." One fact, however, stood out. There were only a small number of persons either from South India or Bihar who thought caste in itself to be a primary indicator of backwardness. The opinion expressed by Chandrika Ram from Bihar was: "Our society is divided into three sections—the higher consisting of that section known as Scheduled Castes and the lowest as Harijans, while the third occupying a middle position between these two and consisting of a larger portion of our people is what may be termed as the Backward Class." Such a view was far less common than that expressed by Dr Dharam Prakash who said: "In fact there is no community which does not have a section of people which is backward, while economically or educationally or socially." (*Constituent Assembly Debates*: 30/11/1949, pp. 680-86).[11] We analyse the extent to which the post-1947 commissions on backward classes used caste as a primary factor in listing the backward classes. It is not only that the Constituent Assembly sought to de-emphasize caste as a denotation of backwardness. Over time, it sought to reduce and finally to abolish caste as an indicator of backwardness. This objective is to be seen not only in the legal abolition of untouchability but also in the Directive Principles of State Policy. Article 38 clearly affirms that "the state shall strive to promote the welfare of the people by securing and protecting as effectively as it may a social order in which justice—social, economic and political—shall inform all the institutions of the national life, and it shall in particular strive to minimize the inequalities in income and endeavour to eliminate inequalities in status, facilities and opportunities not only among individuals but also amongst groups of people residing in different areas or engaged in different vocations." Article 46 also lays down that "the State shali promote with special care the educational and economic interests of the weaker sections of the people and in particular of the Scheduled Castes and the Scheduled Tribes and shall protect them from social injustice and all forms of exploitation." As opposed to the interpretation proposed by Marc Galanter[12] that no specific goal was set to be achieved through the policy of reservations, the goal was clearly stated to be the increased welfare of the weaker sections through a reduction of inequalities in income, education and other status facilities. The clear import of reading together the Constitutional provisions relating directly or indirectly to reservations is that as a device they were supposed to be used over a long period of time, or as long as the majority view was that goals like reduction in inequalities and status had been fully achieved.

Simultaneously reservations were seen by the Constitution makers as a policy which also had some negative aspects and were required to be worked carefully within well-defined limits so as to carry the support of those who would not be able to benefit from it. In the case of reservations of seats in the legislature this consensus was sought to be achieved by limiting, such reservations only to Scheduled Castes/Tribes and then limiting the period of such reservations initially to ten years (Article 334). The really educative part of the proceedings of the Constituent Assembly was that the leaders of the Scheduled Castes sought actively to develop a consensus on the issue of reservations by accepting and even proposing restrictions on the concessions being granted. It is notable that the clause restricting the reservation of seats for the SCs/STs in the legislature to 10 years only was introduced by Dr B.R. Ambedkar who was the *prima donna* among the Harijan leaders. When some of the Scheduled Caste members spoke against the time limit Dr Ambedkar reminded them that they have really no cause for complaint as the decision to limit the thing to ten years was in fact a decision which has been arrived at with their consent. If at the end of the ten years, the Scheduled Castes find that their position has not improved or that they want further extension of this period it will not be beyond their reach to invent new ways of getting the same protection which they are promised. Such a strategy had a position impact on those from among the upper castes who might not have agreed with the policy of reservations for the Scheduled Castes/Tribes. As Jagat Narain Lal from Bihar put it: "If we have accepted this principle of reservation in the case of the Scheduled Castes and the aboriginals, it is because we have seen speaker after speaker rising from among the Scheduled Castes to support a time limit on reservations." The moral of this illustration is that a conscious strategy of accepting a time limit within which a policy of reservations is to be worked, provides a viable mechanism for promoting a consensus in relation to such a policy and hence minimizes the social conflict likely to arise from having to provide preferential treatment to given sections of society, sometimes at the cost of others. In the context of a policy of backward class reservations, we need to renew the search for limits acceptable to the majority social opinion in various parts of the country. Such a framework does not exist within the Constitution nor has one evolved subsequently at the national or local levels, leading to situations of inter-caste social and political conflicts on more than one occasion. The Mandal Judgement (1992) decided to review the list of other backward classes after every ten years.

The 10-year time limit was not the only compromise made by the Scheduled Caste leaders in order to promote a political consensus. In Article 335, which specifically promised that in the making of appointments to service and posts in the Union or a state the claims of the members of the Scheduled Castes and Tribes would be taken into account, a tough qualification was introduced which said that this would be done "consistently with the maintenance of efficiency of administration." This part of Article 335 clearly lays down that unless the criterion of merit is combined with reservation of posts, efficiency would be the likely casualty. In purely formal terms, no such qualification was there in Article 15(4) and 16(4) mentioned above, which refer to reservation of jobs for the backward classes although in practice a minimum level of competence, as is seen in a specific percentage of marks, is needed for any candidate who is entitled to avail of a reserved quota. This defect needs to be rectified since there is no reason why the qualification about efficiency should not apply to both SCs/STs and the OBCs. Further, Dr Ambedkar also fully agreed that in order not to contravene the more fundamental rule about all citizens having an equality of opportunity, the number of jobs or college seats reserved for SCs/STs/OBCs should "be confined to a minority of seats." In fact, in his final summing up of the debate on Article 15(4) and 16(4) he specifically said that the word "backward" had been brought in to limit the number of reservations to a minority of the available seats. In answer to a question by T.T. Krishnamachari whether his view about reservations applying to only a minority of the seats was justiciable, Dr Ambedkar said: "If the local government included in this category of reservations such a large number of seats, one could very well go to the Supreme Court and say that the reservation is of such a magnitude that the rule regarding equality of opportunity has been destroyed."

It is pertinent to stress that, Dr Ambedkar considered the rule about equality of opportunity as being more fundamental and one which an excessive degree of reservations would tend to undermine. The need to be able to limit reservations to a level which does not encroach too greatly upon the principle of providing equality of opportunity needs to be re-emphasized today, when some political leaders visualize a rapid expansion of a system of reservations as a viable welfare strategy through which they can mobilize some quick political support. The point to be stressed upon here is that even if a strategy of expanding reservations were to be politically rewarding, it would still be contrary to the admirable principle laid down by the founders of the Indian Constitution, that reservations can be instituted only if ample safeguards are provided to ensure that equality of opportunity is available to the majority of the population.

Classification of Backward Classes since 1947

After Independence a question was before the Government who should decide a particular group being a Scheduled Caste, Scheduled Tribe or Backward Classes. It was decided that the identification of a particular group as SC, ST or OBC can be decided by the President himself or by a Commission appointed by him. Here, Scheduled Castes and Tribes can be referred to only briefly because the main issue is the criteria implied to determine the OBCs and estimating their population.

The 1931 census had estimated the total of the Depressed Classes to be 39.1 million in British India and 11.1 million in the States and Agencies. The criteria used to identify these castes were not those of theoretical untouchability, i.e., whether a caste, because of its *varna* status, was considered susceptible to touch and distance pollution. Each Provincial Superintendent involved with the 1931 census was told to "reckon as depressed only those castes who definitely suffer from serious social and political handicap due to their degraded position in the Hindu social scheme." The list of Depressed Classes put together by the 1931 census was to form basis for the special electoral representation given to the Depressed Classes in the 1935 Government of India Act. Then the Scheduled Castes order promulgated by the President in 1950 basically re-enacted the 1936 list. It is important to note this fact because it takes away the edge from the criticism that the Scheduled Castes list, as it stands today, is based on narrow political considerations favourable to the Indian National Congress then and the Congress (I) now.

The 1941 census enumerated 12.6 per cent of the total population of undivided India as the Depressed Classes. The 1951 census updated this estimate to 14.5 per cent of the population and according to the 1991 census the Scheduled Castes comprised 16.8 per cent of the population. After the additions and the deletions made by the Scheduled Castes and Scheduled Tribes Lists (Modification) Order 1956, there have been some changes in that list on an all-India basis and latest one in 2002. This policy of relative neutrality in the matter of defining those groups to be included within the Scheduled Caste list contrasts with the changes made by the British government in granting privileges to new groups in order to broaden the narrow social basis of its political support. On this point there is also a contrast between the list of Scheduled Castes and those of the Other Backward Classes (OBCs)—both nationally (which has not been accepted by the government so far) and in those states where reservations exist for the OBCs. There has been a tendency to appoint successive commissions, mostly by governments of different political parties, which have either raised or revised the number of social groups (usually castes) in the OBC lists and the proportion of jobs or places in educational institutions reserved for them.

An interesting example of how the OBC lists tend to be prone to sudden expansion or suggestions for expansion is to be noticed in the comparison between the reports of the First National (Kaka Kalelkar) Commission and the Second (Mandal) Commission on backward classes. According to the Kaka Kalelkar Commission (which reported in 1955), 2399 castes were classified as backward. The Mandal Commission proposed to raise the number of OBCs to 3743 castes. It is not a simple arithmetical increase in number of OBCs over the two decade, but the criteria followed by two Commissions were entirely different. Methodological approaches were too different. The rationale behind this enhanced list was nowhere clearly mentioned and as the Mandal Commission chose not to publish data it had collected through its field surveys, there is no basis for a public debate on this subject. While finalising the Mandal Report the experts were not consulted as it became evident that they disowned the Report, ofcourse after a decade in 1990 when anti reservation agitation was on. It will always remain a trenchant mystery as to why the Mandal Commission data was hidden away from the public eye. In the absence of data with which one can cross-check the classification of OBCs, the Mandal Commission Report ultimately raises the same problems which had stalked the Kaka Kalelkar Commission Report—the unavailability of a firm data base.

The two principal difficulties in classifying backward classes are concerned with the determination of the population of the OBCs and the use of different indices for listing the OBCs. It is necessary to look at these issues in some detail, both at the national and the state levels.

It is a paradox that the commissions appointed and the critics who have analysed their reports have not turned their attention to the complex problem of estimating the population of the OBCs when they are listed caste-wise, as they have been so far. On the face of it, the figures of populations suggested to date scarcely bear comparison and indicate that a more systematic analysis of the report of the backward classes commissions should be undertaken. The Kaka Kalelkar Commission Report estimated the OBC population at 116 million or about 32 per cent of the total population in 1952. The Mandal Commission in 1978 estimated the OBC population at 52 per cent of total population. This included the Hindu OBC castes (43.7 per cent of total population) and the OBCs from among the non-Hindu communities 8.4 per cent of the total population. Incidentally, the Mandal Commission failed to provide the absolute figures of the population involved and it escaped this responsibility in the main body of the report by merely referring to a Table in the Appendices which was not then published!

In effect, the Mandal Commission, like the Kaka Kalelkar Commission, made two distinct calculations: one was a qualitative sample survey to collect its own data for ascertaining the backward classes and the second was a projection of census data from the 1931 census (which was the last census to give a complete breakdown of castewise population figures) in order to generate aggregate caste-wise population figures on an all-India basis. It is evident that the data collected through the sample survey could not provide a clue to overall caste-wise population figures. Even the Mandal Commission, which conducted the largest exercise so far attempted at a socio-educational survey, could cover only two villages and one urban block in each district of India. In addition, it collected information mainly through interviews and from the list of OBCs published by various states. According to the schedule of indices constructed by the commission it then finalized a statewise list of OBCs. There was no certainty, first of all, that the method followed by the Mandal Commission had been able to cover all the castes which claim to exist within the country. Then, given the small size of the sample, the great variations in the mix of castes from one area to another, and differences in fertility patterns within the same caste group and between states and regions, there was little possibility of extrapolating aggregate, all India, castewise figures from the breakdown given by the sample survey. Yet without the aggregate population figures no recommendation could be made as to the overall share of jobs or college seats that should be reserved because since the days of the "Communal G.O." of 1927 in Madras and later the recommendations made by the Kaka Kalelkar Commission, the share of reservations for each group has been, in one way or another, proportional to its overall population.

In order to calculate the overall proportion of different castes or clusters, the Mandal Commission undertook a different exercise. It assumed "that the *inter se* rate of growth of population of different castes, communities and religious groups over the last half a century has remained more or less the same." Then on the strength of its socio-educational survey it culled out from the 1931 census caste/communitywise population figures for those it classified as forward and backward groups. Thereby it obtained the following classifications:

		Percentage of Population
A —	*Scheduled Castes and Tribes*	
A-1	Scheduled Castes (SCs)	15.05
A-2	Scheduled Tribes (STs)	7.51
	Total of A	22.56
B —	*Non-Hindu Communities, Religious Groups, etc.*	
B-1	Muslims (other than STs)	11.19
B-2	Christians (other than STs)	2.16
B-3	Sikhs (other than SCs and STs)	1.67
B-4	Buddhists (other than STs)	0.67
B-5	Jains	0.47
	Total of B	16.16
		Percentage of Total Population of India
C —	*Forward Hindu Castes and Communities*	
C-1	Brahmins (including Bhumihars)	5.52
C-2	Rajputs	3.90
C-3	Marathas	2.21
C-4	Jats	1.00
C-5	Vaishyas, Bania, etc.	1.88
C-6	Kayasthas	1.07
C-7	Other forward Hindu castes/groups	2.00
	Total of C	17.58
	Total A/B/C	56.30
D —	OBCs	
D-1	Backward Hindu castes/groups within OBC	43.7
D-2	52% of religious groups under section B	8.4
D-3	Approximate derived pop. of OBCs rounded off to a unit	52.0

There are many objections as to the procedure used and the results arrived at by the Mandal Commission. Its estimate of backward castes and groups from among the Hindus came to 43.7 per cent of the population. This represents a rise of almost 11 per cent over the estimate of OBC population by the Kaka Kalelkar Commission which only considered the Hindu sections of the population. How is one to explain this rise, especially when the base year for both estimates is the 1931 census and when despite the slowness of the modernization process, the growth of primary, secondary and higher education has more than kept pace with the growth of population in India? It is difficult to argue from any given set of statistics that taking the urban and the rural sector together, socio-economic backwardness now covers proportionately a greater section of the population that it did in 1951. Either the Kaka Kalelkar estimate should be considered to be a gross underestimation or the data on which the Mandal Commission has based its calculations be made available before the estimate of OBCs at 52 per cent of the population can be accepted.

Looking at the methodology followed by the Mandal Commission one can conjecture that its estimates of population could not be correct, even as an approximation. The Mandal Commission assumed that various castes have enjoyed, over the last 50 years, the same rate of growth as the all-India population. This is an impossible assumption to many reasons. Between 1931 and 2001 the annual rate of population growth has shown to be on the rise. However, this increase has been distributed unevenly between the states and a single national percentage for the OBCs would not be applicable to them unless it was an average of the *actual sizes of the OBC population in separate states.*

The second major shortcoming in the Mandal Commission Report is that it entirely neglects differentials within the caste in the matter of population growth, income levels and educational attainments and facilities.

It is clear that the Mandal Commission's figures of OBCs constituting 52 per cent of the population cannot be accepted and needs to be analysed by a committee which will have to design a survey method that will take into account the complexities affecting calculation of population growth in various states.

The additional questions which the report of the Mandal

Commission will have to answer when analyzed in detail, are best illustrated from a close reading of many backward classes commission reports from the states of Karnataka and Gujarat. It should be remembered that when after prolonged debate and consideration it was decided by Pandit Jawaharlal Nehru's government not to accept the Kaka Kalelkar Commission Report (primarily due to its self-confessed weak and unverified data base and unexplained adherence to caste as the principal index of classifying the OBCs), the Cabinet also decided in July 1961 that the state governments should be free to appoint their own commissions in order to make reservations for the backward classes, both under Articles 15(4) and 16(4) of the Constitution. Here one can indicate only typical problems which show the necessity for a detailed and thoroughgoing enquiry.

One of the major paradoxes a researcher is bound to observe when reading successive reports of the backward classes commissions is the absence of any effort by the latter reports to delineate and explain the differences from the earlier ones. In as much as the backward classes commissions claim to base their decisions to provide privileged concessions to certain groups on authentic sociological research and not on any arbitrary dispensation, the contradictions between two reports pertaining to the same area need to be explained and accounted for, especially when they refer to significant aspects of the issues under consideration. The Backward Classes Commission in Karnataka headed by L.G. Havanur took nearly five years to complete its work (1972-77). Subsequently, due to objections raised by many groups before the Supreme Court, the Karnataka government appointed a Second Backward Classes Commission headed by T. Venkataswamy in 1983. This commission submitted its report in 1986. Both the commissions carried out their own surveys and computed their separate lists of OBCs. The determination of caste-wise population by the Havanur Commission was made based on a sample survey in 1972-73 selecting at least one village in each taluka, one division or ward in each town municipality, two divisions in each city municipality and four or five divisions in the city municipal corporations throughout the state. Every individual in the selected 200 villages and 204 blocks was covered under the survey. The Venkataswamy Commission conducted an even more comprehensive door-to-door survey to enumerate the population of the state by religion, caste, and subcaste and to study the existing socio-economic and educational status of the communities.[13] A comparison with the earlier report was however not made and when this exercise was undertaken it showed significant unexplained differences some of which will be described in this chapter.

Evidently, despite its declared intention, the Venkataswamy Commission did not undertake a comprehensive door-to-door survey throughout the state. According to its own estimate published in Annexure 9.2 of Vol. III of the Report, whereas the Karnataka State population according to the 1981 census was 37,135,714 at the 1971-1981 rate of growth, by 1984 it should have risen to 39,920,883. The actual population according to the caste-wise socio-educational survey conducted by the Commission in 1984 was only 36,124,594 or 2.72 per cent less than the figure reported by the 1981 census and 9.15 per cent less than the figure projected on the basis of the 1981 census for 1984. This difference is neither acknowledged nor explained in the text of the report. A comparison with the Havanur Commission Report reveals that one possible reason, when compared to the 1972 survey, is that eight castes with a Scheduled Caste component had been included in the OBC list and were later transferred from it. The population of these 8 castes was 6,42,533. But when the two OBC lists were compared in detail it was observed that the Venkataswamy Commission had altogether omitted another 39 castes which had no Scheduled Caste component and whose population in 1972 was 8,42,221. Among these were substantially numerous castes like the Yadavas (4,46,893), Hanbar (34,001), Kodaga (82,271), Kolayam (20,979) and Koracha (20,164). Again, no mention or explanation of this fact was found in the Venkataswamy Commission's report. Considering that the population figure produced by the 1984 socio-educational survey (36,124,594) was the basis for its recommendations, any future report cannot be considered complete unless and until the following conditions are met: (a) a rigorous comprison is made with the previous reports on the Other Backward Classes commissions to explain differences in assumptions, survey methods and actual data collected; and (b) the data itself are despatched to all the relevant experts, those interviewed by the commission and other connected persons for their comments, and those comments are then taken into account and acted upon before finalizing the report. By implication those reports, e.g., the Mandal Commission and the Venkataswamy Commission reports against which major objections can be raised should not be accepted unless new commissions have analysed their data.

In continuation of the general criticism of the methodology adopted by many commissions, it might also be pointed out that there has as yet not come up any standard means of setting up a scale of indices to measure social and educational backwardness. In its judgement in the famous Balaji case, the Supreme Court had held that if a particular community is to be treated as educationally backward, the divergence between its educational level and that of the state average should not be marginal but substantial. The court considered 50 per cent divergence to be acceptable. It quoted the example of Bihar, where according to the 1971 census, the percentage of illiteracy was 80 per cent. If only those whose social group has a 50 per cent divergence from the state average were to be considered educationally backward then no one in Bihar could be said to be educationally backward since in order to be so, 12 per cent members of a caste/class would have to be uneducated.

The Mandal Commission decided first of all to select about a dozen castes well known for their social and educational backwardness from among its own survey in a state and use the average of their level of achievement as the minimum divergence from the state average. For example, one of the indicators for social backwardness is the rate of student dropouts in the age-group 5-15 years as compared to the state average. As a result of the above tests it was seen that in educationally backward castes this rate is atleast 25 per cent above the state average. Further it was also noticed that this deviation of 25 per cent from the state average in the case of most of the 'indicators' gave satisfactory results. In the light of this, wherever an indicator was based on deviation from the state average, it was fixed at 25 per cent because a deviation of 50 per cent was seen to give wholly unsatisfactory results and at times to create anomalous situations. This should perhaps be regarded one of the more enduring contributions made by the Mandal Commission to the OBC survey methodology.

The one full-scale report on backward classes after the publication of the Mandal Commission Report was the Venkataswamy Commission Report in Karnataka. It was a bit of a regression in this case because instead of adopting the principle of divergence from the state average, the Venkataswamy Commission constructed a schedule of indices in terms of which any deviation above the state average was regarded a sufficient qualification for backwardness. For example, the state average for those not owning any house in Karnataka was 13.11 per cent and for those owning only kuchha houses was 36.52 per cent. Any caste/recognised social group, which registered a percentage higher than this scored one point on the scale of backwardness. Out of 17 such indices, if a group scored nine or more it was considered backward and eight or less it was considered forward. Evidently, the practice of taking a single given figure as the average means that the marginal cases on either side of this limit have to be, in a sense, arbitrarily classified. Out of the thirty-nine Hindu castes and five non-Hindu communities listed by the Venkataswamy Commission, six had an exact score of nine, three had a score of ten, six had a score of eleven and seven had a score of 12. Among those listed as forward, four had a score of 8, six had a score of 7 and nine had a score of 6. Another thirteen castes were assessed on a scale of 18-20 points, an exception which created doubts about the reason for the special treatment awarded to them. A small exercise was done taking the absolute percentages against each caste and in the case of castes listed as backward subtracting three per cent and in the case of the castes listed as forward adding three per cent, to see if this range has affected their classification. Out of a sample of nine castes it was seen that four castes classified as forward would revert to the backward category if the 3 per cent range were applied to them and one caste with a score of nine would move over to the forward category. Clearly, the principle propounded by the Supreme Court and upheld by the Mandal Commission that a divergence of 50 per cent or 25 per cent from the state average should be the criteria for determining backwardness is more definitive and ought to be used in place of a single average figure. The same principle is to be applied in the case of a yardstick like the number of students passing the SSLC or High School exam in a given year being used as a measure for assessing the educational backwardness of a caste. A one-year average is not a decisive index to the cumulative stock of SSLC pass within a caste-group and it is this latter ratio or proportion which need be assessed in the course of a socio-educational survey.

The general trend has been to use caste as one among many indices to assess backwardness. There are many difficulties in concretizing the use of caste as a criterion of backwardness to which attention needs to be drawn. One of the most basic difficulties, which was mentioned as early as the 1931 census in great detail, is the growing dissociation between traditional occupation and caste. As Table 6.3 shows, based on the Imperial Tables of the 1931 census of the 23 castes for whom all-India data is given in 1931, only 33 per cent on an average continued to depend mainly on their traditional occupation. In the case of Bhats and Chamars only 7.7 per cent were wholly dependent on their traditional occupation whereas for the Jat cultivators this figure was 65 per cent, for the weavers 33 per cent, for the potters 37 per cent. This table shows the great requirement for a fresh enquiry into the relationship between caste and occupation in today's circumstances in order to understand how the process of the growth of a modern economy has affected vital features of the caste system.

It is surprising that most of the surveys commissioned by the different backward classes commissions have not undertaken to analyse the existing relationship between caste and occupation. The Mandal Commission Report assumed a more or less static and unchanging relationship between caste and social structure but the data it sought to gather did not even seek to answer the questions contained in its definition of caste. According to the Mandal Commission Report, "When dealing with the living social reality what counts is not the fine metaphysical concepts embodied in great religious works of a people but the homespun ideas that have percolated into the awareness of the masses and become a part of their world view." One of the homespun ideas it propounded was: "In this sense the caste system has meant a division of Hindu society into a number of isolated castes and *Jatis* who marry among themselves, dine among themselves and broadly pursue traditional occupations. Yet neither the data collected, nor the indicators used under the heading for social and educational backwardness, touched on any of these points. The eleven indicators that were used are classified as follows :

I. *Social Indicators*

1. Castes/classes considered as socially backward by others.
2. Castes/classes which mainly depend on manual labour for their livelihood.
3. Castes/classes where a minimum of 25 per cent females and 10 per cent males above the state average get married below 17 years of age in rural areas and at least 10 per cent and 5 per cent males do so in urban areas.
4. Castes/classes where participation of females in work is at least 25 per cent above the state average.

II. *Educational*

5. Castes/classes where the number of children in the age group of 5-15 years who never attended school is a minimum of 25 per cent above the state average.
6. Castes/classes where the rate of student dropout in the age group of 5-15 years is a minimum of 25 per cent above the state average.
7. Castes/classes amongst whom the proportion of matriculates is a minimum 25 per cent below the state average.

III. *Economic*

8. Castes/classes where the average value of family assets is a minimum 25 per cent below the state average.
9. Castes/classes where the number of families living in kuchha houses is a minimum of 25 per cent above the state average.
10. Castes/classes where the source of drinking water is beyond half a kilometre for more than 50 per cent of the households.

11. Castes/classes where the number of households having taken consumption loan is a minimum of 25 per cent above the state average.

Subsequently all the social indicators were given a weightage of three points each; educational indicators a weightage of two points each and economic indicators a weightage of one point each.

What is worth noting is the fact that none of the indicators touched upon the three characteristics earlier said to be the defining characteristics of the caste system namely marriage within the *jati*, inter-caste dining, and traditional occupations. Instead within the criterion 'social' the indicators used were such that they could not tell us much about backwardness. The first criterion,—Castes/ classes considered as socially backward by others—is so relative that it could apply to a majority castes. In local terms sub-castes are arranged in an hierarchical order and in terms of formal language such usage featuring a caste as being below your own persists long after economic and social practice has undermined any real hierarchy. Every sub-caste would be considered backward by the one theoretically occupying a position above it. The second of the social indices pertains to "Castes/classes which mainly depend on manual labour for their livelihood". Now with the fall in the phenomenon of landlordism and a slow increase in the wages of agricultural labourers since 1947 two tendencies have grown stronger—owner-cultivation with a greater involvement of family labour and the opportunity for agricultural labourers to work. Hence the incidence of manual labour in agriculture has gone up. Such manual labour unlike that of the *Bhangis* or bonded labour is economically more rewarding and hence enables one to lead a better life, even to educate one's children. It cannot be counted as a factor of backwardness. The third criterion is even less associated with caste although it does provide a measure for indicating backwardness. This is concerning castes/classes where at least 25 per cent females and 10 per cent males above the state average get married at an age below 17 years in rural areas and at least 10 per cent females and 5 per cent males do so in urban areas. Now clearly there is very little evidence to show that marriage at an early age is determined by caste. It is much more determined by education, the need for children to take part in family work or income mobilization, and one's individual belief in ritual and

TABLE 4.1
CASTE AND TRADITIONAL OCCUPATION, 1931 CENSUS

Caste	*Traditional Occupation (TO)*	*Population earners and working dependents*	*No. of earners whose TO as main means of livelihood*	*Those with TO as percentage of caste population*	*No. of earners whose TO is a subsidiary means of livelihood*	*No. of earners with TO as main but an added subsidiary occupation*	*Those in exploitation of animals and vegetation (farming)*	*Exploitation of minerals*	*Industry*	*Transport*
1	*2*	*3*	*4*	*5*	*6*	*7*	*8*	*9*	*10*	*11*
Barhai	Carpenter	760060	336176	44.2	97270	68920	283300	1694	16518	3905
Bhangi	Scavenger	555829	310983	55.9	52075	10335	118838	972	14324	4841
Bhat	Heralds	50186	371	7.7	786	677	31324	68	991	616
Chamar	Skinners	5075307	386197	7.7	125814	89877	3558939	22015	150606	41420
Darji	Tailors	212359	123687	58	47713	15975	38727	197	4144	554
Dhobi	Washermen	951058	436699	46	89355	93631	345881	2449	14387	4559
Gujar	Herdsmen	711436	269130	38	33504	12362	154073	523	3752	6208
Jat	Cultivators	2687991	1753128	65	179767	77702	147427	1519	37024	27610
Jhinwar	Palki Bearers	933098	252499	27	443966	33467	1946	32404	35691	12868
Khatik	Pig Breeders	103582	22258	21	2864	2844	51699	152	5192	2145
Khatri	Traders	185173	92992	50	9997	2468	17712	319	11288	9090
Kumhar	Potters	995300	369023	37	124191	103091	3090887	16967	12874	
Kurmi	Cultivators	2058580	1335947	65	33693	93090	2193988	1069	150606	8294
Lohar	Blacksmiths	763482	270453	35	65168	77856	268014	3361	331033	4578
Momin	Weavers	1234393	409656	33	51250	41600	520340	8181	49653	12901
Mali	Gardeners	360938	15061	4.2	8466	2056	248823	275	3603	1510
Nai	Barbers	1079229	502552	47	106351	120710	351164	1606	16129	4098
Nat	Dancers	31532	N.A.	N.A.	N.A.	N.A.	N.A.	N.A.	N.A.	N.A.
Od		50320	N.A.	N.A.	N.A.	N.A.	N.A.	N.A.	N.A.	N.A.
Pinjara		1998	N.A.	N.A.	N.A.	N.A.	N.A.	N.A.	N.A.	N.A.
Sansi		10664	N.A.	N.A.	N.A.	N.A.	N.A.	N.A.	N.A.	N.A.
Sonar	Goldsmith	274134	166256	61	16619	35404	53178	251	5590	1228
Koshti	Weavers	427340	181144	42	23107	55340	204915	3964	8258	2715
Teli	Oil Pressers	1783788	383465	22	100904	72321	935926	4405	36999	18299

Source: Census of India, 1931, vol.I, India Part II, Imperial Tables, Table XI.
TO = Traditional Occupation.

religion. These factors are not in all cases determined by caste. The remaining eight criteria are either educational or economic and once again, not linked to caste.

The contradiction between the willingness to use caste as a means of assessing backwardness and the inability to use it in any concrete manner is to be seen in the survey design of the Venkataswamy Commission Report. A five-judge Constitution Bench of the Supreme Court has suggested the use of a caste-cum-means criteria for assessing backwardness. According to them, "we laud and appreciate it (caste-cum-means criteria) as a vital landmark in the march of the Other Backward Classes towards social justice and social equality." Admirable as this desire might appear, it is a revelation to compare the questions actually asked during its survey by the Venkataswamy Commission Report. One then finds that out of the 17 criteria that were applied to collect data, not one referred to the three features considered fundamental by the Mandal Commission in defining the caste system; inter-caste marriage, inter-caste dining and traditional occupation. The indices were divided into negative and positive aspects. In the case of the negative aspects, if a group scored above the state average it indicated backwardness and in the case of the positive aspects this happened when it scored a percentage below the state average. The two indices, each under the rubric of negative and positive social aspects respectively, were whether families belonging to specific castes were houseless/siteless, resided in *kuccha* houses or *pukka* houses and the share of the caste living in urban areas. The rest of the indices once again were related to economic assets, educational achievements, and facilities and share in government employment. This great ambiguity between the use of the word caste and the total absence of empirical criteria for making use of it in accordance with its acceptable sociological definition raises a significant question about how to interpret the word `socially' in the Constitution, which refers to "socially and educationally backward classes". Clearly, the question is not whether a list of OBCs is written down and published in the form of a list of castes to whom an income criterion is then applied, as happens now. The issue is whether in *concrete empirical terms, one can measure or specify backwardness caused by caste in the case of the OBCs and what weight is given to such indices*. Clearly, if we try and use the three criteria recommended by the Mandal Commission, namely inter-caste marriage, inter-caste dining and traditional occupation, these would not be able to give an empirical measure of comparative social backwardness. Either ways are suggested of using these criteria empirically or alternative ways of assessing social backwardness caused by caste are thought of and data collected by future surveys of Other Backward Classes. Alternatively, a likely option is that if no methods are found to link backwardness to caste, the OBC lists are totally drawn up in future according to occupation, where social backwardness is seen in terms of indices referring to education, income, assets, languages spoken, travel, share of female employment outside of the home, age of marriage, access to entertainment, etc. Some of these indices have not been used by the OBC commissions in the past but will be relevant, especially in regions where rural development has or will provide many villagers with facilities now available to urban dwellers.

The inability to effectively make use of the caste criterion led the Karnataka government after it had rejected the recommendations of the Venkataswamy Commission Report, to accord priority to the income criterion. The Government Order specifying the groups of OBCs separately under Article 15(4) and under Article 16(4) listed Groups A to E as shown in the following Table 4.2.

TABLE 4.2

LIST OF OBCs ACCORDING TO KARNATAKA GOVERNMENT ORDER IN FORCE SINCE 13 OCTOBER, 1986

Backward Class	*Under Article 15 (4) (Per cent)*	*Under Article 16 (4) (Per cent)*	*Income limit under both Articles*
Group A	5	5	No income limit
Group B	15	13	Rs. 10,000
Group C	16	16	Rs. 10,000
Group D	9	11	Rs. 10,000
Group E (Backward Special)	5	5	Rs. 8,000
Total	50	50	

N.B. 1. Group A refers to Backward Tribes.
2. Income refers to family income of the citizens and his/her parents/legal guardians.
3. Limit of reservations for OBCs at 50 per cent in addition to the quota for SCs/STs.

What determines the individual's qualification for being able to use the reservation is not caste-determined criteria in this case but an income-oriented criteria, virtually applicable to the entire population subject to a means test. This is especially so since Group E refers to the Backward Special Group which according to the Karnataka government order "shall consist of the following citizens:

(i) an actual cultivator;
(ii) an artisan;
(iii) a petty businessman;
(iv) one holding an appointment either in Government service or corresponding services under private employment including casual labour; and
(v) any person self-employed or engaged in any occupation involving manual labour".

There is no caste qualification as far as the Backward Special Group is concerned. It is to be considered why then there was still a need to list the castes separately in the OBC list. In Karnataka there seems to be tradition of having caste associations. As the examination of the following section would show, the reach of these caste associations is often restricted to the economically well-off sections of the castes. In this sense it is difficult to make caste into a mass issue and as an identity, its mobilizing power creates a greatly diminishing response at the popular level (when one is referring to millions of people) than it does when one is talking of the elite groups, especially at the local levels and in the rural areas (when one is referring to hundreds or thousands of persons). The existence of the Congress and other parties as all-India organisations has already struck hard at the use of caste identities and groups. The rise of regional political parties in India and their substantial success in mobilizing voter support, cutting across caste and other ethnic groups shows the growing strength of identities other than caste. The region as a developmental unit within the nation is gaining a more extensive place in popular consciousness above that of the more localized identities like caste.

This awareness is quite different from that of the region in itself, which was more typical of the princely states of 19th century India. This is a factor that should be considered by those political leaders who might be tempted to see the issue of expanding reservations for the OBCs as a means of winning the political support of "the backward castes". It must after all be remembered that many caste associations have been established at the initiative of political leaders. It was during the tenure of Devraj Urs as Chief Minister of Karnataka that economic and administrative facilities were extended for the organisation of associations of backward castes and more than thirty such new organisations came into existence. If Devraj Urs had hoped to create a long-term base of social or political support, he was to be sadly disillusioned. Once again, the issue raised by the electoral dimension of political behaviour of people takes us back to the relevance of caste, either as an indicator of backwardness or as a powerful lever of mass identification which must continually be forced upon issues like that of defining the `socially and educationally backward classes'. The question of caste needs to be analysed separately before deciding on whether or not to dispense with it entirely in the context of classifying the Other Backward Classes.

Another aspect of social reality which weakens the argument about listing entire caste groups as backward entities is the internal economic and educational variation within the caste groups. The difference in economic conditions, assets and educational standards between castes becomes clear when one analyses the socio-economic data put together by any of the backward classes commissions. Take the example of the tables published in the Report of the Socially and Educationally Backward Classes Commission in Gujarat (1976, Vol. 11). The difference between the average figures shown for different castes reveals how these classified as backward castes themselves have widely varying standards. Each household belonging to the Ghanchi caste spent Rs. 4615 per household, while for the Rajputs this figure was Rs. 3393, for the Bhois Rs. 2871 and for the Bajania Rs. 1318, even while all these castes were classified as backward.

The range of expenditure within the caste group was further indicative of internal economic differentiation, as the following Table of selected castes shows.

These data show that without an income criteria, merely including the entire caste group as backward conceals severe income inequalities. In the case of the Scheduled Castes and Scheduled Tribes where a collective social identity is more developed because of cultural deprivations like untouchability, non-inclusion within Hinduism etc., the better-off might still suffer from psychological and social stigma and complexes. They would then feel need for support of their ethnic groups and would act to give them real leadership on the assumption that without a substantial number of their group achieving a higher status, their own social isolation would not be easily overcome. It is this distinct status of visible group deprivation of a social and cultural type which separates the Scheduled Castes/Tribes from the other backward castes. As one had argued earlier in the case of the OBCs, the commission reports so far have failed to show any caste-governed deprivation as being applicable to "socially and educationally backward classes", and this is especially true of the surveys conducted by the Mandal Commission and the Venkataswamy Commission. If caste is not shown to be the cause of backwardness, the case for applying only cultural, economic and educational criterion to identify the backward classes becomes greatly strengthened.

TABLE 4.3
AVERAGE, MINIMUM AND MAXIMUM ANNUAL EXPENDITURE PER HOUSEHOLD BELONGING TO SELECT CASTES IN GUJARAT

Name of Caste	*Annual Total Expenditure Per HH (Rs)*	*Annual Expenditure Range*	
		Minimum (Rs)	*Maximum (Rs)*
Brahmin (F)	4,070	120	18,500
Darji (B)	3,830	710	15,750
Kanabiheva (F)	4,224	1,100	13,210
Rajput (B)	3,393	120	13,900
Bajania (B)	1,318	350	4,150
Bhoi (B)	2,871	250	2,850
Ghanchi (B)	4,615	1,330	10,750

N.B. (F) Forward, (B) Backward.

Source: Report of the Socially and Educationally Backward Classes Commission, Gujarat, 1976, Vol. II, Appendix XXIX.

Such internal differentiation includes all the castes, also the scheduled castes and tribes. For those two categories the income range was as follows:

Caste/Group	*Annual Expenditure in Rs*	*Minimum*	*Maximum*
Scheduled Castes	3,191	230	36,200
Scheduled Tribes	1,923	210	7,350

Source: Report of the Socially and Educationally Backward Classes Commission, Gujarat, 1976, Vol. II, Appendix XXIX.

A quick survey of the kind of criteria prevailing in the states that have sanctioned reservations for the OBCs shows that most of them already specify an economic criterion. Only, it is applied to specified castes who are not represented within the educational set-up and the government services, in proportion to their population. The application of the income criterion in most states has been chosen without an explanation being given about it and has been changed again without any proper justification on a number of occasions. The Mandal Commission did not specify any income criteria. Instead, it assessed the value of family assets and the proportion of families taking household consumption loans. Clearly, the first criterion, namely the value of family assets, is a difficult rule to apply in the case of household goods and the chances of wrong reporting much more than in the case of current family income. It is also not right to list all families taking household consumption loans, since the value of these loans differs greatly from one household to another. Hence, an income criterion should be used.

A summary of income criteria being applied in different states has been provided by Marc Galanter (1984).[14] It is necessary to consider this data as a starting point for an examination of the income criteria to be used in classifying the OBCs.

TABLE 4.4
INCOME CRITERIA FOR THE OTHER BACKWARD CLASSES

State	*Year*	*Name of Group*	*Criteria*	*Estimate of OBC Population as share of Total Population (Percent)*
1	2	3	4	5
1. Andhra Pradesh	1975	(i) BC (ii) Economically BC	92 listed castes/communities All with income under Rs 1500	38
2. Bihar	1979	BC	Member of list of 128 castes/communities whose annual income is less than Rs 12000/-	50
3. Gujarat	1978	BC	82 listed communities	N.A.
	1972	Economically BC	All with income under Rs 4800 annually.	
4. Jammu & Kashmir	1973	Socially and Educationally BC	1. Occupations 2. 19 communities 3. Border and poor areas	N.A. N.A. 8
5. Karnataka	1986	BC Group A	42 Backward Tribes: No income limit	N.A.
		Group B	95 castes: Within them those having an annual income of Rs 10000	N.A.
		Group C	5 communities: Within them those having an annual income of Rs 10000	N.A.
		Group D	7 castes: Within them those having an annual income of Rs 10000	N.A.

1	2	3	4	5
		Group E	5 occupations: Within them those having an annual income of Rs 8000	N.A.
	1979	(i) BC	List of 16 communities, 129 castes and 62 tribes	45
		(ii) Economically BC	All with annual income under Rs 4800	
6. Kerala	1977	Socially and Educationally BC	Members of listed communities with income less than Rs 10000	N.A.
	1972	Socially and Educationally BC	Members of listed communities with income less than Rs 6000	N.A.
	1970	BC	Members of 560 listed communities with income less than Rs 8000	N.A.
7. Maharashtra	1966	OBC	list of communities	N.A.
8. Tamil Nadu	1972	BC	list of 105 communities	51
9. Uttar Pradesh	1978	BC	list of 58 communities	N.A.

Source: Marc Galanter-Competing Equalities:Law and Backward Classes in India, 1984, Oxford University Press, London, Table 20.

Although Marc Galanter has provided the data on the income criteria actually being used in states, he has said nothing on why these are so varied or why they have been changed over time. The discrepancies in the known statistics for wages reveal that generally the figures are far higher than those prevailing for jobs categorized as badly paid. Few years back the Labour Minister's Conference was held in Delhi that recommended a minimum wage of Rs. 11 per day for agricultural workers. With this as the base it can be noted that in a state like Bihar the annual income of an agricultural labourer would be Rs. 3960. In actual practice, as one knows, the wages paid are often much less than this and so the limit of Rs 12,000 per annum which has been put as a maximum criteria for the backward classes contains many other income levels above that of the agricultural labourers. According to exhaustive data collected by the Ministry of Labour, the wage rates of unskilled labour provides a good basis for assessing the income criterion set up for the backward classes in various states. There is a need to review these income criteria and justify a new one on the ground that it actually covers the educationally backward.

In Karnataka the wage rate mentioned by the Ministry of Labour on 30.1.1985 was Rs. 9.50 to Rs. 14.00 per day, according to class of work and type of land. This gives us an annual income range of Rs. 3420 to Rs. 5040. In comparison, the cutoff points for most groups of backward classes under the latest scheme of the Karnataka Government is Rs 10,000. This is three times the lower figure for unskilled labour and twice the highest salary given to artisans, handicraftsmen, etc. In several states there are no income criteria applicable, for example, Andhra Pradesh in 1975 and Gujarat. Exact estimates of OBC population are also not available in Gujarat, Jammu and Kashmir, Maharashtra, Uttar Pradesh and many other states. At the very least an enquiry is needed to find out the OBC population in those states where a reservation system already exists. Such a demand is likely to arise in the future as this is one of the questions which groups excluded from the OBC list or individuals unable to make use of the reservation system could well ask. It also needs to be answered purely from the point of view of estimating the actual extent of social and educational backwardness and the economic poverty which is linked to it.

Future Policy Perspectives

The question of policy about reservations, as far as the backward classes are concerned, is whether one should argue for an expansion of the reservation system, for cutting down its size, for freezing it as certain levels, for its abolition or for other reforms within it to make it more effective as a means of promoting social equality, without provoking a breakdown of social consensus. It is significant to ask this question now because conflicts over the reservation issue add to other conflicts like communalism, which already threaten to fracture the Indian polity. Besides, the system of reservation had at one time, especially in the latter half of the 1960s and the whole of 1970s, appeared to many political leaders and policy makers as an important instrument of providing an escalator for representatives of deprived social groups or of those with nascent economic wealth but without a reasonable representation in the administration or in the educational world. If political leaders had taken the lead in establishing or extending the reservation for the OBCs expecting to build a stable political base, their calculations have proved to be wrong. In every national election and major state election, those who have been classified as OBCs have clearly shown the capacity and the will to take their own decisions. They have generally been affected by other identities and other issues. Insofar as reservations provide jobs only to a few persons among a particular social group, their usefulness as an avenue of patronage or reward is restricted. This is especially so because the cohesion of social groups like sub-castes—never really existed, and if it did it has now been greatly loosened by a number of factors like language, region, occupation and income, which tend to influence various members of these groups differently.

One kind of political opinion advocates eschewing any discussion or research on the subject of the reservation system in the hope that this will prevent notice being taken of its shortcomings. This is shortsighted for it overlooks the real social factors which will continue to force a discussion about the manner in which the system of reservations is working and the limits that should be imposed on it so as to prevent it from disrupting the social consensus that has characterized its operation for a long time. It is only when these factors are highlighted that it becomes obvious why the reservations issue is likely to be of political relevance for some time to come.

TABLE 4.7
RATES OF LITERACY AND PATTERN OF HIGHER EDUCATION IN SEVERAL STATES

State/ All-India	*Per cent literate Total 1981*	*Per cent literate Urban 1981*	*Per cent literate Rural 1981*	*Number of Colleges Arts, Science and Commerce*		*Total Number of College students 1983/84*
				1981	*Total 1983/84*	
All-India	36.0	57.2	29.6	3652	5246	3359323
Average per state	-	-	-	174	250	159968
Andhra Pradesh	29.7	51.1	23.2	287	420	273176
Bihar	26.1	51.9	22.3	331	473	228441
Gujarat	43.8	60.3	36.3	191	285	204697
Karnataka	38.4	56.4	31.1	314	498	259804
Kerala	69.2	75.0	67.8	128	184	140226
Maharashtra	47.0	63.8	38.0	472	693	397280

Source: 1. Registrar General and Census Commissioner of India, *Census of India*, 1981, Series 1, India, Paper 3, Provisional Population Totals, Workers and Non-Workers, 1981.
2. *University Grants Commission Report*, 1983/84.

The four states where, in the last year, there has been a vigorous discussion about the future course of the OBC reservation system (as well as protests against attempts at expanding it or excluding groups already included in the OBC list) are Gujarat, Karnataka, Andhra Pradesh and Kerala. In addition, during the last so many years, the two states where there have been protests against the expansion of the OBC reservation system and the operation of a reserved seat system for the Scheduled Castes are Bihar and Maharashtra. One common observable characteristic in all these six states is that although they have a different rate of literacy, the number of colleges and the students enrolled within them are far above the all-India average. (Table 4.7)

TABLE 4.8
JOB SEEKERS REGISTERED WITH EMPLOYMENT EXCHANGES (AS ON JUNE 30, 1980 EXCEPT WHERE SPECIFIED OTHERWISE)

(In thousands)

States/ All India	*Matric and above but below graduates*	*Graduates including post-graduates*	*Total*	*Unskilled manual labourers and others*	*Total of all Job Seekers*	*Job Seekers as on May 31, 1985*
All-India	5882	1415	7297	7873	1517	24179
Average per state	196	47	243	262	51	806
Andhra Pradesh & UP	487.6	114	601.6	714.4	1316	2218
Bihar	594.6	117	711.6	1504.4	2216	2650
Gujarat	217	42.3	259.2	118.8	448	652
Karnataka	287.2	76.1	363.3	206.7	570	811
Kerala	639	71.8	711	657	1368	2461
Maharashtra	493.2	101	594	539	1134	2102

Source: *Commerce Research Bureau*, Bombay, October, 1986.

The key ratios to look at are those concerning the total number of students. In Kerala, the number of students in colleges is 12 per cent below the all-India average. In Andhra Pradesh it is 71 per cent higher, in Bihar it is 43 per cent higher, in Gujarat it is 28 per cent higher, in Karnataka 62 per cent and in Maharashtra 148 per cent higher than the all-India average. In Kerala, although the number of students enrolled in colleges is below the all-India average, the relatively greater numbers in the schools make up for this deficiency. It stands to reason that in these states the number of educated job seekers will tend to be higher than in other states or the all-India average. This fact is confirmed by a look at the statistics complied by the Economic Monitoring Service of the Commerce Research Bureau in Bombay. These are reproduced in the Table 4.8.

Statistics on State Economics

The number of job seekers shows the great pressure that exists on the economy to create jobs or some form of self-employment. For those who consider themselves unemployed the sight of more jobs being reserved for specific categories is much less acceptable than the feeling that they have won or lost through a system of open competition. Indeed, our system of education has not been closely associated with the specific manpower needs of the economy and therefore there is every likelihood to produce a surplus of the wrong kind of degree holders. The psychology of the unemployed is not to demand reservations, but to resist its expansion or demand the application of cultural, educational and economic criteria that are not limited by caste. A good example of such a reaction is the loss in popularity experienced by the Congress-led government in Kerala when it did not implement its initial promise to provide a 15 per cent reservation in schools, on the basis of only economic criteria. It would be an interesting exercise to conduct an opinion survey among the job seekers on their opinion of the function and the future of the reservations system. No such surveys have been made so far. One of the elementary facts such a survey may be expected to find out is the spread of educated job seekers over all the different social, religious and linguistic groups.

Another significant reason why the reservation issue is going to remain in focus politically is connected to the question of how the population of the backward classes has been estimated so far. According to the information given by the central government ministries and departments to the Mandal Commission, the latter estimated that the OBCs constitute 12.55 per cent of the total number of government employees, whereas their aggregate population is 52 per cent. Their representation is Class I jobs is only 4.69 per cent, i.e., less than 1/10th of their proportion to the country's total population. As has been revealed at length, the estimates of OBC population, both at the national and state levels, are subject to varying but definite and often a big margins of error. Clearly, if the estimates of OBC population themselves are questionable, then to say that only 12 per cent of OBCs are government employees and compare them against an erroneous population estimate is equally mistaken. Until and unless a reliable estimate of OBC population is provided, other calculations based on such an estimate too will be suspect. The same observation may be made about the more detailed estimates which are often presented by Members of Parliament during the course of several debates. For example, during the discussion on the Mandal Commission Report in the Rajya Sabha in October 1982 one Member of Parliament presented a set of statistics (Table 4.9) which claimed to show the relative position of various categories in different classified services.

TABLE 4.9
RELATIVE POSITION OF VARIOUS CATEGORIES IN CENTRAL GOVERNMENT SERVICES AS PRESENTED BY AN HONOURABLE MP TO THE RAJYA SABHA IN OCTOBER 1982

	Scheduled Castes Percentage	*Other Backward Classes Percentage*
Class I	7.18	2.59
Class II	13.56	3.98
Class III & IV	30.95	8.41
Total Services	16.83	4.83

Source: *Parliamentary Proceedings*, Parliament Library, Vol. XXIV, 11-15 October 1982, pp. 249-50.

The claim made in the above table cannot be a credible one as long as the actual basis for classifying the backward classes is not available. Whereas the MP had claimed that only 4.83 per cent of all central government employees belong to the OBCs, the Mandal Commission had estimated this to be 12.55 per cent. Clearly, such discrepancies come up because in order to strengthen the claims of the backward classes many political leaders are generally prepared to use statistics that underestimate the actual extent of representation of the backward groups.

Some time after the Constitution was enacted, the Supreme Court, in the famous Balaji case, ruled that reservations for Scheduled Castes/Tribes and the Other Backward Classes together should not exceed than 50 per cent of the total available seats. Since it was a ruling of the Supreme Court and not enforceable by law, for some time it was observed by all the states. Soon enough, the 50 per cent barrier was crossed and Karnataka reserve 68 per cent of seats and jobs for SCs/STs/OBCs. Kerala 54 per cent,

Tamil Nadu also 68 per cent Andhra Pradesh approximately 43 per cent, Jammu and Kashmir almost 50 per cent, and Bihar close to 51 per cent. The Constitutional Bench of the Supreme Court has made efforts to rationalize this situation by advising, through a majority decision, that each state can fix its own quotas according to its specific conditions. This is a significant revision and from the standpoint of the letter and spirit of the relevant constitutional provisions an unfortunate one, since it encourages pressures for the further expansion of the reservation system. The government can help to remedy the situation by introducing the 50 per cent limit as a part of the constitutional provisions themselves, emphasizing that a system of reservation must function alongside that based only on merit and not swallow the latter altogether. The share of reservations allocated to the Scheduled Castes and Tribes in this rule should come first and the difference up to 50 per cent be proportionately divided according to the criteria used for classifying the backward classes. The case for such a constitutional amendment is strengthened by the fact that despite estimating the OBC population at 52 per cent, the Mandal Commission recommended that only 27 per cent of the central government jobs be reserved for the OBCs. This figure of 27 per cent was arrived at by deducting the 23 per cent already allocated to the SC/ST from the 50 per cent limit prescribed by the Supreme Court in its ruling in the Balaji case. With this 50 per cent as the maximum limit, states can feel free to adjust the level of reservations at the minimum possible, as per the existing social consensus and demand. Such an arrangement will both be flexible and have the additional advantage of conforming to the known intentions of the Indian Constitution makers to limit the reservations system to a minority share of available places.

Finally, a major policy issue concerning the system of reservations as a whole is one of time limit, which may be a renewable one. Such a time limit exists in the case of Article 340 where reservations of political seats in the legislatures for Scheduled Castes and Tribes is done every ten years. Many of the members of the Constituent Assembly recommended a similar time limit for reservations as a whole. According to them, a time limit, say of twenty years, would provide an occasion for a comprehensive review of progress in the implementation of the reservation quotas and the extent to which they have achieved the goal of social justice and equality. A rigid enforcement of the education and income criteria will automatically provide an entry and exit point for members of a family entitled to use the reservation system. There may be some other kind of entry and exit system. The Venkataswamy Commission had suggested that those families who have used the reservation system for three generations may be disallowed the future use of reservation quotas for some jobs and for college education. Such exclusion may be acceptable if it is also decided that the right to avail of reservations can be restored to families which have not used the reservation system for three generations.

The provision and enforcement of an entry/exit/re-entry system would need a proper monitoring machinery as a part of the regular administration. The Ministries of Personnel may monitor the progress of implementation of reservation policy in Central Ministries/Deptts. and States/Uts. With the growth in the numbers of the educated job seekers such an entry/exit system will prove popular. It would probably face resistance from within those groups/families who have so far been able to use the system of reservations on a more continuous basis. Inorder that such resistance is not excessive and eventually leads to a social consensus, two measures could be advocated. As earlier suggested, the direct descendants of those who left the reservation system after having used it for a specified time could use it again after a certain period of time, if they satisfy the income and other criteria for the users. Secondly, such provisions for entry/exit may be introduced as a part of a package scheme for the welfare of the backward classes, either in the form of rise in the number of scholarships or through schemes for giving loans, etc.

In the present scenario of a growing number of educated job seekers, an expansion of the reservation quotas is not at all desirable. The present levels of reservation is limited to 50 per cent maximum, thereby giving full scope to a system on the merit. The introduction of the reservation system into new areas should also be not allowed since it offers a solution, if at all, to a tiny minority. If such an extension becomes necessary as a concession it should be accompanied by an entry/exit system from the outset. In today's circumstances and those of the foreseeable future, programmes of increased growth, increasing output and mass welfare rather than reservations for small numbers will meet the needs of the people. The adoption of a statutory maximum limit of 50 per cent for all reservations on an all-India basis, an entry/exit system, a more rational criteria of classification and estimate of OBC population and a renewable time limit can provide, as suggested above, a meaningful basis in efforts to build a political consensus on the reservations issue during the coming decade.

References

1. Shah Ghanshyam, "Agitations in Gujarat" in Seminar (375), November, 1990, p. 54.
2. Lamaya, Madhu, "Democratic Weapon" in Seminar (375), November, 1990, pp. 61-62.
3. Ramchander, N., Reservation Policy in India (ed.) by B.A.V. Sharma and K. Reddy, New Delhi: Light and Life, 1983.
4. Census of India 1931: Bombay: Government of India, Vol. VIII, Part I, Statement No. 17.
5. Sharma, G.S., Legislation and Cases on Untouchability and Scheduled Castes in India, New Delhi: Indian Council of Social Sciences Research, 1975.
6. Rao, M.S.A. Social Movements and Social Transformation, New Delhi: Manohar, 1987 (Reprint).
7. Census of India, 1931: Madras. Madras: Government of India.
8. Census of India, 1931: Baroda. Baroda: Government of India.
9. Galanter, Marc, Competing Equalities: Law and the Backward Classes in India, Delhi: Oxford University Press, 1984.
10. Parliamentary Debates, Vol. XII-XIII (Part II) Col. 9830.
11. Constituent Assembly Debates: 30.16.1949, pp. 680-86.
12. Gallanter Marc, *op. cit.*
13. Government of Karnataka Report of the Second Backward Classes Commission, Vol. I, 1986, pp. 141-42.
14. Gallanter Marc, *op. cit.*

Five

Reservational Justice: Problems and Solutions

Indian society is stratified into caste hierarchy. Upper castes which are numerically in minority weild the power in Indian Social structure. By virtue of their position in power structure they become ruling elite and enjoyed all priviledges available in the society. As a result lower caste people who are numerically preponderant and in majority always remained deprived of benefits such as education, economic available in the society. These privileges are available to upper castes. That is the reason why did lower castes SCs, Sts and OBCs raised their demand to get the benefit as a matter of right over a century. In India it is majority which has been deprived of, which is persecuted, and discriminated by a small number of upper caste people who have effective control over levers of power — be it administrative or political. The other distinguishing feature of Indian scene is that positive discrimination does not have its justification in India on the basis of utility. Indian style of justification of reservational justice is based on the ground of constitutional rights. One is sure to get bewildered on the reservational issues in India because of many misgivings arising out of misconceptions of the real involved in it. First, to all numerical majority to secure reservational justice to itself may look strange and give the impression that majority may ensure its own aggrandisement at the cost of others. M.N. Buch, said that, "the virtual monopolisation of power by Brahmins, Rajputs and Kayastha has been commented upon by many authorities. Such a monopoly, however, can only survive under feudal rule in which society is stratified. Democracy, being a game of numbers and as power shifts to elected rather than appointed official, the dominant caste in politics would naturally be the most numerous and not the one which is highest in the social hierarchy."[1] Educated persons belonging to upper castes took benefit of employment opportunities and in Indian politics. There were many other attributes of dominance of upper castes in the society. So far, Indian scene has been dominated by upper caste people in general and single dominant caste people in particular. In class I services of the Union Government upto three decades of the functioning of the Constitution the representation of upper castes has been 89.63 per cent as against the 4.69 per cent representation of backward classes and 5.68 per cent representation of Scheduled Castes/Scheduled Tribes. The representation of the upper castes whose population approximates 25.34 is too high, i.e., more than 3.5 times than the percentage of the population of the community. In comparison, the 4.69 per cent representation of the backward classes constituting 52.10 per cent is too low, i.e., nearly 1/12th of the percentage of the population and 5.68 per cent representation of Scheduled Castes/Scheduled Tribes constituting 22.60 is also considerably low, i.e., 1/4th of the percentage of the population. The poor state of the representation of backward classes in prominent offices becomes obvious in view of the figure presented in the following table:

Sl. No.	*Department/Ministry*	*No. of Class I Officers*	*No. of Backward Class Officers*
1	*2*	*3*	*4*
1.	President Secretariat	48	None
2.	Vice-President Secretariat	7	None
3.	Atomic Energy	35	None
4.	Civil Supply and Co-operative	31	None
5.	Communication	42	None
6.	Health and Social Welfare	240	None
7.	Labour Ministry	74	None
8.	Parliamentary Affairs	18	None
9.	Petroleum and Chemical	121	None
10.	P.M. Office	34	1
11.	Cabinet Secretariat	20	1
12.	Agriculture and Irrigation Ministry	261	14
13.	Defence Ministry	1379	9
14.	Education Social Welfare	259	4
15.	Electronics	92	2
16.	Energy	641	20
17.	Foreign Ministry	649	1
18.	Finance Ministry	1008	1
19.	Home Ministry	409	13

1	2	3	4
20.	Industry Ministry	169	3
21.	Information and Communication	1506	124
22.	Law Department	143	5
23.	Legislative Department	112	2
24.	Company Affairs	247	6
25.	Planning	1262	72
26.	Science and Technology	101	1
27.	Shipping and Roadways	103	1

Source: Udyan Sharma, Arakshana in Ambedkar Centenary Special Issue dated 14.4.92.

The above table gives the measurable position of backward classes in union services and highest representation of upper caste people in the union services.

The position in political affairs is the same. The joint percentage of the population of SCs/STs/OBCs is nearly eighty per cent. Out of 12 PMs so far, there has been only one P.M. from OBCs. Out of 12 PMs, 6 belonged to Brahmin caste, 1 to Bhumihar, 1 to Kayastha, 1 to Jat, 2 to Rajput caste and 1 Bania. The detail is given below:

Sl.	*Name of P.M.*	*Caste*	*Tenure*
1.	Pt. Jawahar Lal Nehru	Brahmin	1947 to 1964 (four times)
2.	Sri Lal Bahadur Shastri	Kayastha	1964—1966
3.	Smt. Indira Gandhi	Brahmin	1966—1977
4.	Sri Morarji Desai	Bania	May 1977 to June 1979
5.	Chaudhary Charan Singh	Jat	June/July 1979 to Dec. 1979
6.	Smt. Indira Gandhi	Brahmin	Jan. 1980 to Oct. 30, 1984
7.	Sri Rajeev Gandhi	Brahmin	Oct. 1984 to Nov. 1989
8.	Sri V.P. Singh	Rajput	Dec. 2, 1989 to Nov. 7, 1990
9.	Sri Chandrashekhar	Rajput	Nov. 7, 1990 to June 1991
10.	Sri P.V. Narshimha Rao	Brahmin	June 1991 — May 16, 1996
11.	Sri Atal Behari Vajpai (Even when he could show support of only 195 M.Ps out of the House of 537 and resigned on 28.5.96 before voting for confidence)	Brahmin	1996
12.	Shri H.D. Dev Gowda	Gowda	June 1, 1996
13.	Shri Indra Kumar Gujral	Forward	
14.	Shri Atal Behari Vajpayee	Brahmin	1998 till date

Political Scene in U.P.

The political dominance in Uttar Pradesh from the beginning was in the hands of forward castes / upper castes most of the times as shown in the numerical order: Brahman (8), Thakur (Rajput) (4), Vaishya (3), Yadav (2), Jat (1), Lodi 91) and SC (1).

Sl.	*Name*	*Community*	*Tenure*
1	*2*	*3*	*4*
1.	Pt. Govind Vallabh Pant	Brahmin	17.7.1937 to 2.11.1939
2.	Pt. Govind Vallabh Pant	Brahmin	14.4.1946 to 20.5.1952
	First Assembly from March 8, 1952 to March 31, 1957 = 5 years 24 days		
3.	Pt. Govind Vallabh Pant	Brahmin	20.5.1952 to 27.12.1954
4.	Dr. Sampurnanand	Kayastha	28.12.1954 to 9.4.1957
	Second Legislative Assembly From April 1, 1957 to March 6, 1962 = 4 years 11 months 6 days		
5.	Dr. Sampurnanand	Kayastha	10.4.1957 to 6.12.1960
6.	Sri Chandrabhan Gupta	Vaishya	7.12.1960 to 14.3.1962
	Third Legislative Assembly From March 6, 1962 to March 9, 1967 = 5 years 3 days		
7.	Sri Chandrabhan Gupta	Vaishya	6.3.1962 to 1.10.1963
8.	Smt. Sucheta Kriplani	Brahmin	2.10.1963 to 13.3.1967
	Fourth Legislative Assembly From 10.3.1967 to 15.4.1968 = 1 year, 1 month, 15 days.		
9.	Sri Chandrabhan Gupta	Vaishya	14.3.1967 to 2.4.1967
10.	Chaudhary Charan Singh	Jat	3.4.1967 to 25.2.1968
	Fifth Legislative Assembly From 26.2.1969 to 4.3.1974 = 5 years 6 days		
11.	Sri Chandrabhan Gupta	Vaishya	26.2.1969 to 17.2.1970
12.	Chaudhary Charan Singh	Jat	18.7.1970 to 1.10.1970
	President Rule 1.10.1970 to 18.10.1970		
13.	Sri Tribhuvan Narain Singh	Thakur	18.10.1970 to 3.4.1971
14.	Pt. Kamla Pati Tripathi	Brahmin	4.4.1971 to 12.6.1973
	President Rule — 13.6.1973 to 8.11.1973		
15.	Sri Hemvati Nandan Bahuguna	Brahmin	8.11.1973 to 4.3.1974
	Sixth Legislative Assembly From 1.3.1974 to 30.4.1977 = 3 years, 1 month, 26 days.		
16.	Sri Hemvati Nandan Bahuguna	Brahmin	15.3.1974 to 29.11.1975
	President Rule 30.11.1975 to 21.1.1976		

Sl.	*Name*	*Community*	*Tenure*
17.	Sri Narayan Dutt Tewari	Brahmin	21.1.1976 to 30.4.1976
	President Rule 30.4.1977 to 23.6.1977		
18.	Sri Ram Naresh Yadav	Backward (Yadav)	23.6.1977 to 27.2.1979
19.	Sri Banarsi Das	Vaishya	28.2.1979 to 19.2.1980
	Eighth Legislative Assembly 9.6.1980 to 10.3.1984 = 4 years 9 months 2 days		
20.	Sri V.P. Singh	Kshatriya	9.6.1980 to 18.7.82
21.	Sri Sripati Mishra	Brahmin	18.7.1982 to 3.8.84
22.	Sri Narayan Dutt Tewari	Brahmin	3.8.1984 to 10.3.1985
	Ninth Legislative Assembly 10.3.1985 to Dec. 1989		
23.	Sri Narayan Dutt Tewari	Brahmin	11.3.1985 to 24.9.1985
24.	Sri Veer Bahadur Singh	Kshatriya	24.9.1985 to 24.6.88
25.	Sri Narayan Dutt Tewari	Brahmin	25.6.1988 to Dec. 89
	Tenth Legislative Assembly Jan. 1988 to Feb. 1991		
26.	Sri Mulayam Singh Yadav	Backward (Yadav)	Jan. 1990 to May 1991
	Eleventh Legislative Assembly June 1991 to 6.12.1992		
27.	Sri Kalayan Singh	Backward (Lodh)	June 1991 to 6.12.92 (dismissed)
	President Rule 6.12.1992 to Nov. 1993		
	Twelfth Legislative Assembly Nov. 1993 to 27.10.1995 = 2 years		
28.	Sri Mulayam Singh Yadav	Backward (Yadav)	Nov. 1993 to 11.6.1995
29.	Km. Mayavati	Scheduled Caste	11.6.1995 to 17.10.1995 = 4 months 10 days
	President Rule 7.10.1995 to 17.10.1996 = 1 Year		
	Again President Rule on 17.10.1996 to 20.3.1997 = 5 months 3 days		
30.	Km. Mayawati	Scheduled Caste	20.3.1997
31.	Sri Kalyan Singh	Backward (Lodh)	
32.	Sri Ram Prakash Gupta	Bania	
33.	Sri Raj Nath Singh	Thakur	
34.	Km. Mayawati	SC	2002-03
35.	Sri Mulayam Singh Yadav	Yadav	2003

Not only CMs even ministers from backward classes did not find adequate representation in the cabinet. For the first time in Sampurnanand Minisry of 1957 to 1960 Ram Swaroop Varma and Jai Ram Verma two deputy ministers were chosen from backward classes. In Chandrabhan Gupta cabinet of 1960 to 1962 only Ram Swaroop Yadav was included as Deputy Minister in Chandrabhan Gupta Ministry of 1962-1963 Shivaraj Singh and Jaya Ram Verma were inducted as deputy ministers, in Sucheta Kriplani Ministry there was only one deputy minister of backward class ; in Chandrabhan Gupta Ministry of 1967 there was not even a single BC minister. For the first time in the Charan Singh Ministry of 1967-68 the backward class was given due representation by inducing 3 cabinet Ministers and 4 Deputy Ministers.[2] It shows that upto 1960s the upper caste dominance continued both in services as well as in ministries. Thus, it would not be justified to say that backwards could safeguard their interests through political power. Political power still remains under the command of upper castes. In West Bengal where it is said that caste plays no role in politics at operational level it is there. For instance in the Left Front State Cabinet in 1984 of the total of 43 members, 17 were from high caste Brahmins, 12 from high caste Kayastha, one high caste Vaisya surname and two upper middle caste surnames.[3] In Southern States where there was developed and long tradition of backward class movement BCs could claim reservations for them on the basis of political clout. Now atleast at State level BCs are asserting their position and strengthening their status in northern states too. There is likelihood that BCs will assert their claims of more and more benefits through legislative process or governmental actions. Tamil Nadu government categorically insisted total reservation for SCs/STs/OBCs and 69 per cent. It passed the law namely the Tamil Nadu Backward classes. Scheduled Castes and Scheduled Tribes (Reservation of Seats in Educational Institutions and of Appointment or Posts in the services under the State Act, 1993 (Tamil Nadu Act, 45 of 1994) and it was put in Ninth Schedule by the Constitution (Seventy-sixth Amendment) Act, 1994. One lurking fear arises that because electoral dominance BCs will add privileges to their aggrandisement at the cost of the others. The fear is not genuine due to two factors. First, on numerical basis BCs may control political power, i.e., government and legislature, but the services are prevailed upon by upper caste people who have always been putting obstacles in effective implementation of reservational provisions on one pretext or the other. Second, numerically backward communities may be in a majority and accordingly it can be said that they will allow aggrandisement for themselves. But in reality the scene is dominated by dominant castes. Laloo Prasad Yadav is an exception who is able to carry on the government for a considerably long time. In UP no BC Chief Minister has been allowed to carry on beyond 2 years. They have fallen victims of high caste politics. The twenty months Mulayam Singh Yadav government went out of power because of BJP conspiracy to dislodge him by alluring Mayawati for Chief Ministership. BJP did install her as CM. But did not tolerate for long and withdrew support within a period of four months few days. The high caste politics killed two birds with one stone. SP and BSP got divided, came at front with daggers drawn and the possibility of Joint front of backwards got frustrated at least for few years. Had SP and BSP combination lasted during 1996 elections they would have swept and BJP would have been no where.

In UP, BSP was either No. 1 or 2 in 22 constituencies and SP was number one or two in 43 constituencies.[4] Had the both remained combined 65 out of 85 seats would have gone to SP BSP combinations. The details of the four constituencies in Gorakhpur Region is given below:

Constituency	*Party which won candidate/votes*	*Candidate No. 2 and votes*	*Candidate No. 3 and votes 1*	*Total of SP + BSP*
1	2	3	4	5
Deoria	Sri Prakash Mani BJP 227155	Nand Kishore Singh JD-SP 180228	Murad Ahmad Lari, BSP 92819	273047
Basti	Sri Ram Chauhan, BJP 199941	Ram Karan Arya, SP 150103	Lalmani, BSP 132513	282616

Padrauna	Ram Nagina Misra, BJP 196903	Kasim Ali SP 153299	Baleshwar Yadav, 116353	269652
Maharajganj	Pankaj Chaudhari, BJP 182850	Harshwardhan, BSP. 149304	Akhilesh Singh SP 119462	268766

1996 UP Assembly election result indicates the same trend.

Somebody may reason that in politics 2 + 2 is not always four. But it is also true that in most of cases it may be or may have unimaginable effect even beyond four by creating strong electoral force as was found in 1977 when Janata Dal won all the 85 Lok Sabha seats in UP and 54 in Bihar. The voters waiting on fences join the forceful current and add to the victory. There is truth in what Mandal Commission observed, "Caste lost on ritual front, it gained on political front." According to Kothari (1973) caste identities which were still strong and distinct provided the principal media of political participation.[5] He writes, "Those who in India complain of casteism in politics are really looking for a sort of politics which has no basis in society."[6] Caste-politics interaction has produced the results—first, the caste system available to the leadership, structural and ideological basis for political mobilisation; second the leadership was forced to concede to local opinion, take its cue from the consensus that existed as regards claims to power. Political parties played their part in educating people of their rights and privileges in general in articulating their support; *third,* the emergence of vertical and horizontal caste associations have become hall mark of political mobilization;[7] *fourth,* through politics caste groups get a chance to claim their identity and to strive for position.[8] It is also true that this is so due to lack of positive avenues for such caste people. He raised a question: "Had other avenues of social advancement and status mobility been available to the aspirant caste groups, it is doubtful whether politics would have been so much impressed by caste as it is... Politics affords to the lower castes an opportunity to achieve through politics what they can not through social instrumentalities."[9] No doubt, caste plays important role in Indian Politics. Earlier Congress exploited the principle of caste in election.[10] Now post emergency awakening has given rise to backward castes/parties. The process of polarisation will take place sometime and in the last phase of stability the slogan of social justice will work as stimulant for backward classes to unite under some solid combinations. Even if backward classes unite there is no danger of aggrandisement according to Judicial outlook.

The Supreme Court ruling of 50 per cent limit of reservation finally approved in the *Mandal Case* in 1992 reveals that balance between the reservational avenues and general or merit pool would be maintained at any cost. The political influence and pressure cannot allow reservation beyond 50 per cent limit. This issue relates to heart burning among all savarnas—Brahmins, Kshatriya, Baniyas, Kayasthas, Bhumihars, etc. due to their wrong thinking that reservation will harm their interest. Reservation policy for Scheduled Castes and Scheduled Tribes is in existence for many years. According to forward castes this policy is anti meritariary. There was no reservation for OBCs in Central Services before 1993. Were all savarnas given the equitable share in services? If not who robbed them? As a matter of fact before 1993 the competition was within the Savarnas themselves. Brahmins made use of their talent and resourcefulness to enormously increase their share in services. With their tradition of learning, their role in freedom struggle and its arrangement of their full return with caste backing led them to capture almost all seats of power. They had competition only with Kayasthas who had tradition of learning. Thakur did not bother about services. Bhumihars were wealthy landlords and did not have much attraction for service, Banias did not aspire for services due to their business mentality.

Social Justice is guiding spirit and therefore in the area of reservational justice merit theory cannot be over emphasized. In words of Hegde, J. the nation's interest will be best served taking a long term view — if the backward classes are helped to march forward and take their placces in a line with the advanced sections of the people.[11] From the long range perspective immediate benefits of the Nation in the effective utilization of talent have to be harmonised with its long-range interests.[12] This justice-oriented concept led Gajendragadkar, J. to say in Balaji case that the interests of weaker sections of society which are a first charge on the States and the Centre have to be accommodated with the interests of the community as a whole.[13] One of such community interest was to erase the caste consciousness. The framers of Constitution did not think that caste will remain for long. Article 15, 16, 29 etc. prohibit discrimination based on caste, religion, race, place of birth etc. But different provisions of the Constitution like Article 26, 29(1) and 30 recognise religion and language or culture and script for special treatment. But caste is not recognised as such identity. Thus, the Court came to conclude that caste can not be sole or dominant criterion. But the problem of some stable criterion of determining backwardness continued. Despite its laudability economic status could not be such an criterion. As soon as a person is given reservational benefit he jumps out and crosses the boundary of backwardness. The Courts had to look at caste as criterion searching the possibility of group identification. In *P. Rajendran v. State of Madras,*[14] Wanchoo, C.J. ruled that caste is also a class of citizens and if the caste as a whole is socially and educationally backward reservation can be made in favour of such a caste. This line of argument dominated in *Triloki Nath v. State of J and K (II),*[15] *Peeriakaruppan v. State of Tamil Nadu,*[16] *State of A.P. v. U.S.V. Balaram.*[17] The emphasis got changed: "a caste has always been recognised as a class". The Court found it a suitable criterion. Desai J. ruled in *K.C. Vasanth Kumar versus State of Karnataka*[18] that caste is the primary index of social backwardness and said that so sadly and oppressively deep-rooted is caste in our society that it has cut across even the barriers of religion. This led Kania, C.J. and Venkatachaliah, Ahmadi and Jeevan Reddy, JJ to conclude that caste is nothing but a social class — a socially homogeneous class.[19] So did Sawant[20] and Pandian, JJ. Thus it forms a solid and stable criterion of backwardness. Louis Dumont felt that the road to abolition of caste system in India is likely to lie in caste action.[21] Likewise D.L. Sheth observes that "there is no sanction in the Constitution for applying economic criteria; either exclusively or primarily for reservations. And there seems to be no escape from using caste as a primary criterion for reservation."[22] However, in *Mandal case,* Thommen, Kuldip Singh and Sahai, JJ said that caste as criterion was not permissible. The harsh reality of Indian social life has come to the surface and the biggest fall out of its assertion is going to be acceptance of reservation for Dalit Christians and Muslims. One may very well agree with comment that in the Indian crucible "all that is solid melts into air...[23] and in the midst of entrenched injustice, it echoes Gramsci's admotion to be a pessimist of the intellect; an optimist of the will.[24]

The judgement of the Supreme Court in *Mandal Case* reveals the extreme tension which the Court wished to solve. The quietness of the Supreme Court was quietness of a storm Centre. The judges were aware of the unabated pro as well as anti-reservation agitations and violent societal disturbances virtually disrupting the normal life. The Court took notice of the fact. It asserted that sitting as a Judge one cannot be swayed either way while interpreting the constitutional provisions to the issues and controversy by the mere reflexes of the opinion of any section of the people or by the turbulence created in the society or by the emotions of the day.[25] The issues taken up by the Court were hypersensitive, highly explosive and extremely delicate. Perhaps India has entered a fundamentally new era, in which courts do not simply respond when problems are left untended by other institutions, but instead, display an ongoing activism that frequently affects the conduct of public policy. Of course, the Court was asked "to finally settle the legal position relating to reservations" but circumstances were not conducive. The nine member Bench in the Mandal Judgement (1992) was division of opinion in ratio of four, three and two. It can be conveniently drawn that majority judgement was over other numerically minority three hair thin and two judges decision. It was good luck of backward classes they won the case by narrow margin and not a matter of victory or joy at large.[26] Many a critic of reservation welcomed the Mandal verdict for the ousting of creamy layer from Backward classes.[27] The verdict will cause heart-burning in some sections but it would be beneficial for the whole society in the long-run.[28] Student Federation of India showed their appreciation for the socially advanced sections among OBCs had been kept outside the purview of the reservation.[29] The other group appreciated the decision with desire that reservation of economically backward should be considered.[30] A section of teaching community saw danger of splitting the Indian society. It is open to debate whether caste-based reservation will split the society or bring cohesiveness. Rajni Kothari expressed the view that "if you want to bring casteism to an end, provide more reservations for the backwards."[31] Likewise Ram Jethmalani is unequivocal on the point when he said, reservations do not perpetuate caste. They destroy its ugly manifestations.[32] Of course, it introduces non-sectarianism in services. One feel inclined to agree with Ghurye that, we are marching towards caste pluralism instead of a casteless society. The issue of creamy layer in absence of empirical study about the percentage of OBCs in services is too much haste. It may be laudable but not at once but when 27 per cent quota is filled in. It would be appropriate to mention the fact many personnel at different levels in government setup hardly understand well-meaning of criteria led down in the order to exclude creamy layer. As a result many genuine OBC persons face great difficulty in getting their OBC certificate. This order needs to be simplified from the present complex and confusing nature.

It is to be noted that wherever the Courts have chosen to decline a certain class to be treated as backward they have insisted on sufficiency of data to prove the backwardness of that class.[33] There is no reason why the Court should not demand data to prove that the share of OBCs is being consumed or grabbed by creamy layer and 27 per cent has already been filled by OBCs? Thus, it is required that a larger full bench (of justices more than nine Judge Mandal bench) be constituted to look into the matter afresh in cool atmosphere free from psychological terror and horror to anti-reservation agitational violence and self-immolation. It is the sole responsibility of Government of India to provide data on OBC. The Government initially decided to include OBC in census 2001 but due to many political pressures and criticism the decision was not implemented.

Protective Discrimination

Protective reservations to SCs/STs/OBCs are the by-product of unwritten reservations of dominant higher castes perpetuating hostility, discrimination and unequal treatment in societal system[34] and in words of Kuldip Singh, J. 'with passage of time this system has become the cancer-cell of the society'.[35] The Hindu caste system conveyed the message, Divided we are—come and rule us and Turks, Mughals and Britishers came and ruled us. The ill-impact of caste system is not limited to the Hinduism. It is perpetuating and has infiltrated even amongst Muslims, Christians, Sikhs or others although it initially had no place in their region.[36] Casteism has become bane of the entire Indian society. And, therefore, we are not very sincere when we say that reservation is a remedy or a cure for the ill effects of historical discrimination which allows compensatory justice or inter-generational justice or when we speak of reservation as a concept having in it the seeds of termination. These are theoretical and principle based assumptions which are far from the practical implications. Discrimination is still going on in the shape of untold or unwritten reservation. It has affected the society in two ways. First, in peculiar Indian conditions reservation can never be self-liquidating because the reasons compelling such concessions will never die. The story of the perpetuation of reservation for SCs/STs in the legislatures originally meant for 10 years is the glaring example. The political parties have not taken enough measures to ensure representation of SCs/STs without reservation and their confidence has not been won. The hard fact is that either there shall be reservation or no representation. And therefore, 10 years figure in Article 334 is being changed after the expiry of the data at the end of each decade. Now it is fifty and by the end of 1949 it will be sixty and so on. Similarly, in services there is no guarantee of the recognition of merit even if backwards do have that. The caste structure of Selection Committees, interview boards and over all control of levers of power rule out the possibility of fair dealing and recognition of merit and merit alone. This tendency alongwith non-commitment to get reservation policy implemented effectively is bound to perpetuate the reservation and perpetuation not liquidation is the fate of reservational justice to OBCs in India. *Second*, India is going to and is bound to pay heavy price of its ingrained caste ridden structure. Max Muller in 1869 declared that Caste cannot be abolished in India, and to attempt it would be one of the most dangerous operations that was ever performed in a political body. As a religious institutions caste will die; as a social institution, it will grow bigger. And in 1980 Mandal

Commission said, 'what caste lost on ritual front it gained on political front'. Infiltration of casteism into other religious communities and continued social tyranny has inspired and led to demand of reservational benefits to dalit Christians and Muslims. Thus, in the light of perpetuation of discriminatory practices the fate of reservation is perpetuation and expansion and not self-liquidation. Had Mandal Commission Report been implemented honestly such acute problems would have been discouraged.

The basic difference in American and Indian social structure attracts different considerations. As pointed out earlier, in America a tiny number of minority of Negroes had suffered discriminatory treatment at the hands of white people. In India the majority of population has suffered discriminatory treatment at the hands of a minority dominant caste people controlling the levers of power. Thus, the American style of justification for positive discrimination or protective discrimination is based on ground of utility as against which the Indian style of justification is based on the ground of constitutional rights[37] under Articles 15(4), 16(4), 46 and so on. The moving spirit behind reservational justice is not equalitarian but equalisational justice.

It is relevant to probe why Scheduled Castes and Scheduled Tribes have not been able to advance them and reach a level par with forward castes in last fifty years or so. One of the important reason is low literacy level among these groups after every decade. There is no appreciable rise in literacy level and especially among females. This has its cause-effect relation of getting reservation benefit in service sector. It is further clarified that when persons of these groups have not acquired minimum educational level required for entry in governmental service at class IV level how could they enjoy taste of fruits of reservation. We should not forget a real fact that those Scheduled Castes (e.g., Chamars) and Scheduled Tribes (e.g., Meenas) have advanced themselves educationally and occupy high position, pass on benefits to their generation only and other not advanced groups remain at the same level. This too applies for OBCs (e.g., Ahirs and Yadavs).

Major area relates to value preference in cases of reservational justice to OBCs. The accent of Article 16(4) is collectivist and not individualist. Reservational Justice to OBCs is not only eminently just but necessary to implement the constitutional aspirations to ensure stability, unity and prosperity of the country. Proper representation in administration of all the sections of society through reservational participation would help "to promote healthy administration of the country avoiding sectarian approaches and securing the requisite talent from all available sources.[38] The harsh reality is that intelligence and administrative capacity is no longer the monopoly of one class, caste or community. There is much weightage in conclusion of Sawant, J. when he says, "there cannot be a more compelling goal than to achieve the Unity of the Country by integration of different social groups of social integration cannot be achieved without giving equal status to all. The administration of the country cannot also be carried on impartially and efficiently without the representation in it of all the social groups and interests, and without the aid and assistance of all the views and social experiences. Neither democracy nor unity will become effective, unless all sections of the society have an equal and effective voice in the affairs and the governance of the country.[39] Thus the provision of Article 16(4) is clear and aims not at amelioration of the conditions of backward people by alleviating poverty but to give the backward classes a fair share in power.[40] Reservation for backward class seeks to achieve the social purpose of sharing in services which had been monopolised by few of the forward classes.[41] Mandal Commission itself visualised three chief merits of reservation to backward classes: First, by increasing the representation of OBCs in Government services, we give them an immediate opportunity of participation in the governance of the country; Second, the presence of OBCs in services has tremendous psychological spin off effect and the entire community of that backward class. Candidates feel socially elevated. The feeling that now it has its own man in the corridor of power acts as morale booster ; and third, the main advantage of reservation is not that it will introduce equalitarianism among OBCs when the whole rest of the Indian society is seized by all sorts of inequalities. But reservation will certainly release the grip of higher castes on the services and enable OBCs in general to have a sense of participation in running the affairs of their country. Sharing of power by the various segment of society has great merit in itself. In words of Sawant, J. "this would help to promote healthy administration of the country avoiding sectarian approaches and securing the requisite talent from all available sources".[42]

Fourth, Supreme Court did not choose to pronounce upon the genuity or ingenuity of Mandal Commission Report due to the fact that the Government had not accepted Mandal Commission Report in toto nor had the Government accepted the list of OBCs in its entirety. Only those classes were selected as to be backward which were common both in Mandal Report and respective State Commission's Report. Thus, the validity of Mandal Commission Report was not controversial. It was the validity of the OM issued on basis of Report which was under challenge which for all practical purposes adopted the respective State Lists, as they obtained on August 13, 1990.[43] Only Kuldip Singh, J. found fault with Mandal[44] and Pandian, J. found merit in it.[45] Whatever be the limitation of the Mandal Commission report, there was over reaction on labelling certain castes belonging to Brahmins and Kshatriyas without any empirical and social basis. To strengthen this argument mere prefixing or suffixing Brahmin, Kshatriya or Vaishya to any caste do not change place and position of a caste to forward caste. This is a biased thinking. For example, Raona Rajput of Rajasthan is a socially backward and included in the Mandal State and Central lists of Backward Classes of the state. Agrahari Vaishya, Kamlapuri Vaishya and Poddar find place in the list of Backward Classes of Bihar. They are not socially advanced castes. There are many such examples. Had it chosen only caste as criterion some denigrated castes of Brahmins and Rajputs would not have found place in the list of OBCs nor non-Hindu communities would have been included in it. Mandal was more prophetic on the point. Mandal took all possible precautions and improved sufficiently over Kaka Kalelkar Commission which had taken into caste considerations. Mandal had taken in view social, economic and educational criterion. Likewise identification of classes was based on the realities prevailing in 1980 and not in 1931. That too on the basis of country-wide socio-educational field survey and census report of 1961. The same method had been followed in section 5 of the Scheduled Castes and Scheduled Tribes Order (Amendment) Act,

1976. Since the census based on Castes was stopped after 1931 census it was but natural that it should have been used for cross examination. Due to higher rate of population growth in lower classes the percentage of population of lower castes would have increased more and more than that of the higher classes. The insufficiency of information furnished by Government was felt by the Commission, that is to say, "No State Government could furnish figures regarding the level of literacy and education among the backward class" (para 9.30) or "No List of OBCs is maintained by the Central Government, nor their particulars are separately compiled in Government offices (para 9.47). This in itself is enough to grant reservation to OBCs in order to make their presence felt in the services. The plea of non-availability of sufficient information or identification of OBCs on improper criterion is taken with a view to frustrate the preferential treatment schemes. Such a move could be seen in *Chhotelal Pandey* v. *State of U.P.*[46] After submission of the Report of Chhedilal Sathi Commission (U.P. Most Backward Classes Commission) in May 1977 suggesting 29.5 per cent reservation of seats/posts for backward classes, the U.P. Government decided to give 15 per cent reservations in departmental promotions vide G.O. No. 2003/40/N/Integration 6-11-77 dated August 20, 1977. In April 1978 U.P. Public Service Commission conducted examinations for 150 posts of Judicial services and composition of reservation of seats was like this — 27 posts for SCs, 3 posts for STs, 8 posts for dependents of Freedom Fighters, 12 posts for deformed military personnel and 23 posts for backward classes. Its validity was challenged in the High Court through Writ Petition No. 2637 of 1978 by Chhotelal Pandey and 6 others. The issue was heard by T.S. Mishra and K.N. Goyal, JJ. and Division Bench declared the Government Order as violative of Articles 15(4) and 16(4). Said, the learned Judges, having given our thoughtful consideration, we are driven to the irresistible conclusion that the Government Orders dated 6th September 1955, 17th September, 1958 and 20th August, 1977 are a fraud on the constitutional power conferred on the State under Articles 15(4) and 16(4) of the Constitution in the sense the expression has been defined in *M.R. Balaji supra*, and are, as such, invalid. It will, of course, be open to the government to pass fresh orders for reservation after identifying the backward classes through proper investigation and inquiry.[47] The Court directed the respondent State to withdraw reservation of posts in U.P., Nayayik Seva to be filled on the basis of competitive examination 1977 for the so-called Backward Classes. In Civil Appeal No. 577 of 1979, i.e., *State of UP v. Chhotelal Pandey*[48] the Supreme Court stayed the High Court order and 15 per cent reservation continued. On August 11, 1978 on final hearing the Court did not have occasion to decide the issue on merit as the government Counsel submitted that government has appointed a Commission to identify backward classes and therefore, the appeal was disallowed on August 11, 1987. The order of the Division Bench consisting of O. Chinnappa Reddy, M.H. Kania and K. Jagannath Shetty, J.J. reads as follows:

> "We think, it is really unnecessary to go into the merits of this appeal. The orders of the Government of Uttar Pradesh identifying the Backward Classes for recruitment to the post of Munsifs struck down on the ground that Backward Classes had not been properly identified.
>
> We are told that subsequently another Commission had been appointed to go into that question and the Commission had submitted a report and it is stated to be under consideration of the State Government. We, therefore, do not think it necessary to go into the merits of the appeal. The appeal is, therefore, dismissed."

Views of Eminent Leaders

The bitter fact is that the U.P. Government did not appoint any Commission after Chhedilal Sathi Commission. Sathi apprehended that the counsel of the government has submitted wrong informations owing to savarna mentality to undo reservation[49] in regime Sri N.D. Tewari government. Due to dismissal of appeal 15 per cent reservation ended on August 11, 1987. The Government had ultimately to nullify the impact of decision by passing U.P. Public Services (Reservation for Backward Classes) Act, 1989 on October 6, 1989 with retrospective effect from August 20, 1977. *Fifth*, the claim of merit, i.e., performance on tests, examinations, interviews etc. cannot rest on the moral deservingness of individual candidates. It rests upon the supposed consequences; those with higher merit will be more efficient or productive; awarding them society's scarce resources will result in more indirect benefits for their fellows. In words of Marc Galanter the argument of merit is an argument for production of more social well-being.

Anyway in every case it is an empirical question whether the test of performance is actually a very good predictor of performance. Many factors are to be taken into considerations. Merit depends upon showing of sufficient grit and determination, intelligence, diligence, potentiality and inclination in performance of duty. *Second,* Dr. Ambedkar's example is worth citing. The obvious conclusion that reservation is not anti-meritarian. The biggest merit of job reservation is sharing of power by OBCs and due to wide participation in administration it ensures avoiding of sectarian approaches. Likewise efficiency means responsive service to the people. It includes sense of belongingness and accountability. Efficiency is not a *mantra* whispered by the Guru in the 'Shishya's ear'. An efficient administrator is the one who possess among other qualities the capacity to understand with sympathy and therefore to tackle bravely the problem of large segment of population constituting the weaker section of the people. To quote Chinnappa Reddy, J. efficiency cannot be permitted to be used as cover, to let the "upper" classes take advantage of the backward classes in its name and to monopolise the services, particularly the higher posts and the professional institutions.[50] *Sixth,* the greatest myth in some services is that open pool appointments are based on merit. In most of the cases it is revealed that merit has no role to play. Considerations other than merit prevail. In most of the cases a candidate with minimum statutory qualification gets appointment of the seat of the selection committee. Worst in career is appointed and best in career is omitted.

The dominant caste power clique and their conspiracy to keep others out of posts becomes successful. There is peculiar tendency. Such people counter reservation as anti-meritarian but they adopt the same anti-meritarian measurements in selections to open posts—more so in the Universities. The dominant caste clique does not want to let go any key administrative posts irrespective of their most vulnerable candidates. This perpetuates injustice and inequalitarianism. Such inequality is more injurious—it does not harm only the unequals but it hurts the whole society. Such discrimination — negative discrimination with a view to help less meritorious dominant caste person and humiliate meritorious OBCs, goes to the root of unwritten reservation.

Seventh, inter-linked to the above issue is the case of promotions. It is myth that everybody becomes equal when he claims for promotion. Promotions depend on a number of factors like favourable evaluation by superior officers who rate subordinate in Confidential Report (CR) as outstanding, very good, good, etc. In most of the cases higher caste bias prevails[51] and promotions are blocked based on unfavourable ratings.[52]

Eighth, many a conclusions relating to higher education and posts are impressionistic. The Hon'ble Court in *Mandal case* ruled that Professor's post[53] should be immune from quota system or best talent should be reserved for teaching job.[54] In spirit and principle this ideal is very high. It is most unfortunate that the essential qualification for the post of a Professor is "any eminent person...." and not formal educational qualification of doctorate degree or even Post-graduate degree in the subject and other conditions applicable to the posts of Readers and Lecturers in the same university as required. Does it ensure that if there is no reservation most talented and meritorious candidates would be appointed? In Universities where there were no reservations during the four decade functioning of the Constitution, steep deterioration in standards is noted. Due to non-sayable unwritten reservations worst have got appointments and best have been denied the chance. The deteriorating standard, mass production of Ph.Ds, without any worth and use, development of non-teaching culture have marred University education. Has non-implementation of reservation in the educational institution, so far, been able to ensure impartiality in searching best talent and best teaching service? It has seen deteriorated standards without reservations from *Pothi Pandits* (well-read teachers) to *Khaini Pandits* (teachers taking Chaitanya Churna or *Surti* in classes). The representation of different caste group without reservation in Gorakhpur University was as follow:

CASTE-WISE POSTS HELD BY TEACHERS IN GORAKHPUR UNIVERSITY (AS ON 31.1.1990), SANCTIONED POSTS: (33 + 76 + 238 + 5 + 4) = 356

Caste category	*Professor*				*Reader*				*Lecturer*	
	Regular	*Personal Promotees*	*Total*	*Per cent*	*Regular*	*Personal Promotees*	*Total*	*Per cent*	*No.*	*Per cent*
1	*2*	*3*	*4*	*5*	*6*	*7*	*8*	*9*	*10*	*11*
A. Upper Caste Forward										
1. Brahmin	10	9	19	43	15	42	57	41.2	51	36.2
2. Thakur	4	1	5	11.3	6	13	19	13	26	18.8
3. Bhumihar	1	—	1	2.3	3	2	5	3.8	4	2.8
Total	15	10	25	56.6	24	57	81	58.0	81	57.8
B. Intermediary Caste Forward										
4. Kayastha	6	5	11	25	6	23	29	20.25	24	17.3
Bania	4	2	6	13.6	4	4	8	6	11	6.8
Total	10	7	17	38.6	10	27	37	26.25	35	24.1
Total A+B	25	17	42	95.2	34	84	118	84.25	116	81.9
C. Backward Castes										
6. Yadav	—	—	—	0	2	2	4	3	2	1.6
7. Others Koeri, Kurmi, Sonar, Nonia Barai, Khatik	—	—	—	0	1	1	2	1.6	12	8.1
Total	—	—	—	0	3	3	6	4.6	14	9.7
D. Minorities										
8. Mohammedan	1	—	1	2.4	2	3	5	3.6	3	2.4
9. Christian	—	—	—	0	—	2	2	1.6	2	1.6
10. Sikh	—	—	—	0	—	3	3	2.1	1	0.8
Total	1	—	1	2.4	2	8	10	7.3	6	4.8
E. SC, ST										
Harijan, Dhobi, etc.	—	—	—	0	—	3	3	2.25	2	1.6
F. Others										
Bengali, Punjabi etc.	1	—	1	2.4	1	1	2	1.6	2	1.6
Grand Total	27	17	44	100.0	40	99	139	100.0	139	100.0

The academic standards are getting further deteriorated in the wake of vicious atmosphere of promotion scheme and with multiplicity of promotion schemes — single promotion, double promotion and triple promotions. Under single promotion scheme a lecturer becomes Reader and a substantive post-holder Reader becomes Professor; under double promotion scheme a lecturer gets elevated to the post of Reader and again as Professor. Under triple promotion scheme an Instructor is elevated as lecturer, then from lecturership to Readership and again from Readership to Professor. In UP Universities one may come across three types of Professor:

I. *Lecturer-Professor* — Professor whose substantive post is that of a lecturer and when he retires from Professorship a lecturer's post becomes vacant.

II. *Reader Professor* — A Professor whose substantive post is that of a Reader and after his retirement Reader's post fall vacant.

III. *Professor in his own right* — A Professor whose substantive post is that of a Professor.

A comparative chart is produced below :

Regular Post	*Substantive post held by incumbent (SPP)*	*Single Personal Promotion*	*Substantive post held by incumbent*	*Double Personal Promotion (DPP)*	*Substantive post held by incumbent*
1	2	3	4	5	6
Professor	Professor	Professor	Reader	Professor	Lecturer
Reader	Reader	Reader	Lecturer	Reader	Lecturer
Lecturer	Lecturer	Selection Grade Lecturer	Lecturer	Lecturer	
		Senior Lecturer			
		Lecturer			

The obvious fallout of promotional avenues in the Universities is that the different schemes have introduced the idea of notional Readership and Professorship. From the angle of the monetary gain ali higher promotions are nothing but the other name of

Lecturership. This 'sure' is not a healthy sign of academics marching towards glorious Twenty-first Century.

How academic atmosphere is polluted and populism has prevailed over academicism is clear from the following trends. First, a promotee or double promotee Professor is elevated on plea of removing of stagnation and thereby frustration and once appointed he enjoys all administrative and other privileges as a regular Professor. Sometimes statutory fraud continues. The First Statutes make use of the word 'temporary addition to the cadre' without equalising promotional posts to the regular posts and continuing legacy of the lower post to the last. Second, the regular posts are not filled in and promotion under compulsion is done on war footing. Is there any advantage of allowing more or less automatic promotions on such a large scale, not filling regular vacancy in fear of reservation quota and necessarily denying right of seniority and administrative posts to open post holders by detaining regular selections? *Third,* a Professor can be appointed without the positive recommendation of the Selection Committee or even against the negative recommendation of the Selection Committee.

Views of Supreme Court

Ninth, the Supreme Court's unequivocal recognition of caste as a class and thereby a basis of identification of other backward classes tells volumes of hard social reality. It affirms that idealism cannot go long and gap between perception and performance cannot last. For a considerable period there has been an ideological tussle in the Supreme Court taking zig-zag path. Dr. Rajeev Dhavan was prompted to comment that "new ideas are being added without discarding the old ideas and generate a kind of doctrinal overload with result that "law does not evolve in the Supreme Court, it meanders".[55] At last, the Supreme Court had to concede the caste system, though predominantly known in Hindu society runs through the entire fabric of the social structure. The caste is a reality. It is stable mark to be relied upon for identification of backwardness. The bogy of caste divisiveness cannot overlook the surface reality for long and salvation of India's problem may lie in allowing all castes presence in all walks of life atleast with a view to avoid sectarian approach of selective casteism of upper caste prevailing since immemorable time and having full-fledged blooming in post-Independence era by converting three per cent pre-constitution participation in central services into 75 per cent within a period of four decades.

The hard reality of Indian life convinced the majority of the nine judges bench that caste-based backwardness has to be eradicated by allowing them participation in administration of the country and therefore certain conclusions have been arrived at : (a) backwardness of OBCs need is unequal to the backwardness of SCs/STs; (b) in determination of backwardness more accent lies on social backwardness as it is direct consequence of caste status; (c) the primary duty to identify backward classes rests with the government on whose shoulder lies the burden of implementing policies; (d) representative government has to ensure reservational justice and therefore it may be either through the parliamentary action or executive orders; (e) to make the effective implementation of the policy of reservational justice OBCs may be subdivided into backward classes and most backward classes; (f) clause (4) of Article 16 is not exception to clause (1) of Article 16. It is an instance of classification implicit in and permitted by clause (1) or an emphatic way of stating a principle implicit in Article 16(1).

Tenth, despite progressive looking Courts and unequivocally recognising Article 16(4) not as exception to Article 16(1) and the claim that it is very much a provision as clause (1) of Article 16 is, the Courts have consciously or unconsciously strengthened status quoist approach and have applied clause (4) to Article 16 more or less as exception to clause (1) Article 16.

Suggestions

In view of the conclusions arrived at on principle based equality tested empirically and realist approaches the following suggestions are given keeping in view to ensure justice to all instead of leaving it at the mercy of unwritten reservationists.

1. The issue of 'creamy layer' among OBCs is not as simple as it has been assumed by majority in *Mandal case.* It must be based on solid empirical grounds which cannot be prepared on impressionistic conclusions sitting in ivory

towers. Few observations need to be verified and tested. *First*, the stress on women education by making the educatedness of mother as relevant factor for determination of backwardness or otherwise may be a welcome move. It is mother which shapes the upbringing of the child and therefore, the emphasis on graduation of mother of a candidate has its own merit. Second, Justice Ramanandan Prasad Committee itself appears to be under influence of the merit of Chinnapa Reddy, J's observation in Vasanth Kumar Case demolishing the criticism that the benefits of reservation are often claimed by the top creamy layer of backward class or caste and observation of Pandian, J. that it is an apt reply to such a criticism.[56] The Committee also cited Pandian, J. to expose the stark reality that reservations for OBCs had not been enforced in Central services and it is after more than five decades since the advent of the Constitution that the Government took steps to implement this scheme of reservation for OBCs under Article 16(4).[57] It also cited S. Sahay "A Moment of Truth" published in the Hindustam Times, Patna Edition, dated 26.11.1992, quoted by R. Prasad, J. para 38, p. 10, to express the fear that after skimming off of creamy layer many posts remain unfilled.[58] And therefore, it suggested that in identification of creamy layer an extraordinary cautious approach is called for, i.e., stability of creamy layer and spreading of cream or more appearance should be the determining factor. Exclusion is to be preferred only if the roots of the ill-effect of backwardness has been eliminated and even its shadow is not visible.[59] Creamy layer does not mean cream in flow but stable layer of cream. The observation of the Committee in para 37 itself hints at the postponement of the exclusion of creamy layer for sometime. The Committee reports : Will it not be just and desirable that the pace needs to be accelerated and before putting the brake some distance be covered? Otherwise it may help status quoist: "There is no enough fruit in the garden and so those who are in want to keep out those who are out." Thus the creamy layer test to skim off the advanced section of backward classes, though laudable in principle, should be postponed till the 4.69 per cent representation in higher services reach the level of 27 per cent. Otherwise, it would amount to taking away with one hand what is given with other and would serve the purpose of upper caste status quoist control of levers of power by denying OBCs the power sharing.

2. In order to make sure that reservations as self-liquidating process and not self perpetuating any semblance of discrimination based on unwritten reservation should not appear. They have to disappear from the services. To quote V.P. Singh, "reservations within our hearts must finally go. The need of governmental reservations will then vanish.[60] Since unwritten reservation is the cause and governmental reservation is the effect, the effect cannot be eliminated unless the cause is removed. That is the message of Sawant, J. who emphatically said in the Mandal Case that "the goals can not be realised unless all sections of society participate in the state power equally irrespective of their caste, community, race, religion and sex and all discrimination in sharing of the State power made on those grounds are eliminated by positive measures.[61] Otherwise, reservation for OBCs will meet the same fate of perpetuation which reservation in legislatures for SCs/STs has met under Article 334 about which it has been observed that if all the political parties make efforts to help as many as Scheduled Caste persons as possible to return to Lok Sabha and Vidhan Sabhas against General Seats, the time will automatically come when the need for separate reservations may disappear.[62] But this stark reality will never happen. Since the cause of conceding reservation under Articles 330 and 332 continues to exist the ten years figure is being repeated after the end of period by another 10 years, being at present 50 and so on. Contrary Article 16(4) is not for any specified period. Unless OBCs are assured of equal treatment based on merit and merit alone and so long as discrimination will continue, the provision of reservation cannot be scrapped. Unless cause of

unwritten reservation is removed the effect of reservational justice to OBCs will continue to remain in operation.

3. Reservation need to be allowed at promotional stages too. The reasons are obvious : First, it is only impressionistic that after initial appointment everybody becomes equal. All may be equal on paper but in practice they are not. A higher caste employee has better chances of promotion than OBC of even better achievements than the upper caste employee. Second, if reservation can be practiced in all services including the top ones, why not to apply it in promotional cases where OBCs may have to suffer the clique of upper caste mania — not to see anybody else on high administrative posts. Third, promotion is also an incidence of appointment and therefore Rangachari ruling despite its overruling in *Mandal case* appears to be quite reasonable. Fourth, reservation is intended to ensure sharing of power in all services and not lower services only. Therefore, reservation should be allowed at promotional stages. The Constitution (Seventy-seventh Amendment) Act, 1995 (assented on 17.6.95) has negated the effect of *Mandal case* on the point in relation to SCs/STs. Newly added clause (4) inserted to Article 16 reads inter alia: "(4A) Nothing in this Article shall prevent the State from making any provision for reservation in matters of promotion to any class or classes of posts in the services under the State in favour of the Scheduled Castes and the Scheduled Tribes which, in the opinion of the State, are not adequately represented in the services under the State". There is no reason why it should not be applicable in the case of OBCs and why at all have they been left out. OBCs also bear upper caste persecution and discrimination. They are under represented in upper posts. And, therefore clause (4A) of Article 16 should be suitably amended to include all backward classes of citizens — SCs/STs and OBCs, not having adequate representation in the services. Fifth, the opinion of the Supreme Court on the issue of promotion is mere *obiter dicta*, as it did not arise in the *Mandal case* and therefore, Rangachari decision allowing reservation in promotion should not be considered as overruled.

4. The *Balaji-Devadasan* formula of 50 per cent limit of reservation is conventional restatement of equalitarian justice with balance between reservational posts and general pool. The controlling spirit behind reservational justice is that as every power must be exercised reasonably and fairly, the power conferred by clause (4) of Article 16 should also be exercised in a fair reasonable manner and within reasonable limit. Normally, it should be within limit of the 50 per cent.
   (a) Reservation to OBCs is over and above the merit pool and is not a guaranteed minimum. Since, the reservation system under Article 16(4) does not operate like communal reservation, i.e., reservation quota fixed for each community as prevailed during British times, reservation has to be over and above the merit, i.e., the OBCs candidates competing others in merit should not be counted within 27 per cent. The 27 per cent limits for OBCs must be over and above those who are chosen in merit pool.
   (b) The 50 per cent limit must apply to vertical reservational categories, i.e., reservation for SCs/STs/OBCs. Horizontal reservations cut across the vertical reservations and are known as interlocking reservations. Reservation under Article 16(1) must be accommodated in percentage of the particular category to which the candidates belong, i.e., general, SC, ST, OBC etc.
   (c) Carry Forward Rule in itself is not a bad idea. It is valid if it comes within 50 per cent limit of the reservation for SCs/STs/OBCs. The Arithmetical limit of 50 per cent in any one year should not be pressed too far because the posts relate to reservational categories left unfilled earlier. Thus, the 50 per cent must include flexibility for application of carry forward rule.
   (d) The percentage of reservation need to be worked out in relation to number of posts in a particular cadre, class, category or grade (unit for the purpose of applying the rule of reservation) and not with respect to vacancies.
   (e) No reservation in certain significant services and super

specialities should be given liberal interpretation. It should be left to the decision of the government to make policy decision whether to apply reservation to such services and super specialities or not. Only merit should be the criteria for selection to such posts.

5. It is in the interest of the country that reservation to OBCs be implemented honestly and sincerely. Government and upper caste clique should not be applied to ineffectuate it. Otherwise, impartiality and non-sectarian approach in administration would always lead to element of doubt.
   (a) The government and political parties should avoid creating confusion in reservational justice to OBCs by alluring people with assurance of reservational benefit to economically backward classes, as it would not be possible due to its flexibility and instable and unconstitutional nature.
   (b) The circumvention of reservation policy by resisting its implementation, circumventing by violating norms should be avoided and stern action should be taken against erring officials.
6. Roster system should be applied effectively. There are two pattern of rosters — (i) the post-wise reservation and (ii) total or cadrewise reservation. The cadrewise reservation may face problem if common selection committee is not ensured. Any roster should be applied in such a way that reservational posts are not lost. Judiciary should interpret roster in order to safeguard the interest of backward classes. It should avoid the policy of literal interpretation like strict recycling in retrenchment cases; filling up unfilled vacancy of reserved category from general category candidates and not by other reserved category candidates in absence of specific provision to that effect and applying running account roster system.
7. Dereservation of posts should be avoided as far as possible. It should be processed only if it is not reasonably possible to fill the post by successive three efforts and that too after due permission of the departmental authorities. Effective means for filling the reserved quota should be adopted.

And instead of dereservation exchange of quota between different reservational categories be preferred, that is to say, if post reserved for ST remains unfilled, it should be filled by SC and if SC's post is unfilled, it should be filled by OBCs.

8. Effective measures should be taken to discourage taking benefit of reservation on the basis of false certificates. Stern action should be taken against such candidates.
9. Central and State Backward Classes Commissions have been established. But they are not properly maintained and lack in staff and resources.

References

1. Buch, M.N., "Caste Aspersions" in The Times of India, dated 30th January, 1994, p. 16.
2. Sathi, Cheddi Lal, Bharat Ki Aam Janta Soshan Mukta Va Adhikaryukta Kaise Ho (in Hindi), 1992, p. 141.
3. Mitra Ashok, "Lower Castes in Bengal are resigned to their Fate" in The Telegraph, dated 25.7.1986. .
4. Dainik Jagran, dated 11.5.1996.
5. Kothari Rajani, "Caste in Indian Politics", New Delhi: Orient Longman Ltd., 1973, p. 16.
6. *Ibid*.
7. Prasad Ishwari, Reservation—Action for Social Equality, New Delhi: Criterion Publication, 1986, p. 49.
8. *Ibid*., pp. 49-50.
9. Kothari Rajani, *op. cit*.
10. Wad, S.B., Caste and Law in India. 1984, p. 73.
11. Vishwanath v. State of Mysore, AIR 1964 Mys. 132 at p. 136.
12. Periakaruppan v. State of Tamil Nadu, AIR 1971 SC 2303 at p. 2309.
13. Balaji v. State of Mysore, AIR 1963 SC 649 at p. 661.
14. (1968) 2 SCR 786, AIR 1968 SC 1012.
15. (1969) 1 SCR 103, AIR 1969 SC 1.
16. (1971) 1 SCC 38.
17. (1972) 1 SCC 660.
18. 1985 Supp. SCC 714.
19. Mandal Case, p. 418.
20. Ibid., p. 272 (para 552).
21. Dumont Louis, Homo Hierarchicus, Granada Publishing House Ltd., London, 1972, p. 270.
22. Seth, D.L., Reservation: Changes in Elite Perception, Financial Express, June 16, 17, 18, 1986.
23. Marx and Engels, Communist Manifesto, Chicago, 1947, p. 17.

24. Cited from Marc Galanter, Law and Society in Modern India, 1989, p. 303.
25. Pandian J., Mandal Case, p. 67 (para 9).
26. The Times of India, Nov. 21, 1992.
27. *Ibid.*
28. *Ibid.*
29. The Times of India, Nov. 21, 1992.
30. The Hindustan Times, 17 Nov., 1992. (President ABVP, Sri Raj Kumar Bhatia).
31. Rajni Kothari, National Herald, Dec. 1989.
32. Jethmalani, Mandal Revised, Indian Bar Review, Vols. 17 and 18 (1991) 393 at p. 396.
33. Ram Krishna Singh v. State of Mysore, AIR 1960 Mys. 338; Sukhdeo v. Government of Andhra Pradesh, 1966 (1) Andh. W.R. 294; Triloki Nath Tikku v. State of J&K, AIR 1967 SC 1283; State of A.P. v. Sagar, AIR 1968 SC 1379.
34. Professor Harold A. Gould, *The Hindu*, Caste System.
35. Per Kuldip Singh, J., Mandal Case, p. 175 (para 333).
36. Per Sahai, J., Mandal Case, p. 313 (para 602); Sawant, J., Ibid., p. 207 (para 400); Pandian, J., ibid., p. 89 (para 84).
37. Per Pandian J., in Mandal Case, p. 110 (para 164).
38. Per Sawant, J., ibid., p. 211 (para 407).
39. Per Sawant, J., ibid, p. 216 (para 420); See also Kania, C.J. and Venkatachaliah, Ahmad and Jeevan Reddy, JJ., ibid., p. 366 (para 634).
40. Per Sawant, J., ibid., p. 245 (para 492).
41. Per Sahai, J., ibid., p. 329 (para 627). But see, Thommen, J. who conceded that reservation affords backward classes of citizens a golden opportunity to serve the nation and thus gain security, status, comparative affluence and influence in decision-making process. But he refused to see it as a mere weapon to capture power. ibid., p. 163 (para 312).
42. Per Sawant, J., in Mandal Case, p. 211 (para 407).
43. Majority Judgement of Jeevan Reddy, J., ibid., p. 464 [para 851(a)].
44. Per Kulwant Singh, J., ibid., pp. 200-204 (para 393).
45. Pandian, J. ibid., pp. 101-103 (para 130-135).
46. AIR 1979 All 135.
47. Ibid., para 58.
48. D/11.8.1987.
49. Sathi Chhedilal, Bharat Ki Am Janta Soshana Mukta va Adhikar Yukta Kaise Ho, 1992, pp. 111-113.
50. K.C. Vasanth Kumar v. State of Karnataka, AIR 1985 SC 1495.
51. RCSCST 1975-777:I, 43-47.
52. Department of Social Welfare 1969: 278.
53. Per Majority, p. 456 (839).
54. Sawant, J., p. 253 (para 508).
55. Jawahar Lal Nehru University v. B.S. Narwal, AIR 1980 SC 1666, (1980) 4 SCC 480, State Bank of India v. Mohd. Mynuddin (19877) 4 SCC 486, Patna University v. Avadh Kishore Pd. Yadav (1994) Supp. 2 SCC 250.
56. Dhavan Rajeev, The Supreme Court of India — A Socio-Legal Critique of its Juristic Techniques, N.M. Tripathi, 1977, pp. 451-452.

57. Paras 35-36 of Ramanandan Committee Report, 1993.
58. Ibid., para 36.
59. Ibid., para 38, (Committee cited S. Sahai, A moment of Truth, The Hindustan Times, 26.11.1992).
60. Ibid., para 34.
61. Singh, V.P., 'Power And Equality', The Times of India, 14.2.1996 (Lucknow ed.) 6.
62. Per Sawant, J., concurring judgement in Mandal Case.

Six

Social Justice, Constitution and Law

Indian society has for centuries been horizontally and vertically split and stratified on the basis of caste. People are born into a caste or sub-caste many of which have traditionally suffered from various kinds of social discrimination and disabilities. These traditionally backward and deprived sections of society are so weak that they have not been able to take equal advantage of equal opportunities compared to the educationally and socially stronger castes or classes. Thus the weaker sections of society have suffered from getting social justice. Social justice denotes overall development of weaker sections. Overall development includes educational development, economic development, political representation, social empowerment at all levels of institutions. The constitution provides benefits to weaker section of society under Article 15(4) and 16(4) mainly related to educational development and employment opportunities in Government services. It is the responsibility of the State to provide educational opportunities and employment opportunities to all including weaker sections of the society on the principle of equality. It was the enormity of inequality that gave rise to various low-caste movements, particularly in the south, right from the beginning of this century. As a result of sustained agitations, specific quotas of seats had been ear marked in medical and engineering colleges in the state. Travancore-Cochin, Madras, Mysore before independence. In post-Independence India, the first important step to remedy this situation was taken with the incorporation of clause 4 under Article 16 of the Constitution which empowered the states to reserve posts in favour of backward classes of citizens. After Independence, Scheduled Castes and Scheduled Tribes have been Constitutionally recognised as groups under the category of weaker sections. They have started getting benefits in educational institutions and employment. Backward castes (OBCs) got recognition in 1993. The present chapter focuses on Constitutional provisions related to various benefits available to these groups.

Social justice is a means to achieve the aim of establishing an egalitarian society and eradicating distribution of power in its several social sections. To achieve the goals of distribution of political, administrative and economic power, the Constitution of India was amended eighty-five times during the last fifty years. The democratic, secular and liberal Constitution of India is doing well under the ethos of social milieu and it is playing a major role in shaping its policies and competing to gain and control political power.

The Indian constitutional law is a unique social document which accepts social pluralism and makes provisions for safeguarding the interests of different social sections. It has been aimed at bringing social equality, social justice and distribution of power along with protection of right to equality. However, in the last few years, it has become imperative for the defenders of the exploitative social order and monopolizers of social, economic and political power to take to the streets and approach the judiciary to create hinderances in the way of social legislation for distribution of power. On the other hand, the leaders of the deprived and disadvantaged social sections have been trying to get benefit of the special provisions made for bringing social justice to the poor and deprived social sections, in order to have a share in the distribution of state power.

The expression 'backward classes' has not been defined anywhere in the Indian Constitution. Backward classes includes Scheduled Castes (SCs) and Scheduled Tribes (STs) and other backward classes (OBCs). The OBCs are other than SCs and STs, and who are also socially and educationally backward in comparison to the other advanced sections of the society.

Articles 15(4) and 340 use the words 'socially and educationally backward classes', It may be mentioned that whereas Article 16(4) refers to "any backward class citizen", in clause (4) of Article 15, the reference is "any socially and educationally backward classes". As Pt. Nehru explained before the select committee, this departure was made to bring the language of Article 15(4) in line with that of Article 340, which provides that Backward Classes Commission may be set up for "socially and educationally backward class citizens."

Perusal of the Parliament debate on this amendment clearly shows that irrespective of the criteria for the classification of backward classes there had to be a list of castes and communities. Pt. Nehru observed, "we want to put an end to ...... all those infinite divisions that have grown up in our social life. We may call them by any name you like, the caste system or religious divisions, etc....." (B.P. Mandal, 1980, p. 24, Vol. I)

Article 16(4) speaks of just 'backward classes', and Article mentions the 'weaker sections of the people'. Even now, the term 'backward classes' is defined differently in the reports of the different backward classes commissions and the judgments of various High Courts and the Supreme Court of India.

Special Provisions

As leader of the Congress Party in the Constituent Assembly of India, Jawaharlal Nehru moved a historic resolution on the aims and objectives of the Constitution. It was regarding provisions for adequate safeguards to the minorities, backward and depressed sections of society. The resolution stated that: "Wherein shall be guaranteed and secured to all the people of India, justice, social, economic and political, equality of status and opportunity before the law, freedom of thought, expression, belief faith, worship, vocation, association and action, subject to law and public morality, and wherein adequate safeguards shall be made available to minorities, backward and tribal areas, and depressed and other backward classes.[1]

The problems of backward classes including the issue of distribution of political and administrative power through policy of reservation and other benefits enjoyed by them till the attainment of independence and the future of these policies were thoroughly debated before appropriate Articles and provisions were incorporated in the Indian Constitution. Despite the divergent views expressed as to the meaning of the term 'backward classes' there was a consensus that the term would include not just the

Scheduled Castes and Scheduled Tribes, but also others who were economically, educationally and socially backward.[2] In India, there are some communities, apart from the Scheduled Castes and Scheduled Tribes, which give a definite impression of social and educational backwardness and inferiority and powerlessness in comparison to the monopoly of social, economic and political power by the traditional upper castes.[3]

The sub-committee on Fundamental Rights had discussed[3] the question of other backward classes in detail. It, however, did not provide reservation and any other special measures to them. It was left it for the State Governments to identify the backward classes in their respective territories and to assist them. Thus, the chance of OBCs to share power in the central services became futile but they became important power brokers at the state level.

Affirmative Action

The Constitution of India made certain provisions for the welfare of deprived social section, known as affirmative action, reservation policy and positive discrimination. The aims and objectives of the Constitution, the general agreement and the compromises reached in the Constituent Assembly are reflected in the different Articles and provisions relating to backward classes, e.g., the Preamble, Articles 38 and 46 of the Directive Principles of State Policy, Articles 14, 15 and 16 of the Fundamental Rights and Articles 338 and 340 of the Constitution of India. The Preamble to the Constitution expresses the determination and aspirations of the people of India in the following terms:

"...Justice, Social Economic and Political,
Liberty of thought, expression, belief, faith and worship:
Equality of status and of opportunity; and
to promote fraternity among them all assuring the dignity of the individual and the unity and integrity of the Nation."

The two objectives: justice—social, economic and political; and equality of status and opportunity of the Preamble are specially relevant and linked to the advancement of the weaker sections and backward classes. In short, the Constitution of India promises not only political democracy, but also social democracy as described by Ambedkar in his speech in the Constitution Assembly: "It means a way of life which recognizes liberty equality and fraternity which are not treated as separate items in a trinity. They form a union of trinity in the sense that to divorce one from the other is to defeat the very purpose of democracy. Liberty cannot be divorced from equality and cannot be divorced from liberty. Nor can liberty and equality be divorced from fraternity.[4]

The Constitution of India includes a number of Articles which deal with compensatory preference for the backward classes. The most important among them are Articles 15(4) and 16(4). Articles 46, 325, 338, 340, 341, 342, 366(24) and 366(25) also have an influence on the subject.

Backward Classes and Directive Principles of State Policy

The Directive Principles of State Policy enshrined in the Articles 38 and 46 of the Indian Constitution make it the duty of the State to strive to promote the welfare of the people in general and weaker sections, including the backward classes, in particular. Article 38 of the Constitution reads thus:

(1) The State shall strive to promote the welfare of the people by securing and protecting as effectively as it may a social order in which justice, social, economic and political, shall inform all the institutions of national life.

(2) The state shall, in particular, strive to minimize the inequalities in income, and endeavour to eliminate inequalities in status, facilities and opportunities, not only amongst individuals but also amongst groups of people residing in different areas or engaged in different vocations.

Thus, the Directive Principles along with the Preamble embody the socio-economic ideals which the nation had set before itself during the freedom movement. It points out to the political mind of the makers of the Constitution who visualized the creation of a new social order in India on the basis of social, economic and political justice, eliminating the evils of the existing socio-economic system. Though the nature of the 'social order' is not defined in the Constitution, but is interpreted to mean a 'welfare state' and 'socialistic pattern of society'. As a part of this objective, the State is directed to remove the existing inequalities of income, status, facilities and opportunities among the individuals and groups in India. Further, Article 46 directs that: "The State shall promote with special care the educational and economic interests of weaker sections of the people, and, in particular, of the Scheduled Castes and Scheduled Tribes, and shall protect them from social injustice and all forms of exploitation."

As can be seen, Article 46 makes the State duty bound to take action to ameliorate the conditions of the weaker sections including the backward classes. They are two-fold: (1) to promote with special care the educational and economic interests by taking 'positive measures'; and (ii) to prevent social injustice and all forms of exploitation by taking 'preventive measures'.

Equality Vs. Inequality

The issue of equality and inequality, the theory that no two persons are equal and the belief that equality of opportunity could do away with the drawbacks which many faced due to their social inferiority have occupied the minds of eminent philosophers such as Locke, Rousseau, Huxley and many others. As Andre Beteille has said "the distinction between natural inequality and social inequality is inherently ambiguous."[2]

However, there was no doubt about the arbitrarily hierarchical and social and economic exploitation through caste system that had guided Indian society till date. At the base of this pyramidal structure lay the masses of economically suppressed, politically disabled and socially deprived Depressed Classes of India. For ages, they had been victimised and at the dawn of freedom, the time had come to begin, an extraordinary phase of the upliftment of the masses of humanity from the state of animals like social existence, deep poverty and inhuman economic exploitation.[3]

Rights of Equality: Legal Provisions

The new constitutional and legal environment emphasized equal participation by every citizen in the functioning of the state. Founding fathers of the constitution tried to eliminate the discrimination of centuries by ensuring universal adult franchise. To reverse the age old oppression of backwards, special constitutional measures were enacted for the SCs who had traditionally been the sufferers of socio-economic oppression. Arnold Toynbee writes "Law's weakness is that its range is not co-extensive with social life. There are many kinds of social relations that cannot be regulated by legislation." Nevertheless, it showed the sincerity and moral commitment of the Constitution makers that they sought to establish a secular democratic set up based on equality for all before the law. Article 15 of the Constitution prohibited discrimination on grounds of religion, race, caste, sex or place of birth and Article 17 sought to abolish untouchability while Articles 330 and 332 ensured the reservation of seats for Scheduled Castes in the Lok Sabha and the Legislative Assemblies of the States. Responding to the needs of the hour, the Constituent Assembly members opted for the policy of reservation or "protective discrimination" towards the Scheduled Castes and Scheduled Tribes.

With the objective of improving the economic and social conditions of the Depressed Classes spread all over the country, the Government of India decided to list them in a Schedule in 1930, in so that accurate estimate of their numbers can be sought and special benefits to them can be provided through legislative and executive action. There was no absolute definition to establish the criteria that branded a particular group or caste as belonging to the "Scheduled Castes", hence the *Census Report of 1931* gave a nine-point test in order to distinguish the Scheduled Castes from others :

From the point of view of the State, the important test is the right to use public conveniences—roads, wells and schools and if this is regarded as the primary test, religions disabilities and the social differences indirectly involved by them may be considered contributory only. Some significance must be attached to them obviously if an ordinary person regards the persons of certain groups so that he wants to keep away from them. Certain persons of those groups do suffer under a serious disability. The list of castes was first released in the Schedule appended to the Government of India Act, 1935 and was later included in the Constitution of India (SC and ST) Order, 1950.[4]

Regarding the tribal population in the country, there were mainly concentrates in the North-Eastern Himalayan Belt, Orissa, Madhya Pradesh, Gujarat, Rajasthan, Bihar, Maharashtra and Himachal Pradesh.[5] The British adopted policies which were designed to keep them separate the tribals from the mainstream as part of their deliberate policy of not developing communications in the tribal areas. This isolation resulted in exploitation by non-tribal moneylenders, contractors, zamindars and middlemen. The few roads that were constructed were only helping contractors to exploit forest produce.

Jawaharlal Nehru suggested that their development be along the lines of their own culture and thoroughly disagreed with the idea that tribals should be considered primitive while the rest thought of themselves as civilised.

Article 46 contains a very significant directive to the state. It says:

"The State shall promote, with special care, the educational and economic interests of the weaker sections of the people and in particular, of the Scheduled Castes and the Scheduled Tribes and shall protect them from social injustice and all forms of exploitation." It is evident that "the weaker sections of the people do include the "backward classes of citizens contemplated by Article 16(4). Article 46 aims at their educational and economic development, Article 164 makes for the appointment of a Minister to look after exclusively tribal interests while Article 224 provides special administration of Scheduled Areas and Tribal Areas ; grants by the Centre to certain States come under Article 235. Reservation of seats for tribals is provided in the Lok Sabha under Article 330 and in the State Assemblies under Article 332. Article 334 grants reservation of seats and special representation, Article 335 grants special claims to service and posts. Article 342 of the Constitution is exclusively about Scheduled Tribes. Many more constitutional provisions were granted subsequently also. Constitutional enactments were followed by administrative structure suitable for safeguarding the interests of the tribals, thereby initiating the age of social and economic change. Interaction between national and tribal leaders as well as social workers and anthropologists helped to the present set-up for tribal upliftment.

The President of India has been constitutionally empowered to appoint a Commissioner for Scheduled Castes and Scheduled Tribes at the national level with the special responsibility of protecting the interests of the tribal population. The Director General of Backward Classes, with the help of Regional Deputy Directors assists in all the tribal welfare acivities, and the Commissioner for Scheduled Castes and Scheduled Tribes submits his annual report to Parliament through the President. At the State level, the Governor and Chief Minister supervise and implement welfare schemes for STs through the Welfare Minister. The Welfare Ministry in turn is advised by the Tribes Advisory Council and the Tribal Research Institutes in formulating policies and programmes for their upliftment. Many religious and academic agencies are also engaged in the act of improving the socio-economic conditions of the tribals in various parts of India.

Although it is blamed that more work for tribals has been done on paper than in the field, it would be wrong to say that very little has been done for tribal upliftment. Alongwith legislation and socio-economic and educational schemes, the most important feature has been the willing effort of both the Central and State governments to provide all assistance in their endeavour to improve the living conditions of the tribals. The 20-Point Economic Programme and the subsequent rural rehabilitation schemes such as IRDP, ITDP, ERRP, abolition of Bonded Labour etc. were clear manifestations of this intentions and acts. Irrespective of whether or not critics, politicians and the tribals themselves feel that not much has been done, it cannot be denied that the government has been determined in its efforts to integrate the tribals into social set up even while enabling them to retain the intrinsic advantages of their own cultures. They have not been thrust within the confines of "Reservations" as the Red Indians in North America and turned into objects of tourist curiosity.

The establishment of Ashram schools, such as those in Orissa, encourage the tribal culture and traditions and creative arts. At the same time at every level of recruitment right from teachers and class IV employees to the Civil Services and Legislatures, seats are reserved for tribal candidates. Four decades after Independence, the system of reservation or affirmative action continues.

After more than forty years of its introduction, the question being asked again and again today is—has the reservation policy achieved its objective and should it now be done away with altogether?

The idea of having 78 and 38 seats in Parliament and 540 and 282 seats in the State for SC and ST candidates was to help them to voice the grievances and rectify the injustices done on them. Whereas there has been no systematic study of the role of reserved candidates in the legislatures, it has been seen that their capacity for decision-making is often marginalised, that they are used by political parties to secure votes and that they have hardly used their status to secure personal benefits. If they are intended to promote the cause of their community they get branded as *Dalit* or *Adivasi* leaders. If they ignore themselves they are accused of betraying the community and adopting elitist attitudes.

Social Justice and Right to Equality

The Constitution of India gives right of equality before law to all citizens of the country irrespective of caste, creed, religion, sex, etc. Article 14 of the Constitution provides rights to citizens of the country. The other Articles of the Constitution, e.g., 15 and 16 provide right of admission to any educational institutions and employment respectively. The question does arises: Are all citizens getting equal opportunity, and enjoying benefits enshrined under various Articles of the Constitution of India? If the answer is yes than why large number of population is still educationally deprived and without any job. If the answer is no, then do they have no right to get social justice under the constitution of India, like those who 'have'.

B.P. Mandal (1980, p. 21, Vol. I) quotes Justice K. Subba Rao's views from "Social Justice and Law" (National, New Delhi) as follows:

> "In a limited sense, the right to social justice may be defined as the right of the weak, aged, destitute, poor, women, children and other under-privileged persons to the protection of the State against the ruthless competition of life. It seeks to give the necessary adventitious aids to the underprivileged so that they may have the equal opportunity with the more advanced in the race of life. It is a bundle of rights; in one sense it is carved of other rights; in another sense it is a preserver of other rights. It is the balancing wheel between haves and havenots."

The doctrine of equality has many facets. It is a dynamic, an evolving concepts. Its main facets relevant to Indian society, have been referred to in the Preamble and the Articles under the sub-heading "Right to equality"—(Articles 14 to 18).

Our Constitution makers were fully conscious of the need for providing safeguards to the weaker sections of society. Whereas Articles 15, 16 and 29 create the overall impression of according equal access to all citizens to educational, employment and other facilities, Clause (4) of Article 16 lays down.

> (4) Nothing in this article shall prevent the State from making any provision for the reservation of appointments or posts in favour of any backward class of citizens which, in the opinion of the State, is not adequately represented in the services under the State.

Subsequently as a result of the Constitution (First Amendment) Act, 1951 a similar clause was added to Article 15 also. Thus, it will be seen that Clauses (4) of both Article 15 and 16 provide special provisions for the advancement of any socially and educationally backward classes. Further, Article 46 enjoins upon the State the obligation to promote with special care the educational and economic interests of the weaker sections of the people.

From the above, it may appear that special safeguards have been provided to weaker sections under Articles 15(4) and 16(4) as fundamental rights to education, employment, etc. But the real power lies with the State and individuals are beneficiaries entitled to take benefits under these articles.

The Fundamental Rights are primarily concerned with the

rights of the individual. Claims of society do not have the same sort of immediately and urgency as the claims of individuals. Wrongs suffered by individuals stick out much more pointedly than the wrongs suffered by the society. In the light of this the exceptions contained under Articles 15(4) and 16(4) appear to confer a privileged status on backward classes which seems out of line with the overall scheme of Fundamental Rights. It is only under Directive Principles of the State Policy that the claims of society in general are given due recognition.

The issues of Fundamental Rights of individuals and Directive Principles of the State Policy became a very common theme of Parliamentary debates and judicial pronouncements in early 1950s. Pandit Nehru during the Parliamentary debates on the Constitution (First Amendment) Bill, 1951, stated:

> "...The Directive Principles of State Policy represent a dynamic move towards a certain objective. The Fundamental Rights represent something static, to preserve certain rights which exist. Both again are right. But somehow and sometime it might so happen that dynamic movement and that static standstill do not quite fit into each other."
>
> "...The result is that the whole purpose behind the Constitution which was meant to be a dynamic Constitution leading to a certain goal step by step is somewhat hampered and hindered by the static element being emphasised a little more than the dynamic element and we have to find out some way of solving it."
>
> "...If in the protection of individual liberty you protect also individual or group inequality, then you come into conflict with that Directive Principle which wants, according to your own Constitution, a gradual advance or let us put it another way, not so gradual but more rapid advance, wherever possible, to a State where there is less and less inequality and more and more equality. If any kind of an appeal to individual liberty and freedom is to mean as an appeal to the continuation of the existing inequality, then you get into difficulties. Then you become static, that ideal of an egalitarian society which I hope most of us aim at."

The dilemma observed by Pandit Nehru is very real and has been faced repeatedly in the course of implementing legislation aimed at creating of a more just social order. Whereas we can take legitimate pride in having set up a Democratic Republic in India, the elitist and unequal character of Indian society cannot be considered as a matter of great satisfaction.

The core issue is to consider the implication of 'Equality in the light of human societies' in the book 'More Equality' (1973). H.G. Gans in his book has observed that three alternative outcomes of 'Equality' are often considered: (i) Equality of opportunity, (ii) Equality of treatment, and (iii) Equality of results. He further elaborate these three alternatives of equality. Equality of opportunity promised under Article 16(1) of the Constitution, is actually a libertarian and not egalitarian principle as it allows the same freedom to everybody in the race of life. "People who start their lives at a disadvantage rarely benefit significantly from equality of opportunity, because, unless they are distinctly superior in skills or upward mobility techniques; they can rarely catch up with the more fortunate and most disadvantaged people never even get access to the supposedly equal opportunity... Equality of opportunity is also an asocial principle, because it neglects the several invisible and cumulative obstacles in the way of disadvantaged in fact, unless the children of the poor are taken from their parents at birth and brought up in middle-class homes, most are condemned to inequality of opportunity."

Gans says equality of treatment, notes Gans, may be interpreted in two ways. "On the one hand, it means treating people as roughly equal in impersonal social intersections . . . On the other hand, it means providing people with the same resources regardless of their current resources of socio-economic position; used in this sense, equality of treatment suffers from the same drawback as equality of opportunity for to treat the disadvantaged uniformly with the advantaged will only prepetuate their disadvantage. Even in the courts which pride themselves on equality of treatment before the law, the defendent who can afford only a poor or overworked lawyer will not often obtain equal treatment from the judge."

In the light of the above considerations, Gans observes

"Consequently, the only truly egalitarian principle is equality of results, which may require unequal opportunity or treatment for the initially disadvantaged so that they eventually wind up equal in resources or rights."

In fact the spirit of Fundamental Rights itself remains unrealised unless proper conditions are created for protecting the legitimate rights of the under-privileged. Soon after Independence every State enacted land reforms legislation, providing security of tenure to tenants and tillers, placed a ceiling on land holdings, etc. As the weak and poor tenants and cultivators did not have the means to enforce their rights and the powerful land owners had the resources and influence to evade ceiling laws, our land measures have fallen far short of their aims. Stronger sections of society keep perpetrating all sorts of atrocities against Dalits and other backward classes and they are often able to get away without any puinishment. Our entire legal apparatus is so expensive and time-consuming that under-privileged sections of society mostly do not have the means or stamina to get justice from law courts. Under these circumstances, the claim of 'Equality before the law' does not carry much conviction with the weaker sections of Indian society. Equality of results being the real acid test of effective equality, there is no running away from the fact that our sovereign democratic republic will remain seriously affected without a fair share of the fruits of freedom. Equality of opportunity and Equality of treatment are also made available to the backward sections of our people. In this connection, Justice K. Subba Rao has noted:

> "...unless adventitious aids are given to the under-privileged people, it would be impossible to suggest that they have equal opportunities with the more advanced people. This is the reason and the justification for the demand of social justice that the under-privileged citizens of the country should be given a preferential treatment in order to give them an equal opportunity with other more advanced sections of the community." *(Ibid.)*

In this connection nothing generates so much heat and genuine indignation as the concept of 'merit'. Whereas no body objects to the grant of special educational facilities and several other concessions to the backward classes, the provision of a reserved quota in educational institutions or services for members of Scheduled Castes, Scheduled Tribes or other Backward Classes gives rise to sharp reaction. This argument can be strongly supported by the well known historical fact when the Janta Dal Government headed by shri V.P. Singh issued order for reservation to OBCs in service in 1990 there was country wide agitation against this decision.

This kind of reaction is based on two considerations: First, it hurts a person's sense of fair play to find that a more 'meritorious' candidate has been omitted in preference to a less 'meritorious' person on purely extraneous grounds. Secondly, it is argued, that by selecting candidates with lower merit against reserved quota vacancies, the nation is being deprived of the services of the best talent that is available to it.

Right to equality—one of the fundamental rights enshrined in the Constitution of India—guarantees every citizen, under Article 14, equality before law or equal protection of laws, and under Article 16(1) equality of opportunity in matters of public appointment. The Constitution prohibits any discrimination that is common to any traditional hierarchical and compartmental society in India. This is explained and specified in Articles 15(1), 16(2) and 29(2). All these are the steps towards the realization and protection of the right to equality. The relevant Articles are mentioned as follows:

As per Article 14 "the state shall not deny any person equality before the law or the equal protection of laws within the territory of India". Similarly, Article 16(1) says that "there shall be equality of opportunity for all citizens in matters relating to employment or appointment to any office under the State".

The Constitution prohibits discrimination, to ensure the equality before law and equality of opportunity and to secure social justice to every citizens. Prohibition of discrimination is the first step towards the realization of the right to equality. This is explained and made specific in Articles 15 and 29. The Constitution, under Article 15(1), prohibits discrimination against any citizens on grounds of religion, race, caste, sex or place of birth either by the State or by any of its citizens. Article 15 reads:

1. The State shall not discriminate against any citizen on grounds only of religion, race, caste, sex, place of birth or any of them.

2. No citizen shall, on grounds only of religion, race, caste, sex, plae of birth or any of them, be subject to any disability, liability, restriction or conditions with regard to:
   (a) access to shops, public restaurants, hotels, places of public entertainment, or
   (b) the use of wells, tanks, bathing ghats, roads, and places of public resort maintained wholly or partly out of State funds or dedicated to the use of the general public.

Article 16(2) prohibits discrimination on grounds only of religion, race, caste, sex, descent, place of birth, residence or any of them with regard to any appointment or office under the State. It lays down that "no citizen shall on grounds only of religion, race, caste, sex, descent, place of birth, residence, or any of them shall be ineligible for or discriminated against in respect of any employment or office under the State".

Article 29(2) also prohibits discrimination on grounds only of religion, race, caste, language or any of them in respect of admission into any educational institution maintained by the State or receiving aid from the State funds. It reads as follows: "No citizen shall be denied admission into any educational institution maintained by the State or receiving aid out of State funds on grounds only of religion, race, caste, language or any of them."

Provisions for Other Backward Classes

Along with the Right to Equality, the Constitution of India provides separate and special provisions for the advancement of backward classes. It is often called compensatory discrimination, protective discrimination and discrimination in reverse. These provisions permit the government to undertake special steps for the upliftment of the backward classes. Article 15(4), which was incorporated into the Indian Constitution under the Constitution (First Amendment) Act, 1951 declares: "Nothing in Article 15 or in Clause (2) of Article 29 shall prevent the State from making any special provision for the advancement of any socially and educationally backward classes of citizens or for the Scheduled Castes and the Scheduled Tribes."

Article 15(4) provides the ground to the State to make special provisions for the backward classes in all the areas within its jurisdiction. The expression 'class' in Article 15(4) means a homogeneous section of the people ground together on account of certain common traits and by being identifiable by some common attributes such as status, rank, occupation, residence in a locality, race and religion. In defining whether a particular section forms a class, caste cannot be totally excluded. At the same time, a test based upon only caste or community cannot be accepted. Article 16(4) which is relevant to government jobs, says: "Nothing in this Article shall prevent the State from making any provision for the reservation of appointments or posts in favour of any backward class of citizens which in the opinion of the State is not adequately represented in the services under the State."

When the Constitution of India came into force with effect from 26th January 1950, Article 15 did not have the Clause (4). Later on, in the light of the judgment of the High Court of Madras and the Supreme Court of India in the famous case Champarkam Dorairajan versus The State of Madras, the Constitution was amended. The Government of India felt that some special provision must be made for the educational advanement of the backward classes, as they could not get any benefit under Article 16(4) of the Constitution. Hence, an amendment to the Constitution was made to reserve seats for the citizens of the backward classes, the Scheduled Castes and the Scheduled Tribes in public services and educational institutions and also undertake other measures for the advancement of the other backward classes. Accordingly, Clause (4) was added to the Article 15 by the first amendment to the Constitution. By this amendment, Article 15 and 29 were brought to become consistent with Articles 16(4) and 340. According to the Supreme Court of India, the above special provisions of the Constitution are in the nature of an enabling provision' and a 'discretionary power' of the State under Articles 15(4) and 16(4) to take any measure for the advancement of socially and educationally backward classes.

For a long time it had been regarded that Articles 15(4) and 16(4) are 'exceptions' to Articles 15(1) and 16(1). According to this view, the claims of the backward classes could be projected only through exceptional Clauses and not outside them. But, in the case of State of Kerala *versus* N.M. Thomas, the Supreme Court by majority rejected this notion of exception and held that the State was free to select any 'means' to achieve equality for these backward classes. It is evident that the Supreme Court has discarded the old way of thinking that Articles 15(4) and 16(4) are exceptions to the equality guaranteed and declared that these Articles are themselves aimed at achieving the goal of equality broadly proclaimed and guaranteed by Articles 14, 15(1) and 16(1).

The prevailing view now is that Article 15(4) of the Constitution authorizes the State to make 'special provision' for the uplift of the socially and educationally backward classes of citizens. So also, Article 16(4) authorizes the State to make 'any provision' for the reservation of appointment in favour of backward classes of citizens, which, in the opinion of the State, are not sufficiently represented in the services under the State. It also permits the government to readily identify a backward class with reference to a person's caste. It is also clear from the decisions of the Supreme Court in the case of Balaji *versus* State of Mysore (1963) and Indira Sawhney *versus* Union of India (1992) that the action envisaged by the Articles 15(4) and 16(4) can be taken either by the Union or the State Government. The policy of reservation subsequently adopted in many States in India is connected to the need for the maintenance of efficiency in administration. This is clear from Article 335 which reads: "The claims of the members of the Scheduled Castes and the Scheduled Tribes shall be taken into consideration, consistently with the maintenance of efficiency of administration, in the making of appointments to services and posts in connection with the affairs of the Union or of a State."

This Article, thus, makes it clear that to get the benefit of reservation a candidate on a post in the government or in a public undertaking would have to fulfil the minimum educational and other qualifications required for the post in consonance with the nature and requirement of that post, so as to maintain efficiency of any organisation.

Reservations for Education

Under Articles 15 (4) and 29, it is compulsory for educational institutions and universities to reserve 20 per cent, i.e., 1/5th of seats for SC and ST candidates, for whom qualifying marks are considerably relaxed. Despite the relaxation, the quotas often remain unfulfilled and many institutions try to avoid reserving seats. At the post-graduate level, number of SC and ST candidates in Engineering and Medical courses remain very low. Moreover, the Report of the Commissioner for Scheduled Castes and Scheduled Tribes 1978-79 reveals that 83 per cent general as against 75 per cent and 66 per cent of SC and ST Children between the ages of 6 and 11 were enrolled in Primary Schools. In addition, the dropout rate at the Primary level of these children was 79 per cent.

Educationally, the SC and ST children face financial problems, hostile social backup, an supp;ortive atmosphere for studies at home and inadequate guidance for academics. Despite the obstacles, the outstanding students among the SC and ST have increased and many occupy positions of power in the buraucracy and elsewhere because of the policy of protective discrimination which enables them to compete, no matter how small the number and how difficult their path to success.

Reservation in Jobs

Under Articles 16(4), 320(4) and 333, 15 per cent and 7 per cent respectively were reserved for SCs and STs at all levels of the public sector. Qualifications for both recruitment and promotion were relaxed in the cases of such candidates. Between 1959 and 1979, the number of SC and ST candidates in Class-I services has risen from 1.18 per cent to 4.75 per cent. At the lower levels, however, they occupy many positions but have little or no scope in the private sector. If a society is to be judged not only for what it is but what it aspires to be, and if the Constitution is considered as the expression of a society's desire to have an ideal set up for all its citizens, then the Indian Constitution is remarkable for its stress on the idea of equality. Not only is the principal of equality incorporated in the Preamble and the Directive Principles of State

Policy and Fundamental Rights, but it has also been protected judicial decisions and legislations enacted over the years. Jurists agree that in its commitment to equality, the Indian Constitution has gone beyond any contemporary Constitution including that of America.

The Background of System of Reservation

The disharmony and turmoil which is presently prevalent is due to the paradox of equality versus the reality of inequality and injustice which still have not vanished from our society. In order to ensure equality under unequal circumstances and in order to discriminate in favour of those who in the past had been discriminated against, a policy of "affirmative action" or protective discrimination was necessary. The factor behind the idea of protective discrimination was that certain sections, castes or groups have special claims on society which cannot be ignored for mere individual excellence. The compensatory principles in which redressal is made for wrongs of past whole classes and groups of people may not always succeed in reversing past injuries and care has to be taken that in destroying old inequalities we do not create fresh ones. Discrimination is a disastrous, no matter how good the intentions are of those who use it and how careful we have to be in using it even for a desirable end.

In adopting, retaining and even extending the range of the policy of protective discrimination, the individual claims as against those of the group, of the reward given to merit as against those of need are important to be balanced. It would be wrongful to think that by making concessions to communities and castes, the needs of every individual is fulfilled. Classification of castes and communities incorporates in itself the concept of discrimination as does classification of individuals into slots and niches. The SCs and STs have already been classified as such and everyday there is further clamour from other backward or economically deprived groups for a portion of the State's resources as recompense for past injuries and/or present needs.

Communal politics, minority politics and the politics of

backwardness were encouraged by the British to the freedom movement and they are a fact of life in contemporary Indian politics, which is heavily dependent on the concept of "vote banks" for the major political parties and their partisan goals. There is no perfect correlation between the ritual status of a caste and their actual material condition. There are many forces which come into play presently which have reduced the association between caste and income, occupation and education. Keeping in mind that the interests of the Scheduled Castes and Scheduled Tribes have been given constitutional protection, it seems anachronistic to increase the scope of positive discrimination to such an extent that an individuals caste become a determining factor in his entitlements.

While including an individual or a community in the list of backward classes in India, one would have to consider both the economic and sociological factors. While the stigma of caste and the isolation of the tribals may continue, even hardened cynics would agree that the feeling of distance and discrimination between castes today has been decreased. However, economic inequality and poverty have not started much decrease, so that visible and glaring evidence of poverty can be seen in both rural areas as well as in urban slums. Poverty, illiteracy and health problems are not the exclusive problems of the SC and ST but for as Jagjivan Ram they are the problems of a poor Brahmin and a poor Harijan are the same.

In many cases, protective discrimination has become a "crutch" for both activating the state and the affected persons themselves, who take little initiative and instead depend on official programmes and policies for advancement and social mobility.

Since the ideology underlying the division of castes into high and low, proved "negative discrimination", reservation in educational, economic and legislative institutions were aimed at removing both gaps and discrimination, with education serving as the important tool of an improved lifestyle. Reservation in jobs and monetary incentives were also designed to both social and financial standing, while political reservation ensured that they shoud be given an adequate participation in the formulation of state policies.

Why the Reservation has been Extended

Why has the policy of reservation which had initially been given for a period of twenty years been again and again extended and why is there at present a clamour to redefine the criteria for reservation ?

With the Scheduled Castes and Scheduled Tribes being an important vote bank, vested political interests could never terminate the policy or end the period of reservation. Despite many economic and educational surveys and studies being undertaken, the observations have not shown that the reservation policy alone has set right all previous hardships and difficulties faced by the "weaker sections". The efforts of the state policy cannot be written off for them has had a psychological impact on the Scheduled Castes and Scheduled Tribes making many of their capable members to come forward. Seeing the benefits of reservation which have reached the SCs or STs an amorphous group of so-called "other backward classes/castes" have used political character and to secure reservation for themselves, e.g., in southern states Karnataka and Andhra Pradesh, where approximately 55 per cent and 45 per cent of the seats are reserved.

Criticism of Reservation Policies

With the rapid rise of India's population from the time of Independence to the present, the pressure on the sufficient, educational and job opportunities have been heavy. Competition has become hard in the educational and professional institutions and the increasing demand for employment opportunities have not kept pace with the growth of the population. Again, a new generation has grown up with a secular, liberal education and for them the existence of caste-based reservation in every sphere seems to be a irrational to the concept of equality and individual capacities.

Caste prejudices may be a reality especially in rural areas but the systematic increase in the percentage of reservation in different states presents a shrinking opportunities to those who are not the so called disadvantaged. In addition, the benefits of reservation are hardly reaching the needy. There is no denial to the children of the reserved category bureaucrats and politicians to continue availing privileges under the quota system. In fact, the reservation-policy has given rise to new pejorative terms such as "quota wallah" SC or ST etc. It is not be wise to view all criticism voiced against reservation as merely the cries of the privileged sections who are scared of losing the upper hand. Rather it should be seen as the mind set that when the country is supposed to be entering into the 21st century, political pressures force the fragmentation of society, yet again into high and low Scheduled Castes and Scheduled Tribes, women and handicapped persons all trying to ease themselves into comfortable slots with the minimum of effort by virtue of birth and through the medium of reservations.

At the same time it would be unjust to attribute the decline in efficiency in the government and the lowering of educational standards to the reservation policy. Initially, lower percentage was reserved for Scheduled Castes and Scheduled Tribes who are still heavily outnumbered by general candidates. It is the increasing reservation to various pressure groups for political expediency which is causing disappointment amongst those who have to sacrifice their chances for members of other sections of society who are not necessarily either the most disadvantaged or deserving candidates in the competitions for the few seats and jobs available in open market. Protective justice for the deprived is a legitimate aim of society but mollycoddling those who are already ahead constitutes an injustice which has to be handled with political will rather than political expediency, if caste rivalries are not to be tended and hatred perpetuated to new generations of Indians.

While the Constitution of India bars any form of discrimination among citizens, yet protective discrimination becomes legal in the context of "reservation". While the Constitution was categorical in reservations for the Scheduled Castes and Scheduled Tribes, it was vague about the other Backward Castes or OBCs. This was due to the ambiguity at that time in identifying the beneficiaries, specifying the type of benefits that would be required as well as implementing this policy of preferential treatment. Several autonomous

Commissions and Committees have therefore looked into the issue of reservation under Articles 15 (4) and 16(4) appointed by the State and Central Governments. While various State governments have appointed nearly seventeen Commissions and Committees, the Central Government form the Kalekar Commission in 1953 and the Mandal Commission in 1979 for deciding the quota of reservation as well as identifying those who needed such protective discrimination. The recommendations are divided in two categories: one adopted caste as the basis for reservation (both the Mandal and Kalekar Commission) and the adopted economic criteria (the State Committees adopted by J & K, West Bengal, Karnataka and Gujarat).

The Mandal Commission focussed on the aspects of reservation—namely, the criteria and percentage of reservation among others. Eleven indicators were grouped under three heads—social, educational and economic indicators were fixed in order to ascertain the socio-economic backwardness of the people. It acted on the principle that economic backwardness was the result of socio-educational backwardness and thus poverty was the result of caste-based handicaps.

Whereas caste has now disappeared in its ritualistic form, it has gained new importance and secured a fresh existence on the political front. This has increased, rather than decreased casteism in the country, as caste-based pressure groups vie with each other to secure certain privileges for themselves. Since a government job carries with it a great deal of social prestige and financial security, it has been thought that caste-based proportional reservation should be provided in the government, the public sector and educational institutions. As the Supreme Court does not favour raising the percentage of reservation beyond 50 per cent, the Mandal Commission was constrained to recommend a 27 per cent reservation for 3,743 castes.

Justice Rane on the other hand, in his report presented before the Gujarat Assembly in March 1985 clearly stated: "It will not only be totally unrealistic but also unpatriotic to make any attempt to assess social backwardness on the basis of caste." Many fact that caste-based reservation would create gaps in society and it would eliminate non-Hindu communities. Already in the fifty years of independence the higher echelons all castes have progressed, due to reservation or otherwise, so it is inevitable to bring in those who are the poorest and most deprived within the ambit of reservation. To meet the need for fixing new criteria in determining backwardness, the Commission suggested that family income and occupation to be the only criterion for determining socio-economic backwardness. In Gujarat, 63 occupations with incomes below Rs. 10,000 per annum were determined as backward.

According to Ishwari Prasad, there must be two conditions in a modern day reservation policy, one, identification should be secular and rational and, two, there should be an in-built mechanism for its dissolution in the course of time.

Financial criteria is acceptable because of its social neutrality. Instead of entering into the controversial issues of the respective positions of the four thousand castes of India, the lone criteria of income will determine the question of special treatment while at the same time eliminating the question of caste and its corresponding social position altogether.

Thirdly, economic criteria will and must be self-abolishing as the increase of income will obviously uplift a person from the purview of reservations. The policy of reservation must have inbuilt deservation which is possible only if economic criteria is the parameter.

Where caste is taken as the factor determining socio-economic backwardness, there will never be any dereservation, as this is a Indian caste society. The phenomenal rise of India's population makes impossible social parity with regard to jobs and education as the resources have not increased sufficiently to absorb this gigantic mass of people.

In the past it was a generally accepted fact of life that different lifestyles were appropriate to different castes of society. With the increase of literacy and education to the Scheduled Castes and Scheduled Tribes, western way of living and a government job are seen as ideals to which they aspire. There is strong desire for white collar jobs among Scheduled Castes and Scheduled Tribes, as in any sphere of Indian society there is great respectability attached to them. Hence a white collar job, whether that of a clerk or a peon, a mark of respectability. For this reason, studies reveal that since these classes were, until recently, excluded from such professions they aspire all the more zealously for government or clerical posts. Due to such state of affair government-run craft training schools do not attract as many students as they should, despite the fact that a manually skilled job would give greater monetary benefits than a clerical one. Westernised education, expansion of caste-free occupations and geographical mobility have all combined to give a thrust to individual social mobility. Urban and semi-urban centres which have become overloaded due to an ever increasing number of people, strains and constraints of caste and hierarchical pressures are missing normally seen in the villages.

Caste politics and pressure groups have formed an unholy combination for getting ahead without due efforts have given voice to the plea for increased reservation. However, reservation may be a prominent method for ensuring social justice and equality, but it cannot and should not be an obstacle for the very urgent needs for concerted economic action, which alone can bring succour to millions in this country.

The Report of the Commissioner for Scheduled Castes says, "Even though recommendations were made for extending the scope of the principle of positive discrimination, greater emphasis was placed on basic structural changes in the economy through formulation of equitous policies and their effective implementation, besides attending to the immediate problems" regarding wages, protection of traditional occupations and equal distribution of land. The Commission regarded that the Central Government's decision not to dereserve, but launch a special drive for filling vacant posts in reserved quotas was a measure with limited scope. Two national level bodies namely, The Tribal Cooperative Marketing Development Federation of India Limited and the National Scheduled Castes and Scheduled Tribes Finance Development Corporation have also been formed to fulfil the needs of the SCs and STs.

Since new generation is hardly aware of the extremely humiliating status of the Scheduled Castes and the isolation of the Tribals, the willingness of the government in distributing largesse to them arouses in the intermediary Backward Classes. The clamour for State-sponsored social mobility and economic and educational security by means of reservation is being asked by OBCs in every state. Politicians are buying peace by extending the scope and percentage of reservations in OBCs every State while the actual task of forming the nation's economy, extending educational facilities and improving the quality of life for the every increasing population remains a dream.

With the reservation policy being routinely renewed so frequently, other "dominant" caste groups such as Kurmi, Yadav, Koeri, Lingayats, Vokkaligas etc. all over the country are demanding backward status and reservation. Due to the benefits which are the outcome of reservation to various communities, each vies with the other in the race for backwardness.

A frequently given argument is that Backward Classes have a low social status, even if they are comparatively well-off. In his landmark work on the *Harijan Elite* Prof. Sachchidananda has included numerous case studies in which interviews were conducted with members of the harijan elite, who had given up their caste-based hierarchal occupations. By connecting themselves from their traditional occupations which had the brand of pollution, untouchability automatically vanished. It was found that status disabilities were mainly led to village only but here too, discrimination at public wells and in temples had decreased to a great extent. Moreover, legislators and public servants were ultimised thereby establishing a direct correlation between the politico-economic status of an individual and his social status. A well off harijan says, "Superior Brahmins come to my residence to conduct each and every family ritual. This privilege, however, is not available to other persons of my caste residing in the same village." Having given up the traditional caste occupation of toddy tapping , healthy social relations and being a vegetarian has made him "acceptable" even to diehard Brahmins in the village.

Eating with Harijans is no longer taboo and in bigger cities there is hardly any discrimination prevailing on this front. The entry of SCs in government or professional institutions is secretly disliked by colleagues because of contempt for Scheduled Castes, growing competition and jealousy because of their weapon of protective discrimination. Some harijan have an inherited inferiority and oversensitiveness so that they frequently infer discrimination or ill-treatment where it is not exercised.

Human nature being what it is, resentment towards those who have been offered special privileges or those who are considered interlopers, as Asian immigrants in the USA and England, are bound to surface.

With respect to the ability of the SC leaders to transform the social set up by virtue of their upgradation to positions of power and prestige, the study shows that large numbers of educated ones both in urban and rural areas and have little active concern with improving conditions of their less fortunate caste fellows. Alienated from traditional professions, their major concern appears to be that of meeting the needs of the immediate family and kin. Some of the leaders who have risen high in the social hierarchy have snapped their ties with their bleak past. While public servants were completely out of concern with their community, social workers and legislators had to work out dual roles of maintaining close relations with the wider community for their own ends, as well as achieving a hold over their own community whose support they required during elections.

The SC leaders perceived that by and large structural distance between the Scheduled Castes and others have reduced significantly especially in cities, where young and educated Scheduled Castes felt no blocks because of the role of education as instrument of change.

While caste Hindus have liberalised their attitudes towards dalits, it has been observed that so called middle range backward castes offer larger resistance to the rising status of the Harijan than the very highest castes. Not only do they perceive a threat to their own positions because of the growing power of the Scheduled Castes but they are also jealous of the benefits and advantages provided to the Scheduled Castes by the Constitution.

As far as politics is concerned, the Harijan leader has to maintain a delicate balance between an image as a receiver of benefits of their own community while ensuring that they do not isolate the rest of their constituency by being too radical or strident in promoting the cause of freedom from oppression.

If the goal of reservation was to integrate the Scheduled Castes and Scheduled Tribes with the rest of the population than the system of quotas in profession, education and politics have only strengthened their separate identity and caused jealousy to members of higher castes who are similarly deprived but are without reservation.

While political expediency has made reservations somewhat permanent. In fact, many members of the Scheduled Castes and Scheduled Tribes are now able to prove the gains of the reservation policy, which has protected them for the last five decades, catapulting many to positions of power, privilege and wealth. But if one looks at the number of SC/ST Secretaries in the government of India or the actual literacy rates and the data of those SCs/STs below the poverty line as compared to the rest, it will repeat the old saying "One swallow does not make a summer." The upliftment of a single individual member of the community does not enhance the economic condition of the rest. While there may be Jagjivan Rams, B.R. Ambedkars, Karpoori Thakurs, Solankis, and K.R. Narayanans, their presence in the highest positions of political and administrative structure seemed to by only psychological strength. Whereas the rise of Indira Gandhi to the premiership of India may have been motivating to women all over the world, her presence did not enhance the status of women. There was no decline in evils pertaining to and atrocities committed on women during her term in office.

Two generations of Indians have tried to redress for the victimisation and low status given to Scheduled Castes and Scheduled Tribes in the past. Sincere efforts have been made to bring these communities on a par with the rest and to extent them socio-psychological support. It has been found that economic progress gets the maximum amount of social progress. The time has come when concrete steps to uplift all the Backward Classes must be taken in the form of free and compulsory education, vocational training, land, housing, health care, family planning and nutrition. A rural thrust such as the one given in the 20-Point Economic Programme, the abolition of bonded labour, the inclusion of tribals in the mainstream and other viable schemes for industrial and agricultural development must be initiated with great sincerity and commitement. What they need is a alternative to the problems of poverty, illness, shelter and illiteracy. Job reservations are only for the communities amongst SCs and STs and job reservations benefit only a handful minority of the downtrodden.

While the determination of one Indira Gandhi led to the withdrawal of a constitutional commitment on princely privileges and privy pauses, similarly the time has come to take political initiative to wish away rather than increase reservation. Reservations help a limited number of people and have no significant overall benefit to the most suppressed in that community.

The acceptance of the Mandal Commission suggestions would serve no purpose other than dividing society along caste lines and awakening caste awareness even where it was existent as in the metropolitan cities and rural areas in every state. The presentation of caste certificates at each platform would lead to further corruption and needless expansion of an already entrenched bureaucracy. By including more and more people within the purview of reservations there will be a mere expansion of non-productive clerical and bureaucratic posts, for which there will be a little scope for individual progress.

Reservation for Scheduled Castes/Scheduled Tribes

The Constitution mentioned only the reservation policy. It did not fix any particular percentage of seats in professional and technical institutions and posts in government and semi-government jobs. In 1950, the Government of India reserved 12.5 per cent seats for the Scheduled Castes and 5 per cent for the Scheduled Tribes in all-India services to be recruited on the basis of open competition. It also relaxed the age limit in their case by three years. In 1952, it relaxed the age limit to five years more than the maximum prescribed for others. Now, in the central and state services, seats and posts are reserved in proportion to population.

In 1970, the Central Government raised the reservation quota for the Scheduled Castes to 15 per cent, and that for the Scheduled Tribes to 7.5 per cent. As for reservation of jobs, the Constitution describes no fixed period. Naturally, the State is supposed to continue such preferential treatment until the SCs, STs and OBCs make substantial progress educationally and economically and reach a level of equality with the rest of the Indian citizens.

It hastened the process of socio-economic changes in India and specially of improving the conditions of the weaker sections and backward classes who constitute a majority of the population. The future of national progress and achievement of an egalitarian society depends on the rapid advancement of these backward sections of the people. The Constitution has set its goal to achieve this social justice and it can be explained in terms representation percentage of employees in the various categories of Central Government services (Table 6.1).

TABLE 6.1
RESERVATION OF OTHER BACKWARD CLASSES, SCHEDULED CASTES/SCHEDULED TRIBES IN CENTRAL GOVERNMENT SERVICES

Class	*Total*	*SC/ST*	*OBC*	*General*
I	174026 (100.00)	9891 (5.68)	8169 (4.69)	155966 (89.63)
II	912925 (100.00)	165982 (18.18)	97063 (10.63)	649880 (71.19)
III & IV	484687 (100.00)	118282 (24.40)	91975 (18.98)	274430 (56.62)
All Classes (excluding sweepers)	1571638 (100.00)	294155 (18.72)	197207 (12.55)	1080276 (68.73)

Source: Government of India Report on the Backward Classes Commission, First Part, Vol. I & II, 1980, Statement No. 1, p. 92.

This statement gives an interesting trend (i) there is decline in percentage of reservation of SCs/STs and OBCs from lower classes to higher class of posts. (ii) there is an increase in percentage of reservation of General Category. This shows a reverse trend, i.e., forward castes held largest share.

The positive impact of the affirmative action taken by the Indian Constitution can also be explained in terms of the educational progress and raising the level of literacy of the SCs and STs in India. At the time of India's independence in 1947, the literacy rate among them was below one per cent and in the last fifty years there has been considerable increase in their literacy rate. It is a fact that almost half of the world's illiterate population lives in India, but slowly the literacy level is going up. The position can be justified on the basis of Table 6.2.

The literacy rate in the case of SCs and STs has constantly gone up during the last five decades. The growth rate of literacy is higher among SCs and STs when compared to the total population. It is also clear from the data that the gap between them and rest of the population has increased. There are also considerable changes in literacy rates among different castes and different tribes. Again, wide interstate and inter-district variations exist in the context of SCs and STs.[6] The special provisions in the Constitution led to the progressive realization of the creation of a new and just social order as visualized by the architects of the Constitution. Further, in view of economic development of the underprivileged section of the society, the Constitution of India has set goals for the eradication of poverty. The First Five Year Plan of India (1952-57) outlined its objects like this. The State shall, in particular, direct its policy towards achieving (a) that the citizens, men and women equally have the right to a fair means of livelihood, and (b) that the ownership and control of the material resources of the community are so distributed as to subserve the common good. In 1954, the Government of India gave recognition to the socialist pattern of society as one of the objects of its economic and social policy. It was focussed to improve the living standards of the masses and provide gainful employment to those living below the poverty line. Many plans failed to end poverty, unemployment and economic inequality. Although there had been a perceptible increases in per capita income and some decline in percentage of the persons living below the poverty line, the magnitude of poverty in India is very high. In the context of SCs and STs, they continue to be socially and educationally backward and form the bottom of socio-economic pyramids. Table 6.3 gives comparative picture of the decline of poverty during the period 1977-78 to 1987-88.

TABLE 6.2
PERCENTAGE GROWTH RATE OF LITERACY AMONG SCs/STs IN INDIA IN 1961, 1971, 1981 AND 1991 CENSUS

Social Sections	*Literacy Rates*				*Growth Rates of Literacy*		
	1961	*1971*	*1981*	*1991*	*1991*	*1971-81*	*1981-91*
Total Population	24.00	29.45	36.23	52.21	22.71	23.02	44.10
SCs	10.27 (3.29)	14.67 (6.44)	21.30 (10.93)	37.41 (23.76)	42.84 (95.44)	45.74 (69.71)	75.76
STs	88.54 (3.16)	11.29 (4.85)	16.35 (8.04)	29.60 (18.19)	32.20 (53.48)	44.82 (65.77)	81.35

Note: Figures in parentheses show percentage of female literacy.
Source: Shymanand Singh, *Tribal Education in India*, Uppal (New Delhi), 1991, p. 7 and Census of India 1991 Series-I SC and ST, p. 14.

TABLE 6.3
PERCENTAGE OF SCs AND STs LIVING BELOW POVERTY LINE

Year	*Total Population*	*Scheduled Castes*	*Scheduled Tribes*
1977-78	51.2	64.6	72.4
1983-84	40.4	53.1	58.4
1987-88	33.4	44.7	52.6

Source: *Eighth Five Year Plan*, 1992-97, Planning Commission, Government of India, 1992 (New Delhi), Vol. II, p. 420.

The data reveal that one-third of Indian population lives in the condition of poverty. They are denied access to the basic needs of life such as sufficient food, clothes, house and medicine. There is no provision of social security for the poor. Now, the process of liberalization and the new economic policy have created a market friendly atmosphere. It could lead to still wider disparities within Indian society. The underprivileged sections will not get benefit of the opportunities, and the competitive market system will wipe out special privileges provided to them. This will increase the gap between the rich and the poor.

In Article 334 of the Indian Constitution reservation of seats in legislatures (Lok Sabha and Vidhan Sabhas) was made initially only for ten years. It was later extended through a series of amendments to the Constitution. The 62nd constitutional amendment in 1989 had extended reservation upto January 2000. In proportion to the population of SCs and STs reservation in legislature provided to them in Indian Parliament and State Legislatures.[7] Table 6.4 presents number of reserved seats alongwith the total seats.

As is clear from the table that out of 543 seats in the Lok Sabha, 46 seats are reserved for the SCs and STs. It provided them an opportunity to take part in the decision-making process of the country and many strong leaders have emerged from amongst them. In the various State Governments reservation in legislature produced capable ministers from them. In absence of these provisions they might not have got opportunity to serve the people and get share in the political process. Thus, reserved seats in legislature became a boom for bringing social justice and social change in India.

TABLE 6.4
STATEWISE NUMBERS OF SEATS RESERVED FOR SCs AND STs IN THE ASSEMBLIES AND PARLIAMENT

	Lok Sabha			*Assemblies*		
	Total	*SC*	*ST*	*Total*	*SC*	*ST*
States						
1. Andhra Pradesh	42	6	2	294	39	15
2. Arunachal Pradesh	2		2	60		59
3. Assam	14	1	2	126	8	16
4. Bihar	54	8	5	324	48	28
5. Gujarat	26	2	4	182	13	26
6. Haryana	10	2	0	90	17	0
7. Himachal Pradesh	4	1	0	68	16	3
8. Jammu & Kashmir	6	0	0	76	6	0
9. Karnataka	28	4	0	224	33	2
10. Kerala	20	2	0	140	13	1
11. Madhya Pradesh	40	6	9	320	44	75
12. Maharashtra	48	3	4	288	18	22
13. Manipur	2	0	1	60	1	19
14. Meghalaya	2	0	2	60	0	55

15. Nagaland	1	0	1	60	0	59
16. Orissa	21	3	5	147	22	34
17. Punjab	13	3	0	117	29	0
18. Rajasthan	25	4	3	200	33	34
19. Sikkim	1	0	0	32	1	15
20. Tamil Nadu	39	7	0	234	42	3
21. Tripura	2	0	1	60	7	17
22. Uttar Pradesh	85	18	0	425	92	1
23. West Bengal	42	8	2	294	59	17
24. Goa	2	0	0	30	1	0
25. Mizoram	1	0	1	40	6	38
26. Delhi	7	1	0	56	9	0
Union Territories						
1. Pondicherry	1	0	0	30	5	0
2. A & N Islands	1	0	0	-	-	-
3. Chandigarh	1	0	0	-	-	-
4. Dadra & Nagar Haveli	1	0	1	-	-	-
5. Daman & Diu	1	0	0	-	-	-
6. Lakshdweep	1	0	1	-	-	-
All India	543	79	46	4037	56	529

Source: *28th Report of the Commission of SC and ST*, Government of India (New Delhi) 1986-87, pp. 242-43.

The tenth Plan document (2002-07) brought out by the Planning Commission quoted representation of SCs, STs, at different level of political institutions (See Table 6.5).

TABLE 6.5

PERCENTAGE GROWTH RATE OF LITERACY AMONG SCs/STs IN INDIA IN 1961, 1971, 1981 AND 1991 CENSUS

Category	1991	1999					
SCs	6	7	3,67,941	18,546	1,822	562	79
	(10.5)	(9.5)	(14.3)	(14.4)	(13.5)	(13.8)	(14.**)
STs	3	3	2,35,445	7,237	1,170	530	4**
	(5.3)	(4.1)	(9.1)	(5.6)	(8.7)	(13.0)	(7.5)
General	48	64	11,76,875	99,798	10,482	2,980	423
Total	57	74	2580261	1,25,581	13,484	4,072	543

1. National Informatics Centre, Parliament House, New Delhi. Figures within paranthesis indicate percentage to total.
2. Election Commission, New Delhi, Department of Rural Development, GOI, New Delhi. NIC, Parliament

Backward Classes Commissions

Article 340 is connected with the appointment of commissions for the investigation of the socio-economic considerations of SCs, STs and OBCs. It makes it obligatory for the appointment of commissions by the President (i) to look into and report on the administration of the scheduled areas and the welfare of the Scheduled Tribes, and (ii) to investigate the conditions of socially and educationally backward classes and to make recommendations as to the step that should be taken by the Union or State Government to ameliorate those conditions. So far two such commissions have been appointed by the President of India under the Article 340 of the Constitution.

The First Commission on Backward Classes under the chairmanship of Kaka Kalelkar gave extremely wide ranging recommendations for upliftment of the backward classes. Some of the most noteworthy recommendations of the Commission were:

(i) Undertaking caste-wise enumeration of population in the census of 1961.

(ii) Relating social backwardness of a class to its low position in the traditional caste hierarchy of Hindu Society.

(iii) Treating all women as a class as 'backward'.

(iv) Reservation of 70 per cent in seats in all technical and professional institutions for qualified students of backward classes.

(v) Minimum reservation of vacancies in all government services and local bodies for OBCs on the following scale:

- Class I (25%), Class II (33.3%), Class III & IV (40%).

The report of the commission was not unanimous; five of its members recorded minutes of dissent. Shri Kaka Kalelkar in his forwarding letter to the President opposed inclusion of caste as a basis for backwardness.

About the caste-based reservations policy as recommended by the Kalelkar Commission, Govind Ballabh Pant, the then Home Minister, noted that the recognition of the specific castes as backward may serve to maintain and even perpetuate the existing distinction based on caste. The Central Government did not implement it and left it for the State Governments to adopt their own criteria. Again, in 1978, the claim of OBCs was referred to the second Backward Classes Commission, headed by B.P. Mandal. The terms of reference Mandal Commission were: (i) to determine the criteria for defining socially and educationally backward classes; (ii) to recommend steps to be taken for the advancement of the socially and educationally backward classes of citizens so identified; (iii) to examine the desirability or otherwise of making provisions for the reservation of appointment of posts in favour of such backward classes of citizens which are not reasonably represented in public services and posts in connection with the affairs of the Union or any State, and (iv) present to the President a report setting out of facts as found by them and making such recommendations as they think proper.

The Mandal Commission also settled upon the routine and ready tool of caste with which to identify backward classes. The research team, appointed to carry out a village level survey, chose family as a unit of observation. The team found as a horizontal segmental division of society spread over a district of a region or the whole state even beyond. In each village, a section of a caste exists largely in vertical relationship with other castes. The survey, thus, neglected the community aspect of caste.[8] The Commission prepared one consolidated list of backward classes L.R. Naik, a Member of the Commission, while giving a dissenting note, recommended that a separate list be prepared for each state and that each list should be in two parts, one part listing the intermediate backward classes and other one the depressed backward classes. The Commission did not accept this suggestion. It even cited the judgment of the Supreme Court of India in Balaji *versus* State of Mysore case, which had *inter alia* stated that in introducing two categories of backward classes, what the impugned order, in substance, purports to do is to devise methods for all the classes of citizens who are less advanced compared to the most advanced in the state, this is not the scope of Article 15(4).

The Commission found that the representation of the backward classes (other than SCs and STs) in the central services in different categories was below that of the SCs and STs although the population of these backward classes was more than double of the SCs and STs. The better representation of the SCs and STs is entirely because of the reservation policy.

The Mandal Commission identified as many as 3,943 castes covering about 52 per cent of the total population of India as OBCs in its report in 1980. It, therefore, suggested reservation for these backward classes in proportion of their population. However, in the context of the legal constraint that total reservation should not exceed 50 per cent for all categories, it restricted this reservation to 27 per cent in government service and in educational institutions. It proposed the following overall scheme of reservation for the OBCs:

(i) Candidates belonging to these classes recruited on the basis of merit in an open competition should be excluded against their reservation quota of 27 per cent.
(ii) Reservation should also be provided in promotions at all levels.
(iii) Any reserved quota remaining unfilled should be carried forward for a period of three years and dereserved thereafter.
(iv) Relaxation in the upper age limit for direct recruitment should be given to candidates of the backward classes as in the case of the SCs and STs.
(v) A roster system for each category of posts should be adopted by the authorities concerned as in the case of the SCs and STs.[9]

The report of the Mandal Commission was placed before Lok Sabha in 1982 for the debate. But the political will for implementation was lacking till the emergence of OBCs as a political force in 1989 parliamentary election. The Mandal Commission's recommendations were implemented by the Janata Dal government led by V.P. Singh on 13th August 1990.[10] This was challenged in the Supreme Court and various High Courts. The Supreme Court issued a stay order on 7th November, 1990. The issue was then examined by the nine-member Constitutional Bench which, on 16th November, 1992, in its majority judgment (4 out of 9) permitted the Central Government to reserve 27 per cent for the OBCs subject to the exclusion of the creamy layer.[11] After the identification of the creamy layer by the Ramanand Prasad Committee in March 1993[12] and their exclusion from becoming the beneficiary of OBCs the Central Government executed the V.P. Singh govenment order of 13th August, 1990 in September 1993. Thus, the constitutional validity of reservation for OBCs in central service was thoroughly examined by the Supreme Court which said that the list of OBCs can be made on the basis of caste as it represents an existing identifiable social group of the country's population. At present, for the three groups of backward classes—SCs, STs and OBCs, 15, 7.5 and 27 per cent of posts respectively are reserved.

The Indian social and political system is moving towards achievement of a trinity of goals of the constitution viz., socialism, secularism and democracy. Now, a situation has been created by the State that all sections of the society can take part in the State power equally, irrespective of their caste, community, race, religion and sex.

Although there are always some groups who conspire, some oppress, some manipulate and equally others expose conspiracy, fight oppression and resist manipulations. The different sides are not evenly matched. But the pluralist Indian society gives protection to all of its divergent interest,[13] under its broad political spectrum and its law is committed to bringing distribution of power, social justice and eradicating poverty of its deprived masses. The economic development as well as the spread egalitarian values has generated a formidable challenge to the old social order and those who were at the bottom of the social and economic order are moving up and are in the process of getting power from the hands of traditional elite.

References

1. Granville Austin, *The Indian Constitution: Corner Stone of a Nation*, Oxford, 1966, p. 50.
2. *Constituent Assembly Debates*, Vol. VII, Government of India (New Delhi) 1947, pp. 696-7.
3. *Ibid.*, p. 304.
4. Marc Galanter, *Competing Equalities: Law and Backward Classes in India*, Oxford (New Delhi), 1984, p. 159.
5. Philip Mason (ed.), *India and Ceylon: Unity and Diversity*, article by Andre Beteille "The future of the Backward Classes: The Competing Demands of Status and Power" Oxford (New York), 1967.

6. M.S. Khan, *Current Problems of Indian Economy*, Ashish (New Delhi) 1994, p. 30.
7. Shyama Nand Singh, *Reservation: Problems and Prospects*, Uppal (New Delhi), 1991, p. 72.
8. *Report of the First Backward Classes Commission* (Chairman: Kaka Kalelkar), Government of India 1955, p. vii.
9. *Report of the Second Backward Classes Commission of India* (Chairman: B.P. Mandal, 1980 (New Delhi), Vol. VII, p. 58.
10. *Official Memorandum of Department of Personnel*, Government of India, 13 August, 1990.
11. *Indra Sawhney vs. Union of India*, SC 16, November 1992.
12. *Report of the Expert Committee for specifying the criteria for identification of socially and educationally backward classes* (Chairman: R.N. Prasad) Government of India, 10th March, 1993.
13. Atul Kohli, *India's Democracy: An Analysis of Changing State-Society Relations*, Orient Longman (New Delhi), 1991, p. 15.

Index

I-3690-A

ENCYCLOPAEDIA OF BACKWARD CASTES: COMMISSIONS

ENCYCLOPAEDIA OF BACKWARD CASTES
(In 4 Volumes)

1. RESERVATION
2. COMMISSIONS
3. MANDAL, MEDIA AND AFTERMATH
4. JUDGEMENTS: BEFORE AND AFTER MANDAL JUDGEMENT

ENCYCLOPAEDIA
OF
BACKWARD CASTES
(In 4 Volumes)

COMMISSIONS
(Volume 2)

M.L. Mathur
Senior Research Officer
Ministry of Social Justice and Empowerment
Government of India, New Delhi.

PUBLICATIONS

KALPAZ PUBLICATIONS
DELHI - 110052

ENCYCLOPAEDIA OF BACKWARD CASTES: COMMISSIONS
[Scheduled Castes and OBCs]

Rs. 3600/- (Set)

ISBN: 81-7835-069-6 (Set)
ISBN: 81-7835-269-9 (Vol. 2)

©M.L. Mathur

This book may not be reproduced in any manner without written permission of the author and the publisher.

Published in 2004 in India by
Kalpaz Publications
C-30, Satyawati Nagar,
Delhi-110052
e-mail: kalpaz@hotmail.com

Laser Typeset at: Alphabet, Delhi
Printed at: Mehra Offset Press, Delhi

Contents

Introduction

There was no policy of reservation for backward classes (Scheduled Castes, Scheduled Tribes, and Other Backward Classes earlier termed "depressed classes" during British rule. It can also be said that only a few castes took benefit of education and employment and that was their monopoly. Consequently non-forward castes remained educationally and economically deprived for centuries. When they realised there was a need to advanced their education and economic level in the society they organized themselves as strong social force. Social force truned into social movements. M.S.A. Rao (1979) work on social movement is a pioneer work covering Non-brahmin movement in Tamil Nadu and Yadav movement in Northern India. Thus in preindependence India Tamil Nadu, Karnataka and Maharashtra are three states in the country where backward classes movement for their right of reservation in government service was noticed. Take for example, of Tamil Nadu. In Tamil Nadu Brahmins were the main beneficiaries of the British System of education and other advantages. Non-Brahmins realized they were deprived of such benefits. South Indian Liberation Federation and Justice Party worked as political force for non-brahmins in Tamil Nadu and movement for reservation began there. A very popular government order of 1927 'communal order' was revised in 1947 which was further struck down by the Supreme Court in 1951. There was no improvement in employment position over the period of twenty-five years, i.e., during 1922 to 1947. (See Table 1). Similar was the education situation at each decade of census in 1911, 1921, 1931. (See Table 2). Let us see the situation in Karnataka. In Karnataka also Brahmins had their monopoly in education and employment. This situation was alike as in Tamil Nadu. As far as back in 1851, Mysore State (now part of Karnataka State) made reservation policy for non-Brahmins. There a system of recruitment through nomination was introduced in 1914. In 1918, Maharaja of Mysore appointed a committee under the Chairmanship of Sir C. Miller to enquire into inadequate representation of non-brahmins in government service. Unlike Tamil Nadu, in Karnataka percentages of posts held by non-Brahmins on gazetted and non-gazetted posts increased gradually over the period of forty years, i.e. from 1918 to 1957 (see Table 3). This was after the policy of reservation was introduced. The third state is Maharashtra where due to emergence of leaders like Jotiba Phule, non-Brahmin movement got momentum. This movement spread from Bombay to Kolhapur. During those days Ambedkar was active fighting for cause of depressed classes. The first chapter presents an overview of non-Brahmin movements in these three states before pre-independence and prevailing conditions of reservation for backward castes in those days.

Chapter Two discusses recommendations given by Commissions and Committees appointed by different states for preparing a list of backward classes and recommended percentage of reservation in government services. As stated earlier three states Tamilnadu (Madras Presidency) Karnataka (Mysore State) and Maharashtra (Bombay Presidency) recognized the demand of non-Brahmins for granting them reservation in government service before independence. The Government of India left it to all states to draw their own lists unlike the list of Scheduled Castes and Scheduled Tribes being prepared by Government of India only. After independence 10 states initiated action by way of appointing Committees and Commissions for giving reservation benefit to other backward classes, when Government of India did not act upon the recommendations of Kaka Kalelker Commission in 1955. Only ten states prepared the list of backward classes based on recommendations of various committees/commissions. These States are Andhra Pradesh, Bihar, Gujarat, Jammu & Kashmir, Karnataka, Kerala, Maharashtra, Punjab, Tamil Nadu and Uttar Pradesh. Further 8 States and Union Territories have notified lists of OBCs for the grant of education, employment and other benefits. These are: Assam, Delhi, Haryana, Himachal Pradesh, Meghalaya, Orissa, Pondicherry and *****. These State Governments and Union Territories mainly relied upon the list of OBCs maintained by them for grant of post-matric scholarships, etc. under the Education Ministry's scheme formulated in 1944 and another list prepared by Commissioner of SC & ST at the time of drafting the First Five Year Plan. Briefly the recommendations given by various States Commissions and Committees were as follows:—

Sl. No.	*State*	*Year*	*Committee/ Commissions*	*Recommedations*
1.	Andhra Pradesh	1968	Manohar Pershad Commission	30% reservation in Govt. service among four categories of OBCs (i) Aboriginal tribes, Vimukta Jatis, Nomadic and Semi nomadic tribes (7%), (ii) Vocational groups (13%), (iii) Harijan Converts (1%) and other classes (9%). Govt. reduced it to 25%.
		1975	Veerapa Committee	25% reservation
		1982	Murlidhar Rao Commission	44% reservation.
2.	Bihar	1951	Govt. of Bihar	A list of 109 castes prepared to give them benefit of scholarships.
		1971	Mungeri Lal Commission	24% seats in medical and other professional institutions, 26% in Govt. and Semi-Govt. jobs.
		1978	Karpoori Thakur	20% reservation in Govt. service.
		1994	U.N. Sinha	Not accepted.

Sl. No.	State	Year	Committee/ Commissions	Recommedations
3.	Gujarat	1972	A.R. Bakshi	82 castes identified, 10% reservation in medical/ engineering and other professional institutions/ Trg. cum Production centres. 10% reservation in Class III and IV posts and 5% in Class I and II posts.
		1981	C.V. Rane	28% reservation in posts and seats.
		1987	R.C. Mankad	Report not submitted.
4.	Haryana	1991	Gurnam Singh	27% reservation in Govt. Service.
5.	Himachal Pradesh	1951	Govt. of H.P.	Followed the list of OBCs declared by erstwhile state Punjab
		1970	Govt. of H.P.	Economic Criteria
		1993	Govt. of H.P.	20% for OBCs.
6.	Jammu & Kashmir	1967	P.B. Gajendra-gadkar Commission	Recommended for high powered Committee to identify castes and communities.
		1969	J.N. Wazir Committee	42% reservation for OBCs.
		1976	A.S. Anand Committee	42% of Govt. jobs and seats in technical institutions and in other institutions.
7.	Karnataka	1918	Sir L.C. Miller	Special facilities to backward communities with regard to education and recruitment in State Services.

Sl. No.	*State*	*Year*	*Committee/ Commissions*	*Recommedations*
		1961	Nagan Gowda Committee	Reservation in professional and Technical institutions (BC-28%, MBC-22%). In Govt. service (BC-21% & MBC-24%)
		1975	Havanur Commission	Reservation for OBCs 16% in education & Govt. service
		1985	Venkataswamy Commission	27% reservation for OBCs.
		1990	Chinnappa Reddy Commission	
8.	Kerala	1961	Vishwanathan Committee	40% of seats in technical and professional colleges and direct recruitment of service Govt. of Kerala restricted to 25%.
		1965	G. Kumara Pillai	40% reservation for OBCs in Govt. jobs.
		1970	M.P. Damodaran	40% reservation in Govt. services for OBCs and further distributed among different communities.
9.	Madhya Pradesh	1980	Ramjee Mahajan	Recommended for 35% reservation for OBCs in educational Institutions and in government service.
		1984	Govt. of M.P.	25% reservation for OBCs.
10.	Maha-rashtra	1961	B.D. Deshmukh	10% reservation for OBCs.

Sl. No.	State	Year	Committee/ Commissions	Recommedations
11.	Punjab	1951	Committee	2% reservation for OBCs.
		1965	Brish Bhan Committee	5% reservation for OBCs in educational institutions and Govt. service.
		1975	Harcharan Singh Commission	15% reservation for OBCs in educational institutions and Govt. service.
12.	Tamilnadu	1885	Provincial Govt.	Grant-in-aid Code 1885 to regulate financial aid to educational institutions.
		1927	Madras Presidency	Communal Government order 25% for OBCs.
		1969	A.N. Sattanathan Commission	17% reservation for backward classes and 16% reservation for most backward classes.
		1982	J.A. Ambashankar Commission	50% for OBC in Government Service.
13.	Uttar Pradesh	1975	Chhedi Lal Sathi Commission	15% reservation for OBCs in government services, technical & professional seats.

At national level the Govt. of India appointed two Commissions Kaka Kalelkar Commission in 1953 and B.P. Mandal Commission in 1978. This volume discusses about these Commissions in separate chapters.

Kaka Kalelkar Commission (1953)

The Government of India appointed a First Backward Classes Commission under the Chairmanship of Kaka Kalelkar in 1953.

This was the first national level Commission to determine criteria for identifying socially and educationally backward classes and their numbers state-wise. The commission identified 2399 backward castes or communities out of these 837 were classified as most backward. The Commission recommended to government for reservation of OBCs in government service in different classes of posts. 25 per cent in class I, 33.3 per cent in Class II, 40 per cent in class III and 40 per cent in Class IV. There were many more recommendations given for upliftment of backward classes. The report of the Commission was not unanimous. The Government of India laid a copy of the report alongwith a memorandum of action taken before each House of Parliament on September 3rd, 1956. The report was not discussed in the Parliament. Finally, the Government of India did not act upon recommendations of the commission thus kept the backward classes to live on hope in future.

B.P. Mandal (1980)

When Janata Party Government came into power in 1977 it appointed a Second Backward Classes Commission in 1978 to fulfil its promises made in the election manifesto. The Commission was asked to determine the criteria for defining the socially and educationally backward classes and recommended steps for their advancement. The Commission gave their report in 1980. The Commission identified 3743 castes as backward castes Depressed backward classes (see Table 2). It also recommended for reservation of 27% for OBCs in Government service.

By the time Janata Party Government thought of implementing the recommendations of Mandal Report in 1980, it went out of power. The Congress government came to power. As it made an attempt by placing the report before the Parliament, the government faced stiff resistance. Feeling the heat and pulse in the Parliament, the Congress government having two-third majority in the Parliament, shelved their effort and put the report in the cold storage. Again the backward castes lost their hopes of getting reservation benefit in government service. After ten years when the National Front Government headed by Shri V.P. Singh came to power in 1989, it announced the implementation of the recommendations of the Mandal Commission in 1990 and issued government order reserving 27% of posts for OBCs in Government service. There was widespread agitations all over the country and backward castes got justice only in 1992 from the Supreme Court upholding G.O. of 1990 with minor modifications.

One

Pre-Independence Backward Classes Movement in states*

The Reform Movement for the Backward Classes in Tamil Nadu

In Tamil Nadu Brahmins were the main beneficiaries of the British System of education and the other advantages. The educated Brahmins captured the largest share of Government service in the state. 'The monopoly situation' in government service created by Brahmins and Montagu-Chelmsford reforms alerted and alarmed non-Brahmins. As a result non-Brahmin elite castes took lead and established first the South Indian Liberal Federation and secondly, the Justice Party in 1916. After coming into power in 1920 this party took steps to loosen the hold of Brahmins on services. It was under communal G.O. of 1927 that compartmental reservation of posts was made for various communities.

An interesting fact is that the Justice party leaders were drawn from the landed classes and were not much keen on broadening their base by including the landless castes within their ranks. The communal G.O. of 1927 represented a victory for the vellala castes, particularly the Mudalliars. This approach eroded the mass base of the Justice Party. Its aloofness from the national movement weakened it further.

In 1947, the communal G.O. of 1927 was revised an important feature of the new order was that for the first time the non-Brahmin castes were bifurcated into non-Brahmins Hindus and non-Brahmin backward Hindus. This compartmental reservation was struck down by the Supreme Court and consequently, the Government issued another order in 1951 making reservations for

---

* This Chapter is based on Government of India Report on Backward Classes Commission, First Part, 1980.

Scheduled Castes, Tribes and other Backward Classes only. This did not give rise to any sharp reaction from the non-Brahmin forward castes as they had become sufficiently powerful to hold out to their benefits and did not have to resort to any kind of protest or backlash.

The reservation policy was initiated during the British rule and was modified time and again. In Madras, the term 'backward' was first used in the Department of Education in payment of stipends to students coming from 'illiterate' and 'indigent' castes. The number of backward classes, which was 39 in 1895, grew to 113 in 1913, 128 in 1920, 152 in 1950, and 253 in 1994. This, of course does not imply that more and more castes became backward as the years passed. It only shows that more and more castes learnt to demand and receive special educational concessions on the basis of several backwardness rather than individual merit.[1] The principle in 1922 was that among the qualified applicants for any job preference should be given to those belonging to the least represented communities. The recruitment to services on a communal basis was regularized and a definite quota for different communities in vacancies under the government was prescribed.

The reservation policy introduced by the Government of India in 1922 brought the expected result in the direction for more jobs for non-Brahmins. In 1947, only 21 per cent gazetted and 20 per cent non-gazetted posts were filled by Brahmins. The non-Brahmins obtained most of the posts.

In 1950, the system of communal representation in the services of the state was further expanded and the benefit of preferential treatment was reserved for the Scheduled Castes, Scheduled Tribes and OBCs. Under the new system, a cycle of twenty recruitments was taken as a unit. Three were reserved for the SCs/STs, five for the backward classes, and the rest were filled by open competition. On the basis of the 1951 census and in the wake of the separation of Andhra Pradesh from Tamil Nadu in 1954, the number of reservation was changed to 16 per cent for the SCs/STs and 25 per cent for the backward classes.

For this purpose, the various communities were combined into five broad categories. This is illustrated below:

Forward Castes	*Backward Castes*
Other Christians (Reddis)	Christian Converts from Scheduled Castes
Muslims (Urdu speaking)	Labbani
Adisawa	Dakhni Muslims
Kargliata	Thuluvallas
Kalavali Vallals, Kamanaidus	Sozhia Vallas
	Ganjam Reddies, Gavara and Vadugar Naidus

The communal government order became the prime point of dispute between the Brahmins and the non-Brahmins. The Brahmins who monopolized the public services for years were getting only two out of twelve posts.[2] They were forced to search jobs in the Central Government and private enterprises. They demanded a review of the policy. It was revised in 1947, but again, it went against them as they were only entitled to get two out of fourteen posts. The proportion of jobs to be given to each category was revised in the manner as shown in Table 1.

TABLE 1

QUOTAS FOR VARIOUS COMMUNITIES IN MADRAS 1927 AND 1947

Categories	*Posts to be Allocated*	
	1922	*1947*
Non-Brahmins Hindu	5 out of 12	6 out of 14
Backward Hindu	—	2 out of 14
Brahmin	2 out of 12	2 out of 14
Muslim	2 out of 12	1 out of 14
Anglo-Indians and Indian Christians	2 out of 12	1 out of 14
Scheduled Castes (Depressed Classes)	1 out of 12	2 out of 14

Source: Report of Tamil Nadu Backward Classes Commission, 1970, p. 39.

The reservation made for the SCs, STs and OBCs under the reforms of 1908 also forced the Muslims to demand reservation in the government services in proportion to their population. The Government of India Act of 1919 (also known as Montague Chelmsford reforms) made arrangement for separate representations in the legislatures for Muslims, Sikhs, Anglo-Indians and Indian Christians. The Government of India Act of 1935 also contained separate electorates for Muslims and the Governor General and Governors were put under the obligation to protect the interests of minorities in the instrument of instructions. But it was not until about 1935 that the Muslims could secure reservation of 25 per cent of the selection to the central services where there was direct recruitment. Some time later quota may kept for Muslims in the civil services through competitive examinations to the extent of 25 per cent.

Table 2 explains the education scenario from 1911 to 1931 of the various communities in Madras presidency.

In the three consecutive censuses of Madras presidency in 1911, 1921, and 1931 the Brahmins population was only 3, 3.5 and 2 per cent respectively. But the percentage of students among them was 35.5, 39.5 and 31 respectively. It shows their keenness for education. In the same case, the non-Brahmins (including Harijans and all other Hindus) were 86, 85.5 and 86 per cent respectively of the total population. The percentage of students among them was only 41.5, 44.5 and 47 respectively. It throws light at some upward mobility of the number of students among them. In comparison to them Brahmins were far ahead. The low level of education among non-Brahmins was responsible for the percentage of employment in government jobs. In 1931, in Madras, 45.75 per cent Brahmins, 29.1 per cent Komatis, 30.8 per cent Nayars, 10 per cent low castes and 1.16 per cent Harijans were literate. Muslims and Christians too had effective percentage in the state and more so among literates. The rate of literacy was only due to number of students of these castes in the schools. Therefore, they started asking better facilities for themselves in planned way.

The preferential treatment given to backward classes is credited to the non-Brahmin movement started in the second decade of the 20th century in Madras presidency. The non-Brahmin leaders with feudal background became aware of educational backwardness of their numbers and the domination of Brahmins in English education and government jobs. The distribution of public offices and political positions among different communities in proportion to their population was demanded by them from the British Government of India. English education made Brahmin capable to join government offices in a large number. They constituted about 3.5 per cent of the total population of old Madras presidency, but occupied more than 70 per cent of the total government posts. The non-Brahmin manifesto of 1916 started a vitriolic tirade against the ritual supremacy,[3] and worldly success of the Brahmins. From then onwards, newly formed Justice Party in 1916 took up the issue and started demanding adequate representation of non-Brahmins in the popular house and in all branches of administration.[4] Newspapers like *Justice, Dravidan* and *Andhra Prakasika* served their cause and repudiated the blames of Brahmins against manifesto of the Justice Party and non-Brahmin movement.

TABLE 2

CASTEWISE LEVEL OF EDUCATION 1911, 1921 AND 1931

Caste	*1911*		*1921*		*1931*	
	per cent of population	*per cent of students*	*per cent of population*	*per cent of students*	*per cent of Population*	*per cent of students*
Brahmin	3.0	35.5	3.5	39.5	2.0	31.0
Non-Brahmin	86.0	41.5	85.5	44.5	86.0	47.0
Muslim	6.5	5.5	6.5	5.0	7.0	6.0
Christian	3.0	13.5	3.0	10.5	4.0	12.0
Others	1.5	4.0	1.5	1.0	1.0	4.0
Total	100.0	100.0	100.0	100.0	100.0	100.0

Source: Census of India, Madras, 1911, Vol. XII, Part II, p. 62, 1921, Vol. XIII, Part II, pp. 62, 161: 1931, Vol. XIV, Part II, pp. 256, 275. Reports on Public Instructions in the Madras Presidency for the years 1911, 1921 and 1931.

This was reconsidered in 1947 and a unit of fourteen was recognized. In the new system, one more seat each was allotted to non-Brahmins and Scheduled Castes. Two out of fourteen posts were reserved for the Scheduled Castes. In 1947, for the first time, backward Hindus came up as a separate category for the purpose of preferential treatment.

Backward Classes Movement in Karnataka

Most parts of the present Karnataka state were parts of the previous Mysore state. Between 1851 to 1881 reservations were made for non-Brahmins as the Brahmins had established monopoly in the services and the professions. In 1895, appointments in police department were made on reserved seats in fixed proportions in favour of Brahmins, Muslims and other Hindu castes. But these previous measures did not seriously affect Brahmin monopoly. In the same year, an order was issued by the Mysore Government reserving some posts for the backward classes. In 1914, a system of recruitment through nomination was introduced by which on posts of Assistant Commissioners were appointed the members of the backward classes, but their position did not improve.

In the year 1882, the Mysore Representative Assembly was constituted on limited franchise to make the people capable to voice their grievances and aspirations, but with no legislative powers. From then, however, political consciousness owned amongst the people and particularly among the dominant castes like Lingayats and Vokkaligas in the state. In 1905, the Mysore Lingayat Education Fund Association and in 1906 the Vokkaliga Sangha were formed in Bangalore and they began to take interest in the education, services and professions of their community members. Their efforts were, however, weak and little supported by the ruling class. But the Representative Assembly was an effective new democratic platform for the people to express their grievances and pass resolutions.

In 1875, mild controversies emerged about the policy of recruitment to public services in Mysore state. In 1912, M. Visweswarayya became the Dewan and advocated for the age-old policy that the best man should secure the job. The Maharaja detested this policy and being influenced by the debates in the Representative Assembly and the representations made by the various caste and community organizations, declared strongly in unequivocal for appointing non-Brahmins into the service.

In 1918, the Maharaja of Mysore felt that there was a large number of Brahmins in public service and that efforts should be made to ensure that all the other important communities in the state also the adequate representation in the services of the state.

For this purpose, the government formed committee in August 1918 under the Chairmanship of Sir Leslie C. Miller, Kt., to enquire and report on the problem. The questions referred to the committee were the following:

I. Changes needed in the then existing rules of recruitment to the public services;

II. Special facilities to promote higher and professional education among the members of backward classes; and

III. Any other special steps which may be taken to enhance the representation of backward communities in the public service without materially affecting the efficiency, due value being paid also to the common good accruing to the state by a wider diffusion of education and sense of increased status which will thereby be created in the backward communities.[5]

The Miller Committee submitted its report in July 1919 which said that even during 1916 and 1918, the condition of the non-Brahmins did not get better. We find that the results obtained have not shown any progressive decrease of the inequality each year, but on the other hand, have actually aggravated it year by year. The report says that the Brahmin percentage in all grades of salary varied from 67 per cent to 82 per cent and even 100 per cent in the grade of Rs. 100 to Rs. 200. The committee suggested that backward classes should include all communities other than the Brahmins, Anglo-Indians and Europeans. The Brahmin community that was just 4.5 per cent of the population enjoyed an overwhelming part in the services. The report had significantly observed, "we think that a large increase in the proportion of officers drawn from communities other than the Brahmins may safely be advocated without any fear that the efficiency of the services as a whole will thereby be materially reduced."

The Miller Committee suggested that (i) within seven years the non-Brahmin strength in the higher services must be increased to one half and in the lower services to two-thirds, (ii) there should be special schools for the depressed class student and that teachers must be drawn from amongst the backward classes, (iii) English must be made compulsory in secondary education, (iv) scholarships should be given to the backward students, (v) hostels should be constructed with both vegetarian and non-vegetarian kitchens, (vi) the Anglo Indian schools must be increased to help them, (vii) age limit for the backward class members must be raised from 25 to 28 years, (viii) competitive examinations must be remove and backward class candidates should be appointed into service by nomination, and (ix) a committee of representative officers should be appointed for selection of candidates. Two members of the committee, namely, C. Srikanteshwara Iyer and M.C. Ranga Iyengar presented dissenting notes disagreeing with most of the recommendations of the committee.

After receiving the Miller report, the government passed orders in May 1921 and, among others, constituted the Central Recruitment Board and reserved 75 per cent of the posts for the backward classes. As a result of this recruitment policy, and six years after, the position started slightly to improve.

In the services of Mysore state, the Brahmins were in large number, it was several years before the Miller Order began to think about the people of apparent impact on the proportion of Brahmins in state services, especially at the gazetted level. Table 3 explains the fact that percentage of Brahmins declined about half from 1918 to 1957 among Gazetted posts and among non-gazetted posts. The Statistical fact is an evidence to say that Miller's recommendation had been implemented.

TABLE 3
CASTE AND PUBLIC EMPLOYMENT IN KARNATAKA, 1918-1957

Year	*Gazetted Posts*		*Non-Gazetted Posts*	
	Total No.	*Brahmins percentage*	*Total No.*	*Brahmins percentage*
1918	370	64.86	13,946	69.64
1936	760	61.32	22,615	49.65
1947	1298	46.89	37,820	37.50
1957	1797	35.72	57,516	27.65

Source: Report of the Second Backward Classes Commission of Karnataka, Bangalore, 1988, p. 18.

For the first time in the modern times, seats in colleges and state services reserved in the Mysore state brought out expected results in the educational development and job prospects of non-Brahmins. It can also be said in terms of decline of Brahmins in the gazetted and non-gazetted services of the state. In 1918, the Brahmins possessed 64.86 per cent of the total gazetted posts. It reduced to 35.72 per cent in 1957. This trend continued even after independence. Similar was the state for non-gazetted posts also. The non-Brahmins were also asking for greater share of political representation. It not only the Government of India Act of 1919 special representation was provided to them, it not only helped in the rise of non-Brahmin political parties in the Madras and Bombay Presidencies, but also the non-Brahmins to develop a system of preferences in the field of education and public employment.

The Movement for Backward Classes Reforms in Maharashtra

In the 19th century, Poona and Kolhapur provided leadership to the emergence of backward castes movement in India. One of the first leaders of Christian missionary education was Jothiba Phule of Poona who came from among the Shudra caste of gardner. Phule (1827-1890) is known as the father of the non-Brahmin movement in India. He wrote several books for the material and spiritual betterment of the lower classes in Marathi. He initiated efforts to assist the low castes. The condition of the untouchables horrified him. He started schools for them. Hurt by caste inequities, Jothiba felt an attraction for Islam and Christianity where the principle of equality was uppermost. He provoked the people to revolt against Hindu casteist Gods and the humiliating religious practices. He preached for the abolition of false beliefs, meaningless rituals and baseless customs. He inspired the lower castes to form their own associations create an espirit de corps and work for their emancipation from the age old taboos pertaining to Shudras in social status, education and religion.

Undaunted by the threats of the Brahmins to belittle the anti-Brahminic stance of the new movement, Jothiba founded the Satya Shodak Mandal to bring together all the backward classes on a common platform. Jothiba preached the principle of adequate representation for members of all castes in public services. On this basis, Ambedkar (1891-1956) led the cause of the depressed castes and asked for reservation of seats for them before the Simon Commission (1927) and the first round table conference (1930-31). The Poona Pact (1932) founded permanent basis for the reserved seats in independent India. Thus, Ambedkar became the symbol of the backward classes.

The non-Brahmin movement generated in Bombay province (now Maharashtra) expanded the Kolhapur—a small Maratha state—under the rule of the Bombay Government by Maharaja Chatrapati Shahu. The Brahmin-non-Brahmin contradictions, Bombay began in 1891 when R.P. Paranjape with the new claim of the Maharaja of Kolhapur, a heir of the Great Shivaji, to Vedic rites, as his Brahmin hereditary priest denied to obtain this, his hereditary landed property and allowances were confiscated and the problem became more severe.

The Maharaja, unhappy with the Brahmins, devoted much of his time to the non-Brahmin movement. He declared in 1902 that he would keep at least half the posts in the state for qualified members of the non-Brahmin communities. Earlier, the Prince had elected as his Prime Minister, a Kayastha Prabhu, Rao Bahadur Sahib. Perhaps he was the first non-Brahmin to be appointed as the Dewan. This appointment as well as the order to reserve half the posts were unacceptable to the Brahmins. Firm in his conviction to give just opportunities to all communities, the Prince started a hostel in Kolhapur city for giving education to Marathas, Muslims and Jain youths, who were studying in the Rajaram College. Kolhapur may be said to be the first state to follow reservation policy, though there had been some ineffective attempts earlier by the British Government itself through to break the monopoly of one community. Kolhapur, therefore, has been a landmark in the backward class movement towards equality.

At National Level

Due to the continuous efforts of Ambedkar, the depressed classes first obtained 8.33 per cent reservation in the central jobs in August 1943 and got it raised to 12.5 per cent in June 1946. It was further increased to 16.66 per cent after independence. After creation of Pakistan on August 14, 1947, reservation for minorities was abolished, but SCs and STs continued to get reservation according to their population. In September 1993, OBCs of India got 27 per cent reserved seats in the central services. They are also struggling to get benefits of reservation in educational institutions run by the Central Government. In many states, the OBCs have been given reservation in seats in educational institutions, specially technical and professional education.[6] In the states where backward classes movement were effective during the British rule, such as Tamil Nadu, Karnataka, Andhra Pradesh, Kerala and Maharashtra, alongwith and STs, the OBCs also got advantages of preferential treatment in the early 1950s. In the states of Bihar, Uttar Pradesh, Gujarat, Punjab, J&K and Himachal Pradesh, the OBCs could get reserved quotas in the 1970s.[7] Now, along with all India services, the OBCs are getting benefit of reserved quotas in all the states and union territories.

References

1. S. Saraswati, *Minorities in Madras State*, Delhi, 1974, p. 108.
2. Marc Galanter, *Competing Equalities: Law and the Backward Classes in India*, Delhi, 1984, p. 157.
3. Pandav Nayak in Iqbal Narain (ed.), *State Politics in India*, Meerut, 1976, p. 409.
4. *Report of the Tamil Nadu Backward Classes Commission* (Chairman: T.A.N. Sattanathan), Madras, 1970, p. 23.
5. *Report of the First Backward Classes Committee of Karnataka*, (Chairman: R. Nagn Gowda), Bangalore, 1961, p. 1.
6. M.N. Srinivas, "On Living in a Revolution", *Economic and Political Weekly* (Bombay), 30th March, 1991, p. 833.
7. Shyama Nand Singh, "Politics of Job Reservation in India", *Mainstream* (New Delhi), 29th July, 1989.

Two

Backward Classes Commission in Various States*

Different approaches in fixing up the criteria for identification of OBCs by different commissions reflect the absence of uniform basis of backwardness. The two Central Commissions had different outlooks. The State Governments' Commissions had different considerations. Wide differences between these Commissions on various issues, in some cases irrational, have not only expressed absence of uniform policy, but it has also become a source of constant bitterness between the two groups of people. Some people though better off are enjoying privileges of backwardness in various States and the Central Government services. Others who really deserve privileges, suffer because they belong to castes outside the jurisdiction of backwards. In this situation, calls for an analysis of different Commissions constituted by the State Governments, in brief, the existing situation and approaches towards the reservation policy for OBCs. The present chapter high lights on this issue.

State Backward Classes Commissions

Andhra Pradesh

Before the organisation of Andhra Pradesh, the OBCs were getting preferential treatment in the State of Madras. In 1966 the Government of Andhra Pradesh notified a list of 112 communities belonging to OBCs and ordered for reservation of seats for them in government services and professional colleges, etc. Several writ

* This chapter is based on the Government of India Report of the Backward Classes Commission, First Part, Vol. I and II, (Chapter II, pp. 5-12), 1980 and all State Backward Classes Commissions Report.

petitions were filed against this order. This order was struck down by the High Court of Andhra Pradesh on the ground that the State could not produce evidence regarding the social and educational backwardness of the listed communities. This decision was upheld by the Supreme Court.

(1) Manohar Pershad Commission, 1968

On 12th April, 1968, the State Government appointed a Backward Classes Commission, chaired by Manohar Pershad, for preparing a list of all the backward classes which were not adequately represented in the services of the State and to make suggestions in regard to (a) the reservation of government posts in favour of such backward classes; and (b) the percentage of proportion of such reservation and the fixed time during which such reservation might be made. The Commission carried out an exhaustive survey of the trades and occupations being pursued by the various classes of people and other matters relevant to the decision of social backwardness. It indicated that only castes or communities, which had traditionally followed unclean and undignified occupations, could be called backward classes. Representatives of these castes demanded reservation upto 40 to 50 per cent. Some of them demanded percentage of reservation in proportion to the population as per the principle adopted by the Government of India in the case of the SCs and the STs.

In its report of 20th June, 1970, the Commission listed 92 classes as other backward classes. Further, it recommended reservation of 30 per cent of the vacancies in government service and educational institutions for candidates belonging to the backward classes. This would be in addition to the seats the backward class candidates might avail in the open competition. The Commission distributed the reserved vacancies among four categories of OBCs: (i) Aboriginal tribes, vimukta jatis, Nomadic and seminomadic tribes (7%), (ii) vocational groups (13%), (iii) Harijan converts (1%) and (iv) other classes (9%). The recommendation of the Commission on these two important items were accounted by the State government reducing it to 25%.

What else, even this was struck down by the Andhra Pradesh High Court on the ground that the list of backward classes had been prepared on the basis of caste alone. The Apex Court, however, in *State of Andhra Pradesh* versus *U.S.V. Balaram* did not accept the judgment of the High Court. It observed that even on the hypothesis that the list is based exclusively on caste it is clear from the materials before the Commission and the reasons given by it in its report that the entire caste was socially and educationally backward. It approved the view that caste was also a class and that reservation in favour of a caste was acceptable if the whole caste was socially and educationally backward.

(2) Veerapa Committee, 1975

Vidhan Sabha of fifth general election in Andhra Pradesh appointed a Committee of the legislature headed by Agisam Veerappa in 1975 to recommend welfare measures for the benefit of the backward classes. The committee, which submitted its report in 1977, suggested the following measures along with 25 per cent reservation: (a) sanction of scholarships from Class I onwards instead of VI standard as was the practice; (b) an increase in the amount of the scholarship; and (c) a lowering of the minimum marks required for students belonging to OBCs for admission from 40 per cent to 35 per cent.

(3) Murlidhar Rao Commission, 1982

The third State Commission, constituted in February, 1982, was headed by Murlidhar Rao. The Commission, in its report in September 1982, suggested 44 per cent reservation of seats and posts for 52 per cent state population of OBCs. The Commission included 10 more castes and sub-castes in the list of OBCs and the total rose to 102. The recommendations could not be implemented by the Congress Party. It was defeated in the elections of state assembly elections in 1983. The ruling Telugu Desham implemented it only in July 1986. The High Court of Andhra Pradesh struck it down on 5th September, 1986. The government decision witnessed public protest against reserving 71 per cent of seats and posts.

Then, the N.T. Rama Rao reservation policy (1986) was designed to benefit the most backward sections of the OBCs. The 44 per cent reservation was distributed among the five categories of the OBCs according to their backwardness and population.

Again, the reservation quota was only available to those with family income of less than Rs.12,000 a year. The dependents of a large number of government employees were not able to enjoy the benefit owing to low income limit. In contrast, the students belonging to the agriculturist and trade background might have been benefitted with fake income certificates.

Bihar

In 1951 the Government of Bihar had prepared a list of 109 backward classes for awarding post-matric scholarships, etc. under a scheme launched by the Ministry of Education, Government of India advised the State Government to draw their own list as they did not accept the recommendations given by Kaka Kalelkar Commission. In 1964 Patna High Court (AIR 1965, Patna 372), in view of Supreme Court's judgement in Balaji's case, declared Bihar government's list of backward classes as invalid as it had relied on caste as the criterion of backward classes. In view of this, the State Government decided that the current educational benefits should be given only to such students of other backward classes mentioned in the 1951 order whose family income was below Rs. 500 per month. For admission to medical colleges, the income limit was fixed at Rs. 250 per month.

Mungerilal Commission, 1971

Bihar government appointed a Backward Classes Commission under the chairmanship of Shri Mungeri Lal in June 1971 and it submitted its report in February 1976. The Commission took note of representation in government and private services, membership in elected bodies, occupation and share in trade, commerce, industry, etc. It began with a list prepared in 1951 for the grant of scholarship to students of the backward and the most backward castes in Bihar. Its enquiry was based on the other backward classes lists prepared by Kalelkar Commission. The Commission, then prepared its own list of socially and educationally backward classes on caste and economic basis. This list contains 128 backward castes, including 94 castes known as 'most backward classes'. In Bihar, it estimated 38.1 per cent population as OBCs. It had received miserable representation in government and semi-government services. It favoured rebate of

10 per cent marks for getting admission in educational institutions, like SCs and STs, maintenance of roster and carry forward policy for reserved quotas in case reserved posts for OBCs are not filled even after fresh advertisement, it should be made available to Scheduled Castes and Scheduled Tribes and not filled from the general category.

Divided into various volumes, the report, the Commission recommended a number of welfare measures for the upliftment of the backward classes. The most important of these measures was the recommendation about reservation of 24 per cent of the seats in medical and other professional institutions and 26 per cent posts in government and semi-governmnt jobs for the other backward classes. It also, viewed that the backward and the most backward classes be considered separately in enforcing the reserved quotas. The Jagannath Mishra Government did not take any action on these recommendations obviously in view of its support base of forward castes.

Karpoori Thakur, 1978

In 1978, the Janata Party government chaired by Karpoori Thakur, implemented the recommendations of Mungerilal Commission. It witnessed street-fighting between the upper castes and backward castes.

The State government accepted the recommendations in October, 1978 and this gave rise to a lot of agitation. Both the forward and the backward communities were dissatisfied with the government. The implementation of Commissions's recommendations also raised lot of controversy. Many recruiting acencies misconstrued the provision for reservation as prescribing the upper limit for the intake of backward class candidates selected on merit. In case OBC candidate is in excess of the reserved quota of 20 per cent got selected in open compitition the actual intake was restricted to 20 per cent only.

Subsequently, the Government of Bihar corrected this misconception in July, 1979 and clarified that the reservation quota indicated the minimum and not the maximum quota for backward class candidates. It was also clarified that the percentage of backward class candidates selected on merit should not be adjusted against their reserved quotas.

U.N. Sinha, 1994

The second Backward Classes Commission, was appointed in 1994 headed by U.N. Sinha. On the basis of recommendations of Sinha Committee even a few OBCs of Bihar do not came under the exclusion of advanced sections as rarely OBCs have annual income of Rs. 10 lakhs per year or urban property of Rs. 20 lakhs. It even recommended inclusion of any well-off sections or individuals availing the benefit of reservation within the recommendations of the Mandal Commission. It is a politically motivated report on the suggestions of the Chief Minister of Bihar to get political benefit out of it. It was planned to checkmate the Samata Dal leader Nitish Kumar's support among the economically advanced sections of OBCs such as Kurmi and Koiri.

Gujarat

In Gujarat State government appointed four Backward Classes Commission for identifying SEBCs or OBCs in the State.

Bakshi Commission, 1972

This Commission was appointed to prepare a list of OBCs and recommended memasures for their amelioration in August 1972 under the chairmanship of A.R. Bakshi, a retired High Court Judge and Chairman of the Law Commission. The Commission submitted its report to Gujarat Government in February 1976. It listed 82 castes and communities as socially and educationally backward and recommended the following steps for their advancement: (a) reservation of 10 per cent of seats in medical, engineering and other professional institutions; (b) reservation of 10 per cent of the Class III and Class IV posts in all government services, (c) reservation of five per cent of all Class I and Class II vacancies in all government services, local bodies, or public undertaking, etc.; (d) reservation of 10 per cent of the seats in training-cum-production centres; and (e) granting of scholarships and other educational facilities, provided the parental income did not exceed Rs. 4,800 per year. This income limit was increased to Rs. 7,200 in the case of nomadic and denotified tribes.

The government run by Janata Party accepted all the recommendations of the Commission in April 1978 and implemented them. Some castes, which the Commission did not accept socially and educationally backward, made representations to the government requesting reconsideration of their castes. Representations were also made by members of those castes which had due to some reasons failed to make representations to the Bakshi Commission.

Rane Commission, 1981

After that, Government appointed the second Backward Classes Commission in April 1981, headed by C.V. Rane, a retired Judge of the High Court of Gujarat, to consider whether there were any other castes/communities/classes which could be included in the category of socially and educationally backward classes. The terms of reference of this commission were the same as those of the Baxi commission. The Commission undertook an extensive tour of all the districts (except the district of Dangs) in the State for gathering information from various sources and recording evidence. It submitted its report to the government in October, 1983.

In view of the Commission, the social backwardness should be determined without reference to caste. It would facilitate promotion of welfare and educational and economic interests of the weaker sections of the people and speed up the process of establishing an egalitarian society. It thought that to enumerate caste for determining socially and educationally backward classes was to exercise casteism. Thus, the Rane Commission was the first Backward Classes Commission to reject the caste yardstick for deciding social backwardness. The Commission also held that the identification of socially and educationally backward classes in terms of caste was not feasible in the case of non-Hindu communities. It pointed out how some sections of people, who were socially and educationally backward, would be left out if socially and educationally backward classes were identified in terms of caste. In reality, only the lower income groups were socially and educationally backward. In the mask of caste the benefits of reservation were appropriated by the top layers of the so-called backward castes. The Commission emphatically stated that there was no backwardness for well-to-do sections or families.

As a parameter, the Commission took occupation in place of caste for identifying backward classes. It felt that there would be no difficulty in ascertaining citizens belonging to socially and educationally backward classes on the grounds of occupation. It declared that occupations considered to be inferior with low income were the main causes of social and educational backwardness. It identified 63 occupations as socially and educationally backward. Therefore, the classes it identified as socially and educationally backward included agricultural labourers, small farmers, marginal farmers, share-croppers, etc. as well as rural and urban artisans. It suggested that only those employed in 63 occupations and receiving less than Rs. 1,000 yearly be treated as backward.

This Commission also recommended reservation of seats/posts in educational institutions and in government services for the socially and educationally backward classes in proportion to their population alongwith a relaxation in the higher age limit in their case for entry into service. The population of the socially and educationally backward classes identified by the Commission was 35.16 per cent of the total population of Bihar. The Commission, however, recommended reservation of only 28 per cent of the posts and seats for them. Even then this meant an 18 per cent increase over the quota of reservation recommended by the Bakshi Commission. In January 1985, the Government of Gujarat reserved 28 per cent of seats and posts for the other backward classes. It did not approve the occupational criteria as suggested by the Rane Commission, but went with the caste criterion. It witnessed anti-reservation protest and withdrawal of increased quota in July 1985.

The government therefore appointed a one-man committee to identify castes/communities other than the 82 castes as backward and asked him to submit the report within 15 days. But before the committee could start working, the students and the middle class opposed the rise in quota and launched an anti-reservations agitation which continued for more than three months. Madhavsingh Solanki had to resign.

Justice Mankad Report

Amar Singh Chaudhary became the Chief Minister of Gujarat in place of Madhav Singh Solanki when the agitation in Gujarat was on. He immediately withdrew the increase of 18 per cent for the OBCs. He also agreed to agitationists to appoint another commission headed by a High Court Judge. Justice R.C. Mankad was appointed in June 1987 and asked to submit its report by December, 1987. He could not do so and finally the existing system under Baxi Commission continued.

Haryana

Haryana was earlier part of the Punjab State till 1966. Two committees were appointed in 1951 and 1961 by the erstwhile Punjab state government to recommend measures for welfare of OBCs. The last committee is known Brish Bhan Committee.

During the year 1969, the Government of Haryana published a list of backward classes without a formal inquiry into their economic backwardness and social status. It declared 10 per cent reservation in government services and 2 per cent in professional and technical institutions. The facilities and concessions awarded were: (a) All members of the backward classes are eligible for the reserved posts at the time of initial appointment, whatever their income is; (b) Reservations included promotions as well in the case of Class III and Class IV posts; (c) Income limit for students of the backward classes to be eligible for scholarships has been raised from Rs. 1,800 to Rs. 4,200 a year.

The State Government had not adopted any specific criterion to classify the people of the State before 1991 as backward. However, on the grounds of their economic backwardness and social status of occupation, certain classes of people have been declared as backward. These incorporated:

(i) All the residents of the State whose family income is less than Rs. 1,000 per annum, irrespective of the truth as to the caste, community or class they belong to and the profession they follow.
(ii) Apart from the above category, certain other communities should also be declared as backward by the State Government. These communities should be such as are socially looked down upon by the other people of the State. All the members belonging to these backward communities, excluding those whose family

income was more than Rs. 1,800 per annum should be entitled to privileges being enjoyed by backward classes.

Facilities and concessions given to backward classes:

(a) No income ceiling has been prescribed for a member of the backward classes for getting the concession of reservation of posts at the time of initial appointment.

(b) There is reservation for promotion posts in Class III and Class IV posts.

Gurman Singh Commission, 1991

In the year 1990, when anti-Mandal agitation was very strong in all parts of Haryana, Jats, the dominant caste of Haryana were asking for inclusion of 'Jat' in the list of OBCs. In early 1991, the first Backward Classes Commission was constituted under the chairmanship of Gurman Singh. The Commission gave its report in 1991 itself in which the most numerous and dominant castes were included in OBCs. These castes are Jat, Ahir, Bishnoi, Gujar, Saini, Rajput, Meo and others. Now, 27 per cent posts are kept reserved for OBCs in Haryana besides 19 per cent to SCs. There is no separate reservation for STs in Haryana. The report has many weaknesses and lack objectivity.

Himachal Pradesh

Like in Haryana, the Government of Himachal Pradesh also followed the list of OBCs declared by the erstwhile State of Punjab for the areas merged in the state of Himachal Pradesh. Official of State government had prepared a list on the basis of economic backwardness and social status. They identified the following sections of people as backward: (a) All the residents of Himachal Pradesh whose annual income is less than Rs. 6,000 are backward whatever their caste or community and whatever their professions or occupation; (b) Members of certain communities are backward if their annual family income is not more than Rs. 6,000.

OBC list is based on both caste and income. The quota of reservation before 1993 was 5 per cent of the vacancies in government services and in educational institutions. Students of the backward classes also receive scholarships, interest-free loans, and the tuition fees paid by them are reimbursed. Besides, they have reservation in promotions to selection posts in Class III under the government.

In 1970, the Government of Himachal Pradesh has, on the basis of 'economic backwardness' and 'social status' of occupation other than castes, identified the following sections of people as backward:

1. (a) All the residents of Himachal Pradesh whose total income is less than Rs. 6,000 per annum, irrespective of the fact as to which caste or community or class they belong to and what professions they are following.
   (b) Alongwith the above category, persons belonging to the communities, listed in the annexure attached to the report, having a family income not exceeding Rs. 6,000 per annum should also be considered as backward in the State.
2. Both 'economy-based' and 'caste-based' backward classes in Himachal Pradesh will receive the following facilities and concessions:
   (a) pre-metric stipends at primary, middle and high/higher secondary stages;
   (b) refund of tuition fees;
   (c) interest-free loans; and
   (d) reservation of two per cent in direct recruitment and in promotions to selection posts in Class III and Class IV services of the government.

On the basis of the Mandal Commission report, the reservation policy in Himachal Pradesh was changed in 1993. Now, 50 per cent jobs are reserved for the 3 categories of backward classes as 25 per cent for SCs, 5 per cent for STs and 20 per cent for OBCs.

Jammu & Kashmir

Reservation Policy in J&K has been a controversial issue between the government and the judiciary. Judicial intervention forced the State Government to appoint three Backward Classes Commissions. In 1956, the State Government passed Civil Services

Rules which provided for reservation for the backward classes in government services without making any special class of people as backward.

Gajendragadkar Commission, 1967

On 6th November, 1967, this Commission was appointed.

(i) On 6th Nov., 1967 - For the purpose of making an assessment of the development programmes apportioned to the various regions of the State and to recommed steps necessary to give assurance that the resources available to the State Government are being shared equitably and also to convey a sense of equal participation in the integrated development of the State; and

(ii) To examine the existing recruitment policies of government and recommend measures for giving an equitable share to the various regions and backward classes in government employment.

In its report, the Gajendragadkar Commission (1968) recommended that a high-power committee should be appointed to make a list of backward classes on the grounds of the following criteria: (a) economic backwardness (based on a suitable ad hoc figure of annual income); (b) the occupation or occupations pursued; (c) area of permanent residence; (d) number of students per thousand of the population; and (e) caste in the case of the Hindus.

Wazir Committee, 1969

Acting on the suggestion of Gajendragadkar Commission, the State Government appointed a committee headed by J.N. Wazir in February 1969. On the recommendation of the Wazir Committee, submitted in November 1969, the government passed the J&K Scheduled Castes and Backward Classes (Reservation) Rules, 1970 and reserved vacancies for the Scheduled Castes and backward classes in each jobs, class category and grade in the State services in accordance with the following ratio: (a) Scheduled Castes eight per cent, and (b) backward classes 42 per cent (including two per cent for the permanent residents of Ladakh). It was challenged in the High Court and the Supreme Court which found fault in the rules.

In its report, the Committee had classified backward classes into six broad categories as follows:

(a) Traditional occupations
(b) Social castes
(c) Cultivators
(d) Pensioners
(e) Areas adjourning the ceasefire line
(f) Bad pockets.

Anand Committee, 1976

In the month of August, 1976, the State Government appointed a Backward Classes Committee headed by Justice Adarsh Sein Anand to advise on the removal of the various anomalies in the Act of 1970 as ordered by the Supreme Court. It asked the Committee to make recommendations with regard to the following issues: (a) to determine the criteria to be followed in deciding backwardness: (b) to identify and prepare a list of backward classes; (c) to categorize backward classes and suggest safeguards for giving benefits to the real deserving only; and (d) to examine the question of reservation in government posts at every stage. The Committee was of the view that the six categories, made by the Wazir Committee, could be cut down to two broad categories as under:

(a) Twenty-two weak and underprivileged classes; and
(b) Residents of backward areas, i.e., (i) bad pockets, and (ii) areas near the line of actual control.

Having undergone a detailed discussion with the cross section of the people at various levels and of various areas, the Committee found the 22 groups of population classified as backward. The Committee regard them weak and underprivileged classes.

The Committee noted the desire of the government to remove the backwardness of certain classes of people of the State so as to enable all groups of the population to live as equals and have equality of opportunity in all spheres of life. It supported preferential representation for the backward classes in government services with due regard being paid to administrative efficiency. It prepared a list of two categories of backward classes: (a) weak and underprivileged sections, and (b) residents of backward areas, i.e., of (i) bad pockets; and (ii) regions within eight kilometres of the line of actual control.

Based on the above recommendations, 42 per cent government jobs and seats in professional and technical institutions and in other institutions of higher learning were reserved for the backward classes. This policy remained in practice till 1993. Now, 9 per cent seats and posts are reserved for SCs, 13 per cent for STs, and 27 per cent for OBCs. All the inhabitants of Ladakh region are considered STs.

Karnataka

Miller Committee, 1918

On the basis of representations received from aggrieved communities in August 1918, the Maharaja of Mysore appointed a Committee under the chairmanship of Sir L.C. Miller then Chief Justice of Mysore to recommend steps for adequate representation for non-Brahmins in the services of the state. The committee was asked to examine the following questions also: (a) changes required in the then rules of recruitment to the public services; (b) special facilities needed to encourage higher and professional education among the members of the backward classes; and (c) any other special steps needed to increase the representation of the backward communities in the public service without materially affecting the efficiency, due regard being paid also to the general well being accruing to the state by a wider diffusion of education and a feeling of increased status which would thereby by produced in the backward communities.

After almost a year in July 1919, the Committee submitted its report. The State Government accepted its recommendation that the term 'backward communities' should be taken to include all communities in the state other than Brahmins, Anglo-Indians, and Christians. On the basis of Miller Committee report, the Government of Mysore issued orders in 1921 extending special facilities to backward communities with regard to education and recruitment in state services. This was the position more or less till the reorganization of states in November 1956. On the basis of lists drawn by Mysore, Coorg, Bombay, Hyderabad and Madras, the present state, i.e., Karnataka state prepared a uniform list of backward classes for the whole of Karnataka state. This list was struck down by the Mysore High Court and a similar attempt made in 1959 also met the same fate.

Nagan Gowda Committee, 1961

The State Government, under the chiefministership of S. Nijalingappa, formed a committee under the chairmanship of Naganna Gowda, in January 1960, the terms of reference being to suggest (a) the criteria to be adopted in determining which sections of people in the State should be treated as socially and educationally backward, and (b) the right manner in which the criteria thus indicated should be followed to enable the State Government to determine the persons, who should secure such preference, as may be determined by government; regarding admissions to technical institutions and appointment to government services.

Through its interim report submitted in February 1960, after examining some criteria, the Committee stated: "Hence, the Committee after prolonged discussion, decided that backward classes should be listed only on the basis of their castes or communities and the backwardness judged on the basis of the percentage of literacy in the community and their representation in government service." The Committee suggested 36 per cent reservation for 35.34 per cent. The final report was given to the government in May 1961, in which some 214 castes under Article 15(4) and 185 castes under Article 16(4) were recommended and the communities were divided as backward and more backward, the former assumed to be 50 per cent for the purpose of Article 15(4) and the latter 45 per cent for the purpose of Article 16(4).

On reservation recommendations were as below, apart from the reservations to SCs and STs.

	Backward in per cent	*More Backward in per cent*	*Total in per cent*
Professional and Technical institutions under Article 15(4)	28	22	50
Government vacancies	21	24	45

Apart from the reservations already existing for the SCs and the STs the total reservation came up to 67 per cent and 63 per cent respectively. The Committee treated the whole of the Lingayat Community as forward as their representation in the jobs and the education level were above the State average. Muslims were included as a whole for the purpose of Article 15(4) only in the backward list. The Lingayats got annoyed over their exclusion from the backward classes list and the government through it fit to include them in the list as they were only slightly higher than the State average in education. Later, the government direction based on the report was challenged and the Supreme Court struck it down in the famous Balaji's case in 1963 on the basis that caste has been treated as the only test for determining backwardness, though the fact was that literacy, educational standard and representation in jobs were conjunctively considered along with the level of caste. The Court also held the reservation total to be excessive and opined that a special provision should be less than fifty per cent.

Havanur Commission, 1975

Being a member of the small community of Ursus, in 1969, D.Devaraj Urs, was the first non-Lingayat and non-Vokkaliga legislator to become the Chief Minister of Mysore State. He remained the Chief Minister till 1980. During his tenure, he sedulously cultivated the faith of minority backward communities without rousing the opposition of the dominant communities. He inaugurated and participated in several caste conferences and many castes organized and founded their own organisations. Devaraj Urs encouraged many caste associations by granting liberal funds for the construction of hostels for the benefit of poor students of those communities.

At last, in 1972, Devaraj Urs constituted the first Backward Classes Commission under the chairmanship of L.G. Havanur in response to the regular demand of the people as the existing occupation-cum-income test of backwardness was most unsatisfactory. The Commission presented its voluminous report in 1975, listing the backward classes under three categories, viz., backward communities, backward castes and backward tribes, and suggested compartmental reservations for each of these groups. In its findings the Commission stated that it had not gone by the criterion of caste in deciding social backwardness of castes and communities. Instead, it had relied on multiple tests, such as economic, residential and occupational factors in determining social backwardness of castes and communities.

The classification of backward classes was done on the basis of the education level. The State average of students passing SSLC examination in April 1972 was 1.69 per thousand of State population. The Commission said that a caste or community whose student average per thousand of its population passing at the April 1972 SSLC examination is less than the State average, should be treated as educationally backward. After satisfying about their social backwardness by applying the multiple tests, castes and communities were categorized into three whose student population was less than State average were: (a) backward communities whose student average per thousand of population was below State average, but fifty per cent of the State average; (b) backward castes, whose student average per thousand of population was below 50 per cent of the State average; and (c) backward tribes whose students average was less than 50 per cent of State average, except Dombars and Voddars and who were nomadic and denotified tribes.

By the commission, the population of the above three groups has been recorded by the Commission as 45 per cent of the State population on the basis of the educational test, though on the social basis as viewed by the Mysore High Court in Viswanath's case the majority of the population may be backward.

As per Article 15(4), the distribution of reservation recommended by Havanur was as below:

Sl.No.		*Per cent of Population*	*Quota of Reservation*
1.	Backward communities	19.20	16%
2.	Backward caste	14.47	10%
3.	Backward tribes	8.00	6%
	Total	41.67	32%

For the purpose of Article 16(4), the distribution of reservation was recommended as below:

Sl.No.		*Per cent of Population*	*Quota of Reservation*
1.	Backward communities	19.20	16%
2.	Backward castes	14.47	10%
3.	Backward tribes	8.00	6%
	Total	41.67	32

Source: Government of India Report of the Backward Classes Commission, Part First (Vol. I and II), 1980, p. 8.

Recommendation of the Commission was that seats/posts unfilled in any one category should be made over to the next higher category and if the backward classes as a whole are not able to fill the places, the unfilled quota should be shifted to the general merit pool. In other words, the carry over system was not recommended.

Here it is important to note that Lingayats, Muslims and Christians were not treated as backward by the Commission on the ground that the former, viz., Lingayats were above the State average in education and had proper representation in employment, and the latter on the ground that in the opinion of the Commission, they are to be treated as religious minorities entitled to be safeguarded separately under other provisions of the Constitution. The Commission was of the firm opinion that 'backward classes' has reference only to the Hindus, even as untouchability is a Hindu peculiarity. Anyway, finding that Muslim strength in the public services was not adequate, and the permissibility to treat the Muslims as a separate and distinct category of minorities, the Commission suggested that in that event reservation to Muslims should not exceed 6 per cent.

The Chief Minister, Devaraj Urs, while accepting the recommendations of the Havanur Commission, thought it fit to include the Muslims as a whole in the first category of backward castes. Same way, he included the Scheduled Caste converts to Christianity up to the second generation in the second category of backward castes. The order on the Havanur report was passed after considerable deliberation on 22nd February, 1977. One more change, made in the order passed on 4th March, 1977, was that only such citizens of these backward classes, whose family income from all sources is Rs. 8,000 (subsequently raised to Rs. 10,000) and less shall be entitled to special treatment under the said Articles.

Again diverting from the recommendations of Havanur Commission, Devaraj Urs raised the quota of reservation for the backward community from 16 to 20 per cent and introduced a new category of backward classes called the 'backward special group' and reserved 5 per cent (later raised to 15 per cent) of the appointments and posts for them raising the total reservation to 68 per cent. The detail about scale of reservation in services and educational institutions for various categories of backward classes were:

Sl. No.	*Name of Backward Classes*	*Percentage of Reservation in*	
		Educational Institutions	*Government Services*
1.	Scheduled Castes	15	15
2.	Scheduled Tribes	3	3
3.	Backward Communities	20	18
4.	Backward Castes	10	10
5.	Backward Tribes	5	5
6.	Special Groups	15	15
	Total	68	66

Source: Government of India Report of the Backward Classes Commission, Part First (Vol. I and II), 1980, p. 8.

As regards the backward special group, the order stated: "The following five categories of citizen shall be considered as a special group and such citizens of this special group whose annual family income is Rs. 4,800 and below shall be eligible for special treatment under these Articles:

(a) an actual cultivator,

(b) an artisan,

(c) a small businessman,

(d) Holder of an appointment either in government or corresponding services under private employment including casual labour, and

(e) Persons engaged in any occupation involving manual labour or self-employed.

This newly special group open to all people irrespective of caste and community was instituted obviously to satisfy the poorer sections of Brahmins, Lingayats, Sikhs, Jains, etc. However this group, based on poverty and low occupations, was the most abused group, for, people not really poor and not given to low occupations, and mostly belonging to the upper castes, have benefitted the most by showing false income certificates.

On Havanur's report of 22nd February, the government orders in 1977 and 4th March, 1977 were challenged in the High Court of Karnataka on many grounds by as many as 252 persons in 1978. Justice K. Jagannatha Shetty and Justice Sh. Venkatachalaiah delivered their judgment on 9th April, 1979, which talked about the plight and misery of the lower classes stricken by poverty, illiteracy and low social status. The Judgment says: "It is for these teeming millions, our Constitution promises justice, social, economic and political and assures among others, equality of status and of opportunity with the dignity of the individual. The salvation of the weakest among the weaker sections, i.e., Harijans was the first charge on the Constitution and advancement of socially and educationally backward classes was the second charge. The constitutional commitment for these classes is reflected in Article 38 which directs that the State shall strive to promote the welfare of the people by securing and protecting as effectively as it may, a social order in which justice, social, economic and political shall inform all the institutions of the national life. Article 46 directs that the State shall promote with special care the educational and economic interests of the weaker sections of the people, and in particular, of the Scheduled Castes and the Scheduled Tribes, and shall protect them from social injustice and all forms of exploitation. The judgment further states, how many of our weaker sections left to themselves, could rise in this manner? With the encumbrances of the past, it would well nigh be impossible without a head start in these days of acute competition in all walks of life, for these people to rise."

This popular legal controversy as to whether Articles 15(4) and 16(4) are exceptions to Clause (1) in each Article, or an independent illustrative provision, was removed in Thomas case (AIR 1976 S.C. 190). The legal position has explained in State of Kerala versus N.M. Thomas may now be taken to be settled, that Article 16(4) is not an exception to Article 16(1) but is an example of one of the methods of achieving equality, that it is not exhaustive of the classification necessary and, therefore, permissible for achieving equality and that the general principles true to situations under Article 14 are equally applicable under Article 16(1).

Venkataswamy Commission, 1985

The Supreme Court, in the judgment of K.C. Vasanth Kumar versus State of Karnataka (1985), asked the Karnataka government to redetermine the whole reservation of seats and posts. After that, in 1985, the Karnataka government constituted the second Backward Classes Commission chaired by a retired Judge, T.Venkataswamy to find out the OBCs in Karnataka and suggest measures for their upliftment. It went into the problem in depth and undertook extensive survey of secondary school leaving certificate students for identifying educational backwardness. It identified 33 per cent of the State population as OBCs, derecognising many castes and suggested 27 per cent reservation for them in place of then 49 per cent. It divided OBCs in four groups (A, B, C and D) in place of prevailing three (backward communities, backward castes and backward tribes). A new 'backward special group' was also given birth. Numerically strong, politically influential and economically better Vokkaligas and 35 other castes were excluded from the list of OBCs by the Commission. It was founded that these castes were well-off to progress without any special treatment.

In this process, Vokkaliga and other excluded castes organized a number of bandhs and pressurized the ruling Janata Party government for rejecting the Commission's report. The Janata legislators belonging to Vokkaliga caste threatened to leave the party if the report was implemented. Ultimately, the Karnataka government rejected the report on 7th October, 1986, and in its place started a new policy which benefited five categories of OBCs covering 73.5 per cent of the State Population by reservation of 50 per cent of jobs for them. In the new policy, annual income limit was Rs. 10,000 except in the case of backward tribes. This was also applicable to the most backward category. Some of the forward caste members engaged in inferior occupations also added in the list of beneficiaries. In all, 5 per cent posts and seats were reserved for them.

Chinnappa Reddy Commission, 1990

This Backward Classes Commission chaired by Chinnappa Reddy, dealt with the question of economic criterion for reservation at some length. It suggested that the following occupational groups may be added in the list of Socially and Educationally Backward Classes for the purpose of benefits of reservation: "Agricultural labourers not owning any land or not owning more than one hectare of rainfed dryland or its equivalent, handloom weavers not owning more than two looms and working for wages or on piece-rate basis, construction workers, automobile drivers, conductors and cleaners, auto and cycle rickshaw drivers, employees in factories and shops and establishments (excluding those employed in managerial, supervisory or ministerial capacity), workers engaged in road, bridge and railway track work and irrigation projects, pushcart, pavement and street hawkers and vendors, carpenters, blacksmith, mechanics, plumbers, electricians and the like employed on wages, hamalis, those engaged in medical occupations such as sweepers, and cobblers, those engaged in the occupations of butchers, fishermen and other offensive or noxious occupation, those engaged in domestic service and all other manual workers employed on daily wages."

Also, the Commission recommended that no one should be deservant to the benefit of reservation under Article 15(4) or under Section 16(4):

(i) Either of whose parents is a Class I or Class II officer in the service of the government or holds an equivalent post in a public sector undertaking or is employed under a private employer and draws a salary which is not less than that of a Class II officer.

(ii) Either of whose parents is a professional, i.e., (a) doctor, (b) lawyer, (c) chartered accountant, (d) income tax consultant, (e) financial or management consultant, (f) dental surgeon and (g) engineer or architect.

(iii) Both of whose parents are graduates.
(iv) Either of whose parents is assessed to sales-tax.
(v) Either of whose parents is assessed to income-tax.
(vi) Either of whose parents or both together own more than 8 hectares of rainfed dryland or its equivalent.

Due to the recommendations of Chinnappa Reddy Commission report in 1994, the reservation policy in Karnataka remained in controversy. On 25th July 1994, the Karnataka government raised reservation for OBCs in the state to 57 per cent which was further raised to 80 per cent. The matter again went to judiciary and the Apex Court withheld the government order on 1st August, 1994. In October 1994, the State Government got the Karnataka Reservation Law for 73 per cent reservation passed by the State Legislative Assembly. The President of India gave his approval to this Act on 23rd October, 1994. Today, the Karnataka reservation policy is similar to that of Tamil Nadu. The 69 per cent reservation violates the Supreme Court guideline for reservation not more than fifty per cent. Now, the Karnataka reservation policy got constitutional protection under Article 31(B) and free from judicial intervention.

Kerala

In the Kerala State of coconuts, i.e., Kerala reservation policy became the subject of an acute judicial controversy so much so that the government appointed one committee and three BC Commissions. The problem is still persistent in the State for inclusion and exclusion in the list of beneficiaries of the preferential treatment and determination of creamy layer. The Muslims of Kerala now do not come under the creamy layer. The All India Muslim League leaders politicized the creamy-layer issue and it became a bone of contentation in political arena.

Vishwanathan Committee, 1961

The Evaluation Committee on Backward Classes was appointed in June 1961, under the chairmanship of V.K. Vishwanathan. The Committee was asked to identify the backward classes and suggest measures for the improvement of their conditions of life and work. The Committee submitted its report in

October 1963. Its prominent recommendations were as follows: (a) 40 per cent of the seats in technical and professional colleges should be reserved for students of the other backward classes and 10 per cent of seats for students belonging to the SCs and STs; (b) The above reservation should be made applicable to all fresh appointment to posts under the State Government also; (c) Appointment of an Expert Committee to go into the question of reclassification of backward communities.

Government of Kerala accepted the recommendations of the committee but restricted reservation at the level of 25 per cent seats for the backward classes. This was challenged in the Kerala High Court in the case *Jacob Mathew* versus *State of Kerala*. The Court found fault with the assessment of the social backwardness of the popular Ezhava caste. The Division Bench supported reservation for Muslims, Ezhavas and Roman Catholics on the basis that they constituted socially and educationally backward classes. At the same time it said that a fact-finding commission be appointd to develop objective criteria for making educational benefits available to the backward classes.

Pillai Commission, 1965

The state government appointed a commission under the chairmanship of Shri G. Kumara Pillai in July 1964 and the commission submitted its report in December, 1965. Its main recommendations were: (i) It classified 91 communities as backward and stipulated that the benefits recommended in the report should be extended only to those members of the backward classes whose aggregate family income was below Rs. 4,200 per year; and (ii) In technical and professional institutions 25 per cent of the seats should be reserved for OBCs. It also indicated separate quotas for various categories of OBCs in the allocation of these seats.

The state government accepted the above recommendations with the modification that the income ceiling of Rs. 4,200 was raised to Rs. 6,000 per annum. It may be noted that the High Court had desired the State Government to institute an enquiry for granting educational benefits to OBCs under Article 15(4) of the Constitution only. In view of this State Government kept reservation at 40 per cent level in government jobs.

Damodaran Commission, 1970

After two years, in 1967, the Kerala High Court suggested the appointment of yet another Backward Classes Commission. The State government then appointed third BC Commission, under the chairmanship of by M.P. Damodaran, in October 1967. This Commission submitted its report in June 1970.

This Commission found the following factors responsible for social backwardness for the purposes of Article 16(4): (a) Absence of requisite educational attainments (test of education); (b) Absence of money or wealth (economic test); (c) absence of ability to appropriate an adequate number of appointments (test of appropriation of appointments); and (d) caste disability, occupational stigma, and social taboos acting as obstacles in the field of education.

Suggestion of the Commission was that the level at which and methods by which each of the tests adopted could be applied:

(a) SSLS and graduate course shall be the levels at which the test of education shall be applied.

(b) The last grade (Class IV), the non-gazetted and gazetted categories of appointments in the jobs under the State shall be the levels at which the test of appropriation of appointment shall be applied.

(c) Rs. 8,000 and below shall be the level of total annual family income at which the economic test shall be applied.

(d) The norm of yardstick with reference to which the attainment or position of each group of citizens, in the field of each of the tests applied, is to be compared (except the test of social backwardness) with the population of that group itself. The comparison of attainment of a group of citizens shall not be made with the attainment of the most developed group of citizens at each of the levels mentioned.

(e) The percentage of student population belonging to each group of citizens at each of the levels as said above, on the total number of such students in Kerala, shall be compared with the norm, namely, the percentage of population of that group itself.

(f) The number of appointments appropriated by each group of citizens in each of the three categories of services, namely, last grade, non-gazetted and gazetted as said above, on the total number of such households in the State, shall be compared with the norm, namely, percentage of population of that group itself.

(g) The percentage of households whose total annual income is Rs. 8,000 or below in each group of citizens on the total number of this type of households in the State shall be compared with the percentage of population of that group itself.

(h) The test of education shall not be applied as a separate test. Similar is the case with the application of other tests.

Despite the suggestions, social backwardness continued to be a matter of controversy in Kerala. Some of the populous and advanced castes like the Ezhavas exerted pressure not to disturb their privileges status as a backward community. The Administrative Reforms Committee (ARC), appointed by the Government of Kerala, realizing the evils and drawbacks of caste as the grounds for backwardness, suggested the economic criterion. This resulted in a prolonged and bitter conflict between the Ezhavas and the Nairs. Further, the dominant castes, irrespective of the fact whether they were actually economically, educationally and socially backward, managed to enjoy the concessions accorded to the backward classes because of their political influence. Owing to political pressure, all the backward communities of Kerala accepted the Ezhavas as backward.

Such communities as passed 4 tests (education, economic, participation in government service and social backwardness for historical reasons), together with families with income below Rs. 8,000 a year, were recommended for considering backward for the purposes of Article 16(4). It included such factors as stigmatized occupations, vestiges of caste discrimination, the custom of *purdah*, and hatred towards education in English. It recommended 40 per cent reservation in government posts for the backward classes for eight groups of backward classes such as Ezhavas, Muslims, OBCs and others as per details given below:

Sl. No.	Name of Group	Reservation for Class IV posts (%)	Reservation for other than class IV posts (%)
1.	Ezhavas	11	14
2.	Muslims	10	12
3.	Latin Catholics and Anglo Indians	4	4
4.	Nadars	1	1
5.	Scheduled Castes converts to Christianity	2	1
6.	22 communities like Asaris, Kammalas, Viwakarmas, etc.	2	3
7.	Dheerva Community	2	1
8.	Other Backward Classes	8	4
	Total	40	40

Source: Government of India Report of the Backward Classes Commission, Part First (Vol. I and II), 1980, p. 9.

Madhya Pradesh

Mahajan Commission, 1980

State Government appointed a Backward Classes Commission under the chairmanship of Ramjee Mahajan in November 1980 for drawing list of backward classes and suggest measures for their upliftment. The Commission, identified 254 castes and sub-castes as backward classes and suggested reservation of 35 per cent of the seats for them in educational institutions. It also wanted the same percentage of government and semi-government services to be reserved for them.

Besides the fact that Commission used the caste criterion for identifying backward classes, it suggested the exclusion of prosperous groups from the benefits of reservations. Thus, it suggested that the benefits of reservation should be extended only to the children of those who were not income-tax payees or who owned below ten acres of irrigated and non-irrigated land. Along with the benefits of reservation, it recommended the grant of scholarships and the provision of hostel facilities.

In year 1984, the State Government announced reservation of 25 per cent of the jobs for the backward classes instead of 35 per cent as suggested by the Commission. The anti-reservationists took the matter to the streets. They also appealed to the judiciary. The Bhopal High Court asked the State Government to refrain from bringing the reservation policy. Change of leadership in Congress(I) (Arjun Singh, who favoured reservation for OBCs was replaced by Motilal Vohra) also supported the anti-reservationists. If the government plan for reservation was executed, it would mean 65 per cent on the basis of caste SCs: 22.5 per cent, STs: 7.5 per cent and OBCs: 35%). The government also proposed to reserve 4 per cent for the economically backward five per cent for ex-servicemen, three per cent for freedom fighters and 'technical' hands and one per cent for miscellaneous categories. On a whole it was 78 per cent reservation of posts and seats. It was not adequate and just on the part of government to leave only 22 per cent seats and posts for open competition. In 1993, the Government of Madhya Pradesh declared that 50 per cent posts will be filled through open competition.

Maharashtra

The movement of Backward class in India has originated in Maharashtra and Tamil Nadu. Omvedt considers Maharashtra and Tamil Nadu to be states where rural improverishment was the maximum. This was why they produced a cultural revolt in India. The *Satya Shodhak Samaj*, founded by Jyotiba Phule, provided organization and leadership to backward castes like Malis, Telis, Kumbis, etc. They struggled against Brahminical dominance and created in the backward classes an awareness of their genuine rights. They prepared the social base for the leadership of Bheemarao Ambedkar.

Deshmukh Committee, 1961

OBCs of Maharashtra whose number grew from 125 in 1953 to 198 in 1967 also mobilized themselves as social groups. The government policy was to shift from the caste to the economic criterion. In November 1961, the State Government appointed a Backward Classes Committee, under the Chairmanship of

B.D. Deshmukh, to report on the reservation of backward classes in government jobs. This committee, in its report of January 1964, grouped backward classes into four categories: (i) Scheduled Castes and neo-Buddhists, (ii) Scheduled Tribes, (iii) denotified and nomadic tribes, and (iv) other backward communities. It also recommended that reservation in government services and educational institutions for different categories of backward classes should be linked to the percentage of their population in the State.

State Government broadly accepted the recommendations and made the reservation in state services and educational institutions for four categories of Backward Classes, viz., the SCs and neo-Buddhists (13 per cent), the Scheduled Tribes (7 per cent), denotified and nomadic tribes (4 per cent), and other backward communities (10 per cent). Subsequently in April, 1979 the state government issued orders that 80 per cent of all vacancies under the state government, local bodies, etc., should be reserved for Economically Weaker Sections of society. These weaker sections were defined as families whose income was less than Rs. 200 per month. Where adequate number of suitably qualified candidates were not available to fill 80 per cent of reserved vacancies from persons with family income below Rs. 200 per month, preference for the balance of reserved seats was to be given to candidates whose family income ranged from Rs. 200 to 400 per month. In this order, it was also clarified that 80 per cent reservation was inclusive of earlier reservations made for other Backward Classes, Scheduled Castes, Scheduled Tribes, etc.

Punjab

In the year 1951, the State Government appointed a committee on Backward Classes to identify the backward classes in the State. The criteria implied for the identification of backward classes were economic, educational and social backwardness. On the basis of its recommendations, the government declared 14 castes as OBC, consisting 2 per cent of the population as backward and suggested the same percentage of reservation. The government accepted the recommendation. Only 2 per cent seats and posts were reserved for OBCs in Punjab. Similar concessions were given in respect of admission to educational institutions.

Brish Bhan Committee, 1965

In 1965, the state government appointed an Evaluation Committee headed by Sh. Brish Bhan to review the concessions given to backward classes. This committee, in its report of 1966, made the following recommendations: (a) The existing list of backward classes should be made rational so that classes or castes which were no longer backward might be excluded. (b) The existing reservation of 2 per cent of the seats in educational institutions should be increased to 5 per cent. The committee also observed that reservation in service was not serving any useful purpose and government should give concessions mainly in matters of education.

Controversy between the two was that the committee was not in favour of extending the reservation policy to government jobs, but the government was. The government raised reservation upto 5 per cent both in services and in educational institutions for sixty-three backward classes irrespective of their religion.

Harcharan Singh Commission, 1975

In its fourth report in 1975-76, Punjjab Vishan Sabha Committee on Welfare of Scheduled Castes, Scheduled Tribes, and the Backward Classes under the chairmanship of Harcharan Singh recommended that 15% reservation should be made for OBCs in services. Finding improper representation of the backward classes in relation to their population, it recommended 15 per cent reservation for them in jobs and education. The government, however, found it difficult to accept this recommendation as it had already provided for reservation upto 25 per cent for the SCs and upto 20 per cent for retired army personnel. It, therefore, continued with its policy of reserving 5 per cent of the seats in educational institutions and 5 per cent of initial appointments in public service. It also provided for two per cent reservation in promotions up to Class I. It further decided to maintain a roster of all vacancies meant for SCs and OBCs and in the form of a running account, year by year, for each category of posts. However, it kept safe its right to de-reserve vacancies at its discretion. In 1993, reservation for OBCs increased to 23 per cent in Punjab.

Tamil Nadu

Tamil Nadu has been the pioneer in providing special concessions to OBCs. For the welfare of depressed or deprived sections of society the first such step was taken by Madras Government with the framing of Grant-in-Aid Code in 1885 to regulate financial aid to educational institutions, providing special facilities for students of depressed classes. Subsequently in 1921, action on a resolution passed by the state legislative council. Madras government took steps for higher representation of non-Brahmins in Government services. The scheme was reviewed in 1927 and the scope of reservation was enlarged further, dividing all the communities in the state into five broad categories and made separate quota for each category.

The Madras (then a State) had passed the Communal Government Order in 1927 and 1947 to distribute the posts and seats among the various communities to strengthen distributive justice and also to break up the monopoly of a few communities. By the time independence was achieved, the services and professions, especially in the southern states, had become to some extent representative of all the important communities of the area. Through the Communal Government Directive, it was intended to achieve fair, just and equal distribution of educational facilities and government jobs, even the Brahmins got 15 per cent of the vacancies reserved for them as against their population of 3 per cent. But, the Communal Government Order was attacked as being *ultra vires* of the Constitution in the famous case of *Champakam Dorairajan* versus *State of Madras*. This system continued till independence. In 1947, in view of mounting pressure from backward classes the government revised their representation as follows.

Sl. No.	*Name of the Group*	*Group quota reserved in 1947*	*Quota reserved in 1947*
1.	Non-Brahmin Hindus	5/12	6/12
2.	Brahmins	2/12	2/14
3.	Scheduled Castes/Depressed Classes	1/12	2/14
4.	Muslims	2/12	1/14
5.	Anglo Indian and Christians	2/14	1/14
6.	Backward Hindus	—	2/14

Source: Government of India Report of the Backward Classes Commission, First Part (Vol. I and II), 1980, p. 10.

After the separation of Andhra Pradesh, the Government of Madras ordered in 1964 that 16 per cent of all posts under the State Government should be reserved for Scheduled Castes and Scheduled Tribes and 25 per cent for Backward Classes. For admission to Medical Colleges, etc., the earlier system of linguistic-cum-district basis was discontinued in 1960 and orders were issued for reserving 15 per cent seats for Scheduled Castes and scheduled Tribes and 25 per cent for Backward Classes.

The above scheme of reservation was struck down by the Supreme Court and subsequently the state Government decided in 1951 that henceforth reservation should be made for Scheduled Castes and Backward classes only.

Depending upon 1951 census and in the wake of the separation of Andhra Pradesh from Tamil Nadu in 1954, the reservation was altered to 15 per cent for SCs and STs and 25 per cent for OBCs.

Sattanathan Commission, 1969

In November 1969, the State Government appointed BC Commission under the chairmanship of A.N. Sattanathan. The Commission, in its report of 1970, used educational and social backwardness and the nature of the occupation continued traditionally by a majority of the members of a caste as the main criterion of backwardness. It held that to guess that there was no social and economic or educational backwardness outside the fold of the Scheduled Castes was to betray a total ignorance of Indian social conditions. As for economic backwardness, it kept most of the backward classes under the occupational categories newly listed by the Mysore government as socially backward, thus: (a) actual cultivators, (b) artisans, (c) petty businessmen, (d) those who perform inferior services, including casual labourers, and (e) those engaged in any other occupation involving manual labour. It recommended 33 per cent reservation for the bckward classes.

Sattanathan Commission divided the backward classes into two parts: (a) backward classes, and (b) most backward classes. It suggested 17 per cent reservation for the backward classes and 16 per cent for the most backward classes. It did not support reservation on the basis of population as in the case of the Scheduled Castes and the Scheduled Tribes. Most of the backward classes have made no progress worth the name and their condition even now is worse than that of the Scheduled Castes. From this viewpoint, the division of the backward classes into two parts was justifiable. Recommendations of the Sattanathan Commission were accepted by the government but made some modifications as required by the Supreme Court judgment in the Balaji case. It took the population of the Scheduled Castes and the Scheduled Tribes as found during the 1971 census, and gave directions that 31 per cent of all posts in government services and seats in educational institutions be reserved for the backward classes and 18 per cent for the SCs and STs. In November 1980, the State Government increased the reservation for the other backward classes from 31 per cent to 50 per cent. This excluded the reservation (18 per cent) made for the Scheduled Castes and the Scheduled Tribes. This increase was introduced, not on the basis of socio-economic and educational backwardness, but on caste basis for political considerations.

M.G. Ramachandran government in 1979, the Tamil Nadu Government proposed to apply an income limit to Rs. 9,000 per year for being eligible for reservation and as this proposal would seriously affect the greater part of the backward classes, it was opposed by the people led by the Dravida Kazhagam and Dravida Munnettra Kazhagam parties. Due to the popular agitation, the Ramachandran Government dropped the economic criterion and raised the percentage of reservation for the backward classes from 32 per cent to 50 per cent, raising the total reservation including that of the SCs and STs to 68 per cent wth effect from 1st February, 1980. Challenging this order a writ was filed in the Apex Court, but as the State Government undertook to look afresh into the policy of reservation, both as regards the caste list and the quota of reservation, by the appointment of a new Commission, the Court reserved its judgment.

Another directive of the government in 1980 dispensed with the ceiling of Rs. 9,000 on the annual family income for eligibility for the concessions provided to the backward classes. The government also scrapped the division of the backward castes and most backward classes. This was also challenged in the Supreme Court which then struck down the move of the government.

Ambashanker Commission, 1982

Following the decision of Supreme Court, the government constituted a 21-member Backward Classes Commission under the chairmanship of J.A. Ambashanker to re-evaluate the classification of backward classes in the State and to re-assess their reservation quota of 50 per cent. The Commission submitted its report in February 1985 and advised for the reserved quota to be slashed to 32 per cent. The Finance Minister announced the Government's acceptance of the Supreme Court's ruling that the reservation for the backward classes and the Scheduled Castes and the Scheduled Tribes in total should not exceed 50 per cent. The Tamil Nadu government, however, passed orders re-affirming the reservation of 50 per cent for OBCs in July 1985.

On the grounds of Indra Sawhney judgment reserved quotas in Tamil Nadu was limited within 50 per cent of the available posts. But it was totally against the political arithmetic of AIADMK and DMK leaders. They asked for exception from the 50 per cent limit and organized public rallies. The Tamil Nadu Legislative Assembly made an enactment of the constitutional amendment and inclusion of its Reservation Act in the 9th Schedule of the Indian Constitution. The 85th Constitutional Amendment was passed to save Tamil Nadu's 50 per cent seats and posts are reserved for OBCs besides 19 per cent for SCs and 1 per cent for STs, bring the total to 70.

Uttar Pradesh

In U.P., in 1945, the Government United Provinces of Agra and Oudh identified 37 Hindu castes and 21 Muslim groupings as backward and gave them educational concessions. In 1950, the Uttar Pradesh government reserved 10 per cent of the jobs in government services and educational institutions for the Scheduled Castes but did nothing specific for the backward classes. In 1955, a cabinet sub-committee drew up two lists of backward classes—one for the purpose of recruitment to the public services and the other for the sanction of educational concessions. The first consisted of 15 and the second of 59 backward castes.

Later in 1958, the State Government prepared another two lists—one containing 37 Hindu castes and the second 21 Muslim groupings. These lists were similar to those of 1945. They were used for the granting of educational concessions. There was no move to reserve posts in government services.

Chhedi Lal Sathi Commission, 1975

Though the efforts for OBC betterment had started long before in UP it was in October 1975 that a Most Backward Classes Commission was constituted under the chairmanship of Cheedi Lal Sethi to consider the position of the 'most backward classes of citizens' as distinguished from the 'backward classes' and to suggest measures for improving their conditions. The Commission used social evils like poverty, illiteracy, housing, occupation, caste, social inequality and representation in government service, industry and commerce as parameters for measuring backwardness. After two years' deliberation it gave its report in June 1977. Classifying backward classes into three categories, it recommended separate quotas in government jobs for each of the three categories.

The list that was first prepared, contained 36 backward castes with a little land or without land (17 per cent), the second had 18 agriculturist castes like Yadavas, Gujars, Kurmis, etc. (10 per cent), and the last one was exclusively for the backward classes from the Muslim community (2½ per cent). The Commission recommended special facilities, scholarships, etc. for the caste and other sections it had designated backward.

Government led by Janta Party partially accepted the recommendations of the Commission and passed orders for the reservation of 15 per cent of government services and seats in technical and professional institutions for candidates of the backward classes. Already 18 per cent of the jobs were reserved for the SCs, 2 per cent each for the STs and handicapped, 5 per cent for the dependents of freedom fighters, and 8 per cent for retired military personnel. With the reservation of 15 per cent of jobs for the backward classes, the total reservation for different social groups reached 30 per cent. This gave birth to an anti-reservationist movement in 1977.

This way, the reservation policy then came up before the Allahabad High Court. The petitioners alleged that many of the so-called backward castes like Ahirs (i.e., Yadavas) and Kurmis were not economically and socially backward, that most of them were well-off big farmers and were prosperous, and that quite a number of them were highly educated and occupied high offices. It would not be right to say, therefore, that the entire Ahir, Kurmi, or other castes included in the government order were backward within the meaning of Article 16(4) of the Constitution of India. Further, the petitioners submitted that all that the Sethi Commission had done was to enlarge the size of the list of the 'most backward classes' identified by the Kaka Kalelkar Commission. They also drew the attention of the High Court to the difference between the report of the Sethi Commission and the defective government order as regards the number of communities. The report had listed 120 communities, while the lists attached to the impugned government order mentioned only 59 communities. It was struck down by the Allahabad High Court.

Later, in March 1994, the Uttar Pradesh government revised its reservation policy in accordance with the Supreme Court judgment on Mandal Commission report. It implemented the Supreme Court order of 16th November, 1992 for 27 per cent reservation in favour of OBCs in the State Governments. It has caused strong protests from the people of eight districts of hilly area of Uttar Pradesh. These districts are popularly known as Uttarkhand and OBCs constitute only 3 per cent population in this region. These districts are dominated by the upper castes and they are agitating from July 1994 for the withdrawal of raised reserved quota. This agitation was also related with the formation of Uttarkhand State which has been constituted but their demand regarding dereservation is yet to be heard.

Other States and Union Territories

Regarding eight other states and union Territories which have notified lists on other Backward Classes without ordering a formal inquiry into their conditions, the position is briefly as follows. Before the implementation of Mandal Commission's recommendations some Indian States like Assam and Union Territories like Pondicherry felt educational backwardness as the most important aspect of backwardness and reserved some seats for the educationally backward in educational institutions. They have made no such reservation in government jobs. Haryana has provided for 10 per cent reservation in government services and 2 per cent in professional and technical institutions for OBCs. Himachal Pradesh has reserved 5 per cent of all posts for OBCs and also extended some educational concessions to Backward class students. Before 1993, in Delhi, Meghalaya, Orissa and Rajasthan, the backward classes were not getting any preferential treatment in the context of appointment to public jobs and admission to educational institutions. But, they do enjoy certain concessions regarding school fees, books, mid-day meals, etc. In 1961, both Delhi and Orissa which had earlier drew the list of OBCs on the ground of caste opted for the economic criterion in place of the caste criterion and dispensed with the lists of backward classes prepared on caste basis. This situation almost continued till 1993. Many other states like Arunachal Pradesh, Mizoram, Nagaland, Sikkim, Tripura and West Bengal had not made any list of other backward classes till 1993. None of the Union Territories has done so. These states do not consider backward classes as calling for State action in respect of their socio-economic conditions. The backward classes have never come up as a political force in these states. Nor that there is no backward class lobby, but it has not acquired and perceptible influence so far. There, OBCs remained out of touch of special treatment. Now 27 per cent jobs have been reserved for them in the central services which prepared background for reservation in all states. It has taken this position even during the Chief Ministers Conference or various other platforms. But now, 22 per cent seats and vacancies are reserved for OBCs in West Bengal also.

State-wise list of backward classes is given at Appendix-I.

Three

Kalelkar Commission*

The Constitution of independent India contained numerous provisions for Scheduled Castes and Scheduled Tribes and economically weaker to bring them in the mainstream. The Other Backward Classes too had high hopes of acquiring benefits in educational institutions and in job reservation, i.e., in recruitment and promotion in jobs like SCs and STs under the new Constitution of their Republic. But to their surprise they got only a promise of help (in the form of Article 340), if the President of India ever thought in his wisdom that such aid was really required by them. What did it really mean? Practically this: when the Article was drafted, the OBCs had no clear case for being helped; they did not suffer from social injustice, or denial in national life; but if any such eventuality occurred to them in future, then the President of the Union would take care of them. Of course, this was a setback to the OBCs. Non-recognition of OBCs in the constitution led these people to form an All-India Backward Classes Federation which came into existence on 26 January 1950. Its headquarters was at Delhi. Next, they opened its branches in almost every state. The crux of the aims and objectives of the organization was to fight for the rights of the OBCs. Punjabrao Deshmukh became its first national president who was a member of the newly created Lok Sabha.

In March1948, for example, he got an amount sanctioned for the award of scholarships for the children of the OBCs as had been done for those of the SCs and STs. The amount was very low in the beginning—Rs. 2.46 lakh in 1949-50, but it was increased about

---

* This chapter is based on Government of India Report of the Backward Classes Commission. Printed in India by the Manager, Government of India Press, Simla, 1955.

tenfold—Rs. 26.51 lakh, by 1953-54. Apart from this, the OBCs were given financial help in some States also as Table 1 indicates below:

TABLE 1
AMOUNT OF EXPENDITURE INCURRED FOR THE OBCS, 1952-53 (STATEWISE)

State	*Amount in lakh (rupees)*
Andhra Pradesh	4.36
Assam	2.49
Bihar	10.26
Bombay	50.15
Madhya Pradesh	0.77
Madras	41.25
Orissa	Nil
Punjab	Nil
Uttar Pradesh	6.29
West Bengal	5.86
Madhya Bharat	Nil
Hyderabad	1.70
Mysore	9.14
P.E.P.S.U.	Nil
Rajasthan	Not available
Saurashtra	6.44
Travancore-Cochin	8.71
Ajmer	Nil
Bhopal	0.05
Coorg	0.06
Delhi	Not available
Himachal Pradesh	Not available
Kutch	3.47
Manipur	Not available
Tripura	Not available
Vindhya Pradesh	Nil
Andaman & Nicobar Islands	Not available
Total	151.00

Heads on which this expenditure could be made: (a) freeships, scholarships and stipends for books and clothing; (b) grants and aids to hostels and construction of hostel buildings; and (c) Donation to social institutions in their expenditure on the welfare of these classes. In some southern states, the OBCs also got some share in the public services and other benefits. The monetary help or government jobs proved too insignificant to satisfy the OBCs, however, and a section of them, especially those who were not under the Congress influence became critical of both the Government and their own organization.

II

The first Backward Classes Commission was set up by a presidential order under Article 340 of the Constitution of India on January 29th, 1953. The first National Level Commission, popularly known as the Backward Classes Commission or the Kalelkar Commission after its Chairman, comprised the following members:

1.	Shri Kakasaheb Kalelkar, M.P.	Chairman
2.	Shri N.S. Kajrolkar	M.P.
3.	Shri Bheekha Bhai	M.P.
4.	Shri Shivdayal Singh Chaurasia	
5.	Shri Rajeshwar Patel	M.P.
6.	Shri Abdul Qaiyum Ansari, (Bihar)	M.L.A.
7.	T. Mariappa, (Mysore)	M.L.A.
8.	Shri Atma Singh Namdhari	M.P.
9.	Lala Jagannath	
10.	Shri N.R.M. Swamy	M.P.
11.	Shri Arunangshu De.	Member-Secretary

Terms of reference of the Commission were:

(a) Determine the criteria to be adopted in considering whether any sections of the people in the territory of India (in addition to the Scheduled Castes and Scheduled Tribes specified by notifications issued under Articles 341 and 342 of the Constitution) should be treated as socially and educationally backward classes; and as per such criteria, prepare a list of such classes setting out also their approximate number and their territorial distribution;

(b) Investigate the conditions of all such socially and educationally backward classes and the difficulties under which they labour;

and make recommendations: (i) as to the steps that should be taken by the Union or any State to remove such difficulties or to improve their condition; and (ii) as to the grants that should be made for the purpose by the Union or any State and the conditions subject to which such grants should be made:

(c) Investigate such other matters as the President may hereafter refer to them; and

(d) Present to the President a report setting out the facts as found by them and making such recommendations as they think proper.

It suffered from serious defects of methodology and internal contradictions. The Commission formulated the following criteria for identifying socially and educationally backward classes:

(i) Low social status in the traditional caste hierarchy of Hindu society;

(ii) Absence of general educational advancement among the major section of a caste or community;

(iii) Inappropriate or no representation in government service; and

(iv) inadequate representation in the field of trade, commerce and industry.

The Commission worked for about two years and submitted a three volume report to the President of India on 30 March 1955. It prepared a list of 2399 backward castes or communities for the entire country and 837 of these were classified as most backward. The registrar General and Census Commissioner of India assigned the commission in making population projections of 930 backward castes and communities.

It is pertinent to mention that the commission could not present an unanimous report. In fact five of its members recorded minutes of dissent. They were: Dr. Anup Singh, Shri Arunangshu De, Shri P.C. Shah, Shri S.D. Chaurasia and Shri T. Mariappa.

(i) Relating social backwardness of a class to its low position in the traditional caste hierarchy of Hindu Society.

(ii) Having taken into account the social position which a community occupied in the social hierarchy, the percentage of literacy and its general educational betterment and its representations in the government service or in the industrial and other economic spheres, 2399 castes comprising about 32 per cent population remaining at a low level in the Indian society as OBCs;

(iii) Treating all Women class as backward;

(iv) Reservation of 70 per cent seats in all technical and professional institutions for qualified students of backward class.

(v) Minimum reservation on all vacancies of government and local bodies on the following scale: Class I: 25%; Class II & III: 33 1/3% and Class IV: 40%.

The recommendations of the commission for the upliftment of the backward classes are extremely wide-ranging and comprehensive. They cover such diverse fields as:

- Extensive Land reforms
- Reorganisation of village Economy
- Bhoodan Movement
- Development of Live Stock
- Dairy Farming
- Cattle Insurance
- Bee-keeping
- Piggery
- Fisheries
- Development of Rural and Cottage Industries
- Rural Housing
- Public Health and Rural water supply
- Adult Literacy
- University Education
- Representation of backward classes in government services, etc.

Some of the most noteworthy recommendations of the commission were:

(i) Undertaking caste-wise enumeration of population in the census of 1961.

TABLE 2

THE OBC POPULATION, 1951

Sl. No.	*State*	*Total Populalation of State (1951)*	*Estimated OBCs Population*	*% of OBC Population to State Population*
1.	Assam	90,43,707	28,65,934	31.6
2.	Bihar	4,02,25,947	1,53,21,746	38.1
3.	Bombay	3,59,56,150	1,10,09,745	30.6
4.	Madhya Pradesh	2,12,47,533	79,02,586	37.2
5.	Madras (including Andhra)	5,70,16,002	1,26,80,945	22.2
6.	Orissa	1,46,45,946	13,56,373	9.3
7.	Punjab	1,26,41,205	25,56,087	20.2
8.	Uttar Pradesh	6,32,15,742	2,60,10,161	42.6
9.	West Bengal	2,48,10,308	22,66,445	9.1
10.	Andhra	Added in Madras		
11.	Hyderabad	1,86,55,108	1,37,66,090	73.8
12.	Madhya Bharat	79,54,154	19,36,980	24.4
13.	Mysore	90,74,972	59,63,902	65.7
14.	Pepsu	34,93,685	4,42,397	12.7
15.	Rajasthan	1,52,90,797	34,31,326	22.4
16.	Saurashtra	41,37,359	12,16,475	29.4
17.	Travancore-Cochin	92,80,425	9,12,272	9.8
18.	Ajmer	6,93,372	2,97,699	42.9
19.	Bhopal	8,36,474	2,94,534	35.2
20.	Himachal Pradesh and Bilaspur	11,09,466	3,15,101	28.4
21.	Coorg.	2,29,405	63,727	27.8
22.	Delhi	17,44,072	3,17,906	18.2
23.	Kutch	5,67,606	2,01,170	35.4
24.	Manipur	5,77,635	35,490	6.1
25.	Tripura	6,39,029	69,432	10.9
26.	Vindhya Pradesh	35,74,690	13,76,307	38.5
27.	Andaman & Nicobar Islands	30,971	-	-
	India	35,68,29,485	11,35,10,830	31.81

*Report of the Backward Classes Commission, 1955, Vol. I, pp. 14-15.

These computations of the population and percentages of the OBCs are not of all the 2399 castes declared to be OBCs by the Commission but of 837 castes only. The actual figures would be much higher than these figures.

Thus was prepared a list of 2,399 castes as belonging to the OBCs on the basis of these criteria. This list had no merit, however, for it had not been shown anywhere how the list was made 'by the application of the criteria'. The same was the case with the state-wise lists. These were based, for the most part, on the basis of a list prepared by the Ministry of Education for educational scholarships kept for 'Other Educationally Backward Classes' in 1949. The Ministry had prepared the lists 'without any special survey for the identification of the OBCs'. Also, it was prepared for 'Other Educationally Backward Classes' and not for 'Socially and Educationally Backward Classes as mentioned in Article 340 of the Constitution. The Commission suggested reserving seats/vacancies in educational institutions, government services, etc. for the OBCs, but again made a similar mistake. It did not give the basis for arriving at the exact percentage of reservations in various categories of jobs and in educational institutions.

Apart from all this, the Commission's work was marked by utter confusion and dissent. On almost every crucial issue, its members spoke in different voices. For example, three of them Dr. Anup Singh, Shri Arunangshu De and Shri P.G. Shah did not agree that caste should determine the backwardness of the people and opposed the reservation of posts on its basis. On the other hand, one member Shri S.D.S. Chaurasia made a forceful argument, in his 67-page note, for including the caste criterion for both these things. Yet another member Shri T. Mariappa was concerned only with the inclusion of a couple of castes in the list of other Backward classes. Shri Kaka Kalelkar, took rather equivocal stand on the issue. Though he did not give a formal minute of dissent. While forwarding the report, he expressed his reservations regarding several recommendations and opposed caste as a basis of backwardness.

Critically speaking, the Commission's identification of the OBCs was faulty. It no doubt 'modified the Education Ministry's original lists of the 'OBCs' in the light of the facts collected by it. But the fact remains that it broadly adopted the lists of Other Educationally Backward Classes prepared by another agency for an entirely different objective passed it on as the list of socially and educationally backward classes of India. This was done without undertaking any field survey to check their validity for the purpose of the Commission. Nor were they examined against the criteria evolved by the Commission for identifying socially and educationally backward classes.

It was also true that we should why give up a thing, anybody can argue, that has served well for thousands of years then? Kakasaheb admitted that high castes have been exploiting the lower castes for centuries, but he told the OBCs who were 'too backward to be introspective and to find out what is faulty with themselves' that their backwardness was not owing to this exploitation as their leaders would have them believe. Their backwardness was in fact the result of their own 'apathy, lethargy and negligence'. The great Gandhian was convinced that the OBCs had very low share in the government service and he proposed to make the following reservations to compensate the deficiency: Class I: 25 per cent, Class II: 33 1/3per cent, and Classes III & IV: 40 per cent. But he negated his proposal without any valid reason in the forwarding note attached in the end of his Report as follows:

> "I am definitely against reservation in government services for any community for the simple reason that the services are not meant for the servants but they are meant for the services of the society as a whole. I believe that in Class I and Class II services (non-Shudra jobs?), the backward classes will stand to gain, both morally and materially if they do not demand a reservation percentage in the vacancies and simply rely on the fairmindedness of the administration (manned by high castes)."

On the question of matter of education also, Kakasaheb went back on his earlier stand that the state should make efforts to remove darkness from the lives of the OBCs. Whatever the *smritis, Shankracharyas or savarnas* might have said or done in this context, the great Gandhian believed that the OBCs have suffered of their own will or choice and thought that they need not be helped;

> It has been stated that if such communities (i.e., OBCs) have neglected education, it is because they had no use for it. Now that they have realised their mistake it is for them to make the necessary effort for making up the leeway.

Not only this, there is much more in the Report and the forwarding note of Kakasaheb to prove our point that caste bias, even in the case of this great Gandhian, worked to force him in taking the *volte face* after preparing the Report. Two small quotes from the Report itself confirm the point. First is a kind of self-admission by Kakasaheb:

> "Even the most intellectual, including those who declared themselves to be enemies of castes, are not often entirely free and consciously and unconsciously they act in a manner which gives a fresh lease of life to the caste system."

Alongwith the above there was also a 'hidden hand' which contributed to the undoing of Kalelkar Report. A Congress activist and a former member of the Indian Parliament from Gurgaon (Haryana) said that Kakasaheb had shared with him that it was Dr. Rajendra Prasad who had asked him 'to give his views in detail' in the controversial note. It was ethically unjust for the first citizen of the Union to have done so. Nothing surprising: Lohia had predicted this to happen about three years earlier (1953) while indicting the President for going to Banaras and openly bathing the feet of two hundred Brahmanas, a majority of whom were of no spiritual or even intellectual character, in the following words:

> "The spirit of which such evil acts are born, can never plan the country's welfare nor adventure with joy. It will ever keep the vast millions lowly and submerged. It will deny them social and economic equality, just as much as it denies them spiritual equality?"

The above is the reality of what happened. The Report was confronted with 'the spirit of which such evil acts are born' almost at every step. To begin with, the Government of India took it very casually and placed it before the Parliament on 3 September 1956 alongwith a lengthy memorandum of action done by Pt. Govind Ballabh Pant which among other things said,

(i) the Commission had not been able to conduct the required objective tests or criteria for identification of the OBCs;

(ii) going for the caste as the basis of the backwardness of the OBCs, the Commission had taken a retrograde step; it cannot be refused that the caste system is the greatest hindrance in the way of our progress towards an egalitarian society, and the recognition of the specified castes as backward may help to maintain and even perpetuate the existing distinctions on the basis of caste;

(iii) If such a large number of castes/communities as the Commission had recommended were to be considered as backward, the really needy would be swamped by the multitude and hardly receive any special attention or proper assistance, nor would such dispensation fulfil the conditions laid down in Article 340 of the Constitution.

Besides this, the Memorandum further added that in view of what has been said above, another exercise be made in this direction so that lacunaes that have been noticed in the findings of the Commission are made good...' But such an exercise be undertaken only, it recommended, if the special needs of the backward classes could not be 'intensively and effectively served by appropriate shifts of stress or by rearrangement of priorities within the framework of the existing programmes being kept in mind by the Planning Commission.

But this should be enough to believe that the Pant Memorandum was as bad if not more a document as the forwarding note of Kaka Kalelkar was. It is impossible to believe that a man of law of the stature of Pant could not discern that the very basis on which his Memorandum stood was illegal and unjust. Economic poverty or backwardness has no direct relevance to the case in point. By giving primacy to 'economic tests' in determining the type of backwardness mentioned to in Article 340(I) of the Constitution, the Government had ignored the Constitutional needs. It may be possible to make out a very plausible case for not accepting caste as a criterion for defining 'social and educational backwardness'. But the substitution of caste by economic examination amounted to ignoring the reasons of social backwardness in the Indian society.

Inspite of the all above, the Parliament did not discuss the Report. This made the OBCs unhappy. A section of them, which was more politically aware, came forward and launched a virtual attack on the powers that be. By matter of chance, Rammanohar Lohia (1910-1967) a person belonging to a forward caste was passionately sympathetic to the downtrodden,—the SCs, STs, OBCs, minorities and women. A critic of both the Congress and the Communist parties, the former for its 'undemocratic ways' and the latter for their 'non-Indian approach', he tried various political ways out but eventually formed his own party and worked to achieve his goal—a truly people's *raj* where no distinction of caste, creed or colour would be allowed. Blessed with a remarkable capacity to articulate the abstract and the real, he was perhaps the only political leader in India after Gandhiji who had reduced the gap almost to none between the precept and practice. And it was perhaps owing to this that he stood up and strove to build a true 'democratic programme' in which caste would be totally non-existent, not by 'big talk', nor by denying its existence, nor by wishing it away, and not even by achievement of economic equality, for economic inequality and caste inequality were twin demons 'which have both to be pushed out'. This work, said Lohia could be done only when the lower castes—the exploited, oppressed deprived masses—were brought to the national mainstream, and offered proper share in the 'four main departments of national activity, business, army, white collored civil services and political parties. Without any concern for merit? Giving a go-bye to the principle of equal opportunity? Yes, said Lohia, for talk of merit and equal opportunity has no meaning in the Indian conditions.

> "The intelligentsia of India, which is overwhelmingly the highcaste, abhors all talk of a mental and social revolution or a radical change in respect of language or caste or the bases of thought. It talks generally and in principle against caste. In fact, it can be most vociferous in its theoretical condemnation of caste, so long as it can be allowed to be equally vociferous in raising the banner of merit and equal opportunity. What it loses in respect of caste by birth, it gains in respect of caste by merit. Its merit concerning speech, grammar, manners, capacity to adjust, routine efficiency is undisputed. Five thousand years have gone into the building of this undisputed merit. A true doctrine

of equal opportunity would have to undo the work of five thousand years by giving preferential treatment to the lower castes over a period of at least a few decades. Congress party was under Nehru's leadership, thoroughly hostile to the award of preferential treatment on any large scale. They denounce it as a caste-motivated measure while they were themselves viciously caste-ridden, perhaps unknowingly. They denounced caste by birth, but in enthroning the principle of merit, they kept secured their privileged positions.

On no account do the high castes comprise more than one-fifth of India's population. But they keep to themselves almost four-fifths of the nation's leadership... When more than four-fifths of a nation's vital leadership is traditionally selected from among one-fifths of its population, a state of atrophy is bound to ensure. Four-fifths of its population sinks into a state of listlessness and inefficiency. The nation is sick and continually on the point of death."

Due to his commitment Lohia became a champion of the cause of the OBCs. Little wonder, then, that a sizeable section of the OBCs was drawn to him at once. The Congress tried its level best to distance them from 'the charmer', but they could not succeed for the reasons given below by a 'concerned man':

"The reactionary policy of the government, such as creating dissensions and divisions in BCF (Backward Classes Federation) movement, overtaxing the members of the backward classes, non-implementation of recommendations of Backward Classes Commission and usurping all their rights, led Indian backward classes to think in terms of organising a political party of their own".

During the general elections, 1957, the Backward Classes Federation was split into two, the All-India Backward Classes Federation controlled by the Congress activists and the Indian National Backward Classes Federation dominated by the Lohiaites. The twin streams were, however, not destined to flow like this for long. On 10 November 1957, the latter merged with the Socialist Party, thinking that with a leader like Lohia to guide them they could fight more effectively for the betterment of the OBCs.

It is a universal fact that splits and divisions harm organizations, but not always. In the present case, for instance, there was some temporary setback, but in the long run the OBCs were at profit: they had two organisations now to fight their battle—one from inside the citadel of power and the other from outside.

All these developments as discussed till now, unnerved the powers that be in Delhi who at once moved to do 'something' for the OBCs. To begin with, they demanded from federal counterparts 'to extend the benefits of various welfare schemes to the OBC's till further orders, using the Ministry of Education lists. This was followed by instructions to the effect that all vacant seats meant for SC and ST students in educational institutions be filled up with those from the OBCs. And finally, an assurance was given to increase the state expenditure on the welfare schemes for the OBCs. Expectedly, even these small moves caused a huge reaction. The high caste vested interest in the government and in the judiciary and legislature, in the press and academic world raised a lot of hue and cry against 'the retrograde goings-on'. There was the desired effect; and soon the 'moves' started moving in the opposite direction. The Backward Classes Commission's Report was removed from the table of the Houses of Parliament (1965). The Deputy Registrar General made an attempt to conduct a pilot survey to see if backwardness could be linked to occupational communities instead of caste. Having got no results, help was sought from the 'representatives of the states' to find way out to the caste-based reservations. Again there was no result. And there the matter ended and the central government washed its hands off everything: no more lists of OBCs, no reservations for them in jobs, no scholarships, or stipends for their children, and no aid to remove their poverty in the national plans. The buck was passed to the states to do whatever they wished for 'the purposes of Articles 15 and 16'.

During this critical situation, the OBCs suffered yet another blow: one of their most influential leaders and president of the All-India Backward Classes Federation, Punjabrao Deshmukh passed away (1965). There was chaos and confusion for some time but soon order was restored. Ch. Brahma Prakash, M.P. former

Chief Minister of Delhi took the presidential reins of the Federation in his hands (1965). The divisive fight, which had made the Federation weak for long, came to subside in the face of the danger to the very existence of the OBCs. Under the influence of the new leadership, almost full of Yadavas, the Yadava Mahasabha, which had become a formidable all-India organization by now acquired control over the Federation in a big way. This infused new blood, new life and vigour into the moribund Federation, signs of which were seen clearly in its very next meeting at Delhi (1966). Attended by over 1,000 delegates from all over the country, it was a different meeting altogether where speaker after speaker gave a clarion call to organize and protest against the 'Brahmana-Bania raj'. They castigated the Union Government for not implementing the recommendations of the Backward Classes Commission and wanted them to do the following things right then:

- (i) Bring in practice the list of 'Other Backward Classes' hitherto followed on the basis of social backwardness and notify under Article 338(3) of the Constitution;
- (ii) Sanction sufficient grants for scholarships to meet the demands of the students of the 'Other Backward Classes';
- (iii) Reserving seats in educational institutions and posts in services in proportions to their populations; and
- (iv) Initiating ameliorative schemes for their economic advancement by organizing separate cooperative institutions, and provide funds to grant loans and also the share capital.

The Federation knew that their demands would not be given effect unless there was a strong popular movement to back them. Hence this resolution was passed.

> "The Federation calls upon all the backward and weaker sections of the people to organize themselves to fight for their progress and social advancement. Our demand for a just and equal treatment should be backed by popular movement. In its absence, our goal has remained unrealized. It is high time we should concentrate all our energies to build up mass sanction for achieving our goal".

Similarly, the Federation, the Socialist Party also worked a great deal, meanwhile, to uplift the OBCs. Lohia, their dynamic leader, launched a virulent attack on the Congress—'the rival of the OBCs, minorities and other have-nots'. As long as this Brahmana-Bania casteist' outfit remained in power, he said, these people would keep on suffering exploitation, oppression and deprivation. He exhorted the sufferers to fight it out with all the might at their disposal.

A large number of the OBCs seems to have been moved by Lohia's call, for we see the Congress facing tough opposition, and defeat from them in many states in the north in the general elections held soon after in 1967. But unlike the states, the Congress continued in the saddle at the centre. As a result, the OBCs continued to be neglected there. But in 1977, when the Congress was replaced by the Janata Dal, things appeared to change for them, for the latter had promised in their election manifesto (a) to formulate a special programme with adequate funds within the time period of the Five Year Plans for the substantial advancement among other weaker sections of the OBCs; (b) to devise a special machinery to implement the programmes for their well-being and welfare and realise the relevant Constitutional guarantees; and (c) to reserve between 25 and 33 per cent of all government jobs for them as suggested by the Kalelkar Commission. But a leopard, it is said, does not change its spots. And so does the high caste vested interest well woven almost everywhere in national life. Otherwise, what else could make the new rulers drag their feet on the fulfilment of the promises made to the OBCs; and, then, when goaded into action, after over one year and nine months, they took recourse to delaying tactics by establishing second commission to examine the whole issue *de novo*?

But the commission (First) had made some recommendation and suggestions in the report. A brief summary of these recommendations will provide an informative insight in the same.

Conclusions and Recommendations: A Summary

I. Census and Caste

Before the process of destruction of disease of caste is started all facts about it have to be noted and classified in a scientific manner as in a clinical record. To this end we suggest that the 1961 Census be remodelled and reorganised so as to secure the required information on the following lines:

1. The Census operation should be carried out as a well-equipped continuous organisation competent to supply information on various topics of sociological importance.
2. The Census Offices must have long lasting ethnologists and sociologists in addition to the economists attached to them.
3. As long as social welfare and social relief have to be administered through castes, classes or groups, full awareness about these groups should be obtained and tabulated.
4. Some of the staff for the census should be appointed from social workers and village-level workers of the Planning and Development Departments.
5. Estimated family income and expenditure should be gathered and tabulated.
6. The Census slips should carry amongst others 'caste' in a separate column. If possible, Census should be conducted in 1957 instead of in 1961.

II. Special Groups

1. *Muslims:* It would be wrong or just to list all Muslims as socially and educationally backward. But there are a number of communities amongst those who are suffering from social inferiority in their own society and consequent education backwardness. Such backward communities are included in the list of OBCs. Various State Govts have mentioned such communities under separate heads of Hindu and Muslim backward communities. But the Commission has pointed at the names of the communities to include those of Muslims and Hindus.
2. *Christians:* Christianity has consistently refused to recognises caste. And yet, in practice, it was found that segregation of converts from the scheduled castes was not successfully handled in certain parts of South India. We have included such communities, especially in the South,

in the list of OBCs. We add that if scheduled caste converts to Christianity in other parts of the country also suffer from any identifiable degree of segregation and social disability their case should be considered for being included in the list of other backward classes.

3. *Anglo-Indians:* The problem of Anglo-Indians does not come strictly within the purview of our investigation. Yet, certain representations were made on their behalf. The Constitution of India guaranteed certain concessions to this community for certain period. Apart from this, this community cannot be classed as backward either educationally or socially.
4. *Eurasians in Travancore-Cochin:* A small community in the extreme south which is truly Eurasian in character is now being called Anglo-Indians in the list published by the Education Ministry, Government of India. This nomenclature is a blunder. It may be renamed Eurasian for the purpose of relief and included in the list of other backward classes of Travancore-Cochin State.
5. *Sikhs:* We opine that the Sikhs constitute an integral part of the broader Hindu religion. Although, in theory, the Sikhs do not subscribe to caste system, in real practice they cling to many Hindu traditions and practices. We recommend that the communities or groups who are treated as untouchables among the Sikhs should be added to the list of SCs. Any distinct community among the Sikhs found to be socially and educationally backward must be included in the list of OBCs.
6. *Gurkhas:* The Gurkhas are socially and culturally an integral part of the Hindu Community. Such of the communities among the Gurkhas found in UP, Bihar and West Bengal, who are educationally and socially backward, are included in the list of other backward classes. In the rest of India they are known to sideline caste and to live as one homogeneous community. Such of those who have settled down in other States (except UP, Bihar and West Bengal) should be added in the list of other backward classes if they are found to be socially and educationally backward.

7. *Bhangis:* The status of Bhangis at present is very miserable. Their living conditions are bad and the tools with which they work should enable them to carry out their work in a more decent and hygienic manner. The Bhangis should not be criticised to live in segregated locations. They should be distributed and given quarters among other groups.
8. *Women:* Women in India have lived under great social handicaps and as a class must be considered backward. But since they do not form a separate community they cannot be included in the list of backward classes. The condition of women among the backward classes is worse. The girls of the backward classes should be given better facilities for leaving. They should be encouraged to live in special hostels for girls of all communities. They should be trained in basic education. Women should have a share in the political life of the country. The following steps are recommended for the advancement of women in general:
   (i) Free education in all stages to all female children whose parents' income is less than Rs. 3,000 per annum.
   (ii) Education for girls belonging to the backward classes.
   (iii) Residential hostels for girl students, with priority for girls of the backward classes.
   (iv) Samata Ashrams for girls of all communities to be managed by trained staffs of women and men.
   (v) Creation of special facilities for girls to study Medicine, Home Science and other subjects specially fit for women.
   (vi) More facilities for training women in the Fine Arts, and in Social Service.
9. *Unfortunate Women:* The administration of the 'Suppression of Immoral Traffic Act' is found to be more punitive than reformative. It is seen that the punished offenders drift back to their old profession in the lack of any properly organised rescue homes where they could find refuge. There is great scope for establishing rescue homes and the Government should be able to help such efforts with finance and legislation. Rescue homes should not be mere shelters for such women. Such homes must be controlled by committees consisting of social workers under government supervision.

Women social workers from rich part of society accept an increasingly larger role in tackling this problem. In addition to providing food and shelter for these unfortunate women, they must be trained in different occupations to enable them to earn a living and become useful members of society. They must also be taught to improve their outlook and to lead normal married lives.

10. *Delinquent Children:* The lower sections of society often ignore their children with the result that the later go astray and sometimes become the victims of greed, cupidity and passions. Such children generally learn all kinds of voices and are trained to offences and crime. The provisions for the rehabilitation of delinquent children are totally faulty. It is not legislation that matters but better provision for the maintenance and education of such children that counts; it is the quality of the reforming agency that is all-important. The State must help persons who volunteer for the work of amelioration of these delinquent children.
11. *Denotified Communities (Ex-Criminal Tribes):* The following measures are recommended for adoption for the upliftment of the conditions of the communities in this groups:
    (i) The Ex-Criminal Tribes should hereafter be called denotified communities (*Vimochit Jatian*).
    (ii) These communities have been classed as SCs, STs or OBCs according to the criterion application to them for the purpose of relief.
    (iii) The nomadic groups should be given facilities for leading an established life. Efforts must be made to distribute them in the towns and villages so that they could slowly be assimilated by society.
    (iv) The children of these groups should be trained in Basic Education. They must also be given training in cottage industries, handicrafts and agriculture. Services of trained psychologists and social workers should be availed to reform these habitual offenders.
    (v) Group criminality should be treated separately from the acquired criminality of individuals.

12. *Backward Areas:* Backward regions in Himachal Pradesh, Uttar Pradesh, Udaipur in Rajasthan, Bastar in Madhya Pradesh, Alirapur and Jobat in Madhya Bharat, Amarakantak in Vindhya Pradesh should be evolved by allocating more community projects, National Extensions Service blocks, Social Welfare Extension projects and other developmental schemes. The proposals of some of the States to identify them as Scheduled Areas may be examined by the Government of India and early action taken.

Parameters of Backwardness

Numerous causes — social, environmental, economic and political — have operated both openly and in a subtle form for centuries to create the present colossal problem of backwardness. Economic backwardness is the outcome and not the cause of many social evils of the present day. Social backwardness, therefore, is not today due to the particular profession of a person. It is not easy to group sections of people under special occupations. There are certain distinct communities who are not confined to any one occupational and it would be difficult to classify them under any known occupation. There are certain castes and sub-castes based on regionalism. The Commission is justified in interpreting the terms of reference as mainly about social hierarchy based on caste. Caste generally depends upon birth; it may also depend upon habits and it may create further cleavage because of conventions and denominational differences.

After a consideration of the social conditions in Indian society and the reasons for the backwardness of a large section of the people, the following criteria were adopted for general guidance:

(a) low social position, in the traditional caste hierarchy of Hindu society;
(b) lack of general educational uplifment among the major section of a caste or community;
(c) improper or no representation in government services;
(d) inadequate representation in the areas of trade, commerce and industry.

Categorisation of Communities

The following aspects were taken into consideration: the social position which a community occupies in the social order, the percentages of literacy and its general educational advancement; and its representation in government jobs or in the industrial sphere. The economic backwardness had also to be kept in view in order to find out the ability of the community to take advantage of the available opportunities as also the recent trends in its progress. The list of OBCs selected by the Education Ministry, Government of India, and the lists furnished by the State Governments form the basis. The options of the representatives of various communities, leaders of public opinion and social workers were also paid attention.

This way, the lists of other backward classes was prepared and also revised the lists of SCs and STs. Every efforts were made to bring in as many communities as possible who fell in the criteria. It was the effort of the Commission to see that no community should be omitted. It was suggested to set up a board for the implementation of the policy for the advancement of all the backward classes. This Board should be authorised to investigate the conditions of the communities who may later seek addition in the list of OBCs.

The names of castes have not been specified as Hindu or Muslim and they should invariably be regarded as caste names common to both.

Level of Backwardness and Steps for their Removal

(a) Political

The framers of the Indian Constitution recognised the historical processes that were at work in India and inconsistent development of the various sections of the Indian population. They have, therefore, made adequate provision for the protection and betterment of OBCs also. Universal adult franchise has given to the masses the most potent and powerful instrument with which to shape their future. What was required was to strengthen their hands through education and not to offer another weapon to feeble hands.

After discussing all aspects of the question, it was concluded that it would be suicidal to accord any additional or special political representation to any community or communities.

(b) Economic and Industrial

Aims should be full employment and the removal of economic inequalities. Maximum production, full employment, the realisation of economic equality and social justice should constitute the accepted objective of planning under the present-day conditions. Unplanned industrial advancement in India, urbanisation and expansion of trade and commerce, growth of towns and large cities and the British educational and industrial policy have disrupted the traditional village economy and have resulted in denuding the rural areas of local talent and leadership.

During the 30 years after 1921 the population has increased by 11 crores, and there is a drop of 25 per cent in the per capita area of cultivated land.

The pressure on land has gone up from decade to decade. The decay of rural industries has aggravated the rural situation. All these factors have contributed to the growth of landless agriculturist families.

Smallness of holdings, primitive system of cultivation, absence of educational facilities, lack of adequate agricultural equipment, decay of rural industries causing unemployment and underemployment have all contributed to the growing poverty of the rural people.

Any plan for economic reconstruction of the country must necessarily include measures designed for the fast uplift of the backward classes. Conditions must be recreated in which the development of these classes takes a natural growth. Removal of economic and social reasons that are operating to their detriment should receive first priority.

No time should be lost in making fuller use of the human resources, available skill and experience of the artisan and occupational classes to produce goods which are required by the community. Improved equipment or improved tools and training in modern methods of production may follow the above steps.

Best solution, therefore, for the speedy uplift of the backward classes in the rural area is not so much to wait for the creation of new opportunities of employment, as to provide favourable conditions in which their lost or decaying occupations could be revived. A large scale employment in old occupations will alone relieve the present pressure on land. It will also help in creating suitable social atmosphere for economic uplift. It is only thereafter that we will have better picture of rural life which will enable us to reorganise rural life on a sound and rational basis.

"The economic policy and the ideology behind the Five-Year Plan do not inspire sufficient confidence. It is realised that even the policies enunciated in the Five-Year Plan have not been properly implemented'. The administrative set up entrusted with the task of implementing the welfare schemes requires a complete reorientation. There was widespread demand from the representatives of the backward classes that high number of their own men should be taken into services to bring about better social contact with the masses.

Remedial Measures

All developmental activities should radiate from central villages of compact blocks consisting of 10 to 15 villages. The country should be divided into compact blocks of such dimensions on a planned basis, and modern comforts should be taken to such *Panchkoshi* units. Causes disturbing rural life such as factious feelings, presence of anti-social elements and the trend of litigation often leading to breaches of peace should be removed to help development of the rural areas.

Land Policy

To ameliorate the backward classes, it is vital to have a proper land policy. It is important that all kinds of intermediary tenures should be eradicated to help in the formulation and implementation of a national land policy.

The land legislation must be simple and easily understandable by the rural population. There should be no gaps in such a legislation that might lead to social conflict. Too many and frequent changes in land legislation create confusion and difficulty and often lead to never ending litigation and exploitation.

Large Landowners and Ceilings on Holdings

An ordinary picture in India is one of numerous small holdings, a large proportion of them being uneconomic, a small number of middle peasants and a sprinkling of substantial owners. If it were only object of policy to reduce the holdings of the large owners with a view to providing for the landless or for increasing the farms of those who now have uneconomic fragments, the facts at present available shows that these aims are not likely to be achieved in any substantial measures. The principle of an upper limit for landholdings must be regarded as in relation to the general economic pattern of the country as a whole, rather than in relation to the possible use that could be made of land in excess of any ceiling limit that may be decided. Fixing a ceiling on landholding is necessary as a social principle to remove the existing inequality of the cultivators' holding in the countryside. But it should be followed almost immediately by putting limits on incomes from other fields of national economy. Only then would it be possible to create a psychological satisfaction among those who are needed to surrender their property for the common good. The ceiling should be different for different types of land and conditions of rainfall, types of crop grown, pressure of population, etc., should be taken into notice in fixing the ceilings.

Distribution of Land

The government land available should firstly be distributed among the landless and then among the owners of uneconomic holdings. To this end land revenue rules should be accordingly amended. Any infringement of this rule should be severely dealt with by State authorities. The excess land resumed after setting the ceilings should also be distributed first among the landless. The distribution of land should be left in the hands of government officers who should be directed to implement the government policy in this behalf.

Small and Middle Owners

All these titled groups include almost all backward communities. Their holdings are uneconomic and seriously fragmented. The general aim should be to bring about consolidation of holdings.

Fragmentation beyond a specified limit should be prohibited by law.

Regulation of Tenancy Rights

What is required is to protect the tenants under large holders from arbitrary eviction and from the levy of unreasonable rent. A limit on the amount of land to be resumed by the owners for personal cultivation is important in all cases where ceilings on holdings are not fixed. In cases where ceilings are fixed the tenants may be given the option to acquire the excess land by payment of adequate price in easy instalments. The quantum of rent to be fixed and the security of tenancy should be determined in relation as per local conditions. In the case of small and middle owners and in cases where ceilings are decided the rights of tenants under such owners should be regulated by simple laws and it must always be open to the owners to resume the land without much problem at the end of the tenancy period, which may be fixed from five to ten years.

Record of Rights

Undoubtedly, peasant proprietorship, however small the holding, will, for some years, be the pattern in most rural areas. The rights of all interests in land should be correctly recorded and maintained.

Structure of Agricultural Class

High number of owner-cultivators is the most important and characteristic feature of our agricultural class structure. The economic conditions of communities involved in agriculture are far from satisfactory and a large majority of them have necessarily to live below subsistence level. Their condition has become such that they are inevitably the helpless victims of exploitation. They need State help in abundant measure, not only to improve agriculture which is their mainstay but to ensure general improvement in their living conditions. It is equally necessary to remove all forms of exploitation from rural life, and set up cooperatives on a planned basis—both functional and regional—manned by proper type of persons who would work devotedly for the advancement of the rural people.

Marketing and Rural Credit

In this whole process, we endorse the integrated scheme of rural credit with State partnership suggested by the All-India Rural Credit Survey.

Rural Indebtedness

In critical condition, agricultural communities habitually run into debt and more so when adverse seasonal conditions prevail. It is important that provision should be made either through land marketing societies or through proposed State for long-term credit to redeem them from the bondage of unconscionable money-lenders. Relief from usurious rates of interest is also needed. Scaling down of the debts of impecunious cultivators is equally desirable.

Marketing Facilities

"In the absence of staying power a large number of small farmers compete with each other and the markets witness conditions of occasional glut and scarcity." They are noctious of exploitation at the hands of money-lenders or mandi-merchants in marketing their produce. It is, therefore, necessary to set-up cooperative marketing societies, regulated markets at suitable centres with warehouse and banking facilities.

Cost Support

In India, the conditions of agricultural communities are largely governed by the price they get for their surplus produce. Minimum fair costs should be guaranteed to the cultivators both from the point of view of increasing agricultural production and of the prosperity of the agricultural communities.

Irrigation

The best method of increasing crop production in India is to provide through irrigation an additional source of water supply to the cultivated land. Small and medium irrigation tasks have an important part to play and they have obvious advantages. In view of the urgency of this problem we recommend that greater attention should be paid to the implementation of small and medium irrigation works and to provide irrigation from wells and rivers wherever it is not feasible to have tanks and anicuts.

Land Tax Policy

It is said that the present system of land taxation has not been equitable and it is especially oppressive in the case of uneconomic holdings. The present system has not been based on the capacity of the cultivator to pay the tax. The system of land taxation in its connection with the capacity of the cultivator should be thoroughly examined and an equitable system of taxation be developed.

Rural Savings

Due to the growing agricultural prosperity there should be scope for effecting savings in rural areas. The villagers have to be educated to practise thrift and economy. There is, thus, need for organising rural savings schemes at village level.

Backward Communities Engaged in the Cultivation of Vegetables and Flowers

Besides the above, there are some distinct communities who are mainly engaged in the cultivation of vegetables and flowers. They are known by different names in different parts of the country. Some steps are recommended below to ameliorate their conditions.

1. Sufficient land should be made available for growing vegetables and fruits. Suburban belts around large towns should be developed for raising fruits and vegetables by organising these communities into cooperatives, particularly for the supply of improved seeds and marketing their produce.
2. Also, the exorbitant rents in all cases of tenancies should be scaled down as in the case of other tenancies.
3. Directions should be issued to the young men of these communities on improved methods of fruit and vegetables cultivation.
4. Stipends and scholarships should be established for the purpose of training qualified students among them in general horticulture.

Communities Engaged in Growing Betel Vine

Irrigation of betel vine is mainly confined to one caste which is found all over the country. It is cultivated on small plots of land

and the community is generally poor. The greatest problem is in the matter of marketing betel leaves. Pan growers have lost these export markets in Pakistan, Ceylon, Burma and Nepal. The following steps are recommended for their amelioration:

1. Sanction of sufficient and suitable land for raising betel vine to members of this community and reduction of oppressive rents.
2. Setting up of cooperatives to grant medium-term loans for the purchase of agricultural implements and manure and for marketing betel leaves.
3. Discovery of foreign markets by the State for betel leaves.
4. Study for the eradication of pests and diseases and for improving the quality of the vines, and the nutritional and medicinal value of pan.

Betterment of Village Economy

For village economy, the First Five-Year Plan advocates cooperative farming for the rapid reorganisation of village economy. The Planning Commission has also recommended cooperatives village management as the ultimate objectives. But the socio-economic structure of the present village life is not congenial for the proper working of cooperatives in rural areas. The basic causes hindering the development of the cooperatives spirit must be vanished before agriculture could be reorganised on cooperative principles. A few essential steps are required to facilitate such a reorganisation. They are:

1. Banning of investment on land as a source of income by persons who are not themselves cultivators or by those who do not live either in the village in which the land is situated or on the farm.
2. Control over land in a village from persons who own the land but who are themselves not agriculturists and do not reside in the village.
3. Checks on alienation of land in favour of a non-agriculturist.
4. Keeping of the required extent of land for grazing purpose and for village plantations.

5. Earliest possible redistribution of the remaining land among the landless agriculturists in the village in the first instance and among the owners of uneconomic holdings next.
6. Convergence of holdings.
7. Introducing mutual aid among agriculturists in farm operations.
8. Formation of multi-purpose cooperative societies for better farming or for distribution of seeds, fertilisers, agricultural equipment for marketing and financing, etc.

Bhoodan Movement

Bhoodan is in nutshell the application of the principle of non-violence for the acquisition and distribution of land among the landless in the country. This movement has pushed a great agrarian revolution, and is creating a necessary psychological climate in the country for the establishment of social ownership of land through voluntary and non-violent means. It attempted to influence the psychology of the 'haves' as regards money, power and prestige and to inculcate in them a feeling of social solidarity by demanding to recognise their duty towards the backward people as members of a vast family. Acharya Vinoba Bhave is teaching the 'haves' to accept the 'have-nots' one's blood brothers. He is, therefore, not only removing the backwardnesses of the 'have-nots' but he is also removing the bitterness which the 'have-nots' in their desperation are nursing. This large agrarian revolution is more spiritual in its content. The scope of Bhoodan Movement is widened to include in its scope. *Sampattidan*, *Shramadan* and *Jeevandan* so important for the establishment of a Sarvodaya society. The commission recommend both to the Government and to the nation that they should take up the work of Bhoodan Movement and spread it to all nooks and corners of India.

Improvement of Livestock

Betterment of agriculture is bound up with the development of livestock, for bullocks are the principal motive power used amonst universally for agricultural operations. It is necessary, therefore, that the cattle wealth of the country should be improved. All communities engaged in agriculture are also engaged in rearing livestock. The prosperity of these communities relies on the development of livestock.

The following steps were suggested:

1. Stratification of all useless and decrepit and cattle and establishment of *Gosadans* for their upkeep.
2. Big arrangements for the castration of useless and scrub bulls, to prevent deterioration in the quality of cattle.
3. Stations to improve the breed of cattle as also to improve the milk-yielding qualities of the cow should be established. All help and encouragement should be provided to local breeders to improve their stock.
4. Measures should be taken to conserve the existing pasture land in the interest of village cattle.
5. Additional veterinary institutions should be established.

Dairy-Farming

In India, small-scale dairying is a general feature in rural areas and brings subsidiary income to the farmers. Efforts should be made to organise these small producers into cooperative milk unions and to give them financial help and other assistance needed for developing dairying.

Insurance of Livestock

In India, cattle are subject to periodical epidemics and loss of cattle during such epidemics renders agriculturists helpless. They have no other source to rely upon for their livelihood when they lose their cattle. It is necessary to protect their interest by sponsoring schemes of cattle insurance.

Sheep and Wool

Community of shepherds is engaged mainly in sheep-breeding. There is great scope for the improvement of sheep both of wool and mutton type. The present state of sheep-breeders are far from satisfactory. Besides establishing regional centres for improving the quality of wool by selective breeding and cross-breeding, it is necessary to make available enough breeding areas to the sheep-breeders in several states. Steps should be taken to save the flocks of sheep from disease and epidemics.

Bee-keeping and Poultry

Bee-keeping and poultry could form an important subsidiary industry for the poorer classes in the rural parts. It would be a source of additional income to them. Improved breeds such as white leghorn, Rhode-Island, etc., should be started in the rural areas. The rural population should also be instructed in the art of bee-keeping and State help extended to popularise it.

Piggery

Groups involved in pig rearing are considered as low castes. Some of them have no fixed place of residence and they move from place to place with their pigs. State Governments should provide more facilities to communities engaged in this occupation and they must be helped to lead a more settled life.

Fisheries

Many communities are engaged both in inland fishing and in sea-fishing. Some of them are regarded as untouchables. In addition to fishing, some of them are involved implying boats and ferries in inland streams or cargo boats along the coastal areas. Their living conditions are highly unsatisfactory and they lead a very hard and strenuous life. Fisheries have to be developed to supply adequate food to the nation. Fishermen should be organised and supported to form multi-purpose cooperative societies. Through these societies they should be helped to build strong boats or buy boats and nets. They should also be enabled to buy steam-launchers so that they can convey their catch to coastal towns. Facilities for quick and cheap transport including facilities for the preservation of fish should be made available to them. The Khalas community could be encouraged to join the Indian Navy.

Agricultural Labour

As per Dr. Radha Kumud Mukherjee, the system of land tenure started by the British in India was responsible for the growth of agricultural labour population in India. The decay of cottage and village industries has also contributed its share. The Agricultural Labour Enquiry had revealed that 30.4 per cent of the population in rural areas was agricultural labour. The same inquiry had disclosed that as many as eighty-nine per cent of them were casual workers and the period of unemployment ranged from 3 to 6 months. Agricultural labour forms the most vulnerable section of the population, and the issue of rehabilitation of communities in this group should receive the earnest consideration of the government—Central and State. Revival of cottage and village industries and reorganisation of agriculture would afford greater opportunities for employment of these communities. The redistribution of land among the landless would further ameliorate the economic condition of these classes.

Minimum Wages

About the agricultural labour, it was felt that barring a few exceptional cases the fixation of the minimum wage was desirable. All the facilities provided to industrial labour should also be extended to agricultural labour. Backward classes have to fulfill the following requirement: (i) minimum wages; (ii) minimum housing; (iii) drinking water supply; (iv) education; (v) health facilities.

Development of Industries

The conflict between heavy industries on the one hand and cottage and rural industries on the other be removed. It is essential in establishing industries to avoid the ugly features of the industrial life of the West. It is equally necessary to avoid heavy concentrations of population around urban areas. Measures should be taken to disperse industries all over the country according to a definite plan.

Communities belonging to backward classes are employed only as unskilled labour in these industries. Training facilities should be provided for these communities to enhance their skill. The principle of recruiting and training suitable men from backward communities to higher ranks of jobs at least in government-controlled industries should be conceded. Introduction of short-term training courses in all industrial establishments is equally necessary.

Cottage Industries in Villages

State of communities engaged in village and cottage industries and other handicrafts are far from satisfactory. During times of unemployment they have to rely either on dole from Government or resort to begging. There is conflict of opinion between the policy-makers and those entrusted with the enforcement of policies. Some of the government servants in the Industries Departments in several states do not appear to have much faith in the survival capacity of cottage and village industries. Their interest is at best lukewarm. The present supervisory, administrative and technical staff employed in Industries Departments are not drawn from communities related to traditional rural industries or occupations.

Scheme of giving subsidies to sustain these industries is at best only a palliative. The only feasible course would be to remove all factors hindering natural development of these industries and recreate favourable circumstances in which these industries could flourish spontaneously. These communities will, by their own exertions try to improve themselves and their conditions if the atmosphere is supportive. With government assistance and help, it will become easier for them not only to improve the technique of production but to organise themselves on modern lines.

Industry of Khadi

Manual spinning and hand-weaving have been India's traditional village industry. "The story of the deterioration and almost total extermination of so universal an industry in Indian villages is documented in blood and tears." Gandhiji made it the central programme of his constructive activity and with the growing tide of nationalism, Khadi gained in importance.

The employment potential of this industry is great. It gives part-time and full employment to lakhs of villagers and especially to the poorer sections of backward classes. There is great scope for the development of khadi industry, particularly in cotton growing areas of the country, particularly where there are no mills. Improved *charkhas* and improved looms should be introduced to cut down cost and to enhance production.

Weaving Industry

Advancement of Indian mill industry has inevitably affected the fortunes of handloom weavers. As the largest cottage industry in India, it occupies a place of prominence in the general economy of the country. Production of handloom cloth has presently been about 1,200 million yards out of a total production in the country of about 6,200 million yards per annum. In spite of great vicissitudes in economic crisis this industry has shown great vitality to survive and continues to sustain millions of people. It is estimated that about 100 lakhs of persons including dependants are supported by this industry. The tradition, experience, and skill of handloom weavers have been long and distinguished. This could be preserved only by checking unfair competition by the mills. The well-being of the communities engaged in handloom weaving depends upon the early rehabilitation of this industry. The following steps are recommended for the resuscitation of this industry:

1. Proper demarcation of spheres of production exclusively for the handloom should be made with immediate effect. Since the weavers are accustomed to produce varieties of clothes like saris, *dhotis* and *lungis*, all these varieties should be exclusively reserved for the handloom industry. The present partial reservation has not pushed the industry to any desirable extent.
2. Continuous and adequate supply of yarn of required counts and colours at reasonable prices should be made to the handloom weavers. (See in this connection Chairman's note on *Ambar* yarn).
3. Handloom operators should be brought into the cooperative fold as soon as possible with a view to protecting them from exploitation by middlemen and master weavers.
4. An adequate and responsible chain of marketing organisation should be formed throughout the country and possibilities should be thoroughly explored for creation of foreign markets for handloom clothes.
5. After full protection and patronage of Khadi, only handloom products should be purchased by Govts. — Central and State — for their requirements.

6. Monetary assistance by the State should be provided to weavers for the improvement of their looms for increased production.
7. Manual weavers are at present living and working in 'shocking conditions of congestion'. A planned programme for improving their housing condition and, where necessary, for ameliorations of weavers' colonies is urgently called for and should be undertaken by Government without any delay.
8. Through the improvement in the technique of production of the handloom industry and increase in its yardage, the textile mills should be required gradually to limit themselves to the production of fabrics of export varieties as well as of luxury fabrics of finest yarn both for export and for internal consumption.

Peculiar characteristics of Cotton and Silk Weaving in Assam and Manipur

States of Assam and Manipur have strong domestic weaving tradition. In these two States handloom weaving is non-commercial in nature. Women of these two states are skilled weavers. The weaving industry here is severely handicapped for want of regular supply of yarn from the mills. There is a great possibility of making Assam and Manipur completely self-sufficient in fabrics. To this end, the entry of mill cloth should be prohibited and the State Governments should give special help to hand-spinning and weaving and also set up a yarn mill with necessary spindleage. Cotton cultivation in some parts of Assam should also be encouraged. These steps should provide a large volume of employment to the backward communities including a great number of tribals.

Industry of Silk Handlooms

Silk handloom weavers in the industry suffer from the hard competition from the mills. Sudden and sharp fluctuations in the price of silk yarn often throws a good number of them out of work. Arrangements should be made for supplying the weavers with silk yarn at reasonable prices. The All India Handlooms

Board should draw programmes for improving the state weavers and marketing their cloth.

Sericulture

It is one of the successful cottage industries giving subsidiary employment to a large population of agricultural communities. The internal production of silk is still not sufficient to meet the country's demand, and the unregulated import of raw silk from abroad causes crises in the local industry. There is great scope both for expansion and for improvement in the method of production of silk. This industry needs stabilisation and only then it can develop sufficiently speed.

Wool Spinning Weaving Industry

The industry of wool spinning and weaving is mainly confined to a community of shepherds who are found all over the country. Severe mill competition has been responsible for the downfall of this industry. Though India is a large producer of wool, a great part of it is exported and the local weaving industry is severely handicapped. Proper organisations should be established, preferably on cooperative lines, in suitable places for the purchase and supply of wool to the spinners and weavers. Marketing facilities for the sale of woollen blankets should be made available so that weavers may get a proper price for their products. It is also necessary to improve the technique of softening wool and of production of both woollen yarn and blankets to suit the changing likes and dislikes of the people. Woollen cloth should be standardised to supply the needs of the Defence Forces and hospitals.

Village Oil Industry

This industry is mainly in the hands of the community of *Telis*. The number of workers engaged in this industry has been falling steadily from decade to decade. The oil mill industry has affected this industry to a great extent and large number of oil workers (*telis*) are either unemployed or have joined the ranks of agricultural labour.

Our country is one of the most important producers of oil

seeds and yet the tragedy of the situation is that the traditional oil pressers find it difficult to sustain their industry in the situation of competition from oil mill industry. Both from the point of view of employment and of improving the conditions of village *telis*, it is necessary to reserve the crushing of edible oil seeds to the village *ghanis*. At first, if the competition is removed and the regular supply of oil seeds ensured, the *telis* themselves will immediately revive the industry. This may follow supply of better *ghanis* and organisation for the supply of oil seeds and for marketing the oil produced by the village oil industry. We would add that immediate steps should be taken to check the use of machinery for crushing edible oil. It is also important to stop further licensing of new oil mills and gradually stop the crushing of edible oils in the existing mills.

Rural Pottery

The section of village potters have preserved the traditional art of producing not only artistic and elegant earthenware but also articles for the routine use of all the poor and backward communities. At present they find no place in the production of modern ceramic wares. The potters should be pushed and supported to improve their methods of production by giving them training and better implements.

Cane and Bamboo Workers

Communities engaged in bamboo and cane workers are known by different names in different states. They are poor and backward, and live in segregated areas in rural parts or in the vicinity of forests. Their main difficulties are lack of raw materials at reasonable prices and proper marketing facilities. In view of the wide variety of bamboo and cane in our country there is great scope for the improvement in the production of articles from bamboo and cane to suit modern tastes. Measures should be taken to encourage these communities by arranging supply of raw materials at reasonable prices and adequate marketing facilities. Proper housing and educational facilities should be provided for improving the conditions of these communities.

Paddy Husking

Setting up of rice mills has greatly affected this important village industry. Paddy husking is a source of employment to a large number of agricultural labourers and it is said that 65 per cent of paddy is still hand-pounded and husked locally. It is desirable to eliminate rice mills altogether from the village areas.

Coir Industry

This industry is still providing a large volume of employment in Travancore-Cochin, but is often subject to periodical depression. The recent establishment of Coir Board is expected to help this industry.

Minor Industries

Communities engaged in preparing leaf-plates, gathering from forests, etc. are poor and backward. Special measures should be taken for their uplift and rehabilitation.

Village Handicrafts

Demands for articles of utility produced by village artisans has always been there. Factory products have affected the production of village artisans. The latter need protection and assistance at the hands of the public and the states. Care must be taken to keep distinction between artisans who produce useful articles and those who produce works of fine arts. Those works of art cannot be produced on a large popular scale. With the disappearance of kings, maharajas, nawabs and zamindars, the traditional patronage is gone. The artisan classes should be helped and encouraged and national museums of art and emporia should be established to patronise these artists. Governments should purchase these articles of art to please the embassies, Parliament and legislatures. The Government of India should assist in building up foreign markets for such articles.

Beedi Industry

The Beedi industry has a great potentiality for the employment of labour. Measures are essential not only to prevent exploitation but also to organise beedi workers on a cooperative basis.

Mill and Factory Competition

Safeguarding cottage and rural industries from unrestricted competition of the mills and factories and decentralisation of industries will greatly contribute towards the rehabilitation of the backward communities.

Communities with Traditional Occupation is Personal Service

Such communities are the washerman, the barber, the *kahar* or the water-carrier and other classes of domestic servants. The conditions of these communities are deplorable. They need special help for ameliorating their conditions.

Nomadic Communities

We have in our country a number of small communities who eke out a precarious existence in the countryside. They have no fixed place of residence and they wonder from place to place in search of food and employment. They believe in witchcraft. Because of the insecurity of their lives, some of these communities are driven to crime. it should be the special responsibility of the State to give them a settled life.

Traditional Beggars

Culture of Ancient India has dignified a life of mendicancy. It enjoined that only those who admitted selfless services as a life mission were entitled to live on alms. This ideal was too good to remain unsullied. People who did not want to work for their bread assumed the name of religion and took to begging. Natural disasters like famines and invasions sometimes created a large band of beggars. Hinduism enjoined feeding the poor as one of the duties of the householder. India, therefore, contentedly nurtured a large body of beggars till at last the institution broke under its own weight. The caste system also must share the responsibility for a large number of beggars. Some communities claim that beggary is their age old profession and that they cannot take to any service occupation or industry. Society has to consider the whole situation and tackle the problem by stressing certain social standards being accepted universally both by those who accept alms and those who give them. What is needed most is that the ideal of self-respect and the idea of the dignity of labour should be instilled into the minds of the people. It is only by direct inculation of social ideals that beggary can be eradicated and the manpower of India fully utilised.

Steps to Prevent Exploitation of the Backward Classes

In India, Backward Classes are subject to various kinds of exploitation. Measures to save them from exploitation are ineviably essential for the improvement of their economic conditions. Adequate institutions must be established for the distribution of wealth produced. A chain of suitable cooperative institutions or government stores is badly needed for this purpose. Measure should be taken to train these communities in running institutions set up for their benefit. The ultimate alternative seems to be that all production and distribution should be on a socialistic basis and that people should be encouraged to establish the essential moral basis and to get trained for the change over.

Communications

Ours is a land of vast distances and unless all kinds of communications are developed it will not be possible to remove either the backwardness of areas distant from urban centres or of people inhabiting these areas.

Public Health and Rural Water Supply

Most of the time required backward communities live in insanitary conditions and in ill-ventilated houses. The ideas of sanitation and public health among them are still primitive. Large-scale preventive measures are required to improve the health of these classes. It is absolutely essential that the rural public should be educated in the necessity of maintaining cleanliness conditions.

Rural water supply in villages should be improved a great deal. Public wells and reservoirs must be built within easy reach of the Harijan quarters for the use of the whole area. These should be kept in sanitary conditions under the supervision of a Village Water Intact Committee with a Harijan as President.

Rural Housing

Conditions of houses of many of the communities belonging to backward classes are far from satisfactory. They live in ill-ventilated mud houses or thatched sheds. These houses are generally populated.

Proper programme of rural housing should be drawn upto provide housing for the poorer sections in proper village layouts. Sites for building houses should be provided to those people either free or at nominal rates. Financial assistance either in the form of subsidies or loans should also be extended to help the backward communities to construct cheap houses. Housing cooperatives may be organised for this purpose.

Social Backwardness and Measures for its Removal

It has been seen that the social backwardness of many communities of the backward class group is due to the undesirable features of the Hindu social system. The sense of caste and prejudices based on social inequality is eating into the vitals of the nation. Modern conditions no doubt are gradually toning down some of those rigid caste ideas but the spirit of caste still permeates major positions of our society. In condemning the iniquitous features of the caste system, it is not suggested that Hinduism should be liquidated. Hinduism could be purified or cleansed of the dross which it has grown up during the course of centuries. Hinduism must re-examine itself in the world context and boldly shed all its undesirable features. It must stop to be medieval in its concept of life; must refresh itself and take a new form which would liberate the spirit of man and enable him to assimilate the best and the noblest that Hinduism has treasured through the centuries. The Hindu view of life was based on a harmonious pursuit of the four chief conceivable objects, viz., *dharma, artha, kama* and *moksha*. It taught the universal brotherhood of human beings or rather the essential unity of mankind, as all individual beings were regarded as part of one Eternal Soul.

Efforts for establishment of equalisation is beset with many hazards. Poverty, ignorance and illiteracy make the task all the more difficult. Therefore, nothing short of strong unit by the entire nation and in particular by the leaders of society to effect a complete revolution in the fundamental social outlook of the people can possibly turn the diverse elements into a homogeneous society. We indicate below, on general lines, the measures that Governments — Central and State — should follow for the eradication of social evils:

1. Visible enunciation and effective implementation of this policy of social solidarity and national progress.
2. Essential legislation on marriage and inheritance laws.
3. Ban by law of social disabilities.
4. Arrangements for the production and distribution of literature on social problems.
5. Moderate use of the Press, films, platform and radio for the removal of social evils.
6. Ban on all observances tending to promote caste feelings in governmental activities.
7. Reorganisation of the educational system with special emphasis on the dignity of manual labour.
8. Complete aid and support to promote education as speedily as possible among the backward classes.
9. Proper representation in government service and government controlled industrial establishments of those sections who had no chance so far.
10. Encouragement to art, literature, special cultural groups and assistance and promotion of cultural activities with this social end in view.

Educational Backwardness and Measures for its Removal

Here are the various causes of educational backwardness of the backward classes:

1. Conventional apathy for education on account of social and environmental conditions or occupational handicaps;
2. Poverty and lack of means of a large number of communities to educate their children;
3. Absence of educational institutions in the rural areas;
4. Living in inaccessible areas and poor facilities of communications;
5. Absence of adequate educational aids in the form of

free-ships, scholarships and monetary grants for the purchase of books and clothing;
6. Absence of residential hostel facilities in places where educational institutions are situated;
7. A large number of unemployed educated youth also damper on the desire of some of the communities to educate their children;
8. Unadequate educational system which does not train students for appropriate occupations and social profession.

The overall progress of literacy in India is slow and literacy among the backward classes is considerably low. Introduction of free and compulsory elementary education is imperative to wipe off illiteracy from among the backward classes. Introduction of free and compulsory education for the age group 6-14 must not mean the extension of the present system of education. Conversion of the existing elementary schools into basic schools wherever there are no schools, is the only solution to the problem.

Teachers for the basic schools should be drawn from the artisan and occupational communities in surrounding areas. They must be trained first in general education and then appointed as teachers. Establishment of basic schools should be planned in the central villages which should be selected for location of senior basic schools so that they could serve all the feeder villages within a radius of five miles. Board or Committee should be formed in each area to see that no child remain without basic education. Hostels should be established on secular grounds and the cost of board and lodging for the poorer sections of the backward classes should be borne by the Government Students of all communities and all religious denominations should be encouraged to live together and to lead a common life. It should be made possible for such teachers and students to live together, work together, and study together.

There should be established special type of *ashram* schools (*samata ashrams*) where teachers with their families live with the students. One such *ashram* school in each one of the 300 and odd districts into which India is divided should be set-up. These *ashrams* should be run by special trained teachers who have equal respect for all religions and who regard all communities as integral part of one human family. The *panchkoshi* schools as also *samata ashrams* will naturally culminate into rural universities of the basic type.

For the purpose of making basic education popular with the masses and to carry conviction with them, it is necessary that Government should categorically declare that in selecting candidates for government jobs especially of the upper grades, students trained in basic education will be given a decided preference. Pre-basic or pre-school education is essential to overcome the initial social handicap under which the backward classes children are suffering.

Next stage of education is vital from the point of view of the educational advancement of the backward classes. Until suitable senior basic schools are set up there is need to start secondary schools in rural areas. Hostels should be attached to the secondary schools on non-communal lines. But it is important that a majority of the places in those hostels should be reserved for the boys belonging to backward classes. The aim should be to make the hostels training houses for developing that common social outlook which is so necessary for the future well-being of the country.

Education in Universities

As the Basic Rural Universities would gradually take their place, the present-day Universities should confine themselves to technical education and research, certain percentage of seats being reserved for qualified students of the backward classes with liberal scholarships being granted to poorer amongst them.

Post-graduate Courses and Research Centres in India and Abroad

Proper provision should be made both by State and the Central Governments for training students of all backward classes in post-graduate courses and in research centres both in India and in other countries.

Adult Education

For the better interests of the backward classes, the scheme of social education should be expanded to cover the whole country, priority being given to those regions where the standard of literacy is very low.

Reading Rooms and Libraries in Rural Areas

In villages, reading rooms and libraries in rural areas should be established and a judicious selection of books made for rural libraries. Important periodicals should be read out in those reading rooms to keep the people in touch with the day-to-day happenings in the country. Also, seminal books should be read out before serious adults and described to them.

All India Institutions for Higher Learning

For the purpose of achieving speedy educational advancement of the backward classes and to create new conditions to root out casteism and regional and linguistic tendencies, special residential institutions of the university grade should be established in various states to inculcate an all-India outlook among the students. These institutions should be manned by professors and lecturers of learning and patriotism. The courses of studies should be suitably set. The medium of instruction should be Hindi but one or two original languages must also be taught. Professors and students drawn from various parts of the country and from all communities should live, study and work in common. Government should spend all money on basic education and only where basic schools cannot be opened for want of teachers money may be spent on orthodox education.

Facilities for Advanced Studies Abroad

Our Government should make necessary provision for award of various scholarships to backward class students.

Scheme of Scholarships in States

1. Provisions for freeships and scholarships should be introduced in all the States for the benefit of students belonging to other backward classes. State Governments should make required provision in their budgets for the purpose.
2. While awarding scholarships the claims of all communities among the backward classes should be taken into consideration and the allotment in the first instance should be on the grounds of population of various communities

in a state, preference being given always to those who are extremely backward, viz., starred communities in the lists made by the Commission.

3. These small committees which consist of representatives of various communities should be constituted for various grades of scholarships in each state to assist the educational authorities to select deserving candidates from among all communities for purposes of award.
4. Annual income of the parents of a student applying for a scholarship should not exceed Rs. 1,800 to enable him to get a scholarship up to the secondary course.
5. For education abroad, the income of the parents of a student should not go beyond Rs. 3,600 per annum for getting a scholarship.

Reservation of Seats in Science, Medicine, Engineering, Agriculture, Veterinary and Other Technical and Technological Institutions of Higher Learning

1. For science, engineering, medicine, agriculture, veterinary and other technical and technological institutions, a reservation of seventy per cent of seats should be made for deserving students of backward classes till such time as accommodation is provided for all the students eligible for admission. The remaining thirty per cent as also all seats unavailed of by backward classes should go to the rest of the students.
2. While making selection to the reserved quota of seats, qualified candidates from extremely backward classes should be taken into consideration first, and while making distribution, the principle of favouring the lower of the two claimants among the candidates from the various communities should be followed.
3. One Selection Committee consisting of some of the representative of all communities (not necessarily of the backward alone) should be set up to help the educational authorities in the selection of deserving candidates.

Representation of OBCs in Government Service — Central and States

1. Status, prestige, power and influence, scales of pay, security of employment and scope to distribute patronage—all these have made government service attractive. So long as it continues to be so, claims of OBCs for proper representation in the service should be recognised by providing reservation of definite quota of vacancies in each class.
2. For reducing the keen desire for government services on the part of the OBCs, one way is to render them as unattractive as possible by decreasing the emoluments attached to them. Social justice and communal harmony both demand that the present alarming inequality between the scales of pay of the lowest and the highest appointments should be reduced. As an immediate step, the ratio between the emoluments of the lowest and those of the highest paid persons may be decreased to 1:20. But this ratio may be ultimately brought down to 1:10.
3. Considering the necessity for maintaining high administrative efficiency in conjunction with social justice to all sections of the population, best candidates should, as per rule, be recruited by means of a competitive examination without any regard to caste considerations.
4. In the sector of reservation, the best amongst the qualified backward classes should be recruited. The method of recruitment to this sector could be either by personal interview and nomination or by general competition. In the latter case the selection should be confined to the best among those satisfying the required standard in the examination despite their lower ranks in the general list.
5. The procedure of recruitment is of any type, whether through selection after personal interview or by limited competition amongst the candidates of backward communities, the reservation specified must be kept safe in favour of candidates of the OBC group. Strict adherence to rules of recruitment, with a severe penalty for any breach thereof, would be the best remedy.

6. The interest of the State, the efficiency and the running of the administrative machinery and the increasing role of welfare which the administrative services have to perform in relation to the masses of the country—all these demand that reservation should, where education is on the high among the communities, be in proportion to the population of the communities of the other backward classes. Taking all these factors into consideration the conclusion made by a majority of the members of the Commission is that in all government and local body service, the minimum basis of representation of OBCs should be as follows:
   (a) Class I : 25 per cent of vacancies;
   (b) Class II : 33-1/3 per cent of vacancies;
   (c) Class III : 40 per cent of vacancies;
   (d) Class IV : 40 per cent of vacancies.

   The above percentage would be over and above that which has already been conceded by Government in the case of Scheduled Castes and Scheduled Tribes.
7. By the competition of 10 years the adequacy of representation of OBCs should be reviewed in the light of the statistics then available as a result of the 1961 or earlier census which may contain all communities listed by the Commission in the OBCs group.
8. To fulfil the objective of distribution of the reserved quota of posts among all the communities comprising the OBCs no hard and fast rule need be followed. The circumstances and the social conditions prevailing in the country require greater consideration for the most backward and unrepresented communities in the group. Some system of rotation worked out in the conditions prevailing in the respective state is demanded. Communities should be conveniently grouped according to the degree of advancement in each state and representation in the reserved quota granted in the beginning with the most unrepresented groups. This method need be followed for all time. After a period of 15 years the position should be reviewed.
9. At the time of recognising the desirability of selecting the best qualified candidates in technical services, the OBCs should be increasing given facilities in educational and more especially in technical institutions. It should be the

clear policy for many years to come that, qualifications being fairly equal, preference should be given to a candidate from among the backward communities.

10. Where there training is needed to impose efficiency among the candidates belonging to backward classes after selection to various posts, they should be provided training for a year or two during the period of probation.
11. In the selection of members for Public Service Commission appointments from among the members of backward classes should carry on as liberal a scale as possible. Caste or community consideration should have no place whatsoever in making the selection. Merit should be the sole criterion.
12. A small body of trained and experienced administrators and social workers should be formed with sufficient powers to enforce full and proper implementation of the policy for recruitment to government service and also to handle any complaints from non-backward classes in the unreserved sector of employment under government service. The precise powers and functions of the Body should be carefully worked out by Government.

Ministry for the Advancement of Backward Classes

1. One special Ministry should be created both at the Centre and in the states similar to the Ministry of Rehabilitation to handle in an effective manner the problems of the upliftment of backward classes and also to prevent anti-social elements from fostering disruptive tendencies among the backward classes by exploiting satisfaction among them.
2. This new Ministry should have sufficient powers to co-ordinate ameliorative measures and welfare work done through different agencies in the various states. Especially, the following should be its special functions:—
   (a) all educational problems;
   (b) rural housing schemes;
   (c) representation in services under government and local bodies;
   (d) administration of grants for welfare measures;
   (e) provision of full employment in rural areas;

(f) drawing up schemes for the advancement of backward classes;

(g) provision of adequate finances for implementation.

3. Another department consisting of distinct sections, each administering separately the affairs of scheduled castes, scheduled tribes and other backward classes should be formed under the new Ministry. Sanctioning of schemes, allotment of funds, coordination of work, training of personnel, etc. would be the main activities of the Department. Funds should be separately earmarked for each of the three categories of the backward classes, namely SCs, STs and OBCs and the expenditure should also be separately debited.
4. Constitution of an Advisory Board

(a) An Advisory Board both at the Centre and in each state to assist the Ministry in the administration of welfare measures should also be established.

(b) Major questions of policy and specific schemes for uplift should be placed before this Board for eliciting opinion.

(c) The powers and functions of the Board should be worked out in detail by the Government of India.

Grants

A statement containing a summary of the recommendations in respect of financial grants required to give effect to various ameliorative measures has been attached at the end of Chapter VIII of the Report....

Conclusion

As is seen in the recommendation, it incorporated suggestions for almost all the backward sections. But due to certain reasons, as mentioned previously, the recommendations could not be implemented. But the biggest contribution and achievement of this was that it opened doors for organised efforts for amelioration of the backward classes.

State-wise list of backward classes prepared by Kaka Kalelkar Commission has been rearranged alphabetically showing their presence in various states is given at Appendix-II.

Four

Mandal Commission

The Congress Party ruled the country for more than twenty five years after the Constitution of India came into existence on 26th January, 1950. During this period the Congress Government at Center appointed the First Commission for Backward Classes, the report of which was not accepted by them having absolute majority in both houses of the Parliament. Both Prime Minister Shri Jawahar Lal Nehru and Smt. Indira Gandhi were powerful leaders but they realised and felt pulse and heat of the public and kept the report in cold storage. After emergency era was over the Janta Party, first non-congress government came into power at centre. During the Janata Party rule, on 20th December, 1978, the then Prime Minister, Mr. Morarji Desai in Parliament announced the decision to appoint a commission for the Backward Classes under the chairmanship of B.P. Mandal. Accordingly, in exercise of the powers conferred by Article 340 of the Constitution, the President of India appointed a Commission for the Backward Classes to investigate the conditions of socially and educationally backward classes within the territory of India.

The composition of the Commission was as follows:

1. B.P. Mandal (Ex-MP) Chairman
2. R.R. Bhole, M.P. Member
3. L.R. Naik (Ex-MP) Member
4. Dewan Mohan Lal Member
5. K. Subramanium Member
6. S.S. Gill Secretary

The Chairman and the members appointed on part-time basis and worked in an honorary capacity. The terms of reference of the Commission were:—

* This chapter is based on Government of India Report of the Backward Classes Commission, 1980, First Part.

(i) to determine the criteria for defining the socially and educationally backward classes;

(ii) to recommend steps to be taken for the advancement of the socially and educationally backward classes of citizens so identified;

(iii) to examine the desirability or otherwise of making provisions for the reservation of appointments or posts in favour of such backward classes of citizens which are not adequately represented in public services and posts in connection with the affairs of the Union or of any state; and

(iv) present to the President a report setting out the facts as found by them and making such recommendations as they think proper.

In this connection, the Commission were also to examine the recommendations of the Backward Classes Commission appointed earlier under the Chairmanship of Kaka Kalelkar and the considerations which stood in the way of the acceptance of its recommendations by Government.

Methodology of Investigation and Data Base

One important reason as to why the Central Government could not accept the recommendations of Kaka Kalelkar Commission was that it had not worked out objective tests and criteria for the proper classification of socially and educationally backward classes. In several petitions filed against reservation order issued by some State Governments the Supreme Court and various High Courts also emphasised the imperative need for an empirical approach to the defining of social and educational backwardness or identification of other Backward Classes. Chapter III Methodology and Data Base of Government of India Report of the Backward Classes Commission (First part, volume I and II, 1980, pp. 12-13) gives details Methodology followed by the Commission. The commission developed different sets of questionnaire for collection of information from state government, central ministries, departments,general public, voluntary organisations. The members of the commission extensively toured states and collected oral evidence from public there. The research planning team of the cpmmission extended their assistance to the commission for determining in a scientific and objjective criteria for defining the socially and educationally backward classes.

To overcome the deficiencies pointed out earlier, the commission associated a team of expert social scientists.

Criteria for Social and Educational Backwardness

As a result of the above exercise, the Commission evolved eleven indicators or criteria for determining social and educational backwardness. These 11 indicators were grouped under three broad heads, i.e., social, educational, and economical. These are as follows:

A. Social

(i) Castes/Classes considered as socially backward by others.

(ii) Castes/Classes which mainly depend on manual labour for their livelihood.

(iii) Castes/Classes where at least 25 per cent females and 10 per cent males above the State average got married at an age below 17 years in rural areas and at least 10 per cent females and 5 per cent males do so in urban areas.

(iv) Castes/Classes where participation of females in work is at least 25 per cent above the State average.

B. Education

(v) Castes/Classes where the number of children in the age group of 5-25 years who never attended school is at least 25 per cent above the State average.

(vi) Castes/Classes where the rate of student dropout in the age group of 5-15 years is at least 25 per cent above the State average.

(vii) Castes/Classes amongst whom the proportion of matriculates is at least 25 per cent below the State average.

C. Economic

(viii) Castes/Classes where the average value of family assets is at least 25 per cent below the State average.

(ix) Castes/Classes where the number of families living in Kutcha house is at least 25 per cent above the State average.

(x) Castes/Classes where the source of drinking water is beyond half a kilometre for more than 50 per cent of the households.

(xi) Castes/Classes where the number of households having taken consumption loan is at least 25 per cent above the State average.

As the above three groups are not of equal importance for the purpose separate weightage was given to indicators in each group. As the social indicators were given a weightage of 3 points each, educational indicators a weightage of 2 points each and economic indicators a weightage of 1 point each. Economic, in addition to social and educational indicators, were considered important as they directly flowed from social and educational backwardness. This also helped to highlights the fact that socially and educationally backward classes are economically backward also.

It will be seen that from the values given to each indicator, the total score adds up to 22. All these 11 indicators were applied to all the castes covered by the survey for a particular State. As a result of this application all castes which had a score of 50 per cent (11 points) for above were listed as socially and educationally backward and the rest were treated as advanced. Further, in case the number of households covered by the survey for any particular caste were below 20, it was left out of consideration, as the sample was considered too small for any dependable inference.

The above system of listing castes as socially and educationally backward on the basis of their score may appear somewhat arbitrary. On the face of it this is a tangible viewpoint. On the other hand, the points scored by a particular caste under the above system actually reflects the number of indicators of backwardness which it satisfies. Secondly, this method has the great merit of objectivity as point system allow no subjective assessment. Thirdly, this method was found to be highly dependable in practice. For instance, as a result of its application, most of the well-known socially and educationally backward castes were identified as backward.

Recommendations of the Commission

The Commission recommended the various welfare measures for these castes listed as socially and educationally backward. These were:

Reservations

Provision of reservation in government services and educational institutions for the candidates of OBCs will certainly snatch away share of forward caste people who were enjoying benefits so far. Reservation as a policy and as a right are two different issues to be examined objectively. It was generally argued that looking to the large population of OBCs (52 per cent) recruitment of a few thousand OBCs every year against reserved vacancies is not going to produce any perceptible change of their overall general condition. On the other hand, the induction of a large proportion of employees against reserved vacancies will considerably impair the quality and efficiency of the government services. This is against merit or anti-meritarian.

It is not at all the contention that by offering a few thousand jobs to OBCs candidates it shall be possible to bring 52 per cent of the Indian population as forward. Here we must recognise that an essential part of the battle against social backwardness is to be fought in the thinking of the backward people. In India, government service has always been looked upon as a symbol of prestige and power. By increasing the representation of OBCs in government services, we give them an immediate feeling of participation in the governance of this country. When a backward class candidate becomes a Collector or a Superintendent of Police, the material benefits accruing from his position are limited to the members of his family only. But the psychological spinoff of this phenomenon is tremendous because the entire community of that backward class candidate feels elevated. Even when no tangible benefits flow to the community at large, the feeling that now it has its own man in the corridors of power acts as a morale booster. But then the question does arise can we change power structure. No, if not then we can uplift them by way of providing education, economic assistance, etc. How many OBCs families or SCs and STs have given up their traditional occupation in last two or three generations. Caste barrier will continie to exist.

In a democratic setup every individual and community has the legitimate right and aspiration to participate in ruling the country. Any situation which results in a near denial of this right to nearly 52 per cent of the country's populations needs to be urgently rectified. (See Table 1 and 2).

Apprehensions regarding drop in the quality of government services owing to large scale inclusion of SC/ST and OBC candidates against reserved posts may be justified only up to a point. But it is possible to maintain that all candidates selected on merit turn out to be honest, efficient, hardworking and dedicated. At present, top echelons of all the government services are manned predominantly by open competition candidates and if the performance of our bureaucracy is any indication, it has not exactly covered itself with glory. Of course, this does not imply that candidates selected against reserved posts will do any better. The chances are that owing to their social and cultural handicaps they may generally be a shade less competent. But otherwise they would have the great advantage of possessing firsthand knowledge of the suffering and problems of the backward sections of society. This is not a small asset for field workers and policy-makers even at the highest level. (See Table 3).

It is no doubt that true that the major benefits of reservations and other welfare measures for OBCs will be cornered by the more advanced sections of the backward communities. But this a universal phenomenon? All reformist remedies have to contend with a slow recovery along the hierarchical gradient, there are no quantum jumps in social reform. Moreover, human nature being what it is, a new class ultimately does emerge even in classless societies. The chief merit of reservation is not that it will introduce egalitarianism amongst OBCs when the rest of the Indian society is seized by all sorts of inequalities. But reservation will certainly erode the hold of higher castes on the services and enable OBCs in general to have a sense of participation in the running of the affairs of their country. Benefits of reservation reaches to only those who have got, not who have not got so far.

Quantum and the Scheme of Reservation

Population of OBCs, both Hindu and non-Hindu, is around 52 per cent of the total population of India. Theoretically, 52 per cent of all posts under the Central Government should be reserved for them. But this provision may go against the law laid down in a number of Supreme Court judgements wherein it has been held that the total quantum of reservation under Articles 15(4) and 16(4) of the Constitution should be below 50 per cent. In view of this the proposed reservation for OBCs would have to be pegged at a figure which, when added to 22.5 per cent for SCs and STs remains below 50 per cent. In view of this legal constraint, the Commission is obliged to recommend a reservation of 27 per cent to them only, even though their population is almost twice this figure.

The States which have already introduced reservation for OBCs exceeding 27 per cent will remain unaffected by this recommendation. With the above general recommendations regarding the quantum of reservation, the Commission proposes the following overall scheme of reservation for OBCs:

(i) Candidates belonging to OBCs recruited on the basis of merit in an open competition should not be adjusted against their reservation quota of 27 per cent.

(ii) The above recommended reservation should also be made applicable to promotion quota at all level.

(iii) Reserved quota remaining unfilled should be carried forward for a period of three years and dereserved thereafter.

(iv) Relaxation in the upper age limit for direct recruitment should be extended to the candidates of OBCs in the same manner as is done in the case of SCs and STs.

(v) A roster system for each categories of posts should be adopted by the concerned authorities in the same manner as is presently done in respect of SC and ST candidates.

The above scheme of reservation in toto should be made applicable to all recruitments to public sector undertakings both under the Central and State Governments, as also to nationalised banks.

All private sector undertakings which have received financial assistance from the government in one form or the other also be obliged to recruit personnel on the aforesaid basis.

All universities and affiliated colleges should also be covered by the above recommended scheme of reservations.

To give proper effect to these recommendations, it is imperative that adequate statutory provisions are made by the government to amend the enactments, rules, procedures, etc. to the extent that they are not in consonance with the same.

Educational Concessions

Various State Governments are giving a number of educational concessions to OBC students like exemption of tuition fees, free supply of books and clothes, mid-day meals, special hostel facilities, stipends, etc. The concessions are all right as far as they go. But they do not go far enough. What is required perhaps is not so much the provision of additional funds as the framing of integrated schemes for creating proper environment and incentives for serious and purposeful studies.

It is a well known fact that most backward class children are irregular and indifferent students and their drop-out rate is very high. There are two main reasons for it. Firstly, these children are brought up in a climate of extreme social and cultural deprivation and, consequently, proper motivation for schooling is generally lacking. Secondly, most of these children come from very poor houses and their parents are forced to press them into doing small chores from a very young age.

An intensive and time-bound programme for adult education should be launched in select pockets that have high concentration of OBC population. This is basically a motivational approach, as only properly motivated parents will take serious interest in educating their children. Secondly, residential schools should be set up for backward class students in these areas to provide a climate specially conducive to serious studies. All facilities in these schools including boarding and lodging should be provided free of cost to attract students from poor and backward homes. Separate government hostels for OBC students with the above facilities will be another step in the right direction.

After all education is the best catalyst of change and educating the backward classes is the surest way to improve their self-image and raise their social status. As OBCs cannot afford the high wastage rates of our educational system, it is very important that their education is highly biased in favour of vocational training. After all reservation in services will absorb only a very small percentage of the educated backward classes and the rest should be suitably equipped with vocational skills to enable them to get a return on having invested several years in education.

It is also obvious that even if all the above facilities are given to OBC students, they will not fully be able to compete on an equal footing with others in securing admission to technical and professional institutions. In view of this it is recommended that seats should be reserved for OBC students in all scientific, technical and professional institutions run by the Central as well as State Governments. This reservation will fall under Article 15(4) of the Constitution and the quantum of reservation should be the same as in the government services, i.e., 27 per cent. Those States which have already reserved more than 27 per cent seats for OBC students will remain unaffected by this recommendation.

While implementing the provision of reservation it should also be ensured that the candidates who are admitted against the reserved quota are enabled to derive full benefit of higher studies. It has been generally noticed that those OBC students who come from an impoverished cultural background are not able to keep abreast of studies in comparison with other students. It is, therefore, very essential that special coaching facilities be arranged for all such students in our technical and professional institutions. The concerned authorities should clearly appreciate that their job is not finished once candidates against reserved quota have been admitted to various institutions. In fact, the real task starts only after it. Unless adequate follow-up action is taken to give special coaching assistance to these students, not only would these young people feel frustrated and humiliated but the country will also be handed with ill-equipped and substandard engineers, doctors, and other professionals.

Financial Assistance

Vocational communities following hereditary occupations have suffered heavily as a result of institutionalisation. Mechanical production and introduction of synthetic materials has robbed the village potter, oil crusher, blacksmith, carpenter, etc. of their traditional means of livelihood and the pauperization of these classes is a well-known phenomenon in the countryside.

It has, therefore, become very necessary that suitable institutional finance and technical assistance is made available to such members of village vocational communities who want to set up small scale industries of their own. Similar assistance should also be provided to those promising OBC candidates who have obtained special vocational training.

Of course, most State Governments have created various financial and technical agencies for the promotion of small and medium scale industries. But it is well-known that only the more influential members of the community are able to derive benefits from these agencies. In view of this, it is very essential that different financial institutions provide financial and technical assistance to backward classes. Some State Governments like Karnataka and Andhra Pradesh have already set up separate financial corporations for OBCs.

Cooperative societies and occupational groups would also help a lot. But due care should be taken that all the office-bearers and members of such societies belong to the concerned hereditary occupational groups and outsiders are not allowed to exploit by infiltrating into such cooperatives.

The share of OBCs in the industrial and business life of the country is negligible and this partly explains their extremely low income levels. As a part of its overall strategy to uplift the backward classes, it is imperative that all State Governments are suitably devised and encouraged to create a separate network of financial and technical institutions to foster business and industrial enterprise among OBCs.

Structural Changes

Reservations in government employment and educational institutions, as also all possible financial assistance will remain mere palliatives unless the problem of backwardness is tackled at its root. The bulk of the small landholders, tenants, agricultural labour, impoverished village artisans, unskilled workers, etc. belong to SCs, STs and OBCs. Apart from social traditions, the dominance by the top peasantry is exercised through recourse to informal bondage which arises mainly through money-lending, leasing out of small bits of land and providing housesites and dwelling space to poor peasants. As most of the functionaries of government are drawn from the top peasantry these practices endure. It also tilts the socio-political balance in favour of the top peasantry and helps it in maintaining its dominance over the lesser beings.

It is the Commission's firm conviction that a radical transformation of the existing production relations is the most important single step that can be taken for the welfare and uplift of all backward classes. Even if this is not possible in the industrial sector for various reasons, in the agricultural sector a change of this nature is both feasible and overdue.

The Commission, therefore, strongly recommends that all the State Governments should be directed to enact and implement progressive land legislation so as to effect basic structural changes in the existing production relations countrywide.

A present surplus land is being allotted to SCs and STs. A part of the surplus land becoming available in future as a result of the operation of land ceiling loans, etc. should also be allotted to the OBC landless labour.

Some Important Miscellaneous Recommendations

(1) Backward Classes Development Corporations should be set up both at the Central and State levels to implement

various socio-educational and economic measures for their advancement.

(2) A separate Ministry/Department for OBCs at the Centre and the States should be created to safeguard their interests.

Central Assistance

At present no Central assistance is available to any State Government for implementing any measures to OBCs. The 18 States and Union Territories which have undertaken such measures have to provide funds from their own resources. During the Commission's tours practically every State Government pointed out that unless the Centre is prepared to liberally finance all special schemes for the uplift of OBCs, it would be beyond the available resources of the States to undertake any worthwhile programme for the benefit of OBCs.

The Commission fully shares the views of the State Governments in this matter and strongly recommends that all development programmes specially designed for OBCs should be financed by the Central Government if not fully, at least in part in the same manner and to the same extent as is done in the case of SCs and STs.

Regarding the period of operation of the Commission's recommendations, the entire scheme should be reviewed after twenty years. It was suggested this span of one generation, as the raising of social consciousness is a generational progress. Any review at a shorter interval would be rather arbitrary and would not give a fair indication of the impact of the recommendations on the prevailing status and lifestyles of OBCs.

Consequences and Aftermath of the Mandal Report

B.K. Roy Burman (1992) was associated as an expert social science member in the Second Backward Classes Commission headed by B.P. Mandal. He critically reviewed the report. He found many deficiencies in the report. Some of which are listed here:

(i) The Mandal Commission did not make any analysis of

the social and political process in the Indian Society and the Indian state, which stood in the way of acceptance of Kalelkar Commission's recommendations by the Central Government in the matter of recognition of SEBC's on the basis of caste.

(ii) He found that the commission compared facts with incomparable facts. For example, the practice of recording the caste in service had been discontinued by 1951. Then, level of education achieved by father or grandfather of the respondent was not recorded. Then how was it possible for the commission to arrive at the conclusion that the particular employee in service belonged to socially and educationally backward and included in the category of OBCs.

(iii) The commissions claim of scrutiny of village monographs have been reputed by Kalla (1990) of Deptt. of Anthropology, University of Delhi, Delhi on the ground that there was no such monograph as mentioned in the Report.

Without any doubt, acceptance of the Mandal Commission recommendation of 27 per cent reservation of jobs in the Central Government and public undertakings for the backward castes is impossible to give peace to any government at the Centre. Job reservation is bound to create a host of problems continually. Some of them would be: (1) To qualify for the 'backward caste' concessions, the government may require a certificate, which is not very difficult to obtain. (2) The Mandal Commission has categorised as many as 3,743 castes as backward in contrast to 2,399 identified by the Kalelkar Commission (1953). Despite this dose of extravagant generosity, more and more castes would clamour for inclusion in the beneficiaries' list, and this would generate unending clash in society. (3) As the backward castes themselves are not homogeneous socially, economically and educationally, most jobs would inevitably be hogged by a few castes — more accurately the elite among the better placed. A demand for fixation of sub-quotas for each caste or cluster of backward castes is likely to be made under the name of true social justice.

Our own stands are self-contradictory, in 1947, we acquired for ourselves a nation called India the colonial clutches. Since then, the challenge has been to make Indians out of us — who are basically Punjabis, Bangalees, Gujaratis, or Brahmins, Thakurs, Jats, Yadavs, Reddys, Khammas, etc. Mandalisation and Indianness cannot get alongwith each other: the former is a centrifugal force while the latter is centripetal. It has been said that an important event tends to repeat itself — first as a tragedy, and next as a farce. The tragedy has happened before our eyes. The farce may yet come. Just as 'backward' countries became 'developing' nations, the 'backward' castes may demand to be called 'developing' castes. They may also find out an 'arch-saint' for themselves, in the form of Kanshi Ram, the president of the Bahujan Samaj Party, Ram Vilas Paswan or Sharad Yadav. A demand may be made to honour B.P. Mandal with award like Bharat Ratna and his birth anniversary may be celebrated as a national holiday but to what extent that may be justified is a question before us.

Societal Concerns

It is wise not to recall any public issue which has aroused so much social controversy, bordering on acrimony, as the Mandal scheme of reservation in employment has done. The Mandal Report has vertically divided the society in India, and the cleavages may not be adhoc. The issue is about the extent to which a government in a democracy could go in the issue of making public policies. Democracy implies a level of sensitivity to the other views even though the task of governance is assigned to a particular party based on majority, or to any minority in a minority government. Democracy has its boundaries, which set a fixed limit to the rulers' options and choice. A government elected for a five-year term has little moral right to fetter and handicap society indefinitely with its myopic actions. Society will have to find out ways of obliging a government to evolve and internalise norms of understanding politeness and circumspection. Curbing the arrogance and obstinacy of the political leader is a major problem for society. One more issue demanding attention. Political parties emerged as ideologically motivated entities but with the passage of time they have been becoming merely organisations for contesting elections with the eye wholly set on winning at the hustings, thus giving a short shrift to ideology or long range interests of society. Today, a political party speaks with a stringed tongue, saying different things at different times to please different groups. All parties resort to populist measures; and in the process ignore nation-building tasks, which are not necessarily populist, more so in a fragmentation-oriented polity like ours.

In principle, job reservation — a denial and negation of merit is indefensible. But when the agitation against the Mandal Report started, no political party was prepared to protest against it openly and directly for fear of alienating the vote banks. The question arises: What is the true role of a political party? Only to be populist and self-serving at the cost of the nation's welfare and survival? Now is the time for the nation to think about proper checks and balances on the political parties of the land as well.

State-wise list prepared by the Mandal Commission has been rearranged alphabetically showing presence of castes in States and is given at Appendix-3.

TABLE 1

PERCENTAGE DISTRIBUTION OF INDIAN POPULATION BY CASTE AND RELIGIOUS GROUPS (1971)

		Name of the group/category	*%age of Total Population*
(I)		Scheduled Castes and Scheduled Tribes	
	A-1	Scheduled Castes	15.05
	A-2	Scheduled Tribes	7.51
		Total of 'A'	22.56
(II)		Non-Hindu Communities, Religious Groups, etc.	
	B-1	Muslims (other than STs)	11.09 (0.02)+
	B-2	Christians (other than STs)	2.16 (0.44)+
	B-3	Sikhs (other than SCs and STs)	1.67 (0.22)+
	B-4	Buddhists (other than STs)	0.67 (0.03)+
	B-5	Jains	0.47
		Total of B'	16.16
(III)		Forward Hindu Castes and Communities	
	C-1	Brahmins (including Bhumihars)	5.52
	C-2	Rajputs	3.90
	C-3	Marathas	2.21
	C-4	Jats	1.00
	C-5	Vaishyas-Bania etc.	1.88
	C-6	Kayasthas	1.07
	C-7	Other forward Hindu castes/groups	2.00
		Total of 'C'	17.58
		Total of 'A', 'B', and 'C'	56.30
(IV)		Backward Hindu Castes and Communities	
	D.	Remaining Hindu castes/groups which come in the category of OBCs	43.70@
(V)		Backward Non-Hindu Communities	
	E.	52 per cent of religious groups under section 'B' may also be treated as OBCs	8.40
	F.	The approximate derived population of other backward classes including non-Hindu communities (Aggregate of D&E rounded).	52%

N.B. It is proposed to divide the population percentage of OBCs mentioned in serials 'D' and 'E' into—
(a) percentage of population of Intermediate Backward Classes
(b) percentage of population of the Depressed Backward Classes

(VI)	'Intermediate Backward Classes' including Non-Hindu Communities	
G-1	Land owner and cultivating castes and communities excluding Marathas and Jats	6.40
G-2	Marketing Gardners	2.06
G-3	Pastoral Castes excluding shepherds Artisans, viz:	2.50
G-4	(a) Vishwakarma	2.10
G-5	(b) Tailors & Dyers	0.18
G-6	(c) Weavers	1.40
G-7	(d) Potters	1.10
G-8	Petty Business-cum-Agricultural Castes	0.50
G-9	Oil Mongers	1.40
G-10	Cmbatants other than Rajputs	1.80
G-11	Heralders	0.10
G-12	Temple servants and Astrologers	0.10
G-13	Non-Hindu communities excluding scavengers, Muslim ex-criminal tribes, Muslim Nomadic tribes and Muslim Shepherds	6.80
	Total og 'G'	26.44
H.	Percentage population of 'Intermediatary Backward Classes + Backward Non-Hindu Communities	26.44
I.	Percentage of population of Depressed Backward classes, i.e., 'F' minus 'H'	20.56@

Source: Government of India Report of the Backward Classes Commission, Second Part 1980, Annexure I, p. 235.

\+ Figures in brackets give the population of SC/ST among these non-Hindu communities.

@ This is a derived figure.

TABLE 2
STATE-WISE BREAK-UP OF NO. OF THE OBCS AND DEPRESSED BACKWARD CLASSES

States	*No. of castes listed as OBCs*	*No. of Depressed Backward Classes*
1. Andhra Pradesh	292	155
2. Assam	135	96
3. Bihar	168	97
4. Gujarat	105	61
5. Haryana	76	40
6. Himachal Pradesh	57	35
7. Jammu & Kashmir	63	40
8. Karnataka	333	204
9. Kerala	208	128
10. Madhya Pradesh	279	160
11. Maharashtra	272	164
12. Manipur	49	35
13. Meghalaya	37	13
14. Nagaland	—	—
15. Orissa	224	181
16. Punjab	83	34
17. Rajasthan	140	85
18. Sikkim	10	10
19. Tamil Nadu	288	*171
20. Tripura	136	76
21. Uttar Pradesh	116	67
22. West Bengal	177	113
23. Andaman & Nicobar Islands	17	8
24. Arunachal Pradesh	10	6
25. Chandigarh	93	54
26. Dadra & Nagar Haveli	10	12
27. Delhi	82	40
28. Goa	18	18
29. Lakshadweep	—	—
30. Mizoram	5	5
31. Pondicherry	260	
Total	3743	2108

Source: Government of India Report of the Backward Classes Commission (Second Part, Vol. VI), 1980, pp. 173-226 and Annexure II, pp. 239-274.

* Including Pondicherry.

TABLE 3

REPRESENTATION OF OTHER BACKWARD CLASSES, SCHEDULED CASTES/SCHEDULED TRIBES IN THE SERVICE OF CENTRAL GOVERNMENT SERVICES

	Class I			*Class II*			*Class III & IV*			*All Classes (Consolidated)*		
Concerns	*Total*	*SCs/STs*	*OBCs*	*Total*	*SCs/STs*	*OBCs*	*Total*	*SCs/STs*	*OBCs*	*Total*	*SCs/STs*	*OBCs*
Govt. Ministries/ Departments	11707	840 (7.18%)	303	43803 (2.59%)	5985 (13.66%)	1742 (3.98%)	17829	5518 (30.95%)	1500 (8.41%)	73339	12313 (16.83%)	3545 (4.83%)
Autonomous Bodies, Attached and Subordinate Offices	81325	5399 (6.64%)	4147 (5.09%)	503337	91431 (18.16%)	59079 (11.74%)	322948	67118 (20.78%)	67786 (20.98%)	907610	163948 (18.06%)	13101 (14.43%)
Public Sector Undertakings	80994	3652 (4.51%)	3719 (4.59%)	365785	68566 (18.74%)	36242 (9.91%)	143910	45646 (31.72%)	22689 (15.77%)	590689	117864 (19.95%)	62650 (10.61%)
Total	174026	9891 (5.68%)	8169 (4.69%)	912925	165982 (18.18%)	97063 (10.63%)	484687	118282 (24.10%)	91975 (18.98%)	1571638	294155 (18.72%)	19720 (12.55%)

Source: Government of India Report of the Backward Classes Commission, New Delhi, 1980, First Part (Vol. I to II), Appendix VIII, Statement No. 1, p. 92.

Appendix-I

State-wise State OBC List

ANDHRA PRADESH

Group 'A'

Aboriginal tribes Vimuktha Jathis Nomadic and Semi Nomadic tribes, etc.

1. Agnikulakshatriya, Palli, Vadabalija, Bestha, Jalari, Gangavar, Gangaputra, Goondla, Vanyakula-Kshatriya (vannekapu, Vannereddi, Pallikapu, Pallireddi, Neyyala and Pattapu)
2. Balasanthu, Bahurupi
3. Bandara
4. Budabukkala
5. Rajaka (Chakalivannar)
6. Dasari (formerly engaged in Bikshatana) (amended vide G.O.Rt.L. No. 32, BCW (MI) Dept., dated 23.2.1995
7. Dommara
8. Gangireddlavaru
9. Jangam, whose traditional occupation is Begging
10. Jogi
11. Kalipapala
12. Korcha
13. (Lambada or Banjara in Telangana area (deleted and included in S.Ts list) vide G.O.Ms No.149, S.W., dt. 3.5.1978)
14. Medari or Mahendra
15. Mondivaru, Mondibanda, Banda
16. Nayee Brahmin (Mangali), Mangala and Bajantri (amended vide G.O.Ms. No.1 BCW (MI) Dept., dated 6.1.1996)
17. Nakkala
18. Vamsharaj (amended vide G.O.Ms. No. 27 BCW (MI) Dept. dated 23.6.1995)
19. Pamula
20. Pardhi (Mirshikari)
21. Pambala
22. Peddammavandlu, Devaravandlu, Yellammavandlu, Mutyalammavandlu
23. Veeramusthi (Nettikotala), Veerabhadreeya, (amended vide G.O.Ms. No. 62, BCW (MI) Dept., dated 10.12.1996.
24. Valmiki, Boya (Boya, Bedar, Kirataka, Nishadi, Yellapi, Peddaboya) Talayari and Chunduvallu (G.O.Ms. No.124, S.W., dated 24.6.1985) Yellapl and Yellapu are one and the same (amended vide G.O.Ms. No. 61, BCW (MI) Dept. dated 5.12.1996.

25. Yerukulas in Telangana area (deleted and included in the list of S.Ts)
26. Gudala
27. Kanjara-Bhatta
28. Kalinga (Kinthala deleted vide G.O.Ms. No. 53 S.W., dated 7.3.1980).
29. Kepmare, or Reddika
30. Mondipatta
31. Nokkar
32. Pariki Muggula
33. Yata
34. Chopemari
35. Kaikadi
36. Joshinandiwalas
37. Odde (Oddilu, Vaddi, Vaddelu)
38. Mandula (Govt). Memo No. 40-VI/70-I, Edn., dated 10.2.1971)
39. Mehtar (Muslim) Govt. Memo. No. 234/VI/72-2, Edn., dt. 5-7-1972)
40. Kunapuli (Govt. Memo. No.1279/P1/74-10 E&SW dated 3-8-1975)

Group-'B'
Vocational

1. Achukatlavandlu
2. Aryakshatriya, Chittari, Giniyar, Chitrakara, Nakhas. (Muchi Telugu speaking) deleted vide G.O.Ms. No. 31, BCW (MI) Dept., dt.11.6.1996)
3. Devanga
4. Goud (Ediga, Gouda (Gamella), Kalalee Goundla, Settibalija of Visakahapatnam, East Godavari, West Godavari and Krishna Dists. and Srisayana (Segidi) (amended vide G.O.Ms. No. 16 BCW (A1) Dept., dated 19.6.1997)
5. Dudekula, Laddaf, Pinjari or Noorbash
6. Gandla, Telikula, Devatilakula (amended vide G.O.Ms. No. 13, BCW (A1) Dept., dated 20-5-1997)
7. Jandra
8. Kummara or Kulala, Salivahana (Salivahana Added vide G.O.Ms. No. 28 BCW (M1) Dept., Dated 24.6.1995)
9. Karikalabhakthulu, Kaikolan or Kaikala (Sengundam or Sengunther)
10. Karnabhakthulu
11. Kuruba or Kuruma
12. Nagavaddilu
13. Neelakanthi
14. Patkar (Khatri)
15. Perika (Perika, Balija, Puragirikshatriya)
16. Nessi or Kurni
17. Padmasali (Sali, Salivan, Pattusali, Senapathulu, Thogata Sali)
18. Srisayana (Segidi) deleted and added to Sl.No. 4 of Group B)
19. Swakulasali

21. Vishwabrahmin, Viswakarma (Ausula or Kamsali, Kammari, Kanchari, Vadla or Vadra or Vadrangi and Silpis) (Viswakarma added vide G.O.Ms. No. 59, BCW (M1) Dept., dated 6.12.1995).

Group - 'C'

Harijan Converts

1. Scheduled Castes converts to Christainity and their progeny (G.O.Ms. No. 5, S.W.Dept., dated 24.1.1981)

Group - 'D'

Other Classes

1. Agaru
2. Arekatika, Katika
3. Atagara
4. Bhatraju
5. Chippolu (Mera)
6. Gavara
7. Godaba
8. Natkar
9. Jakkala
10. Jingar
11. Kandra
12. Koshti
13. Kachi
14. Surya Balija (Kalavanthulu), Ganika (amended vide G.O.Ms. No. 20 BCW (P2) Dept., dated 19.7.1994)
15. Krishnabalija (Dasari, Bukka)
16. Koppulavelama
17. Mathura
18. Mali
19. Mudiraj, Mutrasi, Tenugollu
20. Munnurukapu (Telangana)
21. Nagavamsam (Nagavamsa) (amended vide G.O.Ms. No. 53, BCW (M1) Dept., dated 19.9.1996)
22. Nelli
23. Polinativelamas of Srikakulam and Visakhapatnam districts
24. Poosala
25. Passi
26. Rangrez or Bhavasara Kshatriya
27. Sadhuchetty
28. Satani (Chattadasrivaishnava)
29. Tammali confined to five districts of Nalgonda, Mahaboobnagar, Karimnagar, Nizamabad and Adilabad of Telangana Region only and not to other parts of A.P. (amended vide G.O.Ms. No. 29 BCW (A1) Dept., dated 21.7.1997)
30. Thurpukapus of Gajulakapus of Srikakulam and Visakhapatnam districts who are subject to social Customs of divorce and remarriages among their Women G.O.Ms. No. 65, E&SW, dt. 18.2.1974).
31. Uppara or Sagara
32. Vanjara (Vanjari)
33. Yadava (Golla)

ASSAM

1. Ahom
2. Baria
3. Baruj
4. Barjabi
5. Baroi
6. Chutia
   Chutiya
7. Cheudang
8. Ganak in Districts of Kachar Karimganj and Hailakandi
9. Ghosh
   Gop
   Gowala
   Goal
   Goala
10. Rumai, Rudra Paul of district of Cashar Karimganj and Hailakandi
11. Kupadhar
    Kushiari
    Path
12. Mahisya Das
    Mahisya
13. Manipuri including Manipuri Brahmi and Manipuri Muslim
14. Moran
    Matak
15. Mukhi
16. Napit
17. Nepali (i.e., Thapa, Gurung,
    Lama
    Gains
    Rai
    Chetri, Chatri, Chhetri
    Lihu
    Magar
    Lohar
    Dami
    Sark i.e. (Cobbler)
18. Rajbanshi
    Koch
19. Sudra Das, Dey
20. Saloi
21. Sut, Seet
22. Scheduled Caste persons converted to Christainity
23. Tantripal,
    Tanti,
    Tantri
24. Tea Garden Labourers,
    Tea Garden Tribes,
    Ex-Tea Garden Labourers
    & Ex-Tea Garden

Tribes as listed below:

1. Ahitgroala
2. Arya Mala
3. Asur
4. Barhai
5. Basphor
6. Bhokta
7. Baurl
8. Bowrl
9. Bhayan
10. Bhumij
11. Bedia
12. Beldar
13. Bharaik
14. Bhatta
15. Basor
16. Baiga
17. Baijara
18. Bhil
19. Bondo
20. Binjia
21. Birhar
22. Birjia
23. Beddi
24. Chamar
25. Chowdhari
26. Chero

27. Chick Banik
28. Dandari
29. Dandasi
30. Dusad
31. Dhanwar
32. Ganda
33. Gonda
34. Gond
35. Ghansi
36. Gorait
37. Ghatowar
38. Hari
39. Holra
40. Jolha
41. Keot
42. Koiri
43. Khonyor
44. Kurni
45. Kawar
46. Karmali
47. Korwa
48. Kol
49. Kalabandi
50. Kalihandi
51. Kotval
52. Kharia
53. Kumhar
54. Kherwar
55. Khodal
56. Khond
57. Koya
58. Kondpan
59. Kohar
60. Kormakar
61. Kashan
62. Lahar
63. Lodha
64. Lodhi
65. Madari
66. Mahli
67. Mohali
68. Modi
69. Mahato
70. Malpatharia
71. Manki
72. Majwar
73. Mirdhar
74. Munda
75. Nonia, Nunia
76. Nagasia
77. Nagbansi
78. Nath
79. Oraon
80. Pasi
81. Paidi
82. Pan
83. Panika
84. Parja
85. Patratanti
86. Pradhan
87. Rajwar
88. Sahora
89. Santhal, Santal
90. Sarvera
91. Turi
92. Telenga
93. Tassa
94. Tantubai
95. Teli
96. Tanti

25. Teli
26. Yogi, Jogi, Jugi Nath
27. Maimal (Muslim Fisherman)
28. Maria

Bihar

List-I (List of most backward classes)

1. Kapadia
2. Kanu
3. Kawar
4. Kalandar
5. Kochh

6. Kurmi (Mahto) (Jharkhand Autonomous Council)
7. Kewat (Kaut)
8. Kadar
9. Kaura
10. Korku
11. Kaibart
12. Kumar Bhag Paharia
13. Khatwa
14. (Deleted)
15. Khatouri
16. Khangar
17. Khatik
18. Khelta
19. Khatwe
20. (Deleted)
21. Gorhi (Chhabi)
22. Gangai (Nagesh)
23. Gangota
24. Gour or Gonr
25. Gandharb
26. Gulgalia
27. Gour
28. Chain
29. Chapota
30. Ghandrabansi (Kahar)
31. Tikulhar
32. Dhekaru
33. Tanti (Tatwa)
34. Tamaria
35. Turha
36. Tiar
37. Dharu
38. Dhanuk
39. Dhamin
40. Dhimar
41. Dhanwar
42. Nonia
43. Naiya
44. Nai
45. Namsudar
46. Pandu
47. Pal (Bherihar) (Gareri)
48. Pradhan
49. Pingania
50. Pahira
51. Wari
52. Beldar
53. Bind
54. (Deleted)
55. Shekhra
56. Bagdi
57. Bhuiyar
58. Bhar
59. (Deleted)
60. Bhaskar
61. Mali (Malakar)
62. Mangar
63. Madar
64. Mallah (Surhia)
65. Majhwar
66. Markandey
67. Moriyari
68. Malar (Malhor)
69. Molik
70. Rajdhobi
71. Rajbhar
72. Rangwa
73 Banpar
74. (Deleted)
75. Shota (Shota)
76. Sangatrash (for Nawadah Dist.)
77. Agaria
78. Aghouri
79. Abdal
80. Kasab (Kasai) (Muslim)
81. Chik (Muslim)
82. Dafali (Muslim)
83. Dhunia (Muslim)
84. Dhobi (Muslim)
85 Nut (Muslim)
86. Pamaria (Muslim)

87. Bhathiara (Muslim)
88. Bhat (Muslim)
89. Mehtar, Lalbegia, Halalkhor, Bhangi (Muslim)
90. Miriasia (Muslim)
91. Madari (Muslim)
92. Neershikar (Muslim)
93. Saeen (Muslim)
94. Momin (Muslim)
95. Amat
96. Churihar (Muslim)
97. Parjapati (Kumhar)
98. Raeen or Kunjara (Muslim)
99. Soyar
100. Thakurai (Muslim)
101. Nagar
102. Shershahbadi
103. Bakkho (Muslim)
104. Adarakhi
105. Chhipy
106. Tili
107. Idiris or Darzi (Muslim)
108. Saikalgar (Sikalgar) (Muslim)

Note:The caste or class where Muslims is not mentioned, take it as Hindu and Muslim both, such as Teli means both Hindu and Muslim Teli.]

List-II (List of Backward Classes)

1. (Deleted)
2. Kagji
3. Kamar (Lohar & Karmkar)
4. Kuswaha (Koiri)
5. Kosta
6. Gaddi
7. Ghatwar
8. (Deleted)
9. Chanau
10. Jadupatia
11. Jogi (Jugi)
12. Tamoli
13. Teli
14. Dewhar
15. Nalband (Muslim)
16. (Deleted)
17. Partha
18. Barhi
19. Barai
20. Bania (Sundi, Halwai, Roniar, Pansari, Modi Kasera, Kesarwani, Thathera, Kalwar, (Kalal/ Araqi) (Bihayut Kalwar),Patwa, Kamlapuri Vaishya, Sinduria Bania, Mahuri Vaishya, Awadh Bania, Bangia ,Vaishya, (Bengali Bania), Barnwal, Agrahari Vaishya, Poddar, Kasaodhan, (Gandhbanik).
21. Mukri, (Mukeri) (Muslim)
22. Yadav (Gwala, Ahir, Gora, Ghasi, Mehar Sadgope)
23. Rajbansi (Rasia or Polia)
24. Rangrej (Muslim)
25. Rautia
26. (Deleted)
27. Laheri
28. Shivhari
29. Sonar
30. Sutardhar
31. Sukriar
32. (Deleted)
33. Ishai Dharmawalambi (Harijan)
34. Ishai Dharmawalambi (Pichari Jat)
35. Kurmi (Mahto)
36. Bhat (Hindu)
37. Dangi

38. Kulhaiya

Note:The caste or class where Muslims is not mentioned, take it as Hindu and Muslim both, such as Teli means both Hindu and Muslim Teli.]

Delhi

1. Abbasi, Bhishti, Sakka
2. Agri, Kharwal, Kharol Khariwal
3. Ahir, Yadav, Gwala
4. Arain, Rayoo, Kunjra
5. Badhai, Barhai, Khati, Tarkhan Jangra-Brahmin, Vishwakarma, Porichal, Mathul-Brahmin, Dheeman, Ramgarhia-Sikh.
6. Badi
7. Bairagi
8. Bairwa, Berwa
9. Barai, Bari, Tamboli
10. Bauria/Bawria (excluding those in SCs)
11. Bazigar, Nat., Kalandar (excluding those in SCs)
12. Bharbhooja, Kanu
13. Bhat, Bhatra, Darpi, Ramiya ....
14. Bhatiara
15. Chak
16. Chippi, Tonk, Darzi, Terishi
17. Dakaut, Prade
18. Dhinwar, Jhinwar, Nishad, Kewat/Mallah (excluding those in SCs) Kashyap (Non-Brahmin), Kahar
19. Dhobi (excluding those in SCs)
20. Dhunia, Pinjara, Kandera-Karan, Dhunnewala, Naddaf, Mansoori
21. Fakir
22. Gadaria, Pal, Baghel, Dhangar, Nikhar, Kurba, Gadhori, Gaddi, Garri
23. Ghasiara, Ghosi
24. Gujar, Gurjar
25. Jogi, Goswami, Nath, Yogi, Jugi Gosain
26. Julaha-Ansari (excluding those in SCs)
27. Kachhi, Koeri, Murai, Murao, Maurya, Kush-waha, Shakya, Mahate.
28. Kasai, Qassab, Quraishi
29. Kasara, Tamara, Thathiar
30. Khatguna
31. Khatik (excluding those in SCs)
32. Kumhar, Prajapati
33. Kumri
34. Lakhera, Manihar
35. Lodhi, Lodha, Lodh, Maha-Lodh
36. Luhar, Saifi, Bhubhalia
37. Machi, Machhera
38. Mali, Saini, Southia, Sagarwan, Shimali, Nayak
39. Memar, Raj
40. Mina/Meena
41. Merasi, Miras
42. Mochi (excluding those in SCs)
43. Nai, Hajjam, Nai (Sabita), Sain, Salmani
44. Nalband
45. Naggal
46. Pakhiwara
47. Patwa
48. Pathar, Chera, Sangtarash
49. Rangrez
50. Raya-Tanwar

51. Sunar
52. Teli
53. Rai-Sikh
54. Jat

Goa

1. Kumbhar including Christian Kumbhar
2. Teli
3. Shimpi
4. Christian Mahar
5. Kalaikar/Blacksmith/Tinsmith
6. Pagui/Gabit
7. Christian Barber
8. Satarkar
9. Bhandari Naik

Gujarat

1. Agri
2. Ahir
   Ayar-Boricha
2A. Yadav
3. Bafan (Muslim)
4. Barot
   Vahivancha Charan-Gadhvi.
5. Bavcha (now ST)
6. Bavri or Baori
7. Bawa
   Atit Bawa,
   Goswami,
   Gosai,
   Dashnam Goswami,
   Ramanandi/Ramanandi Bawa/Ramanandi Sadhu.
   Puri,
   Bharti,
   Kapdi,
   Nath Bawa,
   Bharathari,
   Margi,
   Gangajalia,
   Dashnami Baws,
   Giri
8. Bhalia.
9. Bhamta,
   Pardesi Bhamta
10. Bharwad,
   Motabhai Bharwad,
   Nanabhai Bharwad
10A. Kabari Baria Motabhai,
   Chosla,
   Janpda. (where there are not ST)
11. Bhil (now ST)
12. Bhoi,
   Bhoiraj,
   Dhimar,
   Zinga-Bhoi,
   Kevat Bhoi,
   Bhanara Bhoi,
   Machhindra Bhoi,
   Palewar Bhoi,
   Kirat Bhoi,
   Kahar Bhoi,
   Pardeshi Bhoi,
   Srimali Bhoi
13. Charan, Gadhvi or Charan
13A. Bhat
14. Chhara,
   Adodia,
   Sansi
15. Chunara
16. Chuvalia Koli
17. Dabgar
18. Divecha Koli
19. Dafer (Hindu and Muslim)
20. Dhobi
21. Fakir or Faquir (Muslim)
22. Gadhai (Muslim)
23. Gadalia or Gadiluharia
23A. Luhariya/Luvaria
24. Galiara (Muslim)

25. Ganchi (Muslim)
25A. Teli,
Modh Ganchi
26. Ghedia Koli
26A. Gola-Rana
27. Hingora (Muslim)
28A. Hingora (Hindu)
28. Julaya,
Garana,
Taria and Tari (all Muslim)
29A. Julaya (Muslim)
29B. Tariya-Tai/Tariya (Muslim)
Tariya-Tai (Muslim)
30. Jat (Muslim)
31. Kaikadi
32. Kambadia Bhagat
33. Kangasia
34. Katki or Kasai,
Chamadia Khatki,
Halari Khatki (all Muslims)
35. Khatki
36. Khant
37. Kharwa-Bhadela
38. Kristi
Gujarati-Christian
(converts from SC only)
39. Koli
Idaria Koli,
Kharwa-Koli,
Rathwa-Koli,
Baria-Koli,
Dhebaria-Koli
39A. Koli-Malhar,
Koli-Mahadev or Dongar
Koli (where they are not ST)
40. Labana
Mehravat,
Goti,
Hadkashi,
Zod,
Dhinga,
Pelya,
Shatbe,
Baman
41. Lodha
42. Mir, Dadhi,
Langha. Mirasi (all Muslim)
43. Machhi (Hindu)
Kharwa,
Khalas,
Dhimar,
Dhivar,
Bitna,
Tandel,
Mangela,
Khalasi,
Sarang,
Kahar
44. Mandari,
Nath,
Bharathari,
45. Majothi Kumbar,
Darban or Darbar Majothi
(all Muslim)
46. Makrani (Muslim).
47. Matwa or Matwa-Kureshi
(Muslim),
Gavli (Hindu).
48. Me or Meta.
49. Mena (Bhil).
50. Mer
51. Miyana (Muslim)
51A. Miana. Miyana (Hindu)
52. Mochi (now SC)
Jansali,
Sivania,
Myanagar,
Jingar,
Dasania,
Chamadia
Bharatbhara,
Chandlia,
Sonara,
Aari Bharatbhara

53. Nat,
Nat-Bajania, Bajania.
Bajigar,
Natada or Bajania
54. Od
55. Padhar (now ST)
56. Padmashali-Patushali
57. Pinjara, Ganchi,
Mansuri-Pinjara (all Muslim)
57A. Mansuri (Muslim)
58. Rabari,
Bhopa,
Kodiatar
Sorathiya Rabari,
Champya
58A. Charalia,
Charmta,
Luni,
Kushar,
Tank,
Muchhal,
Kadiya Kumbhar
(where they are not S.C.)
59. Rathodia
60. Raval-Ravalia,
Jati or Raval Yogi
Raval Jati, Jagaria
60A. Padat,
Ravar,
Rawalia
61. Salat (excluding Sompura Salat)
Salat Ghera
62. Sandhi (Muslim)
62A. Sandhi (Hindu)
63. Sarania
64. Sargara
65. Shrawan
Sarwan
66. Shikligar
67. Siddi
68. Sipai, Patni Jamat or Turk Jamat. (all Muslim)
69. Talpada Koli/Tarbada Koli
70. Tankar
71. Targala,
Bhavaiya,
Nayak,
Bhojak,
72. Thakarda,
Thakore,
Patanwadia,
Dharala,
Barieya
Baria
72A. Palanwadia
73. Theba (Muslims)
74. Vadi
74A. Jogi Vadi
75. Vahivancha Charan-Gadhavi of Harijan Vankar and Chamar
76. Valand
Nayi and Barbar (Hindu)
Hajam (Hindu)
Khalipha (Muslim)
76A. Vale (Hindu)
77. Vankar/Sadhu
78. Vansfoda,
Vansfodia or Vanza
78A. Vanza (Saurashtra)
79. Vanzara,
Shinagwala (Hindu)
Kangasiwala (Hindu) and
Vanzara (Muslim) of Dang district only
79A. Ra,
Charan Vanzara,
Mathura Vanzara,
Maru Vanzara,
Bhagora Vanzara,
Kangashiya Vanzara,
Bamania Vanzara,

Ladonia Vanzara,
Gavaria Gawalia,
Rohidas Vanzara.
80. Waghari,
Dataniya Vaghari,
Vedu Waghari,
Talpada Waghari,
Gamachiya Waghari,
Godadia Waghari,
Chibhadia Waghari,
Marwada or Marwada Waghari,
Marwadi Waghari,
80A. Waghari Gamichiya,
Wedva Churaliya,
Jakhudia
(where they are not S.T.)
80B. Wadva Waghari or Velva Waghari
81. Wagher (Hindu & Muslim)
82. Wandhara
83. Arab (Muslim)
84. Bhand
85. Burud
86. Chakrawadya Dasar
87. Chaudhari of Hindu Anjana,
Chaudhari or Hindu Aanjana,
Chaudhari or Aanjana,
Aanjana Patel, Aanjana Patidar,
Aanjana Desai, Aanjana Kanbi,
Chaudhari Patel,
Chaudhari Patidar
(where they are not ST)
88. Chamtha
89. Dakaleru
90. Depala
91. Ghantia
92. Ghancha
93. Galkada
94. Gavli
95. Hati
96. Jachak
97. Kalodhia
98. Kotwal
99. Kumbhar,
Biyar,
Kadra Patel,
Lathiya,
Potmaker,
Prajapati
Variya
Varia
or Sorathiya Prajapati,
Kadia Kumbhar,
Vataliya Prajapati,
or Gujjar Kshatriya Kadia
Gurjar Prajapati,
Kshatriya Kadia, Kadia
100. Kharak
101. Khavas
102. Karadiya-Nadoda,
Bhati Rajput,
or Karadiya Rajput,
or Nadoda Rajput.
103. Kasiya
104. Mistri, Gujjar, Mistri Rathod. Mistri Suthar Suthar, Sutar, Suthar Gurjar, Gujjar Suthar. Gurjar Mistri Sutar, Luhar, Panchal, Kadiya Suthar Sai-Suthar
105. Munda
106. Madhaviya
107. Mali/Mali Rami, Marwadi Mali
108. Maiya or Mihiya
109. Palwadia
110. Padhariya
111. Pakhali
112. Sangheda

113. Shingdav or Shingadiya
114. Sochi
115. Sumra (Muslim)
116. Sagar
117. Sathvara/Satvara, or Kadiya-Sathwara or Kadiya Satvara Dalwadi or Kadiya
118. Thakur (Non Rajputs)
119. Timali,
120. Tarak (Muslim)
121. Vajir
122. Kathi
123. Lakhara/Lakhavara/Lakshakar
124. Kalal (Muslim)
125. Jagri
126. Jogi
127. Bahvaiya (Muslim)
128. Nizama (Hindu)
129. Gadriya
130. Kamaliya-Pujara
131. Gari

7. Haryana

Block - 'A'

1. Aheria, Aheri, Heri, Naik Thori or Turi, Hari
2. Barra
3. Beta, Hensi or Hesi
4. Bagria
5. Barwar
6. Barai, Tamboli
7. Baragi, Bairagi
8. Battera
9. Bharbhunja, Bharbhuja
10. Bhat, Bhatra, Darpi, Ramiya
11. Bhuhalia Lohar
12. Changar
13. Chirimar
14. Chang
15. Chimba, Chhipi, Chimpa, Darzi, Rohilla
16. Daiya
17. Dhobis
18. Dakaut
19. Dhimar, Mallah. Kashyap-Rajpoot, Kahar, Jhiwar, Dhinwar, Khewat, Mehra, Nishad
20. Dhosali, Dosali
21. Faquir
22. Gwaria, Gauria or Gwar
23. Ghirath
24. Ghasi, Ghasiara or Ghosi
25. Gorkhas
26. Gawala, Gowala
27. Gadaria, Pal
28. Garhi Lohar
29. Hajjam, Nai, Nais, Sain
30. Jhangra-Brahman, Khati, Suthar, Dhiman, Tarkhan, Barhai, Baddi
31. Joginath, Jogi, Nath, Jangam-Jogi
32. Kanjar or Kanchan
33. Kurmi
34. Kumhars, Prajapati
35. Kamboj
36. Khanghera
37. Kuchband
38. Labana
39. Lakhera, Manihar
40. Lohar, Panchal
41. Madari
42. Mochi
43. Mirasi
44. Nar
45. Noongar
46. Nalband
47. Pinja, Penja
48. Rehar, Rehara or Re
49. Raigar
50. Rai Sikhs
51. Rechband

52. Shorgir, Shergir
53. Soi
54. Singhikant, Singiwala
55. Sunar, Zargar, Soni
56. Thathera, Tamera
57. Teli
58. Banzara, Banjara
59. Weaver (Jullaha)
60. Badi/Badden
61. Bhattu/Chattu
62. Mina
63. Rahbari
64. Charan
65. Chaoraj (Mahabrahman)
66. Udasin
67. Ramgarhia

Block - 'B'

68. Ahir/Yadav
69. Gujjar
70. Lodh/Lodha
71. Saini
72. Meo

Throughout the Himachal Pradesh (A)

1. Aheri, Ahori, Neri, Haik, Thori, Turi
2. Ard pop
3. Beda
4. Bahti
5. Bata, Hensi, or Hosi
6. Bagria
7. Batoerha
8. Baragi, Bairagi,
9. Bharbunha, Bharbhuja
10. Bhat or Bhatta (whether with or without the appendage Brahman), Darpi
11. Bhuhalia
12. Chang
13. Changar
14. Chirimar
15. Dhimar
16. Dhosali, Dosal
17. Daiya
18. Faguir
19. Ghirath including Chang and Bhati
20. Ghasi, Ghasiara or Ghosi
21. Gorkha
22. Ghai
23. Gowala, Gwala
24. Gadaria
25. Gawaria, Gauria or Gwar
26. Hajam, Nai
27. Jhiwar, Dhiwar, Jhinwar, Dhinwar, Jheur, Jheer
28. Keshap Rajput
29. Kahar
30. Kumhar
31. Kangehra
32. Kanjarokanchan
33. Kurmi
34. Labana
35. Mahatam
36. Madari
37. Mirasi
38. Mallah
39. Mehra
40. Nai (Kullen Brahman)
41. Nalband
42. Nar
43. Pinja, Panja
44. Roolband
45. Soi
46. Tarkhan, Badhai, Ramgarhia, Dhiman (excluding Lohar), Vishwakarma. Thawins
47. Vanzara

(B) In Merged area only

1. Keer
2. Gaddi
3. Gujjar

Karnataka

Category- I

1. Agamudi
2. (a) Ambalakaran
   (b) Ambalakarma
3. Bavandhi
4. (a) Bavaji
   (b) Atit
   (c) Bairagi
   (d) Bavani
   (e) Byragi
   (f) Daurigosayi
   (g) Davari
   (h) Gosayi
   (i) Gusai
   (j) Helava
   (k) Helova
   (l) Holeva
   (m) Nandiwala
   (n) Nathapanthi
   (o) Pichigunta
   (p) Pichguntala
   (q) Pichiguntala
   (r) Bava
   (s) Byaragi
5. (a) Bestha
   (b) Ambiga
   (c) Barki
   (d) Besthar
   (e) Bhoyi
   (f) Bunde-Beshtar
   (g) Daaiji
   (h) Daavat
   (i) Gabit
   (j) Galadakonkani
   (k) Gangemakkalu
   (l) Gangakula
   (m) Gangamatha
   (n) Gangamathastha
   (o) Gangaputra
   (p) Gowrimatha
   (q) Bunde Bestha/Gunde Bestha
   (r) Harakanthra
   (s) Jalagara
   (t) Kabbera/Kabber
   (u) Kabbaliga
   (v) Kabbili
   (w) Kahar
   (x) Kharvi
   (y) Koli
   (z) Kolimahadev
   (aa) Maddar
   (ab) Meenagar
   (ac) Mogaveera
   (ad) Moger
   (ae) Mukkavan
   (af) Parivara
   (ag) Siviyar
   (ah) Sunagara
   (ai) Thoreya
6. (a) Bhamta
   (b) Bhompta
   (c) Paradeshi-Bhampta
   (d) Takari
   (e) Bhomptra
   (f) Uchillan
7. Bhatraju
8. (a) Bogad
   (b) Begadi
   (c) Bagali
   (d) Bogadi
9. (a) Budubuduki
   (b) Bududki
   (c) Chhetri
   (d) Devari
   (e) Garadi
   (f) Gidakoni
   (g) Joshi
   (h) Kichagara
   (i) Killikyata
   (j) Modiga
   (k) Pansa
   (1) Panasa
   (m) Pingale

(n) Sadajoshi
(o) Budbudkala
10. Chunchar
11. (a) Dasari
(b) Chakravadya-Dasa
(c) Dang-Dasar
(d) Dombi-Dasaru
12. (a) Devadasi
(b) Basavi
(c) Bhavin
(d) Bogam
(e) Ganika
(f) Kalavant
(g) Nat
(h) Natuva
(i) Patramela
13. (a) Ghisade
(b) Ghisadi
14. (a) Goniga-Mane
(b) 24 Mane Telugu Shetty
(c) Goni Chetty
(d) Sadusetty
(e) Salaparu
15. (a) Gurav
(b) Tamballa
(c) Tambli
16. Gurkha
17. (a) Halawakki Wakkal
(b) Halakki Vakkal
(c) Atte Vokkalu
(d) Gam Gawada
(e) Gam Vokkal
(f) Grama Vokkalu
(g) Halakki Vokkalu
(h) Kare Vokkalu
(i) Kunchavakkal
(j) Shilwakkal
(k) Vakkal
(l) Gavada
(m) Gam Gawda
(n) Gram Vakkal
18. (a) Hawadiga
(b) Hawgar
(c) Howgar
19. (a) Jogi
(b) Brahma Kapali
(c) Jogar
(d) Jogtin
(e) Kapali
(f) Raval
(g) Ravalia
(h) Sanjogi
(i) Sanyasi
(j) Joger
20. (a) Kanjlibhat
(b) Kanjar
(c) Khanjar Bhat
21. (a) Kashikapadi
(b) Kashikapdi
(c) Tirumali
22. (a) Katabar
(b) Katabu
23. (a) Katik
(b) Aray
(c) Are Kasal
(d) Ari Katikelu
(e) Kalal Khatik
(f) Kasab
(g) Kasai
(h) Maratti
(i) Suryavamsha Kshatriya
24. (a) Kolari
(b) Kalayiri
(c) Koleri
25. (a) Kolla
(b) Kollala
26. Kotari
27. Kudubi
28. (a) Kurma
(b) Kurmi
29. (a) Ladaru/Ladara/Ladar
(b) Lad
(c) Yelegal

30. Malaya
31. (a) Medara
    (b) Batter
    (c) Burned
    (d) Gauriga
    (e) Gouriga
    (f) Gowri
    (g) Gowrimaratha
    (h) Gowriga
    (i) Medari
    (j) Burud
32. Mudhar
33. Otari
34. Pamtor
35. (a) Pangual
    (b) Pangusal
36. Panika
37. (a) Raya Rawath
    (b) Ravat
38. Reinudas
39. Sansia
40. Satarkar
41. Siddi
42. (a) Sikkaligara
    (b) Shikalgar
    (c) Shikkaligar
43. (a) Sotmavamsa Arya Kshatriya
    (b) Chitara
    (c) Chitragar
    (d) Digwan
    (e) Jeeragara
    (f) Najabund
    (g) Nalabund
    (h) Tambat
44. Takankar
45. (a) Tewar
    (b) Kalari
    (c) Kallar
    (d) Maravar
46. (a) Tilari
    (b) Tirali
47. (a) Uppara
    (b) Beldar
    (c) Chunar
    (d) Gavadi
    (e) Goundi
    (f) Kallu Kutiga Uppara
    (g) Lonari
    (h) Melu Sakkreyavaru
    (i) Melusakkare
    (j) Namada Uppara
    (k) Padit/Padti
    (l) Padithi
    (m) Padi
    (n) Sagara
    (o) Sunnagara
    (p) Sunna Uppara
    (q) Uppaliga
    (r) Uppaliga Shetty
    (s) Uppaliyan
    (t) Uppera
    (u) Yakalara
    (v) Yekkali
48. Vaidu
49. Vasudev
50. (a) Veer
    (b) Veeramasti
    (c) Vir
51. Yeralu
52. (a) Yerkala
    (b) Erakala
    (c) Kaikadi
    (d) Koragar
    (e) Kormasetty
    (f) Kunchi
    (g) Korwari
    (h) Yerukala
53. (a) Bailpatar
    (b) Bailapatar
    (c) Bilapatar
54. (a) Bajania
    (b) Bajenia
55. Balasanthoshi

56. Bazigar
57. Deria
58. (a) Bhardi
    (b) Bhargi
59. (a) Chara
    (b) Chhar
    (c) Chhara
60. (a) Chapper Band (Muslim)
    (b) Chapper Banda
61. Chitrakathijoshi
62. Darvesu
63. Dholi
64. (a) Durgamurga
    (b) Burburcha
65. (a) Modikara
    (b) Modikar
66. (a) Gondali
    (b) Ghondali
    (c) Gondaliga
    (d) Gondhali
    (e) Gondhalli
67. Vagri
68. (a) Javeri
    (b) Jawari
69. Johari
70. (a) Kamatti
    (b) Kaman
71. (a) Kanjari
    (b) Kanjir
72. (a) Kalkari, Kelkari
    (b) Khelkari
73. (a) Kolhati
    (b) Kolhatigi
74. (a) Masania Yogi
75. Full Mall
76. Sarania
77. (a) Sarordi
    (b) Saroda
78. Vadi
79. Bedaru
80. (a) Golla
    (b) Yadav
    (c) Asthanagolla
    (d) Yadava
    (e) Adavigolla
    (f) Gopala
    (g) Gopali
    (h) Gouli
    (i) Gauli
    (j) Gavali
    (k) Gavli
    (1) Anubaru
    (m) Atanabaru
    (n) Hanabar
    (o) Kavadi
    (p) Kolayan
    (q) Konar
    (r) Konnur
    (s) Krishna Golla
    (t) Maniyani
    (u) Urali
81. (a) Banjari
    (b) Brinjari
    (c) Vanjara
    (d) Wanjari
    (e) Lambaid
    (f) Gore or Goria
82. (a) Bendar
    (b) Berad
    (c) Boya
    (d) Naikamakkalu
    (e) Naikwadi
    (f) Palegar
    (g) Remoshi
    (h) Talawar/Talwar-Boya
    (i) Valmikimakkalu
    (j) Vedan
    (k) Parivara Nayaka
    (l) Myasa Nayaka
    (m) Urs Nayaka
    (n) Byada
    (o) Haranshikari
    (p) Chigari Betagar

(q) Vaghri
(r) Wagiri
(s) Nirshikari
(t) Bargi
(u) Baori
(v) Phasachari
(w) Hirshikari

83. Daveri
84. (a) Garudi
    (b) Garudiga
    (c) Garadiga
85. Paradhis
86. (a) Girni Waddar
    (b) Tudug-Woddar
    (c) Kallu Vaddar
    (d) Mannu Voddar
    (e) Bhandi Voddar
87. (a) Bhot
    (b) Boyi
    (c) Harikanthra
    (d) Kharia
    (e) Bovi
88. Pinjara
89. S.C. converts to Christianity

Category-II (A)

1. (a) Agasa
   (b) Chakala
   (c) Dhobi
   (d) Madivala
   (e) Mannan
   (f) Parit
   (g) Rajaka
   (h) Sakala
   (i) Vannan
   (j) Velluthedan
   (k) Sakalavadu
2. (a) Devadiga
   (b) Devali
   (c) Moyili
   (d) Padiar
   (e) Seregara
   (f) Servegar
   (g) Sheregar
   (h) Suplig
3. (a) Idiga
   (b) Bandhari
   (c) Belehad
   (d) Billava
   (e) Deevar
   (f) Desha Bhandari
   (g) Devar
   (h) Devaramakkalu/Divara Makkalu
   (i) Ediga
   (j) Eliga
   (k) Ezhava
   (l) Gamalla
   (m) Goundla
   (n) Halepaikaru
   (o) Hale Paik
   (p) Illavan
   (q) Kalal
   (r) Malayali Billava
   (s) Nadar
   (t) Namadhari
   (u) Thiyan
   (v) Iliga
   (w) Goondla
   (x) Tiyan
4. (a) Kumbara
   (b) Chakrasali
   (c) Gunaga
   (d) Ganagi
   (e) Koyava
   (f) Kula
   (g) Kulala
   (h) Kumbar
   (i) Kumbard
   (j) Kummara
   (k) Kusavan
   (1) Moolya
   (m) Sajjan Kumbara
   (n) Khumara

(o) Kumbhar
(p) Khumbhar
(q) Kulalar

5. (a) Kuruba
(b) Bharwad
(c) Dhanagar
(d) Goraya
(e) Halumatha
(f) Kurab
(g) Kuruban
(h) Kurumba
(i) Kurub
(j) Kurumban

6. (a) Nayinda
(b) Ambattan
(c) Bajanthri
(d) Bandari
(e) Chouriya
(f) Hadapada
(g) Hajama
(h) Kavutian
(i) Kelasi
(j) Kshaurika
(k) Kshowrad
(l) Mahale
(m) Mangala
(n) Melagara
(o) Nadiga
(p) Napitha
(q) Navalig
(r) Navi
(s) Nayanaja Kshatriya
(t) Nhavi
(u) Savitha
(v) Nayanaja Kshatri
(w) Nadig
(x) Kshowrik
(y) Kshowrika

7. Buddhists

8. (a) Tigala
(b) Agni Vamsha Kshatriya
(c) Agnivanni
(d) Agnikula Kshatriya
(e) Dharmaraja Kapu
(f) Palli
(g) Shambhukula Kshatriya
(h) Thigala
(i) Vanniar
(j) Vannikula Kshatriya
(k) Tigler
(1) Kurovan

9. (a) Viswakarma
(b) Achari
(c) Akkasale
(d) Ausala
(e) Badigar
(f) Badiwadla
(g) Bailapatar
(h) Bailu Akkasali
(i) Bailu Kammara
(j) Bogara
(k) Chaptegar
(1) Charodi
(m) Daivagnya Brahmin
(n) Gejjigara
(o) Kambar
(p) Kammalan
(q) Kammara
(r) Kamsala
(s) Kamsan
(t) Kanehagar
(u) Kanehora
(v) Kanehori
(w) Kanehugara
(x) Kansar
(y) Kasar
(z) Luhar
(aa) Mesta
(ab) Panchal
(ac) Pattar
(ad) Silpi
(ae) Sohagar

(af) Sonar
(ag) Sony
(ah) Sutar
(ai) Tacehan
(aj) Viswa Brahmin
(ak) Thattan
(al) Aksali
(am) Kamsal
(an) Badagi

10. (a) Aghori
 (b) Karkarmunda
11. Agnani
12. Ambalavasi
13. Anduran
14. (a) Atari
 (b) Athari
15. Bahurupi
16. Bakadra
17. (a) Bathal
 (b) Battal
 (c) Batter
18. Bawtar
19. (a) Bhaat
 (b) Bohrot
20. Binapatta
21. Bingi
22. (a) Bagadi
 (b) Bagaadi
 (c) Bagdi
23. (a) Chaliyan
 (b) Teruvan
 (c) Challiya
24. Chamboti
25. Chambukutti
26. Mestha
27. Jingar
28. Ghadi
29. (a) Ghadsi
 (b) Ghadshi
30. (a) Pingle
31. (a) Gosavi
 (b) Gosain
32. (a) Gujar
 (b) Guzar
33. (a) Gurava
 (b) Gurou
34. (a) Gabbit
 (b) Gapit
 (c) Gaabit
 (d) Daalija
35. (a) Hanbar
 (b) Hanabaru
36. Handevazir
37. Handervut
38. Honniyar
39. (a) Hoovadiga
 (b) Hugar
 (c) Hoogar
 (d) Maalgar
 (e) Mali
 (f) Phool Mali
 (g) Phul Mali
 (h) Phulari
 (i) Phoolari
 (j) Jeer
40. Kadu Konkani
41. Karikudumbi
42. Karuva
43 (a) Khatik
 (b) Katuka
 (c) Katuga
44. Bogar
45. Kasbin
46. (a) Kolayiri
 (b) Kolyiri
47. (a) Kanisan
 (b) Kaniyar
 (c) Kaniyaru
 (d) Kaniya
 (e) Kaniyan
 (Other than Kollegal Tq. of Mysore District)
 (f) Kanyan
48. (a) Kanbi

(b) Kulwadi
(c) Kunbi
49. Kutuma
50. Marta
51. (a) Marayan
(b) Maravan
52. Murrari
53. (a) Nadora
(b) Uppu Nadar
(c) Torke Nador
(d) Nador
(e) Nadavar
(f) Nadava
(g) Uppunador
54. Nalki
55. Osthan
56. (a) Pandaram
(b) Pandar
(c) Pandara
57. Panaba
58. Pannekara Konkani
59. Patra
60. Pichati
61. Pallavan
62. (a) Rajapuri
(b) Rajpur
(c) Balavalikar
63. Saniyaar
64. Shanan
65. (a) Sudir
(b) Sudra
66. Sutsali
67. Techayiri
68. Tilvi
69. (a) Gavandi
(b) Govandi
70. Vettuvan
71. (a) Yeklar
(b) Yaklar
(c) Egalika
72. (a) Gatti/Gattiyavaru
(b) Poledava/Poladavaru
73. Gudigara
74. (a) Darzi
(b) Bhavasar Kshatriya
(c) Chippi
(d) Chippiga
(e) Simpi
(f) Shimpi
(g) Sai
(h) Mirai
(i) Rangari
(j) Rangrez
(k) Nilari
(1) Namdev
(m) Namdev Simpi
(n) Rangare
(o) Neelagar
75. (a) Devanga
(b) Devang
(c) Koshti
(d) Hutgar/Hutkar
(e) Jed
(f) Winkar
(g) Julohi
(h) Hulkar
(i) Hatagar
76. (a) Neygi
(b) Kuruhina Setty
(c) Bill Magga
(d) Thogata
(e) Soniga
(f) Jam Khana
(g) Ayiri
(h) Avir
(i) Sale
(j) Padma Sale
(k) Saale
(l) Kaikolan
(m) Neikar
(n) Jadar
(o) Jandra
(p) Sakula Sale
77. (a) Pategar
(b) Pattekari
(c) Patiegar

(d) Somavamsha Sahasrarjuna Kshatriya
78. (a) Ganiga
(b) Teli
(c) Gandla
(d) Vaniyan
79. Rajput
80. Amman Kodava
81. Anappan
82. (a) Andi
(b) Andipandaram
83. Baandhi
84. (a) Bolaballala
(b) Baliala
85. (a) Bhatial
(b) Bhattia
86. (a) Chakkan
87. Dogra
88. Gulli
89. Hindu Sardu/Sadaru
90. (a) Jatti. Jetty
(b) Mallaru Malla Kshatriya
(c) Mushtiga
91. (a) Kalavanthi
(b) Bhogam/Teluga
92. (a) Kanakan
(b) Kanakar
93. (a) Kotegara
(b) Koteyar
(c) Kothati
(d) Kottegara
(e) Kotteyara
(f) Kumara Kshatriya
(g) Kumara Panth/Komarpant
(h) Rama Kshatriya
(i) Rama Raj Kshatriya
(j) Serugara (North Kanara)
(k) Servgar (South Kanara)
(l) Kote Kshatriya
94. (a) Kshatriya/Kshatri
95. Malawa
96. Maleya
97. Aryan
98. (a) Raju Kshatriya
(b) Raju-Raju
(c) Rajuwar/Rajavar/Rachevar
99. Somavamsha Kshatriya
100. Stanika
101. (a) Tulu
(b) Tuluva

Category - II (b)

1. Muslim

Category - III (a)

1. (a) Vokkaliga
(b) Vakkaliga
(c) Sarpa Vokkaliga
(d) Hallikar Vokkaliga
(e) Namdhari Vokkaliga
(f) Gangadkar Vokkaliga
(g) Das Vokkaliga
(h) Reddy Vokkaliga
(i) Marasu Vokkaliga
(j) Reddy
(k) Hallikar
(1) Kunchitiga
(m) Gouda
(n) Kapu
(o) Heggade
(p) Kamma
(q) Raddy
(r) Gownder
2. Kodagaru
3. (a) Balija
(b) Balajiga/Banajiga
(c) Naidu
(d) Bogam Teluga
(e) Telaga Balija
(f) Setty Balija

(g) Kasban
(h) Mannur-Munnar
(i) Mutrasi
(j) Maracha
(k) Janappan
(1) Balegara
(m) Banagara

Category - III (b)

1. (a) Veerashaiva Lingayath
   (b) Lingayath Sub-Groups of Helava, Ambiga, Bhoyi, Gangamata, Sunagara, Agasa, Madivala, Kumbara. Kuruba, Bajanthri, Bandari, Hadapada, Kshaurika, Navalig, Navi, Akkasale, Badigar, Kammara, Kamsala, Pancltal, Medara, Uppara, Gowli
2. (a) Maratha, Marata
   (b) Are Kshatri, Are Maratha, Arya Maratha.
   (c) Arya, Aryaru
   (d) Konkan Maratha
   (e) Kshatriaya Maratha
   (f) Kulavadi
3. Christian
4. (a) Bunt/Bant
   (b) Parivara Bant
5. Jains (Digambaras)
6. (a) Satani
   (b) Chattada Srivaislmava
   (c) Kadri Vaislinava
   (d) Sameraya
   (e) Sattandaval
   (f) Sattadavan
   (g) Vaislmavd

Kerala

I Throughout the State

1. Agoan
2. Ambalakkaran
3. Anglo Indian
4. xxxx
5. xxxx
6. Aremahratl
7. Arya
8. Bandarl
9. Billava
10. Chakkala
11. xxxx
12. Chavalakkaran
13. Chattlos (Kottar Chottios, Parakko, Chottles, Elur Chattios. Attingal Chatiles, Pudukkada Chettlos Iranlal Chattlos, S Pondare Cliattlos, Telugu Chottlas, Udnyamkulengara Chettles; Paroorkada Chattles. Sudliu Chettles, Manol Chottles. Wynadan Chottles and Kalavara Chettles).
14. Devadiga
15. Devenga

15A. Dheevare (Areyan) (Valan) (Nulayan), (Mukkuvan Arayavathi) Valinjion (??) Panlakkal, Mekaya and Mukaveeran (??)

16. Ezhavas and Thiyyas
17. Ezhavathl
18. Ezhuthachan
19. Ganika
20. Gatti
21. Gowdn
22. Hegde
23. xxxx
24. lzhuvan (Liluvan or Ezhuvan)

25. Jogi
26. Kaduppattan
27. Kaikalan
28. Kolasi (Kalasi Panicker)
29. Kalari Kuiup or Kalari Panicker 30. Viswakar mas including Assari. Chaptegra, Kallasarl, Kalthachan, Kanunala, Kamsele. Kannan Keruvan, Kitaren, Kollan, Malayalo Kammala, Moosari, Pandikammala, Pandithattan, Perumkollan. Thachan. Thattan, Vilkurup. Villasan, Viswabrahmanan or viswabrahmanai and Viswakarmala)
31. Kannadiyans
32. Kanisu or Koniyat Panicker. Kani or Kaniyan (Ganaka) or Kanisan or Kamnan
33. Kavuthiyan
34. Kavudiyaru
35. xxxx
36. Koteyar
37. Krishnanvaka
38. Kerala Mudalis
39. Kudumbis
40. Kusavan (Kulala, Kulals Nair or Andhra Nair or Anthuru Nair)
41. Kumbarans
42. Latin Catholics
43. Medivals
44. Mappila
45. Maravans
46. Maruthuvar
47. xxxx
48. Muslim
49. Nadars (Hindu Nadara and Nadars Included in S.I.U.C.)
50. Nalkkang
51 Odans
52. Scheduled Caste Converts to Christianity
53. Pandithars
54. Panniyar
55. Pattariyas
56. xxxx
57. Peruvannan(Varanavar)
58. Pulluvan
59. Rajapur
60. Chakravar Sacravar (Kavathi)
61. Sourashtras
62. Saliyas
63. Senai Thalavar (Elavaniar)

2. In Malabar District

1. x x x x
2. Boyan
3. Ganjam Reddis
4. Vishavan

3. Throughout the State except Malabar District

1. Kammara
2. x x x x
3. Malayekandi
4. Roddlars

4. Throughout the State except Kasargod Taluk of Malabar District Marati

Explanation - In this Schedule, Malabar District shall mean the Malabar District releted to in sub-section (2) of Section 5 of the States Reorganisation Act. 1956.

64. S.I.U.C. (excluding Nadars spacifiod in.Item 49)

64A. Thachar)

65. Tholkolans
66. Thoaian
67. Vaduvans. Vadugans, Vadukars and Vadukas (Vadukans).
68. xxxx
69. Velaans (Valaan. Velaar)
70. Vanians (Vanika, Vanika Vaisya. Vanibha Chetty. Vania Chetty, Ayiravar, Nagarathar and Vanlyan).
71. Vaniyar
72. Vakkaliga
73. Veerasaivas (Yogis and Yogesware)
74. Veluthedathu Nair (Veluthedan and Vannathan)
75. Vilakkithala Nair (Vilakkithalavan)
76. Yadavas (Kolaya, Ayar, Mayar. Manlyanl and Iruman)

Orissa

1. Agltaria, Agaria. Aghria
2. Aranedan
3. Asur
4. Badhal. Barhai, Bindhania, Sutradhar, Badhira and Badltria.
5. Badasuda
6. Baipari
7. Baira. Barai
8. Bairagi
9. Bariji or Barui
10. Barika, Bliandari. Napit and Nai
11. Bellara
12. Bentkar
13. Bhatua
14. Bania/Putulibandlia Vaisya Sunari/Sunaree/Viswa Brahman/Putuli Bania/ Vashya Bania Vaishya Vaisya Bania/Vashya/ Bania/Vashya Banik/ Vaishya Banik/Potali Bania/Gandha Bania/ Vaishya Putuli Bania. Paudar Bania/Podar Bania. Kamila /Astalohi / Astalohi Karmakar / Subarna Banik / Sunari Bania / Swarnakar / Subarna Bania /Sunari Bania.
15. Bhogta
16. Bhokta
17. Bliujan
18. Bhuliya
19. Birjliia
20. Bissoy-Barangi Jodia. Bennangi. Daduva. Frangi, Hollar, Jhoriya, Kollai, Konde. Paranga, Pengajodia, Sodojodia & Takoara.
21. Binedhanies
22. Bogada
23. Bolodhia
24. Buruashankar/Barna Suankar
25. Byagari
26. Chaupal
27. Chasa, Pradhan/ Padhan/ Odapadhan/ Odachasa
28. Chero
29. Cheruman
30. Chikbaraik

31. Chik
32. Chitra, Chitrakar, Chitrasilpi
33. Churia
34. Dahalia
35. Darji
36. Damal
37. Dangua
38. Dehuri
39. Dhakkada
40. Dhaner
41. Dumala, Dumal
42. Ghatwar
43. Girigiris
44. Godda
45. Gola, Golla, Gope, Sadgope, Ahir, Gour, Gouda, Goudo, Mekala Golla Puunu Golla, Yadav, Mathurapuria, Gouda, Gopapuria Gouda, Nanda Gouda, Jhadua Gouda, Dumala Gouda, Naria Gouda, Bashya Gopa, Maha Bhoi, Gandu, Nepalies, Gorkha Gopal, Sholakhandia, Magadha Gouda Mahakul/ Mahakud, Laxminarayan Gola, Goudia Gola.
46. Gudia or Guria, Gurja, Gunju
47. Gosangi
48. Gondu-Bato, Bhirthya, Dudho Kouriya, Hato, Jatako and Joria
49. Habra
50. Hansi, Dera, Dewanga, Kosta, Vina, Tula Bhina, Tanti, Patsalia, Buna, Rangani, Bunakara, Salia, Sukuli, Saraka/Saraka Tanti, Hativansa Tanti/ Asina Tanti/ Aswina Tanti/ Ashani Tanti/Aswinna Tanti/ Bangali Tanti/ Bangiya Tanti, Rangani Tanti/Rangani Tantes/ Tanganee Tantee/Rangini Tanti/Ranguni Tanti
51. Holeya
52. Irula
53. Jadapus
54. Jaintrapans
55. Jogi or Yogi
56. Jyotish Jyotisha Abadhan, Jyotish Nayak
57. Jensan
58. Kalladi
59. Kammara, Kamara, Kamar, Kammaro, Muli, Loharo, Loharo, Astolohi Kamar
60. Kanakkan
61. Kandarpa
62. Kanjar
63. Kapudia
64. Karhara/Kachara/Kachera
65. Karimpalan
66. Karmali
67. Kattunayakan
68. Khaira
69. Khuria/Thoria/ Throdia/ Thudia/Thura
70 Khandnals/Khandal, Khandual
71. Khatti-Khatti
72. Khatua
73. Khodra/Khadura/ Kharuda
74. Khetauri
75. Koda, Kuda
76. Koilar
77. Kolam
78. Kond (Kul)
79. Konda Kapu/Gagula Kapu, Kapu, Kampo
80. Kondareddy, Reddy dhakas and Reddy

81. Koraga
82. Kosalya, Goudus, Bosotheriya Goudus, Chiti Goudus, Dangayath Goudus, Doddu Kamariya/Dudu Kamaro, Ladiya Goudus and Pullo Soriya Goudus
83. Kota
84. Kudiya
85. Kudubl
86. Kudumban
87. Kumbhar, Kulal, Kumhar, Kumbharo
88. Kundamatia
89. Kulta
90. Kurariar
91. Kuravan
92. Kurichchan
93. Kuruman (Kurumba)
94. Lakhra
95. Lambadi
96. Luhura
97. Machua
98. Maghi or Meghia
99. Magura
100. Mahunta
101. Magatha Goudus, Bermia Goudus, Boodo Magatha, Dongayath Goudh, Ladya Goudu, Poona Magatha and Sana Magatha
102. Magadhi Goral
103. Maila
104. Maladasu
105. Malasar
106. Mali, Phulia, Sagbaris, Bhajemali, Muni
107. Malis-Korchia Malis, Paido Malis and Pedda Malis
108. Mal Paharia
109. Manna Dhora
110. Maune
111. Marathi
112. Matangi
113. Mavilan
114. Minka
115. Moger
116. Mukhadora-Mokka Dhora
117. Muliya
118. Mundala
119. Muria
120. Nahaf
121. Nalakeyava
122. Nat
123. Nagavasam, Mahisya, and Saunties, Mahesh, Maheshya
124. Nayadi
125. Nolia
126. Nuhura, Nuhuraj
127. Nuniya
128. Ojula or Metta, Kamasalie
129. Omeyita
130. Padaria, Pamaria, Pandara
131. Pagadia
132. Paigarapu
133. Paltan
134. Paky
135. Pal
136. Palasi
137. Paliyan
138. Paiko, Khandayat, Chasa Paiko, Paikali, Khandayat, Kalingi Sudra Khandayat, Alia, Mahanayak Sudra, and Baisya Karan
139. Palli
140. Pulayan
141. Pambada
142. Paniyan
143. Panjira
144. Panniandi
145. Paraiyan

146. Paravan
147. Parhaiya
148. Pathuria
149. Patara, Asini Patara/Asivini Patara/Ashini Patara, Goudia Patara
150. Pogua
151. Pita
152. Raneyar
153. Ronas/Rana
154. Routia
155. Sagarpasha
156. Samban
157. Sankhari
158. Sanyasi, Moembram
159. Seerithi Goudu
160. Semman
161. Sholagar
162. Sauria Paharia
163. Sinke/Sinko
164. Suda
165. Sulia
166. Sunri/Sundi/Sundhi
167. Tana
168. Teli, Telli, Kubera, Talakar, Sahu, Bahaldia Ekadas Teli, Tailik Baishya
169. Telaga, Pamula/Teloga, Telugu, Telanga, Telenga and Telugu Kachara
170. Thanu
171. Thatari/Kansari
172. Thoti
173. Tiruvalluvar
174. Tivoro
175. Toda
176. Valluvan
177. Vannan
178. Vettuvan
179. Yandi
180. Yerna Golta
181. Yerukula
182. Kurmi, Kuruma Chasa, Kudumi, Kurma, Kurmi Mahto, Kurmi Khetriya, Kurumi and Kudumi Kshyatriya, Kurum
183. Bhanja Puran
184. Bhopa and Raula
185. Mahla and Mahlar
186. Kalanji, Khandayat Kalanji, Odra Khandayat Kalanji, Kalinga, Kalingi and Kaliji
187. Shudra
188. Belama
189. Dalapati/Dalua
190. Rajasri Balasi/Balasi
191. Raju
192. Segidi, Srisayan
193. Dambo-Christian, Pano-Christian, Ganda-Christian
194. Kandha-Kumbhar
195. Dalakhandayat & Dalua-Paik
196. Kapala Velama, Kapulu Elama, Koppala Velama, Koppala Elama, Kappula Elama, Kupala Velama, Kapala Elama & Kapala Elaga
197. Banka
198. Kshitibansa Matibansa Ojha, Kshitibansa Naik, Ojhakaran, Kshitibansa Nayak, Matibansa, Matibansa Abadhan
199. Arua
200. Hatua
201. Kalar
202. Banayat Oriya, Benayat Oriya, Beneyit Odia, Banayat, Banayat Odia, Odia and Udia

Punjab

1. Aheria, Aheri, Heri, Naik, Thori or Turi
2. Barra
3. Beta, Hensi or Hesi
4. Changar
5. Chirimar
6. Daiya
7. Gwaria, Gauria or Gwar
8. Kanjar or Kanohan
9. Kurmi
10. Nar
11. Rehar, Rahara or Re
12. Ghirath including Chang and Bahti
13. Kahar, Jhinwar or Dhinwar
14. Ghasi, Ghasiara or Ghosi
15. Bagria
16. Raigar
17. Weaver Jullaha).
18. Labana
19. Gorkhas
20. Kumhars
21. Nais
22. Dhobis
23. Kamboj
24. Rai Sikhs
25. Barwar
26. Barai, Tamoli
27. Baragi, Bairagi
28. Battera
29. Bharbhunja, Bharbhuja
30. Bhat, Bhatra, Darpi, Ramiya
31. Bhuhalia Lohar
32. Chahang
33. Chimba, Chhippi, Chimba, Derzi Tonk
34. Dakaut
35. Dhimar, Mallah, Kashyap Rajputs
36. Faquir
37. Dhosali, Dosali
38. Gawala, Gowala
39. Gaddaria
40. Jhangra Brahman
41. Hajjam, Nari
42. Jogi Nath
43. Khati
44. Rechhanad
45. Khanghera
46. Kucha band
47. Thathera, Tamera
48. Lakhera, Manihar
49. Vanzara
50. Madari
51. Lohar
52. Mochi
53. Mirasi
54. Noongarh
55. Nalband
56. Shorgir
57. Pinja, Penja
58. Soi
59. Singh
60. Teli
61. Christians
62. Daula or Soni
63. Gujjar
64. Arain
65. Sanyasi Sadhu / Sanyasi Bawa
66. Buzroos
67. Mehra Rajputs
68. Soni Rajputs

Sikkim

1. Bhujel
2. Gurung
3. Limboo
4. Rai
5. Manger
6. Sunuwar
7. Tamang

   Explanation I - The expression 'Limboo' includes Tsong, Subba and Yakthngba

Explanation II - The expression 'Sunuwar' includes Koincha/ Mukhia

Tamil Nadu

Backward Classes (Others than Most Backward Classes and Denotified Communities

1. Agamudayar including Thozhu or Thuuva Vollala
2. Agaram Vellan Chottiar
3. Alwar, Azhavar and Alavar (in Kannyakumari District and Shencottah Taluk or Tirunvelveli-Kottabomman District).
4. Servai (except Tiruchirapalli and Pudukkottai District).
5. Ansar
6. Arayar, Nulayar (in Kanniyakumari District and Shencottah taluk of Tirunelveli-Kattabomman District)
7. Archakarai Vellala
8. Aryavathi (in Kanniyakumari District and Shencottah Taluk of Tirunelveli-Kattabomman District).
9. Ayira Vaisyar
10. Baoagar
11. Billava
12. Bondil
13. Boyas (except Tiruchirapalli, Pudukottai, The Nilgiris, Salem and Dharmapuri Districts) Pedda Boyar (except Tiruchirapalli and Pudukottai District) Oddars (except Thanjavur, Nagapattinam Quaid-e-Milleth, Tiruchirapalli, Pudukottai and Madurai, Dindigul-Anna Districts) Kaloddars (except Chengalpattu-MGR, Ramanathapuram, Pasutnpon Muthuramalinga Thavar, Kamarajar, Madurai, Dindigul Anna, Puddukottai, Tiruchirappalli, Tirunelveli Kattabomman, Chidambaranar and Salem Districts)
    Nellorapet Oddars (except North Arcot Ambedkar and Tiruvannamalai Sambuvarayar Districts)
    Sooramari Oddar's (except North Arcot Ambedkar and Tiruvannamalai Sambuvarayar Districts)
14. Chakkala (except Pasuntpon Muthuramalinga Thevar, Kamarajar, Ramanathapuram, Thanjavur, Nagapattinam Quaid-e-Millath, Pudukkottai, Tiruchirappalli, Madurai. Dindigul Anna and The Nilgiris Districts)
15. Chavalakarar (in Kannyakumari District and Shencottah taluk of Tirunelveli-Kattabomman District).
16. Chettu or Chetty (including

Kottar Chetty, Elur Chetty Pathira Chetty, Vadayalchetty, Padukkdai Chetty) (in Kanniyakumari District and Shencottah Taluk of Tirunelveli Kattabomman Districts)

17. Chowdhry
18. Converts to Christianity from Scheduled Castes irrespective of the generation of conversion for the purpose of reservation of seats in Educational Institutions and for seats in Public Services.
19. C.S.I. formerly S.I.U.C. (in Kanniyakumari District and Shencottah Taluk of Tirunelveli Kattabomman District).
20. Donga Dasaris (except Chengalpattu-MGR, Tiruchirapalli, Pudukottai, Madras and Salem Districts)
21. Dakkani Muslims
22. Devangar, Sedar
    Sooramani Oddar (except North Arcot Ambedkar and Tiruvannamalai Sombuvaryar Districts
23. Domos' (except Puduckottai and Tiruchirapalli Districts) Dommars (except Thanjavur, Nagapactinam Quaid-a-Milleth, Pudukkottai, North Arcot Ambedkar and Tiruvannamalai Sambuvarayar Districts).
24. Dudekula
25. Enadi
26. Ezhavathy (in Kanniyakumari District and Shencottah Taluk of Tirunelveli-Kattabomman District)
27. Ezhuthachar (in Kanniyakumari District and Shencottah Taluk of Tirunelveli-Kattabomman District)
28. Ezhuva (in Kanniyakumari District and Shencottah Taluk of Tirunelveli-Kattabomman District).
29. Gangavar
30. Gavara, Gavarai and Vadugar (Vaduvar) (other than Kamma, Kapu Balija and Reddi)
31. Gounde
32. Gowda (including Gammala, Kalali and Anuppa Gounder).
33. Hegde
34. Idiga
35. Itlathu Pillaimar, Illuvar, Ezhuvar and Illathar
36. Jhetty
37. Jogis (except Chengalpattu-MGR, Madurai, Dindigul Anna, South Arcot Vallalar, Villupuram Ramasami Padayachiyar, North Arcot Ambedkar and Tiruvannamalai Sambuvarayar Districts)
38. Kabbera
39. Kaikolar, Sengunthar
40. Kaladi (except Pasumpon Muthuramalinga Thevar,

Kamarajar, Ramanathapuram, Madurai, Dindigul Anna, Thanjavur Nagapattinam Quaid-e-Milleth. Pudukkottai and Tiruchirappalli District)

41. Kalari Kurup including Kazlari Panicker (in Kanniyakumari District and Shencottah Taluk of Tirunelveli-Kattabomman District)
42. Kalingi
43. Kallar (including Easanattu Kallar, Gandarvakottai Kallars (except Thanjavur, Nagapattinam Quaid-e-Milleth and Pudukkottai Districts)

    Koottappal Kallars (except Pudukkottai and Tiruchirappalli Districts) Piramalai Kallars (except Pasumpon Muthuramalinga Thevar, Ramarajar, Ramanathapuram Madurai, Dindigul Anna, Puddukkottai and Thanjavur, Nagapattinam Quaid-e-Milleth Districts) Periyasooriyur Kallars (except Tiruchirappalli and Pudukuottai Districts)
44. Kallar Kula Thondaman
45. Kalveli Gounder
46. Kamar
47. Kammalar or Viswakarma, Viswakarmala (including Thattar, Porkolla Kannar, Karamar, Kollar, Thacher, Kal Thacher Kamsala and Viswabrahmin).
48. Kani, Kanisu, Kaulyar Panikkar
49. Kaniyala Vellalar
50. Kannada Saineegar, Kannadiyar (Throughout the State) and Dasapalanjika (Coimbatore, Periyar and the Nilgiris Districts)
51. Kannadiya Naidu
52. Karpoorachattiar
53. Karuneegar (Seer Karuneegar, Sri Karuneegar, Sarattu Karuneegar, Kaikatti, Karuneegar, Machuvazhi Kanakkar, Sozhi Kanakkar and Sunnambu Karuneegar)
54. Kasuakara Chettiar
55. Katesar, Pattamkatti
56. Kavuthiyar
57. Kerala Mudali
58. Kharvi
59. Khatri
60. Kongu Vaishnava
61. Kongu Vellalars (including Vellala Gounder, Nattu Gounder, Narambukkatoi Gounder, Tirumudi Vellalar, Thondu Vellalar, Pala Gounder, Poosari Gounder, Anuppa Vellala Gounder, Kurumba Gounder, Padaithalai Gounder, Chendalai Gounder, Pavalankatti Vellala Gounder, Pala Vellala Gounder, Sanku Vellala Gounder and Rachinagiri Gounder)
62. Koppala Valama

63. Koteyar
64. Krisinauvaka (in Kanniyakumari District and Shencottah Taluk of Tirunelveli - Kattabomman District)
65. Kudikara Vellalar
66. Kudumbi (in Kanniyakumari District and Shencottah Taluk of Tirunelveli - Kattabomman District)
67. Kuga Vellalar
68. Kunchidigar
69. Labbais including Rowthar and Marakayar (whether their spoken language is Tamil or Urdu)
70. Lambadi
71. Latin Catholics (in Kanniyakumari District and Shencottah Taluk of Tirunelveli - Kattabomman District)
72. Lingayat (Jangama)
73. Mahratta (non-Brahmin) (including Namdev Mahratta)
74. Malayar
75. Male
76. Maniagar
77. Mapilla
78. Maravars (except Thanjavur, Nagapattinam Quaid-e-Milleth, Pudukkottai, Ramanathapuram, Pasumpon Muthuramalinga Thevar, Kamarajar, Tirunelveli Kattabomman and Chidambaranar Districts) including Karumaravars, Appanad Kondayamkottai Maravar (except Pasumpon Mathuramalinga Thevar, Kamarajar, Ramanathapuram, Madurai and Dindigul-Anna Districts) and Sembanad Maravars (except Pasumpon Muthuramalinga Thevar, Kamarajar and Ramanathapuram Districts)
79. Moondrumandai Enbathunalu (84) Ur. Sozhia Vellalar
80. Mooppan
81. Muthuraja, Muthuracha, Muttiriyar, Muthiriyar, Mutharaiyar
82. Nadar, Shanar and Gramani (including Christian Nadar Christian Shanar and Christian Gramani)
83. Nagaram
84. Naikkar (in Kanniyakumari District and Shencottah Taluk of Tirunelveli-Kattabomman District)
85. Nangudi Vellalar
86. Nanjil Mudali (in Kanniyakumari District and Shencottah Taluk of Tirunelveli-Kattabomman District)
87. Odar (in Kanniyakumari District and Shencottah Taluk of Tirunelveli Kattabomman District)
88. Odiya.
89. Oottruvalanattu Vellalar

90. O.P.S. Vellalar
91. Ovachar
92. Paiyur Kotta Vellalar
93. Pamulu
94. Panar (except in Kanniyakumari District and Shencottah Taluk of Tirunelveli -Kattabomman District where the community is a scheduled-caste)
95. Panisaivan (including Virakodi Vellala)
96. Kathikarar in Kanniyakumari District
97. Pannirandam Chettiar or Uthama Chettiar
98. Parkavakulam (including Surithimar, Nathamar, Malayamar, Moopanar and Nainar)
99. Perike (including Perike Balija)
100. Perumkollar (in Kanniyakumari District and Shencottah Taluk of Tirunelveli Kattabomman District)
101. Podikara Vellalar
102. Pooluva Gounder
103. Poraya
104. Pulavar (in Coimbatore and Periyar Districts)
105. Pulluvar or Pooluvar
106. Pusala
107. Reddy (Ganjam)
108. Sadhu Chetty (including Telugu Chetty, Twenty four Manai Telugu Chetty).
109. Sakkaravar or Kavathi (in Kanniyakumari District and Shencottah taluk of Tirunelveli Kattabomman District)
110. Salivagana
111. Saliyar, Padmasaliyan, Pattusaliyar, Pattariyar and Adhaviyar
112. Savalakkarar
113. Senaithalaivar, Senaikudiyar and Illaivaniar
114. Sheik.
115. Sourashtra (Patnulkarar)
116. Sozhia Vellalar (including Sozha Vellalar, Vetrilaikarar, Kodikalkarar and Keeraikarar)
117. Srisayar
118. Sundaram Chetty
119. Syed
120. Thogatta Veerakshatriya
121. Tholkollar (in Kanniyakumari District and Shencottah Taluk at Tirunelveli - Kattabomman District)
122. Tholuva Naicker and Vetalakara Naicker
123. Thoraiyar
124. Thoriyar
125. Ukkirakula Kshatriya Naicker
126. Uppara, Uppillia and Sagara
127. Urali Gounder (except Tiruchirapalli and Pudukottai Districts) and Orudaya Gounder or Oorudaya Gounder (in Madurai, Dindigul-Anna. Coimbatore, Periyar, Tiruchirapalli, Pudukottai and Salem District)

128. Urikkara Nayakkar
129. Vallambar
130. Valmiki
131. Vaniyar, Vania Chettiar including Gandla, Gandvad, Telikula and Chekkalar)
132. Veduvar and Vedar (except in Kanniyakumari District and Shencottah Taluk of Tirunelveli-Kattabomman District where the community is a Scheduled Caste)
133. Veerasaiva (in Kanniyakumari District and Shencottah Taluk of Tirunelveli - Kattabomman District)
134. Velar
135. Vellan Chettiar
136. Veluthodathu Nair (in Kanniyakumari District and Shencottah Taluk of Tirunelveli-Kattabomman
137. Vokkaligar (including Vakkaligar, Okkaligar, Kappillgar/ Kappaliya, Okkaliga Gowda, Okkaliya, Gowda, Okkaliya Gowder, Okkaliya Gowda)
138. Wynad Chetty (The Nilgiris District)
139. Yadhava (including Idaiyar. Telugu Speaking Idaiyar known as Vaduga Ayar or Vaduga Idaiyar or Golla and Asthanthra Golla).
140. Yavana
141. Yerukula
142. Converts to Christianity from any Hindu Backward Classes Community or Most Backward Classes Community of Denotified Communities except the Converts to Christianity from Meenavar, Parvatha-rajukulam, Pattanavar, Sembadavar, Mukkuvar or Mukayar and Paravar.
143. Orphans and destitute children who have lost their parents before reaching the age of ten and are destitutes; and who have nobody else to take care of them either by law or custom; and also who are admitted into any of the schools or orphanages run by the Government of recognised by the Government.

Part - B. Most Backward Classes

1. Ambalakarar
2. Andipandaram
3. Bestha, Siviar
4. Bhatraju (Other than Kshatriya Raju)
5. Boyar, Oddar
6. Dasari
7. Dommara
8. Eravallar (except in Kanniyakumari district and Shencottah Taluk of Tirunelveli Kattabomman District where the Community is a Scheduled Tribe)
9. Isaivellalar
10. Jambuvanodai
11. Jangam

12. Jogi
13. Kongu Chettiar (in Coimbatore and Periyar Districts only)
14. Koracha
15. Kulala (including Kuyavar and Kumbarar)
16. Kunnuvar Mannadi
17. Kurumba
18. Kuruhini Chetty
19. Maruthuvar, Navithar, Mangala, Velakattalavar, Velakatalanair and Pronopakari
20. Mond Golla
21. Moundadan chetty
22. Mahendra, Medara
23. Mutlakarnpatti
24. Narikoravar
25. Nokkar
26. Vanniakula Kshatriya (including Vanniya, Vanniya, Vannia-Gounder, Gounder of Kander, Padayachi, Palli and Agnikula-Kshatriya)
27. Paravar (except in Kanniyakumari District and Shencottah Taluk of Tirunelveli Kattabomman district where the community is Scheduled Caste) (including Converts to Christianity)
28. Meenavar (Parvatliarajakulam, Pattanavar, Sembadavar) (including Converts to Christianity)
29. Mukkuvar or Mukayar (including Converts to Christianity)
30. Punnan Vettuva Gounder
31. Pannayar (other than Kathikarar in Kanniyakumari District)
32. Sathatha Sri Vaishanava (including Sathani, Chattadi and Chattada Srivaishnava)
33. Sezhia Chetty
34. Telugupatty Chetty
35. Thottja Naicker (including Rajakambalatn Gollavar, Sillavar, Thockalavar and Thozhuva Naicker)
36. Thondaman
37. Valaiyar (including Chettinad Valayars)
38. Vannar (Salaivai Thozhilalar) (including Agasa, Madivala, Ekali, Rajakula. Veluthadar and Rajaka) (except in Kanniyakumari District and Shencottah Taluk of Tirunelveli Kattabomman District where the community is a Scheduled Caste)
39. Vettaikarar
40. Vettuva Gounder
41. Yogeeswarar

Tripura

1. Acharji (Ganak)
2. Badyakar, Dliuli. Nagarchi, Sabdakar
3. Baishnab
4. Barui. Barujibi
5. Bauri
6. Bhar, Rajbhar
7. Bhumij, Bumij
8. Bin

9. Bind
10. Chouhan
11. Dosadh. Dosad
12. Gara
13. Gareri
14. Goala, Gope, Yadav, Aheer
15. Haledas, Halladas; Haloadas
16. Jhara
17. Kandh
18. Kapali
19. Karmakar, Kamar
20. Kairi
21. Kumbhakar, Kumar, Rudrapal
22. Kuri
23. Kurmi
24. Lohar
25. Manipuri, Bishnupriya. Manipuri
26. Marai
27. Modak
28. Mat, Natta
29. Napit, Shill
30. Nayak
31. Nepali (Limbo, Matwali, Rai)
32. Puniya, Nunia
33. Pan
34. Pankli, Painak
35. Pasi
36. Rai (Orlya)
37. Raily
38. Sutradhar
39. Telenga
40. Tanti, Tati
41. Teli (Oriya)
42. Yogi, Jogi, Nath

West Bengal

1. Kapali
2. Baishya Kapali
3. Kurni
4. Sutradhar
5. Karmakar
6. Kumbhakar, Kumar
7. Swarnakar
8. Teli, Kolu
9. Napit
10. Yogi-Nath
11. Goala-Gope (Pallav Gope, Ballav Gope, Yadav Gope, Gope Ahir, Yadav)
12. Moira-Modak (Halwai)
13. Barujibi, Barui
14. Satchasi
15. Malakar
16. Tanti
17. Kansari
18. Shankhakar
19. Koori/Koiri
20. Raju
21. Tamboli/Tamli
22. Nagar
23. Karani
24. Dhanuk
25. Sarak
26. Jolah (Ansari-Momin)
27. Roniwar
28. Kosta/Kostha
29. Christians

Converted from Scheduled Castes

30. Bhujel
31. Newar
32. Mangar (Thapa, Rana)
33. Nembang
34. Sampang
35. Bunchheng
36. Thami
37. Yogi
38. Dhimal
39. Lakhera/Lahera
40. Fakir, Sain
41. Kahar

42. Tamang
43. Betkar (Bentkar)
44. Chitrakar
45. Hawari
46. Tuhra
47. Bhar
48. Dhunia
49. Khandait
50. Patidar
51. Gangot
52. Kasai
53. Hele-Helia-Chasi Kaibarta
54. Banshi-Barman
55. Nashya-Sekh
56. Pahadia Muslim
57. Khen
58. Sukli
59. Sunuwar
60. Bharbhuja

Chandigarh

1. Ahoria, Aheri, Hori. Naik, Thori or Turi
2. Borrer/Barra
3. Bota/Tota, Hansi/Hensi or Hesi
4. Chamgar/Changar
5. Chirimar/Chrimar
6. Daiya
7. Gwaria, Gauria or Gwar
8. Kanjur or Kanchan/Kunchan
9. Kummi/Kurmi
10. Nar
11. Rohar, Rehare/Rohard or Ree/Re
12. Ghirath including Chahng and Bahti
13. Kahar, Jhinwar or Dhinwar/Dhinear
14. Ghani/Ghazi, Goasiara/Ghasiara or Ghosi/Ghosia
15. Bagria
16. Weavers (Jullaha)
17. Labana
18. Kumhar/Kumahars
19. Nais
20. Dhobis
21. Kamboj
22. Rai Sikh
23. Barwar
24. Barai, Tarboli/Tomboji
25. Batera/Battera
26. Bairagi, Baregi/Baragi
27. Bharbunja. Bharbhuja/Bharbhuria
28. Bhat, Bhatra, Darpi, Amiya
29. Bhuhalia-Lohar
30. Chahang/Chang
31. Chimba/Chiba/Chhimba, Chipi, Chhippi/Chimpa/Darji/ Darj, Tank
32. Dahakaut/Dakuat
33. Dhimar, Mallah/Mallah, Kashyap Rajput/Kasya Rajputs
34. Faquir
35. Dhosali/Bhosali, Dosali
36. Gawla/Gawala, Gowala/Gowala
37. Gadderia/Gadaria
38. Jhangara Brahaman/Jhangra Brahman/Jangra Brahman
39. Hazam Nai/Hajjam Nai
40. Jogi Nath
41. Khati
42. Rachban/Rechhand
43. Khanghera
44. Kuchband/Kuch Band
45. Ththera/Thethera, Tamera
46. Lakhora, Kamhar/Maninar
47. Vanzara
48. Madari

49. Lohar
50. Mochi
51. Mhasi
52. Noonga
53. Nalband
54. Shorgie
55. Pinja, Pomja/Ponja
56. Soi
57. Singhliar/Singhikant, Singhwala/Singhiwala
58. Toll
59. Christian converted from Scheduled Castes
60. Dauln, Soni Barderi/Soni

Daman & Diu

1. Bhandari
1A. Banjara, Lambadi, Lamani. Sugali
2. Christian Chamar
3. Christian Mahar
4. Dhangar
5. Dhobi
6. Dhor
7. Gauda
8. Goggi
9. Gosavi
10. Kasar
11. Koli
12. Kumbi
13. Mitna
14. Naidu
15. Nath, Jogi
16. Rhavi, Nai
17. Sagar
18. Yadav, Gavli

Pondicherry

[Notified vide Gazette of the UT dated 19th February, 2001]

1. Agamudiyas (including Thuluva Vellalas)
2. Ayeeravaisiar - confined to Acharapakkam Chettiar, Beri Chettiar, Manjapudoor Chettiar. Vadambar Chettiar
3. Converts to Christianity from and Hindu Backward Classes Community irrespective of the Generation of Conversion
4. Converts to Christianity from Scheduled Castes irrespective of the Generation of Conversion
5. Dekkani Muslims (Pondicherry and Karaikal Regions only)
6. Gramani/Sanar/Nadar/Ezhava/Tiyya
7. Irular/Vettaikarar/Kattunaicker
8. Isai Vellalar
9. Jangam/ Jangamar
10. Kalavanthula
11. Kamsali
12. Kannada Devanga/ Telugu Devanga
13. Karuneegar/Kannakkupillai
14. Khatriyas
15. Konda Reddiar
16. Kongu Vellalar
17. Kuyavar/Kulalar/Kumbarar/Kummari - including Mannudayar, Pathar, Poonul Kuyavar, Velaar
18. Latin Catholics
19. Mahratta (Non-Brahmin) including Khatik
20. Mappila
21. Marudha Naidu

22. Maruthuvar/Nayee Brahmin/Mangali - including Ambattan Navithar, Pandithar, Pariyari, Pronopakari
23. Meenavar/Agnikulakshatriya/Mukkuvan - including Chettiar, Chinna Pattinavar. Meenava Chettiar, Nattar, Paravar, Parvatharajakulam, Pattinavar, Pattinava Chettiar, Periya Pattinavar, Sembadavar
24. Lubbai including Maricar, Ravuthar, Saibu, Shaik, Syed
25. Mukkulathor/Devar - including Agamudaya Devar, Kallar, Maravar
26. Nainar
27. Ottar
28. Padmasaliar/ Padmasali/ Saliar/ Salian/Pattu Saliar/ Saliars
29. Palayapattu Naidu
30. Parkavakulam - including Malayaman, Nathaman, Parkavakula Pillai, Parakavakula Udayar, Suruthiman
31. Pattu Chettiar
32. Reddy (Ganjam)
33. Sadhu Chetty/24 Manai Telugu Chetty/ Telugupatty Chetty
34. Salia Chettiar
35. Senai Thalaivar
36. Sengunthar/Kaikolar
37. Settibalija
38. Sozhia Vellalar
39. Vadamalai Chettiar
40. Valayal Naidu/Balija Naidu/Cavara Naidu/ Gavaralu
41. Vandayar
42. Vaniar/Vaniya Chetty
43. Vannan/Vannar/Ekali/ Mannan/Rajaka/ Chakkali
44. Vanniakula Kshatriya - including Gounder, Naicker, Padayatchi, Palli, Vanniar
45. Vellala Chettiar
46. Viswakarma/ Kammalar/ Thatchar/Porkollar/ Karumar/ Kannar/ Kalthatchar/ Thattar/ Viswakarmala/ Pathar
47. Yadava/Gollalu -including Idayar, Konar, Sambar Yadava, Yadava Pillai
48. Yadava Naidu
49. Yerukula

Appendix - II

List of Other Backward Classes Recommended by the First Backward Classes Commission (Kalelkar)

Alphabetical List to Facilitate users to Identify the Backward Class in Respective States.

Abbreviations used for the States

Ajmer	AJ
Andhra State	AP
Assam	AS
Bhopal	BH
Bihar	BI
Bombay	BO
Coorg	CO
Delhi	DE
Himachal Pradesh	HP
Hyderabad State	HY
Kutch	KU
Madhya Bharat	MB
Madhya Pradesh	MP
Madras	MD
Manipur	MA
Mysore State	MY
Orissa	OR
Patiala and Punjab States Union	PP
Punjab	PU
Rajasthan	RA
Saurashtra	SA
Travancore-Cochin	TC
Tripura	TR
Uttar Pradesh	UP
Vindhya Pradesh	VP
West Bangal	WB

Abbasi, Bhishti, Sakka (DE)
Abdal (BI)
Acharaj (RA)
Acharaj, Dakaut, Gujru (HP)
Acharaj, Panchal Brahman, Changar (PU)
Acharja (PP)
Acharji, Agariya (WB)
Acharya, Acharji (WB)
Ad-Bhopa (RA)
Adhori (VP)
Adi-Saiva (MD)
Adi-Telaga (AP)
Adodia (SA)
Agamudaiyan (Excluding, Vellala) (MD)
Agaria Aghria, Aghria (OR)
Agasa (BO)
Agasa (HY)
Agasa (MD)
Agasa (MY)
Aghore (WB)
Aghori (BI)
Agnikula Kashatriya, Pallekapu, Pallereddi, Palli, Vannireddi, Vanni Kapu, Vannikula Kshatriya (AP)
Agnikula Kshatriya, Palli, Vanniyakula Kshatriya (MD)
Agradana, Agradani, Agradani (WB)
Agrahari (UP)
Agrahari Vaishya (BI)
Agri (BO)
Agri Kharwal (DE)
Ahar (UP)
Aheri, Aheria, Heri, Naik, Thori, Tori, Aheria (PP)
Aheria, Aheri Heri, Naik, Thori, Turi, Aheri (PU)
Ahibasi (UP)
Ahir (AJ)
Ahir (BH)
Ahir (KU)
Ahir (MA)
Ahir (MB)
Ahir (PU)
Ahir (RA)
Ahir (SA)
Ahir, Ahir Sonar, Ahir Sonar (BO)
Ahir, Bargahi Brijbasi, Jadav (VP)
Ahir, Bargahi, Bhurtiya (UP)
Ahir, Ghosh, Goala, Jadav, Yadv (WB)
Ahir, Ghosi (DE)
Ahir, Gola, Golla, Mekala Golla, Punnu Golla, and Yadava (OR)
Ahir, Gola, Yadav, Gaura, Goala Bagal, Ghosi, Gaddi (BI)
Ahir, Jadav (MP)
Ahom (AS)
Airavar, Ayiravaisya (MD)
Aiyarakulu (AP)
Akkasalig Sonar (BO)
Akkasaliga (HY)
Alia (OR)
Alitkar (BO)
Alkari (BO)
Alwar (TC)
Amaguntamala (AP)
Amanatiya (OR)
Amant, Amat, Amath, Amat Amath (WB)
Amat (BI)
Ambalakaran (MD)
Ambigaru (BO)
Ambika (MD)
Amma Kodaga (CO)
Anarpay Mala (AP)
Andhiya Domb, Chonel, Domb, Christian Domb, Dombo, Mirgani Domb, Ponaka Domb, Telaga, Telaga, Ummia, Audiniya Domba (AP)

Andhiyadiya Domb, Audiniya Domb, Chonel Domb, christian Domb, Domb, Mirgani Domb, Ponaka Domb, Telaga, Ummia (MD)
Andi Pandaram (MD)
Anglo-Indians (Eurasians) (TC)
Annadan (MD)
Anne Boyina Palli (AP)
Annupagoundar (Ramnad, Coimbatore, Madura, Tinnevelly) (MD)
Ansar, Julaha, Momin (UP)
Arab (SA)
Arain Rayee, Kunjra (DE)
Arain, Kunjra, Rayee, Bhandi Waddar, Dandhi Dasa, Dhunia, Ghatti Waddar, (BO)
Arakalu (AP)
Arakh (UP)
Arakh (VP)
Archukatlavandu (AP)
Are Maharati (AP)
Are Maharati (S.Kanara) (MD)
Arekatika (HY)
Arer (BO)
Arya (S.Kanara) (MD)
Arya Kshatriya (AP)
Arya Sarollu, Daruwala, Sharigaru (HY)
Arya Vaishya (CO)
Asara (MB)
Asthana Golla (Coimbatore and Malabar Distts.) (MD)
Atagara, Devanga, Audiniya Domb (AP)
Atagora, Devanga, Audiniya Domb, Ayira Vaisya (MD)
Atari (BO)
Atashbaz, Tirgar (UP)
Atishbaz (HP)
Atit (UP)
Atith, Gosain (BI)
Atte Vikkal (BO)
Audhia (MP)
Audhias (Oudhias) (UP)
Audhie, Avadhi, Avadhi (VP)
Ausula (HY)
Ayer (KU) Bagal (WB)
Ayodha Kapu (AP)
Ayodhareddi, Kambalathar, Kendi, Kottai Reddi, Rajakambala Naicker, Reddi, Ganiga (MD)
Ayri (CO)

Babar, Nai, Ved, Hajam (RA)
Babria (BO)
Badahi, Barhi, Barhai, Viswakarma, Bagal (BI)
Badaka (MP)
Badani (BO)
Badasuda (OR)
Badera (RA)
Badgi (BO)
Badgujar (BO)
Badhai (BO)
Badhair, Barhai, Bindhani, Sutradhar and Badhira, Badhira (OR)
Badhi, Barhai Dhiman, Brahman (PU)
Badi (Nepali) (AS)
Badi (Nepali) (MA)
Badi (Nepali) (WB)
Badiga (HY)
Badigar (VP)
Badwa Goswami (UP)
Badyakar, Dhuli, Nagarchi, Sabdakar (TR)
Bagadi (BO)
Bagaria, Barhai (PU)
Bagaria, Beldia (RA)
Bagdi (BI)
Baghia, Baree, Bawar, Payak, Singhiwala, Vaidyanai (MB)

Baghwan, Mali (UP)
Bagri (VP)
Bagri, Gujarat Baori, Marwar Baori, Marwar Waghri, Salat Waghri (BO)
Bagria (PP)
Bahari (PU)
Bahurupi (BO)
Bahurupi (MP)
Bairagi (BH)
Bairagi (BI)
Bairagi (DE)
Bairagi (MY)
Bairagi (VP)
Bairagi, Baragi, Baragi (PP)
Bairagi, Bava, Gosavi, Gosai (BO)
Bairagi, Bawa (KU)
Bairagi, Jogi (RA)
Bairagi, Nath, Gossain (HP)
Bairwa (Berwa, Jatiya, Bola, Meghwanshi (AJ)
Bairwa (DE)
Baishnab (TR)
Baishya Kapali, Kapali (WB)
(Bajadar, bajania, Bedey, Bediya (excluding, Bediya in S.C.), Bajania (WB)
Bajania, Kannatia (MB)
Bajenia (BO)
Bajir (BO)
Balasanthosh (HY)
Balasanthu (HY)
Balasi (OR)
Baldhia Bhat (RA)
Balegar (HY)
Balija, Oda, Balija, Togara, Kita Balia (OR)
Baloch (if settled in Saurashtra) (SA)
Balolika (MD)
Balsantoshi (BO)
Banajiga (MY)
Bandekar, Komti, Kudale, Maratha Vani, Pednekar, Sangameshwari, Narwekar, Patne (BO)
Bandhara (BO)
Bandhara Khati (SA)
Bandi (BO)
Banerwala (DE)
Banjara (BH)
Banjara, Baldia (RA)
Banjara, Berwa, Bola (AJ)
Banjara, Kuta (UP)
Banjara, Labana (MB)
Banjara, Lamana, Baragahi (VP)
Banjara/Vanjari, Labhan, Lamane, Mathura, Nayak/Nayakda, Thuria (MP)
Banka (OR)
Banna (CO)
Banoudhiya Rajputs (PU)
Banua, Buna, Bunna, Buno (WB)
Baori (RA)
Bara (SA)
Baragi, Bairagi, Bairagi (PU)
Barai, Bargahi (UP)
Barai, Tamboli (BH)
Barai, Tamboli (DE)
Barai, Tamboli (PU)
Barai, Tamboli, Tamoli, Chaurasia, Barhai, Barhi (BI)
Baraik (TR)
Baraji, Barui, Barhai (OR)
Barcha (BO)
Barchain, Chai, Chain (WB)
Barhai (UP)
Barhai, Carpenters, Baree (MB)
Barhai, Khati, Tarkhan (DE)
Barhai, Kundera, Sutar (VP)
Barhai, Tarkhan (PP)
Barhunda (BH)
Bari (BI)
Bari (BO)

Bari (DE)
Bari (MP)
Bari (RA)
Bari (UP)
Bari, Baria, Baria (VP)
Bari, Tamboli (MP)
Baria (AS)
Baria, Koli Baria (BO)
Barika, Bhandhari, Beja, Napit and Nai, Barui (OR)
Barker (BO)
Barmera, Bava (BO)
Bama Brahman, Patit, Brahman (WB)
Bamwal Bania (BI)
Baroi Chauraia, Kumavat, panwari, Purabia, Tamboli, Bawar (MB)
Baroi, Barui, Barujibi, Barui, Barujibi (AS)
Barot, Bawa (KU)
Barra (PU)
Baruasankar, Beja (OR)
Barui (TR)
Barui, Barujibi, Barujibi, Bedey, Bediya (WB)
barwar (PU)
Basdewa/Vasdeo/Vasudewa (MP)
Baseda (RA)
Basudev, Harbola, Jaga, Kaparia Kapdi (VP)
Batham (BI)
Bathi (PP)
Bathi (PU)
Battada (AP)
Battada (MD)
Battal (BO)
Batterha (PU)
Batwal (PU)
Bauri (TR)
Baver (MB)
Bawa, Barber (SA)
Bawaji (MY)
Bawaria (UP)
Bazigar (BO)
Bazigar, Nat, Qalandar, (Excluding those in, S.C.) (DE)
Beda (MY)
Bedar, Berad, Naikmakkalu, Naikwadi, Nayakaru, Talvar, Valmiki (BO)
Bedia (TR)
Bedia/Beria/Biria, Dukar-Kolhati, Kolhati (MP)
Bediya, Sapera (BI)
Bega (HP)
Behna (VP)
Behna, Dhunia, Pinjara (MB)
Behna, Pinjara (BH)
Beldar (BI)
Beldar, Berad (BO)
Beldar, Kharol (MB)
Beldar, Telegu-Munnarkapu (MP)
Benata Oriya, Benati, Benati (OR)
Bentkar, Bentkars, Bentkars (OR)
Beparla (SA)
Beragi (UP)
Beria (UP)
Beria, Bedia, Bedia (RA)
Beria, Chhara, Dass, Gujarathi Kolhati, Kanjar Bhat, Kanjari, Kanjar, Sansia (BO)
Beria, Kasera (PU)
Berua (WB)
Besfa, Gangaputra (HY)
Bestar (BO)
Bestha (AP)
Bestha (MD)
Beta, Hensi, Hesi (PU)
Betera, Betra, Betra, Bhandari (OR)
Betru (HP)
Bhaat, Bhat, Bhat (HY)
Bhabhulia (DE)
Bhadbhuja (BO)
Bhadbhunja (by caste) (MP)

Bhadhuja (MB)
Bhadi-Waddar, Matti-Wadder, Waddar (MP)
Bhadre (MP)
Bhagat (RA)
Bhagat (UP)
Bhagia (BO)
Bhaitia (BO)
Bhakta (TR)
Bhal (BO)
Bhalya (BO)
Bhampta, Bhampta (Rajput), Dong-Dasar, Ghantichor, Uchlia, Bhampta (Rajput) (BO)
Bhamta, Bhamti, Bhamti (MB)
Bhand (BO)
Bhand (DE)
Bhand (PP)
Bhand (PU)
Bhand (UP)
Bhand, Bhavaya (SA)
Bhandari (AP)
Bhandari (MD)
Bhandari, Bhandara (in Gujarat), Bhandara (in Gujarat) (BO)
Bhangi (WB)
Bhangi, Dom (UP)
Bhangi, Halalkhor, Lalbegi and Mehtar (Excluding those in S.C.) (BI)
Bhangi, Hela (MB)
Bhania (OR)
Bhanja Purana (OR)
Bhanjara Dhai (PU)
Bhanmati, Bhanta/Bhamta, Bhanta/Bhamta (MP)
Bhansali (KU)
Bhant (WB)
Bhantu (MB)
Bhar (BI)
Bhar (MP)
Bhar (TR)
Bhar (WB)
Bhar, Rajbhar (UP)
Bharadi (BO)
Bharari (MB)
Bharawa (RA)
Bharbhooja (DE)
Bharbhuja (MB)
Bharbhuja (PP)
Bharbhuja (VP)
Bharbhuja, Bhurji, Kandu (UP)
Bharbhunja (BH)
Bharbhunja (PU)
Bharbhunja (RA)
Bharewa (VP)
Bharia-Bharihar (MP)
Bharwad (KU)
Bharwad (outside Nesses, area in the forests of, Alech, Gir and Barada), Bhopa Rabari (SA)
Bharwad, Rabari (BO)
Bhaskar (BI)
Bhat (BH)
Bhat (BI)
Bhat (BO)
Bhat (DE)
Bhat (KU)
Bhat (WB)
Bhat, Bhatra, Darpi, Ramaiya, Bhatra (PU)
Bhat, Charan (RA)
Bhat, Charan, Maru, Sotiya, Salvi (MB)
Bhat, Deti (HP)
Bhat, Jasondhi (VP)
Bhat, Sanghadia (SA)
Bhat, Taga Bhat (UP)
Bhat/Brahmabhat, Charan (MP)
Bhatarajula (OR)
Bhathiara (BI)
Bhathiara, Rizzaqi (WB)
Bhati Rajput, Karadia, Pardoda, Bhoyan, Bhoyah, Bhoy (SA)

Bhati, Chang, Ghirath (PU)
Bhatiara (RA)
Bhatiara, Bhisti (DE)
Bhatiya (WB)
Bhatiyara (MB)
Bhatiyara (UP)
Bhatraja (HY)
Bhatraju (AP)
Bhatraju (MD)
Bhatraju (MY)
Bhatua (OR)
Bhavaiya, Targala (BO)
Bhavasar (RA)
Bhavasar Kshtriya (AP)
Bhavin (BO)
Bhavsar (BO)
Bhavsar (KU)
Bhavsar, Chippa, Nilgar, Nirali, Rangari (MP)
Bhawasar, Rangari, Rangrez (HY)
Bherihar, Gareri, Gadaria (BI)
Bhil (SA)
Bhilaya (SA)
Bhima (VP)
Bhinhar (TR)
Bhinjia (TR)
Bhiro (RA)
Bhishti (BH)
Bhishti (MB)
Bhishti (UP)
Bhishti (VP)
Bhishti, Sakka (RA)
Bhisti, Bhurji, Bhurtiya (UP)
Bhisti, Pakhali (BO)
Bhisty (MP)
Bhogam, Ganika, Kalavanthula (HY)
Bhogam, Sani, Kalavantulu, Devdasi (OR)
Bhoi (BO)
Bhoi (HY)
Bhoi (KU)
Bhoi, Bhoyan, Bhoyah, Bhoy (SA)
Bhoi, Dhiwar, Kahar, Mallah, Navda (MB)
Bhoi, Ezingabhui, Kahar, Turha (MP)
Bhoi, Kahar, Kewat, Mallah, Dhimar (BH)
Bhoi, Sagarwanshi Mali, Mali, Saini (RA)
Bhojak, Sevak (RA)
Bhojki (PU)
Bhokta (OR)
Bhopa, Manbhao (MB)
Bhoyar (MP)
Bhuhalia, Lohar (PU)
Bhuiya (TR)
Bhujan (OR)
Bhujru, Chang, Changar (PU)
Bhujwa (VP)
Bhuk (BO)
Bhuliya, Bindhani (OR)
Bhunji (BI)
Bhunvaya, Bhavaiya, Bhawari, Bhavaiya, Bhawari (RA)
Bhupar (BO)
Bhura Brahman (PU)
Bhurtiya (VP)
Bhute (BO)
Bhutia, Brijbasi (VP)
Bidia (MB)
Bikak (BO)
Bilas Naik (BO)
Bilimagga (CO)
Billava (CO)
Billava Maliah Billava (MD)
Biloch (PU)
Bin (TR)
Bind (BI)
Bind (TR)
Bind (UP)
Binjara, Vanjari, Vanjara (BO)
Binjhia, Binjhwar, Birjia, Brijia, Binjhwar (WB)

Birhor, Birjia, Brijia, Buna, Bunna, Buno (WB)
Birjhia (OR)
Bisati (UP)
Bissoy (AP)
Bogada (OR)
Bogari (BO)
Boldari (RA)
Bolodhia (OR)
Bondil (AP)
Bondil (MD)
Bondili (HY)
Bondili (OR)
Boreka, Gopal, Carpenters, Charan, Chaurasia (MB)
Boriabaf, Rassiban (HY)
Botakusuda (OR)
Botehra (PU)
Bowariya (MP)
Boya (AP)
Boya (CO)
Boya (HY)
Boya (MD)
Brahman (in Kangra District) (PU)
Britia, Kahar (VP)
Budabukkala (AP)
Budbudkala (HY)
Budbudki (BO)
Budubudike (MY)
Bugri (BO)
Bujhri (Brahman) (HP)
Bukka (HY)
Bukkitgar (BO)
Bumij (TR)
Bundabestha (MY)
Burud (HY)
Burud, Medar (BO)

Chack, Chai, Chain (WB)
Chai, Kewat, Mallah, Sorahiya (UP)
Chain (BI)
Chak (DE)
Chakala (AP)
Chakala (HY)
Chakar, Daroga, Hazuri, Lambuat, Charan (RA)
Chakkala (TC)
Chamadia (BO)
Chamadia Khatki (SA)
Chamta (RA)
Chamtha (BO)
Chamtha (SA)
Chanara (KU)
Chandal, Namasudra (BI)
Chandlagara (BO)
Chandor (RA)
Changar (PP)
Chaniatia, Daya Maha-Brahman, Gujargaod, Brahman (RA)
Chapota, Chaurasia (BI)
Chapparband (BO)
Chaptogara (S. Kanara) (MD)
Charan (KU)
Charan, Gadhavi (BO)
Charan, Maldhari (outside, Nesses area in the forests, of Alech, Gir and Barada) (SA)
Charg (PU)
Charodi, Chhara (BO)
Chasadhoba Haladhar, Halari, Satchasi (WB)
Chatada, Chattada, Srivaishnava, Chattada, Srivaishnava, Chonel Domb, Christian Domb (MD)
Chatadi, Chattada, Sri Vaishnava, Chattadasri Vaishnava, Chonel Domb, Christian Domb (AP)
Chauhan, Chippa (MP)
Chaukalshi (BO)
Chaurasi, Tamboli (VP)
Chaurth (BO)
Chavalakkaran (TC)
Cheeta (RA)
Chhadipti (UP)

Chhimba, Chhipi, Chhipa (PU)
Chhimba, chimpa, Darzi, Tank, Chimpa (PP)
Chhimba, Darzi, Dakaut, Darzi, Deti (HP)
Chhipa (AJ)
Chhipa (MB)
Chhipa (RA)
Chhipi (UP)
Chhipi, Tank (DE)
Chhippa (UP)
Chigari Betegar (BO)
Chik (BI)
Chik (OR)
Chik, Chikwa, Kasai, Kassab, Chikwa (WB)
Chikwa, Qussab (UP)
Chikwa, Qussab (VP)
Chipa (VP)
Chipar (BH)
Chipi, Darzi (VP)
Chippa (in Gujarat) (BO)
Chippa, Kuntulu (HY)
Chippar, Rangrez (BH)
Chippollu, Mera (HY)
Chirimar (DE)
Chirimar (PU)
Chirimar (WB)
Chirimar, Darzi (PP)
Chimar, Mirshikar (BI)
Chita (AJ)
Chitari (MP)
Chitari, Naqqashi (HY)
Chitra (OR)
Chitrakar (OR)
Chitrakathi (BO)
Chittrakar (WB)
Choodi Farosh, Daruwala (HY)
Choongar (BH)
Choudang (AS)
Chunari, Lonari (BO)
Chunera (SA)
Chunkar, Sunkar (MP)
Chunvalia Koli, Chunvaidia, Chunvadia (SA)
Churia (OR)
Churigar, Lakhera (RA)
Churihar, Manihar (UP)
Churihara (BI)
Churihara, Lahera (WB)
Chutiya (AS)

Dabagar (BO)
Dabgar (SA)
Dafali (BI)
Dafali (DE)
Dafali (UP)
Dafali (WB)
Dafali, Dholi (BH)
Daffer (SA)
Dahalias (OR)
Dahej (VP)
Daibagya, Daivagna, Ganak (AS)
Daiya, Darpi (PU)
Daiya, Dhaiya (DE)
Dakaut (AJ)
Dakaut (PU)
Dakaut, Prade, Daiya (DE)
Dakot, Garo, Gakudia (RA)
Dalera (UP)
Damai (Nepali) (MA)
Damai (Nepali), Daivagna (AS)
Damami (Dholi, Nagarchi), Dholi (AJ)
Damami, Daroga (RA)
Dana (VP)
Dandrolu, Dyandrawar (AP)
Dangi (BH)
Dangi (BI)
Dangi (UP)
Dangi, Darzi (VP)
Dangi, Daya Maha Brahman (RA)
Dangua (OR)
Danwar (of Gorakhpur) (UP)

Darji (OR)
Darji, Meru (MP)
Darji, Shimpi, Dasa (BO)
Daroga (AJ)
Darzi (BH)
Darzi (DE)
Darzi (MB)
Darzi (MY)
Darzi (RA)
Darzi (SA)
Darzi (UP)
Darzi, Idrisi (BI)
Darzi, Idrisi (WB)
Dasari (AP)
Dasari (HY)
Dasari (MD)
Dasari (MY)
Dasari (OR)
Davari, Davari Gosavi, Nath Panthi, Davari Gosavi (BO)
Debhar (BI)
Deevanga (HY)
Deha, Dhaya, Dhea, Dhaya, Dhea (PP)
Dehuri (OR)
Deons, Devadasi (OR)
Depala (BO)
Depala Dhobi (KU)
Depala, Dhobi, Dhobi (SA)
Desali, Dhuli (TR)
Deshwali, Mina (MB)
Devadasi Caste, Natuva (HY)
Devadika (S. Kanara), Devanga, Domb (MD)
Devakuditalayari, Devanga (AP)
Devali (BO)
Devalkar (AP)
Devanga (CO)
Devanga (MY)
Devangi, Dora (OR)
Devdig (BO)
Dewang, Jandra, Koskati, Lingayat, Dukar-Kolhati (MP)
Dey, Sudra Das (AS)
Dhakad (BH)
Dhakad, Keer, Kirar (MB)
Dhakar (AJ)
Dhamin (BI)
Dhanak, Dhai (PU)
Dhanak, Dhanka, Dhanuk, Gokhi Dhanka, Dhanuk (RA)
Dhandi, Dhadhi, Dhadhi (RA)
Dhaner (OR)
Dhangar (BH)
Dhangar (HY)
Dhangar, Dhiwar (MB)
Dhangar, Gadri/Gadaria, Hatgar/Hatkar, Kurmar, Mirdha (MP)
Dhangar, Kurbar (BO)
Dhanka (MP)
Dhanuk (BI)
Dharala, Patanwadia (BO)
Dharhi, Pawaria, Singharia Tanwar (UP)
Dhasa (WB)
Dhavad (BO)
Dhebra, Dhimar, Dhivar, Gabit, Harkantra, Mangeli, Mangela, Page, Sankuri, Dhimar, Dhivar (BO)
Dheh (PU)
Dhekaru (BI)
Dhekaru (WB)
Dhenuar (WB)
Dhimar (BI)
Dhimar, Dhinwar, Jhinwar, Kahar, Mallah, Dhiman Brahman, Dhinwar (PU)
Dhimar, Dhiver, Dhiver (UP)
Dhimar, Kewat (MP)
Dhinwar, Jheet, Jhinwar, Kahar (HP)
Dhinwar, Jhinwar, Kahar, Mallah (PP)
Dhinwar, Jhinwar, Kahar, Nishar (DE)

Dhobi (DE)
Dhobi (excluding those in S.C.), Dhimar (BH)
Dhobi (excluding those in S.C.) (OR)
Dhobi (HY)
Dhobi (MP)
Dhobi (PP)
Dhobi (PU)
Dhobi (RA)
Dhobi (UP)
Dhobi (VP)
Dhobi, Hawari, (excluding those in S.C.) (BI)
Dhobi, Parit (BO)
Dhogri (PU)
Dhoki (BO)
Dholi (BO)
Dholi (MP)
Dholi, Nagarchi (RA)
Dhosali (PU)
Dhukkar (BO)
Dhulia, Kosti/Kushta/, Kosthi, Lingayat, Hatgar, Charan (MP)
Dhunia, Dhunkar, Dhunkar, Dora (OR)
Dhunia, Dhunkar, Ezingabhui (MP)
Dhunia, Mansoori, Naddaf, Gadaria, Gaddi (BI)
Dhunia, Masoori (WB)
Dhunia, Naddaf (BH)
Dhunia, Naddaf, Dom (UP)
Dhunia, Pinjara, Kadhera, Dhunnewala, Dhunnewala (DE)
Dhunkar, Kadore, Dhunia (MB)
Doga (MY)
Dombara (HY)
Dombara (MY)
Dombari (HY)
Dombari, Dong-Dasar (BO)
Dombo, Dombo (AP)
Dommara (AP)
Dommara (HY)
Dommara (MD)
Donga Dasari (AP)
Donga Yata (AP)
Doodekula (HY)
Dosad (TR)
Dosali (PP)
Drazi, Sai (KU)
Dudekula (MD)
Dudekula, Dyandrawar (AP)
Dudekulu (OR)
Dumal (OR)
Durgamurogeru (BO)

Eediga (HY)
Eeliga (HY)
Elmar (BO)
Eravallar (MD)
Erragoala (OR)
Eshava, Thiya (TC)
Ex-Tea-Garden Labourers (AS)
Ex-Tea-Garden Labourers (TR)
Ezhavathy, Vathi (TC)
Ezhuthasan (TC)
Ezhuvan, Illuvan (Malabar) (MD)

Fakir (BH)
Fakir (DE)
Fakir (KU)
Fakir (OR)
Fakir (RA)
Fakir, Sain (VP)
Fakir, Sain (WB)
Fakir-Bandarwala, Gadri/Gadaria (MP)
Faqeer (HY)
Faqir (PU)
Faqir (UP)
Faquir (MB)
Futgudi, Gabit, Gadhavi (BO)

Gach, Mandewala (DE)
Gachaki (MP)
Gadaria (DE)
Gadaria (PP)
Gadaria (PU)
Gadaria (RA)
Gadaria, Gadri, Gari, Gadri, Gari (BH)
Gadariya (VP)
Gadariya, Gauriya (UP)
Gadariya, Ghosi (MB)
Gaddi, Garri (DE)
Gaddi, Ghosi (UP)
Gaddi, Ghosi (WB)
Gadhai (SA)
Gadheri (BI)
Gadheri, Garri (DE)
Gadic Lohar, Gadolia, Lohar, Lohar, Garo (RA)
Gadlia (SA)
Gadole, Gaddoli, Longoliha, Lohpita, Gaddoli (MB)
Gadolia (Gadodia), Gadodia (AJ)
Gahamandi (MP)
Gahelra (BO)
Gain (WB)
Gainey (Nepali) (MA)
Gainey (Nepali), Ganak (AS)
Gajula (HY)
Gajulu (OR)
Galada Konkani (MD)
Galkata (SA)
Gam Vakkal (BO)
Gamalla, Gowda, Kalali (AP)
Gamalla, Gowda, Kalali (MD)
Gamantiya (OR)
Ganda (WB)
Gandharap (BO)
Gandharb (BI)
Gandharp (UP)
Gandhi (UP)
Gandhila (UP)
Gandhiya, Gauriya (UP)
Gandla (AP)
Gandla (MD)
Gandla, Gangaputra (HY)
Gangai, Ganesh (BI)
Gangakula (MY)
Ganguata, Gangota, Gangota (BI)
Gangavar (AP)
Gangavar (Coimbatore, Distt) (MD)
Gangelddulavar (HY)
Gangi Reddula (AP)
Gangin (TR)
Gangwar, Ganesh, Gareri, Ghosi, Gaura, Goala, Gola (BI)
Ganiga (CO)
Ganiga (MY)
Ganiga, Ganika (HY)
Ganiga, Ghanchi, Teli (BO)
Ganiga, Nagavamsam (AP)
Ganika Nagavamsam (MD)
Ganika, Kaniyan (TC)
Ganjam Reddi (Ramned, Madura, Tinnevelly, Distts) (MD)
Ganju (TR)
Ganju, Gunju (OR)
Gaoli, Gwal (BH)
Gaoli, Lingayat-Gaoli (MP)
Garadiga (MY)
Garai, Kalu (WB)
Garasia (in Gujarat) (BO)
Gareri (TR)
Garhwal (MP)
Garpagari, Nath (MP)
Garudi (KU)
Garudi (SA)
Garudi, Modikar (BO)
Garwadi/Garaddi (MP)
Gatti (S. Kanara) (MD)
Gauria, Gwar, Gwaria (PU)
Gavada, Gavdi, Gavdi (BO)
Gavandhi (BO)
Gavandi (HY)

Gavara (AP)
Gavli (BO)
Gavli (SA)
Gawaria (AJ)
Gawaria, Gadolia Lohar, Garudia (RA)
Gayari (MB)
Gayari (RA)
Gazula Balija (AP)
Gend (BO)
Gengettinavaru (HY)
Ghadi (BO)
Ghadshi, Ghanchi (BO)
Ghai (HP)
Ghai (PU)
Ghami (MB)
Ghancha (KU)
Ghanchani, Rangaswami (RA)
Ghanchi, Ghancha, Ghanacha, Ghancha, Ghanacha (RA)
Ghanchi, Ghancha, Ghancha (SA)
Ghandaria, Ghantichor (BO)
Ghantia (SA)
Ghariya (VP)
Gharuk (BO)
Gharuk, Kahar, Kamkar, Ghosi (UP)
Gharwali (BO)
Ghasiara (PP)
Ghasiara (RA)
Ghasiara, Ghirath (PU)
Ghasiara, Ghosi (DE)
Chatti Ghare, Ghosi, Gopal (MB)
Ghatwal, Ghosh, Ghosi, Goala (WB)
Ghisadi (BO)
Ghosh, Gop, Gowala, Gop (AS)
Ghosi (MP)
Ghosi (PP)
Ghosi (PU)
Ghosi (VP)
Ghosi, Gnosi, Gnosi (BH)
Ghosi, Gokhi, Gujar Goad Brahman, Hajam (RA)
Ghur (MY)
Gingra (OR)
Gir (BO)
Giri (UP)
Girigiria, Gola, Golla (OR)
Gimi-Waddar (BO)
Goala (TR)
Goala, Gopala, and Gowdo, Gopala, Gowdo (OR)
Godaba (AP)
Golarana (BO)
Golla (CO)
Golla (MY)
Golla, Gol, Gol (BO)
Golla, Iddayar Konar, Yadav, Gowda (MD)
Golla, Iddayar, Konar, Yadav (AP)
Golla, Yadav (HY)
Gond (WB)
Gonda (WB)
Gondaliga (MY)
Gonde, Gowda (AP)
Gondhali (BO)
Gondhali (HY)
Gondhali (MP)
Gondhaliga (HY)
Gongadikar (BO)
Goniga (MY)
Gontia (VP)
Goondla (HY)
Gopal, Gosavi, Gosai (BO)
Gopal, Pangala Gopal (MP)
Gorhi, Gosain (BI)
Gorkha (UP)
Gorkha, Gosain, Gujru (HP)
Gorkhodu, Gowala (AS)
Gosain (BH)
Gosain (VP)
Gosangiwar (MP)
Gosayi (MY)

Gossain (UP)
Goundla, Gowda, Gowda (HY)
Gowala (PP)
Gowda (CO)
Gowli (HY)
Gowliga (CO)
Gowliga (HY)
Grahabipra Brahman, Jyotish Sakaldarpee, Brahman (OR)
Gramani, Shanan (MD)
Gudheri (WB)
Gudia, Gurja, Gunja, Gujra (OR)
Gudigar, Gujarat-Baori (BO)
Gudigara, Iddayar (MD)
Guhar, Jatiya (AJ)
Gujar (AJ)
Gujar (DE)
Gujar (MB)
Gujar (MY)
Gujar (UP)
Gujar Kadia, Kadia (in, Gujarat,) Gujarati Kolhati (BO)
Gujar, Gwal (BH)
Gujar, Harbola (VP)
Gulgulia (BI)
Gunagi (BO)
Gundi (TR)
Gurav (BO)
Gurav (MP)
Guri (TR)
Gurira (BO)
Gurkha (MY)
Gurou (HY)
Gwala (DE)
Gwala, Gwar, Gwaria (PU)
Habbu (BO)
Habra (OR)
Habura (MP)
Hadi (PU)
Hajam (KU)
Hajam, Ibrahimi, Haladhar, Halari (WB)
Hajam, Kalseru Navaliga, Kelashi, Nabhik, Nai, Nhavi (BO)
Hajam, Navai, Nai, Barber (SA)
Hajjam (HY)
Hajjam (MB)
Hajjam (MP)
Hajjam (OR)
Hajjam (UP)
Hajjam, Ibrahimi, Halalkhor (BI)
Hajjam, Nai (DE)
Hajjam, Nai (PU)
Hajjam, Nai, Heri Hajuri Daroga, Hela (PP)
Halalkhor (excluding those in S.C. List) (WB)
Halalkhor (UP)
Halalkhor, Hazuri (RA)
Halepaik (BO)
Hali Kaibartta (AS)
Hali, Heri, Hensi, Hesi (PU)
Hallikar (MY)
Halvakki Vakkal (BO)
Halwai (MA)
Halwai (UP)
Halwai (WB)
Halwai, Kandu, Kanu, Hawari, Ibrahimi, Idrisi (BI)
Hammal (MB)
Hanbar (BO)
Hansi (OR)
Haranshikari (BO)
Hari (PP)
Haridas (in East, Khandesh) (BO)
Harikalyan, Harkantra (BO)
Harjala (UP)
Hami, Hatgar/Hatkar (MP)
Hassimi (UP)
Hati (BO)
Hati (SA)
Hatkar (HY)
Hawari (WB)
Hegde, Kuruba (AP)

Heggade (CO)
Hela (RA)
Hela (VP)
Hela, Ibrahimi, Idrisi, Jadav (WB)
Helav (BO)
Herbi (DE)
Higer (BO)
Hijra (DE)
Hijra (UP)
Hill Tribes of Himalaya and Chittagong, Hill Tracts (WB)
Hingora (KU)
Hiragar, Sargara (BO)
Holar, Valhar (BO)
Hollar, Jadav, Jandra (MP)
Hoogar (HY)
Huga Lohar, Lohar, Lohpeta, Jadav, Jaga (VP)
Idiga (MY)
Idiga, Setti Balija (AP)
Idiga, Setti-Balija (MD)
Ilgar (BO)
Illathar, Pannikkar, Pillamar, Sarayakara, Sirkudipillai, Illuvan (MD)
Irulan (MD)
Isaivellalar, Melakarar, (Tanjore Distt.) (MD)
Jachak Mir Dhadhi (SA)
Jachak Mir Dhadi (KU)
Jada, Nekar (HY)
Jadupatia (BI)
Jaga (BO)
Jagaria (BO)
Jagiasi (from Sind) (BO)
Jagyasi (AJ)
Jagyasi Bhagat, Jogi (RA)
Jain (MY)
Jajak (From Sind) (BO)
Jajri (BO)
Jakhria Jakreja (BO)
Jakkula (Guntur Dist.) (AP)
Jalari (AP)
Jallad (DE)
Jambovanodai (AP)
Jambuvanodai (MD)
Janappa Chetty (AP)
Jandara (AP)
Jandara (MD)
Jandra (HY)
Jangalu (OR)
Jangam (AP)
Jangam (MD)
Jangam (MP)
Jangra, Lodhi, Jasondhi (VP)
Jarugamalli (AP)
Jat (BH)
Jat (BI)
Jat (BO)
Jat (HP)
Jat (KU)
Jat (MB)
Jat (SA)
Jatia (BO)
Jatigar (BO)
Jaunpuri Bania (BI)
Javeri, Johari (BO)
Jeoni (WB)
Jethi Mal (KU)
Jetty (AP)
Jetty (MD)
Jetty (MY)
Jhandi, Sonar (MP)
Jhangra Brahman, Khati (PU)
Jhara (TR)
Jhatkia Sikh, Jhinwar (DE)
Jhatkia, Kasab, Jhinwar (PP)
Jhodia (OR)
Jhoja (UP)
Jilaya (SA)
Jingar (BO)
Jingar (HY)
Jingar (MB)
Jogde (MB)

Jogi (AP)
Jogi (BH)
Jogi (BO)
Jogi (DE)
Jogi (HY)
Jogi (MD)
Jogi (MY)
Jogi (VP)
Jogi Nath, Jhinwar (PU)
Jogi Vadi (SA)
Jogi, Jugi, Jugi (BI)
Jogi, Jullaha (UP)
Jogi, Nath, Yogi (TR)
Jogi, Yogi (OR)
Jogin (BO)
Joginath (MB)
Jogivadi (KU)
Jogtin, Johari (BO)
Jolaha, Momin (AS)
Jolaha, Momin, Jyotish, Kalavantulu (OR)
Jonakan (TC)
Joshi (BO)
Joshi (MB)
Joshi (VP)
Julaha (AJ)
Julaha (excluding those in Scheduled Castes), Kahar (PU)
Julaha (if not Harijans), Jhinwar, Jheer, Kahar (HP)
Julaha (RA)
Julaha, Kahar (PP)
Julaha, Momin (BH)
Julaha, Momin (HY)
Julaha, Momin (MB)
Julaha, Momin (VP)
Julaha, Momin, (excluding those in S. C.), Kahar (DE)
Julaha, Momin, Kassab, Kasai, Kunjra, Kharwi, Laddaf, Lad Vanjari, Mann Waddar, Matti Waddar, Maratha Kolhati, Mitha, Momin, Naddaf, Pardeshi Bhoi, Raj Bhoi, Rajput Lamani, Rajput Vanjari, Rayee, Shilavat (BO)
Jyotshi Brahman (UP)

Kaasaar, Kasar (HY)
Kabad, Kabadia, Kamad, Kamadia, Kabadia, Kamad, Kamadia (RA)
Kabar, Kaleari, Kabari (VP)
Kabariya (UP)
Kabbaliga Kabberu, Kabberu (HY)
Kabbaligar (BO)
Kabbera (S. Kanara) (MD)
Kabirpanthi, Ramdasiya, Ravidasia (MB)
Kacchi (UP)
Kachagandhivaru (HY)
Kachari (BO)
Kachchi, Kahar (BH)
Kachera, Lakhera (MP)
Kachhi (MP)
Kachhi (RA)
Kachhi (VP)
Kachhi Koeri, Murai, Murao (DE)
Kachhi, Kushwaha Kshatriya, Kadore, Kahar (MB)
Kachhia, Kachi, Kachi, Kadia (in Gujarat) (BO)
Kachi (HY)
Kadar (BI)
Kadera (VP)
Kadera, Kahar (MP)
Kadera, Kahar (VP)
Kadhere, Kahar (UP)
Kadia (SA)
Kaduppatan (Malabar, Distt.) (MD)
Kaghzi (BI)
Kagzi (WB)
Kahar (AJ)
Kahar (BO)
Khar (MY)

Khar (RA)
Kahar, Kalu (WB)
Kahar, Rawani (BI)
Kaibertta (BI)
Kaikadi, Kalavanthulu (HY)
Kaikadi, Pamlor (BO)
Kaikolan, Songunthur, Kalali (MD)
Kaikollan (TC)
Kaikollan, Kalali (AP)
Kaiserwani, Kasera, Thathera (BI)
Kakal, Kakar, Kakar (KU)
Kalal (BO)
Kalal (HP)
Kalal (RA)
Kalal, Kalar, Kalar (BH)
Kalal, Kalar, Kalar (MB)
Kalal, Kalwar, Kalwar, Kadhera (DE)
Kalandar (BI)
Kalar, Kapdi, Kaparia (VP)
Kalar, Khatri-Maratha (MP)
Kalari Kurup Kalari, Panickar, Kalaripanicker (TC)
Kalavant (BO)
Kalavanthula (AP)
Kalavanthula (MD)
Kalawati (HY)
Kalbelia (BH)
Kalbi, Kulbi, Kangshia (RA)
Kalingi (AP)
Kalingi, Kintala-Kalingi (OR)
Kalkutika (HY)
Kall-Waddar, Kalseru Navaliga (BO)
Kallan, Kaniyan (TC)
Kallan, Parimalai Kallan, Kambalathar (MD)
Kallunder, Kannatia (MB)
Kalota (BH)
Kalwar (AS)
Kalwar (UP)
Kalwar Bania (BI)
Kamalapuri Vaishya, Teli (UP)
Kamar (OR)
Kamar, Karmakar (AS)
Kamar, Karmakar (WB)
Kamar, Karmakar, Karmakar (TR)
Kamar, Lohar, Karamkar (BI)
Kamati (BO)
Kambar (HY)
Kamboh, Kamkar, Kandu (UP)
Kamboj, Kamboh, Kamboh (PU)
Kami (Nepali) (AS)
Kami (Napali) (MA)
Kamlapuri Vaish Teli, Kandu, Kanu, Karamkar, Kasera (BI)
Kamli (BO)
Kammalan, (Kamsala, Viswa Brahman, Viswa), Kamsala (AP)
Kammalan, Kamsala, Viswabrahmin, Viswakarma, Kamsala (MD)
Kammar (BO)
Kammari (HY)
Kammari (OR)
Kammi (BO)
Kan (WB)
Kanada (BO)
Kanbi, (except Lova Kanbi otherwise styled as Patidar of the Kaira Distt. and the, North and South Daskroi Talukas of the Ahmedabad, Distt.) (BO)
Kanbi, Karadia Nardoda (SA)
Kanchagar, Kanjari, Kanjar, Kanjar Bhat (BO)
Kanchan, Kanjar (PP)
Kanchari (AP)
Kanchari (HY)
Kanchari (OR)
Kanchugar (HY)
Kandarpa (OR)
Kandera (BH)
Kandh (WB)

Kandu (WB)
Kandu, Kamakar (AS)
Kandu, Kanu, Kanu (MA)
Kanera, Khangar (UP)
Kenet Rajput (HP)
Kangar (DE)
Kangar Batwalo (MP)
Kangashia (SA)
Kangehra (PU)
Kangerha, Kanjar, Kasab (PP)
Kangh (TR)
Kangi, Kangshia (RA)
Kanisu, Kaniyar Pannikkar, Kanitha Pulaver, Kanitha Pulaver, Kaniyar Pannikkar (MD)
Kaniyar (MY)
Kanjar (MP)
Kanjar, Kanchan, Rachband, Kanchan (PU)
Kanjar, Sansia (VP)
Kannadiyar (MD)
Kannaeli (DE)
Kansara (BO)
Kansari (OR)
Kansari, Kangsakar, Kangsakar, Kapali (WB)
Kanuh (BO)
Kanvi (RA)
Kaora (BI)
Kapali (TR)
Kapdi (BO)
Kapu (Srikakulam and Vizag Distt.) (AP)
Kapu, Koppulakapu (OR)
Kapudia (OR)
Kapuria (WB)
Karad (RA)
Karani (WB)
Karar, Kirar (VP)
Karaun (BI)
Kare Vakkal (BO)
Karha, Karmaker (WB)
Karhara (OR)
Karia (BO)
Karikala Bhaktulu, Karni, Bhaktula, Pattusali, Padmasali, Sale, Sali Saliyan, Senapathulu, Thogata (MD)
Karnataka - Vishwa Brahman, Panchal (BO)
Kartias (OR)
Karush (UP)
Karvi (BO)
Karwal Nut (BI)
Karwal Nut, Nat, Kasai (WB)
Kasaar, Kasar (HY)
Kasab (Qasab) (AP)
Kasab, Kasai, Quraishi, Kasai (OR)
Kasab, Kasai, Qureshi, Kasai (BI)
Kasai (AJ)
Kasai (KU)
Kasai (MY)
Kasai (SA)
Kasai Maji, Kassab (WB)
Kasai, Kassab, Quraishi, Kassab (AS)
Kasai, Qussab, Quraishi (DE)
Kasar (BO)
Kasar, Kasera, Otari, Tamera/ Tambatkar, Thathera (MP)
Kasarwani (UP)
Kasaundhan (UP)
Kasbi, Kasera, Kewat (MP)
Kasera, Keer (MB)
Kasera, Kewat (BH)
Kasera, Tamera (VP)
Kasera, Tamera, Thathera (PP)
Kasera, Thathera (RA)
Kasera, Thathera (UP)
Kasgar (UP)
Kashikapdi, Timali (BO)
Kasia (BO)
Kasodan Bania (BI)

Kassab (BH)
Kassab (HP)
Kassab, Kasai, Quraishi, Khatik (MP)
Kassab, Khati (PU)
Kassab, Qassab, Kasai, Kasai (RA)
Katabu, Killiket (BO)
Katari (BO)
Kathgara (MY)
Kathi, Kelashi (BO)
Kathodia, Kherwa (RA)
Kathputli Nachanewala (DE)
Katipapala (HY)
Kauri, Kori (VP)
Kavathi, Kerala-Muthali, Sakravar, Kerala Muthali (TC)
Kavuthiyan, Kendi (MD)
Kechai (TR)
Keer (AJ)
Keer, Kirar, Kewat (UP)
Keot, Keuta, Keute, Keuata, Keuta, Keuata, Keute (OR)
Kepmari (AP)
Kesera, Temara, Thathera, Thathiar (DE)
Keut, Kewat, Kewat (BI)
Kewat, Kundera (VP)
Khagi, Khangar, Kirar (UP)
Khajirin (OR)
Khalasi (KU)
Khalasi (SA)
Khamgara, Khatri-Maratha (MP)
Khandual (OR)
Khangar (BH)
Khangar (BI)
Khangar, Mirdha, Kirar (VP)
Khangar, Mirdhan, Kharol, Kirar (MB)
Khant (SA)
Khant, Khorwa (RA)
Kharadi (BO)
Kharak (BO)
Kharak (SA)
Kharga (WB)
Kharia (WB)
Kharol (AJ)
Kharol (RA)
Kharur, Kharwa, Kharwa (BO)
Kharvi (S. Kanara) (MD)
Kharwa (KU)
Kharwa (SA)
Kharwar, Kherwar, Khewar (WB)
Khasia (SA)
Khatgune, Khati (DE)
Khathi (HY)
Khati (AJ)
Khati (from Sind) (BO)
Khati (OR)
Khatia (MP)
Khatik (only Suryavanshi) (PP)
Khatik (only Suryavanshi), Koeri (DE)
Khatri (AP)
Khatri (MD)
Khattri (BO)
Khatua (OR)
Khatwe (BI)
Khavas (BO)
Khawas (KU)
Khawas (SA)
Khelkari, Kolhati (BO)
Kheltas (BI)
Khetauri (BI)
Khetri, Killiket (BO)
Khodra, Kintala Kalingi, Kita Balija (OR)
Khondal (OR)
Khumbhakar (TR)
Khurdalta (RA)
Khyara (WB)
Kichha (KU)
Kintala Kalinga, Konar (AP)
Kirad, Kolhati (BO)
Kirar (BH)

Kirar/Kirad, Kolhati (MP)
Kisan (UP)
Koch (BI)
Koch, Rajbanshi (AS)
Koda (OR)
Kodaga of Yedavanar and, Suriabinads (CO)
Kodar, Kori (VP)
Koeri (BI)
Koeri (UP)
Kohli (PP)
Kohli (PU)
Koiri (WB)
Kolari, Muniyani (South Kanara) (MD)
Kolasi (S. Kanara) (MD)
Kolhati, Kolhatni (HY)
Koli (SA)
Koli (Son) (BO)
Koli Malhar (BO)
Koli Suryavanshi (BO)
Koli, Koli Bariya (BO)
Koli, Koskati, Kosti/Kushta/Kashti (MP)
Koli, Kuli (OR)
Koliy, Urali Nair (MD)
Kollar, Kuli, Koppula Kapu (OR)
Komarpaik (BO)
Komarpantha, Komti (BO)
Konar (TC)
Konchi Korava (HY)
Kongadi (BO)
Kongu Chettiar (Coimbatore Distt.) Konar (S) (MD)
Koppala Velama (AP)
Koracha (AP)
Koracha (MD)
Koranga (BI)
Korava (HY)
Korcha (BO)
Kori (from Sind) (BO)
Korku (BI)
Korva (BO)
Korvanji (BO)
Koshi (BO)
Koshti (HY)
Koshti (MB)
Kot (BO)
Koteyar, Sheragara, Kshatriya (S. Karana), Kettai Reddi (MD)
Kotil (MP)
Kotwal Kotwalia, Kotwalia (BO)
Kotwal, Kutwar (BH)
Kuccharia (from Sind), Kudale (BO)
Kuchband (PU)
Kuchbandha (MP)
Kuchbandhia (BI)
Kuchbandiya (MB)
Kuda (OR)
Kudal Desahasti Gowd (MD)
Kudamatia (OR)
Kudavakkal (BO)
Kuduma (OR)
Kudumbi (TC)
Kulait (PU)
Kulal, Kumbhar, Kumbar (OR)
Kulala (MD)
Kulala, Kummari, Kummari, Kuruba (AP)
Kulama (BO)
Kulbandhiya, Kumavat (MB)
Kulta, Kumbhar, Kumhar (OR)
Kuluva (TC)
Kumahar (BH)
Kumar (BH)
Kumar, Khumbhakar, Kumhar, Kumbhakar, Kumhar (WB)
Kumar, Rudra Paul of, Chachar (AS)
Kumara Kshatriya (MD)
Kumbara (CO)
Kumbara (HY)
Kumbara (MY)
Kumbaran (TC)

Kumbhakar, Kumhar, Prajapati, Kumhar (BI)
Kumbhar (BO)
Kumbhar (HY)
Kumbhar, Kulbi (RA)
Kumbhar, Prajapati (SA)
Kumhar (AJ)
Kumhar (HP)
Kumhar (KU)
Kumhar (MB)
Kumhar (PP)
Kumhar (UP)
Kumar, Prajapati (PU)
Kumhar, Prajapati, Kunjra (DE)
Kumhar/Kumbhar (MP)
Kummara (HY)
Kunbi (BH)
Kunbi (Maratha) (MB)
Kunbi Tillori (in the Ratnagiri and Kolaba Distts.) (BO)
Kunbi, Kurmar (MP)
Kunchavakkal (BO)
Kunchi Korava (BO)
Kunchita Kapu (AP)
Kunchitiga (MY)
Kundigar (UP)
Kunjra (RA)
Kunjra (VP)
Kunjra, Kashwaha Kshatriya (MB)
Kunjra, Rain (UP)
Kunjra, Rayeen (BI)
Kunjra, Rayeen (WB)
Kunnuvar Mannadi (MD)
Kupadhar Kushiari Rarh, Kushiari (AS)
Kurba (HY)
Kurma (HY)
Kurmi (DE)
Kurmi (MA)
Kurmi (MP)
Kurmi (OR)
Kurmi (PP)
Kurmi (PU)
Kurmi (TR)
Kurmi (VP)
Kurmi, Kurbar (BO)
Kurmi, Kurmi Mahto, Kurmi Mahto (BI)
Kurmi, Kuta (UP)
Kurmi, Kutwar (BH)
Kurmi, Labana (MB)
Kurmi, Lahera (WB)
Kuruba (BO)
Kuruba (MY)
Kuruba, Kurumba (MD)
Kuruhini Chetty, Kurumba (MD)
Kusavan (TC)
Kuvinchetty (HY)

Labana (AJ)
Labana (DE)
Labana (HP)
Labana, Lakhera, Lambuat, Lohar (RA)
Lobana, Vanzara (PU)
Labbai (MD)
Labbai (MY)
Labbai (TC)
Lad, Lad Sonar, Lad Sonar (BO)
Ladar (MY)
Laddaf (HY)
Ladia/Ladhia/Laria, Lakhera, Lingayat, Lingayat-Gaoli, Lingayat, Hatgar (MP)
Lahakar, Laheri, Laheri, Lalbegui (BI)
Lahera (UP)
Lakhera (AJ)
Lakhera (BH)
Lakhera, Lamana (VP)
Lakhera, Langoliha (MB)
Lakhera, Manihar (DE)
Lakhera, Manihar (PP)
Lakhera, Manihar, Lohar (PU)

Lakheri (BO)
Lakhra (OR)
Lakshmir (BO)
Lalbegi (PP)
Lamani, Lambada, Lambada (BO)
Langha (KU)
Langha (SA)
Larai (BO)
Larhia, Lodhi, Lohar, Lohpeta (VP)
Laskar (TR)
Liari, Radhi, Niari (OR)
Lingayat (CO)
Lingayod (only of, rural areas) (MY)
Lobana (UP)
Lodh (UP)
Lodha (AJ)
Lodha (BO)
Lodha (HY)
Lodha (RA)
Lodha (SA)
Lodha (TR)
Lodha, Lodhi, Lodhi (BH)
Lodha, Lodhi, Lodhi, Lohpita (MB)
Lodha, Lohar (BI)
Lodhi (MP)
Lodhi, Lodh, Lodha, Maha Lodh, Lodh, Lodha (DE)
Lohar (AJ)
Lohar (BO)
Lohar (HY)
Lohar (if not Harijan) (HP)
Lohar (MA)
Lohar (MP)
Lohar (PP)
Lohar (TR)
Lohar, Luhura, Luhura (OR)
Lohar, Vishwakarma (UP)
Loi (MA)
Lok, Lonari (BO)
Lome (VP)
Lonari (HY)
Lonia, Lunia, Ode, Odiya, Lunia (MB)
Lubana (BO)
Lubana (PP)
Luhar (BH)
Luhar (DE)
Luhar (in Gujarat) (BO)
Luharia, Luvaria, Lunvaria, Luhar, Luvaria, Lunvaria, Luhar (SA)
Lund (BO)
Lunia, Murha, Nunia (VP)
Lunia, Nonia (MP)
Lunia, Nunia (BH)
Lunia, Nunia, Mali, Mallah, Manihar (UP)
Luvaria, Luharia, Lohar, Luharia, Lohar (KU)

Machhi, Machhera, Machhera (DE)
Machhi, Mali, Mali, Mallah, Manbhao (MB)
Machhi, Tandel (BO)
Machhua (OR)
Machhua (WB)
Machula (BO)
Madambi (MD)
Madari (BI)
Madari (KU)
Madari (PP)
Madari (PU)
Madari (SA)
Madhvia (SA)
Madivala (AP)
Madivala (CO)
Madivala (MD)
Madugar, Medavar, Mahendra, Medara, Mahendra (MD)
Magadha, Magadhi-Goral, Magadhi Goral (OR)
Magar, Mangar, Mangar, Mansoori (BI)
Maghi, Maghia, Maghia (OR)

Magura (OR)
Maha Brahman, Mali (RA)
Mahadarda (WB)
Mahajir (BO)
Mahali (HY)
Mahata (WB)
Mahatam, Rai Sikh (PU)
Mahatam, Rai, Mallah, Manihar (PP)
Mahato (WB)
Mahawat (RA)
Mahendra, Medara (AP)
Mahendra, Medari (HY)
Mahesya (OR)
Mahia (BO)
Mahind (BO)
Mahisya, Mahisya Das, Mahisya Das (AS)
Mahratta (MY)
Mahratta (non-Brahmin) (AP)
Mahratta (non-brahmin) (MD)
Mahunta (OR)
Mahuriya (BI)
Mairal (BO)
Maiya, Mahiya, Mahiya (SA)
Majhwar (BI)
Makarani (KU)
Makhar (BO)
Makrani (SA)
Mala (MP)
Malakar Mali (BI)
Malakar, Mali, Mali (WB)
Malal, Malhor, Malhor (BI)
Malayali (MY)
Malayaman, Moopanar, Nainar, Nathaman, Parakavakulam, Surithiman, Maliah, Billava (MD)
Malayan (Malabar) (MD)
Male (AP)
Male (S. Karana) (MD)
Maleya (CO)
Malhar (BI)
Mali (AJ)
Mali (BO)
Mali (HY)
Mali (KU)
Mali (OR)
Mali (SA)
Mali (VP)
Mali, Mali Korchia, Paddamali, Paikomali, Mali Korchia (AP)
Mali, Mali Korchia, Paiko Mali Peddamali, Mali Korchia (MD)
Mali, Mallah (BH)
Mali, Marar (MP)
Mali, Phool Mali, Saini, Mallah, Manihar (PU)
Mali, Saini, Pholl Mali (HP)
Mali, Saini, Sauthia, Sagarwanshi Mali, Nayak, Maha Lodh, Mandewala, Manihar (DE)
Mallah (except those in the list of S.C.), Mali (BI)
Mallah, Mansoori (WB)
Managali (OR)
Manbhav, Mangela, Mangel, Maratha Vani (BO)
Manbhav/Mahanubhav, Purohit (MP)
Mandatan Chetty (MD)
Mandulavaru (HY)
Mangala (HY)
Mangala (MD)
Mangala, Medara (AP)
Mangaria (BO)
Manghli (OR)
Manigar (HY)
Manihar (VP)
Manihar, Maratha (Kunbi), Maru Sotiya (MB)
Manipuri (AS)
Manipuri, Nagarchi (TR)
Manjar, Marar, Mathura, Matti-Waddar, Meru (MP)

Manjhi (UP)
Manka Kanbi (KU)
Mapilla (CO)
Mappila (TC)
Mappilla (MD)
Marasi (UP)
Maratha (HY)
Marati (CO)
Maravan (MY)
Maravan (TC)
Maravar (MD)
Mari (SA)
Marich, Marwar Baori, Marwar Waghri, (17) (BO)
Markanda (BI)
Maruthuvar Medara, Medavar, Melakarar Mirgani Domb (MD)
Marwada (KU)
Marwada, Maldhari (SA)
Masan Jogi, Medari (HY)
Masania Jogi (DE)
Matak Moran (AS)
Mathuiar (BI)
Matial (WB)
Matva (SA)
Maulik (BI)
Mauriari (BI)
Mavi (MB)
Me (KU)
Me, Medar (BO)
Meda (MY)
Medara, Mehtar (BI)
Medara, Mekala Golla (OR)
Meengar (fishermen in, Karnataka) (HY)
Mehara (RA)
Mehrat, Meghwanshi (AJ)
Mehtar (Muslim), Mera, Momin (HY)
Mehtar, Mirdha, Momin (VP)
Memar, Raj (DE)
Mena (outside Alwar, Bundi, Bharatpur, Dholpur and Udaipur Division, excuding Jahajpur Tehsil, Miras (RA)
Meo, Mewati, Mewati (DE)
Mer (BO)
Mer (KU)
Mer (SA)
Merani (KU)
Merasi, Miras (RA)
Merasi, Mirasi, Mirasi (DE)
Merat (RA)
Merh Rajput (PU)
Meru Kshatriya, Mirgani Domb (AP)
Met (RA)
Metapathi Pandaram-Veerasaiva, Vairagi, Vairavi, Veerasaiva, Yogeswar (TC)
Mettan (TC)
Mewati (BH)
Mewati, Mina (MB)
Mewati, Momin, Murai, Naddaf, Nai, Naik, Naqqal, Nandbai, Nat, Naiyaria, Nunia (UP)
Mewati, Rachband (PU)
Mhali, Nai/Nhavi (MP)
Mina (BH)
Mina (BO)
Mina (PP)
Mina (PU)
Mina, Mirdha (MP)
Mina, Nagarchi (AJ)
Minka, Momin (OR)
Mirasi (PP)
Mirasi (PU)
Mirasi, Mirdhan, Momin (MB)
Mirdha, Momin, Naddaf (BH)
Miriasin, Mirshikar (BI)
Mirshikar (WB)
Miyana (KU)
Miyana, Sanghadi (SA)
Mochi (excluding those, in S.C.),

Momin, Murai, Murao, Nat (excluding those in S.C.), Nai (DE)
Mochi (in Gujarat), Modikar (BO)
Mochi (KU)
Mochi (PU)
Mochi (SA)
Mochi, Naik, Nai (PP)
Modak, Momin, Moran (AS)
Modakmera, Modi, Nichundia Modi, Modi (BI)
Modi Banda (MD)
Modi Randa (AP)
Mogaveera (S. Kanara) (MD)
Moger (BO)
Mogia, Nagarchi, Nai (RA)
Mohani (BI)
Moili (S. Kanara) (MD)
Momin (BI)
Momin (WB)
Momin, Julaha, Nai/Nhavi (MP)
Mond-Golla (MD)
Mondi-Vogola (AP)
Mondiwaru (HY)
Moniagar (Tinnevelly, Madura Distts), Moopanar (MD)
Moothakammala Musuka, Balija (MD)
Moranjhiria (BO)
Morao, Murai (UP)
Morapora Brahmin (WB)
Moria (AS)
Muchhia (MB)
Mudiraj, Mutharasi (HY)
Muduva (MD)
Mug (WB)
Mukhari (MD)
Mukhi (AS)
Muli, Muliya, Muliya, Muniyani (MD)
Multani (HY)
Multani (MY)
Multani (RA)
Mund Patta (AP)
Munda (SA)
Mundama, Naddaf (BI)
Munnoorwar, Munnoorkapu, Munnoorkapu (BO)
Munnur, Munnurkapu, Munnurkapu, Mutharasi (HY)
Murli Vaghya (BO)
Murraha, Murha (VP)
Mussavar (PU)
Musukunta Nadu Vellala, (Tanjore Distt.) (MD)
Mutracha (MD)
Mutracha, Nagavamsam (AP)
Muttakkampatti (MD)
Muttiriyan (MD)
Myadara (HY)

Nabha (BO)
Nadar Hindu (TC)
Nador (BO)
Nagaram (AP)
Nagaram, Nagavamsam (MD)
Nagartha (MY)
Naghori, Nai, Naikmakkalu, Naikwadi (BO)
Nahar, Nai, Napit, Niari (OR)
Nai (AJ)
Nai (BH)
Nai (MB)
Nai, Nath (HP)
Nai, Nunia (VP)
Naicken (TC)
Naik (MB)
Naik (RA)
Naiko (TR)
Naita, Nayata (MB)
Naiya, Namasudra (BI)
Najjar, Naqqashi, Natuva (HY)
Nakkale (AP)
Nalband (BI)

Nalband (PU)
Nalband (WB)
Nalband, Nayak (DE)
Namdev Maharatta (North, Arcot Distt.) Nainar (MD)
Namdev Mahratta (AP)
Namdhari, Namdhari Paik, Numdhari Paik (BO)
Nandiwale (BO)
Nanga (BO)
Nangar (BO)
Nangraj, Narwekar (BO)
Napit (AS)
Napit (TR)
Napit, Nai, Nai (MA)
Napit, Nat (WB)
Napita (CO)
Naqqal, Nishad (DE)
Nar, Nai, Naik (PU)
Narikoravan, Nathanman (MD)
Nat (BH)
Nat (BO)
Nat and Nattadas, Nath (TR)
Nat, Nath (MP)
Nat, Navda, Nayata (MB)
Nat, Nichundia Modi (BI)
Nat-Bajania Bajigar (SA)
Nat-Bajania-Bzigar (KU)
Nath, Nath Panthi, Nayakaru (BO)
Nath, Nunia (BH)
Nath, Yogi (AS)
Nath, Yogi (WB)
Nathbawa (KU)
Nathbawa, Nhavi (SA)
Natuva (MY)
Navudian (MD)
Nayak (AJ)
Nayak (TR)
Nayak/Nayakda (MP)
Nayar (MY)
Nayer, Nhavi (BO)
Nayidaru (HY)
Nayinda (MY)
Neeli (HY)
Neelkanti, Nekar (HY)
Neria, Ode, Odiya (MB)
Neygi (MY)
Neyyalu (AP)
Nhavi (HY)
Niaria (RA)
Nilara (BO)
Nilgar (BO)
Nilgar, Rangrez (RA)
Nirshikari (AP)
Nirshikari (BO)
Nishad (Mallah Tyar, Bind, Khulvat Goria, Vankar, Bathua, Kewat, Manjhi), Quraish, Rajbanshi, Rarh, Rudra Paul of Cachar only (AS)
Noila (OR)
Nokkar (MD)
Noniya (BI)
Noongar, Panchal Brahman, Phool Mali (PU)
Nuhura, Nuhuraj, Nuhuraj, Oda Balifa (OR)
Nunia (TR)
Nut, Pinjara (BH)
Od (AJ)
Od (BO)
Od (KU)
Od (SA)
Odan (TC)
Oddar, Odde, Vadde, Veddai, Vodde, Odde (MD)
Odde, Odder, Vadde, Veddai, Vodde, (AP)
Odiya, A, Paddamali (AP)
Ojha (VP)
Omeyita (OR)
Oshthama (BO)
Otari (BO)
Otta Nicken, Pandaram Veerasaiva (TC)

Padamsali, Sali (BO)
Padaria, Pamaria, Pandara, Pandara, Pamaria (OR)
Padayachi (Villayan, Kuppan) (South Arcot, and Salem Distts.), Padmasali, Paiko Mali, Panikkar, Palli (MD)
Padhar, Padhiar (outside, Jhalawad District), Padhiar (SA)
Padharia (BO)
Padiar (BO)
Padka (MP)
Padmasali, Sali, Saliyan, Swakulasali (MY)
Padmasali, Sali/Sutsali, Salewer (MP)
Padmashali, Sale (HY)
Padti, Page (BO)
Pagi (In Karwar), Thakarda, Pakhali, Pamlor, Panchal (BO)
Pahar, Panwari, Payak, Pinjara, Purabia (MB)
Paidee, Paikomali (AP)
Paik (TR)
Paiko (OR)
Paisari Bania (BI)
Pakhali Bhisti (KU)
Pakhali-Bhisti (SA)
Pal (OR)
Pala Ekari (AP)
Palavyakula Kshatriya, Palle Kapu, Palle Reddi (AP)
Palhari (MP)
Palli (OR)
Pamaria (BI)
Pamaria (UP)
Pamula (AP)
Pan (TR)
Panchkalashi (BO)
Pancholi (BO)
Panda (of Uttarakhand, only) (UP)
Pandaram (MY)
Pandaran (TC)
Pandither (TC)
Pando (BI)
Pangadikara (AP)
Pangania (BI)
Panguas (OR)
Pangul (BO)
Pangul (HY)
Panjira (OR)
Panka (MP)
Panka (VP)
Panki (TR)
Pannayar, Panniyar, Panniyar, Parakavakulam (MD)
Panthi, Patit, Brahmin (WB)
Panura (BO)
Parasher (MP)
Paravathara Jakulam, Pattanavan, Sambadavar (MD)
Pardeshi Bhampta (BO)
Pardeshi Thakur, Parit (BO)
Pardhi (HY)
Pareet (HY)
Parel Madivala, Parimalaikallan (MD)
Pargha (BI)
Parivar (MY)
Parivarbunt (MD)
Parkha, Patanwadia (BO)
Parthi (MP)
Parumban (TC)
Pasi (TR)
Patara, Patra (OR)
Pategar (BO)
Pathara (UP)
Patharphora, Sangtarash, Prajapati, Prade, Panjara, Qalandar, Qussab, Quraishi (DE)
Patharvat (BO)
Patharwat (HY)
Pathrut, Patne (BO)
Pathuria, Patra (OR)

Patka/Patki, Patwa, Patwa (MP)
Patkar (HY)
Patnulkaran, Pattanavan (MD)
Patradavaru (BO)
Pattaria, Saliya (TC)
Pattariyar (Tinnevelly and Madura Distts.), Pattusali, Paddamali (MD)
Pattasali, Pattusali, Pattusali (OR)
Pattunulkaran (AP)
Patua (WB)
Paturia (UP)
Patvekar (BO)
Patwa (DE)
Patwa Bania (BI)
Patwa, Pawaria, Qassab (UP)
Patwa, Phadal (RA)
Patwa, Qussab (VP)
Pavaiya, Pednekar (BO)
Payak (RA)
Pedditti Golla (AP)
Peeris (TC)
Pendhari (BO)
Penja, Pinja, Pinja, Rai (PP)
Perika (HY)
Perike (AP)
Perike Balija (AP)
Perki (MP)
Peruvannan (MD)
Phasechari (BO)
Phool Mali (HY)
Phudgi (BO)
Phulari (HY)
Licchigunta, Ponaka Domb (AP)
Pichakuntla (HY)
Pico Higunta, Pillamar, Ponaka Domb (MD)
Pindara (MP)
Pinja, Prajapati, Ramaiya, Rai Sikh (PU)
Pinjara (HY)
Pinjara, Pinjari, Pinjari (BO)
Pinjara, Prajapati (SA)
Pinjara, Qassab, Rangaswami, Rangrez (RA)
Pinjari (HY)
Pinjari (MY)
Pinje, Phool Mali, Saini (HP)
Piraj Pota (BO)
Pirali (WB)
Pita, Punnu Golla, Quraishi, Radhi (OR)
Polia, Rajbansi, Resiya, Prajapati Qureshi, Rajbanshi (BI)
Poosala (HY)
Poraya (Coimbatore Distt.) (MD)
Powar (MP)
Pradhan, Rangrez (BH)
Pulluvan (Malabar Distt.) (MD)
Punnan Vettuva Gowndar, Rajakambala Naicker (MD)
Puragiri Kshatriya (AP)
Pusala, Pusalavadu, Pusalavadu (AP)
Putligar (MP)

Qasa, Qassab, Quarashi, Qassab, Quraishi, Rangari, Rangrez, Rassiban (HY)
Qassab, Ramdasiya (MB)
Quraish, Rabari (BO)

Rabari (KU)
Rabari, Bhopa Rabari, (outside the Nesses area, in the forests of Alech, Gir and Barada) (SA)
Rachawar (MY)
Rachevar (BO)
Raddi (BO)
Radha (UP)
Raghvi, Raghvanshi (MP)
Ragwai, Rain, Rajbhar (UP)
Rai, Rehbari (RA)
Raighatwal (TR)

Raikari (BO)
Raj Pardhi (BO)
Rajaka (AP)
Rajamuria, Rangari (MP)
Rajapur (S. Karana), Reddi Ganiga (MD)
Rajgir (VP)
Rajput (CO)
Rajput (only in Kangra District) (PU)
Ramaiya (UP)
Rami Mali (BO)
Ramoshi (BO)
Rangaraju (in Kurnool Dist.) (AP)
Rangari (BO)
Rangraz (UP)
Rangraz, Raj, Rayee, Saini, Sagarwanshi Mali (DE)
Rangredh, Rangraz, Rangrez, Sain, Sansia (VP)
Rangres, Rayeens, Razzaqi (WB)
Rangrez (BI)
Rangrez (MP)
Rangrez (UP)
Rangrez, Ravidasiya (MB)
Ranguni (OR)
Rao (BH)
Raot/Rawt, Raoti (MP)
Rar (UP)
Raul, Ravalia, Rawal, Rawalyogi, Ravalia, Rawal, Rawalyogi (BO)
Rauniyar (UP)
Rautara, Sonar (UP)
Rautia, Rawani, Rayeen, Resiya (BI)
Raval (KU)
Raval (SA)
Rawa (UP)
Rawat (AJ)
Rawat (BO)
Rawat (MY)
Rawat (RA)
Rebari (AJ)
Reddi (Ganjam) (AP)
Reddi of Reddika origin (AP)
Reddi, Reddika, Reddika (OR)
Rehar, Rehara, Rer, Rehara, Rer, Saini (PU)
Rengi Reju (OR)
Rohangia, Roshangia, Roshangia (WB)
Rohar (MP)
Rona (AP)
Rona (MD)
Rona (OR)
Routia (OR)
Ruchbandhia (MP)
Runiar Bania (BI)
Rupai, Sabdakar (TR)

Sad, Santia, Santia (RA)
Sadar, Sali, Saliyan (MY)
Sadh, Singharia (UP)
Sadhu (AJ)
Sadhu Chetty, 24 Manai, Teluga Chetty, Teluga, Chetty (AP)
Sadhu Chetty, Teluga, Chetty, 24 Manai Telugu, Chetty, 24 Manai Telugu Chetty (MD)
Sagar (BO)
Sagar (SA)
Sagar, Uppara (HY)
Sagara, Uppara (AP)
Sagara, Uppara, Sarayakara, Sale, Sali, Saliyan, Sambadavar (MD)
Sagarpesha, Sakaldarpee Brahman (OR)
Saha, Sahu, Suri, Sahu (AS)
Saha, Sain (WB)
Sahadev Joshi (BO)
Sain (BI)
Saini (BO)
Sais/Sayees, Shis, Salewar, Sali/Sutsali (MP)
Saisutar, Zalawadi (BO)

Saiz, Sakka, Sangtarash, Santhia (DE)
Sakka (HP)
Sakka, Sagarvanshi Mali, Saini (RA)
Sakravar, Saliya (TC)
Sakulashali, Sale (HY)
Salat (excluding Sompur, Salat) (SA)
Salat (excluding Sompura, Salat) (KU)
Salat, Salat Waghri, Sali Sangameshwari (BO)
Sali, Salia, Salia, Sani (OR)
Sali, Salvi (MB)
Saliyan (Padamsali, Pattusali, Senapathulu, Kauni Bhaktulu, Sale, (Thogata, Sali, Kerikal, Bhaktulu) (AP)
Saloi (AS)
Sandhi (SA)
Sangar (BO)
Sanghar, Sai (KU)
Sangtrash (HY)
Saniyar (MY)
Sanjogi, Sankuri, Sansia (BO)
Sankhakar, Sankheru, Sankheru, Satchasi (WB)
Sankhari (OR)
Sanoria (BH)
Sansi (OR)
Sanyasi, Sapera (BI)
Sapera (AJ)
Sarania (BO)
Sarania (SA)
Saranjia (MP)
Sarbaria (BI)
Sarekari, Sargara (BO)
Sarki (Nepali) (AS)
Sarki (Nepali) (MA)
Saroda (BO)
Sarvade (BO)
Sarwan (BO)
Satani, Sharigaru (HY)
Satani, Swakulsali (MY)
Satarkar (BO)
Sathwara (KU)
Sathwara (SA)
Satiaya, Sindhi (RA)
Saunta, Sauta, Saita (BI)
Sauntis (OR)
Savar, Sayar, Sayar (WB)
Scheduled Castes converted to Christianity (AP)
Scheduled Castes converted to Christianity (MY)
Scheduled Castes converted to Christianity (TC)
Scheduled Castes converted to Christianity (VP)
Scheduled Castes converted to Christianity (HY)
Scheduled Castes, converted to Christianity (MD)
Scheduled Tribes in three areas when they leave, their habitat and settle, in other parts of Assam (AS)
Sedar (MD)
Seerithigoudu, Senapathulu (MD)
Segidi (OR)
Sehar, Sonsi, Sevak, Sindhi (RA)
Senaikudyan, Senaithalaivar, Senaithalaivar (MD)
Senia, Setti Balija, Shanan, Sheragara Kshatriya of, S. Kanara, Sirkudi Pillai (MD)
Setti Ralija (of Vizag, East and West Godavari, Krishna Distts.), Setti Balija (AP)
Shedia (KU)
Sheikhars (BI)
Sherogar (BO)
Shikari (BO)

Shikkaligar, Shimpi (BO)
Shimpi (HY)
Shimpi (KU)
Shimpiga (HY)
Shorgir (PP)
Shorgir (PU)
Siddi (BO)
Siddi (outside Nesses, area in the forests of, Alech, Gir and Barada) (SA)
Sidi (KU)
Sikh (AJ)
Sikh (KU)
Sikh (TC)
Sikh Harijan (AP)
Sikh Harijan (AS)
Sikh Harijan (MA)
Sikh Harijans (BH)
Sikh Harijans (BI)
Sikh Harijans (CO)
Sikh Harijans (HY)
Sikh Harijans (MY)
Sikh Harijans (OR)
Sikh Scheduled Castes (MD)
Sikhs (BO)
Sikhs (DE)
Sikhs (PP)
Sikhs (PU)
Sikhs (RA)
Sikhs (SA)
Sikhs (TR)
Sikhs (VP)
Sikhs (WB)
Sikligar (AJ)
Sikligar (PU)
Sikligar (RA)
Sikligar (VP)
Sikligar, Singhiwala (MB)
Singhikaut, Singhiwals, Singhiwals, Tamera, Tank, Tarkhan (PP)
Singhiwala, Singhikaut, Singhikaut (PU)
Singiwala, Sonar, Sunkar (MP)
Sinkos (OR)
Sirkiwala, Sonsi (RA)
Sithula (OR)
Sitria (OR)
Situlia (OR)
Siviar (Coimbatore, Distt.) (MD)
Siyal (BO)
Siyane (MB)
Soeri, Sonar, Sorahiya (UP)
Soi, Tamboli (PU)
Solangi (BO)
Somakshatriya (HY)
Sonar (DE)
Sonar (HY)
Sonar (MB)
Sonar, Sunar, Sunar (MA)
Sonar, Sutar, Tamboli, Tamera (VP)
Sonar, Swamakar (WB)
Sonar, Swamakar, Swamakar (BI)
Sondhia, Tamboli (MB)
Soni (KU)
Sonowal, Sudra Das, Suri (AS)
Sourashtra (TC)
Sourashtra, Surithimar, Telaga, Teluga Chetty (MD)
Sourastera (AP)
Sozhia Chetty (MD)
Srisayana (AP)
Suda (OR)
Sudgadsidda (BO)
Sudugadusiddha (HY)
Sukiar (BI)
Sukuli, Tanti (OR)
Suleru (BO)
Sulia (OR)
Sumra (KU)
Sumra (SA)
Sunagar (BO)
Sunar, Tamboli (BH)
Sundi (BI)
Sundi, Sutradhar (OR)

Sunkar (MP)
Sunkar, Taga Bhat (UP)
Suppalig (BO)
Surabhi Janga (HY)
Surhi Bania, Tamboli, Tamoli, Thathera (BI)
Sut (AS)
Sutar (RA)
Sutar, Suthar, Suthar (BO)
Sutar, Tamboli, Tamera/ Tambatkar, Telugu Mannarkapu (MP)
Sutar, Wadhai (HY)
Suthar (SA)
Suthria (from Sind) (BO)
Sutradhar (TR)
Sutradhar, Swarnakar (WB)
Suwar (BO)
Swakula Sali (AP)

Taga, Tagah, Tagah, Tank, Tarkhan, Tamboli (DE)
Taga, Vanzara (PU)
Tak Bodar, Telaga (AP)
Takankar, Talvar Including Kanade, Talvar (BO)
Takari (BO)
Tamadia Purana (OR)
Tambat (BO)
Tamboli (RA)
Tamboli, Tamuli, Tamuli (MA)
Tamboli, Tandel, Targala (BO)
Tambuli, Tamli, Tamli (WB)
Tamil (OR)
Tammali (HY)
Tamoli (UP)
Tana, Tanti (OR)
Tank (AJ)
Tanti, Tantri, Tantripal, Tantri, Tantripal (AS)
Tanti, Tantubaya, Tantubaya (WB)
Tantuvai, Tatwan, Tanwar, Tatwan, Teli, Thathera, Tirgar (UP)
Tapodhan Brahmin (BO)
Targala Bhavaya (KU)
Targala, Bhavaya (SA)
Tariatai (KU)
Tariatai (SA)
Tarkada (SA)
Tarkhan (if not Harijan) (HP)
Tarkhan (PU)
Taru (BO)
Tatapu (AP)
Tati, Tanti, Tanti (TR)
Tatiyajan (AS)
Tavate (BO)
Tawaif (MB)
Tea-garden labourers (AS)
Tea-garden labourers (TR)
Telaga (CO)
Telaga (OR)
Telaga of Telagu (HY)
Telaga Pamula (AP)
Telegu Banjig (BO)
Telegu Madiraj (BO)
Telegu Munnoorwar, Teli (BO)
Telenga Pamola (OR)
Teli (AJ)
Teli (BH)
Teli (BI)
Teli (HY)
Teli (if not Harijan) (HP)
Teli (MA)
Teli (MB)
Teli (Nepali) (AS)
Teli (Nepali) (MA)
Teli (Nepali) (WB)
Teli (OR)
Teli (PU)
Teli (VP)
Teli (WB)
Teli, Temara, Thathera, Thathiar (DE)
Teli, Thathera (MP)
Teli, Thathera, Thori, Tori (PP)

Teli, Thathera, Ved (RA)
Teli, Yogi (AS)
Telikula, Teluga Chetty (AP)
Telunga Patty Chetty (MD)
Tenugollu (HY)
Thakar, Thakarda (BO)
Thakarda (KU)
Thakarda (SA)
Thakurhar (BO)
Thambat (HY)
Thambatgar (HY)
Thami (HP)
Thami, Vaidyanai (MB)
Thandal Vannan, Thiya (TC)
Thanwar, Wasdeo (VP)
Thanwin (HP)
Thanwin (PU)
Thatari (OR)
Thathera, Kasera, Thori, Turi (PU)
Theba (KU)
Thegotaveerkshatriya (AP)
Thetwar (MP)
Thiyya (Malabar Distt.), Thogata (MD)
Thogti (HY)
Tholuva-Naicker, Vettala, Karanaicker (MD)
Thondaiman (TC)
Thori (BO)
Thoroya (CO)
Thoti Burud, Thuria (MP)
Thottai Naickan (MD)
Thottiyar (TC)
Thuria (OR)
Thurpu Kapu (AP)
Thurpukapu (MD)
Tiar (BI)
Tigala (BO)
Tigala (Tigla), Tigla, Ummia, Uppara (AP)
Tigala, Tigla, Tigla (MD)
Tigala, Vanniya Kulu, Kashatriya (MY)
Tikulhara, Vishwakarma, Yadav (BI)
Tili (MB)
Timaliya (BO)
Tippera (WB)
Tirgar (BO)
Tirguli, Tirmali (BO)
Tirmale (MP)
Tirwalli, Turha, Waddar (MP)
Tiyar (UP)
Tiyaro, Togara (OR)
Tondaman, Ummia, Uppara (MD)
Traditional Buddhists (WB)
Tudug-Waddar, Uchlia (BO)
Tulleru, Uppara (HY)
Tulukkan (TC)
Tuha (BI)
Turha, Yadav, Yogi (WB)
Turi, Yogi (TR)

Udasi (BO)
Ulra (BO)
Umar Bania, Vishwakarma (UP)
Uppar (BO)
Uppara, Vanniyakula Kashatriya (MY)
Ural Goundan, Urali Nair, Vadde (MD)

Vada Baliza of Ganjam, and Vizag Distts., Veddai, Vadde (AP)
Vaddar (BO)
Vadhala (KU)
Vadhala (SA)
Vadi (BO)
Vadugan Vaduvan, Vaduvan (MD)
Vadugan, Vaduvan, Vaduvan (AP)
Vadukan, Vairagi, Vairavi (TC)
Vagher (BO)
Vagher (KU)
Vagher (SA)
Vaghra (KU)

Vaghri (BO)
Vaghri (SA)
Vaidu (BO)
Vaishya Thakur (BO)
Vaiti (BO)
Vakkal (in Kanara Distt.), Valhar, Valmiki, Vanjara, Vanjari (BO)
Vakkaliga (MD)
Valaian (MD)
Valan (N. Malabar) (MD)
Valand (KU)
Valand (SA)
Valimiki of Rayalaseema, Vanne Reddi (AP)
Valla Nagam, Veddai (MD)
Vaniar (MD)
Vaniyan, Vathi (TC)
Vanjara (SA)
Vankar Khatri (BO)
Vannan, Vanniyakula Kshatriya (MD)
Vanniar, Vanni Kapu, Vanni Kulakshatriya, Vishwa Brahman, Vishwakarma, Vodde (AP)
Vanza (BO)
Vanza (KU)
Vanza (SA)
Vanzara (KU)
Varala (HY)
Vasudeo (HY)
Vasudev (BO)
Vathi (MD)
Vavad (SA)
Vedva Gaghri (SA)
Velaan, Veera Saiva (TC)
Velakatalavan (MD)
Velama (OR)
Veluthadan (Malabar) (MD)
Veluthdan, Veluthedathu, Nair (TC)
Vema Golla (OR)
Vettikaran, Vettalakara Naickers (MD)
Vettuva Gownder (MD)
Vidur (BO)
Vijantri (BO)
Vilakkathala Nair (TC)
Vilakkathalavan (TC)
Vilkurup (MD)
Vilkurup (TC)
Vina Tulavina, Yadava, Yogi (OR)
Vir (BO)
Virakodi Vellalar, Viswa Brahmin, Viswakarma, Vodde, Yadava (MD)
Viramushti (HY)
Viswakarma (MY)
Viswakarmala (TC)
Vokkaliga (CO)
Vokkaliga (only from, rural areas) (MY)
Vokkaliga, Wodayar, Yadava (AP)
Vyasokta (WB)

Wadar (HY)
Wadari (BO)
Waddar (HY)
Waddara, Wadhai (HY)
Wadla (HY)
Waghri Pardhi (BO)
Wanha (MP)
Wanham (BO)
Wansfoda (BO)
Warthi, Yadav (HY)

Yadava (MY)
Yadava, Yogoeswarar (TC)
Yaklar, Zalawadi (BO)
Yerkilwar, Yerkula (MP)
Yoggeeswara (MD)

Zharekari (BO)

Appendix - III

The List of Backward Castes Enumerated in the Second Backward Classes Commission (Mandal)

Alphabatical list to facilitate users to identify the backward class in respective States.

Abbreviations used for the States

Andaman & Nicobar Islands	AN
Andhra Pradesh	AP
Arunachal Pradesh	AR
Assam	AS
Bihar	BI
Chandigarh	CH
Dadra and Nagar Haveli	DN
Delhi	DE
Goa, Daman & Diu	GD
Gujarat	GU
Haryana	HR
Himachal Pradesh	HP
Jammu & Kashmir	JK
Karnataka	KA
Kerala	KE
Madhya Pradesh	MP
Maharashtra	MR
Manipur	MA
Meghalaya	ME
Mizoram	MI
Orissa	OR
Pondicherry	PO
Punjab	PU
Rajasthan	RA
Sikkim	SI
Tamil Nadu	TN
Tripura	TR
Uttar Pradesh	UP
West Bengal	WB

Abbas., Bhishti, Sakka (DE)
Abdal (BI)
Acharaj, Panchal-Brahman, Changar (CH)
Achari, Viswakarma, Kammalar, Thattan, Thatchan, Porkollar, Assari, Chary (TN)
Acharya, Acharji (WB)
Achukatlavandhu (AP)
Achukatlavandlu (PO)
Adhiri (BI)
Adhori (MP)
Adi Karnataka (AP)
Adi-Dravida (OR)
Adi-Karnataka (OR)
Adidharmi (MP)
Adikari (WB)
Adikarnataka (MP)
Adiya (excluding Coorg District) (KA)
Adodia (GU)
Agamudayar of Southern Tamil Distts. belonging to Mukkulathers, Agamudayar of Northern Tamil Distts., Thozhu or Thuluva Vellala (TN)
Agamudiyas (including Thuluva Vellalas) (PO)
Agamundi (AP)
Agaria, Agariya (TR)
Agaria, Agariya (WB)
Agariya (BI)
Agaru (AP)
Agaru, Jurakula (PO)
Agasa (KE)
Agasa (PO)
Agasa, Madivala, Sakala, Sakalavadu, Shakala, Tsakala, Vannan, Dhobi, Parit, Rajaka (KA)
Ager (RA)
Aghamudayar, Vellari, Madali Agahamudaya, Aghambadiar, Barichatty, Kondaliyar, Palegaru (AP)
Agharia, Agaria, Aghria (OR)
Aghore (WB)
Aghori, Karkarmunda (KA)
Agnani (KA)
Agnikula Kshatriya (Pallekapu, Palloreddi, Vannekapu, Vannereddi) (PO)
Agradana, Agradani (WB)
Agri (DN)
Agri (GU)
Agri (UP)
Agri Kharwal (DE)
Agri, Agale or Kolan (MR)
Aguri - Vaishya, Sudi, Halwai, Roniyar, Pansari, Modi, Kasera, Kesarwani, Kathera, Siduriya - Bania, Mahuro-Vaishya-Awadh-Bania, Kaith-Bania (BI)
Aheri (MP)
Aheria, Aheri, Heri, Naik, Thori, Turi (HP)
Aheria, Aheri, Heri, Naik, Thori, Turi (PU)
Aheria, Aheri, Naik, Heri (CH)
Aheria, Aheriya (UP)
Aheria, Ahiria, Heri, Aheri, Naik, Thori, Turi (HR)
Ahir (Yadav, Gope) (RA)
Ahir, Ayar-Boricha, Yadav (GU)
Ahir, Bharvad, Yadav (DN)
Ahir, Gavala, Goala, Gwal, Kansa, Thakur, Jadav, Yadav (MP)
Ahir, Gawala, Gowala, Rao, Yadav (HR)
Ahir, Ghosi, Gwala, Yaduvanshi/ Yadav (UP)
Ahir, Goala, Gope, Sadgope, Yadav, Gola, Gawar (WB)
Ahir, Yadav, Gowli (MR)

Ahir, Yadav, Gwala (CH)
Ahir, Yadav, Gwala (DE)
Ahir, Yadav, Gwala (MA)
Ahom (AS)
Ahom (ME)
Aiyanavar (TN)
Ajila (AP)
Ajila (OR)
Alavan (KE)
Alavan, Alavar, Alwar and Azhavar (TN)
Alitkar (MR)
Alwar (PO)
Amaat (BI)
Amant, Amat, Amath (WB)
Ambalagars (TN)
Ambalakaran (PO)
Ambalakaran, Ambalakarar, Vallamber (TN)
Ambalakarma, Ambalakaran (KA)
Ambalakkaran (KE)
Ambika (PO)
Amblar, Ambathan, Ambithan, Ezhavatery, Kalrrikurup, Maruthuvar, Naiken, Pandithar Villakkitha-lanavi (KE)
Ampattan (KE)
Ampattari (TN)
Anandan (PO)
Andh (KA)
Andipandaram (TN)
Andipandaran (PO)
Anduram (KA)
Anglo Indian (PO)
Anglo-Indian (KE)
Ansari (Muslim) (WB)
Ansari (UP)
Ansari, Julai (Muslims) (KA)
Apatani (MI)
Arain (PU)
Arain, Rayee, Kunjra (DE)
Arakh (UP)
Aranadan (KA)
Aranedan (OR)
Aravala (AP)
Arayan (Nulayan), Araya (PO)
Arayan, Arayar (Nulayar) (TN)
Arayas (KE)
Arayavathi (TN)
Arayavathis (KE)
Archak Brahmins (AP)
Archakari Vellala (TN)
Archakatalavandu (PO)
Ard-Pop (HP)
Are Mahrati (PO)
Are-Marathi (AP)
Arekatika, Katika (AP)
Aremaharti (KE)
Arundatilu (H) (AN)
Arunthutiyar (OR)
Arya (KE)
Arya (PO)
Arya Mala (AS)
Arya, Dingra (HP)
Aryakshatriya, Chittari, Chitrakara, Giniyar, Nakahs (AP)
Aryan (KE)
Aryavathi Nairuseri (PO)
Asada (RA)
Asara (MP)
Asur (AS)
Asur (OR)
Asur (TR)
Atagara (AP)
Atagara, Atagora (PO)
Atar (AP)
Atar (KA)
Atar (MR)
Atazri (KA)
Athiya (MP)
Audhie, Avadhi (MP)
Audhiya (MP)
Audhiya (MR)

Auji (UP)
Ayyanavar (where they are not Scheduled Castes) (TN)

Baagawan Tamboli (Muslims) (KA)
Badaga (AP)
Badaga (KA)
Badaga (KE)
Badaga (OR)
Badaga (PO)
Badaga (TN)
Badagar (TN)
Badak (MP)
Badak (MR)
Badak (UP)
Badaka (MP)
Badasuda (OR)
Badera (RA)
Badhai, Ade-Gaur, Chaurasia, Pansari, Sutar, Suthar, Tudolia, Viswakarma (MP)
Badhai, Badai, Barahi, Dhiman, Jhangra-Brahman, Khati, Kondal, Ramgarhia, Tarkhan, Taryal, Vishwakarma (HP)
Badhai, Barhai, Bindhania, Sutradhar, Badhira and Badhria (OR)
Badhai, Barhai, Khati, Tarkhan, Jangra-Brahmin, Viswakarma (DE)
Badhi, Barhai, Dhiman-Brahman (CH)
Badi (DE)
Badi (MP)
Badi (Nepali) (MA)
Badi (Nepali) (WB)
Badi, Chinaora, Melori, Odmata, Uranamara (HP)
Badia (MR)
Badia, Beaja, Biria, Dukar, Kolthati, Kolhati (MP)
Badigar (MP)
Badwa (RA)
Badyakar, Dhuli, Nagarchi, Sabdakar (TR)
Bafan (Muslims) (GU)
Baffand (JK)
Bag (WB)
Bagal (WB)
Bagal, Batalian, Bhut, Dangi, Dhame, Hir, Harbansia, Jalaria, Kaushal, Manadia, Marbansia, Manem, Masaun, Mehton, Mule, Nagia, Parmar, Sangutva, Sial, Thunalia (PU)
Bagalu (AP)
Bagalu (KA)
Bagalu (MR)
Bagaria (CH)
Bagaria (HR)
Bagata (KA)
Bagata (KE)
Bagata (TN)
Bagdi (Marwar Baori, Marwar, Waghri, Salat Waghri) (MR)
Bagdiya (RA)
Bagdo (BI)
Baghia, Baree, Bawar, Payak, Vaidyanai (MP)
Bagria (HP)
Bagria, Bagaria (PU)
Bahari (CH)
Bahelia (TR)
Bahti (HP)
Bahurupi (MP)
Bahurupi (MR)
Baiga (AS)
Baijara (AS)
Bailapatar, Bailaptar, Bikapatar (KA)
Baipari (OR)
Baira (KA)
Baira (OR)

Bairagi (DE)
Bairagi (MP)
Bairagi (OR)
Bairagi (UP)
Bairagi, Baregi (PU)
Bairagi, Bava, Bavaji, Byragi, Bavani (KA)
Bairagi, Gosai, Udasi (MR)
Bairi (UP)
Bairwa, Berwa (DE)
Baishnab (TR)
Baishya Kapali (WB)
Baiti (TR)
Bajadar, Bajania, Bedey (WB)
Bajania (MR)
Bajania, Bajenia (KA)
Bajania, Kannatia (MP)
Bajel (SI)
Bajgar (MP)
Bajigar (MR)
Bajigar (UP)
Bakad, Bant (RA)
Bakadra (KA)
Bakerwal, Bakkarwal (JK)
Bakharia (UP)
Bakuda (AP)
Bakuda (OR)
Balasanthanam (AP)
Balasanthanam (KA)
Balasanthanam (MR)
Balasanthoshi (KA)
Balasanthu, Bahurupi (AP)
Balasaria, Bhagat, Bhara, Gagan, Kanwan, Kawandal, Kawdeya, Khiri, Kunkani, Loda, Lodha, Lodia, Mandi, Niwan, Ramka, Thira (HR)
Balija (AN)
Balija, Bajajiga, Naidu, Bogam Telaga, Telaga, Balaja, Setty Balija, Kasban, Munnur, Mutrasi, Matracha, Janapan, Balegara (KA)
Balolika (PO)
Banchada (RA)
Bandara (AP)
Bandari (KE)
Bandi (AP)
Bandi (MR)
Bandi (OR)
Bandi (UP)
Banerwala (DE)
Banjara (AS)
Banjara (WB)
Banjara, Banjara Nats, Lobana, Vanjara, Kanjar, Kanchan (HR)
Banjara, Banjare, Nal, Naik, Nayak, Kangi, Sirkiband, Labana, Dhan-Kute Banjara, Banjara Sikh, Brijwasi (UP)
Banjara, Banjari, Vanjara, Mathura Banjara (A), Goar Banjara, Lambada/Lambara, Lambhani, Charan Banjara, Labhan, Mathura Labhani, Kuchikiwale Banjaras, Laman Banjara, Laman/Lamani, Laban, Dhali/ Dhalia, Dhadi/Dhari, Singaris, Navi Banjaras, Jogi Banjaras,Banjari, Shingde, Banjara, Lambade, Phanade Banjara, Sunar Banjara, Dhalya-Banjara, Shingadya Banjara (MR)
Banjara, Gamalia, Baladia, Sirkiwala, Labana or Labhana, Manu Banjara, Bamania Banjara, Bagora, Digora (RA)
Banjara, Goar Banjara, Lambana/ Lambara, Lambhani, Charan Banjara, Labham, Mathura Labhan, Kachitiwala Banjara, Laman Banjara, Laman/ Lambani, Laban, Dhali/Dhalia, Dhadi/Dhari, Singari, Navi

Banjara, Jogi Banjara, Banjari, Mathura Banjari, Bamania Banjara (MP)
Banjara, Gour (TR)
Banjara, Gour, Badi, Labana (JK)
Banjara, Lambadi, Lamani, Sugali (GD)
Banjogi (TR)
Banjogi (WB)
Banka (OR)
Banna, Bannagar (KA)
Banoudhiya-Rajput (CH)
Banpar (BI)
Bansphor (MA)
Bant (excluding Belgaum, Bijapur, Dharwar and North Kanara District) (KA)
Bantu (AP)
Bantu (KA)
Bantu (MR)
Banua, Buna, Bunna, Buno (WB)
Baoria (MP)
Baoria (MR)
Baragahi, Labana, Labhan, Lamame, Mathura, Nayakda, Thuria (MP)
Baragi, Bairagi (CH)
Baragi, Bairagi (HP)
Baragi, Bairagi (HR)
Baragiri (WB)
Barahar, Basod (RA)
Barai (BI)
Barai Jambali (MP)
Barai, Atwasa, Badhai, Baiwal, Dagesar, Dingar, Jungid-Brahman, Jhangra-Brahman, Kavigar, Khati, Kliokar, Mayal, Suthar, Tarkhan, Vishwakarma (RA)
Barai, Tamboli (CH)
Barai, Tamboli (DE)
Barai, Tamboli (HR)
Barai, Tarboli, Tamboli (PU)
Baraik (TR)
Barar (MP)
Barar (RA)
Barar (Umati) (AN)
Barari (MP)
Barchain, Chai, Chain (WB)
Barda (KA)
Barda (RA)
Bargi (MP)
Bargunda (RA)
Barhai (AS)
Barhai, Badhai, Barai, Chauvasia, Jangid-Brahman, Khati, Kolash, Lote, Panchal, Tarkhan, Vishwakarma (UP)
Barhai, Kundera, Barhai Sutar (MP)
Barhi, Badhai, Bishwakarma, Khati, Sutradhar (WB)
Barhi, Bimrao, Dadoi, Dhawal, Dhiman, Jangiar, Jangid-Brahman, Jangra- Brahmin, Khati, Kashyap, Manithiya, Rajotia, Ramgarhia, Suthar, Tarkhan, Viswakarma (HR)
Barhunda (MP)
Bari (BI)
Bari (DE)
Bari (UP)
Bari or Barai (MR)
Bari, Baree (MP)
Baria (AP)
Baria (AS)
Baria (MP)
Baria, Koli Baria (MR)
Bariji or Barui (OR)
Barika, Bhandari, Beja, Napit and Nai (OR)
Bariki (KA)
Bariki (KE)
Bariki (TN)
Barjubi (AS)

Barjubi (ME)
Barlur (KA)
Barma (HR)
Bama-Brahmin, Patit-Brahmin (WB)
Baro (WB)
Baroi (AS)
Baroi (MP)
Baroi, Barui (ME)
Barot, Vahivancha (GU)
Barra (CH)
Barra (HR)
Barui (AS)
Barui (TR)
Barui, Barujibi (WB)
Barwar (CH)
Barwar (HR)
Barwar (PU)
Basdewa, Vasdev, Vasudewa (MP)
Basor (AS)
Basor (RA)
Baspher (TR)
Basphor (AS)
Basphor (BI)
Basudev, Harbola, Jaga, Kaparia, Kapdi (MP)
Batera (PU)
Bathal, Battal, Batler, Battar (KA)
Bathi (CH)
Bathini (AP)
Bathini (KA)
Bathini (MR)
Bathudi (WB)
Battada (AP)
Battada (KA)
Battada (KE)
Battada (OR)
Battada (TN)
Battera (HR)
Batterha (CH)
Batterha (HP)
Baura (UP)
Bauri (AS)
Bauri (TR)
Bauria (DE)
Bauriah (UP)
Bavacha, Bamcha (RA)
Bavcha (MR)
Baver (MP)
Bavocha (GU)
Bavri or Baori (GU)
Bavuri (KA)
Bavuri (KE)
Bavuri (TN)
Bawa, Atit Bawa, Bharathari, Bharti, Deshnami Bawa, Dhashnam, Gangajalia, Giri, Gosai, Goswami, Ramanandi, Kapdi, Margi, Nath Bawa, Puri, Vairagi Bawa (GU)
Bawari (RA)
Bawaria (MP)
Bawtar (KA)
Bayar (UP)
Bazgar, Bazigar (UP)
Bazigar (JK)
Bazigar (KA)
Bazigar, Nat, Kalandar (excluding those in SC) (DE)
Beda (Drum-beaters/Pipers) (JK)
Beda (HP)
Beda, Bedaru, Valimiki, Barki Bedar, Privara, Bendar, Boya, Bedar, Nayaka, Bedar Nayak, Naikomakkalu, Naikwadi, Palegar, Romoshi, Talwar, Valmiki, Valmikimakkalu, Vedan (KA)
Beddi (AS)
Bedia (AS)
Bedia (UP)
Bedia, Bediya (TR)
Begari (AP)
Begari (KA)

Begari, Bedar, Berad, Naikawadi, Talwar, Walmiki (MR)
Behana (UP)
Behha, Pinjara, Dhunia (MP)
Behurupi (KA)
Bekhada (BI)
Beldar (AS)
Beldar (TR)
Beldar, Bachgotra (BI)
Beldiya (BI)
Bellara (AP)
Bellara (KA)
Bellara (OR)
Bemariha (MP)
Bengali (MP)
Bentkar (BI)
Bentkar (OR)
Bentkar (WB)
Berad (Bedar) (KA)
Beri (Muslims) (KA)
Beria (CH)
Beria (HR)
Beria (KA)
Beria (MP)
Beria (PU)
Beriah (UP)
Berrer (PU)
Berua (TR)
Berua (WB)
Besdewa (MR)
Beshtar, Bunde-Bestar (KA)
Bestar, Sachaluwaddar (MR)
Bestha, Beztha (Jalarula Nagavadaity) (PO)
Bestha, Siviar (TN)
Bestha-Anikali, Jelare, Ratna Balaji, Uppila, Vade Balaji (AP)
Beta, Hensi, Hesi (CH)
Beta, Hensi, Hesi (HP)
Beta, Hensi, Hesi (PU)
Beta, Hersi or Hesi (HR)
Betare or Betra (OR)
Bhaat (MR)
Bhadbhunja (MR)
Bhadi-Waddar, Matti-Waddar, Waddar (MP)
Bhadre (MP)
Bhaduja (MP)
Bhaduria (MP)
Bhakta (TR)
Bhalia (GU)
Bhampta or Ghantichore or Pardesi, Pong, Dasar, Uchila, Rajput-Bhamta, Bhamta, Bhamti, Kumati, Pathrut, Takari, Uchale (MR)
Bhampta, Ghantichor, Pardesi-Bhampta (RA)
Bhamta (AP)
Bhamta, Bhamti, Bhanmate, Bhanta, Bhanmate (MP)
Bhamta, Bhompta, Pradeshi, Bhampta, Bhomtra, Takari, Uchillian, Rajput Bhamta (KA)
Bhamta, Pardeshi Bhamta (GU)
Bhand (CH)
Bhand (DE)
Bhand (JK)
Bhand (MP)
Bhand (MR)
Bhandari (GD)
Bhandari (MR)
Bhandura, Billawar (MR)
Bhangi (excluding those in Scheduled Caste) (WB)
Bhangi, Khakrob (Sweepers) (JK)
Bhania (OR)
Bhant (WB)
Bhanta (MR)
Bhantu (MP)
Bhanumati (RA)
Bhaot, Bhatraju, Bhatraj, Bohrot (KA)
Bhar (BI)

Bhar (TR)
Bhar (UP)
Bhar (WB)
Bharadi, Balasantoshi, Kinggriwale, Nathbava, Nath Jogi, Nath Panthi, Davari Gosavi (MR)
Bharai Tarkhan (JK)
Bharaik (AS)
Bharari (MP)
Bharatar (where they are not Scheduled Castes) (TN)
Bharbhooja (DE)
Bharbhuja (BI)
Bharbhuja (MP)
Bharbhuja, Bharbhunja, Kalenera (HR)
Bharbhuja, Bhujawala (WB)
Bharbhunja (CH)
Bharbhunja, Bharbhuja (HP)
Bharbhunja, Bharbhuja (PU)
Bhardi, Bharagi (KA)
Bharewa (MP)
Bhari, Rode (PU)
Bharia, Bharihar (MP)
Bharud (MP)
Bharud (RA)
Bharunja (JK)
Bharwad, Mota Bhai Bharwad, Nana Bhai Bharwad, Kabari, Baria Mota Bhai, Chosla, Janapada (where they are not Scheduled Tribes) (GU)
Bhaskar (BI)
Bhat (DE)
Bhat (JK)
Bhat (WB)
Bhat, Bhatra, Charan, Darpi, Ramiya (HR)
Bhat, Bhatra, Darpi (HP)
Bhat, Bhatra, Darpi, Ramiya (CH)
Bhat, Charan (RA)
Bhat, Charan, Brahmbhat, Jasondhi, Mary, Maru, Sotiya, Salui, Salvi (MP)
Bhat/Bhatt (BI)
Bhathiara (Muslims) (BI)
Bhathiara (UP)
Bhathiara, Razzaqi (WB)
Bhati, Chang, Ghirath (CH)
Bhatiara (DE)
Bhatiya (TR)
Bhatiya (WB)
Bhatiyara (MP)
Bhatra, Bhat, Darpi, Digpal, Ramiya, Rana, Rathore, Rau, Swali (PU)
Bhatraju (AP)
Bhatraju (other than Kshatriya Raju) (TN)
Bhatraju (PO)
Bhatta (AS)
Bhatu Turka (AP)
Bhatua (OR)
Bhauh (Sagavanshi-Mali) (RA)
Bhavaiya or Targala (MR)
Bhavassar Kshatriya, Banagarajulu, Rongare, Darji, Simpi (PO)
Bhavin (KA)
Bhavin (MR)
Bhavsar, Chippa, Nilgar, Nirali, Rangrez, Rangari (MP)
Bhil (AS)
Bhil (UP)
Bhillala (MR)
Bhillava (KE)
Bhima (MP)
Bhina Koya (MR)
Bhinhar (TR)
Bhinjia (TR)
Bhir (TR)
Bhishti, Bhisty (MP)
Bhisti or Pakhali (MR)
Bhogta (OR)

Bhoi (MP)
Bhoi, Bhoiraj, Dhimar, Zinga-Bhoi, Kevat-Bhoi, Bhanara Bhoi, Kirat Bhoi, Machhindra Bhoi, Palewar Bhoi, Kahar Bhoi, Pardeshi Bhoi, Shrimali Bhoi (GU)
Bhoi, Kharvi, Dhiwar Bhoi, Zinga Bhoi, Pardeshi Bhoi, Raj Bhoi, Kahar, Gadia Kahar, Kirat, Machwa, Manzi, Jatia, Kewat, Dhiwar, Dheewar, Dhimar, Palewr, Machhendra, Navadi, Malhar, Malhav, Gadhav Bhoi, Khadi Bhoi, Khare Bhoi, Dhevra Dhuria Kahar (MR)
Bhojki (CH)
Bhokta (AS)
Bhokta (OR)
Bhot (MP)
Bhotia (WB)
Bhottadas, Boto Bhottada, Muria Bhottad, Sano Bhottada (KA)
Bhottadas-Bodo Bhottada, Muria Bhottad and Sano Bhottada (TN)
Bhottadas-Bodo Bhottada, Muria bhattada and Sano Bhottada (AP)
Bhottadas-Bodo-Bhottada, Muria-Bhottada, and Sano Bhottada (KE)
Bhottodas-Bodo Bottadu, Muria Bhottada and Sano Bhottada (PO)
Bhoyar (MP)
Bhoyar (Pawra) (MR)
Bhrhmi (DN)
Bhubalia-Lohar (CH)
Bhubalia-Lohar, Garhi-Lohar (HR)
Bhubhalia (DE)
Bhugal (WB)
Bhuhalia (HP)
Bhuhalia (PU)
Bhuihar, Bhuiyar (BI)
Bhuiya (TR)
Bhujan (OR)
Bhuji, Bharbhuja (RA)
Bhujru (CH)
Bhujwa (MP)
Bhul (UP)
Bhuliya (OR)
Bhumias, Bado Bhumias and Bhuri Bhumia (PO)
Bhumias-Bhumia and Bodo Bhumia (KE)
Bhumias-Bhuri Bhumia and Bodo Bhumia (TN)
Bhumias-Bhuri Bhumia and Bodo Bhumia (AP)
Bhumias-Bhuri-Bhumia and Bodo Bhumia (KA)
Bhumij (AS)
Bhumij (MA)
Bhumij (ME)
Bhumij, Bumij (TR)
Bhundari (PO)
Bhura-Brahman (CH)
Bhura-Brahman (HR)
Bhura-Brahman (PU)
Bhurji, Bharbhuja, Bharbhunja, Bhunj, Bhunjia, Kandu, Kashodhay (UP)
Bhurtiya (MP)
Bhute, Bhope (MR)
Bhutia (MP)
Bhuyan (AS)
Bidakia (MP)
Bidia (MP)
Bijoria (MP)
Billava (PO)
Billava (TN)
Biloch (CH)
Bin (TR)
Bin (WB)
Binapatta (KA)

Bind (BI)
Bind (TR)
Bind (UP)
Bindli (AP)
Bindli (KA)
Bindli (MR)
Binedhanies (OR)
Bingi (KA)
Binjhawar (WB)
Binjhia (TR)
Binjhia (WB)
Binjia (AS)
Binjina (BI)
Binjina (WB)
Birarea (RA)
Birhor (AS)
Birhor (TR)
Birjhia (OR)
Birjia (AS)
Bissoy (PO)
Bissoy, Barangi Jodia, Bennagi, Dadua, Frangi, Hollar, Jhoriya, Kollai, Konde, Paranga, Penga Jodia, Sodo and Takora (KA)
Bissoy-Barangi Jodia, Bannangi, Daduva, Frangi, Hollar, Jhoriya, Kollai, Konde, Paranga, Penga-Jodia, Sodo Jodia and Takora (TN)
Bissoy-Barangi Jodia, Bannangi, Daduva, Godo Jodia, Hollar, Jheriya, Kollai Konde, Paranga, Pergajodia, Prangi, Takora (AP)
Bissoy-Barangi Jodia, Bennangi, Bollar, Daduva, Frangi, Jhoriya Kollai, Konde Pranga, Penga Jodia, Sodo Jodia and Takora (KE)
Bi-soy-Barangi Jodia, Bennangi, Daduva, Frangi, Hollar, Jhoriya, Kollai, Konde, Paranga, Pengajodia, Sodo Jodia and Takoara (OR)
Bogad-Bogadi, Bagodi, Bagadi, Bagdi, Bogodi (KA)
Bogada (OR)
Bolodhia (OR)
Bondil (TN)
Bondili (PO)
Bondo (AS)
Bonya (PO)
Boreka, Gopal (MP)
Boro, Boro Kachari (MA)
Boro-Kachari (ME)
Botehra (CH)
Bowri (AS)
Bowria (JK)
Boya, Balmiki (AP)
Boyan (PO)
Boyar, Oddar (TN)
Boyas (TN)
Brijbasi (MP)
Brijia (TR)
Brijia (WB)
Budabukhalas (TN)
Budabukkalas (AP)
Budbukk (AP)
Budbukk, Budbudki, Budbukala, Devari, Joshi, Burbook (KA)
Bukka (AP)
Burbook (AP)
Burbook (MR)
Barganakaliga (AP)
Buruashankar/Barna Shankar, Beja (OR)
Burud (GU)
Burud, Medar (MR)
Batakusuda (OR)
Buttal (MR)
Byagari (KA)
Byagari (KE)
Byagari (OR)
Byagari (PO)
Byagari (TN)

C.S.I. (formerly S.I.U.C.) (TN)
Caulota, Kolota (MP)
Chaak (WB)
Chachati (KA)
Chachati (KE)
Chackaravar (KE)
Chackaravar (TN)
Chadar (MR)
Chagar (HR)
Chahang (PU)
Chain, Chayeen (BI)
Chak (DE)
Chakala, Chawla, Dhobi, Rajaka, Chakali, Vannar (AP)
Chakkala (KE)
Chakkala (PO)
Chakkiliyan (AP)
Chakkiliyan (OR)
Chakrawadya Dasar (GU)
Chakrawadya Dasar (KA)
Chakrawadya-Dasar (MR)
Chakrawadya-Dasar (RA)
Chalavadi (KE)
Chalavadi, Chalvadi (OR)
Chalvadi, Chamnayya (RA)
Cham Bukutti (KA)
Chamana (RA)
Chamar (AS)
Chamboti (KA)
Chamling (WB)
Chamtha (MR)
Chanal (UP)
Chanchati (TN)
Chandal (KA)
Chandal (HR)
Chandalagade (MR)
Chandra Vedia (MP)
Chandrabhanshi Kahar (BI)
Chang (HR)
Chang, Chahang (HP)
Changar (HP)
Channan, Chaliya (KE)
Chanou (BI)
Chantia (GU)
Chapota (BI)
Chapparband, Chapparbandsa (Muslims)
Chaptegar, Chaptegara (KA)
Chaptegra (KE)
Chaptogra (PO)
Chara, Chhar, Chhara (KA)
Charan Banjaras (AP)
Charan or Gadhavi (MR)
Charan, Charan Gadhavi (where they are not Scheduled Tribes) (GU)
Charan, Gadvi (DE)
Charg (CH)
Charodi, Chhara (MR)
Charodi, Mestha (KA)
Chasadadhoba, Haladhar, Halari, Satchasi (WB)
Chasi-Kaibartta (TR)
Chasi-Kaibartta (WB)
Chatadi (Chattada or Srivaishnava) (PO)
Chatiyar, Chakkale Chattiyar, Telegu, Vanikavaisya, Vanniar (KE)
Chatri-Agnikulaksatryya, Bombili (AP)
Chatti (KE)
Chatwal (BI)
Chaudhari (where they are not Scheduled Tribes) (GU)
Chaupal (OR)
Chavalakaranas (PO)
Chavalakkaran (KE)
Chavalakkaran, Chavalakkarar (TN)
Chayakkaran (KE)
Chayakkaran (TN)
Cheeta (RA)
Chekkalas whose normal occupation is oil crushing like Cap Vaniyans (PO)

Chelapa (HP)
Chena-Dasaru, Chenna-Dasar, Holaya-Dasar (RA)
Chenchu (KE)
Chenchu (TN)
Chenchu or Chanchwar (MR)
Chenchulu (AP)
Chere (AS)
Chero (OR)
Cheruman (AP)
Cheruman (OR)
Chettadara (PO)
Chetties (Kottar, Chetties, Parakka Chetties, Elur Chetties, Attingal Chetties Pudrakkada Chetties, Iraniel Chetties, Sri Pandara Chetties, Telugu Chetties, Udayamkulangara Chetties, Wynadan Chetties and Palavara Chetties (KE)
Chettu or Chetty (including Kottar Chetty, Elur Chetty, Pathira Chetty, Pudukkadai Chetty,Valayal Chetty) (TN)
Chetty/Balija (AN)
Chhapparband (MR)
Chhara, Adodia, Sansi (GU)
Chhara Kanjar, Nat (MR)
Chhimba Chhipi (CH)
Chhimba, Chimba Darzi, Soi (HR)
Chhipa, Apurba, Bhati, Bhagarwal, Chauhan, Chippa, Dayer, Jasod, Nama Namdeo, Padihar, Pamsar, Solanki, Surage (RA)
Chhipi, Bhata, Mochela Pandla, Rohita, Untal (HR)
Chhipi Tank (DE)
Chick Banik (AS)
Chidar (RA)
Chik (Muslims) (BI)
Chik (OR)
Chik (UP)
Chik, Chikwa, Kasai, Kassab (WB)
Chikbaraik (OR)
Chikwa (Kassab) (UP)
Chimbe Battu Brah Chhimbe, Chhipi, Chimba, Chimpa, Darzi, Dhami, Jassal, Kareer, Kainth, Madahar, Purba, Rekhroy, Sappal, Sarao, Siria, Srao, Tank (PU)
Chimbe, Chipi, Chimpa, Darzi, Soi (HP)
Chimur (MR)
Chintala (AP)
Chintala (KA)
Chintala (MR)
Chipar (MP)
Chipi Darzi, Meru (MP)
Chippa (MR)
Chirath (including Chabang and Bahri) (PU)
Chirimar (CH)
Chirimar (DE)
Chirimar (HP)
Chirimar (HR)
Chirimar (PU)
Chirimar (WB)
Chitari (MP)
Chitra, Chitrakar (OR)
Chitra, Chitrkar (KA)
Chitrakar (WB)
Chitrakathi (MR)
Chitrakathi-Joshi (KA)
Chodhara (RA)
Chodhra (MR)
Choongar, Chunka (MP)
Chopan (JK)
Chopemari (AP)
Choudang (AS)
Choudang (ME)
Chouhan (TR)
Chowdhari (AS)
Christian Chamar (GD)

Christian Mahar (GD)
Christians converted from Scheduled Castes (MR)
Chuhar or Chuhra (KA)
Chunal (UP)
Chunara (GU)
Chunchar (KA)
Chunera (UP)
Chuppolu (Mera) (AP)
Churia (OR)
Churihara, Lakhera, Lahera (WB)
Churihara, Manihar (BI)
Chutia, Chutiya (AS)
Chutiya (ME)
Chuvalia Koli (GU)
Converted Christians from Scheduled Caste (PU)
Converts to Christianity from Scheduled Castes irrespective of the generation of conversion (TN)
Converts to Christianity from Scheduled Castes (PO)

Dabgar (GU)
Dabgar (MP)
Dabgar (MR)
Dafalange (Muslim) (BI)
Dafale (Muslim) (BI)
Dafali (DE)
Dafali (WB)
Dafali, Dholi (MP)
Dafer (Hindus and Muslims) (GU)
Dafla (MA)
Dafoli (UP)
Dahalia (OR)
Dahez (MP)
Daiya (CH)
Daiya, (HP)
Daiya (PU)
Daiya Dhaiya (DE)
Dakalaru (RA)
Dakaleru (GU)
Dakaleru (MR)
Dakaut (CH)
Dakaut (RA)
Dakaut, Bhargava, Dakot, Jyotshi, Ransahab (HR)
Dakaut, Dahkaut (PU)
Dakaut Prade (DE)
Dalera (UP)
Dalu (TR)
Dalu (WB)
Damai (Nepali) (MA)
Damai (TR)
Dernal (OR)
Damala (AP)
Damali-Faqir (JK)
Damami (RA)
Dana (MP)
Dandari (AS)
Dandasa, Dandasi (KE)
Dandasi (AS)
Dandasi (KA)
Dandasi (TN)
Dang-Dasar (KA)
Dangi (BI)
Dangi (MP)
Dangua (OR)
Daoli, Daola (HR)
Daoli, Daola (PU)
Daoli Doala (CH)
Darji (OR)
Darji, Bhavasara, Hindumera, Maratha, Merti, Rangari, Rangrez (AP)
Daroga (RA)
Darvesa (KA)
Darzi (DE)
Darzi (Hindu and Muslim), Bhavasar, Kshatriya, Chippi, Chippiga, Simpi, Shimpi, Shiv Shimpi, Sai, Miai, Rangari, Rangrez, Nilari, Namdev, Rangare, Neelagar (KA)

Darzi (MR)
Darzi (RA)
Darzi, Chhipe, Chhipi, Damdo, Surjia (UP)
Darzi, Idrisi (WB)
Das or Dangdidas (MR)
Dasari (AP)
Dasari (TN)
Dasari, Desri (KA)
Dasaris (Donga and Gudu) (AP)
Daula, Soni-Braderi (PU)
Davadiga, Devadigar, Moili, Moyili, Devadig, Devaili Sappaliga, Sheregar, Servegar, Suplig, Ambalavasi (KA)
Davendrakulathan (KE)
Deha, Dhaya, Dhea (CH)
Dehuri (OR)
Dekkani Muslims (TN)
Deons (OR)
Deoris (MA)
Depala (MR)
Desali (TR)
Desari (PO)
Deshantri (RA)
Deshwa, Deshwalu (MP)
Deshwali, Dewang, Jandra, Koskati (MP)
Deva-Telikula, Gondla, Teli (AP)
Devadiga (KE)
Devadiga (PO)
Devang, Challiyan, Chilliyan, Koshti, Hutgar, Jed, Winkar, Julahi, Hutkar, Hatgar (KA)
Devanga (AP)
Devanga (KE)
Devanga (MR)
Devanga, Devangan (PO)
Devangar (Sedar) (TN)
Devar (KE)
Devari, Gosavi, Nath Panthi (MR)
Devendra Kulathan (AP)
Devendra Kulathan (OR)
Devhar (BI)
Devig (MR)
Deuli (MR)
Dey, Sudra Das (ME)
Dhadi (RA)
Dhai (CH)
Dhakad (RA)
Dhakad, Bhandari, Nagar, Singhavi, Talaya (MP)
Dhakkada (AP)
Dhakkada (KE)
Dhakkada (OR)
Dhakkada (PO)
Dhakkada (TN)
Dhamai (AS)
Dhamin (BI)
Dhaner (OR)
Dhangar (GD)
Dhangar, Bagla, Gadri, Gadaria, Hatgar, Hatkar, Kurmar, Pal (MP)
Dhangar, Kuruba, Kurubar (MR)
Dhanka including Tadvi, Tetaria and Valvi (KA)
Dhankar (BI)
Dhankia, Dhanka (MP)
Dhanohi (RA)
Dhanuk, Purwa (BI)
Dhanwar (AS)
Dhanwar (BI)
Dhanwar (HR)
Dhar (Muslims) (JK)
Dhari (BI)
Dhari (UP)
Dhasa (WB)
Dhaya, Dheya, Daiya (HR)
Dhekaru (B1)
Dhekaru (WB)
Dhemaru (TR)
Dhenuar (WB)
Dhenwar (CH)

Dhenwar (PU)
Dher (AP)
Dher (KA)
Dhimar (BI)
Dhimar (RA)
Dhimar, Dhinwar, Jhinwar, Kahar, Mallah (CH)
Dhimar, Dhivar, Gabit, Harkantra, Mangeli, Mangele, Page, Sanduri (MR)
Dhimar, Dhiwar, Dhinwar, Jheevar, Jhinwar, Kahar, Kashyap-Rajput, Mallah (HP)
Dhimar, Dhiwa, Dhinwar, Jheevar, Jhinwar, Kahar, Kashyap, Rajput, Mallah (PU)
Dhimar, Mallah, Kashyap Rajput (HR)
Dhimen (MP)
Dhimer, Benua, Banawar, Bhorji, Dhimar, Kewat, Raikar, Raikwar, Saimari (MP)
Dhinwar, Jhinwar, Nishad (DE)
Dhirkar (MP)
Dhirwar Britia, Navada, Ezingabhui (MP)
Dhobi (AN)
Dhobi (CH)
Dhobi (DN)
Dhobi (excluding those in S/C) (MP)
Dhobi (excluding those in S.C.) (DE)
Dhobi (GD)
Dhobi (GU)
Dhobi (Muslims) (KA)
Dhobi (RA)
Dhobi (Washermen) (JK)
Dhobi, Batham, Chauhan-Bhatti, Khurdania, Monson, Rajpar, Tanwar (HR)
Dhobi, Qasab (PU)
Dhobi, Rajak (excluding those in S.C.) (UP)
Dhobi, Vannan (TN)
Dhobi, Parit, Watts, Madwal, Rajak (MR)
Dhodia (KA)
Dhodia (RA)
Dholi (KA)
Dholi (MP)
Dholi (MR)
Dholi (UP)
Dholwala (JK)
Dhor (GD)
Dhor, Kakkayya, Kankayya (RA)
Dhosali (CH)
Dhosali, Dosali (HR)
Dhosali, Dosali (PU)
Dhosali, Sosal (HP)
Dhunia, Dhumian (BI)
Dhunia, Kathoria, Naddaf (UP)
Dhunia, Mansoori (WB)
Dhunia, Naddaf (MP)
Dhunia, Pinjara, Kadher Dhunnewala (DE)
Dhunkar, Kadore (MP)
Dilpali (WB)
Divachakoli (GU)
Diwan (AR)
Doai (TR)
Dom, Dombara, Paidi or Pano (KE)
Domb-Andhiya Domb, Audiniya Domb, Chonel Domb, Christian Domb, Mirgani Domb, Oriya Domb, Ponaka Domb, Telegaga Domb and Ummia Domb (KE)
Domb-Andhiya Domb, Audiniya Domb, Chonel Domb, Christian Domb, Mirgani Domb, Oriya Domb, Ponaka Domb, Telega Domb and Ummia Domb (OR)
Dombidasa (KA)
Dombo (AP)

Dombo (KE)
Dombo (TN)
Dombs, Andhiya Dombs, Chonel-Dombs, Oriya Dombs, Ponaka Dombs, Telaga Dombs and Ummia Dombs (TN)
Dombs, Andhiya, Dombs, Audiniya Dombs, Chonel Dombs, Christian Dombs, Nirgani Dombs, Oriya Dombs, Poraka Dombs, Telaga Dombs, Ummia Dombs (AP)
Dombs-Andhiya, Dombs-Audiniya, Dombs-Chonel, Dombs-Christian, Dombs-Nirgani, Dombs-Oriya, Dombs-Poraka, Dombs-Telega, Dombs-Ummia (KA)
Dommara (AP)
Dommara (MR)
Dommara (PO)
Dommera (TN)
Donga Yatas (TN)
Donga Yerukalas (KA)
DongaYathas (AP)
Doom, Dooma, Ganai/Qusab (excluding those in SC) (JK)
Dosadh, Dosad (TR)
Dosali (JK)
Dovalkar (PO)
Drain (PU)
Duari (TR)
Dubla (RA)
Dudekula (TN)
Dudekula, Laddaf, Pinjari or Noor-Bash (AP)
Dudokula, Pinjari (PO)
Dudubi (PO)
Dugla, Dholi (MA)
Dumala, Dumal (OR)
Duraj (WB)
Durgamurga-Burburchal (KA)
Dusad (AS)

Easlija, Daavat (KA)
Ediga, Gowda (Gammalla, Kalalee), Goundla, Settibalija (AP)
Eluvaln (AN)
Enadi (PO)
Enadi (TN)
Eravaliar (PO)
Eravallar (TN)
Ethayar, Idayar, Konar and Udayar (TN)
Exhava (Exhuva, Ezhava Illuvan) (PO)
Exhuthachan (PO)
Ezhavas (KE)
Ezhavathi (KE)
Ezhavathy (TN)
Ezhavathy (Vathi) (PO)
Ezhuthachan (KE)
Ezhuthachans (PO)
Ezhyva (TN)
Ezuthachar (TN)

Fakir (DE)
Fakir Bandarwala (MR)
Fakir or Faquir (Muslims) (GU)
Fakir, Faquir, Sain (MP)
Fakir, Sain (WB)
Fakir-Bandarwala (MP)
Faqir (CH)
Faqir (Muslims) (BI)
Faqir (Muslims) (KA)
Faqir (PU)
Faqir (UP)
Faquir (HP)
Farda (JK)
Fishermen (JK)
Futgudi (MR)

Gaadla, Gaadavars (PO)
Gaalda Kankani (PO)
Gabada or Godba (MR)

Gach, Mandewala (DE)
Gadaba (BI)
Gadaba (WB)
Gadaba, Gadabasboda, Gadaba-Cerilam, Gadaba-Franji, Gadaba Jodia, Gadaba Olaro, Gadaba Pangi (KA)
Gadabas-Boda Gadaba, Cerllam Gadaba, Olarao Gadaba and Pranga Gadaba and Grangi Gadaba, Jodiagadaba (TN)
Gadabas-Bodo Gadaba, Cellan Gadaba, Franji Gadaba, Jodia Gadaba, Olaro Gadaba, Pangi Gadaba and Pranga Gadaba (KE)
Gadalia or Gadiluharia (GU)
Gadaria (CH)
Gadaria (MR)
Gadaria, Banghela, Barela, Biar, Bilra, Hiranwal, Kalanlia, Pondowal, Pal, Shiviya (HR)
Gadaria, Chandalia, Gadaria, Gavala, Ghosi, Kabiria (RA)
Gadaria, Gaddi, Gaderia, Gareria, Pal (UP)
Gadderia. Gadaria (PU)
Gaddi (BI)
Gaddi (CH)
Gaddi (excluding the areas where specified as Scheduled Tribe) (HP)
Gaddi (HR)
Gaddi (JK)
Gaddi, Garri (DE)
Gaddi, Ghosi (WB)
Gaddi, Guddi (PU)
Gaderia (DE)
Gaderia (HP)
Gadhai (Muslims) (GU)
Gadhavi (MR)
Gadheri (DE)
Gadhia (UP)
Gadia-Lohar (RA)
Gadihar (Muslim) (BI)
Gadole, Gaddoli, Langoliha, Lehpita (MP)
Gadolia (RA)
Gadri (CH)
Gadri (MR)
Gadri, Gari (MP)
Gahamandi (MP)
Gain (WB)
Gainey (Nepali) (MA)
Galiara (Muslims) (GU)
Gamit, Gamtak Gavit (including Mavchi, Padvi, Vasava, Vasave and Valvi) (RA)
Ganaka (KE)
Ganali or Gandali (MR)
Ganda (AS)
Ganda (BI)
Ganda (WB)
Gandharap (MR)
Gandharb (BI)
Gandbarva, Bhatu (UP)
Gandhila (UP)
Gandia (MP)
Gandla (PO)
Gandla, Teli (KA)
Gandla, Telikula (AP)
Gandwal, Gangwa (HR)
Gangai (Nagesh) (BI)
Gangakule, Gangemakkalu, Gowrimatha, Ambig, Ambiga, Kabbaliga, Kabbili, Kabber, Kabbera, Kharvi, Bhoyi, Boyi, Thoreya, Harakanthra, Harikanthra, Kahar, Meenagar, Kharia, Sunnagar, Siviyar, Bestha, Gangamatha, Gangaputra, Bhoi, Parivara, Eravva, Brudcbestaru, Mogaveera (KA)

Gangam Reddi (KE)
Gangani (AP)
Gangani (MR)
Gangani, Gabit, Gabbit, Gapit, Gasbit (KA)
Gangavar (TN)
Gangavars (PO)
Gangin (TR)
Gangota, Gangoth (BI)
Ganiga, Chakkam, Teli (KA)
Ganigredlavaru (AP)
Ganika (including Nagavamasam) (PO)
Ganju (TR)
Gankak in Cachar only (AS)
Ganobha (RA)
Ganshi (AS)
Gaoli, Lingayat-Gaoli (MP)
Gara (Blacksmiths) (JK)
Gara (TR)
Garai (WB)
Gareri (TR)
Garhwal (MP)
Gari (TR)
Gari, Kamlivagan, Phylanwar, Purvia (MP)
Garo (MA)
Garodi (AP)
Garodi, Garudi (MR)
Garpagari (MR)
Garpagri, Nath (MP)
Garwadi, Garradi (MP)
Gatti (KA)
Gatti (KE)
Gatti (PO)
Gauda (GD)
Gauria, Gwar, Gwaria (CH)
Gavandi (MR)
Gavara (AP)
Gavara (PO)
Gavarai (Kavarai) and Vadugar (Vaduvar) other than Kamma, Kapu, Balija and Reddy (TN)
Gawala, Ghosh, Goal, Goala, Gop, Gowala, Ahir (AS)
Gawala, Gowala, Yadav, Yaduvanshi, Ahir, Gwar (PU)
Gawari, Gauria, Gwar (HR)
Gawaria (MP)
Gawaria, Gauria (HP)
Gayari (MP)
Gazula Balija, Gazulasetti (Gajula) (PO)
Ghadi (KA)
Ghadshi (MR)
Ghadsi, Ghadshi (KA)
Ghai (CH)
Ghai (HP)
Ghai (PU)
Ghami (MP)
Ghanchi (Muslims) (GU)
Gharati (JK)
Ghariya (MP)
Ghasi or Haddi, Relli Sachandi (KE)
Ghasi or Haddi, Relli, Sachandi, Ghasi, Boda Ghasi and Sanghasi (KA)
Ghasi, Ghasiara, Ghosi (HP)
Ghasi, Ghasiara, Ghosi (PU)
Ghasi, Ghasiyara, Ghosi (HR)
Ghasi, Haddi, Relli and Sachandi (TN)
Ghasiara (CH)
Ghasiara (DE) -
Ghasis-Boda Ghasis and San Ghasis (KE)
Ghati, Ghare Ghatti, Ghasi (MP)
Ghatowar (AS)
Ghatuar (AS)
Ghatwal (WB)
Ghatwar (BI)
Ghatwar (OR)
Ghatwar (WB)
Ghiradh, Ghirath (HR)
Ghirath, Ghrit, Grith-Bahti, Chang (HP)

Ghisadi (KA)
Ghisadi, Ghisadi Lohar, Gadi Lohar, Ghitodi Lohar, Rajput Lohar (MR)
Ghondali, Gondaliga, Gondhali, Gondhalli (KA)
Ghosh, Gopa, Gawala, Yadav (ME)
Ghosi (CH)
Ghosi (DE)
Ghusuria (BI)
Ghusuria (WB)
Giddildki, Pingle, Pingale (KA)
Gidhiya (UP)
Gidigar (KA)
Gingra (OR)
Giri (UP)
Giri, Goswami, Gosain (RA)
Girigiris (OR)
Goala, Gope, Yadav (TR)
Gobba (PO)
Gochaki (MP)
Gochaki (MR)
Godaba (AP)
Godaba (PO)
Godagali (KA)
Godari (KA)
Godari (KE)
Gadari (TN)
Godda (AP)
Godda (OR)
Godhi (MP)
Godi (Muslim) (RA)
Godo (Chhavo), Godhi (BI)
Godri (HR)
Godra (BI)
Godra (WB)
Godra (HP)
Godri (PU)
Goggi (GD)
Gogra (KA)
Gokha (BI)
Gokha (WB)
Gola, Golla, Gope, Sadgope Ahir, Gour, Gouda, Goudo, Mekala Golla, Punnu Golla and Yadav (OR)
Gola-Rana (GU)
Golla, Dhangar, Iddayar, Konar, Kurba Kurwa, Yadav, Yerragella (AP)
Golla, Gollewar, Goler, Golkar, Goller (MR)
Golla, Gouli, Gopal, Yadava Asthana Golla, Yadava, Advai Golla, Gopala, Gopali, Hanabaru, Krishna Golla, Anubaru, Atanaburu, Hanbar, Hanabar, Dudhigola (KA)
Gond (KE)
Gond (ME)
Gond (RA)
Gond (TN)
Gond-i-Modya-Gond & Rajo Gond (OR)
Gonda (AS)
Gonda (TR)
Gonda (WB)
Gondali (KA)
Gondhali (MP)
Gondhali, Gondala (MR)
Gondi, Modya Gond and Rajo, Gonda (PO)
Gondi-Modya Goad and Rajo Gond (KE)
Gondi-Modya Gond and Rajongond (KA)
Gonds (AS)
Gondu-Bato, Bhirthya, Dudho Kouriya, Hato, Jatako and Joria (OR)
Gondus-bato, Bhirithya, Dudho, Kouria, Hato Jatako and Joria (KA)
Goniga, Sadusetty (KA)

Gonrh (UP)
Gonrh, Gorh, Gothahum (BI)
Gonrhi (TR)
Gontia (MP)
Gopal, Gopal Bhorpis, Khelkari (MR)
Gopal, Pangala-Gopal (MP)
Gor (AS)
Gorait (AS)
Gorang (TR)
Gore (WB)
Gore-khans (JK)
Gorkha (HP)
Gorkha (HR)
Gorkha (PU)
Gorkha (WB)
Gorkhali (ME)
Gosain (UP)
Gosain, Bharti, Geria, Gosai, Gowsami, Gosaib (MP)
Gosangi (OR)
Gosangiwar (MP)
Gosavi (GD)
Gosavi Bava, Bairagi, Bharati, Girigosavi, Bharati Gosavi, Saraswati Parbat, Sagar, Ban or Van, Teerth Ashram, Aranya Gharbhari, Sanyasi, Nath Panthi Gosavi (MR)
Gosavi, Gosayi, Gosain, Atit (KA)
Goudu (AP)
Goudus Bato, Bhirithya, Dodhokouria, Hato, Jatako and Joria (PO)
Goudus, Bato, Bhirithya, Dudhokouria, Hato, Tatako and Joria (TN)
Goudus-Bato (Bhirithya, Dudhokuria, Hats, Jatako and Joria) (AP)
Goudus-Bato, Bhivthiya, Dudho Kouria, Hato, Jatako and Joria (KE)
Gound (BI)
Gound or Gowdi, Machhus, Pal, Paiko Patra or Patara, Sundi or Telli, Tanti, Yeranagollas, Oriya or Veddy Samantho, Oriya Backward Classes, Badhai Bhokta, Darji, Gour (PO)
Gounder, Padayachi, Vanniya, Kulaksativa, Vallalar, Vanniar (TN)
Gounder, Pillai (KE)
Goundu (BI)
Gowala, Gwala, Gwar, Yadav, Ahir (HP)
Gowar (WB)
Gowda (including Gammala Kalali and Gounder) (TN)
Gowda (KE)
Gowda, Gouda (including Gamalla or Kalali) (PO)
Gowtia (MP)
Gramani, Shanar, Nadar (TN)
Grammani, Shanan and Nadar (PO)
Gratie (JK)
Gudala (AP)
Gudheri (WB)
Gudia or Guria, Gurja, Gunju (OR)
Gudigara (PO)
Gujar (UP)
Gujar, Bad-Gujar, Dagar-Dahabi, Dasa, Davari, Gawr, Giyar-Gaur, Kansana, Malhli-Gujar, Harbola (MP)
Gujar, Bahar, Barwal, Bhanot, Char, Kalsan, Magria, Padaji, Rawal, Sangi (HR)
Gujar, Bhumla, Gujjar, Ninwalia, Thakur (PU)
Gujar, Gujjar (RA)
Gujar, Gurjar (DE)
Gujar, Guzar (Masons) (KA)

Gujjar (JK)
Gujjar, Gujar (excluding the areas where specified as Scheduled Tribe) (HP)
Gujrath Baori (MR)
Gujree (JK)
Gujula Balija, Dasar, Musoku, Perika Baloa (AP)
Gulgaliya (BI)
Gumtian (HP)
Gunar (TR)
Gundi (TR)
Gurav, Gurou (MR)
Gurav, Gurov, Tambli, Tamballa, Gurava, Gurout, Gurrat (KA)
Guraw (MP)
Guri (TR)
Gurkha (MI)
Gurung (SI)
Gutka Jat, Chillon Jat (CH)
Gutka Jat, Chillon Jat (HR)
Gwaria, Gauria, Gwar (PU)
Habra (OR)
Habura (MP)
Habura (MR)
Haddi (KE)
Hadi (CH)
Hadi (TR)
Hadi (WB)
Hajjam (MP)
Hajjam (Awadhiya, Kanaujia, Kawa, Nai, Naiya, Napit, Naya, Thakur) (BI)
Hajjam, Nai (Barbers) (JK)
Hajjam, Nai (CH)
Hajong (MA)
Hajuri Daroga (MP)
Halalkhor (excluding those in Scheduled Caste) (WB)
Halalkhor (TR)
Halalkhor (UP)
Halawakki, Wakkal, Vakkal, Gram Vakkal, Gam-Gowda, Gam-Gawada, Gvada, Karevakkal Kunchavakal, Attevakkal, Shilwakkal, Halakkivakkal (KA)
Halepaik (MR)
Hali (CH)
Halleer (RA)
Hallfee (KA)
Halsar, Haslar, Hulasvar, Halasvar (RA)
Halwai (UP)
Halwai (WB)
Halwai, Halwayee, Kanyakubj, Vaish (MP)
Halwari (WB)
Handervut (KA)
Handevazir (KA)
Hangie (Manjhi Boatmen and rowing class excluding houseboat owners) (JK)
Hankiya (UP)
Hansi (OR)
Haranshikari, Chigaribetegar, Vaghri, Wagiri, Nirshikari, Bagri, Baori, Phasachari, Vagri (KA)
Hari (AS)
Harni (CH)
Harni (DE)
Harni (HP)
Harni (HR)
Harni (MP)
Harni (MR)
Harni (PU)
Hasla (AP)
Hasla (OR)
Hasla (TN)
Hatkar (AP)
Hatkar (MR)
Hazuri (RA)
Hdiga (including Settibalijas of East and West Godavari Distt.) (PO)

Hedge (PO)
Hegde (KE)
Hegde (TN)
Hela (MP)
Hela (RA)
Hela (WB)
Helava (KA)
Helva (PO)
Helve, Hilav (MR)
Herbi (DE)
Hilka/Mason (JK)
Hill Pulaya (TN)
Hill Reddi (KA)
Hill-Reddis (MR)
Hima, Karanjia, Qassar (Muslims) (BI)
Hingora (Hindu and Muslims) (GU)
Hira (MA)
Ho (TR)
Holar, Valhar (RA)
Holaya, Holer (RA)
Holeva (KA)
Holeya (OR)
Holra (AS)
Holva (KE)
Holva (TN)
Holva, Helava, Helavamallur, Helvagolla, Handihelva, Pitchiguntalu, Helvaru (KA)
Honniyar (KA)
Hovadiga, Hugar, Hoogar, Mallgar, Mali, Phoolmali, Phulmati, Phulari, Pholari, Jeer (KA)
Howgar, Hawagar, Howadiga (KA)
Huga, Lohar, Lohpeta, Jadav, Jaga, Jandza (MP)
Hurkiya (UP)
Ibrahimi (WB)
Idiga (including Sett Balija) (PO)
Idiga (TN)
Idiroso or Darzi (Muslim) (BI)
Iilavathi (TN)
Iliga, Halepaik, Billaava, Devar, Malayali-Billava, Deevar, Divaramakkalu, Namdhari, Goondle, Goundla, Thiyar, Tiyan, Idiga-Kalal, Diviga, Eliga, Kommarpaik (KA)
Illathu Pillaimar (Luvar, Ishuvar Illathar) (TN)
Illavan (KE)
Illavathi (KE)
Illuvan (Ezhvan) (PO)
Ilovan (TN)
Irika (BI)
Irika (WB)
Irula (AP)
Irula (OR)
Irulas (PO)
Isai Vallalar or Melakarar (PO)
Isaivallalar (TN)
Izhuven (Illuvan) (KE)
Jadapu (TN)
Jadapus (KA)
Jadapus (KE)
Jadapus (OR)
Jadapus (PO)
Jadup (BI)
Jaggal (KA)
Jaggali (KE)
Jagiasi (MR)
Jaintrapans (OR)
Jajak (MR)
Jakkala (AP)
Jakkulas (PO)
Jalarlu (PO)
Jallad (DE)
Jambuvandondai (PO)
Jambuvanodai (TN)
Jambuvulu (KE)
Jambuvulu (OR)
Jamoria (UP)

Jandara (PO)
Jandra, Kuruvina Setty (AP)
Jangalla (AP)
Jangam (AP)
Jangam (MP)
Jangam (MR)
Jangam (PO)
Jangama, Jangam (TN)
Jangra, Jasondhi, Janms-Lodhi (MP)
Janira (AP)
Janwa (RA)
Jat (Gutka and Chillon) (PU)
Jat (Muslims) (GU)
Jatapu (TN)
Jatapus (KA)
Jatapus (KE)
Jatigar (MR)
Jatiya (MR)
Javeri, Jawari, Johari (KA)
Javeri Johari (MR)
Jeoni (WB)
Jetty (AP)
Jetty (PO)
Jhadi (MR)
Jhadi, Sonar (MP)
Jhala, Malo (MA)
Jhalo, Malo (TR)
Jhamral (MP)
Jhangara Brahmin, Khati, Viswrakarma (PU)
Jhangra-Brahman, Khati (CH)
Jhara (TR)
Jhari (MP)
Jhatkia-Sikh (DE)
Jheevar (AN)
Jheevar (TN)
Jheewar (JK)
Jhetty (TN)
Jhimar, Atlas, Bidran, Bire, Dhinwar, Duglan, Dora, Chitre, Jhewar, Jhinwar, Jimar, Kahar, Kimal, Lamsar, Malri, Radhav, Tala (HR)
Jhodia (OR)
Jhojha (UP)
Jingar (AP)
Jingar (MP)
Jingar (MR)
Jogde (MP)
Jogi (AP)
Jogi (JK)
Jogi (KE)
Jogi (MP)
Jogi (PO)
Jogi (TN)
Jogi (UP)
Jogi or Yogi (OR)
Jogi, Bans, Chillar, Faqir, Gandi, Galiya, Nath, Padha, Powar, Riwal, Ruel, Tanwar, Toor, Sihag (HR)
Jogi, Goswami (DE)
Jogi, Jogar, Sanjogi, Joger Sanyasi (KA)
Jogi, Jogo, Jugi (BI)
Jogi, Jugi, Nath,Yogi (AS)
Jogi, Nath (CH)
Jogi, Nath (PU)
Jogi, Nath (RA)
Jogi, Nath, Nathjogi, Gosai, Devori (MR)
Jogin (MR)
Joginath (MP)
Jogulas (TN)
Jolha (AS)
Jori (HP)
Joshi, Bududki, Damruwale, Kudmude, Medhangi, Sarode, Sahadev Joshi, Sarvade, Saroda, (MR)
Joshinandiwalas (AP)
Juang (BI)
Juang (WB)

Julaha (BI)
Julaha (excluding those in SC) (CH)
Julaha (Hindu and Muslim) (RA)
Julaha (Weaver) (HR)
Julaha, Dhaver, Dhuna Kabirpanthi (excluding those in S/C) (PU)
Julaha, Momin (excluding those in S.C.) (DE)
Julaha, Momin (MP)
Julaha, Winkar, Vankar, Vanya, Vankar (MR)
Julaya, Garana, Taria and Tari (Muslims) (GU)
Jullaha (JK)
Jyotish, Grahbipra Brahman, Sakaldarpee Brahman (OR)
Kabar, Kaleari, Kabari (MP)
Kabari (BI)
Kabaria (UP)
Kabbara (PO)
Kabbora (TN)
Kabirpanthi (RA)
Kabirpanthi, Ramdasiya, Ravidasia (MP)
Kachari (MA)
Kachari (TR)
Kachari (WB)
Kacher (MP)
Kachera, Lakhera (MP)
Kachhi (RA)
Kachhi, Koeri, Murai, Murao (DE)
Kachhi, Kouri, Kushwa, Mauriya, Murar, Naldih, Nardiha (UP)
Kachhi, Kushwoha, Kshatriya-Kadore (MP)
Kachi (AP)
Kachi, Kachhia (MR)
Kachora (MR)
Kadaiyan (PO)
Kadan (AP)
Kadan (KA)
Kadan (OR)
Kadan (PO)
Kadan (TN)
Kadar (BI)
Kadar (KA)
Kadar (TR)
Kadera (MR)
Kadera, Kamwal (MP)
Kadore (MP)
Kadu-Konkani (KA)
Kadupattan (KE)
Kadupattan (PO)
Kadupattar (Malabar) (TN)
Kaghzi (BI)
Kaghzi (WB)
Kahar (MP)
Kahar (WB)
Kahar, Bhoi (RA)
Kahar, Chandraborai, Chatrapati, Chatra Bansi, Ramani, Rawani, Paneri (BI)
Kahar, Dhadhan, Dhimer, Dhiver, Dhuru, Godia, Kashyap, Mehra (UP)
Kahar, Kashyap (DE)
Kahar, Kumbhar (DN)
Kaibartta (BI)
Kaibartta, Jaliya (MA)
Kaikadi (AP)
Kaikadi (or Korva) (AP)
Kaikadi (where they are not SC), Korach, Dhontle, Korva or Kochi Korva, Makadwale, Padlor, Korvi (MR)
Kaikadi or Korach (GU)
Kaikadi, Korach (RA)
Kaikadi, Koragar, Yerkala, Erakala,
Kunchi, Korva, Koramasetty, Yerukala (KA)
Kaikala (AP)
Kaikari (MP)
Kaikolan Kammara (excluding the areas comprising old Malabar District) (KE)

Kaikolan, Kaikolar, Sengunthar (TN)
Kaira (TR)
Kaira (WB)
Kakhera, Manihar (DE)
Kakkalan (where they are not Sch. Castes) (TN)
Kaladis (TN)
Kalahandi (AS)
Kalai (TR)
Kalal, Kalar, Kapdi (MP)
Kalal, Kalar, Lad, Ladwak, Gond Kalal, Shivhare (MR)
Kalal, Kalwar (DE)
Kalandar (BI)
Kalandar (UP)
Kalar (UP)
Kalari Kurup (Kalari Panich) (TN)
Kalarikurups (Kairal Panicker) (PO)
Kalavanthula (PO)
Kalavanthulu, Baggala, Ganika (AP)
Kalel (RA)
Kalhodia (GU)
Kalihandi (AS)
Kalingi (PO)
Kalingi (TN)
Kalladi (OR)
Kalladi, Kalwar (AP)
Kallan (PO)
Kallar (PO)
Kallar, Vellalar (TN)
Kalloda (KA)
Kallundar (MP)
Kalota (MP)
Kalu (TR)
Kalu, Teli, Garai, Mondal, Sadhukhan, Pal, Patra, Sadhu, Barik (WB)
Kalveli Gounder (TN)
Kalwar (BI)
Kalwar (OR)
Kalwar (TR)
Kalwar (WB)
Kamalas (Viswakarmala) (PO)
Kamar (WB)
Kamar, Barhai, Kakit, Maggia, Maghaiya, Mistri, Nagbansi, Viswakarma (BI)
Kamati (MR)
Kamanti, Kanian (KA)
Kambadia Bhagat (GU)
Kambar (TN)
Kamboj, Bala, Kamboh, Masok, Nande,Thand (PU)
Kamboj, Bangwa, Bangwai, Chimde, Gadhi, Gagwaik, Jangla, Kamboth, Lagle, Padhe, Pradhan (HR)
Kamboj, Kamboh (CH)
Kami (Nepali) (MA)
Kamkar (BI)
Kammalana (Kamsalas, Viswav-Brahman and Viswa Karma Karuvaw) (PO)
Kammalar-Kamsala-Viswa Brahmin and Viswakarmala (including Thattar or Porkollar, Kannar, Karumer or Kollar Thacher and Kalthacher) (TN)
Kammalas, Viswa Karmalas (Viswa Karma Karuvan Agari, Moosari, Thattan Vilkurup or Villasan, Viswabrahmanar, Viswam) (KE)
Kammara (excluding Kollegal taluk of Mysore Distt.) (KA)
Kammara, Kamara, Kamar, Kammaro, Muli, Lohuru, Loharo (OR)
Kammi (MR)
Kamriya (MP)
Kan, Kanu (WB)
Kannakan (AP)

Kanakkan (OR)
Kanate (KA)
Kanbi, Kulwadi, Kunbi (KA)
Kanchan (CH)
Kandarpa (OR)
Kandel (MR)
Kandera (MP)
Kandera (RA)
Kandh (TR)
Kandh (WB)
Kandhal (AS)
Kandra (AP)
Kandra (BI)
Kandra (PO)
Kandra (TR)
Kandu (WB)
Kandu, Kanu (MA)
Kaner (MP)
Kangar (DE)
Kangar, Batwalo (MP)
Kangasia (GU)
Kangh (TR)
Kanghara (CH)
Kanghera (HP)
Kangi, Kangiwala (RA)
Kani or Kanisu or Kaniyar Pannikkar (TN)
Kani, Kanian or Kaniyan and Kanisu or Kaniyar Panikkar, Ganka, Kanisy (PU)
Kanikaran Kannikar (where they are not Sch. Tribes) (TN)
Kanisan (KE)
Kanisan, Kaniyan, Kanyan, (excluding Kollegal Taluk of Mysore Distt.), Kaniyar (KA)
Kanisu or Kaniyar Panicher, Kani or Kaniyan (Ganaka) (KE)
Kaniyan (KE)
Kaniyan (OR)
Kanjar (AP)
Kanjar (CH)
Kanjar (KE)
Kanjar (OR)
Kanjar (TN)
Kanjar, Kanchan (HP)
Kanjar, Kanchan (PU)
Kanjar, Kanjari, Kanjir, Khanjarbhat (KA)
Kanjara-Bhatta (AP)
Kanjra (BI)
Kanmaeli (DE)
Kannada Saineegar, Kamadiyar and Dasapalanjika (TN)
Kannadiyan (KE)
Kannakan, Padanna (where they are not Sch. Castes) (TN)
Kannatia (MP)
Kansari, Kansyakar (WB)
Kanu (BI)
Kanvi (RA)
Kanwar (Jaiswal) (AP)
Kaora (TR)
Kapadia (BI)
Kapadia (MP)
Kapali (TR)
Kapali (WB)
Kapdi (DN)
Kapdi (MR)
Kapmare or Reddika (Redika) (AP)
Kapudia (OR)
Kapumaries (AP)
Kapumaries (KA)
Kapumaries (KE)
Kapumaries (TN)
Kapuria (TR)
Kapuria (WB)
Karan (MP)
Karani (WB)
Karar, Keer (MP)
Karbi (AS)
Karenga (TR)
Karha (WB)
Karhara (OR)

Kari (TR)
Karikalabhakthulu Kaikala or Kaikolan (Sengundam or Sangunther) (AP)
Karikudumbi (KA)
Karimpalan (AP)
Karimpalan (KA)
Karinpalan (OR)
Karmakar (WB)
Karmakar, Kamar (TR)
Karmali (AS)
Karmali (OR)
Karnabhakthulu (AP)
Karnaveegar (Karnam), Kanaka Pillais (AP)
Karneegar, Karnam (TN)
Karuneegar (Seer Karuneegar, Srikaruneegar, Satrattu Karuneegar, Kaikatti Karuneegar, Mathu Vazhi Kanakkar, Sozhi Kanakkar and Sunnambu Karuneegar) (TN)
Karuva (KA)
Karwalnat, Karwalnuts (WB)
Karwalnut (BI)
Kasab, Kassab, Kasai, Quraishi, Qussab, Qassab (MP)
Kasai (UP)
Kasai, Katik, Khatik, Katuka, Katuga, Kasab, Aray, Kulal (KA)
Kasai, Khatik, Kasab (MR)
Kasai, Qassab, Quraishi (DE)
Kasai-Maji (WB)
Kasar (GD)
Kasar, Kansar, Kancheri, Kanchara, Kanchugara, Bogar (KA)
Kasar, Kasera (MR)
Kasbi (MP)
Kasbi (MR)
Kasbin (KA)
Kasera, Jamera, Kasar (MP)
Kasera, Temara, Thathera, Thathiar (DE)
Kasgar (UP)
Kashan (AS)
Kashikappi, Kashi Kapadi, Tirumali (KA)
Kasikapadi (MR)
Kassab (CH)
Kassab (Kasai) (Muslim) (BI)
Kasta (WB)
Kasta, Kastha (TR)
Kastha (WB)
Katabu (MR)
Katabu, Katabar (KA)
Katesar or Pattamkatti (TN)
Kathar Katharwani, Kanthaharwani (Lingayatwani or Ladwani excluded) (MR)
Kathi-Khati (MR)
Kathikkaran (KE)
Kathikkaran (TN)
Kathputli-Nachanewala (DE)
Katika, Kasai (AP)
Katipamula (AP)
Katipamula (MR)
Katipapala (AP)
Katipaula (KA)
Katri-Rajulu (AP)
Kaitunayakan (OR)
Kauathi (KE)
Kaura (BI)
Kauri, Kori, Kodar (MP)
Kavadi (KA)
Kavara (where they are not Scheduled Castes) (TN)
Kavathi (TN)
Kavatiyan (KA)
Kavudiyaru (KE)
Kavuthiyan (KE)
Kavuthiyan (PO)
Kavuthiyar (TN)
Kawar (AS)
Kawar (BI)
Kayasth-Kaiti Brahmin (AP)

Kayastha (Bengali) (AS)
Kechai (TR)
Keer (RA)
Kehal (CH)
Kehal (HP)
Kehal (HR)
Kehal (PU)
Kela (BI)
Kela (WB)
Kelasi (Kalasi Panicker) (KE)
Kelasi (PO)
Kelkari, Khelkari (KA)
Keot (AS)
Keot (BI)
Kerala Kudeli (TN)
Kerala Mudali, Kerala Muthali (PO)
Kerala Mudalis (KE)
Kerala Muthali (TN)
Kesar (JK)
Kewat, Bansi, Chai, Jalehar, Kharsa, Majhi, Mallah, Nishad (UP)
Kewat, Mallah (DE)
Khadwar (BI)
Khaira (OR)
Khaira (TR)
Khairwa (UP)
Khamgara (MP)
Khami (TR)
Khami (WB)
Khampti, Khamti (MA)
Khamti (AS)
Khamti (ME)
Khandait (TN)
Khandait (WB)
Khandnals (OR)
Khangar (BI)
Khangar (UP)
Khanghera (HR)
Khanghera (PU)
Khanjiman (OR)
Khant (GU)
Khant (RA)
Kharag (WB)
Kharia (AN)
Kharia (AS)
Kharia (WB)
Kharol (RA)
Kharol, Telugu-Munar, Kapu (MP)
Kharot (UP)
Kharvi (PO)
Kharvi (TN)
Kharwa or Kharwi (MR)
Kharwa-Bhardela (GU)
Kharwar (MP)
Khasi (MA)
Khatana (JK)
Khatgune (DE)
Khatik (BI)
Khatik (excluding those in S.C.) (DE)
Khatik (GU)
Khatik (TR)
Khatka (RA)
Khatka, Khatia (MP)
Khatki or Kasai, Chamadia or Khatki, Halarikhatki (Muslims) (GU)
Khatri (TN)
Khatti-Khatti (OR)
Khattia-Khatti, Kommarao and Lohara (TN)
Khattis, Khatti, Kommorao and Lohara (KE)
Khattis-Khatti, Kammarao and Lohara (PO)
Khattis-Khatti, Kommarao and Lohara (AP)
Khatua (OR)
Khatwa (BI)
Khatwe (BI)
Khelta (BI)
Khemcha (TR)
Khen (TR)
Khen (WB)

Kherwar (AS)
Kherwar (WB)
Khetauri (BI)
Khetauri (OR)
Khetauri (WB)
Khodal (AS)
Khodra (OR)
Kholie (JK)
Khond (AP)
Khond (AS)
Khond (KA)
Khond (KE)
Khond (ME)
Khond (TN)
Khondal (OR)
Khonyor (AS)
Khristi Gujarati Christian (converts from Scheduled Castes only) (GU)
Khuangsai (MA)
Khyang (TR)
Khyang (WB)
Khyara (WB)
Kichagara (KA)
Kichak (TR)
Kichak (WB)
Kingharia (UP)
Kintali Kalinga (TN)
Kinthala Kalinga (AP)
Kintoli Kalinga (AP)
Kir (MP)
Kirad (MR)
Kirar (RA)
Kirar, Dhakar (MP)
Kirar, Kirad (MP)
Kisan (UP)
Kisarwaki (WB)
Kishar (BI)
Kitara (PO)
Kitara (KE)
Knowar (TR)
Koch (ME)
Kochh (BI)
Kochi (AP)
Koda (TR)
Koda (WB)
Koda, Kuda (OR)
Kodalo (AP)
Kodalo (KA)
Kodalo (KE)
Kodalo (TN)
Kodar (MP)
Kodu (KA)
Kodu (KE)
Kodu (PO)
Kodu (TN)
Koeri, Koiri (WB)
Kohdala (PO)
Kohli (CH)
Kohor (AS)
Koikolan or Koikola (Sengunthar, Sengundar) (PO)
Koilar (OR)
Koiri (AS)
Koiri (TR)
Koiri, Koeri (UP)
Kol (AS)
Kol (RA)
Kol (WB)
Kolaga (HP)
Kolaga (Misal) (DN)
Kolalar, Davar, Thevar (TN)
Kolam (OR)
Kolarios or Munivanies (PO)
Kolayanurali (KA)
Kolayiri, Kolari (KA)
Kolhati, Dombari (MR)
Koli (BI)
Koli (DN)
Koli (GD)
Koli (UP)
Koli (WB)
Koli Mahadeo (KA)
Koli, Koli Malhar, Koli Mahadev or Dongar Koli, Ghedia Koli, Idaria Koli, Kharwa Koli,

Rathwa Koli, Baria Koli, Dbebaria Koli, Talpada Koli (where they are not Scheduled Tribes) (GU)

Koli, Koli-Suryawanshi, Malhar Koli, Christian Koli (MR)

Koli-Mahadev (RA)

Kolinga, Baragana Kalinga (AP)

Kolla, Kollahab (KA)

Kolta (UP)

Kolthati Kolhatigi (KA)

Kolu (WB)

Komakapu (AP)

Komakapu (MR)

Komakpu (KA)

Komar (OR)

Komer (TR)

Kommar (AP)

Kommar (KA)

Kommar (KE)

Kommar (PO)

Kommar, Kommara (TN)

Konai (TR)

Kond (Kui) (AP)

Kond (Kui) (KA)

Kond (Kui) (KE)

Kond (Kul) (OR)

Kond Danoars (KE)

Konda Dhera, Kond (Kui) (TN)

Konda Dhora, Konda Reddis (KA)

Konda Dora (KE)

Konda Kapu (OR)

Konda Reddi (OR)

Kondh, Desaya, Kondhs, Dongria, Kondhs, Kuttiya, Kondhs, Tikiria (KA)

Kondh-Desaya Kondh, Dongria Kondh, Kuttiya Kondh, Tikiria Kondh and Yamity Kondh (TN)

Kondh-Desaya Kondh, Dongriya Kondh, Kuttiya Kondh, Tikiria Kondh and Yanity Kondh (OR)

Kondhs-Desaya Kondh, Dongria Kondhs, Kuttiya Mondhs, Tikiria Kondhs and Yemity Kondhs (KE)

Kondpan (AS)

Kondu (MR)

Konga, Kongadi (KA)

Kongadi (MR)

Kongu Chattiar (TN)

Kongu Malayan (KE)

Kongu Vellalar (including Anupa Vellala Gounder, Chendalai Gounder, Harambukatti Gounder, Kurumba, Gounder, Nattu Gounder, Padaithalaj, Poosari, Paualankatti Vellala Gounder, Pala Gounder, Rathinagiri Gounder, Sanku Vellala Gounder, Tirumudi Vellala, Thondu Vellalar, Vellala Gotunder (TN)

Konkna Yenity (KA)

Koosa (AP)

Koosa (OR)

Kootan, Koodan (where they are not Scheduled Castes) (TN)

Koppala Velama (TN)

Kopplavalamas (PO)

Koppulavelama (AP)

Koracha (Keravars) (AP)

Koracha (PO)

Koracha Koravar, Yerukala (TN)

Korachas (or Koravar or Yerukala) (KE)

Korachas or Yerkula or Korvay (MR)

Koraga (AP)

Koraga (OR)

Korchar (MR)

Koria (MP)

Korku (BI)

Korku (RA)

Kormakar (AS)
Korwa (AS)
Korwa (TR)
Korwa including Kodaku (MR)
Kosalya Coudus, Bosotheriya Goudus, Chiti Goudus, Dangayath Goudus, Doddu Kamariya, Dudu Kamaro, Ladiya Goudus and Pullo Soriya Goudus (OR)
Kosalya Goudus, Bosothoriya Goudus, Chitti Goudus, Dangayath Goundus, Doddu, Kamariya, Dudu Komaro, Ladiya Goudus and Pullosoriya Goudus (PO)
Kosalya Goudus, Bosothoriya Goudus, Chitti Goudus, Dangayath Goudas, Dodukamariya, Dodukamaro, Adiya Goudus and Pullosariya Goudus (KA)
Kosalya Goudus, Bosothoriya Goudus, Chitti Goudus, Dangayath Goudus, Doddu Kamariya, Dudu Kamarok, Ladiya Gouds and Pullsoriya Goudus (KE)
Kosalya Goudus, Bosothoriya Goudus, Chith Goudus, Dangayath Goudus, Doddu Kammariya, Dudu Kamaro, Laddiya Goudus and Fullo Soriya Goudus (TN)
Kosalyagoudus - (Bass Theriya Groundus, Chitti Groundus, Dangayath Goundus Doddu, Dudu Kamaro Ludiya, Komariya Goundus and Pullo Sariya Goundus) (AP)
Kosavans, Kuyauar (PO)
Koshta (BI)
Koshta (UP)
Koshti (AP)
Koshti (MP)
Koshti (RA)
Koshti, Kashkoti-Devanga (MR)
Kosti, Chaudhry, Kusata, Koli-Keskati (MP)
Kota (AP)
Kota (OR)
Kota (TN)
Kotari, Kottari (KA)
Kotayar (Shoragara Kushatriya) (PO)
Kotekshatriya (KA)
Koteyar (KE)
Koteyar (TN)
Kotia-Bartika, Bantho Oriya, Dhulia or Dulia, Holva, Paiko, Putiya Sanrona and Sidho Paiko (TN)
Kotia-Bartika, Bentho Oriya Dhulia or Dulia, Holva Paiko, Putiya, Sahrona and Sidho Paiko (KE)
Kotia-Bartika, Benthooriya, Dhulia or Dulia, Holva Paiko, Putiya, Sanrona and Sidho Paiko (KA)
Kotil (MP)
Kotwal (AS)
Kotwal (RA)
Kotwal or Kotwalia (GU)
Kotwar (UP)
Koya (AS)
Koya or Goud (with its subsesects Raj or Rasha Koyas, Linga Dhari Koya (ordinary) and Kottukoya (TN)
Koya or Goud, with its subsects Raj or Rasha Koya, Kottu Koya and Lingadhari Koya (KE)
Koyava (KA)
Koyi (AP)
Koyi (KE)

Koyi (OR)
Koyi (TN)
Krishnabalija (Dasari Bakka) (AP)
Krishnanyaka (KE)
Krishnavaka (PO)
Krishnavaka (TN)
Kritiria (BI)
Kshatriya (AR)
Kshattriya (AS)
Kshattriya (ME)
Kubbora (TN)
Kuchband (CH)
Kuchband (HR)
Kuchband, Kuchhband (PU)
Kuchbandh (MR)
Kuchhria (MR)
Kudiya (AP)
Kudiya (OR)
Kudubi (AP)
Kudubi (OR)
Kudubi (TN)
Kudubi, Kudubi-Koyi (KA)
Kudubi, Kudumbis (KE)
Kudumban (AP)
Kudunban (OR)
Kudumbi (PO)
Kudumbi (TN)
Kuki (MA)
Kuki (WB)
Kul-Faqir (JK)
Kulait (CH)
Kulala (including Kumbarar and Kyyavar) (TN)
Kulbandhiya, Kumavat (MP)
Kulela, Kulala, Kummari (PO)
Kulta (OR)
Kumahari, Kumbhar, Kumhar (excluding those in SC) (MP)
Kumar (MP)
Kumar, Rudra Paul (ME)
Kumar, Rudra Paul of Cachar (AS)
Kumarbhag Pahadia (BI)
Kumbar-Kulla, Salivahana (AP)
Kumbara, Kummara, Khumbhar,Kambhar, Kulala, Kulalar, Moolya, Kusavan (KA)
Kumbaran (PO)
Kumbhakar, Kumbhar (TR)
Kumbhakshatriya (AP)
Kumbhar (Biyar, Kadra Patel, Pathiya, Potmaker, Prajapati, Sakariya Variya, Varia) (GU)
Kumbhar, Kulal, Kumhar, Kumbharo (OR)
Kumbhar, Kumar, Kumbhakar, Kumhar, Kumrakar, Rudra (WB)
Kumbhar, Kumhar (MR)
Kumbi, Kurmar (MP)
Kunhar (AS)
Kumhar (Potters) (JK)
Kumhar (RA)
Kumhar, Ahitan, Ghamar, Ghumar, Hansanwal, Jopa, Keer, Langotra, Lehri, Narlia, Prajapat, Sanmare, Sohal, Talephail, Zalaf (PU)
Kumhar, Chakbya, Chakire, Kohar, Kumbhar, Prajapati (UP)
Kumhar, Chotrapati, Kobhalkar, Kumbhar, Kumbhakar, Prajapati (BI)
Kumhar, Prajapati (CH)
Kumhar, Prajapati (DE)
Kumhar, Prajapati (HP)
Kumhar, Prajapati (HR)
Kummara or Kulala (AP)
Kunapili (AP)
Kundi (GD)
Kunbi (MR)
Kunchetigara (AP)
Kunchi Korwa (KA)
Kunchidigar (TN)
Kundamatia (OR)

Kunduma/Kuduma (OR)
Kunjra (MP)
Kunjra, Rayeen (UP)
Kunjra, Rayeen (WB)
Kunnuvar Mannadi (PO)
Kunnuvar Monnadi (TN)
Kupadhar, Kushiar, Rarh (ME)
Kupadhar, Kushiari, Rarh (AS)
Kuraban, Kurumban, Kurumba, Hulumatha, Dhangar Bharwad, Gorava (KA)
Kurakula (AP)
Kurariar (OR)
Kurariar (TR)
Kuravan (AP)
Kuravan (OR)
Kuravar (TN)
Kurhini Chetty (TN)
Kurhinshetty (MR)
Kurichchan (AP)
Kurichchan (KA)
Kurichchan (OR)
Kurma, Kurmi (KA)
Kurmar (MR)
Kurmi (AR)
Kurmi (AS)
Kurmi (BI)
Kurmi (CH)
Kurmi (DE)
Kurmi (HP)
Kurmi (HR)
Kurmi (OR)
Kurmi (PU)
Kurmi (TR)
Kurmi (UP)
Kurmi (WB)
Kuruba or Kuruma, Hegde (AP)
Kuruman (Kurumba) (AP)
Kuruman (Kurumba) (OR)
Kurumans (AP)
Kurumba (where are no Scheduled Tribes) (TN)
Kurumba, Kuruba, Kurubar, Kuruva (PO)
Kurumbaravas (TN)
Kuruva, Kurub, Kurab, Kurubar (KA)
Kusavan (Kulala, Andhra Nair or Anthuru Nair) (KE)
Kusavan (PO)
Kushwaha (Koeri) (BI)
Kuta (UP)
Kutuma (KA)
Kutwar, Kotwal (excluding those in S/C) (MP)

Labana (HP)
Labana, Mahravat, Goti, Hadkashi, Zod, Dhinga, Pelya, Shatbai, Baman (GU)
Labana, Vanzara, Lobana Banjara (CH)
Labbai (PO)
Labbai (TN)
Labera (RA)
Labha (MR)
Ladaff, Laddaf (MR)
Ladar, Lad, Ladaru, Yelegar (KA)
Ladha-Lohar (RA)
Ladia, Ladhia, Laria (MP)
Ladia, Ladhia, Laria (MR)
Lahana (DE)
Lahar (AS)
Lahara (AS)
Laher (OR)
Laheri (BI)
Lakar (WB)
Lakhera (RA)
Lakhera, Chhan, Manihar, Panihar, Paniar (HR)
Lakhera, Kanihar, Manihar (PU)
Lakhera, Lakhari (MR)
Lakhera, Manihar (CH)
Lakhra (OR)

Laka (WB)
Lalbegi (MA)
Lalbegi (TR)
Lalbegi, Bhangi (Muslim) (BI)
Lalung (MA)
Lambadi (OR)
Lambadi (PO)
Lambadi, Banjara, Sugadi (TN)
Lambadi, Banjara, Sugali, Gavara (KE)
Lambana, Bhagtava, Ghotra, Kaknia, Khasrin, Labana, Lohana, Lobana, Vanzara, Lavana, Pelia (PU)
Langoliha (MP)
Lanzad (MR)
Larhia (MP)
Laskar, Lashkar (TR)
Latin Catholics (KE)
Latin Catholics (TN)
Lek (RA)
Liamei-Naga (MA)
Limbo, Limbu (ME)
Limboo, Limbu (SI)
Lingabalija (AP)
Lingader (RA)
Lingayat Sections namely Shimpi, Shivashimpi, Neelagar, Koshti, Hatagar, Jeda, Bilijeda, Neygi, Kumhinashetty, Bilimagga, Nayinda, Navi, Kshonrada, Kelasi, Hadapad, Nadig, Mangala, Kummar Badagi, Agasa, Modivala, Rajaka, Gurav, Tambli, Kumbar, Kambhar, Kulal, Banagar, Nagalika, Gowli, (Cowherd), Hugar, Jeer, Malagar, Teligar, Pujar, Mathapatis amongst Jangams, Ganigar, Shuddhashiva Shivarechka, Jhammadi (KA)
Lippara (KA)
Lobana, Labana, (same as in S.No. 5) (HR)
Lodha (AS)
Lodha (BI)
Lodha (GU)
Lodha (TR)
Lodha, Lodh (UP)
Lodhi (AS)
Lodhi (RS)
Lodhi, Hardha, Parihar, Lodha (MP)
Lodhi, Lodha, Lodh, Maha Lodh (DE)
Lohar (BI)
Lohar (JK)
Lohar (MA)
Lohar (MP)
Lohar (TR)
Lohar, Abangar, Luhar, Mistri, Ruriya (UP)
Lohar, Bakhon, Bamsa, Bhati, Bhuhi, Birdi, Channa, Jhita, Luhar, Phul, Roopra, Sandhu, Sehami, Virdi (PU)
Lohar, Jaradi, Khuadi, Khutwal, Lohargiri, Malvi, Panchal, Pancholi, Thurawar, Zaradi (RA)
Lohar, Lohar-Gada, Dodi, Khatwali, Panchal (MR)
Loi (AS)
Loi (ME)
Lome (MP)
Lonari (KA)
Lonari, Chunari (MR)
Lone (JK)
Lonia, Lunia, Nunia, Nonia (MP)
Luhar (DE)
Luhar, Gahelot, Jeva, Kariyar, Kawigar, Luckman, Madwar, Vishwakarma (MP)

Luhar, Lohar (HR)
Luhura (OR)
Luniya, Lonia (UP)
Lushei (WB)

Machhi (Hindu), Bitna, Dhimar, Dhivar, Kahar, Khalas, Khalasi, Kharwal,Mangela,Sarang, Tandel (GU)
Machhi, Machhera (DE)
Machhi, Mali, Marar (MP)
Machhi, Tandel (MR)
Machhua (WB)
Machi, Aaribharatbhara, Bharatbhata, Chamadia, Chandlia, Dasania, Jansali, Jingar, Myangar, Sonari, Sivania (GU)
Machua (OR)
Madar (BI)
Madara (KE)
Madari (AS)
Madari (CH)
Madari (HP)
Madari (HR)
Madari (JK)
Madari (KE)
Madari (Muslim) (BI)
Madari (PU)
Madari, Bharathari, Nath (GU)
Madgi (MP)
Madiga (KE)
Madivala (KE)
Madri (AP)
Madugar or Modavar or Vethakkara (PO)
Maga (MR)
Magadhi Goral (OR)
Magatha Goudu, Bemia Goudu, Boodu Magatha, Dongayath Goudu, Ponna Magatha, Sana Magatha and Yadya Goudu (TN)
Magatha Goudus, Bermia Goudus, Boodo, Magatha, Dongayath Goudu, Ladya Goudu, Poona Magatha and Sana Magatha (OR)
Magatha Goudus, Bemia-Goudus, Boodo Magatha, Dongayath Goudu, Lady Goudu, Pona Magatha and Sana Magatha (KA)
Magatha, Goudus-Bernis, Goudus Boodo, Magatha, Dongaath Goudus, Ladya Goudu, Ponna Magatha and Sanna Magatha (KE)
Maghaiya-Dome (TR)
Maghi or Meghia (OR)
Maghya (HR)
Magura (OR)
Maga-Brahman (RA)
Mahadarda (WB)
Mahaedra, Mahandra, Medara (PO)
Mahali, Mahli (MR)
Mahandra, Medara (TN)
Mahapatra (DE)
Mahar (TR)
Mahara (MA)
Mahasari (AP)
Mahasari (KA)
Mahasha, Bajgal, Sahunta (PU)
Mahata (WB)
Mahatam (CH)
Mahatam (HP)
Mahatam (HR)
Mahatam (PU)
Mahatar (Muslims) (AP)
Mahato (AS)
Mahato (WB)
Mahigir (JK)
Mahil (MR)
Mahishtya (WB)
Mahishya (BI)

Mahisya Das, Mahisya (ME)
Mahisya-Das, Mahisya (AS)
Mahli (AS)
Mahli (TR)
Mahratta (non-Brahmin) (including Namdev Mahratta) (TN)
Mahto (BI)
Mahunta (OR)
Mahuria (BI)
Mahuria (WB)
Maidhasi (KA)
Maidhasi (MR)
Maila (AP)
Maila (OR)
Maimals (Muslim fishermen) (AS)
Mairal, Dangat, Vir (MR)
Maiti (AR)
Majhabi (MP)
Majhi, Deshwali-Majhi (WB)
Majhiara (AR)
Majhwar (BI)
Majhwar (MR)
Majothi Kumbhar, Darbar or Darban Majothi (Muslims) (GU)
Majwar (AS)
Makrana (Muslim) (DN)
Makrani (Muslim) (GU)
Mal (TR)
Mal Paharia (OR)
Mala (MP)
Mala Dasu (KE)
Mala Dasu (TN)
Mala Pantaram (KE)
Mala Pulayan, Karavali Puluyan, Kurumba Pulayan and Paubu Pulayan (KE)
Maladasu (OR)
Malakar (WB)
Malapantaram (TN)
Malapulayan, Kurumbapulayan, Keravalipulayan, Pambupulayam (TN)
Malar (Malhor) (BI)
Malas or Agency Malas, Valmikies (KE)
Malasdar (AP)
Malasar (OR)
Malayali (where they are not Scheduled Tribes) (TN)
Malayan, Malayar (TN)
Malayavayan (TN)
Malayekandi (KE)
Male (PO)
Male (TN)
Malhar (RA)
Mali (Malakar) (BI)
Mali (RA)
Mali (WB)
Mali (where they are not Scheduled Tribes) (AP)
Mali, Bhuimali, Bhuinmali (MA)
Mali, Phoolmali (MR)
Mali, Phoolmali, Saini (CH)
Mali, Phuli, Sagbaria, Bhajemali (OR)
Mali, Saini (UP)
Mali, Saini, Southia, Sagarwanshi-Mali, Nayak (DE)
Mali/Mondi Patta (AP)
Malia-Korchia Malis, Paiko Malis and Pedda Malis (TN)
Malis, Korchiamalis, Paiko Malis and Pedda Malis (KA)
Malis—Korchia Malis, Paido Malis and Pedda Malis (OR)
Mali—Kerchia Mali, Paiko Mali and Peddamali (AP)
Malla Malasar (KE)
Mallah (MP)
Mallah (TR)
Mallah, Birhar, Gayotri, Ghetwel, Jalwar, Kewat, Kurwaha, Maheta, Majhi, Muriyoni, Masuria, Phutant, Purhia, Nisad, Goshi, Dhiwar, Jhiwar, Jhimar (BI)

Mallik (TR)
Malpaharia (AS)
Malphariya (TR)
Malyar (JK)
Manavans (KE)
Manbhav (MR)
Mandula (AP)
Manga (MP)
Mangala (AP)
Mangala (MR)
Mangala (Nayee-Brahman) (PO)
Mangali-Nayi Brahmin (AP)
Mangan (BI)
Mangan (WB)
Mangar (Magar) (BI)
Mangar (WB)
Mangli (OR)
Mangtha Goundus, Bana Megatha, Beraia Goundu, Boodo Magatha, Gongayath Goundu, Ladya Gounda and Pennagagatha (AP)
Maniha (MP)
Manihar, Lakhera (UP)
Manipuri (including Manipuri Brahmins, Manipuri Muslims and Meteis) (AS)
Manipuri (MI)
Manipuri (TR)
Maniyan (AP)
Maniyani, Muniyani (KA)
Manjar, Mara, Mathwaddar (MP)
Manjhi (UP)
Mankar (MP)
Mankar Khalu (MP)
Manki (AS)
Manna Dhora (KA)
Manna Dhora (KE)
Manna Dhora (OR)
Manna Dhora (TN)
Mannan (KA)
Mannan, Vannan, Pathiyar (where they are not Scheduled Castes) (TN)
Mannus (PO)
Mansari (Muslims) (GU)
Manula (AP)
Manurukapu (Telangana), Munnor-Kapu (AP)
Mapilla (TN)
Mappila (KE)
Mappila (PO)
Marakkan (KE)
Marakkan (TN)
Marameri, Gramani (TN)
Marar (TN)
Marar (TR)
Marasi (HP)
Marathi (AP)
Marathi (excluding South Kanara Distt.) (KA)
Marathi (OR)
Marathi (PO)
Marathi (TN)
Marathi, Marati (KE)
Marauan (KE)
Maravan (TN)
Maravans (KE)
Maravar, Maravaw (PO)
Maravars (Sembanad and Appanad KondayanKottai) (TN)
Marayan, Maravanr (KA)
Marchha (UP)
Maria (AS)
Markande (BI)
Marta (KA)
Maru Sotiya (MP)
Maruar, Marumaravar (TN)
Maruthuvar (PO)
Maruthuvar, Navithar (TN)
Marwar Baori (MR)
Marwari, Budhiya (TN)
Masania-Jogi (DE)
Masaniayogi (KA)
Masanjogi, Sudga-Dsiddha, Mapanjogi (MR)

Matangi (KE)
Matangi (OR)
Matangi (TN)
Mathura (AP)
Mathura (MR)
Matial (WB)
Matiara, Matihara (MR)
Matwa or Matwa-Kureshi (Muslims), Gavli (Hindus) (GU)
Maulik (BI)
Maune (AP)
Maune (KE)
Maune (OR)
Maune (TN)
Mauria (MP)
Mauriaro (BI)
Mavi (MP)
Mavilan (AP)
Mavilan (OR)
Mawati (HR)
Mdivla, Madivala (PO)
Me (MR)
Me or Meta (GU)
Mech (MA) Changar (PU)
Mech (TR)
Medara (KE)
Medara (TN)
Medara, Medari, Burud, Gauriga, Medara (KA)
Medari or Mahendra (AP)
Meena, Mina (CH)
Meena, Mina (HR)
Meena, Mina (PU)
Meenavar, Parvatha, Rajakulam, Sembadaran, Patanavan (TN)
Meghaiya-Domes (WB)
Mehra (HP)
Mehra (RA)
Mehtar, Bhungi (MA)
Meitei And Meitei Pangal (MA)
Melakudi or Kudiyan (PO)
Memar, Raj (DE)
Mena (Bhil) (GU)
Meo, Mewati (DE)
Mer (GU)
Mer (RA)
Merasi, Mirasi (DE)
Merasi, Mirasi (RA)
Merat (RA)
Merat-Gorat (RA)
Merat-Kathat (RA)
Merh-Kajpoot (CH)
Meru (MP)
Mewati (CH)
Mewati (MP)
Mewati (PU)
Mewati (UP)
Mhali, Nai, Navi, Nhavi (MP)
Miana, Miyana (Hindus and Muslims) (GU)
Michi (CH)
Mikir (MA)
Mina (DE)
Mina (MR)
Minka (OR)
Mir (JK)
Mir, Dhadhi, Langha, Mirasi (Muslims) (GU)
Mirasi (CH)
Mirasi (JK)
Mirasi (MP)
Mirasi (PU)
Mirasi, Gathala, Halwe, Kuchra, Simrachhukar (HR)
Mirasi, Merasi (UP)
Mirhdar (AS)
Miri (MA)
Miriasin (Muslim) (BI)
Mirshikar (Muslim) (BI)
Mirshikar (WB)
Mishmi (MA)
Mistri, Gujar, Mistri Rathod, Mistri Suthar (GU)
Mitha (MR)

Mitha Ayyalvar (KA)
Mitna (GD)
Mochi (excluding those in S.C.) (PU)
Mochi (excluding those in S.C.) (UP)
Mochi (excluding those in S.C.) (DE)
Mochi (HR)
Mochi, Saraj (Shoe-Repairers) (JK)
Modi (AS)
Modi Bans (PO)
Modiga, Modikara, Modikar (KA)
Modugar or Muduvan (KA)
Mogaveera (KE)
Moraveera (PO)
Moger (AP)
Moger (OR)
Moger, Morgau (WB)
Moghia (RA)
Mogia (RA)
Mohli (AS)
Moili, Moli (PO)
Momin (Asar) (UP)
Momin (Muslim) (BI)
Momin (WB)
Momin (Weaver) (MR)
Mon (Drum-beaters) (JK)
Mondgolla (PO)
Mondivaru, Mondi Banda, Banda (AP)
Mondiwar (AP)
Mondiwar, Mondiwaru (KA)
Mondiwar, Mondiwaru (MR)
Mongar (SI)
Mongola (PO)
Moniagar (PO)
Moniagar (TN)
Moopar (TN)
Moran, Matak (AS)
Moran, Matak (ME)
Morapora-Brahmin (WB)
Moundadan (PO)
Moundadan Chetty (TN)
Mro (TR)
Muchhia (MP)
Mudava/Muduga (PO)
Mudhar (KA)
Mudiraj, Mutrasi, Tenugollu (AP)
Mug (WB)
Mukha Dhora or Nooka-Dhora (KA)
Mukha Dhora, Nooka Dhora (TN)
Mukhadora-Mokka Dhora (OR)
Mukhari (PO)
Mukhi (AS)
Mukhi (ME)
Mukkavan (KA)
Mukkuvan Mukkuvar (TN)
Mukkuvan or Kukayan, Mogayan, Logavan (including Bovis) (PO)
Mukkuvan, Mukaya (KE)
Mukri (RA)
Mukro (Mukero) (Muslim) (BI)
Muliya (AP)
Muliya (KE)
Muliya (OR)
Muliya (TN)
Muliya, Muria (KA)
Munda (AN)
Munda (AS)
Munda (MA)
Munda (ME)
Munda (MR)
Mundala (OR)
Mundas (AS)
Mura (AS)
Murao, Murai (UP)
Muria (AP)
Muria (KE)
Muria (OR)
Muria (PO)
Muria (TN)
Muria Bhottada (KE)

Murraha, Murha (MP)
Murrari (KA)
Musavar (CH)
Muslim Banjara (UP)
Muslim-Kayastha (UP)
Mutherachas (AP)
Muthuraja (Muthuracha, Muthiriyar and Muttiriyar (TN)
Muthuraja (PO)
Muthursi-Bania, Ganga Putra, Mudiraj, Muthuraja, Telenga, Tenugu (AP)
Mutlakampatti (PO)
Mutlakampatti (TN)
Muttiriyan/Muthiriyar (PO)

Naar (CH)
Naar (HR)
Nadafs, Ladafs, Dhunya, Mansuri, Pinjar or Pinjari (Muslims) (KA)
Nadar (KE)
Nadar (PO)
Naddaf, Pinja (CH)
Nadia, Hadi (RA)
Nadkal (UP)
Nadora, Nadar, Uppunador, Troke Nador (KA)
Nag Bansi (AS)
Naga (MA)
Nagar (TR)
Nagar (WB)
Nagaralu (AP)
Nagaralu (PO)
Nagaram (PO)
Nagaram (TN)
Nagarchi (RA)
Nagasia (AS)
Nagatha Goudus-Bemia Goudub, Boodo Magatha, Dengoyath, Dengoyath Goudo, Ladya Goudu, Ponna Magatha And Sana Magatha (PO)
Nagavaddilu (AP)
Nagavaddily (PO)
Nagavasam (Nagavamsa), Nagbansh (AP)
Nagesia (TR)
Nahar (OR)
Nai (RA)
Nai (Valand) (DN)
Nai, Amrewal, Banbiro, Didhia, Hajjam, Mandi, Jadowal, Japi, Juvwa, Kaikan, Kaila, Kaith, Kuleen-Brahman, Matwal, Napit, Navki, Neogi, Panwar, Rajwan, Thakur (HR)
Nai, Bamneru, Hajam Kuleen-Brahman, Patiyal (HP)
Nai, Banvaru, Dhanwal, Dhari Ghangas, Ghiri, Hajjam, Hazam, Hergun, Jallan, Lekha, Nagi, Naisikh, Palan, Panju, Patara, Raja (PU)
Nai, Bij, Hajjam, Napit (AS)
Nai, Hajjam, Naiya, Napit (WB)
Nai, Hazzam, Nai (Sabita) (DE)
Nai, Jakur, Hajjam, Khawa, Napit, Nau, Orrey, Sarivas, Savita (UP)
Naidu (GD)
Naidu (Vadulu, Karare, Naicker, Thayya, Nambiar) (AN)
Naidu Balija Gouda, Vadugan (KE)
Naidu Gavara (PO)
Naik (AP)
Naik (RA)
Naik, Nayak, Nayaka, (Non-Brahmin) (MP)
Naikapu (AP)
Naiker, Vanniya (PO)
Naikkans (KE)
Naikkans, Naicken (PO)
Naikkar (TN)
Naiko (TR)
Naita, Nayata, Nata, Navta (MP)

Naiya (TR)
Nakkala (PO)
Nakkalas (AP)
Nakkalas (TN)
Nal Band (JK)
Nalakeyava (OR)
Nalakodava (PO)
Nalband (BI)
Nalband (CH)
Nalband (DE)
Nalband (HP)
Nalband (HR)
Nalband (Muslims) (KA)
Nalband (PU)
Nalband (WB)
Nalis, Korchia Malis, Paikonalis and Pedda Malis (KE)
Nalki (KA)
Namasudra, Adhikari, Sarkar, Dhati, Bala, Hira, Baidai, Maji, Daligbi, Bodoi, Diskas, Poddar, Hindal Roy, Das, Hadder, Manji, Basi, Manser, Biri, Neg, Bairagi, Bhatra, (Baidya) (AN)
Namdev (MP)
Namdev, Simpi (PO)
Namdhari, Paik (MR)
Namshudra (BI)
Namsudra (MP)
Nandiwala, Fullmali (KA)
Nandiwala, Tirmal (MR)
Naniar (PO)
Nanijil Mudali (TN)
Napit (ME)
Napit (TR)
Napit, Nai (MA)
Naqashi (MR)
Naqqal (DE)
Nar (HP)
Nar (PU)
Narikoravan (PO)
Narikoravar (TN)
Nat (Muslim) (BI)
Nat (OR)
Nat, Nat-Bajania, Natada, Bajigar (GU)
Nat, Nattadas (TR)
Nat, Natuva (KA)
Nath (AS)
Nath (MP)
Nath, Jogi (GD)
Nath, Yogi (WB)
Nathpanthi, Dauri Gosavi (KA)
Nattu Malayans (KE)
Nav-Buddhists, Neo-Buddhists (KA)
Nav-Buddhists, Neo-Buddhists (TN)
Nav-Buddhists, Neo-Buddhists (UP)
Nav-Buddhists, Neo-Buddhists (WB)
Nav-Buddhists, Neo-Buddhists (BI)
Nav-Buddhists, Neo-Buddhists (GU)
Nav-Buddhists, Neo-Buddhists (PU)
Nav-Buddhists, Neo-Buddhists (RA)
Navda (MP)
Navi, Nhavi, Hajam, Kalseru Navaliga, Kelashi, Nabhik, Nai (MR)
Navundian (PO)
Nayadi (AP)
Nayadi (OR)
Nayak (AP)
Nayak (AS)
Nayak (TR)
Nayinda, Nayanaja, Kshatriya, Hajjam, Nhavi, Nadig, Ambettam Mangala, Kelasi, Kshowrad, Ksihowrik, Chouriya, Navaliga, Napitha, Bhandari (KA)

Nayor (AR)
Neelakanthi (AP)
Neeli (MR)
Neelkanti (MR)
Nekar, Jada (MR)
Nelakanavaru (KA)
Neo-Buddhists, Nav-Buddhists (MR)
Neo-Buddhists, Nav-Buddhists (MP)
Nepali (Chatri, Chhetri, Dami, Gaine, Gurung, Lama, Lihu, Lohar, Magar, Rai, Sarki, i.e. Cobbler, Thapa) (AS)
Nepali (Damai, Gaine, Gurung, Lama, Lohar, Newar, Rai, Sarki, i.e. Cobbler, Thapa) (ME)
Nepali (Limbo, Matwali, Rai) (TR)
Nepali Lama (AR)
Merali (MP)
Neria (MP)
Neriya (RA)
Nessi or Kurni (AP)
Nethura (MR)
New Buddhists, Nav-Buddhists (PO)
Newar (WB)
Neygi, Kuruhingsetti, Bilamagga, Thogata, Soniga, Jamkhana, Ayiri, Avir, Sale, Saale, Kaikolan, Neikar, Jadar, Jandra Swakulasale (KA)
Neyyala (AP)
Nhavi (AP)
Nhavi, Nai (GD)
Nilgar (MP)
Nilgar, Nirali (MR)
Nirshikari (MR)
Nirshikaris (AP)
Nirshikaris (TN)
Nokka (PO)
Nokkar (AP)
Nokkars (TN)
Nolakeyava (AP)
Nolia (OR)
Nolli (AP)
Nonia (MR)
Nonia, Kharwat, Nunia (BI)
Nonia, Nunia (AS)
Noongar (CH)
Noongar, Mungar (HR)
Noongar, Nungar (PU)
Nuhura, Nuhuraj (OR)
Nulayan (KE)
Nulayan (TN)
Nuniya (OR)
Nuniya, Nunia (TR)
Nut (excluding those in S.C.) (UP)

Od (GU)
Odans (Andhra Nair or Anthuru Nair) (KE)
Odans, Odde, Vaddoo, or Vadda or Veddai, Odon (Donga), Odiya (PO)
Odar, Oddar, Woddar, Odiya (TN)
Odd (RA)
Oddar (or Weddars), Odde, Odder, Vadde, Oddilu, Vaddi, Vadde (AP)
Ode, Wader, Waddar, Odiya (MP)
Odhia (UP)
Oinlu (PO)
Ojulu or Metta, Kamasalie (OR)
Ojulus or Metta, Komsalies (KE)
Ojulus or Motta, Komsalis (AP)
Ojulus, Metall, Komasalies (TN)
Omanaito (KE)
Omanaito (PO)
Omeyita (OR)
Ommaite (AP)
Oraon (AS)
Oraon (MA)
Oraon (ME)

Oraon (TR)
Orh. Od (UP)
Ostha (KA)
Otari (KA)
Otari, Otankar, Otkar, Vatari, Ojhari (MR)
Ottanaickan (PO)
Ovachar (TN)

Pacha Bhotla (AP)
Pacha Bhotla, Pacha Botla (KA)
Pachabhotla, Pachabotla (MR)
Pachabotla (AP)
Padampari (AP)
Padampari (KA)
Padampari (MR)
Padamsali-Margude, Setty, Devanga (KA)
Padannan (ehere they are not Scheduled Castes) (TN)
Padaria, Pamaria, Pandara (OR)
Padarti (KA)
Padayachi (PO)
Pademsali, Salewar, Sali/Sutsali (MP)
Padhar (where they are not Scheduled Tribes) (GU)
Padharia (MR)
Padia, Padiyar (KA)
Padiar (MR)
Padit (KA)
Padka (MP)
Padmasali, (Pattusali, Sali, Salivan, Seanapathulu, Thogata, Sali) (AP)
Padmasali (PO)
Padmashali-Pattushali (GU)
Pagadai (AP)
Pagadai (KA)
Pagadai (KE)
Pagadai (OR)
Pahar (MP)
Pahira (BI)
Pahri (UP)
Paidi (AS)
Paidi (KE)
Paidi (TN)
Paigarapu (AP)
Paigarapu (KA)
Paigarapu (KE)
Paigarapu (OR)
Paigarapu (PO)
Paigarapu (TN)
Paiko (OR)
Painda (AP)
Painda (KA)
Painda (KE)
Painda (PO)
Painda (TN)
Paite (MI)
Pakhali, Bhisti (MR)
Pakhiwara (CH)
Pakhiwara (DE)
Pakhiwara (HP)
Pakhiwara (HR)
Pakhiwara (PU)
Paky (KA)
Paky (KE)
Paky (OR)
Paky (TN)
Pal (Bherihar - Gaderi), Gaderia (BI)
Pal (OR)
Pal Pardhi (MR)
Palaekari (PO)
Palakari (AP)
Palanwadia (GU)
Palasi (KA)
Palasi (KE)
Palasi (OR)
Palasi (PO)
Palasi (TN)
Palhari (MP)
Paliyan (OR)
Paliye (TR)

Palk (TR)
Palla, Pallikari, Pallikarullu, Agnikela (AP)
Pallan (AP)
Pallan (OR)
Palli (AP)
Palli (KA)
Palli (OR)
Palli (PO)
Palli (TN)
Palli - Vada Balika, Gangawar, Goondla, Valari, Vanyakulak - Shatriya
(Vannokapu, Venneredd Nayyala and Pattapu) (AP)
Palwadia (GU)
Pamaria (Muslim) (BI)
Pambada (OR)
Pambala (AP)
Pamidi (KA)
Pamidi (KE)
Pamidi (TN)
Pamula (AP)
Pamula (KA)
Pamula (PO)
Pamula, Panchal (MR)
Pamulu (TN)
Pan (ME)
Pan (TR)
Pan Davakulan (KA)
Panaba (KA)
Panan (KA)
Panan (where they are not Scheduled Castes) (TN)
Panar (TN)
Panasa, Panssa (KA)
Panchama (MR)
Panda (MR)
Pandara (AP)
Pandaram, Pandar, Pandara (KA)
Pandaran, Maniakar (KE)
Pandi (BI)
Pandi Thattan (PO)
Pandithar (Anpattan, Pranopkari and Nasivan) (PO)
Pandithavs (KE)
Pangul (MR)
Panika (AS)
Panika, Panikkar (KA)
Panikkan (KE)
Panikkan (TN)
Paniyan (AP)
Paniyan (OR)
Panjira (OR)
Panka (MR)
Panki (TR)
Pannagadikara (PO)
Pannaiyar or Pannayar (PO)
Pannan Vettuva Goundor (PO)
Pannayar (TN)
Panniandi (AP)
Panniandi (KE)
Panniandi (OR)
Pannirandam Chettiar or Uthama Chettiar (TN)
Panniyar (KE)
Pano (KE)
Pano (TN)
Pans (AS)
Panthi (WB)
Panwari (MP)
Papmelara Konkani (KA)
Para (JK)
Paradhi, Pardhi, Pardhi-Raj, Advichincher, Phase Pardhi (where they are not Scheduled Tribes) (GU)
Paraiyan (OR)
Paralayan (AP)
Paramban (PO)
Parashar (MP)
Paravan (AP)
Paravan (Christians) (PO)
Paravan (OR)

Paravan, Paravar (where they are not Scheduled Castes) (TN)
Pardhan (KA)
Pardhi (including Advichincher and Phanse-Pardhi) (RA)
Pardhi (Nirshikari) (AP)
Pardies (AP)
Parhaiya (OR)
Pariki Muggula (AP)
Pariyas (Vengur and Vappur) (TN)
Parja (AS)
Parkavakulam Suruthinar, Malayamar, Nathamar (TN)
Parna, Perna (JK)
Parol Madivala (PO)
Parrakavakulam (Surithinaman) Malayanan, Nathaman, Moopanar and Nainar (PO)
Parthi (MP)
Parya (BI)
Pasi (AS)
Pasi (KA)
Pasi (TR)
Passi (AP)
Pathar Chera, Sangtarash (DE)
Patherkut, Bachigolia (BI)
Pathir (JK)
Pathiyan (where they are not Scheduled Castes) (TN)
Pathukudi (PO)
Pathuria (OR)
Patka, Patki (MP)
Patkar (Khatri) (AP)
Patkar (MR)
Patnaik (BI)
Patnulkaran (PO)
Patra (AP)
Patra (KA)
Patradaveru (MR)
Patramela (KA)
Patratanti (AS)
Patrikulam, Patrakulam (PO)
Patro (OR)
Patta avam (PO)
Pattariya (KE)
Pattariyas or Pattarias (PO)
Pattulakaran (PO)
Patua (WB)
Patvekari, Pategar, Pattegar (KA)
Patwa (BI)
Patwa (DE)
Patwa (Phadal) (RA)
Patwa, Namdev, Pathakar, Sipiya (MP)
Pauan (AP)
Pauri (UP)
Pawariya (UP)
Payak (MP)
Peddammavandlu, Davaravandiu, Yellamma Vandlu, Mutyalamma Vandlu (AP)
Peer (JK)
Pengua (OR)
Pentia (KA)
Pentia (KE)
Pentias (PO)
Perika (Perike Balija, Puragiri Kshatriya) (AP)
Perikalu, Reddy (AP)
Perike (Perike Balija) (TN)
Perike, Perike balija, Piragiri Kshatriya (PO)
Perki (MP)
Perki (MR)
Perumannan (TN)
Perumbadlan (PO)
Perumkollans (KE)
Perumkollans (PO)
Perumkollar (TN)
Peruvannan (PO)
Peruvannan (Vearanacvar) (KE)
Petias (AP)
Petias (TN)
Phar (MR)

Phasechari (MR)
Phudgi (MR)
Phulari (MR)
Phutdhar (BI)
Picchigunta (PO)
Picharis (AP)
Pichati, Pichari (KA)
Pichgunta, Picchiguntala, Pichuguntala (KA)
Pielai (PO)
Pillai (KE)
Pillai, Vilaler, Vellalar, Karabhattu, Karanbattu (AN)
Pillava (PO)
Pindara (MP)
Pindaras or Pendaris (Muslims) (KA)
Pinganiya (BI)
Pinja, Penja (HP)
Pinja, Penja (PU)
Pinjali, Pinja (HR)
Pinjara (RA)
Pinjara, Ghanchi, Mansuri-Panjara (Muslims) (GU)
Pinjara, Pinjari (MR)
Pinjare (MP)
Pirali (WB)
Pita (OR)
Pitchiguntala (AP)
Pod (TR)
Poligars (AP)
Polinativalma of Srikakulam and Visakhapatanam Distt (PO)
Polinativelamas (AP)
Pomla (KA)
Pomla (RA)
Pomnala (PO)
Pony-Men-Mule-Men (JK)
Poosala (AP)
Poraya (PO)
Poraya (TN)
Porja-Bado, Bonda, Daruva, Didva, Jodia, Mundil, Sano, Pengu, Pydi, Saliya, Sodia and Pareng (OR)
Porja-Bodo, Bonda, Daruva, Diduva, Jodia, Mundili Pengiyi, Pydi and Proja (KE)
Porjas or Porajas-Bodo, Bonda, Daruva, Didua, Jodia, Mundili, Pareng, Pydi, Salliya, Sano and Sodia (TN)
Porjas, Bonda, Daruva, Didua, Mundili, Pengu, Pundi and Saliva (KA)
Poroja (KE)
Poroja-Boda, Poroja, Sodia Poroja, Sano, Poroja, Joddia Poroja and Parenga, Poroja (KA)
Porojas-Bodo Poroja or Sodia, Sano Poroja, Jodia Poroja and Pareng Saliya (KE)
Poroja- Bado Peroja or Sodia, Jodia Perjoa, Pareng Peroja and Sona Paroja (AP)
Powar (MP)
Powara (KA)
Powara (RA)
Powra (GU)
Pradhan (AS)
Pradhan (BI)
Pradhan (OR)
Praravatharajakulam (PO)
Pukhali (MR)
Pulaya (KE)
Pulayan (AP)
Pulayan (KA)
Pulayan (OR)
Pullavan (KA)
Pulluvan (KE)
Pulluvan (PO)
Pulluvan, Pulluvar (TN)
Pundari (TR)
Pundari (WB)

Punnan Vettuva Gounder (TN)
Pusala, Pusalavaan, Pusalvandlu (PO)
Pusale (TN)
Puthirai Vannan (KA)
Puthiraj Vannan (AP)
Putligar (MP)
Putligar (MR)
Puttnul, Karan (AP)

Qureshi (Kassab) Muslims (KA)

Rabari, Sorthia, Charalia, Charmta, Luni, Kushar, Tank, Muchhal Kadiyakumbhar, (where they are not Scheduled Tribes) (GU)
Rabha (MA)
Rabha (ME)
Rabha (TR)
Rachband (CH)
Rachband (HR)
Rachband, Rechband (PU)
Rachbandhia (MR)
Rachevar (MR)
Rachkoya (AP)
Rachkoya (MR)
Radhi or Niari (OR)
Raghavi (MR)
Raghavi, Raghvanshi (MP)
Rai (SI)
Rai-Sikh (CH)
Rai-Sikh (HR)
Rai-Sikh (PU)
Raighatwal (TR)
Raika (RA)
Raikari (MR)
Raj (UP)
Raj Pardhi, Gaon Pardhi, Haran Shikari (MR)
Rajaka (PO)
Rajamuria, Rangari (MP)
Rajapow (KE)
Rajapuri (TN)
Rajapuri, Rajpur, Balavalikar (KA)
Rajapuri, Raju (PO)
Rajbanshi (ME)
Rajbanshi, Koch (AS)
Rajbanshi, Rajbansi (TR)
Rajbhar (BI)
Rajboshi (Risiya and Poliya) (BI)
Rajdhobi (BI)
Rajgir (MP)
Rajgond (MP)
Rajput (AS)
Rajput (KA)
Rajput Bhamta, Pardeshi Bhamta, Pardeshi Bhamti (MR)
Raju (TR)
Raju (WB)
Rajwar (AS)
Rajwar (OR)
Rajwar (TR)
Rakhal (WB)
Ralte (MI)
Ramgharia, Bimra, Brar, Bumral, Chan, Dhiman, Kalsi, Matharoo, Murway, Ramgarhia, Saggu, Sahota, San, Saran, Tarkhan (PU)
Ramoshi (MR)
Rana (WB)
Ranbari (RA)
Raneyar (AP)
Raneyar (OR)
Rangari, Rangrez, Bhawsar (MR)
Rangrez (DE)
Rangrez (Muslim) (BI)
Rangrez (UP)
Rangrez (WB)
Rangrez, Rangarej, Rangraz, Ramgari, Rangredh (MP)
Rangwa (BI)
Rao (AN)
Rao (MP)

Rao (RA)
Raot, Rautia, Rawt (MR)
Raot, Rawt, Raoti (MP)
Rasali (WB)
Rathawa (RA)
Rathodia (GU)
Raulo (AP)
Rauther (PO)
Rautia (MP)
Rautia (MR)
Rauttiya (BI)
Raval, Raval or Raval Yogi (MR)
Raval, Ravalia Raul, (KA)
Raval-Ravalia, Jati or Raval Yogi, Rawal Jati, Jagaria, Padat, Ravar Rawalia (GU)
Ravana-Rajput (RA)
Rawal (MP)
Rawat (RA)
Rawat, Beder, Gahira, Rast, Rawar, Thethwar (MP)
Rawat, Raya, Rewath (KA)
Rayakwar (DE)
Rayeen (BI)
Rebari (RA)
Rechband (HP)
Reddi Dhokas (OR)
Reddi Dhora (KA)
Reddi Dhoras (TN)
Reddian (KE)
Reddikas (AP)
Reddiyar (Reddiyar, Jhothi, Reddyar) (AN)
Reddy Dhora (KE)
Rehar, Behara, Rer, Rihar (CH)
Rehar, Rehara, Rihar, Rea (HR)
Reinudas (KA)
Relli or Sachandi (KE)
Relli Orsachandi (KA)
Relli, Sachndi (TN)
Rhar (MP)
Riaigar (PU)
Rihar, Rehar, Rehare (PU)
Rohade, Sujharia (MP)
Rohangia, Roshangia (WB)
Rohar (MP)
Rohit (GU)
Rona (KA)
Rona (KE)
Rona (PO)
Rona (TN)
Ronas (OR)
Roniaur (UP)
Routia (OR)
Ruchhandhia (MP)
Rupai (TR)

S.C. (Converted to Christianity) (KA)
S.I.U.C (KE)
Sad-Sausi (Sehar) (RA)
Sadajoshi (KA)
Sadan, Dedan (PO)
Sadhu (RA)
Sadhu Chetty (including Telugu Chetty, Telugupatty Chetty, Twenty four Mani Telugu Chetty) (TN)
Sadhuchetty (AP)
Sagalis (PO)
Sagar (GD)
Sagarpasha (OR)
Sagra (HP)
Saha (WB)
Sahabar (OR)
Sahis, Sais, Shis (MR)
Sahora (AS)
Sahte (MA)
Sain (MP)
Saini (HR)
Saini (PU)
Sais, Sayees, Shis (MP)
Saiva vellalan (PO)
Saiz (DE)

Sajalang (AR)
Sakaravar (Kavathi) (KE)
Sakkarvar (Kavathi) (TN)
Sakravar (Kavathi) (PO)
Salat (where they are not Scheduled Tribes) (GU)
Sali, Padamshali, Swakulsali (MR)
Salian (Pattarayan), Saliyas, Saliyan, Pattusali, Senapathulu, Kamithoktulu, Sale, Jhogata Sali (PO)
Salivahana, Salivagana (TN)
Saliyar (Padmasaliyar, Adhaviyar, Pattariyar) (TN)
Saliyas (KE)
Saloi (AS)
Saloi (ME)
Salvi, Sali (MP)
Samban (OR)
Sambavan (Tamil) (KE)
Sanaithalaivar (Senaikudiyan) (PO)
Sandhi (Hindus and Muslims) (GU)
Sangar (MR)
Sangari (AP)
Sangari (KA)
Sangari (MR)
Sangatrash (BI)
Sangheda (GU)
Sangtrash (JK)
Saniyar (KA)
Sanjogi (MR)
Sankhakar, Sarkheru (WB)
Sankhari (OR)
Sanoria (MP)
Sansi (GU)
Sansi (JK)
Sansi (KA)
Sansia (KA)
Santal (KA)
Santal (MA)
Santal (MR)
Santhal (ME)
Santhal, Santal (AS)
Sanyasi, Mambram (OR)
Sao-Teli (MR)
Saonta or Saunta (MR)
Saora (AP)
Saora (KA)
Saora (KE)
Saora (TN)
Sapari (AP)
Sapari (KE)
Sapera (MR)
Sapera, Kalbelia (UP)
Sarabara (RA)
Saraj (JK)
Sarania (GU)
Sarania (KA)
Sarania (MR)
Saranjia (MP)
Sarbhangi (MP)
Sare (AP)
Sare (KA)
Sare (MR)
Sargara (GU)
Sarki (Nepali) (MA)
Sarodi, Saroda (KA)
Satani (Chattada Srivaishnava Chatadi) (AP)
Satani, Chattada, Srivaishnava (KA)
Satarkar (KA)
Sathatha Srivaishnava (including Sathani Chattadi Chattada) (TN)
Satiya-Sindhi (RA)
Saun (UP)
Sauria Paharia (OR)
Sausashtra (Pathulkarar) (TN)
Sauta (Sota) (BI)
Savalakarar (TN)
Savara (KE)
Savara-Kapu, Savara, Khutto Savara, Mallya Savara (OR)
Savaras-Kapusavaras, Khotto Savaras and Maliya Savaras (KE)

Savaras-Kopu Savaras, Khutto Savaras and Maliya Savaras (TN)
Savare (ME)
Savarsa, Kapusavara, Khuttosavara, Maliya Savara (KA)
Saya Pillaimar (TN)
Sayar (WB)
Sayee (Muslim) (BI)
Scheduled Caste converted to Christianity (WB)
Scheduled Caste converted to Christianity (CH)
Scheduled Caste converts to Christianity and their children (AP)
Scheduled Castes converted to Christianity (KE)
Scheduled Castes converted to Christianity (MP)
Seela-Ventham (AP)
Seerithi Goudu (KA)
Seerithi Goudu (OR)
Seerithi Goudus (AP)
Seerithi Goudus (KE)
Seerithi Goudus (TN)
Semman (AP)
Semman (KA)
Semman (OR)
Senai Thalavar (Elavaniar) (KE)
Senai Thalvivar (Elavabanias) (PO)
Senaithalaivar, Illaivaniar and Senaikudiyar (TN)
Senatal (AP)
Server, Agamudyar (AN)
Sestakarnam (AP)
Setti Balija (PO)
Shagird Pesha (WB)
Shagirdpesha (TR)
Shaksaz (JK)
Shanan (KA)
Sharia (MP)
Shenva, Chenva, Sedma, Ravat, Shindhaya (RA)
Shikkaligar of Sikkaligar (KA)
Shikligar (GU)
Shilavat (MR)
Shimpi, Bhavgar, Shiv Shimpi, Namdeo (MR)
Shin (JK)
Shingdav or Shingadya (GU)
Shingdav or Shingadya (KA)
Shingdav or Shingadya (MR)
Shingdev, Shingadya (RA)
Shivhari (BI)
Sholaga (AP)
Sholaga (KE)
Sholagar (AP)
Sholagar (KA)
Sholagar (KE)
Sholagar (OR)
Shorgir (CH)
Shorgir (HR)
Shorgir (PU)
Shrawan, Sarwan (GU)
Shupri Wattal (excluding those in S.C.) (JK)
Siddi (where they are not Scheduled Tribes) (GU)
Sikkalgar, Kotari (MR)
Sikligar (JK)
Sikligħar (RA)
Silkigar (MP)
Sindhor (AP)
Sindhor (KA)
Sindhor (MR)
Singalu (AP)
Singhikat, Singhiwala (PU)
Singhiwala, Singhikaut (CH)
Singikant, Singiwala (HR)
Singiwala (MP)
Singiwala (MR)
Singpho (MA)

Sinke (OR)
Sipai, Patni-Jamat or Turk Jamat (Muslims) (GU)
Sirkiwal (RA)
Sistakkaranm (PO)
Sithuria, Sitaria, Situlia (OR)
Siyal (BI)
Siyal (WB)
Siyane (MP)
Sochi (GU)
Sochi (KA)
Sochi (RA)
Sochies (JK)
Sodhi (MP)
Soi (CH)
Soi (PU)
Soir, Soyer (BI)
Soliga (KA)
Sollar (PO)
Sonar (MR)
Sonar, Arya (Koli) (KA)
Sonar, Sunar (MA)
Sonar, Sunar, Swarnakar (UP)
Sonar, Swarnakar (WB)
Sondhiya, Chandel (MP)
Sondi, Soundika (AP)
Sore (AP)
Sore (KA)
Sore (MR)
Sorollo (Somavansha Kshatriya) (AP)
Sourashtras (KE)
Soveras (AS)
Sozhia Chetty (TN)
Sozhia Vellalar (including Keerakarar, Kodikalarar, Sozhia Vellalar and Vatrilaikaran) (TN)
Srehde (AR)
Sri Sayama, Segidi (AP)
Srisayana (PO)
Srisayar (TN)
Sthai (DE)
Suba (SI)
Suda (OR)
Sudha Salva Shivarchka (AP)
Sudir, Sudra (KA)
Sudra Das, Dey (AS)
Sukli (TR)
Sukli (WB)
Sukuli, Tanti (OR)
Sulia (OR)
Sumra (GU)
Sunar (AR)
Sunar (DE)
Sunar (SI)
Sunar, Ashta, Chaganara, Dawar, Kangra, Karod, Katcviriya, Lamba, Mahij, Mandwa, Saraf, Shirisiwan, Sirsohal, Sona, Soni, Swamkar, Thingo, Urwal (HR)
Sunar, Ashtat, Bhatti, Dhume, Jure, Kande, Karwar, Sheen, Suniara, Sur, Swamkar (PU)
Sunar, Bakwar, Sonar, Swamkar (BI)
Sunar, Jargar, Kapila, Soni Swamkar, Tonk (HP)
Sunar, Sonar (MP)
Sunna (AP)
Sunna (MR)
Sunna, Sunnai (KA)
Sunnai (AP)
Sunnai, Sutharia (MR)
Sunri (BI)
Sunri (TR)
Sunri/Sundi (OR)
Suppalig (MR)
Surava (KA)
Surehra (HP)
Sut (ME)
Sut, Soot (AS)
Sutar, Bhadai, Wadai (MR)
Sutari (AP)
Sutradhar (TR)

Sutsali (KA)
Swakulasali (AP)
Swami (RA)
Swarankar (RA)
Sweepers (Muslims) (KA)
Synteng (MA)

Tachavire (KA)
Tadavi (MP)
Taga (CH)
Taga (HR)
Taga (PU)
Taga, Tagah (DE)
Taga-Bhat (UP)
Tak (RA)
Takankar (KA)
Takankar (MR)
Takaras (Muslims) (KA)
Takari (MR)
Talabia (GU)
Talavia (KA)
Talayari (AP)
Talwar Kanade (MR)
Tamang (SI)
Tamang (WB)
Tamariya (BI)
Tambat (MR)
Tamboli (AP)
Tamboli (BI)
Tamboli (MR)
Tamboli, Jamboli, Kumavat, Purabia (MP)
Tamboli, Tamali, Tamuli (WB)
Tamboli, Tamuli (MA)
Tameli (UP)
Tamera, Tambatkar, Thatera (MP)
Tammali (AP)
Tamoli (BI)
Tamta (UP)
Tana (OR)
Tankar (GU)
Tanti, Tantubaya (WB)
Tanti, Tati (TR)
Tanti, Tati, Tatin, Tatwa, Swati (BI)
Tanti, Tatwa, Tantripal, Patwa (UP)
Tantripal, Tanti, Tantri (AS)
Tantripal, Tanti, Tantri (ME)
Tantubai (AS)
Tapoli (BI)
Tarakan (PO)
Targala (MR)
Targala, Bhayiya, Bhojak, Nayak (GU)
Tarkhan (CH)
Tatapux (PO)
Tausa (AS)
Tei, Modh Ganchi (GU)
Telaga (KA)
Telaga Pamula (OR)
Telaga Pamula, Peddati Gollas (TN)
Telega, Kamma (AP)
Telenga (AS)
Teli (AS)
Teli (BI)
Teli (CH)
Teli (DE)
Teli (JK)
Teli (MA)
Teli (ME)
Teli (PU)
Teli (RA)
Teli (TR)
Teli, Badbaik, Balu, Rathore (MP)
Teli, Ganiga, Ghanchi (MR)
Teli, Hansarti, Kanala (HR)
Teti, Sahu (Hindu and Muslim both) (UP)
Teli, Telli, Kubara, Talakar, Sahu, Bahaldia (OR)
Tellunga, Palatti Chattris (TN)
Teruvan, Chillya (KA)
Thai-Chanhari (AS)
Thakaroa, Baria, Dharala, Patanwadia, Thakore (GU)

Thakkar (MR)
Thakur (Nai) (AN)
Thakur (Non-Rajputs) (GU)
Thakurai (Muslim) (BI)
Thami (MP)
Thandal Vannan (PO)
Thandan (where they are not Scheduled Castes) (TN)
Thanta Pulayan (KE)
Thantapulayan (TN)
Thanu (OR)
Thanwar (MP)
Thanwin (CH)
Thapa (WB)
Tharu (BI)
Tharu (WB)
Thatari (OR)
Thathera (BI)
Thathera (RA)
Thathera, Kasera (CH)
Thathera, Tamera (PU)
Thathera, Tamera, Thater, Kasera,Tamkar (HR)
Thathers, Kasera (UP)
Thawin (HP)
Theba (Muslims) (GU)
Thelari (MR)
Thetwar (MR)
Thevar (TN)
Thiya, Elhura, Thiyyas (PO)
Thiyya (TN)
Thiyyas (KE)
Thogata Veerakashatriya (TN)
Thogata, Thogati or Thogataveera Kshatriya (AP)
Thogatta Veerakshatriya (PO)
Thogti, Thogati (MR)
Tholko Lans (KE)
Tholkollans (PO)
Tholkollar (TN)
Tholuva Naicker and Vettalakara Naicker (TN)
Tholuva Naicker and Vetalakara Nairko (PO)
Thondaiman (PO)
Thondaman (TN)
Thontaman (KE)
Thoraiyan (PO)
Thori (MP)
Thori, Turi (CH)
Thoria (MR)
Thoriyar (TN)
Thotewadu (KA)
Thotewadu (MR)
Thoti (OR)
Thoti, Burad (MP)
Thottai Naicks (TN)
Thottia Naick (KE)
Thottia Naicken (including Rajakambalam, Gollavar, Sillayar,
Thokalavar and Tholuva Naikar) (PO)
Thottia Naicks (AP)
Thottia-Naicks (KA)
Thottian (KE)
Thottiya Naicker (including Gollavar, Silavar, Rajakambalam, Thockalavar and Tholuva Naicker) (TN)
Thottiyar (PO)
Thulva - Vellala, Agamu - Daiyan (AP)
Thunnan (PO)
Thuria (MP)
Thuria (OR)
Thurpur Kapus, Casula Kapus (PO)
Tigala (Tigla) (PO)
Tigala, Thigala, Tigler, Vannikula Kshatriya, Shanbhukula, Kshatriya, Dharmaraja, Kapu, Kuravana, Pallai Agnikula Kshatriya (KA)
Tikulhar (BI)

Tilari, Tirali (KA)
Tili (WB)
Tilvi (KA)
Timali (GU)
Timali (KA)
Timali (MR)
Timali (RA)
Tipara (ME)
Tipara (TR)
Tipara (WB)
Tipara, Tipera (AS)
Tipera (MA)
Tippera (WB)
Tirgar (MP)
Tirmale (MP)
Tiruvalluvan (KA)
Tiruvalluvar (AP)
Tiruvalluvar (KE)
Tiruvalluvar (OR)
Tirwa (UP)
Tirwalli (MP)
Tivoro (OR)
Tiyar (BI)
Tiyar (OR)
Tiyar (TR)
Toda (AP)
Toda (KE)
Toda (OR)
Toda (TN)
Tolikula (PO)
Tonla Gaud (OR)
Toto (TR)
Tsong (SI)
Turha (MP)
Turha (WB)
Turha, Sao (B1)
Turi (AS)
Turi (KA)
Turi (TR)
Turi (UP)
Turupukapus (AP)
Ulladam (TN)
Ullatan (TN)
Upasara (AP)
Uppaliga Settey-Reey (KA)
Uppara (PO)
Uppara (Upplillia Sagara) (TN)
Uppara or Sagara (AP)
Uppara, Uppear, Uppiliyan, Beldar, Sagara, Chunar, Gavandi, Govandi, Govadi, Goundi, Melusakkare (KA)
Urali Goundan (PO)
Urali Gounders (TN)
Urao, Bandot, Haro, Karkata, Luidu, Shitheo, Tigga, Tirki (WB)

Vada Balija, Vadava (Golla or Kondri) (PO)
Vadder-Bevi, Upparilu (AP)
Vadi (GU)
Vadi (KA)
Vadra or Vaddara (PO)
Vadugan (AP)
Vadukan, Vadagan, Vadugan, Vaduvan (PO)
Vaduvan (KE)
Vaghri, Vaghari, Salat, Salat Vaghri (MR)
Vaghri-Gamicho, Vedva Churalia, Jakhudia (where they are not Scheduled Tribes) (GU)
Vagri, Vaghri, Pradhan (MP)
Vaidu (KA)
Vaidu (MR)
Vaidyanai (MP)
Vaiti (MR)
Vajluthedan (KA)
Vakkaliga (KE)
Valaiyars (TN)
Valakatalavan (PO)
Valan (TN)

Valans (PO)
Valayar (KA)
Vale, Valand, Nai (Hindus), Hajjam, Khalipha (Muslims) (GU)
Vallamber (TN)
Valluvan (AP)
Valluvan (OR)
Valmiki (AP)
Valmiki (KE)
Valmiki (PO)
Valmiki (TN)
Valmiki Boya (Boya,Bedar, Kirataka, Nishadi, Vellapi Pedda Boya), Talayari and Chundu Vallu (AP)
Valvai (KA)
Valvai (MR)
Vanadi (MR)
Vanian (Vanika, Vanika Vaisya, Vanikha Chetty, Vaniya Chetty, Ayiravar,
Nagarthar and Vaniyan) (KE)
Vaniar (KE)
Vaniyan or Vaniar (Vanika,Vanika-Vaisya, Vaisyachetty, Vanibaacherry, Ayiravar and Nagarathar) (PO)
Vaniyar (PO)
Vaniyar, Vania Chettiar (including Gandala, Ganika, Chekkalar and Telugula) (TN)
Vanjara (Vanjari) (AP)
Vanjara, Banjara, Charan Banjara, Mathura Banjara, Maru Banjara, Bagora Banjara, Kangashiya Banjara, Bamania Banjara, Ladonia Banjara, Gavaria or Gawalia, Rohidas Banjara (GU)
Vanjari, Vanjar (MR)
Vanjari, Vanjara (MP)
Vankar Sadhu (GU)
Vannan (Mannan, Pathiyan) (TN)
Vannan (OR)
Vannan, Vannar (PO)
Vannar, Rajakula Veluthadar (where the community is not a Scheduled Caste) (TN)
Vanniyakula Kshatriya (including Vanniya Vanniyar, Vannia Gounder, Gounder or Kander, Pidayachi Palli, Agniguia Kshatriya) (TN) _.
Vanniyakula Kshatriya, including Vanniar or Vanniyar Gounder, Kondar or Vannia Gounder and Vannikandar (other than Vella Gounder belonging to Vanni Vanniyakula Kshatriya Caste) (PO)
Vans-Foda, Vansfodia or Vanza, Wansfoda (GU)
Varala, Thogra, Bholla, Baliga (AP)
Varli (RA)
Varnavar (KE)
Varnavar (TN)
Vasawa (MR)
Vasudeo (MR)
Vasudev (KA)
Vathiriyan (KA)
Vathis (PO)
Vedar (TN)
Veeramushti (Nettikotala) (AP)
Veerasaivas (Yogeeswara and Yogis) (KE)
Veerassiva (Fandaram, Matapathi, Vairagi, Vairavi, Yogiswarar) (PO)
Veetasaiva (TN)
Velaan (KE)
Velaiyar (TN)
Velakkithalanayar (TN)
Velan, Vollan (PO)
Vellala Pillai, (Nanjinad Vellala) (PO)
Vellan Chettiar (TN)

Vellayan-Kuppam Pandayaochis (TN)
Veluthadanayar, Veluthonathunayar (TN)
Veluthedathu Nair (Veluthedan and Vannathan) (KE)
Veluthsdan, Veluthedathu Nair (PO)
Vetan (where they are not Scheduled Castes) (TN)
Vettai Karans, Vettaikarar (TN)
Vettaikaran (PO)
Vettakkaran (KE)
Vettakkaran (TN)
Vetturan (PO)
Vettuva Goundar (PO)
Vettuva Goundus (TN)
Vettuvan (AP)
Vettuvan (KA)
Vettuvan (OR)
Vettuvan (PO)
Vidiki, Niyogi (AP)
Vikurup (PO)
Vilakkathala Nairs (Velakkathalavan) (PO)
Vilakkethal Nair (Vilakkathalavan) (KE)
Vina Tulavina (OR)
Vir, Veer, Veeramasti (KA)
Virakadi Veklalar (PO)
Virakod Vellaa-la (TN)
Virasivalingayat (AP)
Vishavan (KE)
Vishavan (Malankudi) (TN)
Vishavan (TN)
Vishnoi (MP)
Vishwa Brahman, Sarpa, Daivagnya-Brahman, Kammar, Ausala, Kammalan, Kamsal, Kamsala, Panchal, Panchala, Sutar, Badagi, Badiwadli, Soni, Pattar, Gejjigar, Silipi (KA)
Vishwakarma-Luhar, Akkasale, Achari, Sivachar, Ahru (KA)
Vishya (MP)
Viswabrahmin (Ausula or Kamsali, Kammari, Kanchari, Vedia or Vadra or Vadrangi and Silpis) (AP)
Vitholia (KA)
Vitholia (MR)
Vitholia (RA)
Vitolia, Kotwalia, Barodia (RA)
Vizhavan (Malankhdi) (KE)
Vokkaliga (Rural areas only) (KA)
Vokkaligar (including Gounder, Gowda, Kappiliyr, Kappliyar, Oklaligar, Okkaliya, Vakkaligar) (TN)
Vyasokta (WB)
Waddar or Kala Waddars or Pathrods (AP)
Wadder, Wadder (Kalawader or Patharod), Beldar, Od, Gimi Waddar, Vaddar, Gaddi Vaddar, Jati Vaddar, Mati Vaddar, Patharvat (MR)
Wadi (MR)
Wadla (AP)
Wadwa Waghari (GU)
Waghari, Dataniya, Waghari, Vodu Waghari, Talapada, Waghari,
Gamachia Waghari, Godadia Waghari, Chibhadia Waghari (GU)
Wagher (Hindus and Muslims) (GU)
Wandhara (GU)
Wanha (MP)
Wanjari, Wanjara (MR)
Wansfoda (MR)
Warthi (MR)
Wasdeo (MP)
Wynad Chetty (TN)

Yadav (Gwala, Ahir. Gope, Sadgope, Ghasi) (BI)
Yadav, Gavli (GD)
Yadav, Rolal Kollubhatti, Konar (AN)
Yadava (Iruman, Kolaya, Muniyani, Ayar) (KE)
Yadava (Konar, Kolaya, Ayar, Mayar, Muniyan, Eruman) (PO)
Yadavan (Idayan) (KE)
Yadavan (Idayan) or Yadava (including Idaiyar, Telugu speaking Idaiyar known as Vaduga Ayar or Vaduga Idaiyar or Golla, Mond Golla, Asthanthra Golla) (TN)
Yakthungba (SI)
Yanadi (KE)
Yanady, Yenadi (TN)
Yandi (KA)
Yandi (OR)
Yaras (AP)
Yashkun (JK)
Yata (AP)
Yavane (TN)
Yedu Kulam (AP)
Yeklar, Yaklar, Yekkali, Egalika (KA)
Yenadiwads (MR)
Yenadiwaos (KA)
Yenadiwards (AP)
Yeragolawad of Thella Pamalwads (MR)
Yeragolawad or Thella Pamalwada (KA)
Yeralu (KA)
Yerkilwar, Yerkula (MP)
Yerna Golta (OR)
Yerukula (KE)
Yerukula (OR)
Yerukula (TN)
Yetla (AP)
Yogeswaran (TN)
Yoggeswaran (PO)
Yogi, Jogi, Nath (TR)
Yogi, Jugi, Nath (MA)
Yogi, Jugi, Nath (ME)
Yorukula (PO)
Yuarulau (AP)

Zamral (RA)
Zargars/(Muslims) (KA)

The List of Depressed Backward Classes Enumerated in the Second Backward Classes Commission (Mandal)

Alphabetical List to Facilitate users to Identify the Backward Class in Respective States.

Abbreviations used for the States

Andaman & Nicobar Islands	AN
Andhra Pradesh	AP
Arunachal Pradesh	AR
Assam	AS
Bihar	BI
Chandigarh	CH
Dadra And Nagar Haveli	DN
Delhi	DE
Goa, Daman & Diu	GD
Gujarat	GU
Haryana	HR
Himachal Pradesh	HP
Jammu & Kashmir	JK
Karnataka	KA
Kerala	KE
Madhya Pradesh	MP
Maharashtra	MR
Manipur	MA
Meghalaya	ME
Mizoram	MI
Orissa	OR
Punjab	PU
Rajasthan	RA
Sikkim	SI
Tamil Nadu And Pondicherry	TP
Tripura	TR
Uttar Pradesh	UP
West Bengal	WB

Abbasi, Bhisti, Sakka (DE)
Abdal (BI)
Achukatalavandhu (AP)
Adhiri (BI)
Adhori (MP)
Adi Karnatak (AP)
Adi-Dravida (OR)
Adi-Karnataka (OR)
Adidharmi (MP)
Adikari (WB)
Adiya (excluding Coorg District) (KA)
Adodia (GU)
Agaria, Agariya (TR)
Agaria, Agariya (VVB)
Agariya (BI)
Agasa (KE)
Agasa, Madivala, Tsakala, Sakalayadu, Shakala, Vannan, Mannan, Dhobi, Parit, Rajaka, Puthirajvannan,Velluthedan (KA)
Ager (RA)
Agharia, Agaria, Aghria (OR)
Aghore (WB)
Aghore, Karkarmunda (KA)
Agri (DN)
Agri (GU)
Agri (UP)
Agri Kherwal (DE)
Agri, Agala or Kalan (MR)
Aheri (MP)
Aheria, Aheri, Heri, Naik, Thori, Turi (HP)
Aheria, Aheri, Heri, Naik, Thori, Turi (PU)
Aheria, Aheriya (UP)
Aheria, Ahiria, Heri, Aheri, Naik, Thori, Turi (HR)
Ahir (DN)
Ahir, Yadav (CH) (CH)
Ajila (OR)
Alavan (KE)
Alitkar (MR)
Amaat (BI)
Amant, Amat, Amath (WB)
Ambalakkaran (KE)
Amblar, Ambathan, Ambithan, Eshavatory, Kalrrikurup, Maruthuver, Naiken, Pandithar Villakkithatanavi (KE)
Ampattan (TP)
Apatani (M1)
Arakh (UP)
Aranadan (KA)
Aranedan (OR)
Arayan (KE)
Arayan, Arayar (Nulayar) (TP)
Arayavathis (KE)
Ard-Pop (HP)
Arematharti (KE)
Arundatilu (H) (AN)
Arunthuthiyar (OR)
Arupatun (KE)
Aruthuthiyar (KA)
Arya Mala (AS)
Aryakshatriya, Chittari, Chitrakara, Giniyar, Nkha (AP)
Asada (RA)
Asara (MP)
Asur (AS)
Asur (OR)
Asur (TR)
Ataari (KA)
Atar (KA)
Atar (MR)
Athiya (MP)
Audhie, Avadhi (MP)
Audhiya (MP)
Audhiya (MR)
Auji (UP)

Badabukkala (AP)
Badaga (KA)

Badaga (OR)
Badaga (TP)
Badagar (TP)
Badak (MP)
Badak (UP)
Badaka (MP)
Badasuda (OR)
Badera, Baoria (RA)
Badi (MP)
Badi, Chinsoras, Meloris, Odmata, Uramamara (HP)
Badia (HP)
Badia (MR)
Badia (UP)
Badia (WB)
Badia, Sapera (MP)
Badyakar, Dhuli, Nagarchi, Sabdakar (TR)
Bag (WB)
Bagad-Bogadi, Bagodi, Bagadi, Bogodi (KA)
Bagalu (KA)
Bagalu (MR)
Bagari, Bedar, Borad, Beldar (MR)
Bagari, Byageri (KA)
Bagaria (CH) (CH)
Bagaria (HR)
Bagata (KA)
Bagata (KE)
Bagata (KE)
Bagata (TP)
Bagdi (Gujarati Boori, Marwar Boori, Marwar Waghri, Salat Waghri) (MR)
Bagdiya, Bawaria (RA)
Bagdo (BI)
Baghta, Baree, Bawar, Payak, Vaidyanai (MP)
Bagria (HP)
Bagria, Bagaria (PU)
Bahari (CH) (CH)
Bahelia (TR)
Bahti (HP)
Bahurupi (MP)
Bahurupi (MR)
Baiga (AS)
Baijara (AS)
Bailapatar, Bailaptar, Bikapatar (KA)
Baira (KA)
Baira (OR)
Bairagi (MP)
Bairi (UP)
Baishnab (TR)
Baiti (TR)
Bajadar, Bajania, Bedey (WB)
Bajania (MR)
Bajania, Bajonia (KA)
Bajania, Kannatia (MP)
Bajel (SI)
Bajgar, Bajigar (MP)
Bajigar (BI)
Bajigar (HP)
Bajigar (MR)
Bajigar (UP)
Bajikar (CH) (CH)
Baked, Bant (RA)
Bakuda (OR)
Balasanthanam (MR)
Balasanthu, Bahurupi (AP)
Balasantoshi (KA)
Balpari (OR)
Banchada (RA)
Banda (AP)
Bandara (AP)
Bandara (AP)
Bandi (MR)
Bandi (OR)
Bandi (UP)
Bangala (JK)
Bangalo (BI)
Bangela, Badia, Perna Sapera (DE)
Banjara (WB)
Banjara badi Lobana (JK)

Banjara, Banjari, Labana, Bamania Banjara, Mathura Banjara (MP)
Banjara, Banjari, Vanjara, Mathura Banjaras (A) Goar Banjars, Lambada/Lambara, Lambhani, Charan Bangarao, Labhan, Mathura Labhan, Kachikiwale, Sanjaros, Laman Banjaras, Laman/Iamani, Laban, Dhali/ Dhaia, Dhadi/Dhari, Singaris, Navi Banjaras, Jogi Banjaras, Banjari (MR)
Banjara, Gawaria, Kangiwala, Kangi, Baladia, Sirkiwala, Labana, Labhana Maru Banjara, Bamama Banjara, Bayora, Digora (RA)
Banjara, Gor, Ladenia, Gamalia, Osaria, Mathura, Labana, Labhana, Dhanakuta Banjora, Brajawasi Banjara, Banjara nut Gwar, Banjara Sikh (UP)
Banjara, Lambadi, Lamani Sugali (GD)
Banjara, Vanjara, Gwar, Badi (HR)
Banjara, Vanraja, Charan Banjara, Mathura Banjarah, Maru Banjara, Bagora Banjara, Kangashia Banjara, Bamania Banjara, Gavaria, Gavalia, Rohidas Banjara (GU)
Banjogi (TR)
Banjogi (WB)
Banka (OR)
Banpar (BI)
Bansphor (MR)
Bant (excluding Belgaum, Bijapur, Dharwar and North Kanara Distt.) (KA)
Bantu (KA)
Bantu (MR)
Banus, Buna, Bunna, Buno (WB)
Baoria (MP)
Baoria, (MR)
Bara, Barra (HR)
Barad (JK)
Barad (MP)
Baragiri (WB)
Barahar, Basod (RA)
Barai, Tarboli, Tamboli (PU)
Barar (RA)
Barar (Umati) (AN)
Barasa, Labana, Labhan, Lamame, Mathura, Nayakda (MP)
Barchain, Chai, Chain (WB)
Barda (KA)
Barda, Dhia (RA)
Barer (PU)
Bargi (MP)
Bargunda (RA)
Bari (BI)
Bari (MP)
Bari (UP)
Baria (AS)
Baria (MP)
Baria, Koli Bari (MR)
Barika, Bhandari, Beja, Napit and Nai (OR)
Bariki (KE)
Bariki (TP)
Barjubi (AS)
Barlur (KA)
Barma (HR)
Baro (WB)
Barot, Vahivancha, Charan Gadhvi (GU)
Barra (CH) (CH)
Barthunda (MP)
Barwar (CH) (CH)
Barwar (HR)
Barwar (PU)
Basigar (KA)
Basor (AS)
Basor (RA)

Basphor (AS)
Basphor (BI)
Bastar Sanchaluwaddar (MR)
Batahini (KA)
Bateri (PU)
Bathai, Battal, Batler, Battar (KA)
Bathi (CH) (CH)
Bathini (AP)
Bathini (MR)
Bathudi (WB)
Battada (AP)
Battada (KA)
Battada (KE)
Battada (OR)
Battera (HR)
Batterha (CH) (CH)
Batterha MP)
Baura (UP)
Bauri (AS)
Bauri (TR)
Bauria (DE)
Bauriah (UP)
Bavcha (MR)
Baver (MP)
Bavri or Baori (GU)
Bavuri (KA)
Bavuri (KE)
Bavuri (TP)
Bawaria (MP)
Bawrtar (KA)
Bayar (UP)
Bazigar, Nat, Kalendar (excluding those in SC) (DE)
Beda (HP)
Beda, Bedaru, Bedar, Naik, Bedar Nayaka, Naika Makkalu, Naikwara, Palegar, Talwar, Valmiki,Valmikimakkalu, Boya, Vedan, Berad, Ramoshi (KA)
Bedak (MR)
Bedia (AS)
Bedia (JK)
Bedia (UP)
Bedia, Bediya (TR)
Beetha, Siviar (TP)
Begal (WB)
Begari (AP)
Bekewal, Bakkarwal (JK)
Bekhada (BI)
Beldar (AS)
Beldar (TR)
Beldar, Bachgotra, Sapera (BI)
Beldar/OD (MR)
Beldiya (BI)
Bellara (AP)
Bellara (KA)
Bellara (OR)
Bemariha (MP)
Bendari (KE)
Bentkar (BI)
Bentkar (OR)
Bentkar (WB)
Beri (DE)
Beria (CH) (CH)
Beria (HR)
Beria (KA)
Beria (MP)
Beria (PU)
Beriah (UP)
Berua (TR)
Berua (WB)
Bestha, Gangamatha, Gangaputra Bhoi, Parivara, Kabbera Kabbaligar, Bariki, Bariker, Mogaverra, Besthar, Bunde, Besthar, Gangamakkalu, Gowari Matha, Ambiga, Ambig, Kharvi, Bhoi Boyi, Thoreya, Harakantra, Kahar, Meenagar, Sunnagar, Koli, Gabit, Daavat, Kanet (KA)
Bestna, Jelare, Vade-Balaji, Neyyalu, Agnikula-Kshatriya, Palli, Gangaputragoondla, Parvatharajakulam, Gangavar (AP)

Beta, Hensi, Hesi (CH) (CH)
Beta, Hensi, Hesi (PU)
Beta, Hensi, Hosi (HP)
Beta, Herai or Hesi (HR)
Betere or Betra (OR)
Bettada (TP)
Bezigar (JK)
Bhadbhunja (MR)
Bhadre (MP)
Bhadre (MP)
Bhaduja (MP)
Bhaduria (MP)
Bhakta (TR)
Bhalia (GU)
Bhampta or Ghantichote or Pardesi Pong, Baser Uchale (MR)
Bhampta, Ghantichor, Pardasi-Bhampt (RA)
Bhamta (AP)
Bhamta, Bhampta, Paradesi, Bhampata, Takari, Uchillian, Rajaput, Bhampta (KA)
Bhamta, Bhamti, Bhanmate, Bhanta, Bhammate (MP)
Bhamta, Pardeshi Bhamta (GU)
Bhand (CH) (CH)
Bhand (DE)
Bhand (JK)
Bhand (MP)
Bhand (MR)
Bhandari (GD)
Bhangi (excluding those in Scheduled Caste) (WB)
Bhangi, Khokrob, (Sweepers) (excluding those in S.C.) (JK)
Bhant (WB)
Bhanta (MR)
Bhantu, Sansi (MP)
Bhanumati (RA)
Bhaot, Bhatraj, Bhatraju (KA)
Bhar (BI)
Bhar (TR)
Bhar (UP)
Bhar (WB)
Bhar (WB)
Bharadi, Balasantoshi, Kinggriwale, Nathbava, Nath Jogi, Nath Panthi (MR)
Bharai-Bharibar (MP)
Bharaik (AS)
Bharari (MP)
Bharatar (TP)
Bharbhooja (DE)
Bharbhuja (BI)
Bharbhuja (MP)
Bharbhuja, Bharbhunja, Kalanera (HR)
Bharbhunja (CH) (CH)
Bharbhunja, Bharbhuja (HP)
Bharbunja, Bharbhuja (PU)
Bhardi, Bharagi (KA)
Bharewa (MP)
Bhari, Rode (PU)
Bharud (MP)
Bharud (RA)
Bharunja (JK)
Bharwad (DN)
Bharwad (excluding Nesses of forest of Alech Barada and Gir) (GU)
Bhathiara (UP)
Bhatiara, Basgaqi (WB)
Bhatraju (other than Kshatriya Raju) (TP)
Bhatua (OR)
Bhavaiya or Targala (MR)
Bhettadas-Bodo, Bhottads, Muriabhattada and Sano Bhottads (AP)
Bhil (AS)
Bhil (UP)
Bhilava (KE)
Bhina Koya (MR)
Bhinbar (TR)

Bhisti or Pakhali (MR)
Bhogta (OR)
Bhoi (MP)
Bhoi, Bhoiraj, Dhimar, Zingabhoi, Kevat, Bhoi, Bhanara Bhoi, Manchhindra Bhoi, Palewar Bhoi, Kirat Bhoi, Keher Bhoi, Pardesh Bhoi, Shrimali Bhoi (GU)
Bhoi, Kharvi, Dhiwar Bhoi, Zinga Bhoi, Pardeshi Bhoi, Raj Bhoi, Bhoi, Kahar, Tadia Kahar, Kirat, Machwa, Manzi, Jatia, Kewat, Dhiwar, Dheewar, Dhimar, Palowar, Mechhendra, Navadi, Malhar, Malhav, Gadhav Bhoi, Khadi Bhoi, Khare Bhoi, Dhevra, Dhuria Kabar (MR)
Bhokta (AS)
Bhokta (OR)
Bhotia (WB)
Bhottadas-Boda-Bottada, Muria-Bhottada and Sano Bhottada (KE)
Bhottadash-Bodo Bhettada, Muria Bhottada and Sane Bhottada (TP)
Bhottads, Boto Bhattad, Muria Bhottada, Sano Bhatatda (KA)
Bhoyar (MP)
Bhoyar (Pawra) (MR)
Bhubhalia (DE)
Bhugal (WB)
Bhuhalia (HP)
Bhuhalia (PU)
Bhuihar, Bhuiyar, Bhubhalia (BI)
Bhujan (OR)
Bhujru (CH) (CH)
Bhujwa (MP)
Bhul (UP)
Bhuliya (OR)
Bhumaao-Bhuri, Bhumia Bodo-Bhumia (KA)
Bhumias-Bhumia and Bodo Bhumia (KE)
Bhumias-Bhuri Bhumia and Bodo Bhumia (TP)
Bhumij (AS)
Bhumij (AS)
Bhumij (MR)
Bhumij, Bhmij (TR)
Bhumji (ME)
Bhurji, Bharbjuja, Bharbhunja, Bhunj, Bhunjia, Kandu, Kashodhay (UP)
Bhurtiya (MP)
Bhuta, Bhopa (MR)
Bhutia (MP)
Bhuyan (AS)
Bhuyan (AS)
Bidarkia (MP)
Bijoria (MP)
Billava (TP)
Bin (TR)
Bin (WB)
Binapatta (KA)
Bind (BI)
Bind (TR)
Bind (UP)
Bindili (KA)
Binedhany (OR)
Bingi (KA)
Binjhawar (WB)
Binjhia (TR)
Binjhia (WB)
Binjia (AS)
Binjina (BI)
Binjina (WB)
Birhor (AS)
Birjhia (OR)
Birjia (AS)
Bissey, Barangi Jodia, Bennagi, Dadus, Frangi, Bollar, Theoriya, Kollal, Konde, Paranga Jodia, Sodo and Takora (KA)

Bissoy-Barangi Jodia, Bannangi, Daduva, Godo Jodia, Hollar, Jheriya, Kollai, Konde, Paranga, Pergajodia, Prangi, Takora (AP)
Bissoy-Barangi Jodia, Bannagi, Daduva, Frangi, Mollar, Jheriya, Kollai, Konde, Paranga, Panga-Jodia, Sodo Jodia and Takore (TP)
Bissoy-Barangi Jodia, Bennangi, Daduva, Frangi, Hollar, Jhoriya, Kollai, Konde, Paranga, Pengajodia, Sodo Jodia and Takoara (OR)
Bissoy-Barangi, Jodia, Bennangi, Bollar, Daduval, Frangi, Jhoriya Kollai, Konda Pranga, Ponga, Jodia, Sodo Jodia and Takora (KE)
Bogada (OR)
Bolodhia (OR)
Bondil (TP)
Bondo (AS)
Boro, Bore Kachari (MR)
Boro-Kachari (ME)
Botehra (CH) (CH)
Bowri (AS)
Boya (TP)
Boya, Valmiki (AP)
Boyar, Oddar (TP)
Brahmi (DN)
Brijia (WB)
Budabukhala (TP)
Budbukhi, Bubdkala, Devari (KA)
Budbukk (AP)
Bududki, Damruwale, Kudmude, Madhangi, Sarodo, Sahdev Joshi, Sarvade, Sarode (MR)
Bukadra (KA)
Bukka (AP)
Burbook (AP)
Burbook (MR)
Buruashankar/Barna Suarkar, Beja (OR)
Burud (GU)
Burud, Madar (MR)
Butakusuda (OR)
Buttal (MR)
Byagari (KE)
Byagari (TP)

Chaak (WB)
Chachati (KE)
Chackaravar (KE)
Chadar (MR)
Chahang (PU)
Chain, Chayeen (BI)
Chak (DE)
Chakala, Chawla, Dhobi, Rajaka, Chakali, Vannar (AP)
Chakkala (KE)
Chakkiliyan (OR)
Chakrawadya Dasar (GU)
Chakrawadya Dasar (KA)
Chakrawadya-Dasar (RA)
Chalavadi (OR)
Chalavdi (KE)
Chalvadi, Chamnayya (RA)
Chamana (RA)
Chamar (AS)
Chamlong (WB)
Chamtha (MR)
Chanal (UP)
Chanchati (TP)
Chandal (MR)
Chandalagade (MR)
Chandrabanshi (Kahar) (BI)
Chang, Chahang (HP)
Changar (HP)
Chanou (BI)
Chaparband (Muslim) (KA)
Chapota (BI)
Charg (CH) (CH)
Chasadhoba, Haladhar, Halari, Satchasi (WB)

Chatri-Agnikulaksatryya, Bombili (AP)
Chatwal (BI)
Chavalakkaran (KE)
Chavalakkaran, Chavalakkarer (TP)
Cheeta (RA)
Chelopa (HP)
Chemchu or Chanchwar (MR)
Chenchu (KE)
Chenchu (TP)
Chene-Dasaru (RA)
Chenna-Dasar, Holaya (RA)
Chere (AS)
Chero (OR)
Cheruman (AP)
Cheruman (OR)
Chhara, Adodia, Sansi (GU)
Chick Banik (AS)
Chidar (RA)
Chik (OR)
Chik (UP)
Chik, Chikwa, Kasai, Kassab (WB)
Chikbaraik (OR)
Chintala (AP)
Chintala (KA)
Chintala (MR)
Chirimar (CH) (CH)
Chirimar (DE)
Chirimar (WB)
Chitra, Chitrakar (KA)
Chitra, Chitrakar (OR)
Chitrakar (WB)
Chitrakathi-Joshi (KA)
Choongar (MP)
Chopemari (AP)
Choudang (AS)
Choudang (ME)
Chouhan (TR)
Christian Chamar (GD)
Christian Mahar (GD)
Chuhat or Chuhra (KA)
Chumpa (UP)
Chunal (UP)
Chunara (GU)
Chunkar (MP)
Churia (OR)
Churihara, Lakhera, Lahera (WB)
Churima (HR)
Chutia, Chutiya (AS)
Chutiya (ME)
Chuvalia Koli (GU)

Dabgar (GU)
Dabgar (MP)
Dabgar (MR)
Dafali, Dholi (MP)
Dafla (MR)
Dahalia (OR)
Dahez (MP)
Daiya (CH) (CH)
Daiya (PU)
Dakalaru (RA)
Dakaleru (MR)
Dakaut (CH) (CH)
Dakaut, Dahkaut (PU)
Dakaut, Dakot, Jyotshi (HR)
Dakot, Garo, Gakudia (RA)
Dalera (UP)
Dalu (TR)
Dalu (WB)
Damai (Nepali) (MR)
Damai (TR)
Damal (OR)
Damala (AP)
Damami (RA)
Dana (MP)
Danasi (KE)
Dandari (AS)
Dandasi (AS)
Dandasi (KA)
Dandasi (TP)
Dandesa (KE)
Dang-Dasar (KA)
Dangua (OR)
Daoli, Daola (HR)

Daoli, Deola (PU)
Daoli, Doala (CH) (CH)
Dapala (MR)
Dasari (AP)
Dasari (Donga & Gudu) (AP)
Dasari (TP)
Dasari, Desari (KA)
Dasir Dangdidas (MR)
Daula, Soni-Braderi (PU)
Daya, Dhaiya, Jallad (DE)
Deha, Dhaya, Dhea (CH) (CH)
Dehuri (OR)
Dekaleru (GU)
Deons (OR)
Deoria (MR)
Desali (TR)
Devari, Gosavi, Nath, Panthi (MR)
Devhar (BI)
Devli (MR)
Dey, Sudra Das (ME)
Dhadi (RA)
Dhai (CH) (CH)
Dhakad Dhanak Dhanaka, Dhanuk Gokhi (RA)
Dhakad, Bhandari, Nagar Singhavi, Talaya (MP)
Dhakaru (WB)
Dhakkada (AP)
Dhakkada (OR)
Dhakkada (TP)
Dhamai (AS)
Dhamin (BI)
Dhanchi (RA)
Dhaner (OR)
Dhangar (GD)
Dhangar, Gadri, Gadaraia, Hatgar, Hatkar, Kurmar, Pal Bagala (MP)
Dhangar, Kruba, Kurubar (MR)
Dhanka including Tadvi, Tataria and Valvi (KA)
Dhankar (BI)
Dhankia (MP)
Dhanwar (AS)
Dhanwar (BI)
Dhanwar (HR)
Dhaon (WB)
Dhar (MR)
Dhari (BI)
Dhari (UP)
Dheevara (KE)
Dheha (BI)
Dheha (JK)
Dheha (JK)
Dhekaru (BI)
Dhemaru (TR)
Dhenuar (WB)
Dhenwar (CH) (CH)
Dhenwar (PU)
Dher (AP)
Dher (KA)
Dhimar (BI)
Dhimar (RA)
Dhimar, Dhinwar, Jhinwar, Kahar, Mallah (CH) (CH)
Dhimar, Dhivar, Gabit, Harkantra, Mangali, Mangale, Page, Sankuri (MR)
Dhimar, Dhiwar, Dhinwar, Jheevar, Jhinwar, Kahar, Mallah, Kashyap, Rajput (HP)
Dhimar, Dhiwar, Dhinwar, Jheevar, Jhinwar, Kahar, Kashyap, Rajput, Mallah (PU)
Dhimar, Mallah, Kaashyap Rajput (HR)
Dhimer, Benmu, Banawar, Bhorji, Dhimar, Kewat, Raikar, Raikwar Saimari (MP)
Dhinwar, Jhinwar, Nishad (DE)
Dhirkar (MP)
Dhiwar, Britia, Navada, Ezingabhuti (MP)
Dhobi (AN)

Dhobi (CH) (CH)
Dhobi (DN)
Dhobi (excluding those in S.C.) (DE)
Dhobi (GD)
Dhobi (GU)
Dhobi (including those in S.C.) (MP)
Dhobi (RA)
Dhobi (Washermen) (JK)
Dhobi, Batham, Chauhan-Bhatti, Khurdania, Monson, Rajpar, Tanwar (HR)
Dhobi, Parit, Watts, Madwal, Rajak (MR)
Dhobi, Quasab (PU)
Dhobi, Rajak (excluding those in S.C.) (UP)
Dhobi, Vannan (TP)
Dhodia (KA)
Dhodia (RA)
Dholi (Dholi) (UP)
Dholi (KA)
Dholi (MR)
Dholi (RA)
Dholwala (JK)
Dhor (GD)
Dhor, Kakkayya, Kankayya (RA)
Dhosali (CH) (CH)
Dhosali, Dosali (HR)
Dhosali, Dosali (PU)
Dhosali, Sosal (HP)
Dhunia, Dhumian (BI)
Dhunia, Katheria, Naddaf (UP)
Dhunkar, Kadore (MP)
Dibbipuria (HR)
Digwan, Jinger (KA)
Dilpali (WB)
Divachakoli (GU)
Diwan (AR)
Dom, Dombara, Paidi or Pano (KE)
Domb-Andhiya Dombs, Audiniya Dombs, Chonel Dombs, Christian Dombs, Mirgani Dombs, Oriya Dombs, Ponaka Dombs, Telgaga Dombs and Ummia Dombs (KE)
Domb-Andhiya Dombs, Audiniya Dombs, Chonel Dombs, Christian Dombs, Mirgani Dombs, Oriya Dombs, Ponaka Dombs, Telega Dombs and Ummia Dombs (OR)
Domba (TP)
Domba, Dommara, Domba-Audhiya, Domba-Audiniya, Domba-Christian, Domba-Chonal, Domba-Nirgani, Domba-Oriya, Domba-Ponaka, Domba-Telaga, Domba (KA)
Domba-Adhiya Domba, Chonel Domba, Oriya, Domba, Poneka Domba, Telaga Domba and Ummia Domba (TP)
Dombidasa (KA)
Dombo (AP)
Dombo (KE)
Dombs-Andhiya Dombs, Audiniya Dombs, Chonel Dombs, Christian Dombs, Nirgani Dombs, Oriya Dombs, Ponaka Dombs, Telaga Dombs, Ummia Dombs (AP)
Dommara (AP)
Dommara (AP)
Dommara (MR)
Dommara (TP)
Donga Vata (TP)
Donga Yerukala (KA)
Dongayatha (AP)
Doom, Dooma Gansi/Quash (excluding those in S.C.) (JK)
Dosali (JK)
Dubla (RA)

Dudakula (TP)
Dugla, Dholi (MR)
Dumala, Dumal (OR)
Duraj (WB)
Durgamurga, Burburchal (KA)
Dusad (AS)

Eakkarauar (Kavathi) (TP)
Eluvain (AN)
Enadi (TP)
Eravallar (TP)
Eshavathi (KE)
Eshuthachan (KE)
Ezhava (KE)
Ezhavathy (TP)
Ezhuthachar (TP)
Ezhvva (TP)

Faqir (UP)
Fishermen (JK)

Gadaba (BI)
Gadaba (WB)
Gadaba or Godba (MR)
Gadaba, Gadababoda, Gadaba-Garilum, Gadaba-Franji, Gadaba Jodia, Gadaba Olaro, Gadaba Pangi (KA)
Gadabas, Boda Gadaba, Garlas Gadaba, Olarao Gadaba and Frangi Gadaba, Jodia Gadaba (TP)
Gadabas-Boda Gadaba, Cellan Gadaba, Franji Gadaba, Jodia Gadaba, Olaro Gadaba, Pangi Gadaba, Pranga Gadaba (KE)
Gadaria (CH) (CH)
Gadaria (MR)
Gadaria, Baghela, Berela, Biar, Hiranwal, Kalanlia, Padnowal, Pal, Shiviya (HR)
Gadaria, Chandalia, Gadaria, Gavala, Ghosi, Kabiria (RA)
Gadaria, Geddi, Gaderia, Gaerria (UP)
Gadderia, Gadaria (PU)
Gaddi (CH) (CH)
Gaddi (HR)
Gaddi (JK)
Gaddi, Garri (DE)
Gaddi, Guddi (PU)
Gaderia (DE)
Gaderria (HP)
Gadhavi (MR)
Gadheri, Ghandila (DE)
Gadhia (UP)
Gadi (KA)
Gadilohar (DE)
Gadolia (RA)
Gadri (CH) (CH)
Gadri (MR)
Gadri, Gari (MP)
Gahamandi (MP)
Gahtowar (AS)
Gain (WB)
Gamit, Gamta, Gavit (including Mavchi, Padvi, Vassva, Vasava and Valvi) (RA)
Ganali or Gandali (MR)
Ganda (AS)
Ganda (WB)
Gandharap (MR)
Gandharb (BI)
Gandharva, Bhatu Sausi (UP)
Gandhila (UP)
Gandia (MP)
Gangani (AP)
Gangani (KA)
Gangani (MR)
Gangavar (TP)
Gangin (TR)
Ganju (TR)
Gara (MR)
Gara (TR)
Garai (WB)

Gareri (TR)
Garodi (AP)
Garodi (MR)
Garpageri (MR)
Garudi, Garudiga, Modiga, Modikara, Modikar, (KA)
Garvdi (MR)
Gatti (KE)
Gaude (GD)
Gaudhila (JK)
Gavandi (MR)
Gavara (AP)
Geddi (excluding the areas where specified as S.T.) (HP)
Ghadi-Waddar, Matti-Waddar, Waddar, Ode, Odiya (MP)
Ghadsi, Ghadshi (KA)
Ghagi, Haddi, Relli and Sachandi (TP)
Ghandshi (MR)
Ghansi (AS)
Ghantia (GU)
Ghariya (MP)
Ghasi or Haddi, Relli, Sachandi (KE)
Ghasi, Ghasiara, Ghosi (PU)
Ghasi, Ghasiyara, Ghosi (HR)
Ghasi, Haddi, Relli, Sachhandi, Boda, Ghasia and Sanghasia (KA)
Ghasiara (DE)
Ghasis-Boda Ghasis and Sen Ghasis (KE)
Ghassi, Ghasiara, Ghosi (HP)
Ghati, Ghare (MP)
Ghatuar (AS)
Ghatwal (WB)
Ghatwar (B1)
Ghatwar (OR)
Ghatwar (WB)
Ghiradh, Ghirath (HR)
Ghisadi (KA)
Ghondali, Gondaliga, Ghondali, Gondahalli (KA)
Ghosi (CH) (CH)
Ghusuria (BI)
Ghusuria (WB)
Giddibidki, Pingle, Pingale (KA)
Gidhiya (UP)
Gingra (OR)
Giri (UP)
Girigiri (OR)
Gisadi, Ghisadi, Lohar Gadi Lohar, Chitodi Lohar, Rajput Lohar (MR)
Goala (TR)
Godaba (AP)
Godala (AP)
Godali (KA)
Godari (KA)
Godari (KE)
Godari (TP)
Godda (OR)
Godhi (MP)
Godo (Chhavo), Godhi (BI)
Godra (BI)
Godra (WB)
Godri (HP)
Godri (HR)
Goehaki (MP)
Goggi (GD)
Gogra (KA)
Gokha (WB)
Golla, Hawu Golla, Dudi Golla, Adavi Golla, Kishna Golla, Handi Golla (KA)
Gond (KE)
Gond (RA)
Gond (TP)
Gonda (AS)
Gonda (TR)
Gonda (WB)
Gondali (KA)
Gondhali (MP)

Gondi-Modya Gond and Rajo Gond (OR)
Gondi-Modya Gond and Rajo Gond (KE)
Gonds (AS)
Gondu-Bato, Bhirtiya Dubho, Kouria, Bato Jatako and Joria (KA)
Gondu-Rato, Bhirthya, Dudho Kouriya, Hato, Jatako and Joria (OR)
Goniga (KA)
Gonrh (UP)
Gonrh, Gorh, Godh, Gothahum (B1)
Gonrhi (TR)
Gontia (MP)
Gor (AS)
Gora (WB)
Gorait (AS)
Gorang (TR)
Gorkha (HR)
Gorkhali (ME)
Gosavi (GD)
Gosavi Bava, Dairgai, Bharati, Girigosavi, Bharati Gosavi Saraswati Parbat, Sagar, Ben or Ven (MR)
Goskha (BI)
Goud (BI)
Goudu, Bato, Bhirithya, Dudhokouria, Hato, Tatake and Jori (TP)
Goudus-Bato (Bhirithya) Dudhokuria, Hats, Jatako and Joria (AP)
Gowtia (MP)
Gramani, Sahnar, Nadar (TP)
Gudala (AP)
Gudheri (WB)
Gudigar (KA)
Gujarath Baori (MR)
Gulgaliya (BI)
Gumtian (HP)
Gunar (TR)
Gundi (TR)
Guri (TR)
Gurjamar (JK)
Gurjamar (JK)
Gurkha (MI)
Gurung (SI)
Gutgudi (MR)

Habra (OR)
Habura (MP)
Habura (MR)
Hadi (CH) (CH)
Hadi (TR)
Hadi (WB)
Hajjam (MP)
Hajjam, Nai (CH) (CH)
Hajong (MR)
Halalkhor (excluding those in Scheduled Caste) (WB)
Halalkhor (RA)
Halalkhor (TR)
Halalkhor (UP)
Halavakki Vakkal, Gramvakkal, Gam-Gowda, Gavada, Karevakkal Attevakkal, Halakkivakkal (North Canara Distt) (KA)
Halepaik, Deevar, Namadhari, Billava, Kalal, Kumarpaik (KA)
Hali (CH) (CH)
Halleer (RA)
Hallpaik (MR)
Halsar, Haslar, Hulasvar, Halssvar (RA)
Halve, Hilav (MR)
Hangie (Manjhi Boatmen and rowing class excluding house-boat owners) (JK)
Hankiya (UP)

Hansi (OR)
Haranshikari, Chigaribetegar, Vaghri, Wagriri, Nirshikaro, Bagri, Baori, Phasa Chard, Vagri (KA)
Hari (AS)
Hari (TR)
Harni (CH) (CH)
Harni (DE)
Harni (HP)
Harni (PU)
Hasla (AP)
Hasla (OR)
Hasla (TP)
Hawari (WB)
Hela (WB)
Helar (RA)
Helva, Helava, Helava Mallar, Hevagolla, Handi Helva, Helvaru, Pitchosuntala (KA)
Herbi, Hori (DE)
Hika/Mason (JK)
Hill Puleya (TP)
Hingora (GU)
Hira (MR)
Hirhor (TR)
Ho (TR)
Holar, Valhar (RA)
Holaya, Holer (RA)
Holeya (OR)
Holra (AS)
Holve (TP)
Honniyar (KA)
Hoobhudish (WB)
Hovan (TP)
Howgar, Hawagar, Howadiya (KA)
Hurkiya (UP)

Irika (BI)
Irika (WB)
Irula (AP)
Irula (OR)

Jadapu (KA)
Jadapus (OR)
Jadup (BI)
Jaggale (KA)
Jaintrapans (OR)
Jambavanodai (TP)
Jambuvulu (OR)
Jatapua (TP)
Jatgar (KA)
Jatigar (MR)
Jatiya (MR)
Javeri, Jawari (KA)
Jhadi (MR)
Jhala, Malo (MR)
Jhamral (MP)
Jhari (MP)
Jheewar (JK)
Jhimar, Atlas, Bidran, Bire, Bhinwar, Duglan, Dora, Ghitra, Jhewar, Jhinwar
Jimar, Kahar, Kimal, Lamsar, Malri, Radhav, Tala (HR)
Jhodia (OR)
Jingar (MP)
Jingar (MR)
Jodapue (TP)
Jogde (MP)
Jogi (AP)
Jogi (DE)
Jogi (MP)
Jogi (TP)
Jogi (UP)
Jogi or Yogi (OR)
Jogi, Joger, Sanjogi (KA)
Jogi, Jogo, Jugi (BI)
Jogi, Nath (CH) (CH)
Jogi, Nath (PU)
Jogi, Nath, Nathjogi (MR)
Jogin (MR)
Joginath (MP)
Jogula (TP)
Joshinadidala (AP)
Juang (BI)

Juang (WB)

Kabari (BI)
Kabbore (TP)
Kadan (AP)
Kadan (KA)
Kadan (OR)
Kadan (TP)
Kadar (BI)
Kadera (MR)
Kadera Karnwal (MP)
Kadore (MP)
Kadupattar (Malabar) (TP)
Kahar (DN)
Kahar (HP)
Kahar (MP)
Kahar (WB)
Kahar, Chandraborai, Chatrapati, Chotra-Bansi, Ramani, Rawani, Paneri (BI)
Kahar, Dhiver, Dhuru, Godia, Kashyap (UP)
Kahar, Kashyap (DE)
Kahar, Shoi (RA)
Kaibartta, Jaliya (MR)
Kaikadi (GU)
Kaikadi (or Korach), Dhontle, Korve or Kochi Korva, Makadwale, Padler Korvi, Kuchbauda, Gharo (MR)
Kaikadi (or Koracha or Korvav) (AP)
Kaikadi, Korech (RA)
Kaikari (MP)
Kaira (WB)
Kakkalan (TP)
Kala (WB)
Kaladi (OR)
Kaladi (TP)
Kalahandi (AS)
Kalar (MP)
Kalbodia (GU)
Kalihandi (AS)
Kalladi, Kalwar (AP)
Kalloda (KA)
Kalwar (BI)
Kalwar (BI)
Kalwar (OR)
Kalwar (WB)
Kamkar (BI)
Kammar Kumbhar (where they are not S.T.) (KA)
Kampmare or Reddika (AP)
Kamriya (MP)
Kanakkan (AP)
Kanchan (CH) (CH)
Kandarpa (OR)
Kandel (MR)
Kandera (MP)
Kanders (RA)
Kandh (WB)
Kandhai (AS)
Kandra (AP)
Kandra (BI)
Kaner (MP)
Kangasia (GU)
Kanghera (CH) (CH)
Kanghera (HP)
Kani or Kanisu or Kaniyar Panikker (TP)
Kanikaran, Kanaikar (TP)
Kaniyan (AP)
Kaniyan (OR)
Kanjar (AP)
Kanjar (CH) (CH)
Kanjar (OR)
Kanjar (TP)
Kanjar Bhat, Chhera, Kanjar, Nat (MR)
Kanjar, Ghair Kuchbanda, Singikat (DE)
Kanjar, Kanchan (PU)
Kanjar, Knajari, Kanjir, Khangarbhat (KA)

Kanjara-Bhatta (AP)
Kanjra Ghara (BI)
Kannakan, Padanna (TP)
Kanvi (RA)
Kapadi (DN)
Kapadia (BI)
Kapdi (MR)
Kapudia (OR)
Kapumari (KA)
Kapumarie (TP)
Kapumaries (AP)
Kapuria (WB)
Karani (WB)
Karawal (DE)
Karbi (AS)
Karha (WB)
Karhara (OR)
Kari Kudumbi (KA)
Karimpalan (AP)
Karimpalan (KA)
Karimpalan (OR)
Karmali (OR)
Karwalant, Karwalnut (WB)
Karwalnut (BI)
Kasar (GD)
Kashan (AS)
Kashikaffi, Kashi-Kapadi, Tirmali (KA)
Kastha (WB)
Katabu (MR)
Katabu, Katabar (KA)
Katesar or Pattamkatti (TP)
Katipamul (MR)
Katipamula (AP)
Katipaula (KA)
Kattunayakan (OR)
Kauri, Kori (MP)
Kavadi (KA)
Kavara (TP)
Kavathi (TP)
Kavuthiyar (TP)
Kawar (AS)
Keer (RA)
Keet (BI)
Kehal (CH) (CH)
Kehal (HP)
Kehal (HR)
Kehal (PU)
Kela (BI)
Kelkari, Khelkari (KA)
Kenchoro (MR)
Keot (AS)
Kerala Muthali (TP)
Kewat (DE)
Kewat, Bansi, Chai, Jalehar, Kharsa, Majhi, Mallah, Bishad (UP)
Khadwar (BI)
Khaia (OR)
Khairwa (UP)
Khamgara (MP)
Khandait (TR)
Khandnals (OR)
Khangar (BI)
Khanghera (HR)
Khanjiman (OR)
Khant (GU)
Khant (RA)
Kharag (WB)
Kharia (AN)
Kharia (AS)
Kharia (WB)
Kharol (RA)
Kharol, Telugu-Munar, Beldar, Ghara (MP)
Kharot (UP)
Kharvi (TP)
Kharwa Bhadela (GU)
Kharwa or Kharwi (MR)
Kharwar (MP)
Khasi (MR)
Khatgune (DE)
Khatik (BI)
Khatik (excluding those in SC) (DE)
Khatik (GU)
Khatik (TR)
Khatti (OR)

Khatua (OR)
Khemcha (TR)
Khen (TR)
Khen (WB)
Kherwar (AS)
Kherwar (WB)
Khilarger, Marathi Dhanagar (KA)
Khodal (AS)
Khodra (OR)
Kholie (JK)
Khand (AP)
Khond (AS)
Khond (KE)
Khond (TP)
Khondal (OR)
Khonyor (AS)
Khuangsal (MR)
Khyang (TR)
Khyang (WB)
Khyara, Ghara (WB)
Kichak (TR)
Kichak (WB)
Kingharia (UP)
Kinisan (KA)
Kirad (MP)
Kirar (RA)
Kitaran (KE)
Kochi (AP)
Koda (TR)
Koda (WB)
Kodalo (AP)
Kodalo (KE)
Kodar (MP)
Kodu (KE)
Kodu (TP)
Kohli (CH) (CH)
Kohor (AS)
Koilar (OR)
Koiri (TR)
Kol (AS)
Kol (WB)
Kolaga (HP)
Kolaga (Muslim) (DN)
Kolalar, Devar, Thevar (TP)
Kolam (OR)
Kolhari, Dombari (MR)
Koli (BI)
Koli (DN)
Koli (GD)
Koli (UP)
Koli (WB)
Koli Mahadev (RA)
Kolla, Kollah (KA)
Kolthats, Kolthating (KA)
Kolu (WB)
Komakapu (KA)
Komakapu (MR)
Komar (OR)
Kond (Kui) (AP)
Kond (Kui) (KE)
Kond (Kul) (OR)
Kond Danogara (KE)
Konda (Kui) (TP)
Konda Dhera (TP)
Konda Dhora, Kondh Desaya, Kondh Dongria, Kondh Dongria, Kondh
Kuttiya, Kond Tikiriya, Nokka Dhora Manna-Dhora, Makka Dhora (KA)
Konda Dora (KE)
Kondalo (TP)
Kondha-Besaya Kondha, Dangria Kondha, Kuttiya, Kondha, Tikiria Kondha and Yamity Kondha (TP)
Kondha-Dessya Kondha, Kongria Kondha, Kuttiya Kondha, Tikiria Kondha and Venity Kondha (KE)
Kondh-Desaya Kondhs, Dongriya Kondhs, Kuttiya Kondhs, Tikiria Konds and Yanity Kondhs (OR)
Kondpan (AS)
Kongadi (MR)

Kongu Malayan (KE)
Konkna Yenity (KA)
Koosa (AP)
Koosa (OR)
Kora, Juda (OR)
Koracha, Koravar, Yerukale (TP)
Korachas (or Koravar or Yerukala) (KE)
Koraga (AP)
Koraga (OR)
Koraoha or Yerkula or Korva (MR)
Korchar (MR)
Koria (MP)
Korku (BI)
Korku (RA)
Kormakar (AS)
Korwa (AS)
Korwa (TR)
Korwa including Kodaku (MR)
Kosalya Goudu, Bosothoriya Goudu Chitti Goudui, Dangayath Goudus Doddu Kamariya, Dudu Kamaro, Kadiya Gouds and Pullseriya Goudus (KE)
Kosalya Goudus, Bosothe Riya Goudus, Chiti Goudus, Dangayath Goudus, Doddu Kamariya, Dudu Kamaro, Ladiya, Goudus and Pullo Soriya Goudus (OR)
Koselya Goudu, Bosotholya Goudu, Chith Goudu, Dangayath Goodu, Doddu Kammariya, Dudu Kamaro, Laddiya Goudu and Fullo Soriya Goudu (TP)
Kota (AP)
Kota (OR)
Kotari, Kottari (KA)
Kote (TP)
Koteyar (TP)
Koti (AP)
Kotia-Bartika, Bantho, Oriya, Dhulia or Dulia, Holva Paiko, Putiya, Sanrona and Sindho Paiko (TP)
Kotia-Bartika, Beatho Oriya Dhulia or Dulla, Holva Paiko, Putiya, Senrona and Sidho Paiko (KE)
Kotia-Bartika, Bonth-Oriya, Dhulia, Dulia, Holva Paiko, Putiya, Sanrona and Sidho-Paiko (KA)
Kotil (MP)
Kotoyar (KE)
Kottan, Koodan (TP)
Kotwal (AS)
Kotwal or Kotwalia (GU)
Kotwar (UP)
Koya (AS)
Koya or Goud (with its subsects Raj or Resha Koya, Linga Dhari Koya (ordinary) and Kottukoya) (TP)
Koya or Goud, with its sub-sects Raj or Rasha Koyas, Kottu Koyas and Limgadhari Koyas (KE)
Koyava (KA)
Koyi (KE)
Koyi (OR)
Koyi (TP)
Kramali (AS)
Krar, Dhakar (MP)
Krishnabalija (Dasari Bukka) (AP)
Krishnanyoka (KE)
Krishnaveka (TP)
Kritiria (BI)
Kshatriya (AR)
Kubbora, Kukuvan (TP)
Kuchband, Kuchhband (PU)
Kuchhria (MR)
Kudiya (AP)
Kudiya (OR)
Kudubi (AP)
Kudubi (KA)
Kudubi (KE)

Kudubi (OR)
Kudubi (TP)
kudubi Koyi (KA)
Kudumban (AP)
Kudumban (OR)
Kudumbi (KE)
Kudumbi (TP)
Kuki (MR)
Kuki (WB)
Kul (RA)
Kulbandhiya (MP)
Kuli, Koli (OR)
Kulta (OR)
Kumarbhag Pahadia (BI)
Kumbhar (DN)
Kunbi (GD)
Kunchi Korwar, Kaidadi, Koraggar, Yerkala, Erakala, Kunchi Korva, Koramasehy, Yerakala (KA)
Kundamatia (OR)
Kunduma/Kuduma (OR)
Kunjra (MP)
Kunjra, Rayeen (UP)
Kunjra, Rayeen (WB)
Kurakula (AP)
Kurariar (OR)
Kuravan (AP)
Kuravan (OR)
Kuravar (TP)
Kurichchan (AP)
Kurichchan (KA)
Kurichchan (OR)
Kurmar (MR)
Kurmi (AR)
Kurubar, Kurub, Kurab, Kuruba (KA)
Kurul Kuruboru, Halamath (KA)
Kuruman (Kurumba) (OR)
Kurumba (TP)
Kurumbarava (TP)
Kutwar (MP)

Labana (HP)
Labana (HR)
Labana, Lobana, Vanzara, Banjara, Banjari (CH) (CH)
Ladar, Lad, Ladaru, Yelyar (KA)
Laher (OR)
Lakhra (OR)
Lakra (WB)
Lalbagi (MR)
Lalbegi (TR)
Lalbegi, Bhangi (Muslim) (BI)
Lalli (DE)
Lalli (HP)
Lalli (HR)
Lalli (JK)
Lalung (MR)
Lambadi (OR)
Lambadi, Bajara, Lambadi Sugali (TP)
Lambodi, Banjara, Subali (KE)
Liamei-Naga (MR)
Limboo, Limbu (SI)
Lippara (KA)
Lobana, Banjara, Vanjara (PU)
Lohar (TR)
Lonari, Chunari (MR)
Lonia, Lunia, Nunia, Nonia (MP)
Luhura (OR)
Luniya, Lonia (UP)
Lushei (WB)

Machhi (Hindu), Bitna, Dhimar, Dhivar, Kahar, Khalas Khalasi, Kharawl, Mangela, Sarang, Tendal (GU)
Machhi, Machhera, Mali, Saini, Southia, Sagarwanshi-Mali, Nayak (DE)
Machhi, Tandel (MR)
Machhu (WB)
Machi, Aaribharatbhara, Bharadbhara, Ghamadia, Chamadia, Chandilia, Dasania, Jansali, Jingar, Myangar, Sonari, Sivania (GU)

Machua (OR)
Madar (BI)
Madara (KE)
Madara (TP)
Madari (AS)
Madari (CH) (CH)
Madari (HP)
Madari (HR)
Madari (JK)
Madari (KE)
Madari (PU)
Madari, Bharsthari, Nath (GU)
Madgi (MP)
Madiga (KE)
Madivala (KE)
Madri (AP)
Magatha Goddus-Bemia Goudus Boodo Magatha, Dongayath Goudus Ladya Goudu, Poana Magatha and Sama Magatha (KE)
Magatha Goudo, Bamia Goudu, Boodu Magatha, Dongayath Goudu, Ponne Magetha, Sana Magetha and Yadya Goudu (TP)
Magaveera (KE)
Magha Doom (WB)
Maghaiya-Domes (TR)
Maghaiya-Domes (WB)
Maghi or Meghia (OR)
Maghya (HR)
Magura (OR)
Mahadarda (WB)
Mahali, Mahli (MR)
Mahandra, Medara (TP)
Mahar (TR)
Mahara (MR)
Mahasari (KA)
Mahigir (JK)
Mahil (MR)
Mahli (AS)
Mahli (TR)
Mahravat, Goti, Hadkashi, Zod, Dhingd, Pelya, Shatbai, Baman (GU)
Mahunta (OR)
Mahuria (BI)
Maidhasi (KA)
Maila (AP)
Maila (OR)
Mairal, Dangat, Vir (MR)
Maiti (AR)
Majhabi (MP)
Majhiara (AR)
Majhwar (BI)
Majhwar (MR)
Majwar (AS)
Makrana (Muslim) (DN)
Mal (TR)
Mal Paharia (OR)
Mala (MP)
Mala Dasu (KE)
Mala Dasu (TP)
Mala Pantaram (KE)
Mala Pulayan, Kravali, Pulayan Kurumba, Pulayam and Panbu Pulayan (KE)
Maladasu (OR)
Malapantaram (TP)
Malapulayan, Kurumbapalayan, Koravalipulayan, Pambupalayan (TP)
Malas or Agency Malas Valmikies (KE)
Malasar (AP)
Malasar (OR)
Malayakandi (KE)
Malayali (TP)
Male (TP)
Malhar (RA)
Mali (excluding the areas where treated as Scheduled Tribe) (AP)
Mali (Malakar) (BI)
Mali, Bhuimali, Bhuinmali (MR)

Mali, Korchia Mali, Paiko Mali and Padda Mali (TP)
Mali, Korchimale, Paikomali and Pedda Mali (KA)
Mali, Marar (MP)
Malis Korchis Malis, Palkomolis and Pedda Malis (KE)
Malis-Kerchia Malis, Paiko Malis and Peddarmali (AP)
Malis-Korchia Malis, Paido Malis and Pedda Mal (OR)
Malla Malasar (KE)
Mallah (MP)
Mallah (TR)
Mallah (WB)
Mallah Birha, Goyatri, Ghetwel, Jalwar, Kewat, Kurwaha Maheta, Majhi
Muriyoni, Masuria, Phutant, Purbia, Nisad, Goshi, Dhiwar, Jhiwar, Jhimar (BI)
Malnar (Malhor) (BI)
Malpaharia (AS)
Malyar (JK)
Mandula (AP)
Manga (MP)
Mangan (BI)
Mangan (WB),
Mangar{Magar) (BI)
Mangar (WB)
Mangar Batwal (MP)
Mangli (OR)
Manipuri (MI)
Maniyani, Muniyani (KA)
Manjar (MP)
Manki (AS)
Manna Dhora (KE)
Mannan, Vannan, Pathiyar (TP)
Manne Dhora (TP)
Manula (AP)
Marakkan (KE)
Marakkan (TP)
Maramori, Gramani (TP)
Marathi (TP)
Marathi, Marati (KE)
Maria (AS)
Mariya (RA)
Markande (BI)
Marni (HR)
Maru Sotiya (MP)
Maruthuvar, Navithar (TP)
Marwar Bouria (MR)
Marwari Bauria (BI)
Marwari Bauria (WB)
Masania-Jogi (DE)
Masanjogi, Sadgadsiddha, Mapanjogi (MR)
Metangi (OR)
Matial (WB)
Maugala (AP)
Mauna (TP)
Mauria (MP)
Mavi (MP)
Me or Meta (GU)
Mech (MR)
Medara (KE)
Medari or Mahendra (AP)
Medu Medar, Buruk (KA)
Meena, Mina (CH) (CH)
Meena, Mina (HR)
Mehara (RA)
Mehra (HP)
Mehtar, Bhungi (MR)
Mena (Bhil) (GU)
Meo, Mewati (DE)
Mer (GU)
Merasi, Miras (RA)
Meriasi, Mirasi (DE)
Meru (MP)
Mewati (CH) (CH)
Mewati (MP)
Mhali, Naim Navi, Nhavi (MP)
Mikir (MR)
Mina (MR)

Minks (OR)
Mir (JK)
Mirasi (HP)
Mirasi (HR)
Mirasi (JK)
Mirasi (MR)
Mirasi (PU)
Mirdhar (AS)
Miri (MR)
Mirshikar (WB)
Mishmi (MR)
Mitha (MR)
Mitha Dyyalvar (KA)
Mitna (GD)
Mochi (CH) (CH)
Mochi (excluding those in S.C.) (PU)
Mochi (excluding those in S.C.) (DE)
Mochi (excluding those in S.C.) (UP)
Mochi (HR)
Mochi, Saraj (JK)
Moger (AP)
Moger (OR)
Moghia (RA)
Mogia (RA)
Mohli (AS)
Mondi Patta (AP)
Mondivaru, Mondi Banda, Banda (AP)
Mondiwar (AP)
Mondiwar, Mondiwaru (KA)
Mondiwar, Mondiwaru (MR)
Monduvar Muduvan (KA)
Mongar (SI)
Moniagar (TP)
Moran, Matak (AS)
Moran, Matak (ME)
Mug (WB)
Mukha Dhora, Nooka Dhora (TP)
Mukhadora-Mokka Dhora (OR)
Mukhi (AS)
Mukhi (ME)
Mukkuvan, Mukkuvar (TP)
Mukkuven, Mukaya (KE)
Mukri (RA)
Muliya (AP)
Muliya (KA)
Muliya (KE)
Muliya (OR)
Muliya (TP)
Munda (AN)
Munda (AS)
Munda (MR)
Munda (MR)
Mundala (OR)
Mundas (AS)
Mura (AS)
Muria (AP)
Muria (KA)
Muria (KE)
Muria (OR)
Muria (TP)
Muria Bhottada (KE)
Muriaro (BI)
Musavar (CH) (CH)
Muslim Banjara (UP)
Muslim Banjara, Muslim Gujar (HP)

Naar (CH) (CH)
Naar (HR)
Nadar (KE)
Nadia, Hadi (RA)
Nadkal (UP)
Naga (MR)
Nagasia (AS)
Nagavaddilu (AP)
Nahvi (AP)
Nai (DE)
Nai Thakur (AN)
Nai, Banvaru, Dhanwal, Dhari, Ghangas, Ghiri, Hajjam, Hazam,

Hergun, Jallan, Lekha, Nagi, Naisikh, Palan, Panju, Patara, Raja (PU)
Nai, Bij, Hajjam, Napit (AS)
Nai, Valand (DN)
Naidu (GD)
Naik (AP)
Naik (RA)
Naik, Heri, Aheri (CH) (CH)
Naik, Nom (MP)
Naikappu (AP)
Naikawadi, Talwar, Walmiki (MR)
Naikkan (KE)
Naikkar (TP)
Naita, Nayata (MP)
Naiya (TR)
Nakkala (TP)
Nakkalas (AP)
Nalband (DE)
Nalki (KA)
Namasudra, Adhikari, Sarkar, Dhati, Bala, Hira, Baidal, Maji, Daligbi, Bodoi, Diskas, Poddar, Hindal, Roy, Dass, Hadder, Manji, Basi, Manser, Biri, Nag, Bairagi, Bhatra (Badiya) (AN)
Namdhari, Paik (MR)
Namshudra (BI)
Namsudra (MP)
Napit (TR)
Napit, Nai (MR)
Narikeravar (TP)
Nat (OR)
Nat, Nat-Banjania, Natada, Bajigar (GU)
Nat, Natsansi (RA)
Nat, Nattadas (TR)
Nat, Natuvan (KA)
Nath (AS)
Nath (MP)
Nath, Jogi (GD)
Nath, Jogi (RA)
Nattu Malayana (KE)
Navda (MP)
Navi, Nhavi, Hajam, Kalaseru Navaliga, Kalashi, Nambik, Nai, Narrbhllish (MR)
Navilan (OR)
Nayadi (AP)
Nayadi (OR)
Nayak (TR)
Nayak, Naik (UP)
Nayinda, Nayanaja, Kshatriya, Hajjam, Nhavi, Nadig, Ambattan, Mangala, Kelasi Kshowrad, Kshowrik, Navaliga, Napitha, Bhandari, Panikkan, Kavathiyan (KA)
Nayor (AR)
Neelakanthi (AP)
Neeli (MR)
Nelakanvam (KA)
Nepali (Limbo, Matwali, Rai) (TR)
Nepali, (Damai, Gaine, Gurung, Lama, Limbu, Lohar, Newar, Rai, Sarki, i.e., Cobbler, Thapa) (ME)
Nerali (MP)
Neria (MP)
Newati (UP)
Neyyala (AP)
Nhavi, Nai (GD)
Nilgar (MP)
Nirshikari (MR)
Nirshikaris (AP)
Nokkar (AP)
Nokkare (TP)
Nolakeyava (AP)
Nolia (OR)
Nolli (AP)
Nonia (MR)
Nonia, Kharwat, Nunia (BI)
Nonia, Nunia (AS)
Noongar (CH) (CH)

Noongar, Nungar (HR)
Nuhura, Nuhuraj (OR)
Nulayan (KE)
Nulayan (TP)
Nuniya (OR)
Nuniya, Nunia (TR)
Nut (excluding those in S.C.) (UP)

Od (GU)
Odd (RA)
Oddars (or Weddars) (AP)
Odde, Odder, Vadde, Oddilu, Vaddi, Vadde (AP)
Odhia (UP)
Omanaito (AP)
Omeyita (OR)
Onamsica (KE)
Oraon (AS)
Oraon (AS)
Oraon (MR)
Oraon (TR)
Orh, Od (UP)
Otare (KA)
Otari (MP)

Pacha Bhatla, Pacha Botla (KA)
Pacha Bhotala (AP)
Pachabhotla, Pachabotla (MR)
Pachabotla (AP)
Pachbandhia (MR)
Padampari (AP)
Padampari (KA)
Padampari (MR)
Padaria, Pamaria, Pandara (OR)
Padarti (KA)
Padhar (GU)
Padharia (MR)
Padia, Padiyar (KA)
Padiar (MR)
Pagadai (AP)
Pagadai (KA)
Pagadai (OR)
Pagadi (KE)
Pahar (MP)
Pahira (BI)
Pahri (UP)
Pahy (KE)
Paidi (AS)
Paidi (KE)
Paidi (TP)
Paigarapu (AP)
Paigarapu (KA)
Paigarapu (KE)
Paigarapu (OR)
Paigarapu (TP)
Paik (TR)
Paiko (OR)
Painda (AP)
Painda (KA)
Painda (KE)
Paite (MI)
Pakhali, Bhisti (MR)
Paky (KA)
Paky (OR)
Paky (TP)
Pal (Bherihar-Gaderi) (BI)
Pal Pardhi (MR)
Palakari (AP)
Palasi (KA)
Palasi (KE)
Palasi (OR)
Palasi (TP)
Palhari (MP)
Paliyan (OR)
Paliye (TR)
Paliye (TR)
Pallan (AP)
Pallan (OR)
Palluvaw (KE)
Pambada (OR)
Pambala (AP)
Pamide (KA)
Pamidi (TP)
Pamula (AP)
Pamula (KA)
Pamulu (TP)

Pan (TR)
Panabas (KA)
Panan (AP)
Panan (TP)
Panar (TP)
Panasa, Pansa, (KA)
Panchama (MR)
Pangul (MR)
Panidi (KE)
Panika (AS)
Panika (KA)
Panikkan (TP)
Paniyan (AP)
Paniyan (OR)
Panjira (OR)
Panka (MR)
Panki (TR)
Pannan (KA)
Panniandi (AP)
Panniandi (OR)
Panniyar (KE)
Pano (KE)
Pano (TP)
Pans (AS)
Pantias (KE)
Panwari (MP)
Parai (JK)
Paradhi (excluding Kutch District) (GU)
Paraiyan (OR)
Parashar (MP)
Paravan (AP)
Paravan (OR)
Paravan, Paravar, Kabbora, Parvatharajakulani, Pattanavan (TP)
Pardhi (including Adwishincher and Phase-Pardhi) (RA)
Pardhi (Nirshikari) (AP)
Pardhi Advichincher (In districts of Amerali, Bhavnagar, Jamnagar, Junagarbh, Kutch, Rajkot, Surendra Nagar) (GU)
Pareiyan (AP)
Parhaiya (OR)
Panki Muggula (AP)
Pariyas (Vengur and Vappur) (TP)
Parja (AS)
Parjas, Bonda, Daruba, Mundile, Pengu, Pundi and Saliya, Poroja, Bodo-Poroja, Sodia Poroja, Jodia Poroja and Parenga Poroja (KA)
Parkavakulam Suruthinar, Malayamar, Nathamar (TP)
Parki (MR)
Parthi (NIP)
Parya (BI)
Pasi (AS)
Pasi (TR)
Passi (AP)
Pathekut, Bachigolia (BI)
Patherphers, Sangtarash (DE)
Pathira (OR)
Pathiyan (TP)
Patia (TP)
Patka, Patki (MP)
Patra, Patramela (KA)
Pattariyas (KE)
Patua (WB)
Patwa (BI)
Patwa (DE)
Patwa (Phadal) (RA)
Patwa, Pathakar, Sipiya (MP)
Pauri (UP)
Pawariya (UP)
Payak (MP)
Pengua (OR)
Pentia (KA)
Perika (AP)
Perki (MP)
Perunkollons (KE)
Petias (AP)
Phudgi (MR)
Pichari (KA)
Picharis (AP)

Pichasunta, Pichiguntala, Pichuguntala (KA)
Pichati (KA)
Pinganiya (BI)
Pirali (WB)
Pirna (JK)
Pita (OR)
Pitchiguntala (AP)
Pod (TR)
Poligars (AP)
Polli or Sachandi (KE)
Pomla (KA)
Pomla (RA)
Pondara (AP)
Poosala (AP)
Poraya (TP)
Porjas or Poraja-Boda, Bonda, Daruva, Didua, Jodia, Mundili, Parang, Pyadi, Salliya, Sanoand Sodia (TP)
Porjas-Bado, Bonda, Daruva, Didva, Jodia, Mundil, Sano, Pengu, Pydi, Saliya, Sodia and Pareng (OR)
Porogas Bodo, Prooja or Sodia, Sano Poraja, Jadia Poroja and Pareng Proja (KE)
Poroja (KE)
Poroja-Bado, Perojaor Sodia, Jodia Peroja, Pareng Peroja and Sono Poroja (AP)
Powara (KA)
Powara (RA)
Proja-Boda, Nonda, Daruva, Didava, Jodia, Kundili, Pengll, Phdi and Saliya (KE)
Pulaya (KE)
Pulayan (AP)
Pulayan (KA)
Pulayan (OR)
Pullavan (KA)
Pulluvan, Pulluvar (TP)
Pusuale (TP)
Puthiraj Vannan (AP)
Putligar (MP)
Rabari, Sorthia Charalia, Charmta, Luni, Kushar Tank Muchhal kadiyakumbhar (excluding the Nesses of the forest of Alech, Barada and Gir) (GU)
Rabha (ME)
Rabha (MR)
Rabha (TR)
Rachband (CH) (CH)
Rachband (HR)
Rachevar (MR)
Rachkoya (AP)
Rachkoya (MR)
Rai (SI)
Rai-Sikh (CH) (CH)
Raika (RA)
Raikari (MR)
Raj (UP)
Raj Pardhi, Gaon Pradhi, Haranshikari (MR)
Rajdhobi (BI)
Rajgir (MP)
Rajgond (MP)
Rajput Bhamta, Pardeshi, Bhamta, Pardesh Bhamti (MR)
Raju (TR)
Rajwar (OR)
Rajwar (TR)
Rakhal (WB)
Ramoshi (MR)
Raneyar (AP)
Raneyar (OR)
Rangwa (BI)
Raot, Rautia, Rawt (MR)
Rasali (WB)
Rathodia (GU)
Raulo (AP)
Rautia (MP)
Raval, Raval or Raval Yogi (MR)
Raval-Ravalia, Jati or Raval Yogi, Rawal Jati, Jagaria, Padat, Ravar Rawalia (GU)
Rawal (MP)

Rawal, Ravalia, Paul (KA)
Rawat (RA)
Rawat, Bedar. Gahira, Rast, Rawar, Thethwar (MP)
Rawat, Raya, Rewath (KA)
Rebbari (RA)
Rehar, Rehara, Rer, Rihar (CH) (CH)
Rehar, Rehara, Rihar, Rea (HR)
Reinudas (KA)
Relli Orachanji (KA)
Relli, Sachndi (TP)
Relse (MI)
Rhar (MP)
Rohade, Sujharia (MP)
Rohangia, Roshangia (WB)
Rohit (GU)
Rona (KA)
Rona (KE)
Rona (TP)
Ronas (OR)
Routia (OR)
Ruchbandhia (MP)
Rupai (TR)

Saara (KA)
Sacra (KE)
Sad-Sausi (Sehar) (RA)
Sadhumatha (KA)
Sagar (GD)
Sagarpasha (OR)
Sahora (AS)
Sahte (MR)
Sakaravar (Kavathi) (KE)
Sakka (RA)
Salat (GU)
Saloi (ME)
Sanai Thalavar (Elavaniar) (KE)
Sangare (KA)
Sangastrash (BI)
Sangheda (GU)
Sangtrash (JK)
Saniyar (KA)
Sanji (MR)
Sanjogi (MR)
Sankhari (OR)
Sansi (GU)
Sansi (JK)
Sansi (KA)
Sansi (WB)
Sansia (KA)
Santal (KA)
Santal (MR)
Santal (MR)
Santhal, Santal (AS)
Santhals (AS)
Saora (AP)
Sapari (AP)
Sapari (KE)
Sapera (JK)
Sapera (MR)
Sapera, Kalbedia (UP)
Sarabara (RA)
Sarania (GU)
Sarania (MR)
Saranjia (MP)
Sarbhangi (MP)
Sare (AP)
Sare (KA)
Sargara (GU)
Saroa (TP)
Sarodi, Sarada (KA)
Satarkar (KA)
Saunsi (UP)
Sauria Paharia (OR)
Sauta (Sota) (BI)
Savara (KE)
Savara Kopu Savara, Khutto Savara and Maliya Savara (TP)
Savara, Kapusavara, Kuttusavara Maliya Savara (KA)
Savara-Kapu Savaras, Khutto Savaras, Mallya Savaras (OR)
Savaras-Kapusavaras, Khutto Savaras and Maliya Devaras (KE)

Sayar (WB)
Semban (OR)
Semman (KA)
Semman (OR)
Senatal (AP)
Severas (AS)
Shagird Pesha (WB)
Sharia (MP)
Shikkaligar (KA)
Shikligar (GU)
Shingdev or Shingadhya (MR)
Shingdev or Shingadya (KA)
Sholaga (AP)
Sholaga (KE)
Sholagar (KA)
Sholagar (KE)
Sholagar (OR)
Sholager (AP)
Shorgir (HR)
Shorigir (CH) (CH)
Shorigir (PU)
Shypri, Wattal (excluding those in S.C.) (JK)
Sikkalgar, Katari (MR)
Sikliagr (JK)
Sikligar (MP)
Siklighar, Gadi Lohar (RA)
Sindhor (AP)
Sindli (MR)
Singalu (AP)
Singhiwala, Singhikaut (CH) (CH)
Singiwala (MP)
Singiwala (MR)
Singpho (MR)
Sinkes (OR)
Sirkiwala (RA)
Siyal (WB)
Siyane (MP)
Soir, Soyar (BI)
Soliga (KA)
Sondhiya, Chandel (MP)
Sonsi (RA)
Sore (AP)
Sore (MR)
Suba (SI)
Sud (OR)
Sudra Das, Dey (AS)
Sulia (OR)
Sumra (GU)
Sunar (SI)
Sundi (OR)
Sunna (AP)
Sunna, Sunnai (KA)
Sunri (B1)
Sunri (TR)
Surera (HP)
Suriman, Gunjamar (DE)
Surimar (JK)
Surva (KA)
Sut (ME)
Sut, Soot (AS)
Synteng (MR)

Tachavira (KA)
Tahkar (GU)
Takankar (KA)
Takankar (MR)
Talabia (GU)
Talavia (KA)
Taleyari (AP)
Talwar Kanade (MR)
Tamang (SI)
Tamang (WB)
Tamariya (BI)
Tans (OR)
Targala (MR)
Targala, Bhaviya, Bhojai, Nayak (GU)
Tausa (AS)
Telega, Pamula, Paddati Golla (TP)
Thakaroa, Baria, Dharala, Patanwadia, Thakore (GU)
Thami (MP)
Thandan (TP)

Thanta Pulayan (KE)
Thantapulayan (TP)
Thanu (OR)
Thanwar (MP)
Tharu (BI)
Tharu (WB)
Tharu (WB)
Thatari (OR)
Thathera (BI)
Thavar (TP)
Thawin (HP)
Thelari (MR)
Thettia Naick (KE)
Thetwar (MR)
Thiyaa (TP)
Thiyya (KE)
Thogra, Bholla baliga (AP)
Tholko Laus (KE)
Tholuva, Naicker and Vetalakara Naickar (TP)
Thondaman (TP)
Thontoman (KE)
Thori (MP)
Thori, Turi (CH) (CH)
Thoria (MR)
Thoriyar (TP)
Thotawadu (KA)
Thotewadu (MR)
Thoti (OR)
Thoti, Burud (MP)
Thotien (KE)
Thottai Naicka (TP)
Thattia Naicks (AP)
Thottia Naik (KA)
Thottiya Naicker (including Gollavar, Silavar, Rajakambalam, Thockalavar and Tholuva Naicker) (TP)
Thuria (MP)
Thuria (OR)
Tilari, Tirate (KA)
Timali (KA)
Timali (MR)
Timali (RA)
Tipara (ME)
Tipara (WB)
Tipara, Tipera (AS)
Tipera (MR)
Tippera (WB)
Tirgar (MP)
Tirmale (MP)
Tiruvalluvan (KA)
Tirwalli (MP)
Tiyar (BI)
Tiyar (OR)
Tiyar (TR)
Tiyar (WB)
Toda (KE)
Toda (OR)
Toda (TP)
Tonla Gaul (OR)
Tsong (SI)
Turha (MP)
Turha (WB)
Turha, Sao (BI)
Turi (AS)
Turi (KA)
Turi (UP)

Ulladan (TP)
Ullatan (TP)
Uppaliga, Uppara, Uppaliyan, Mannu-Upper, Gavandi, Gavandi, Goundi, Veldar, Sagara, Chunar, Lonari, Mclusakkare, Agri, Lama (KA)
Uppar, Sagar (AP)
Uppars (Upplillia Segara) (TP)
Urali Gounders (TP)
Urao, Bandot, Haro, Karkata, Luidu, Shitheo, Tigga, Tirki (WB)

Vadder-Bevi, Upparilu (AP)
Vadi (KA)
Vaghari, Salat, Salat Vaghri (MR)

Vaghri (KA)
Vaghri (MR)
Vaghri-Gamicho, Vedva Churalia Jakhudia (excluding Kutch Distt) (GU)
Vahivancha Charan Gadhvi or Harijan, Vankar and Chamar (GU)
Vaidu (KA)
Vaidu (MR)
Vaiti (MR)
Vala (GU)
Valaan (KE)
Valaiyar (TP)
Valan (TP)
Valand and Nai (Hindu) Hajjam, Khalipha (Muslims) (GU)
Valayar (KA)
Valiayar (TP)
Valluvan (AP)
Valluvan (OR)
Valmiki (AP)
Valmiki (KE)
Valmiki (TP)
Valmiki Boya (Boya, Bedar, Kirataka, Nishadi, Yellapi Pedda Boya) Talayari and Ghundu Vallu (AP)
Valuthadanayar Valuthanathwanayar (TP)
Valvai (MR)
Valve (KA)
Vannan (Mannan, Bathiyan) (TP)
Vannar, Rajakula Valuthadar (where the community is a S.C. Agasa Madivala mali) (TP)
Vans-foda, Vansfodia or Vanza (GU)
Varli (RA)
Vathiriyan (KA)
Ved (RA)
Vedar (TP)
Vetan (IP)
Vettuvan (AP)
Vettuvan (OR)
Vilathethal Nair (Velakkithalavan) (KE)
Vina Tulavina (OR)
Vitholia (KA)
Voluthadathu Nai (Veluthedan and Vennathan) (KE)
Vottakkaran (KE)

Waddar or Kala Waddars or Pathrods (AP)
Waddar, Wadders (Kalawaders or Patharods) (MR)
Wadla (AP)
Wadwa Waghari (GU)
Waghari, Dataniya, Waghari, Vodu Waghari, Talapada, Waghari, Gamachia, Godalia Wgahari, Chibhadia Waghari, Morawad Waghari (GU)
Waghri (DE)
Waghri (RA)
Wanha (MP)
Warthi (MR)

Yadavan (Idayan) (KE)
Yakthungba (SI)
Yanadi (MR)
Yanadi (TP)
Yanady (TP)
Yandi (KA)
Yandi (OR)
Yanudi (KE)
Yaras (AP)
Yarukula (KE)
Yarukula (TP)
Yashkun (JK)
Yata (AP)
Yavana (TP)
Yeklar, Yeklar, Yekkali, Egalika (KA)

Yenadiwad (KA)
Yenadiwad (MR)
Yeragolawad or Thella Pamalawade (MR)
Yeralu (KA)
Yerasolawadorthella, Pamalwada (KA)
Yerkilwar, Yerkula (MP)
Yerna Golla (OR)
Yerukula (OR)
Yetla (AP)
Yoda (AP)
Yogi, Jogi, Nath (TR)
Yueruleu (AP)

Zemrol (RA)

Index

GYAN Books

ENCYCLOPAEDIA OF BACKWARD CASTES: MANDAL, MEDIA & AFTERMATH

ENCYCLOPAEDIA OF BACKWARD CASTES

(In 4 Volumes)

1. RESERVATION
2. COMMISSIONS
3. MANDAL, MEDIA AND AFTERMATH
4. JUDGEMENTS: BEFORE AND AFTER MANDAL JUDGEMENT

ENCYCLOPAEDIA
OF
BACKWARD CASTES

(In 4 Volumes)

MANDAL, MEDIA & AFTERMATH

(Volume 3)

M.L. Mathur

Senior Research Officer

Ministry of Social Justice and Empowerment

Government of India, New Delhi.

PUBLICATIONS

KALPAZ PUBLICATIONS

DELHI - 110052

ENCYCLOPAEDIA OF BACKWARD CASTES:
MANDAL, MEDIA AND AFTERMATH
[Scheduled Castes and OBCs]

Rs. 3600/- (Set)

ISBN: 81-7835-069-6 (Set)
ISBN: 81-7835-270-2 (Vol. 3)

©M.L. Mathur

This book may not be reproduced in any manner without written permission of the author and the publisher.

Published in 2004 in India by
Kalpaz Publications
C-30, Satyawati Nagar,
Delhi-110052
e-mail: kalpaz@hotmail.com

Laser Typeset at: Alphabet, Delhi
Printed at: Mehra Offset Press, Delhi

Contents

Introduction

The first non-Congress government came to power in 1977 after the draconian emergency era. The Janta Party government made promises in their election manifesto. To fullfil the promises made to backward classes the Janta Party Government headed by Shri Morarji Desai appointed the Second Backward Classes Commission in 1978. Shri B.P. Mandal was the Chairman of the Commission. He submitted the report on Backward Classes in 1980. The Janta Party government could not act upon the report and lost the power at the Centre. Then Congress government again came to power and placed the report before the Parliament for implementation of recommendation of the Mandal Commission. There was a strong protest in both Houses of the Parliament. The Govt. shelved its efforts and placed the report in cold storage. It is worth mentioning that the Congress party having two-third majority could not dare to implement the recommendations on backward classes; first in 1955 of Kaka Kalelkar Commission and second in 1981 of B.P. Mandal. Consequently, backward castes continued to suffer from their rights as deprived.

The second non-Congress government National Front Government headed by V.P. Singh came to power in 1989. The National Front Government also made the promises in their election manifesto to implement the recommendations of the Mandal Commission. V.P. Singh announced in the Parliament to implement the recommendations of the Mandal Commission in 1990. The political situation at that time was coalition government. Was V.P. Singh right in taking this decision, the issue which was always on hotbed? Were there any political compulsions? Were there any political forces working against him? What were his political compulsions in implementation of recommendations of the Mandal

Commission? The first Chapter traces political developments which took place in the Country during that period. During that period regional social forces and regional parties emerged as strong political force in national politics. Bhartiya Kisan Union (BKU), Bahujan Samaj Party (BSP) and Telugu Desam Party (TDP) were actively playing their decisive and affirmative role in national politics. Media projected the Devilal's Kissan rally and L.K. Advani's Rath Yatra from Somnath to Ayodhya, to counter the point of political imbalance in Indian Polity.

Under the current of emerging political forces at national level V.P. Singh hurriedly announced on 7 August, 1990, 27% reservation for OBCs in govt. service and thus implementing recommendations of the Mandal Report. Major political parties Congress (I), CPI(M), questioned the political expediency of National Front Government and V.P. Singh to announce his decision. There was protest in both houses of the Parliament. Outside the House, there was widespread agitation all over the country.

This volume presents viewpoints of cross sections of society on this very important issue. Bureaucrats, legal experts, journalists, politicians and social scientists expressed their viewpoints for and against the quota of reservation. S.S. Gill was Secretary in the Mandal Commission. He opined that backward castes person suffered at the hand of forward castes. During his field tour he noted that caste was a passport to status in the society. Govind Narain was of the view that caste cannot be the sole criterion in determining backwardness of a caste. P.P. Rao said caste was a relevant factor in determining the backwardness of a person and identification of backward classes. Reservation on caste basis is vicious and it should not be extended beyond 10 years. Madhu Limaye, a veteran social leader expressed that reservation would create a new social order. Nani Palkhiwala, an eminent lawyer said Govt. move violets basic structure of the Constitution. Former Supreme Court Judge H.M. Seervai was of the opinion that efficiency had no relevance in public service when govt. announced reservation for OBCs.

There were many issues involved in implementation of recommendation of the Mandal Report. The issues are of technical, political and sociological in nature. B. K. Roy Burman was associated with the Mandal Commission as one of the expert social scientists. He disowned the report as there were 'missing data'. Like him another two experts, M. N. Srinivas and Yogendra Singh also disowned the report as they were not consulted.

Some of journalists also expressed their views. Arun Shourie a well known journalist (presently the Minister in the National Democratic Alliance Government) termed the definition of backward caste 'sub-standard'. He questioned the criterion used by the Mandal Commission in identification of a caste backward. A N Sen and Kuldeep Kumar said announcement of 27 per cent reservation for OBCs has mandalised India. There was a need to have consensus at all levels. Ashok Guha said reservation will boost inefficiency. The situation was in confrontation and the Nikhil Chakravortty cautioned that the outcome of such situation would be ghasty.

While different walks of people reacted differently on the issue of 27 per cent reservation in OBCs. The country came into grip of agitations and violence throughout the country. There were cases of arson, self-immolation and what not?

Political developments in the country during 1990 which led to agitations all over the country against the decision of the National Front Government for implementation of recommendations of the Mandal Report. Chaudhary Devi Lal, a Octogenerian Kisan Leader of Haryana, and V.P. Singh a seasoned politician and a man often known for 'ideal' and issue based politics engaged themselves against each other forgetting national agenda, and brought the OBC issue on the forefront. None of them ever thought their calculation would go wrong, i.e., their decision would not be welcomed by all and there would be opposition. Political analysis reveal that V.P. Singh choose time of announcement of the decision before Devi Lal's Kissan rally. Sharad Yadav, Ram Vilas Paswan and V.P. Singh polarized the nation in the backdrop of this issue.

Just in a week of announcement of V.P. Singh's decision for 27% reservation for OBCs, Mr. Ujjal Singh President of the All-India Anti-Reservation Morcha Filed a writ petition challenging the decision of the Union Government in the Supreme Court. A similar petition was filed in the Allahabad High Court. So one side there were spate of writ petitions filed in different High Courts of the country.

On the other side agitations against the decision began in different parts of the country. Orissa, Himachal Pradesh, West Bengal, Sikkim, Maharashtra, Jammu & Kashmir, Uttar Pradesh, Bihar, Rajasthan, Gujarat, Delhi, Madhya Pradesh reported violence, arson, self immolation cases throughout in their states. Peaceful states like Himachal Pradesh and Rajasthan were burning under fire. 12 states out of 25 states were burning. It was really a serious matter and threat to the social fabric of the society. Interestingly there was no such incidence reported from Southern States. Because backward castes pre-dominate in the State and forward castes like Brahmins have recognized the right of backward castes there.

What was the psychology behind the agitation? V.P. Singh took the decision to counter his political opponents. Those who engineered large scale agitation wanted to gain political capital out of it and forgot that more than 200 students died in the course of agitation were in the age groups of 16-25 years. They were quite innocent and ignorant about who were backward and who were not backward? Ultimately this decision has created social cleavages between forward and backward castes. People have in fact forgotten social distance between these two real groups over the period of more than four decades. K.M. Pannicker attributed the prevailing anarchy to the fact that the Mandal Report agitation was much more than a struggle against reservation. Mandal merely provided a peg for the students to articulate the sense of deprivation which has been snow balling over the years. The reaction was very strong in urban areas than in rural areas. Question also cropped up in mind of many people when there were so many illiterates among backward castes, Scheduled Castes & Scheduled Tribes how could they dream for employment in govt. service. In less than a year the govt. fell Supreme Court admitted the writ petition of *Indira Sawhney & Others* vs *Union of India & Others*.

One

Implementing the Mandal Commission Report: Compulsion and Causes

This chapter traces politico-historical reality which led the then government in power to take out Mandal Report on Backward classes from the dustbin almost for a decade. Why did V.P. Singh Government take a sudden decision to implement recommendations given by B.P. Mandal in 1980 for welfare of Backward Classes? Did he suddenly become Mesiah of backward classes. What were his compulsions? What were causes and its effects after math? Why did the National Front Government take more than a year to announce implementation of Mandal Report which was part of their election manifesto? Let us go into all details to answer all these questions.

The Mandal Commission was set up by the Janta Government as the 1977 poll result was largely brought about by the swing in backward class votes who had by that time become aware of their political importance (Sachidananda, 1990).[1] B.P. Mandal submitted his report on Backward classes in 1980 and gave many recommendations for welfare of backward classes. It was the first time in India non-Congress party, i.e., Janta Party ruled the country after the emergency era was over in 1977. The Janta Party Government did not take any action realising there was strong opposition to implementation of the report on Backward Classes though the Janta Dal in its election manifesto committed implementation of the Mandal Report. Then Charan Singh (Ram) and Raj Narain (Hanuman) played their decisive role and pulled down the Janta Party Government headed by Shri Morarji Desai. Shri Y.B. Chavan could not form the Government. These political developments gave the Congress an opportunity and Indira Gandhi came back to power at centre.

It is an important fact that when Congress government having absolute majority during Indira Gandhi regime did not find implementation of the recommendations of Mandal Commission Report (1980) proper, feeling heat of opposition of forward castes as well as other political forces and compulsions but only shelved.

After assasination of Indira Gandhi on October 31st, 1984, Rajiv Gandhi held the mentor of Congress Party. He had no political background earlier, whatever he saw and learnt about politics was internalization during his upbringing all over the years of his development. He was a pilot and circumstances turned him to become head of the largest Political Party Congress and also head the nation as Prime Minister of the country. He made good beginning and formed his image of 'Mr. Clean'. Later part of his political career was 'thorny' and with political upheavals. When the Bofor issue was on forefront Shri V.P. Singh was a cabinet collegue of Rajjiv Gandhi, headed Ministry of Finance and Defence during those days. He raised his voice against this issue and finally he quit first as a cabinet minister and then left the Congress Party.

When the news of the alleged Bofors kickbacks were announced over Swedish Radio in '87, it came as a lethal blow to pull down the original Mr. Clean from his pedestal. It marked the beginning of Rajiv's fall as an admired public figure and his new *avatar* as a target for vilification by the Press and political opponents.

The Bofors gun deal and its possible connection right up to the Gandhi family provided a vital breakthrough for the Opposition parties. Here at last was a stick with which they could beat Rajiv and when the Haryana elections took place in June '87 it brought in a new period of abusive politics, inflammatory rhetoric and irresponsible populism.

Haryana's "burley, gravel-voiced patriarach and arch Rajiv baiter"[1] Devi Lal and his Green Brigade of Kisan supporters ushered in a very low level of abusive politics in the Haryana. Winning an overwhelming majority on the basis of innuendos and aspersions regarding the Bofors gun deal and the Loan Waiver Scheme of writing off loans taken by farmers, Devi Lal and his rhetoric found no match in his Congress opponents. At his 75th birthday celebrations near India Gate in New Delhi, where hired trucks had flooded the capital with farmers from Haryana, Punjab, Rajasthan, Bihar and Uttar Pradesh, at a deliberate display of rural muscle and political power, the leaders of the Opposition conglomerate united on their one point objective—Rajiv must go. Crudely attacking Rajiv, Devi Lal said, *Italy ka damad, tumhare baska Hindustan nahi. Jiske biwi, Sala, paye ho videshi, woh kaisa swadeshi?* (Italy's son-in-law, Hindustan is beyond your capacity. What kind of Indian is a man who has a foreign wife and relations?)

Since the ruling national emotion was spite and people had made up their minds that they had enough of Rajiv's stint as Prime Ministership, the crowds were regaled by such rhetoric. During the election campaign of 1989, it was a part of the Janata Dal strategy to harp on the *Desi* vs. *Videshi* concept and to convey to the people that the nation had been sold to foreign interests. Such slogans were cried *Gali gali me shor hai, Rajiv Gandhi chor hai* (In every street there is a cry that Rajiv Gandhi is a cheat) and "Bofors *ka dalal kaun hai*? Rajiv Gandhi (who is the middleman for Bofors?) In last so many years the Government could not bring out the truth before the public who is the real culprit in bofors?

Everywhere in northern India V.P. Singh with his mantle of honesty, idealism and self-righteousness evoked an overwhelming response from the public which was disillusioned with the Congress and Rajiv Gandhi personally. Nothing that he told them was convincing. The Congress posters which forecast death, destruction and discord in the country if the Opposition were voted to power drew a negative respose from the public. The people had already made up their minds that V.P. Singh was their new *messiah* and that he would bring in a new era in which prices would come down, national honour restored and corruption weeded out. The public was not interested in verifying the record or the antecedents of either V.P. Singh or his National Front, consisting of such controversial members as Arun Nehru, Ramakrishna Hegde, Devi Lal and N.T. Rama Rao. None of these gentlemen were pure as driven snow. However, it was no easy to analyse an electoral wave and it was undoubtedly a tidal wave of electrified public support which enabled the National Front to form a government in December 1989, supported incongruously by the leftist Communist parties and the rightist Bharatiya Janata Party all coming together owing to a strong hatred for Rajiv Gandhi and the Congress. With the Congress Party dwindling down to becoming a virtually one-man organisation and as Rajiv was personally associated with the Congress Party he was nailed for all the failures of his five year administration.

Such was the level of hysteria and miasma of doubt prevailing at the time that it was genuinely felt, even by responsible, intelligent citizens that on being defeat Rajiv would either declare an Emergency or that he would leave country in a plane which was already on standby alert at Indira Gandhi International Airport! Only when the reigns of government were formally handed over to V.P. Singh, with Rajiv being the first Indian Prime Minister to witness the swearing in of his successor, did people actually breathe easily and understood that perhaps all the negatives attributed to Rajiv Gandhi were not true.

Regional Social Forces and Regional Parties: Its Emergence and Role in National Politics

Bhartiya Kisan Union

Besides Bofors and the issue of Rajiv Gandhi himself, the vexed controversy over the Ram Janambhoomi-Babri Masjid, the *Panchayati Raj Bill*, the wooing of the new segment of the electorate in the age group of eligible voters being reduced to eighteen, the inflation and the question of whether the motley group of desperate leaders who formed the National Front would be able to administer the nation, two underlying factors were also present during the elections of 1989. These two factors were the rise of the Bharatiya Kisan Union and the Bahujan Samaj Party. In a country where numbers and vote banks assume great significance during elections, these two pressure groups emerged as factors which could influence the outcome of the polls. The Bharatiya Kisan Union and its maverick leader Mahendra Singh Tikait claimed to be an apolitical organisation of farmers who wanted all agricultural cess and other dues by farmers waived. Flooding the capital at India Gate in an effort to *gherao* the government he nevertheless gave ample proof of the sheer number of peasants who could summon at an instant's notice and that farmers could no longer be neglected or pushed around by the government. Despite his avowed apolitical intentions, politicians nevertheless flocked to Tikait to gain his support.

The new militancy in the arming community was not limited to Tikait and the BKU in Uttar Pradesh but extended to Sharad Joshi's Shetkari Sanghathan in Maharashtra and Gujarat and M.D. Nanjandaswamy in Karnataka. The lowering of power tariffs, increased power supply, loan waivers as in Haryana, the withdrawal of all police cases against farmers who had unlawfully *gheraoed* the Vidhan Sabha in Lucknow and higher remuneration—the farmers' demands, several of which were conceded.

M.L. Dantwala, former Chairman of the Agricultural Prices Commission says, "High prices are the biggest enemy of the poor. Half the rural households are net purchasers of food. If wheat prices go up by 50 per cent tomorrow, the number of poor will increase by ten per cent. The loan waiver and refusal to pay cess and other taxes in addition to the farmers' united bid to get higher prices would have according to Dantwala terrible consequences and would unsettle the whole banking system. In any other country, these leaders would have been arrested for economic treason.[2]

However, Indian history is replete with examples of people who thought nothing of surrendering the greater national good for narrow sectarian ends. During elections, it was a question of pondering to the wishes of the masses to achieve short-term electoral gains and never mind the consequences to the nation. It was not feasible to alienate vote banks specially when all their real or imagined grievances had not been alleviated.

Bahujan Samaj Party

The Bahujan Samaj Party had made a spectacular debut in UP and Punjab assembly elections but suffered a setback in the Haryana elections of 1987 in which Devi Lal and his Green Brigade stormed to power. The supremo of the Bahujan Samaj Party, Kanshi Ram, claimed to represent the 6000 backward castes of India, his chief objective being to secure for them a share of that national cake in proportion to their numbers. Kanshi Ram's definition of backward castes encompasses not only the Scheduled Castes and Scheduled

Tribes but the other Backward Classes, as also the minorities who may feel a sense of deprivation or discrimination. By applying the common factors of economic deprivation and social discrimination Kanshi Ram's attempt was to draw all the 'have not castes' under the protective umbrella of the BSP. S.S. Gill,[3] the Secretary to the controversial Mandal Commission stated categorically, "These days it is more often the intermediate landed castes like the Yadavs, Kurmis, Ahirs, and Koeris who perpetrate Harijan atrocities rather than the upper castes like the Brahman and Rajputs". He adds, "Ram Manohar Lohia realised a long time back that the most effective strategy to dislodge the Congress from power was to mobilise the depressed castes for political action. But the inner contradiction of this sort of alliance are so sharp and irreconciliable that such an attempt would always fail. And it cannot be otherwise if you try to build a large national edifice on the foundations of caste, which is basically a divisive force." Nevertheless, the BSP successfully cut into both the Janata Dal and Congress vote bank with their 72 candidates securing thirteen per cent of the votes in the '89 Parliamentary Elections in Uttar Pradesh. The avowedly casteist politics and policies of the Bahujan Samaj had succeeded. The present position is different in Uttar Pradesh where BSP and BJP formed a coalition of government after heavily relying upon forward castes votes by BSP and SC, ST, OBC and Muslim votes by BJP. The changed scenario is an indication of shift in political equilibrium according to need of hour and caste equation of political parties.

Perhaps the Congress Party also felt the requirement to renew their commitment to their traditional supporters of the Harijans, tribals and weaker sections and therefore a national drive to fill in all vacancies for Scheduled Castes and Scheduled Tribes was vigorously undertaken by the government and public sector undertaking in 1989. It was also declared that in those cases where no suitable candidate could be found, the post would not be de-reserved as was the case in the past, but would be kept vacant or carried over to the following year.

Election 1989

As the elections were announced and as the campaigning went on, it became evident that the despite having the benefits of incumbency and a captive Doordarshan, the initiative on all issues had been wrested from the Congress by the Opposition parties. Whether on corruption or communalism, inflation or caste based violence, the Opposition especially Vishwanath Pratap Singh and the Bharatiya Janata Party held the upper hand. Neither Rajiv Gandhi nor the Congress Party could effectively deal with the Opposition. They were unable to highlight the positive achievements of the five years of the Congress Government at the Centre, with its success in dealing with the fissiparous tendencies in the country, its effective foreign policy, the tackling of the worst drought in a century and role in the technological and consumer boom were not inconsiderable. Writing on the elections, *India Today*[4] remarked: "All the key elements of the Congress (I) campaign communal strategy, its manifesto seem to be boomeranging... The Opposition has succeeded in carrying out a strategy, it had publicly trumpeted months ago making Rajiv Gandhi the prime target. And he had no credible rebutal or answer to the scathing and convincingly orchestrated attacks being mounted on him in every corner of the country... Obviously the Opposition used V.P. Singh better than the Congress (I) used Rajiv." Continuing on the same lines the article pointed out that "it is not as if the Opposition has suddenly turned into a paradigm of cohesiveness and democratic virtue. It still retains its contradictions and groupism, for example, while most of it is reconciled to V.P. Singh becoming Prime Minister in case of victory, a Janata Dal faction led by Chandra Sekhar and Om Prakash Chautala, Devi Lal's son, make it a point to publicly project Devi Lal as Prime Minister. And the possibility of an internecine struggle breaking out after the elections is cause for trepidation about the stability of a government led by the National Front."

However, during the final lap of campaigning, the Opposition was outgunning and outmarshalling the Congress (I). The Congress (I) slogans were parodied and ridiculed across the country. This image was trivialised as Rajiv Gandhi suddenly turned from star attraction to become the party's greatest liability, becoming the object of widespread scurrilous lampooning.

The article concluded, "And the difference this time is that the country overdosed in the political paranoia of the 'who after

Nehru?' 'Who after Indira?' syndrome does not panic anymore at the prospect of change. The voter's attitude may well be, after Rajiv whoever. The voter is increasingly realising that for all its awesome power, he is bigger than the government, that if he can change it, then he can also make the one he chooses bend to his will and perform in his interests. These are signs of a maturing of democracy."

Intoxicated by a sense of their own power, both the Indian voter and the media seemed to have been overcome by hurbis as the election results and its aftermath led to unprecedented turmoil and uncertainty to the country.

V.P. Singh

Tearing down Rajiv Gandhi, albeit with only 143 votes, conniving with Devi Lal to pull down Chandra Shekhar in the race for premiership, Vishwanath Pratap Singh for all his denials and moral posturings, finally rose to become Prime Minister of India. *India Today*[5] commented: "The events preceding the formation of the government—blackmail, brinkmanship rumour, tantrums—indicated a rocky road ahead... The Congress (I) advertisement of fighting roosters may have backfired during the election campaign, but it began to hit home with an ironic fury in the developments that marked the post-election power struggle in the Janata Dal."

In assessing the '89 elections in which the electoral campaign had been a negative one with each party only trying to destruct its opponents, many could forsee that those who grabbed power under these norms would leave the country more fractured politically and communally than ever before.

Despite the murkey start to his premiership, V.P. Singh did his best to maintain the myth of his disinterest in the lure of office. He sought to dismantle the elaborate security apparatus which had been built up to protect Rajiv and expressed his willingness to remain in his Lodi Estate accommodation rather than shift to the Prime Minister's residence on Nos. 5 and 7 Race Course Road. However, the Prime Minister's yen for simplicity proved to be an expensive proposition, with security arrangements and an adjacent house having to be acquired in order to accommodate the paraphernalia of office. After the kidnapping and subsequent release of the Home Minister Mufti Mohammed Sayyed's daughter Sayeeda, in exchange for terrorists being released in Jammu and Kashmir, security around V.P. Singh and his Cabinet colleagues were again tightened although not to the levels of the gun toting regalia which accompanied all ministers of the previous government.

The manner of his accession to the post of Prime Minister and the Centre's role in releasing terrorists in Kashmir, in exchange for the Home Minister's daughter, made the government a target for criticism when ten days passed and the names of those who had allegedly received kickbacks in the Bofors gun deal were not released some doubts began to creep in, but the real cracks appeared with the unprecedented demand for the mass resignations and sacking of selected State governors.

Although the role of the State governors and their prestige had received a jolt during Indira Gandhi's tenure, as part of the process she had adopted of belittling respected institutions, what happened now represented the nadir of gubernotorial prestige. The role of Barar, Governor of Haryana, is a case in point, as in his eagerness to curry favour with the father-son team of Haryana politics, he did not regard the importance of swearing in the new Chief Minister, Om Prakash Chautala at Haryana Bhawan in New Delhi rather than at Chandigarh. However, he had lowered both his personal dignity and the prestige of his high office, as he too was forced to resign and his resignation was accepted in the purging of State governors.

Paying his obeisance at the Golden Temple in Amritsar and riding through the streets in an open jeep, V.P. Singh felt that he had solved the Punjab problem. Nirmal Mukharji was appointed Governor but as security measures were relaxed, the incidents of killing and violence increased and he too was removed.

In their eagerness to distance themselves from the Rajiv Gandhi administration, the government hastened the process of withdrawal of the Indian Peace Keeping Force in Sri Lanka. Commenting on his formal loyal subordinate and ministerial colleague, Rajiv Gandhi said, "The problem is that our Prime Minister does not have any goals. He has no vision for the country.

He has no principles. We thought he had values. Now he says he does not even have that. He only has issues.... When you tackle the issues without having any goals or principles, you are only tackling the immediate. You are fire-fighting."[5]

And that is exactly what Vishwanath Pratap Singh's tenure became—a series of crises caused by the totally unprincipled coupling of the Left and Right, of Devi Lal and Ramakrishna Hegde, of P. Upendra outdoing K.K. Tewari in misusing and slanting Doordarshan coverage and of his ardent supporters in the Press, especially Arun Shourie finally breaking with him.

The Media: Its View Point

If the Selling of a President could be achieved in the United States when the "Tricky Dick" Nixon of the 1950s and 1960s was packaged and sold through the media as the country's best political candidate in 1968, the Indian Press were equally successful in portraying V.P. Singh as a clean and principled leader who would revive the Gandhian value-based politics to the country. His support of Mrs. Gandhi even during the Emergency, his emotional resignation as Chief Minister of U.P. when he failed to contain the dacoit menace, his unleashing of a "raid raj" during his tenure as Finance Minister when such respected and senior industrial magnates as S.L. Kirloskar were harassed, and his rapid transition from singing paens of praise to Rajiv Gandhi and then becoming his bitterest and most abusive adversary were overlooked. The enigma and insecurity of V.P. Singh, brought about perhaps because of an unsettled childhood, when he left his real parents and was adopted by the childless Raja of Manda, left deep scars on his psyche. An offshoot of these was his obsession with portraying the "right image". Persons who worked with him could hardly expect any favours from V.P. Singh, who always guarded his image zealously and did not prefer to give the impression of either having favourites or using his influence to help a friend. Janardhan Thakur in his book *The Quest for Power*[7] portrayed some facts related to V.P. Singh's political equlibrium during those days. The aftermath of the '89 election went down as a watershed in India's political history not only for the villainous role played by politicians but also because of the machinations of the media which played an overly zealous role, and a partisan one, in the Bofors issue and on the question of Rajiv vs. V.P. Singh.

It was ironic that after the Mandal explosion, V.P. Singh himself stood exposed and villified. As Vinod Mehta wrote in *Sunday*[6] I do not think in the last ten years a Prime Minister has been as mercilessly mauled as V.P. Singh has been over Mandal." Later, Madhu Kishtwar, Chitra Subramaniam, N. Ram, Arun Shourie and V. Gangadhar would expose the in-fighting within the Press. In an article entitled "Value-based editing" Gangadhar[8] wrote, "We now have one-value based editor gunning for Hegde and occasionally soft on Devi Lal. Another hotshot crusading editor is all for Hegde, and has consigned Devi Lal to the devil. Both are rumoured to hanker for a Rajya Sabha nomination. So politicised is our `free press'...." That respected and balanced journalist S. Nihal Singh[9] warned that while it was tempting to play God, ultimately the credibility of the newspaper and the entire Press suffered. This was a pointed reference to the *Indian Express* in which a cartoon by Rajendra claimed that the paper had "successfully captured the scalps of two former Prime Ministers, a former Home Minister, a former Lok Sabha Speaker and even that of the former Deputy Prime Minister."[7]

Meham

And then came the Meham by election when the favourite son of *Tau* Chaudhury Devi Lal fought in the by-election so that he could be elected within the stipulated six months of taking over as Chief Minister. Pitted against him was the rebel Janata Dal candidate Anand Singh Dangi who had worked at the grassroots level and had secured the support of the powerful Meham Chaubise, the influential Jat Panchayat covering 24 of the thirty villages in the Constituency.

Meham and the subsequent mayhem that followed now stands as a black spot in India's democracy. The use of brute force was open and Chautala personally led hordes of gun-wielding hoodlums of the Green Brigade. Ballot boxes were stuffed and booths captured with impunity and there was enough evidence that on February 27th and 28th Chautala's son Abhay Singh, in connivance with senior DIGs and SPs, intimidated voters, terrorised

Dangi's polling agents and made efforts mislead the press and the presiding officers by pretending to be Dangi supporters!

The blatant cooperation of the Police was apparently to keep the *izzat* or honour of the *Tau*. However, not only was Devi Lal and his son splattered by the blood and outrage after the Meham violence but so also was V.P. Singh himself. The Meham election and its aftermath brought out three factors which the value-based National Front government abhorred in the previous regime—the use of money and muscle power during elections, lack of principles and dynastic succession. When questioned about the open and blatant rigging Chautala replied with some inane comments like there being a universal plot by the Press, the Congress (I) and capitalists to defame him and Devi Lal and that the Press was "anti-Jat"!

The Election Commission decided to countermand the election in light of the violence and alleged rigging. There was an outcry both in the Press as well as within the Janata Dal as Om Prakash Chauthala and his cohorts had made a mockery of the Party's value-based ideals. Moreover, the Election Commission had given direction to the Haryana Government to order a probe into the role of the police and the failure of the poll machinery in having a free and fair contest in Meham.

Police officials were concerned that they would be made scapegoats but Chautala could not afford to alienate the police as a murder charge had been framed against his son Abhay Singh. At the height of the Meham violence, a senior police officer had forced a junior constable to exchange his clothes with Abhay Singh while he was trying to rig votes at a polling booth in Bainsi on February 26th. Harbans Singh was lynched by Dangi's supporters who thought him to be Abhay Singh.

Such murky goings-ons during the Meham by-election cast their shadow over Chautala, Devi Lal and the National Front government as well. Despite the dangers of hitting out at Devi Lal and the pregnant silence of V.P. Singh, a five member committee consisting of Ajit Singh, Madhu Dandavate, George Fernandes, Sharad Yadav and Yashwant Sinha conveyed to V.P. Singh by March 3, 1990 that Chautala should resign as Chief Minister of Haryana.[8]

Tau Devi Lal, the patriarch of Haryana politics, the representative of rural India who had vanquished Rajiv Gandhi sitting on his *charpoy* or travelling in his Vijay Rath, now came under attack from his partymen. As the kingmaker who made V.P. Singh Prime Minister, *Tau* wanted to stride the country like a Collosus and this he had been doing with impunity, addressing the Press, causing a rural-urban divide, enunciating all manner of policy pronouncement and creating confusion all around, yet unperturbed by the storms he left in his wake.

The final straw, besides minor irritants in the jockeying for spheres of influence within the Janata Dal, was the visit of arch Jat rival Ajit Singh to Meham and his demand for Chautala's resignation.

On March 16 at a Political Affairs Committee meeting Devi Lal crossed swords with Arun Nehru and Ajit Singh and stormed out of the meeting, resigning for sixty hours while the National Front government came across its first major crisis. Devi Lal found that despite his calculations, there were not many within the Party who shared his blind love for Om Prakash Chautala. Realising that he had picked the wrong moment and the wrong issue to flex his musles within the Party, and disappointed that neither Chief Ministers nor MPs loyal to him were willing to sacrifice their chairs for him, the *Tau* agreed to withdraw his resignation. The master strategist V.P. Singh maintained an enigmatic neutrality as he was sure that Devi Lal's antics would gradually erode his support within the Party and that he would continue to make gaffes and blunders so that one day V.P. Singh would be able to remove his Deputy Prime Minister without a murmur of protest from either within or outside the government.

The May 20th Elections for the post of Interim President of the Janata Dal showed the schisms in the Party. Once again the Devi Lal-Chautala combine rallied behind former Karnataka Chief Minister S.R. Bommai who won against V.P.'s nominee Jaipal Reddy, in spite of the Prime Minister's professed and conspicuous neutrality.

Unlike February when V.P. Singh hesitated to beard the lion in its den by May 19th, he decided that Chautala would have to resign from the Chief Ministership of Haryana. Amiri Singh, an independent candidate, had been shot dead and this time a 10-member Janata Dal Political Affairs Committee had resolved that should Chautala fail to resign he would be expelled from the Party. If Devi Lal resigned he would be allowed to do so as V.P. Singh had enlisted the support both of the Left Parties as well as that of the BJP which made his resolve firm taking firm steps in Haryana.

As Party President V.P. Singh made Bommai bell the cat. Both father and son were told of the party's decision, reiterated by Biju Patnaik and Chimanbhai Patel who were considered part of the Devi Lal faction. For once the father son duo were unable to extricate themselves from the crisis and Om Prakash Chautala had to make way for Banarsi Das Gupta as Chief Minister of Haryana. The folly of dynastic politics once more became evident when the feud between Devi Lal's two sons, Ranjit and Om Prakash, came to the fore and Devi Lal felt that Ranjit Singh was part of the conspiracy to defame and humiliate him.[9]

The farce, drama and factional politics of the National Front government went on while the Nation watched the 1977 Janata Party nightmare being repeated. Devi Lal attacked Arun Nehru and Arif Mohammed Khan, Ramakrishna Hegde resigned, V.P. Singh submitted his resignation to Party President S.R. Bommai and sheepishly took it back, Chautala was reinstated as Haryana Chief Minister and then forced to resign. And so it continued as forewarned by Rajiv Gandhi that if installed to govern, the National Front dramas would be as entertaining as a "nautanki"! But the acrimonious exchanges, deeply embedded rivalries and groupism of the Party and Cabinet did not abate as an injured Devi Lal came back from his sojourn at a nature cure resort in Bangalore to turn afresh on his bete noires, Arun Nehru and finally V.P. Singh himself. With despite individuals from different political ideologies and idiosyncracies trying to blend together to lead the country harmoniously, supported by the extreme left and the extreme Right, V.P. Singh had to exercise all his machiavellian and manipulative skills at his command to keep the government from capsizing.

In the end, it all degenerated into an unsavoury episode of who did what to whom. Did Devi Lal and V.P. Singh agreed to Chautala's reinstallation? Did Ajit Singh's pretensions as Jat leader annoy Devi Lal? Why did Arun Nehru and Devi Lal become implacable foes? Did the *Tau* call V.P. Singh "spineless?" Were Chandra Sekhar and Mulayam Singh supporting the *Tau* to secure their own political ends against the Prime Minister? These and some other questions, endless speculations and permutations and combinations provided the columinists, cartoonists and mischief-makers with more than enough material than they could handle.

On 29th July 1990 the Cabinet meeting discussed the forged letter forwarded to the Prime Minister by Devi Lal. V.P. Singh sought the Deputy Prime Minister's explanation for these and the *Illustrated Weekly* interview. Devi Lal realised that he had little support and Arun Nehru became emboldened to stick to his threat of resigning unless the *Tau* made his exit from the Cabinet. Cornered, V.P. Singh was forced to ask a written explanation from Devi Lal who now vacillated between regret and sullen defiance. Devi Lal's interview with *Illustrated Weekly* was full of injudicious, intemperate and indiscreet remarks about his Cabinet colleagues—"Arun Nehru represents the selfish interests of the urban lobby and big business. So does that chap Arif. Gujral is a wimp. Satyapal Mallick is a useless cheer leader... But we carry them along as extra baggage because V.P. Singh does not have the political will—and the spine—to stand by what is right."

Shedding his customary "everything is fine and we are stronger because of the crisis" routine, V.P. Singh finally admitted to newsmen that there was a crisis within the Party. By August 1st, after consulting his senior party colleagues such as S.R. Bommai, Arun Nehru, George Fernandes, Sharad Yadav and Biju Patnaik amongst others, V.P. Singh resorted to the extreme step of asking the President to dismiss the Deputy Prime Minister.

Devi Lal had refused to eat humble pie and said that his explanation was tantamount to an apology. Why should he be made victim by the urban clique and bring evidence to substantiate allegations against Arif Mohammed and Arun Nehru? It was an irony of fate that one of the prime architects of the Janata Dal and V.P. Singh's rise to premiership should now say:

"They are asking me for evidence against Arun Nehru. Could they produce any evidence against Rajiv Gandhi on the Bofors issue? They won the election on the basis of innunedo."

After consulting, ironically enough, Chandra Shekhar against whom he had conspired in making V.P. Singh the Prime Minister. Devi Lal decided to address the Press corps saying that he would hold a farmers' rally at the Boat Club on August 9. Besides his sons Ranjit Singh and Om Prakash Chautala, Jagdeep Dhankad (who resigned from the Ministry in protest), Mahendra Singh Tikait, the maverick leader of the Bharatiya Kisan Union, was aiso consulted.

V.P. Singh was concerned at the *Tau's* belligerence and manoeuvred to have a meeting of the National Front parliamentary party to affirm their faith in his leadership. Although Devi Lal and Chandra Shekhar also attended this meeting they kept away during the show of hands, otherwise maintaining a cool facade. Taking a leaf out of the Raja's own book when V.P. Singh affirmed "Rajiv is my leader", the *Tau* did not hold V.P. Singh responsible for his dismissal but declared him to be "innocent and trapped", surrounded by conspirators who did not desire the government to complete its five-year tenure!

This line was a cleverly planned move adopted by Chandra Shekhar and Mulayam Singh Yadav. Mahendra Singh Tikait was also on Devi Lal's side, along with 28 MPs who signed a letter of protest at the manner of the *Tau's* dismissal. The Haryana government headed by Hukam Singh, a Chautala stooge, was also clearly on the Chaudhury's side and Devi Lal became an epicentre for dissident moves against V.P. Singh.

V.P. Singh made attempts to initiate some moves to dislodge the Hukam Singh ministry in Haryana so that he could deprive Devi Lal of the vital support of the Haryana government, crucial to him at this juncture. He also put off the Cabinet expansion so that MP's would tag on with V.P. in the hope of a ministerial berth.

The facade of the National Front government crumbled as rival factions declared an open war on each other. Each side had to beat the other in a shameful game of one upmanship in which the economy, foreign policy and all other significant issues took a back seat. The government and its Prime Minister were so preoccupied by their political manoeuvers that the takeover of Kuwait by Iraq on August 2 hardly elicited a suitable reaction from the government.

The conflict between Devi Lal and V.P. Singh, stemming as it did from a Dhritarashtra-like obsession for his son to remain Chief Minister of Haryana, now spilled over to the body politic and assumed the hue of a rural-urban, English-Hindi, farmers-office goers and caste-based issue. All eyes were now focussed on Devi Lal's Boat Club rally on August 9 which would decide the political viability of India's rural leader. V.P. Singh and Rajiv Gandhi were also invited to address the rally, although the Prime Minister abstained as he thought Rajiv Gandhi would be present.

The power struggle which could have been labelled either rural versus urban, Jan Morcha versus Lok Dal, feudalism versus liberalism was in fact a clash between a wrestler and a chess player. Devi Lal was given the midnight sack and was literally caught napping, V.P. Singh's image had been lily white but craftily cultivated with the aid of the Press who attributed to him a messianic role. Now Devi Lal's bluff had been called, the dubious role of his sons exposed and his pretensions to inherit Charan Singh's mantle questioned. Devi Lal was not unique among Indian politicians due to nepotism, a blinkered world vision or his bullying ways. What did him in was his blunt tongue and the impression that he was out to destabilise the government.

Faced with this challenge, the real V.P. Singh had to shed his carefully crafted skin and come to the fore. This response to the challenge was evident in his speech to the Parliamentary Party when he spoke about the requirement of a proper agricultural policy, land reforms and concessions for the Backward and Scheduled Castes.

As a fallout of Devi Lal's exit there was a question mark over the AJGAR factor the famous Ahir, Jat, Gujar, Rajput combine which formed the support base of the Janata Dal. During the November '89 elections, Mr. Ram Vilas Paswan had said, It is actually Homajgar, our base includes Harijans and Muslims" and ignoring the crudely casteist slant he reiterated. "And never mind the criticism, this combination, whatever you call it, includes the majority of our people."[10]

With just 137 seats in the Lok Sabha and a mere percentage of the votes V.P. Singh and his Janata Dal were on a sticky wicket and hence the constant insecurity. Devi Lal was not to be allowed to walk away with a segment of the Janata Dal vote block. For all his folksy tales and rustic manners, Devi Lal represented the rural rich, the kulak who did not pay income tax, yet presented a sharp contrast to the poor peasant who had been reduced to the status of an agricultural labourer eking out a precarious existence. As Nikhil Chakravarty observed, "this bogey of rural India being suppressed by the urbanites is thoroughly bogus and moreover a social survey would indicate" that it is the veto of the rich farmers that decides the fate of all social legislations "whether it is on the question of dowry, child marriage, temple entry or the persistence of sati and untouchability, the accussing finger of any social reformer has to be pointed to the entrenched class of the rural rich." The question of a dowry-related suicide was earlier hushed up in Devi Lal's family when his grand daughter-in-law committed suicide.

All these aspects of the *Tau* were now forgotten and he was projected as an injured victim who would tell his tale of woes to the lakhs of farmers being rushed to the capital in a show of solidarity for his farmers' leader whose "pagri" had been disgraced.

The above political development causing political inequilibrium within National Front Party forced V.P. Singh to tactically use trump card of backward classes and implemented recommendations of the Mandal Commission Report by issuing an executive order.

Implementing the Report

The decision to implement the Mandal Commission Report was tucked away in a remote corner of the National Front election manifesto, along with the intention of "substantial reservation in employment, education and public offices to Backward Classes." However, the timing of V.P. Singh's announcement of the government's decision to accept the Mandal Report in the Lok Sabha on August 7, 1990 raised a question over his actual motives in making such a declaration, and that too without any discussion either within the party or with its supporters, the Leftists and the BJP.

The Mandal Commission was set up by the Morarji Desai Janata government in 1977, probably as an offshoot of the analysis of Indira Gandhi's poll debacle, which proved that her overwhelming defeat was chiefly brought about by *en masse* voting of the politically awakened Backward Classes. Ram Manohar Lohia provided the ideological thrust to this move to cultivate the Backward Classes and cause a new equation between class conflict and caste contradictions.

Because of the political upheavals which beset the first non-Congress government at the Centre and the Assembly and Lok Sabha elections which followed in quick succession, the Mandal Report was submitted only in December 1980 to Indira Gandhi. Mrs. Gandhi neither shelved the Report nor did she accept it. Rather, she discreetly set it aside and the Opposition also equally judiciously let it remain on the shelf for the reason that they also felt a sense of uneasiness handling it.

The Mandal Report itself touched upon the fact that like the proverbial cat with nine lives, the all-powerful caste system too has the immense capacity to survive and take shape according to contemporary needs so that even centuries of social reformers have not been able to eradicate its prenicious hold over Indian society. While every Prime Minister from Jawaharlal Nehru, Shastri, Indira Gandhi, Morarji Desai, and Charan Singh to Rajiv Gandhi had the option of caste-fragmentaion, coupled with the established constitutional precedent of reservation for Scheduled Castes and Scheduled Tribes, none till the arrival of V.P. Singh had used it so blatantly and for such narrow partisan ends. It was evident therefore that this new-found empathy for the Backward Classes was motivated purely by political arithmetic and as a weapon to seize the political initiative from Devi Lal and all his other political opponents, for it would be political suicide for any politician to oppose the Report.

If a man's true calibre is tested during times of stress and challenge, then the real V.P. Singh finally stood exposed as he was, without the image of *messiah* and idealist thrust on him by the Press. It was not a *volte face*, merely a question of the quintessential V.P. Singh finally revealing himself to the public for what he was—a self-centred politician ready for any alliance, any proposal and any compromise for one more day in power. Since he had a great capacity for self-righteousness, even the basest motive could be camoulflaged by high-sounding rhetoric. Since several people and especially the Press had portrayed him as a knight in shining armour, a David who slayed Goliath, a man imbued with great idealism, the transition or transformation from myth to reality came as a shock. Hence the violence and villification, especially by the printed media. It was sad that V.P. Singh was now called the "Artful Dodger", and the only politician/Prime Minister "who does not look you in the eye." Had people recognised the real V.P. Singh earlier instead of perpetrating and idolising a myth, the nation would have been saved a great deal of trauma and bloodshed. But it was now too late. Like the spoken word or the sped arrow, the vote once cast cannot be reversed in a hurry and the people and the Press had to pay the price for their actions.[11]

The Lok Sabha Announcement

While Ram Avedesh Singh had his day, V.P. Singh announced in the Lok Sabha on August 7, 1990 the decision to reserve 27 per cent jobs for socially and educationally Backward Classes in Central Government services and public sector undertakings. Based on the Mandal Report the reservation would be applicable, in the first phase, to castes which are common to both the Mandal Commission lists and those prepared by the State governments. This was being done so that the experience of these States in successfully preparing lists of the socially and economically Backward Classes could be utilised to make sure "harmonious and quick implementation" of the policy.

Describing it as a "momentous decision of social justice," the Prime Minister said this step fulfilled the National Front's commitment to the people. He further added, "It is a negation of the basic structure of our Constitution that till now this requirement was not fulfilled," as he noted that the Constitution envisaged that the problems of the socially and economically Backward Classes be identified and eradicated.

He also referred to his announcement of April 4, 1990 and designated the Ambedkar centenary as the "Year of Social Justice." In addition, the government would take further steps for uplifting the Scheduled Castes, Scheduled Tribes and weaker sections.

In a letter dated August 6, which was flashed in the Press on August 10 and August 11, 1990, circulated to Members of

Parliament Vishwanath Pratap Singh mentioned that the government proposed to enact legislation providing for reservations for SCs and STs in Central government services which are presently enforced through executive instructions, as legislation would carry greater respect and led to more effective enforcement. In addition, he said that the government was ready to come up with a Constitution amendment bill to reserve 40 per cent of the seats in Parliament and in the State Assemblies for the poor.

Although the Parliamentary debate on the Prime Minister's Mandal announcement revealed that all members who congratulated the decision mostly belonged to the Backward Classes irrespective of party affiliation such as P. Shiv Shankar and Madhavsingh Solanki of the Congress (I), Pramod Mahajan (BJP), Ram Avadesh Singh (LD), Khalilur Rehman (IDP), S.P. Malviya (JD), the timing was universally condemned as being hypocritical and politically motivated.

The Devi Lal Rally

On August 9, 1990 all roads led to the Boat Club rally at India Gate.[12] A larger-than-life cardboard cutout of Devi Lal and the colour green dominated the scene as lakhs of farmers from Delhi, Haryana, Rajasthan and Uttar Pradesh marched in to support their leader. While the Intelligence Bureau conservatively estimated the number of farmers at 1,30,000 more realistic estimates said that between two to five lakh were in attendance. Aided by the Bharatiya Kisan Union's (BKU) Mahendra Singh Tikait and the Bahujan Samaj Party's (BSP's) Kanshi Ram, an impressive turnout had been organised and it was clear that the *Tau* had pulled off a major victory.

Encouraged by the large crowds, Devi Lal gave a speech which was full of anecdotes and witticisms designed to go down well with rural folk. Although he did not openly attack V.P. Singh, he did so indirectly saying that he had lost confidence in those he had elevated to office. However, others were not so subtle with Mahendra Singh Tikait threatening to gauge out V.P. Singh eyes and others calling him Raja Jaichand and Capitalist crony. Other stalwarts in attendance included Chandra Shekhar, Prakash Singh Badal, Hukam Deo Narayan Yadav, H.D. Deva Gowda and Jagdeep

Dhankad. Even an overcast sky and brief spells of sharp showers could not act as a deterrent.

Devi Lal exhorted the farmers to realise their power and appealed to them to collect a rupee from each voter and send it to him by money order so that he could conduct the struggle for a fair deal to farmers and workers. With their assistance he boasted that the Janata Dal would secure 328 out of 542 seats in the next parliamentary polls.

V.P. Singh's Efforts to Sabotage the Rally

Showing his desperation, V.P. Singh inducted Ajit Singh to make sure that the Kisan rally flopped. Ajit Singh, angling for the post of Deputy Prime Minister on the formula of Jat replacing Jat, was found too willing to oblige. A Sabotage Committee comprising Sharad Yadav (Textile minister), George Fernandes (Railways), Ram Vilas Paswan (Labour) and Ajit Singh (Industries) was constituted to subtly defuse the threat from Devi Lal.[13]

Speaking to all District Magistrates and Superintendents of Police in western U.P. and instructing them to thwart the rally organisers, Ajit Singh also called upon the President of the Haryana Truck Owners Union and asked him not to give any vehicles to the rally supporters. The U.P. administration announced the cancellation of all trains to Delhi and also issued instructions to private bus owners not to allow their vehicles to be hired for carting people to Delhi.

When Vasant Sathe of Congress (I) alleged in Parliament that trains via Ghaziabad and Sahibabad were cancelled to stop people from attending Devi Lal's rally, the former Railway Minister Madhav Rao Scindia commented that perhaps for the first time the railways had joined politics. However, this was not surprising as under the guise of value-based politics all kinds of firsts were taking place under the National Front government.[14] At 6 p.m. the Railway Minister demolished the allegations, however, by declaring that trains on the line had been diverted resulting in a delay of three to seven hours as the scheduled remodelling scheme was being implemented. He also held that it was not the government's intention to continue the tradition of stalling any political or Kisan rallies, in an obvious dig at the previous regime.

Despite these protestations however, and with the announcement of the Mandal Commission's implementation to secure the support of the Backward Classes, the attempts to declare the rally a flop continued. At noon, Ajit Singh passed a slip to V.P. Singh in the Lok Sabha saying that at noon there were just 25,000 people. But as reports by the I.B. and Janata Dal MP's who had visited the scene of action came in, it was not possible to neglect the presence of between three to five lakh farmers.

A livid Raja summoned Ajit Singh and gave him a piece of his mind. Ajit Singh's plea that he had been in charge of only western U.P. and that a majority of farmers had come in from Haryana and Rajasthan could cut no ice with the Raja. In fact as many as seventeen buses had come from Ajit Singh's constituency Baghpat alone.

The "flip-flop" man of the Janata Dal was a loser both ways as he had lost face with the Prime Minister and destroyed his standing with the Jat masses by conspiring against their two *messiahs*—Devi Lal and Tikhait.

Post-Rally Scenario

Although Devi Lal's dismissal did not lead to a split in the party, the success of the Rally nevertheless proved that he could summon vast multitudes to his side if needed and that he could not be neglected or insulted without repercussions following suit.

On 10th August, the Janata Dal luminaries huddled at 7, Race Course Road, and V.P. Singh, Bommai and others decided that a compromise would have to be made with the *Tau*. The Principal Crisis Manager (PCM) of the Party, Orissa Chief Minister Biju Patnaik was asked to mediate and work out a compromise formula in which the *Tau* would be reinstated, his son Ranjit Singh accommodated and efforts to destabilise the Haryana government of Hukam Singh would be discontinued.

Emboldened and bolstered by the success of the Rally, Devi Lal was now no longer in a mood to see reason. Rather, he declared his intention of organising farmers' rallies throughout the country to acquaint people with the government's anti-farmer and anti-poor policies. Vishwanath Pratap Singh had to shed his enigmatic silence and tackle a belligerent *Tau*. The race for irresponsible populism and dangerous concessions to every possible vote bank had started and August 15, 1990 saw V.P. Singh shedding one image and adopting another as he unfurlled the national flag at Red Fort and submitted himself to utilising the occasion to a partisan election manifesto, as though in preparation for a mid term poll. The Devi Lal Rally had proved that the *Tau* was wounded but not maimed and even while remaining within the Party, the former Deputy Prime Minister was determined to attack those who presided over the nation's destiny.

In August 1990, the Nation was not in a hurry to go back to Congress rule and despite the *Tau's* dismissal there was no genuine threat to Vishwanath Pratap Singh. However the strained relationship between *Tau* and V.P. Singh, the steep rise in prices, the Gulf crisis and the other feuds within the Janata Dal made the Prime Minister insecure and he felt compelled to enhance his personal appeal. Neither a confrontation nor a reconciliation and the reinstatement of Devi Lal was possible. Psychologically, V.P. Singh had always been a loner and before he combined the Opposition into a political alternative, it appeared that he was a Don Quixote tilting at windmills. Having rallied the people and a fragmented opposition into a winning proposition V.P. Singh did not want to lose his hard earned achievements so early. At all times he was determined to retain the political initiative—whether by floating the idea of a national government, by resigning or by taking recourse to such populist gimmicks as *amiri rekha*, Kisan Decade, a National Commission for Women or the declaration of a national holiday on Prophet Mohammed's birthday. It was only when he hastily announced the acceptance of the Mandal Commission Report that V.P. Singh, like the proverbal spider, became enmeshed in his own web. For the first time his calculations went wrong and he had bitten off more than what he could chew.

The 15th August Speech

The speech by Vishwanath Pratap Singh from the ramparts of the historic Red Fort revealed him to be "the classic Hindi-belt demagogue",[15] who in his 75-minute mawkishly emotional speech poetry, promises, populism and platitudes as he pulled out a populist plum for nearly every section that had access to a ballot paper.

Not only were the viewers on national television who witnessed this astonishing speech shocked, but so too was the media. *The Indian Express*[16] which had its own contribution to the election of V.P. Singh denounced the Prime Minister in its editorial saying that the political platform he was constructing in preparation for the mid-term poll would "plunge the country into great trouble...Palpable in all this is an attempt to weave together a coalition of the Muslims and the Scheduled Castes along with the Other Backward Classes (OBCs) who have been presented with the decision to implement the Mandal Commission's Report. To leave nothing to chance, the farmers in general are sought to be won over by the declaration that the 1990's would be observed as a `kisan decade' and women, by the promise of legislation this year to reserve 30 per cent of the seats in Panchayats for them."

The editorial continued that such politics were a continuation of the old KHAM and AJGAR ideas which had incensed both caste and communal passions in states like Gujarat, Bihar and Uttar Pradesh. They expressed disappointment that instead of addressing to national issues from a national perspective the Prime Minister had sought " to give to politics at the national level the parochial and therefore disastrous character which has brought Bihar and Uttar Pradesh to their present pass."

The sense of shock and injury pervading the tone of the *Express* editorial was all the more ironic in light of its role in propelling V.P. Singh to the forefront of national politics. However, V.P. Singh had himself stated that he would be a "disaster as Prime Minister" and his tenure made his apprehension a reality. The *Telegraph*[17] panned the timing and motives behind the implementation of the Mandal Report as did several other newspapers and magazines throughout the country. The political opportunism and the man whose "vision of the country was that of a policeman's" stood exposed.

Populism and political gimmickry which had been made into a fine art by Indira Gandhi had now degenerated into blatant, destructive political opportunism for selfish and sectarian ends. The rag-tag band of men who boasted of themselves as leaders were in fact, intellectual pygmies with narrow and selfish ends. When Devi Lal spoke of the urban versus rural population his heart represented not landless labour, the sharecropper or the rural artisan but the greedy kulaks. When the Agricultural Prices Commission, at the *Tau*'s behest, raised the purchase price of sugarcane in Uttar Pradesh from Rs. 21.50 to Rs. 42.00 it served to benefit a mere three per cent of sugar farmers, mostly in the Jat belt. Same way, the rise in the procurement prices of rice and wheat hit the small farmers in unirrigated areas with near starvation. The *Tau's* eagerness to have a head count of Ambassadors, Governors, MPs and IAS Officers hailing from village post-office addresses was an extension of the Kulaks' desire to have their own *biradari* in the bureaucracy. And Mulayam Singh Yadav's allergy for English stemmed not only from his lack of proficiency in the language but also from pure political logic and an understanding of the numbers game. Approximately 110 million rural youth were there on the job market but were unfit for employment either in a purely rural or urban environment. They are, in reality, the semi-educated youth who cannot till the land as their fathers did due to the drudgery and hard work involved, yet who have been corrupted by the TV - Video values to hanker for the "easy life" and easy money of the big city. The obsession with abolishing English, reserving jobs and harping on the urban-rural divide by politicians are all undertaken with an eye on the opportunity of securing votes and grabbing power. It is this segment of the youth who are too good for the professions of their forefathers but not good enough to compete in urban areas who turned to terrorist activity in the Punjab or serve as the political *goondas* and hangers-on of the politicians. Instead of addressing themselves to some very genuine problems faced by this section of the youth who need employment, guidance and rural industries to channelise their energies, selfish politicians champion their causes for their self-aggrandisement.[18]

Given the background of V.P. Singh's shaky accession to power, the lack of cohesion and high ideals among the leaders of the Janata Dal, the hasty decision on the Mandal Commission was only to be expected. If politics were to be a game of calculation then V.P. Singh was master of the game. But politics goes beyond the calculation of even the wiliest or most powerful politician. In implementing the Mandal Report V.P. Singh's carefully thought out schemes backfired on him and in stirring the cauldron of caste he had gone too far to return. He never anticipated the violence, the demonstrations and the self-immolations in which hundreds lost their lives and which ultimately led to the fall of his government. V.P. Singh's sympathy for the poor and downtrodden were not Gandhian and thus as Gandhi would have said, the ends cannot justify the means and even good intentions become vitiated if the means used are not pure. More than any other factor, the Mandal Report exposed V.P. Singh as a politician who went to any lengths to cling to power, with the ultimate disgrace of being voted out of office on the floor of Parliament. However, such is the resilience of politicians and so short is public memory that the fires which he stoked from August to October 1990 may ignite again. A recurrence of such fragmentation in the name of justice for the Backward Classes may be used in the future with grave consequences for the nation and all its people.

Office Memorandum of P.V. Narasimha Rao Government

"No. 36012/31/90—Estt (SCT)

Government of India

Ministry of Personnel, Public Grievances & Pensions

(Deptt. of Personnel & Training)

Office Memorandum

New Delhi, the 25th September, 1991

Subject: Recommendation of the Second Backward Classes Commission (Mandal Report)—Reservation for Socially and Educationally Backward Classes in Service under the Government of India.

The undersigned is directed to invite the attention to O.M. of even number dated the 13th August, 1990 on the above sections of the SEBCs to receive the benefits of reservation on a preferential basis and to provide reservation for other economically backward section of the people not covered by any of the existing schemes of reservation, Government have decided to amend the said Memorandum with immediate effect as follows :

2. (i) Within the 27 per cent of the vacancies in civil posts and services under the Government of India reserved for SEBCs, preference shall be given to candidates belonging

to the poorer sections of the SEBCs. In case sufficient number of such candidates are not available, unfilled vacancies shall be filled by the other SEBC candidates.

(ii) 10 per cent of the vacancies in civil posts and services under the Government of India shall be reserved for other economically backward sections of the people who are not covered by any of the existing schemes of reservation.

(iii) The criteria for determining the poorer sections of the SEBCs or the other economically backward sections of the people who are not covered by any of the existing schemes of reservations are being issued separately.

3. The O.M. of even number dated the 13th August 1990, shall be deemed to have been amended to the extent specified above.

Sd/-
(A.K. Harit)
Deputy Secretary to the Govt. of India"

References

1. *India Today*, June 30, 1989, p. 52.
2. *Ibid.*, Nov. 30, 1987, pp. 70-72.
3. *The Illustrated Weekly of India*, pp. 32-33, Bahujan Samaj Party 'Will It Survive?' Nov. 15, 1987, S.S. Gill.
4. *India Today*, Nov. 30, 1989.
5. *Sunday*, Aug. 19-25, 1990, p. 27.
6. *Sunday*, Sept. 16-22, 1990.
7. *India Today*, S. Nihal Singh, "Playing Politics", p. 167.
8. *India Today*, March 31, 1990, pp. 30-33.
9. *Sunday*, Aug. 12-18, 1990, pp. 26-33 and p. 12.
10. *The Telegraph*, Aug. 12, 1990, 'The Ajgar Cracks', Sankarshan Thakur, p. 9.
11. *The Times of India*, Aug. 8, 1990.
12. *The Telegraph*, Aug. 10, 1990/*The Indian Express*, Aug. 10, 1990/*The Telegraph*, Aug. 10, 1990.
13. *Sunday*, Aug. 19-25, 1990.
14. *The Telegraph*, Aug. 9, 1990.
15. *Sunday*, Aug. 26-1 Sept., 1990, pp. 23-28.
16. *The Indian Express*, Aug. 17, 1990.
17. *The Telegraph*, Aug. 9, 1990.
18. *The Times of India*, Sunil Sethi, "Who Does Devi Lal's Heart Bleed For?"

Two

Mandal and Media: Views of Cross Sections of Society

Govt. accepts Mandal panel report
27 per cent job quota for Backward Classes
Indian Express, New Delhi, Aug. 8, 1990

The National Front Government has decided, for the first time since independence, to give job reservation to socially and educationally backward classes (SEBCs) in the country in pursuance of the Mandal Commission recommendations.

This was announced by the Prime Minister, Mr. Vishwanath Pratap Singh, in both Houses of Parliament on Tuesday, amid much applause from all sections, cutting across party lines.

In his suo motu statement, the Prime Minister said the reservation for the SEBCs — Government of India and Public Sector Undertakings - would be 27 per cent.

This raises to 49.5 per cent the total reservation of jobs for various classes, since there is already a reservation of 15 per cent for the Scheduled Castes and 7.5 per cent for the Scheduled Tribes. This is in keeping with a Supreme Court directive in 1980 not to exceed the reservations by 50 per cent.

In his statement, Mr. Singh pointed out that in order to avail of the benefit of the long experience of a number of states in preparing lists of SEBCs and in order to ensure harmonious and quick implementation, the Government had decided to adopt, in the first phase, the castes common to both the Mandal list as well as the State lists.

The Prime Minister said the second Backward Classes Commission under the chairmanship of the late Mr. B.P. Mandal, which was appointed on January 1, 1979, submitted its report on

December 31, 1980. "In accordance with our commitment before the people we included this in our action plan. After examining various aspects of it, I am glad to announce that my Government has taken these decisions on the Mandal Commission's report."

Expressing his happiness over what he called a momentous decision of social justice, the Prime Minister recalled the Constitutional provisions envisaging that socially and educationally backward classes be identified, their difficulties removed and their conditions improved in terms of Article 340(1) read with Article 15(4) as well as Article 16(4). It was a negation of the basic structure of the Constitution that till now this requirement was not fulfilled, he added.

The suo motu statement of the Prime Minister was, however, not without opposition from the Congress-I benches.

The leader of the opposition, Mr. P. Shiv Shankar, said, even before the Prime Minister made his statement, that it could wait till Wednesday noon since the House was occupied with the ongoing debate on the price situation. He said he did not want to minimise the importance of the Government's decisions on the Mandal Commission report. Mr. Shiv Shankar also pointed out that as the House business time for the day had been fixed till 5 p.m., he would like to appeal to the Prime Minister to make the statement the next day.

The leader of the House, Mr. M.S. Gurupadaswamy, did not agree with Mr. Shiv Shankar and said that there was no precedent when the Prime Minister had been stopped from making a statement.

He wondered whether there were some other reasons behind the request of the Congress-I for a postponement of the statement.

Mr Gurudas Das Gupta (CPI) also said it was up to the House to decide on the duration of the sitting and never before had the freedom of a Prime Minister to make a statement been questioned by any member.

Mr. M.C. Bhandare (Cong-I) said the matter had not come up suddenly warranting an immediate Government statement. It was not possible to make off-the-cuff clarifications at a short notice unless making a statement was unavoidable, he said.

The issue generated much heat during which several other Congress-I members vociferously pleaded for the postponement of the statement until Wednesday while the treasury benches wanted that the same should be done on Tuesday itself.

The Deputy Chairperson, Dr Najma Heptullah, ruled that the Prime Minister could make the statement while the members could seek clarifications on Wednesday. Both sides then agreed to the Chair's ruling.

Dr Heptullah said a supplementary list of business was circulated in the afternoon indicating that a suo motu statement would be made by the Prime Minister at 4.30 p.m. but this could not be done because of the Business Advisory Committee meeting scheduled at the same time.

The Prime Minister, who was allowed to make his statement after the noisy scenes which lasted for 25 minutes, concluded his statement by reminding the House that on April 14 this year at a function to celebrate the late Dr. Ambedkar's birthday, he had announced that the Ambedkar centenary year would be observed as the "Year of Social Justice"

He said a number of measures aimed at improving the lot of weaker sections had been announced in keeping with the same. "The present decisions are in the same line and belong to the tradition of this Government's dedication to the cause of the Scheduled Castes, Scheduled Tribes, Socially and Educationally Backward Classes and other weaker sections," he added.

The Prime Minister made an identical statement on the Mandal Commission in the Lok Sabha before the House was adjourned for the day.

The presidium of the National Union of Backward Classes, Scheduled Castes, Scheduled Tribes and Minorities on Tuesday congratulated the Prime Minister for implementation the Mandal Commission's recommendations.

In a statement here, the president of the Presidium and former Union Agriculture Minister, Choudhary Brahm Prakash said that the implementation of the Mandal Commission was long overdue.

He said that the National Front Government had fulfilled

yet another of its commitments by raising the reservation quota for Backward Classes including Scheduled Castes and Tribes and other backward classes.

Mandal: Champion of backward classes?

Indian Express, Patna, Aug 19, 1990

The late Bindeshwari Prasad Mandal, whose eponymous report on reservation for Backward Classes in Central services has become a hot topic of debate all over the country, was a curious amalgam of pride and prejudice, tinged with fierce individualism.

Scion of a zamindari family of undivided Saharsa district, Mandal was a survivor of the troubled waters of the State's politics the waves of which buffeted him from the Congress to the Sanyukta Socialist Party (SSP) of those days.

After remaining with the Congress from 1952 to 1964, he attained the dubious distinction of being the first MLA to cross the floor and go over to the opposition. He chose a good cause - but more of that later.

He also had the distinction of being the second Backward Class politician to become Chief Minister of Bihar, succumbing to the temptation of the Congress bigwigs, led by the intrepid Mr. K. Sahay, who had months ago been thrown out of power following the rout of the Congress in the 1967 Assembly Elections which resulted in the installation of the first United Front Government in the State.

This was perhaps the stormiest period in his life when, after he defected from the first non-Congress Government in Bihar, he became the butt of ridicule for some but a messiah for the Backward Classes.

Ironical

The irony of it all is that he was elected to the Lok Sabha in the 1967 election and hankered after a ministerial berth in the United Front outfit, headed by the late Mahamaya Prasad Sinha, who then belonged to the Jana Kranti Dal, of which Mr. Mohan Singh Oberoi, of the famed chain of hotels, was a member.

In those days, Dr. Ram Manohar Lohia, who was the guiding

star of the SSP, was dead-set against party members quitting the Lok Sabha and joining ministries in the State. His arguments were to no avail, however, and Mandal became Health Minister.

The Sinha Ministry was in office for barely six months when, in October, the Government constituted, by a notification, the Aiyar Commission of inquiry to probe charges of corruption against six top leaders of the Bihar Congress - K.B. Sahay, Maheshwar Prasad Sinha, Ambika Sharan Singh, Raghavendra Prasad Singh, Mr. Satyendra Narain Sinha and Mr. Ram Lakhan Singh Yadav.

The first four have since passed away. Five of the "accused" were indicted by the commission, Mr. Satyendra Narain Sinha escaping by the skin of his teeth.

Boiling with rage, the Congress leaders started scratching their heads to find out how the Ministry could be brought down. It was K.B. Sahay who struck upon the brights idea of drawing out Mandal and other backward class MLAs, who were then wooed intensively.

So it was that Mandal and 39 of his supporters broke away to form the "Shoshit Dal Ministry which ruled the roost for 49 days.

But Mandal could not immediately become Chief Minister. Mr Satish Prasad Singh, a staunch Mandal supporter was sworn in as Chief Minister as a stop-gap device. Mandal, meanwhile, was nominated as a member of The Legislative Council, whereupon Mr. Singh dutifully resigned and paved the way for Mandal who then became the second Backward Class Chief Minister of the State.

Penchant for Trouble

But the Congress got divided when over a dozen of its leaders quit to form the Lok Tantric Dal. Along with help from the constituents of the United Front, the Mandal Ministry, was brought down.

In 1972, Mandal was elected to the State Assembly. The 1974 JP movement was anathema to him, more so because he was against the SSP members resigning en masse from the Assembly to join the crusade against the Congress-I. In those days he lost no opportunity to berate Lok Nayak, even calling him 'a "dictator" at one point.

Mandal also had a penchant for creating a furore. Those were the days when the then Railway Minister, Lalit Narain Mishra's star was on the ascendant. But the Maithili Brahman members of the Assembly rose to a man and joined issue with him. The reason because he recited a salacious couplet - "gaya gach jis par bagula baitha gaya raj jis par Maithili baitha" (Gone is the tree on which a swallow perched. Gone is the throne on which a Maithili sat). In common parlance, Maithili stands for a Brahman of the Mithila region of Bihar.

JP, however, ignored Mandal's rantings against him and persuaded him to quit the Assembly, following his party's directive. The advice went home. The emergency was clamped, then lifted. The stormy petrel was elected to the Lok Sabha in 1977. He chose not to take a ministership at the State level this time.

Offer spurned

At the Centre, after lengthy confabulations, the setting-up of the Mandal Commission was announced on January 1, 1979. The report was submitted on December 13, 1980, when Indira Gandhi was Prime Minister.

According to vintage SSP leaders here, Mandal spurned the offer of a gubernatorial assignment made by Indira Gandhi if he incorporated "economic criterion" in his report.

A word more about his floor-crossing. Way back in 1964-65, there was an incident in which Koeris, a backward caste, were at the receiving end of violence in Para village in Saharsa district.

Mandal spoke vehemently against the "oppressors of the upper castes". There was a slanging match between the Congress and opposition members, with the then Chief Minister, Mr. K.B. Sahay keeping xnum. Infuriated by this Mandal, then in the Congress, crossed the floor to the accompaniment of greetings from the opposition members. It was the first time any member had crossed the floor in the State Assembly.

Mandal died a couple of years after submitting the report. He would have enjoyed the controversy generated by the Centre's decisions to implement his report.

Arun Shourie: Mandal: What he says and on what basis
Sub-Standard, by definition
Indian Express, 22.8.1990

It isn't just that by the grace of Mandal and of course the edict of V. P. Singh, half the posts throughout government are to be handed out on the basis of caste. It is that they are to be handed out to those who by definition are not qualified to man them.

For in addition to saying that 27 per cent of all posts in the government must be reserved for "Other Backward Classes" — a Goebbelsian euphemism if ever there was one, a euphemism to which I shall return-Mandal lays down that "Candidates belonging to OBCs recruited on the basis of merit in an open competition should NOT be adjusted against their reservation quota of 27 per cent." In other words, only those who do NOT qualify for the job on merit are to be counted to filling the quotas.

That will hold naturally not just for "Other Backward Classes" but also for the Scheduled Castes and Tribes for whom 22.5 per cent of all posts are already reserved.

And this quota is to apply not just at the time of entrance to a service but also "to promotion at all levels".

Furthermore, if a sufficient number of sub-standard candidates do not become available in a particular year to fill the quota; the unfilled margin is to be carried forward for three years.

A moment's reflection will show the consequence. Assume 100 candidates are to be recruited to a service every year. Under the new dispensation 50 are to be recruited on the basis of caste-plus-lack-of-merit. Assume — and that is the most conservative assumption one can make going by what Mandal says is the condition of these castes — assume that only 40 are available for the first few years who fit the twin criteria. In the second year the quota to be filled by those who by definition do not qualify to do so is not fifty but sixty, in the second year it is seventy, in third eighty!

And this scheme is to be mandatory not just for central government but also for all public sector undertakings, of both the central and state governments, the nationalised banks, "all private sector undertakings which have received financial assistance from the government in one form or the other", as well as "all universities and affiliated colleges."

And that is just one aspect of the matter. Mandal insists that government set up separate financial institutions which will cater exclusively to these "Other Backward Classes"; that it "advise and encourage" all State governments "to create a separate network of financial and technical institutions to foster business and industrial enterprise among OBCs"; that it set up a separate Backward Classes Development Corporation; that separate ministries be created at the Centre and in every state to "safeguard the interests" of the OBCs; .... that "all development programmes specially designed for Other Backward Classes should be financed by the Central Government in the same manner and to the same extent as (is) done in the case of Scheduled Castes and Tribes."

Thus: those who by definition do not qualify .for the job; recruitment as well as promotion; government service, public sector as well as the private sector; financial institutions as well as development allocations on the basis of caste.

Now, V.P. Singh insists that he is bound by the commitment on the Mandal Commission made by the National Front in its manifesto. But that commitment was not limited to reservations. It read:

"The recommendations (that means all the recommendations) of the Mandal Commission on Scheduled Castes and backward classes would be implemented expeditiously".

We must assume, therefore, that we are in for this entire chamber of lunacies. Unless, of course, we assume that V.P. Singh is one who keeps only half his word.

How does he get there?

But who are the "Other Backward Classes"? And how does Mandal identify them?

He is punctilious in setting standards. Criticising the First Backward Classes Commission set up in 1953 he notes that the Commission specified certain criteria for adjudging backwardness and then proceeded to list 2399 castes as backward. "But" he says, "it is not clear from the report as to how the lists of backward classes were derived from the application of that criteria".

"Repeated reminders", he says, "and contacts at personal level did not materially alter the situation".

"Several questions in this section", he records, "pertained to the representation of Other Backward Classes in elected bodies, services, etc. A couple of states have replied to these questions and even these replies are scrappy and inadequate."

"Only Gujarat has furnished information regarding representation of OBCs in local bodies ...," he says.

"Regarding the representation of OBCs in higher public services" he laments, "only a couple of states have given some information.."

"The above information is too sketchy and scrappy," he says, "for any meaningful inference which may be valid for the country as a whole."

"This section (entitled `Census')", he records, "sought to collect information on various demographic aspects of Other Backward Classes, denotified tribes, advanced castes and to compare lists of Other Backward Classes prepared by Kaka Kalelkar Commission with those notified by various state governments. The information supplied was very inadequate."

He notes the vast disparities in even the number of castes recognised as backward by the Kalelkar Commission and by the state governments: 124 versus 95 in Andhra; 44 versus 119 in Assam; 88 versus 64 in Haryana; 27 versus 48 in Himachal; 64 versus 181 in Karnataka; 48 versus 76 in Kerala; 360 versus 196 in Maharashtra; 148 versus 111 in Orissa; 88 versus 62 in Punjab; 156 versus 124 in Tamil Nadu; 120 versus 56 in UP.

The main reason for this; Mandal says, is that while the state governments "prepared their lists on the basis of some sort of field survey and investigation" the Kalelkar Commission "had mostly borrowed the lists prepared by the Ministry of Education for the award of post-Matric Scholarships"! Even that claim about "some sort of field survey and investigation" in the case of the former does not hold: just a few pages earlier Mandal himself says, as we noted a moment ago, that among these very states, Haryana, Himachal, Assam, Orissa had notified their lists "without ordering a formal inquiry into their conditions".

The second reason Mandal lists for the different numbers tells the tale even better: "Secondly", he records, "the pressure of field situation and local factors may have also influenced the judgment of state governments in the preparation of these lists".

To assess the position of the castes, Mandal needs data on their education levels. He asks the states, "No state government"; he says, "could furnish figures regarding the level of literacy and education amongst Other Backward Classes."

He needs data on their employment, the occupations on which they are dependent. "No state government could furnish any precise information on this point," he says.

And so on.

The Survey

He also orders a field survey to identify the backward castes. It is done under the supervision of the NSS, etc. But Mandal himself is very modest about its worth.

This is how he puts it:

"In the end it may be emphasised that this survey has no pretentions to being a piece of academic research. It has been conducted by the administrative machinery of the government and used as a rough and ready tool for evolving a set of simple criteria for identifying social and educational backwardness. Throughout this survey our approach has been conditioned by practical considerations, realities of field conditions, constraints of resources and trained manpower and paucity of time. All these factors obviously militate against the requirements of a technically sophisticated and academically satisfying operation."

But there is a further problem. The survey uses eleven criteria to assess whether a caste is backward. Whether it is considered socially backward by others; whether it depends mainly on manual labour; whether at least 25 per cent females and 10 per cent males above the state's average get married at an age less than 17 years m rural areas and at least 10 per cent females and 5 per cent males do so in urban areas; whether female participation in work is at least 25 per cent above the state average — these four are the "social indicators". There are three "educational indicators"; indices about attendance in schools, about drop out from schools, and the proportion of matriculates. And four economic ones: the average value of family assets, the proportion living in kuchcha houses, the distance from source of drinking water, and consumption loans taken by households.

Each caste is assessed on each criterion. And in regard — to the quantifiable criteria it gets a point if its deviation from the state's average exceeds 25 per cent.

But how are the eleven indices to be combined into a composite score? The social indicators are given a weightage of 3 points each, the educational indicators 2 points each, and the economic ones 1 point each. These are then totalled for the caste. The maximum score that a caste can pile up is 22. Thus by Mandalian logic a caste that scores eleven or more is backward!

The simple question that needed an answer the simplest question, that is — was: how robust is the classification of a caste as backward? To what extent does it alter if some other — equally justifiable — criteria are used rather than these eleven? To what extent does it alter when the relative weights attached to the individual criteria — three each to numbers (i) to (iv), two each to numbers (v) to (vii), one each to numbers (viii) to (xi) are altered?

Quite apart from the reliability of the data collected in the survey, and the choice of these criteria rather than some others, much would turn on the relative weights which are attached to the eleven criteria. What is the explanation Mandal gives for the "3 each social", "2 each for educational", and "one each for economic" formula? Two cryptic sentences — "Economic, in addition to social and educational indicators, were considered important as they directly flowed from social and educational backwardness. This also helped to highlight the fact that socially and educationally backward classes are economically backward also".

Two sentences which don't even address the question.

The Result

On page 53 Mandal extols the virtues of his criteria, his survey, his method of aggregation: ".. Thirdly, this method was found to be highly dependable in practice. For instance; as a result of its application, most of the well-known socially and educationally backward castes were identified as backward."

But on the very next page he invokes the need to apply additional criteria: "In view of the foregoing," he writes:

"The Commission has also applied some other tests like stigmas of low occupation, criminality, nomadism, beggary and untouchability to identify social backwardness. Inadequate representation in public services was taken as another important test."

And by the next page he is embarrassingly candid:

"In this context it may also be stated that in some cases, the findings based on socio-educational field survey happened to be inconsistent with the living social reality. For example, the social status of Kasera caste in Bihar, Dhobi in Gujarat, Agasa in Karnataka, Kumbhar in Rajasthan, Badager in Tamil Nadu, etc. is known to be very low. Yet these castes scored below 11 points and, thus qualified for ranking as forward. Such aberrations are bound to occur in any sociological survey which is based on statistical methods owing to lopsidedness of the sample covered. The only corrective to these aberrations is the intimate personal knowledge of local conditions and the use of massive public evidence produced before the Commission. The results of the field survey have been carefully scrutinised and such aberrations rectified as far as possible."

The survey results are thus improved by "personal knowledge gained through extensive touring of the country and receipt of voluminous public evidences ...."

And the very "Lists of OBCs notified by various state governments" about which Mandal himself as we have seen has so much to say:

And by such magic mixing together of unknown portions in unknown quantities we have the list that is now gospel to this Government: a list of 3743 castes. And that largely among the

Hindus. Most of the non-Hindu ones are still to be put together, says Mandal.

B.K. Roy Burman: Mandal Commission: The Issues Involved
Indian Express, 29.10.1990

The Supreme Court is seized of the various issues concerning the Mandal Commission. Obviously the issues emanate from the context of the appointment of the Commission and from its terms of reference.

The context can be perceived in terms of surface-level facts, it can also be perceived in terms of interplay of deeper processes. At the surface level, one has the heritage of the freedom struggle with its stated and unstated promises for various sections of population and the ethos of welfare state focussing on the principles of equity and social justice.

At the deeper level of social reality, one sees the persistence of feudal and semi-feudal relations in different parts of the country, emergence of rich peasantry through land reforms, state-subsidised new technology and ancillary measures. Side by side with this there is pauperisation of the under-classes. Most of the neo-rich peasants belong to middle strata in the caste system and many in the under classes are members of the Scheduled Castes and Scheduled Tribes and minorities. The dispossessed 'landlords and traditional elites (many of them belonging to upper castes) have moved over to state services and the professions. Some of them have come up as regional level industrial and commercial entrepreneurs and contractors. Besides, by taking advantage, of state supported infrastructure and through pillage of resources from rural and tribal areas, monopolies have deeply entrenched themselves at the national level. They face, from time to time, both competition and seductive nod from the multinationals. In this context they can accommodate regional level industrial and commercial competitors to some extent. But in the post cold-war era, they are likely to be marginalised at the global level and their capacity to accommodate regional interests is shrinking rapidly. This coupled with growing militancy of the under-classes finds the rural and urban elites handicapped in establishing their hegemonic sway. Simultaneously in the world context the political bases of the nation states are being progressively eroded:

Crucial Importance

In such a complex situation, capture of administrative and technical decision-making power, in addition to political power, is of crucial importance for all the competing economic interests.

Against the backdrop of this social reality, the issues related to the Mandal Commission and its report are to be considered.

The Mandal Commission (Second Backward Classes Commission) was get up in 1978 under Article 340 of the Constitution. The first Backward Classes Commission was set in 1953 with Kaka Kalelkar as Chairman. The terms of reference of the two Commissions were not identical. The Kalelkar Commission was required not only to determine the criteria to be adopted in considering whether any sections of people in the territory of India (in addition to the Scheduled Castes and Scheduled Tribes specified by notifications issued under Articles 341 and 342 of the Constitution) should be treated as socially and educationally backward classes. The terms of reference did not vest the Commission with any mandate to prepare a list of OBC. Secondly, whereas the Mandal Commission was required to examine the desirability or otherwise of providing for reservation of jobs in favour of such backward classes which were not adequately represented in the public services and posts in connection with affairs of the Union or any of the States, the Kalelkar Commission was not hedged by any such condition. The terms of reference (with slight differences in language) common to both the Commissions are as follows: (1) to recommend steps to be taken for the advancement of OBC (2) to present to the President a report setting out the facts as found by the Commissions and making such recommendations as they thought proper.

It may be mentioned that the Mandal Commission has gone beyond its terms of reference by giving a list of OBC, quantifying them and by quantifying the extent to which public jobs and appointments are to be reserved for them.

The issues to be considered can be categorised as technical, political and sociological.

Dubious Data

On the technical side there is an empirical and interpretative dimension as also a legal dimension.

At the empirical level, the Mandal Commission has failed to provide requisite information in support of its recommendations. It has claimed to have generated 31 tables based on a socio-educational survey, but has not included these in the report submitted to the President. It has given questionable data about the numerical strength of the OBC and given obviously dubious data about the representation of the OBC in services. On the other hand, it has not shown convincingly which sections of the OBC deserve assistance in the form of job reservation. Last but not the least, except for a passing reference to the recommendations of the Kalelkar Commission and almost a muted discussion about concessions in the field of education, it has neglected the task of recommending the steps to be taken for the advancement of OBC, after a critical examination of the existing programmes and supporting action. It has, however, recommended the creation of a number of techno-bureaucratic agencies which will only benefit the upper strata of the OBC. In view of all these failures in satisfying the term's of reference, the issues to be considered at the very outset are whether (a) the report as a whole, in its present form should be struck down (b) the list of the OBC as prepared by the Commission and the consequential matters, should be struck down or whether (c) the court should give a directive to the Government to make public all the 31 tables and other materials claimed to have been collected by the Commission, so that experts and the public at large can evaluate the data and help the court before it takes a final decision.

Even if the court strikes down the Report wholly or partially, the question of determination of the criteria for identifying the OBC remains, so that the constitutional commitments particularly those postulated in Articles 46, 16(4), 15(4) and 29(2) can be fulfilled. The issue is whether the indicators listed in para 11.23 of the Report can by themselves be treated as criteria for determination of the OBC in view of the fact that in para 2 of Appendix VII, it has been clearly stated that the criteria would be evolved not only on the basis of the indicators obtained from socio-educational survey, but on examination of data called from various agencies.

If the court decides that the indicators for the treatment of the socio-educational survey data by themselves constitute the criteria, two issues arise, namely, the merit of the criteria and the problem of their tie-up with variables as occupation requiring child labour, representation in public sector services or in professions, as suggested, by the Planning Team.

For considering the merit of the criteria, the Expert Panel had prepared Household Schedules as Locality' Schedules. These criteria, which were "refined" and which thus deviated from the indicators suggested by the Technical Sub-Committee of Experts, relate only to the household schedule. So far as the survey is concerned the Expert Panel envisaged "backwardness" in its spatial and social milieu. The importance of the same was spelt out by the Research Planning Team in para 9, Appendix XII. By deviating from the framework given by the Team and the Expert Panel, the Commission has made the criteria meaningless.

If the court agrees with this view, the issue will be whether viable criteria can be generated from the various suggestions given by the Research Planning Team and from the information contained in the Report of Tata Institute of Social Sciences, which has been included in Vol. IV of the Report. It seems that a start can be made, provided that the criteria for identification of OBC are not considered as rigid frames and are treated as reflections of the evolving processes of society. For shortage of space, it will not be possible to go into the details here.

There is a technical issue of caste/ class relations, but that will be discussed while examining the sociological issues.

The legal dimension has been intermeshed with the technical dimension and need not be recapitulated.

Government Infringement

The political issue is that of "Right to Information". The Mandal Commission, after claiming that it has generated massive data of various types, has not included the same in the Report. The Government, by its acceptance of the Report, even though it did not obtain the data through the constitutionally laid down channel; has — infringed on the political right of the people to information.

It is a political right and if it is not justiciable, perhaps, the people will have to assert at the political level.

The sociological issues are quite a few: (a) caste-class relations (b) efficiency of public services (c) reverse discrimination against merit (d) encouragement to primordial loyalties (e) weakening the unity of the country faced with multiple challenges.

As regards caste-class relations, by and large in most parts of the country castes of certain categories provide the basis for social interaction and access to economic resources. But the ideology of class (in Marxian or liberal sociological sense) and the ideology of caste are not identical. Hence caste cannot be always equated with class. At the same time it should not be ignored that frequently intermediate and up-per-strata castes use their caste platforms to suppress the under-classes, thereby forcing the oppressed classes also to operate on caste platforms.

As Andre Beteille has mentioned, any cluster sharing common traits can be described as a class, although in non-sociological sense. Hence some castes can be treated as OBC, provided that they satisfy the agreed criteria. But caste, need not be the only criterion. The Mandal Commission itself suggested in Appendix VII para (b) 2, economic status as one of the parameters for determination of OBC. Besides, in para 1.10 it has recorded attempts to define OBC on the basis of occupation. The document prepared by Tata Institute also makes a mention of non-caste criteria in several States. There is no evidence to show that Mandal Commission has done any serious exercises to follow up the information which was at it disposal.

Affirmative Actions

Efficiency in public services, particularly in a welfare state, is to be considered not only in terms of the system's efficiency. Broad-based participation of different segments of population, particularly the disadvantaged ones, is likely to augment the system's efficiency in a certain sense. For such broad-based participation; reservation in services is; however, only one of the instruments, though a necessary instrument for the more deprived section. But it should not be indiscriminately extended to all sections of OBC. For those who have already attained some degree of economic and social power, as well as for the more vulnerable sections of society, affirmative actions, particularly centering on educational opportunities, and opportunities to break the monopolistic trends at the regional, national and international levels in industry, in economic and ancillary activities should be carefully planned and promoted.

The question of reverse discrimination, as a result of which individuals with proved merit are kept out is certainly an important issue, though one should not ignore the viability of otherwise or the conventional instruments of measuring merit. The problem has become acute because the pattern of "development" that has been operative in India, primarily to serve the interest of the ruling class prodded and reinforced by various international agencies.

The issue cannot be considered in isolation. The problem of primordial loyalties arise out of patterns of distorted development which cover the underlying stagnation of social relations. Besides, while primordial loyalties are negative features, the moral binding of social formations against inherently alienating state power should not be confused with the same. In the long run all regulatory processes through moral binding contain in their ambit the potentials of universal man. India of Mahatma Gandhi should look in this direction for answers to the questions that have come up as a sequel to Mandal Quandary. In operative term it means real democratic decentralisation which is a continuous process and not a structure bestowed by the rulers.

Arun Shourie: Mandal's Report: The Juggernaut

Indian Express, 24.8.1990

A perverse report, an idiotic one.

No one reads it.

And suddenly it is not just gospel, it is law.

The Juggernaut

There is an inexorability about such a Juggernaut, an ineluctable inner logic:

- Introduced as an exception, the measure swallows the rule;
- Given as a concession to one, perhaps deserving group it is grabbed by one group after another, by one progressively more undeserving group after another;
- Introduced in one sphere it spreads to others, exactly as a cancer cell taking root in-one organ multiplies and invades others;
- In its application to the' original group, as well as to its appropriation by others, in its application to the original sphere as well as in its extension to others, it suffers progressive, rapid debasement;
- At first efforts are made to arrest the rotting; to ensure that the measure adheres to the purposes for which it was meant, to pare away the manifest excesses, some brave souls even attempt to introduce an element or two of reform; the Juggernaut crushes the attempts, and soon even the effort at reform is abandoned, even the pretence that what is being done has some nexus with the objective for which the exception was originally made is shed;
- A concession becomes a right, a ceiling beyond which it is not to be given becomes the floor - the level which it is any case the right of everyone who can grab to have;
- Guardians, such as the courts, who are meant to ensure that the exception shall subserve the end for which it was meant instead take to rationalising the advance of the Juggernaut;
- What was meant to be a temporary exception thus becomes a permanent millstone, in the end one that pulls the entire society down.

The communal Award was such. V.P. Singh's decision on Mandal is such.

Progressively Backward!

Reservations under Articles 15(4) in educational institutions and under Articles 16(4) and 335 in services were introduced originally for the Scheduled Castes and Tribes alone.

More and more castes and tribes forced their way into the Schedule.

They were later extended to "Other Backward Classes". More and more castes, indeed more and more powerful and prosperous castes have been able to force society and the State to annoint them as Backward. Dr. P. Radhakrishnan, Fellow of the Madras Institute of Development Studies, records that the list of Backward Castes in Tamil Nadu grew from 11 in 1883 to 39 in 1893 to 46 in 1903 to 122 in 1913 to 131 in 1923 to 182 in 1933 to 238 in 1943 to 270 in 1953. Mandal lists 288 for that state, a state from which those not fortunate enough to be Backward have been well nigh driven.

Now here is a country that is progressing, rapidly so if we go by the proclamations of successive governments. But more and more communities keep becoming Backward!

fifty per cent.

Notice next this whole business of 50 per cent being the limit up to which reservations can be made in services. Everyone takes it as axiomatic, as if it is something which has been not just sanctioned but sanctified by the courts, if not the Constitution itself.

But the case in which the figure originates had nothing to do with reservations in services. And even in that case the figure was put out not as the result of an analysis of what the profession required or of what would be fait and just. It came in as a remark to illustrate the proposition that an exception to a rule cannot be so large as to swallow the rule itself.

As we have seen, Article 15(1) of the Constitution forbids any discrimination on grounds of religion, race, caste, sex, place of birth. Article 15(4) says that notwithstanding this general rule the State may make "any special provision for the advancement of any socially and educationally backward classes of citizens or for the Scheduled Castes and the Scheduled Tribes."

Mysore already had reserved 15 per cent of the seats in medical and engineering colleges and other technical institutes for the Scheduled Castes, and 3 per cent for the Scheduled Tribes. It passed a new order reserving another 50 per cent for "Other Backward Castes". (I will henceforth drop the euphemism "classes" if you don't mind.) That meant that the exception - that is reservations under Article 15(4) - became larger than the rule - the prohibition that is in Article 15(1) against discrimination on grounds of caste, etc.

It is in illustrating this matter that the Supreme Court talked of 50 per cent. It did so illustratively, tentatively, "speaking generally and in a broad way", as it said in the case that ensued and which is the basic reference point on the whole question, *Balaji* v. *State of Mysore*:

- "Speaking generally and in a broad way," Mandal himself quotes the Supreme Court as saying, "a special provision should be less than 50 per cent, how much less than 50 per cent would depend upon the relevant prevailing circumstances in each case."

The language itself shows that the Court was merely illustrating the arithmetical point. Its view of what was being sought to be done was stern:

- "Therefore, what is true in regard to Article 15(4) is equally true in regard to Article 16(4) ... that the Constitution makers assumed, ... that while making adequate reservation under Article 16(4), care would be taken not to provide for unreasonable, excessive or extravagant reservation, for that would, by eliminating general competition in a large field and by creating wide-spread dissatisfaction amongst the employees, materially affect efficiency. Therefore, like the special provision improperly made under Article 15(4), reservation made under Article 16(4) beyond the permissible and legitimate limits would be liable to be challenged as a fraud on the Constitution."

But that arithmetical illustration became the norm. First the ceiling.

And then the floor, the minimum which everyone takes to be

a right, indeed a right which has already been wrested and which is therefore now the base from which one should fight for more.

Notice too that the case was about reservations of seats in medical and engineering colleges. Even in regard to these as we have seen the 50 per cent figure was not the result of any detailed analysis of what the protected communities needed, to say nothing of what the country needed. But more important, the figure, and the stray remarks the Court let fall on reservations which might be made under Article 16(4) in the services, became the norm in assessing the extent of reservations in services also.

Now, this somnambulant adoption, by the courts as much as others, of the figure was just not permissible under the Constitution. Taking Articles 16(4) and 335 together it was clear that reservations in services could be made only "consistently with the requirements of efficiency in administration". No authority, much less any court, had, nor has one till today, concluded on the basis of any study whatsoever that doling out half the jobs in government would not impair the efficiency of administration. But clearly the 50 per cent figure could NOT be extended to reservations in services till it had been shown to be permissible by such inquiry.

Yet it has not just been extended. It is the norm.

Indeed it is the norm which is routinely exceeded, and with impunity.

Reservations in educational institutions as well as in services exceed not just half, they exceed two-thirds in state after state.

The Supreme Court itself has considered instances where seats have been reserved far in excess of this limit - 70 per cent on the basis of residence, 68 per cent on the basis of caste - and it has not struck them down as it was bound even by the construction which had been put on Balaji to do.

Promotions

Similarly reservations when they were first introduced were only for entrance into a service. They have since been extended to promotions. Mandal wants them extended, and V.P. Singh, being as committed to Mandal as he says he is, will extend them to promotions at all levels.

In the Central as well as every state government. In every public sector organisation. In every private enterprise which has taken financial assistance from the State or from a state financial institution - that is, the entire private sector: large, small, and much of the one in cottages too!

The practice is grotesque. There is no other word for it. The procedure Mandal wants all to adopt is called *The Roster System*. It is in operation in states like 'Gujarat and Karnataka where it has already led to rupturing one department after another. Here it is. Posts in each category and at different levels are entered on to a roster. Posts at specified serial numbers are earmarked to be filled *Only By Persons* belonging, to, say, the Scheduled Castes or Tribes, that is one of the categories for which there is reservation. Thus, for instance, in a department post number one may be designated to be filled only by a member of a Scheduled Caste; post number four to be filled only by a member of Scheduled Tribe, etc. Persons from castes which are not entitled to reservations must wait till numbers two or three fall vacant. And when these fall vacant they must of course contend with the Scheduled Castes and Tribes employees who are entitled naturally as much as anyone else to fill these "general" posts.

Nor is that all. In some states the roster is minutely classified. It is not just that posts number 2 and 4 and ... may be filled only by, say, a member of the "Backward Castes". The Backward Castes have themselves been further classified into groups - five in Karnataka. So that post number 2 or 7 as the case may be must be filled not just by a member of the Backward Castes but by a member of Group A of the Backward Castes.

In this way many an employee leap-frogs — my colleague M.K. Mistry in Ahmedabad illustrates the consequence with the case of a Backward Caste employee getting two promotions *In One Day* - while others languish. Here in Delhi we are told of person who joins the service in 1957. Regarded efficient by all, he today works under a young lady who was *Born In 1966*. And so on.

First: reservations at the point of entry.

Then: reservations in promotions.

Then: reservations in promotions in accordance with minutely classified rosters.

And all this in the face of judgments of the Supreme Court which denounce reservation quotas in promotions for in fact having become a device for "exempting persons from possessing the necessary qualifications", which declare that to grant such wholesale exemptions for long periods from the qualifications necessary for the satisfactory discharge of duties would militate against efficiency of administration and doing so is thus violative of Article 335 of the Constitution: which find that quotas in promotions have been harmful from the point of view of efficiency of the Railways, etc. (For the relevant illustrations see the lucid discussion of *Thomas* v *Kerala* and *General Manager, Southern Railway* v *Rangachari* in H.M. Seervai, *Constitutional Law of India*, 1983, Vol. I, pp. 429-30, 464).

Debasement

It isn't just that the concession is appropriated by those who are less and less deserving of it. It isn't just that it is carried into spheres far removed from the one for which it was intended. It is that it is debased.

The use which has been made of Article 15(4) to wrest reservations is itself a debasement. Recall that the Article does not speak of reservations as such. It speaks of the State making "any special provision for the advancement of ...."

That would mean a host of measures: overwhelmingly so of measures which are called "affirmatives action". Extra tuition, better and subsidised text books, subsidised nourishment or whatever. Reservations could be one in this vast gamut. But it is reservations which the Article has been used most to wrest. And public debate has also been preoccupied most on this use of the Article. And the debasement marks every sphere of the use of such Articles even for this singular purpose.

The courts have repeatedly held for instance that it is only after the most thorough and objective inquiry that a caste or a group can be declared to be entitled to reservations, that mere declarations by a government that such an inquiry had been made will not suffice. See how emphatically the Supreme Court for instance puts the matter in *P. Sagar* v. *State of Andhra Pradesh*:

"....The assertion by the State that the officers or the State had taken into consideration the criteria which had been adopted by the courts ... or that the authorities had acted in good faith in determining the socially and educationally backward classes of citizens would not be sufficient to sustain such a claim .... Article 15 guarantees by the first Clause a fundamental right of far-reaching importance to the public generally. Within certain defined limits an exception has been engrafted upon the guarantee of the freedom in clause: (1), but being in the nature of an exception, the conditions which justify departure must be strictly shown to exist".

Mandal himself recalls the admonition. In fact, he cites the very passage. And having done so we have seen how he arrives at his list of 3743 castes!

Similarly, it has been held repeatedly that the object of selection - to a medical college, to a service - is to select the candidates who are most qualified to benefit from the studies, who are most qualified to discharge the duties in question; that standards must not be compromised; that the mandatory requirement of Article 335 - namely, the effect the step is going to have on efficiency of administration must not be lost sight of. But in fact in state after state:

- Norms are relaxed for candidates who are from castes which are entitled to reservations - these relaxations range from age limits to cut-off marks;
- Easier questions - in fact, questions so easy that they are farces of questions — are asked, in interviews, for instance, of these candidates while others are subjected to the normally tough questions;
- Separate examinations are held.

Indeed in many instances examinations are dispensed with altogether! My colleague M.K. Das informs me that just yesterday, i.e., on Wednesday - the Government of Kerala has decided to extend to local bodies the exemption which is already available to Scheduled Caste, and Tribes employees in government service from passing departmental tests for purposes of promotions. The exemption will be in force till the end of the year.

V.P. Singh is not behind anyone in this matter. He declared the other day that whatever the backlog in the filling of quotas reserved for Scheduled Castes and Tribes, it will all be filled forthwith. That, in addition to the portrait in Parliament, of course, being his homage to Ambedkar. And where candidates are not available who qualify by the norms which are in force, the norms will be "relaxed".

Impervious to Improvement

A concession once made cannot be retrieved, a standard once relaxed cannot be restored. The courts say - for instance, the Supreme Court in *A Periakaruppan* v. *Tamil Nadu* — that the list of castes which are entitled to reservations must be kept constantly under review, that the very object of reservations would be defeated if having been recognised as backward and hence entitled to reservations once, the caste were to be treated or to remain backward in perpetuity. The very object of giving special facilities like reservations to it after all is that it may overcome its backwardness.

The point is reiterated often. "The object of reservations will be defeated", Mandal himself reports the Allahabad High Court as declaring in *Chote Lal and Others* v. *State of Uttar Pradesh*.

"If on the inclusion of a class in a list of backward classes, the class is treated as backward for all times to come. Hence the State should keep under constant periodical review the list of backward classes and the quantum of the reservation of seats for the classes determined to be backward at a point of time."

But while hundreds of castes have gone on being added to the list of Backwards, every attempt to delete any from among those which have once made it to the list has been set at nought by agitations and the like. A typical case, one which is set out by Mare Galanter in one of the principal works on the subject, Competing Equalities. The government appoints a committee in June 1965 under the Law Secretary, B.N. Lokur, to review the list of Scheduled Castes and Tribes who are entitled to reservations, etc. It lists 14 tribes and 28 Scheduled Castes which the evidence it has received leads it to believe have since their, inclusion become "relatively forward".

A storm ensues. Ostensibly to give effect to Lokur's recommendations the government introduces the bill to amend the lists on 17 August, 1967. It does not leave out any of the tribe, or castes which Lokur's evidence suggested had become "relatively forward"!

The bill is referred to a Joint Parliamentary Committee. It reports in November, 1969. Among other changes it suggests an exclusion - that those who convert to Christianity or Islam should no longer be taken to qualify for reservations. Another storm ensues. A bill is introduced. It lapses. A bill that is eventually passed in the emergency in August 1976 has many things, but no exclusion!

The fate of every attempt to introduce a means test - a meaningful means test that is, not a farcical one like 'OBCs who do not pay income tax' which for one thing leaves out every rich farmer in the country - has been unvarying: it got nowhere.

The Supreme Court's attempt to temper exorbitant reservations in medical colleges for residents of the state in which the college was situated ended in a tragi-comedy the history of which has to be read to be believed. (It is set out with great relish and sparkle in H.M. Seervai, *Constitutional Law of India*, Supplement, 1988, pp. 320-339).

The Expedient becomes a Fixture

The Supreme Court declares:

"... all the same the Government should not proceed on the basis that once a class is considered as a backward class, it should continue to be backward class for all times. Such an approach would defeat the very purpose of the reservation because once a class reaches a stage of progress which some modern writers call as take off stage then competition is necessary for their future progress. The. Government should always keep under review the question of reservation of seats and only the classes which are really socially and educationally backward should be allowed to have the benefit of reservation. Reservation of seats should not be allowed to become a vested interest. The fact that candidates of backward classes have secured about 50 per cent of the seats in the general pool does show that the time has come for a *de novo* comprehensive examination of the question. It must be remembered that the Government's decision in this regard is open to judicial review."

That was in *A. Periakaruppan. Twenty Years Ago.*

It declares again:

"If freedom, justice and equal opportunity to unfold one's own personality belong alike to bhangi and brahmin, prince and pauper, if the panchama proletariate is to feel the social transformation Article 16(4) promises, the State must apply equalising techniques which will enlarge their opportunities and thereby progressively diminish the need for props. The success of State action under Article 16(4) consists in the speed with which result-oriented reservation withers away as no longer a need, not in the ever-widening and everlasting operation of an exception (Article 16(4)) as if it were a super-fundamental right to continue backward all the time. To lend immortality to the reservation policy is to defeat its *raison d'etre*; to politicise this provision for communal support and Party ends is to subvert the solemn undertaking of Article 16(1); to casteify 'reservation' even beyond the dismal groups of backward-most people, euphemistically described as SC amd ST, is to run a grave constitutional risk. Caste, *ipso facto*, is not class in a secular State."

That was in *Karamchari Sangh. Ten Years Ago.*

What was to be a temporary expedient has become a permanent feature. What was to be a concession for a few has become the right of hordes, a right they wrest by might. What was to be a facility made available to the extent that this could be done consistently with the efficient functioning of the State has been debased to the point that it now bears no resemblance at all to what the Constitution had intended.

And this wretchedness, V.P. Singh and his colleagues have now, in a fit of commitment we are to believe, decreed, must be adopted by the entire Central Government, by the entire public sector, by the banks, by the private sector.

The Juggernaut that will crush us ....

Arun Shourie: The Mandal report: 'This way lies not only folly, but disaster'

Indian Express, 25.8.1990

Half the entire State structure is thus to be manned by persons who are BY DEFINITION not qualified for the job.

"Arey bhai, but what is government work?", one of these leaders said the other day as I demurred on what his leader had done. "It is just pushing files." That is what we have made it. And that is one of the major reasons on account of which we are in the pits. And you now want to take it as desideratum, as the way things should be. And to set up a recruitment system - a stuffing system really - which will congeal the structure further in this immobilisme.

Just "Pushing Files"?

Governance is Not "just pushing files." Government impinges on every aspect of our existence, it is vital for many aspects, in fact in regard to many of them everything turns on how well the structure of State performs.

Fighting terrorism? From among the DSPs will you promote 'X' as SP and put him in charge of operations because he has the expertise to counter the terrorist or because he belongs to sub-caste 'Z' which falls in Group B of the Backward Castes' list and the post that is, to be filled is Number 9 on the Roster, the Number 9 which is reserved for a person from sub-caste 'Z'?

Look around the world and see the hurricane-pace at which new products are coming up, at which new technologies are being adopted to produce them. For good or ill in societies like ours the State is an important actor in determining which products will be encouraged, which discouraged, which technologies will be adopted, which not.

Does that not require specialised, upto-the-minute knowledge? "But do you mean the existing fellows have it?" Assume they don't. Isn't the answer to this to ensure selection procedures and promotion criteria which will select those who do possess the expertise? Or is the answer that as the existing ones don't have as much expertise as the tasks require let us stuff half the posts with persons who by definition do not have the expertise, let us promote persons because they belong to this sub-caste rather than that?

The V.P. Singhs when they have handled these ministries - for instance, when he handled Commerce and was in charge of making our products competitive in the world - these very persons have themselves extolled as the model a ministry such as Japan's MITI. They have extolled the intimate and up-to-date knowledge of the officials of that ministry - their expertise, their innovativeness.

And now? "Arey Mail, but what is government work? ....

Only for "Super-specialities"?

Nor is the need for expertise and excellence limited to one or two ministries. It is the imperative in every nook and corner of the structure. Borrowing in international markets, assessing weapons systems for the defence services, assessing the environmental impact of the Tehri Dam, assessing products to determine whether they are carciogenic, assessing the relative merits of atomic v. thermal v. hydro-electric power plants .... These are routine functions of ministries today. Which of them does not require expert knowledge?

And please remember that Mandal and V. P. Singh are not going to stuff ministries only. Madhu Dandavate has just now declared in Parliament that the recommendations of the Mandal Commission shall be implemented "without any dilution". We can therefore take it that the reservations are to be for the entire Central Government, the entire structure of every state government, for every unit of the public sector, for every institution like the banks, for every unit of the private sector which has availed of assistance from the government or a governmental institution.

Now, Indian Airlines, Air India, the Atomic Energy plants, the Indian Space Research Organisation .... all these are Central Government bodies too. Should half the posts to them be manned by persons not because they know the job but because they are from this caste or that sub-caste?

Nor can any scheme to "draw the line" work. The Supreme Court tried to do this in the case of reservations in medical colleges, to farcical effect. Having been forced to reconcile itself to what had already been done, having tried to push that back a little bit only to retreat within months in subsequent cases, the Court tried in *Pradeep Jain* v. *Union* to do at least something: But, of course, so far as "... super-specialities such as neuro-surgery and cardiology are concerned," it declared, "there should be no reservation at all on the basis of institution preference and admission should be granted purely on merit on all India basis...."

I am not at the moment on the point that little came of even this effort, but on the attempt to differentiate specialities. How is treatment of cancer, or operating on the liver, or replacing knee caps or hip joints ... how is any of these less of a speciality than neurosurgery and cardiology? In fact, how is managing a hospital so that specialists in it have the requisite environment and infrastructure to conduct these specialised operations any less in need of specialization and expertise? A fortriori how is the ministry that shall control, or direct, or intervene in the affairs of the hospitals taken together less in need of excellence and expertise?

In which arena will "pushing files" suffice in this day and age? And notice too that we are no longer a conglomeration of isolated, self-sufficient "village republics". The structure - of the economy, of the State - is organically interlinked, inter-dependent. You can't have substandard functioning in one area - the management of our economic relation with the, rest of the world, say - or casteism to one department - the police, say - without the entire structure getting enfeebled and incapacitated to that extent.

Compelling Merit to Stay Away

Notice too that reservations do not have an impact just at entry. It is not just that the deserving will be excluded in V.P. Singh's scheme from half the jobs in government.

It is that as promotions, etc. too will be determined by caste and sub-caste those with merit will Stay Away From government and every institution with which it has anything to do. For the meritorious will certainly know that even if he makes it to the general pool at the point of entry, his career may be stalled, indeed derailed at any point if he does not happen to be from the caste or sub-caste from which alone post number nine on the roster can at that conjucture of time and place be filled.

"But do you mean backward caste boys and girls just do not have talent and merit?"

Not at all.

The point is not that there is something genetically wrong with anyone. But that at this time the group we are talking about - and that group is not "boys and girls from the backward castes", but "boys and girls from these castes who have got the jobs because those jobs are reserved" - the point is that at this time they are not by definition qualified for the job.

This is evident from two facts which Mandal himself stresses, and around which he frames his fatal recommendations, recommendations which Dandavate declares will be implemented "without dilution":

- These are the persons who do not qualify on merit; those who do are not to be counted against the reserved quota;
- These persons will continue to need reservations to advance in their careers, that is the reason why Mandal insists that there be reservations not just at the point of entry but in promotion also.

So, at this time they are not qualified for the job. And that job has to be done now.

Breaking the Structure

Nor are the mal-effects of the Mandal-V.P. Singh scheme going to be limited to the fact that the meritorious will be discouraged from even seeking to enter government service, that they will be excluded from half the jobs in it should they be foolish enough to still seek to enter it.

Services and departments are bound to rupture along caste lines. And as the scheme will apply to all government services, all governments, the fault-lines will extend beyond the individual department or ministry. They will war the entire structure.

A police official orders firing... Five are killed... His fate will depend on whether his superior is from his caste or from one that is hostile to his caste, on whether the officer in the Home

Department is from this caste or that... And then on the caste of the magistrate or the judge.

Fanciful? But that is what things have already come to in a state like Bihar.

And V.P. Singh would reduce the entire country to that condition.

There is another, and equally enervating consequence of such schemes.

A job should be something one has to work to get, something which one has to do one's utmost to retain and advance in. It should not be, advancement in it must not be anyone's by right.

But this latter is exactly the ethos which reservations entail, that the job, the promotion is mine by right, and that too because of my birth, not work.

How can a modern society survive, let alone grow with this as its ethos?

How are they helped

"I am definitely against reservation in Government Services for any Community for the simple reason that the services are not meant for the servants but they are meant for the service of society as a whole ....."

A pregnant remark. From Kaka Saheb Kalelkar's letter forwarding the report of the First Backward Classes Commission. Mandal reproduces it. And as from all the other things he reproduces learns not a whit from it.

It bears reflection. For so many bleeding heart liberals, to say nothing of the hypocrites who snatch at anything that might be made to appear a progressive plume, so many of them are misled into supporting ruinous schemes such as the present one merely because they are said to be for the "Backwards".

I have already pointed out that on the evidence put out by Mandal himself and naturally he must have used all the camouflage he could to hide it, the sections to whom the scheme is being made available are not "Backward". They are the dominant, the prosperous sections. Indeed, as Mandal himself points out they are the exploiters in large regions of our country, the ones who are suppressing agricultural labourers, who are heaping atrocities on the Harijans.

But assume for a moment that we are talking only of the genuinely "Backward", of say the poor.

A steel mill is set up. How are they best helped? By ensuring that it is manned by the ones who are best and truly qualified for executing the tasks it requires and is thereby run at optimum capacity? Or by decreeing that half of the jobs in it must be packed with persons who are By Definition not qualified to man them, and thereby having it work at half its capacity?

In fact, I will be surprised if a steel mill half manned on the Mandal-V.P. Singh formula can be made to function at half its capacity.

Are the poor helped better by a State structure functioning well and thereby enabling progress in a myriad directions, or by their being given half the jobs which exist in it at the moment and which they are not at the moment for whatever reason qualified to do? Unqualified not because they are poor. But because under the Mandal-V.P. Singh formula only those among them who are by definition not qualified for the jobs can be given them.

"27 per cent of one per cent"

"Arun, why are you so upset? Central government employment is only one per cent of total employment. Giving 27 per cent of one per cent is not going to bring down the heavens".

It was Madhu Dandavate the other day. I was saddened beyond belief. Not only because he prefaced this with the remark, "Not all of us can hate your courage" - even though I knew of course that he was just mocking me, and not saying anything about himself or his colleagues.

Not only because his argument showed that he, the one person in the cabinet we would expect to read and reflect, had not read the report.

Not only because he of all persons surely knows that the effect of packing half the jobs in the structure of governance is to introduce a virus - and in a massive dose - that will incapacitate the entire body.

But because the argument actually proved the opposite. After all, how is 52 per cent of the country's population going to be materially helped by being given 27 per cent of one per cent of jobs?

Society Itself

Indeed, the consequences transcend the economy, even the State. They will rend society itself. For the scheme gives entire communities, and lethally aggressive communities at that, an interest in perpetuating, nay sharpening their separateness.

Reservations in legislatures on the basis of caste. Seeking votes on the basis of caste. Just these two things and we have seen how they have reinvigorated casteism throughout the length and breadth of our country.

V.P. Singh is now seeking to inject, - O, all right, not to "inject" as you say it is already there, he is seeking to intensify - and that in a virulent dose, casteism in the administrative apparatus of the State, in the apparatus that is with which the citizen must deal not once in five years but every day, with which he must deal not just for endorsing one candidate rather than another but for a myriad things that he needs to get through life.

The move marks a regression in another way too:

- Individuals are to get advantage because they are members of a group;
- Not just because they are members of any group, but because they are members of a caste;
- And the advantage they are going to get is to be better able to grab at the State.

Each of these features will have evil consequences. When one secures a gain not because of what he does but because he is a member of a group, he works to strengthen that group.

And, as Mancur Olson has shown in his vital work, *The Rise and Decline of Nations*, such a group is anti-the whole. As he shows it is just not rational for members of the group to devote themselves to the interests they have in common with the rest of society. If they did so they would have to take on the whole or a disproportionate proportion of the cost of realising those interests while securing only a small part of the benefits. The interests it can pursue most profitably are those which are exclusive to its members. (The calculus holds true for the atomic individual *a fortriori*. e. But he cannot as an individual impede the structure the way group not just can, but ever so obviously does). It is when such groups multiply and acquire power that society is immobilised. It is locked in rigidities. Britain of the fifties, sixties and seventies. The effect of many of our trade unions on our industry, of caste and religious groups on our polity. But that regression towards immobility is exactly what will be intensified by the move under consideration.

And that at the precise time when innovation, adaptability, nimbleness is what our society, our economy, our State need. Indeed, the interests in this case are not just exclusive to the members of the group, they are explicitly at the expense of the rest in society, for the jobs the members of the group get are jobs that others are excluded from.

And this at the precise time when harmony, a coming closer is what our country so desperately needs.

Worse, the group which the citizen will be propelled by the move to fortify is not just any group. It is biz caste qua caste.

The very thing everyone has been screaming, the progressives most of all, is the curse of our society.

And then there is the nature of what he is being given. What he is being given for being a member of the group, the caste, is not say a once-over cash prize. He is being given an office of State. What will this do except to intensify the notion that the State, that everything in it, that everything that flows from it, that everything that can be made to flow from it is one's to grab? Has this notion of the State not already all but brought the structure to a halt that it needed another boost from V.P. Singh?

Principles

Therefore as Panditji said 30 years ago in his letter to the Chief Ministers, which we reproduced the other day, "This way lies not only folly, but disaster." It is not just that this way we will be consigning our country, as Panditji feared, to being second-rate. We will be incapacitating it to the point that it will not be able to handle even the problem it has of its own, to say nothing of handling the consequences of developments in the rest of the world.

It is not a question of locating an ameliorative. "Introduce an economic criteria in addition to the caste" - that is the bleat of intellectuals and politicians wanting to have it both ways - to not support this horror but at the same time to not sully their progressive image.

A token economic criterion will be introduced: "Only those members of Backward Castes will be eligible for reservations whose families do not pay income tax".

And a fat lot that will exclude.

The whole thing must be reversed.

Employment, most specially in the structure of governance, must be reorganised on the following principles:

- The individual qua individual must be the unit, not as the member of same group;
- The disadvantaged must be identified as individuals, and that by assessing their economic condition;
- They must be given all the help society can afford to overcome disabilities, to acquire the requisite abilities; but this must be done through "affirmative action" - free and extra tuition, subsidised and extra nourishment, residential accommodation, whatever;
- But once at the test no one should have an easier time of it than any one else;
- After entry, and throughout the career performance and whether the person has the abilities which that level on the next level requires alone should govern continuance and advancement;
- At the point of entry as well as at every subsequent post of advancement the standards must be those which the proper discharge of duties at that level requires;
- These should most certainly be appropriate to the job, they should test the person in the abilities that are needed for the job; if necessary, the methods of assessment should be continually honed so that more and more appropriate persons are selected; but
- at no time and at no level should the standards in force be "relaxed";
- whatever the standards which have been retained as the best available at that moment, they must apply equally to all, and strictly to all.

This Time a Very Difficult Task

But this time the task is a most onerous one. The movement to reverse all this has not to contend with a mere Prime Minister, as in Rajiv's time. It has not to contend with a mere government, as in Mrs Gandhi's time.

It has to contend with the political establishment as such. Witness the silence, at best the mumbling of the other political parties as well. Witness too the silence of their students' organisations as a consequence.

But even the fact that the movement must contend with the entire political establishment, that it must seek to rouse the people in the face of the indifference, where it is not the active hostility of this establishment is not all.

This time the movement must contend with entire communities, communities which have been given the opportunity to grab the State and all that they can wrest by grabbing it.

Arun Shourie: Three Sets of Facts on Mandal
Rank 413? So sorry. Rank 14246? But of course....
Indian Express, 1.9.1990.

Kerala conducts a common examination for entrance to medical and engineering colleges. Marks scored in this examination are not normally revealed. Ranks, however, are available.

This year about 20,000 candidates wrote the examination for the 700 MBBS seats available in the state.

A candidate having been born to a "forward caste" had to rank 412 or higher to get in. A candidate from the Ezhava caste - recognised as a Backward one in Kerala - however, got a seat though his rank was 1605. A Muslim candidate - Kerala has reservations for Muslim "OBCs" - got in although he ranked 1752. A Latin Catholic, again an "OBC", got in although he ranked 2653. A Scheduled Caste candidate got in although he ranked 4409. The really fortunate one of course was the candidate who could register against the quota for Scheduled Tribes. He got a seat although he ranked 14246.

Some way to select doctors. Some way to encourage our youth to strive for excellence. The pattern is repeated in state after state, my colleagues report from the state capitals. To qualify in the corresponding examination in Andhra a candidate from a caste for which there is no reservation must secure a minimum of 45 per cent, a candidate from a caste for which there are reservations has no minimum to cross.

Chandigarh's prestigious Post-Graduate Institute of Medical Education and Research (PGI) is no exception. The general category candidate must secure at least 50 per cent marks, candidates from the Scheduled Caste, backward castes and Scheduled Tribes: have no minimum to cross. They may get in with 20 per cent or 15 per cent or 11 per cent as they have to compete only amongst themselves, i.e., only among those among themselves who do not qualify on merit.

In Karnataka a Scheduled Caste candidate need score only 67 per cent to qualify for the medical colleges, an "OBC" candidate 75 per cent, but the one whose caste has not been anointed in this way must score a minimum of 90 per cent.

In Madhya Pradesh this year the cut-off mark for general candidates seeking admission in medical and engineering colleges was 66.6 per cent, but for candidates from the Scheduled Castes it was 35.7 per cent. Nominally the minimum marks for passing in the state are 40 per cent.

In Rajasthan the corresponding figures this year were 65 per cent for general category candidates, 48 per cent for OBC candidates and 42 per cent for Scheduled Caste candidates; in Punjab 50 per cent for the general category and 25 per cent for the Scheduled Castes; to Gujarat 60 per cent and 45 per cent: in Goa 79 per cent and 48 per cent.

For seats to UP's engineering colleges the cut-off mark for the merit quota was 64.3 per cent this year, it was lowered first to 60 per cent and eventually to 58.3 per cent. Even so, it remained two and a third times the cut-off mark for candidates in the reserved category which was 25 per cent!

Tightening for Meritorious, Letting Go for Others

It is not just that the lowest qualifying marks for the reserved seats are 10 to 15 to 25 per cent lower in state after state. It is that in practice because of the intense competition for the ever dwindling proportion of seats in the open category the marks a candidate must secure to bag one of these far exceed the qualifying barrier, because of the paucity of candidates from castes which have wrested reservations the marks that a person aiming for one of the reserved seats fall lower and lower by the year, in many years well below what has been prescribed as the "minimum qualifying percentage."

Thus in Bihar the minimum qualifying marks for admission to medical colleges are 50 per cent and 40 per cent for the open and reserved categories. In actual fact candidates had to secure 70 per cent and more to make it in the former category, while in the latter case the qualifying marks themselves have had to be lowered to 35 per cent, to 33 per cent to fill in the quotas available.

In UP the qualifying marks for the medical colleges are 55 per cent for the general category and 40 per cent for the reserved quota. In actual fact candidates in the former category getting below 77 per cent could not get a seat, while to the latter those with 48 per cent did so.

In Madhya Pradesh the qualifying mark in the examinations held five years ago was 40 per cent. This year to fill the reservation quotas in medical and engineering colleges the minimum acceptable mark has been lowered to 25 per cent.

In Punjab also the minimum qualifying marks for Scheduled Caste candidates for medical colleges have been lowered from 40 per cent to 25 per cent. In brief:

- Vast differences in what is required of candidates merely on account of their birth:
- Severe competition for the seats in the general category leading to high qualifying marks, and on the other hand progressive relaxation of the requisite standards to fill up reserved quotas;
- The later relaxations being carried to frightful low levels.

Subsequent Performance

My colleagues tried next to obtain data on the comparative performance in subsequent examinations of students who had entered on merit and those who had entered on the reserved quotas. Precise figures were not available though authorities in several of the colleges they visited said that the latter continued to fare poorly: they do not strive as hard, the authorities said, even when they had comparable facilities for coping - hostel accommodation, nourishment, etc; they take more years, and a larger number of trials to complete the courses; and eventually they score substantially lower marks in the completion examinations.

Promotions

Move now to the other end of the spectrum: from entry to colleges not just to entry to government service but to advancement in it. At present most states reserve seats not only at entry to government service but also in promotions. Some parts of the Central Government also do so, the railways for instance.

My colleagues report the ill-effects this has had in state after state, department after department. The railways, the medical services in UP, the education set-up in Kerala — in each instance they found widespread demoralization and resentment among the general category employees and bitterness between them and the reserved category employees.

Apart from the general vitiation, several specific features stand out.

The first feature arises from the fact that in spite of relaxed standards, special recruitment drives and all, it has been extremely difficult to fill the quotas set aside for these castes. Naturally, the lucky ones who get in at this stage leap-frog to the higher posts. Thus, for instance, in spite of strenuous efforts to locate doctors from Scheduled Castes and Tribes it has been possible to fill only about 6 per cent of the posts in UP's Medical and Health Department with persons from these castes. But the law prescribes that 20 per cent of promotions too shall be reserved for doctors from these castes. As a result Dr. 'A' - there is no point in giving the names though these are available - was promoted to the post of Joint Director superseding 100 doctors; Dr. 'B' was promoted to that post superseding 500 doctors, Dr. 'C' superseding 900 doctors, Doctor 'D' received the scale superseding 1600 doctors, Dr. 'E' was appointed Chief Medical Officer of a large city superseding

1100 doctors. Dr. 'F' was appointed Chief Medical Officer of another large city near Delhi superseding 1500 doctors .... The result? "The Medical and Health Department of the UP government," writes my colleague S.K. Tripathi from Lucknow, "has been seething with resentment because of large scale supersessions which have resulted from having the 20 per cent quota even in promotions..."

Four consequences follow:

- They take far fewer years to reach the higher posts than the general category of employees;
- They reach much higher posts by retirement than the latter;
- As they ascend to higher posts when they are still young, the promotion prospects of others - the general category ones over whom they have leap-frogged - are blocked, permanently as far as this generation of employees is concerned;
- Because of these accelerated promotions, because of crash recruitment drives in which persons from reserved castes are inducted directly to higher posts, and because of the pernicious workings of the Roster System, in several departments an overwhelming proportion of the top posts are now occupied by persons who have climbed up the reserved route. The figures are startling in many instances: all but three of the twenty top posts in the General Education Department in a state, reports a colleague; six of six posts in the highest grade in a Claims Office in South Eastern Railways, railway employees report on the basis of documents lodged in courts, 21 out of 29 posts in the next highest grade; 16 of 26 posts of Office Superintendents in a Chief Works Manager's office in Western Railways ....

As the Roster binds the department or enterprise to fill posts numbered such and thus only by persons from the reserved castes, the minimum requirements which have been laid for those posts - for instance, that the person must have served X number of years in the preceding post - are routinely put :aside for these employees. As are mandatory departmental examinations which are meant to ensure that the person has at least the minimum abilities necessary for the job at the level to which he is being promoted. The railway employees draw our attention to specific cases. 'A' joins as a casual waterman in August 1958; by 1980 he is Office Superintendent, the highest post in Grade III, not because he has acquired additional skills which his peers do not have but because of his caste; he would have gone much higher by now but for the fat that he is not even a matriculate .... 'B' is appointed Clerk in mid 1958, ranking 84 in the seniority list"; by 1974 July, having secured four promotions within grade III, he is promoted as Assistant Personal Officer to Grade II; by March 1982 he is Divisional Personal Officer; he is on the verge today of being promoted to the post of Junior Administrative Officer - again not because he has gathered additional qualifications, over the railway officers, but because of his caste.... 'C' joins Railways as a safaiwala; he is appointed a Clerk against a reserved quota post; he ranks 131 in the "seniority list" at this time; within years, leap-frogging over others, he is Senior Clerk...; he too, a matriculate, is going to make it to being a Class I Officer; again not because....

The consequences for efficient administration can be easily imagined.

Only two facts need to be added. These are consequences which have ensued when reservations have been only 22.5 per cent or thereabouts. V.P. Singh is now set to enlarge them to 50, if he has his way to 60 per cent, indeed with his proclaimed eagerness to have reservations for minorities also, to a figure indefinitely higher than even 60 per cent.

Second, in most states thus far, the quota in promotions has been limited to Classes II, III and IV alone. One can avail of these accelerated channels only unto the starting point of Class I. Mandal prescribes that quotas shall he set aside for promotions "at all levels." And V.P. Singh, Madhu Dandavate, etc. have all sworn that Mandal's recommendations will be implemented "without dilution". Imagine the situation then when posts of Secretaries and Additional Secretaries to government are packed in this way, and to this extent - as they must inevitably be when the Roster is put in operation, when they are packed that is by persons who by definition lack the qualifications necessary for the job.

And to imagine that it Prime Minister and his colleagues have set us on this ruinous course without so much as reading the report, and, on the, telling of a minister like Sharad Yadav himself because it is a master-stroke for consolidating some vote hank.

Identification

It is evident that whether one has or not been born into one of the castes which have been able to wrest reservations makes a great deal of difference to one's being able to avail of admissions, of jobs, of jobs at higher levels, etc. - that is of things that are very, very scarce in India.

A great deal therefore turns on which castes have been recognised as backward enough to merit reservations. The courts have struck down lists prepared by states on occasion. Mandal himself cites the Supreme Court's key decision on the point in *State of A.P.* v. *P. Sagar* (AIR 1968 SC 1379). The High Court of Andhra had struck down the list the state government was operating on. The state came to the Supreme Court in appeal. The Supreme Court too declared the list to be without basis and hence invalid. Its observations on the occasion were definite and stern-laying down both the high norms such lists must live up to as well as the reason why they must do so.

The observations are indeed worth reading. The observations when contrasted with what prevails even today, i.e., twenty-two years after the Supreme Court laid down the law so emphatically—are enough to invalidate the entire paraphernalia of reservations, the entire structure rests after all on lists of castes recognised as backward, etc.

Here is what the Supreme Court said in *State of AP* v. *Sagar*:

- "Article 15 guarantees by the first clause a fundamental right of far reaching importance to the public generally. Within certain defined lists an exception has been engrafted upon the guarantee of the freedom in cause (1), but being in the nature of an exception, the conditions which justify departure must be strictly shown to exist. When a dispute is raised before a Court that a particular law which is inconsistent with the guarantee against discrimination is valid on the plea that it is permitted under Clause (4) of Article 15, the assertion by the State that the officers of the State had taken into consideration the criteria which has been adopted by the Courts for determining who the socially and educationally backward classes of the Society are, or that the authorities had acted in good faith in determining the socially and educationally backward classes of citizens, would not be sufficient to sustain the validity of the claim. The Courts of the country are invested with the power to determine the validity of the law which infringes the fundamental rights of citizens and others and when a question arises whether a law which prima facie infringes a guaranteed fundamental right is within an exception the validity of that law has to be determined by the Courts on materials placed before them. By merely asserting that law was made after full consideration of the relevant evidence and criteria which have a bearing thereon, and was within the exception, the jurisdiction of the Courts to determine whether by making the law is a fundamental right has been infringed is not excluded.

"The High Court has repeatedly observed in the course of their judgement that no materials at all were placed on the record to enable them to decide whether the criteria laid down by this Court for determining that the list prepared by the Government conformed to the requirements of Clause (4) of Article 15 were followed. On behalf of the State it was merely asserted that an enquiry was in fact made with the aid of expert officers and the Law Secretary and the question was examined from all points of view by the officers of the State, by the Cabinet Sub-Committee and by the Cabinet. But whether in that examination the correct criteria were applied is not a matter on which any assumption 'could be made especially when the list prepared is ex facie based on castes or communities and is substantially the list which was struck down by the High Court in P. Stakhadev's case 1966-I

Andh W.R. 294. Honesty of purpose of those who prepared and published the list was not and is not challenged but the validity of a law which apparently infringes the fundamental rights of citizens cannot be upheld merely because the law maker was satisfied that what he did was right or that he believes that he acted in manner consistent with the constitutional guarantees of the citizen. The test of the validity of a law alleged to infringe 'the fundamental rights of a citizen or any act done in execution of that law lies not in the belief of the maker of the law or of the person executing the law, but in the demonstration by evidence and argument before the Courts that the guaranteed right is not infringed."

We have already seen that this enunciation, which, of course, he cites in full, had not the slightest effect on Mandal.

- He incorporated wholesale lists that were in use in states which, as we have seen earlier, on his own telling had little basis;
- He ordered an enormous survey. Professor B.K. Roy-Burman who headed the team has revealed (*Indian Express*, August 31, 1990) that each of the suggestions of the experts was ignored; that instead of 151 tables suggested by them being used, 31 were used; that the data collected were concealed from the experts; that while experts had concluded that occupation was a better criteria of backwardness, or at best a blend of occupation and caste, Mandal plummeted for caste alone; that the tampering, commenced precisely after a pilot survey in West Bengal showed that only two occupational groups—blacksmiths and potters—could properly be regarded as "backward"; that the weights arrived at by the experts for the different criteria were arbitrarily dumped and another set fabricated; that the Commission has inflated its estimate of the proportion backwards are of the population by imaginative triple counting; and so on.
- Mandal has himself recorded that the survey the Commission conducted, by excluding the experts it now turns out, yielded incredible results, and that therefore the Commission modified them using its own "intimate

personal knowledge"-of course he does not disclose in how many cases and to what extent the results were thus modified.

The results are therefore of indeterminate worth. In his letter to the Prime Minister, Mr Biju Patnaik has pointed to some laughable aspects of the list Mandal furnishes in the case of Orissa. Twenty-odd castes which he has listed as being "Other Backward Castes" are in fact already recognised as Scheduled Castes! The Commission lists as castes entities which are just surnames, and surnames at that which are used by high caste persons too!! some castes he lists are untraceable in Orissa.

The West Bengal government too has said, that it is not able to even trace some of the "castes" the Commission has listed.

In the cases of UP, Bihar etc. we have seen earlier that the Commission has listed as "backward" castes which are in fact dominant, and domineering. That is as far as his report goes.

The Decade Since

Mandal submitted his report a decade ago. Has the situation changed in the intervening ten years? Is the list in use in your state based on some systematic survey, I asked my colleagues. They contacted the authorities. Here are the answers they received:

• *Andhra:* No survey in the strict sense has been conducted; castes have been identified on the basis of the report submitted by a committee headed by K.N. Anantaraman in June 1970, that is twenty years ago.

• *Assam:* Of all things Mandal's list has been adopted, plus the results of "some sort of rough, survey", in this survey "geographical remoteness, food habits, living patterns, economic standard and educational status" were used as criteria "but they were followed very loosely."

• *Bihar:* Castes have been added to the list periodically; it is said that apart from other things the government has for this purpose used results of the work of two research institutions in the state.

• *Goa:* A survey was the basis of identifying Scheduled Castes no survey was undertaken for identifying Other Backward Castes, instead castes were recognised as backward "on the basis of projections made by OBC leaders".

• *Gujarat:* A mixture of "claims and suggestions and the results of a survey conducted by the Baxi Committee in 1972-76, i.e., about fifteen years ago.

• *Haryana:* No survey was ever carried out to determine who constitute the OBCs, nor are there any definite criteria or guidelines to determine backwardness; officers affirm that castes are recognised as backward "on the suggestions or recommendations of politicians and leaders".

• *Jammu & Kashmir:* Surveys are said to have been done; in the troubled conditions at this time it is not possible to verify their worth, etc.

• *Karnataka:* It is the one state in which a comprehensive survey is said to have been done; but see below for what happened to major entries in it.

• *Kerala:* The list was prepared by the Nettoor Commission years ago: it was not based on any comprehensive survey; "information provided by heads of departments and institutions was used .... a few random sample surveys in villages and towns were used .... scanty police records and newspaper reports of untouchability served to determine historically backward classes .... " reports my colleague.

• *Madhya Pradesh:* No organised survey; guidelines for identification of a caste as backward are also vague; educational and social criteria are said to have been used "which the present set of bureaucrats is not able to elaborate".

• *Maharashtra:* No comprehensive survey; list in use originated primarily from the recommendations of a committee headed by an MLA which submitted its report in November 1961, i.e., almost thirty years ago.

• *Orissa:* As the Chief Minister has stated, the state has no list of OBCs at all.

• *Punjab:* Periodic surveys of indeterminate thoroughness and comparability are said to be the basis.

• *Rajasthan:* No survey has been made to identify OBCs, and the concerned departments of the state government do not have any list of OBCs to operate from.

• ***West Bengal:*** The state government does not seem to have any information about identifying OBCs.

• ***Tamil Nadu:*** From British days castes have from time to time been recognised as backward on the basis of petitions and departmental assessments; no surveys were done, the fate of the Enumeration Commission which was set up in January 1938 is noted below.

• ***Uttar Pradesh:*** No survey; instead recommendations of the Chedilal Sathi Committee which reported in 1975 and of all things, the Mandal Commission seem to be the main sources for the list.

Thus, apart from Karnataka and two-three other states hardly a survey to speak ad hoc additions. A host of criteria, varying from committee to committee, from state to state, and these combined with varying, in most cases unknown weightages.

The Real Determinant

And supervening over all these, muscle power.

The Havanur Commission removes Lingayats from the list of Backward Classes in Karnataka. The Venkataswamy Commission removes the Vokkaligas too. Violence follows. The government restores both to the list.

In September, 1987, the Vanniyar Sangham in Tamil Nadu claims that 65 lakh Vanniyars in the state constitute a fifth of the state's population, and therefore deserve an exclusive reservation of 20 per cent. It launches a violent agitation. This triggers off a fresh wave of demands from other caste-based organisations, and during his last days MGR holds discussions, more accurately these are held on his behalf with about 100 of them. The process of examining their demands comes to nought as the population figures projected by each of them, when added up, far exceed the total population of the state!

In January, 1988 the state comes under President's Rule. After discussions with the Vanniyar Sangham, both at the central and state level, the Tamil Nadu government accepts in principle the need for exclusive reservations for the most backward castes, including the Vanniyars, as distinct from backward castes in general. An Enumeration Commission headed by P.V.

Venkatakrishnan is set up to conduct a census of the most backward castes, including the Vanniyars. The latter are not assuaged and demand an interim reservation for themselves. Karunanidhi comes to power in 1989, and announces in the Assembly that he has wound up the Enumeration Commission so as to decide the issue at the earliest as the Vanniyars have given him an "ultimatum" in this regard. On March 13, 1989, he announces 20 per cent reservation for the Most Backward Castes, including the Vanniyars. Karunanidhi's caste is naturally among the Most Backward Castes.

This is the manner in which additions and deletions to the list, indeed reservations themselves have been wrested. Such is the appalling basis of Mandal's list. Such that of the state lists. And V.P. Singh, in announcing that whichever caste is in Mandal's list and a state list, will be entitled to the new reservations, has embraced both.

His commitment, he says.

Arun Shourie: The Same Sequence Deserves the Same Answer
Indian Express, 28.8.1990

One day, suddenly: "Twenty seven per cent of jobs will be reserved for OBCs."

"And if the courts come in the way, I am sure with your help we will..."

The next, "No, I didn't mean that. I was just saying..." - Could you make out what he was saying about what he had said?

And the next, "The recommendations of the Mandal Commission will be implemented without dilution..."

And the next, "...540 members are not the country."

And the next: "Prime Minister regrets the outburst of his minister..."

And the next, a call: "Hit the streets and give a befitting reply".

And the next: "Cabinet panel meets: 5-10 per cent quota proposed for poor in addition to the 27 per cent already decided for the "Other Backward Castes ... ", the latter being in addition to the 22.5 per cent that already exists for the Scheduled Castes and Tribes.

The new total thus is to be 55 to 60 per cent of all jobs in government, at the Centre and in the states, the public sector, every educational institution, and every unit in the private sector which has availed of assistance from the government or any governmental institution.

The 50 per cent limit the courts are said to have laid down?

But that only brings in back to the first day's proclamation: "And if the courts come in the way, I am sure with your help we will.."

And to the call, "Hit the streets and give a befitting reply..."

What are these? Offices of state? Or assets of a family "trust" to be disposed of at whim?

The Same Sequence

We are seeing again the unvarying sequence.

A ruler is catapulted to power.

For the first few months he is overawed by the responsibilities: Mrs Gandhi in 1967-68 Rajiv in the first three or four months, V.P. Singh till February-March.

But soon the paraphernalia around him, the fact that in his immediate environment everything responds to his directions, indeed to his wishes, the deference of everyone, to say nothing of the flattery, as yet only tentative, exploratory, of the sychophants - all these transform his psyche. The earlier hesitation becomes, "The job is easier than they said."

And that within months, "I am born to it." And that within weeks, "I am better at it than Panditji was."

Again one has just to think back a little and one can pinpoint almost to the month the metamorphosis.

This is the phase in which the ruler is all for openness, for freedom, for inner-party democracy, for participation, this is when he is tossing one "unconventional" idea after another into the public arena, the phase in which he doesn't just proclaim, he comes to hold an expansive, generous view of others. The press? "O, don't worry about them. Boys will be boys after all." Civil servants? "All that was just rot, I tell you. They are most cooperative in fact eager to do well by the country. And they know what they are talking about.

And then some mistakes occur. The ruler, by now convinced of his worth, makes light of them. He doesn't just believe that he is clever, but that cleverness will do.

But the first changes surface: some snide remarks about a colleague or two who "misled" him, a secretary who "thinks too much of himself and needs to be put in his place", and that fellow in the press, "Who does he think he is?"...

Things drift. And then the big mistake - Mrs Gandhi's nationalisation of the wholesale trade in wheat, Rajiv's Muslim Women's Bill. And suddenly a siege mentality. And a new set of arguments: "If we yield now, people will think we are weak..." "These fellows are elitist..." "It is an issue only in the cities..."

And the sychophants are by now thick, their syrup is doubly thick; the leader's difficulty is their opportunity.

And they are joined now by those who had urged the leader to take the step in the first place.

"All these congenital whiners are just a handful of reactionaries, McNamara's boys," the progressives around her were telling Mrs. Gandhi in the days following wheat trade nationalisation. "The masses hate no one more than the traders. Nothing has enthused them as much as this measure... In any case having struck such a mighty blow, governments cannot retreat... Who will obey orders tomorrow if we draw back in the face of a mere agitation?"

"These are just communalists," the fellows around him told Rajiv even as they left him stranded to take the rap for the Muslim Women's Bill. "The Muslims are ours for ever... Now all that we have to do is to do something for the Harijans and we are through... And look at the fantastic impact in the Arab world..."

"All that talk of Punjab... Where is it now?" And, of course, that conclusive argument: "To retreat in the face of this mob will be fatal. We will not only forfeit our claims to be secular, we will be seen as a government that can be pushed around..." The leader thus suddenly turns, *dheeth*, obstinate, "I'll show them..."

"Let it be clear, this government does not give in...," he proclaims.

The Very Things

And all the things he himself had been saying were sickening in, the previous regime commence:

- Staged rallies - trucks rounded up, supporters paid with money collected from the same businessmen in the same black ways...;
- Management of news — blacking facts out from TV and radio, planting stories and "analyses" in the press;
- Unable to answer any of the arguments or facts cited by those who oppose the measure, resort to pasting motives on the critics;
- Use of the IB, of the rest of the apparatus to divide the movement that is building up;
- Some trumped up characters ostensibly from the ranks of the critics with whom a "dialogue" is commenced;
- Some formula... the chant then, "These are just destabilisers, they are not interested in the issue; see, they are refusing to even discuss the matter..." And then the high ground, the moral indignation, "Is it democratic to refuse to even talk? That proves that these so-called critics of the measure are not interested in the measure at all..."
- At first the pooh-poohing of the movement: "Just a handful of professional agitationists...." "The people are solidly with us." Then the frenzy of abuse and distortion: "Vested interests are behind the stir .... Big business houses and sections of the press who want to run the government are using innocent students... Foreign agents ...."
- The proclamation of victory each time the people are unable to stand up to the might of the State, or you succeed in dividing them; a contrived call for a bandh, and then the glee, "...Bandh call a flop ...."

And behind-the-scenes? One "compromise formula" after another .... The desperate search for someone who will negotiate... The plea for mercy, "Arey bhai, you are the ones who created this government. Jo hone tha voh to ho gaya, what had to happen has happened. You must help find a way out ...."

As these don't work, the ruler becomes not just obstinate, he becomes obstinate with a vengeance, his statements become shriller, he bares the more venomous among his colleagues, he rushes the pace of the measure... "You say this is too much? Here are three more things I will do.. Let's see what you gutter-snipes can do..."

Mrs Gandhi on the nationalisation of wholesale trade in wheat .... Mrs Gandhi on her colleagues as their misdeeds became the talk... Mrs Gandhi on Assam... and then on the Punjab... Rajiv on the Muslim Women's Bill... Rajiv on his coterie... Rajiv on the Defamation Bill ....

V.P. Singh Enters that Phase

V.P. Singh has entered this phase.

You object to reservations?

I'll have them from August 7.

You want a discussion?

I'll have them implemented without dilution.

You say 49.5 per cent is too much?

I'll force 55 per cent, even 60 per cent.

And the same management of news: compare the blackout of the unrest that has swept entire regions, the systematic blackout of it on Doordarshan, with the stir against the Defamation Bill and the blackout and misrepresentation of that under Rajiv.

The threatening calls of Paswan and Sharad Yadav ....

The same arguments in V.P. Singh's circle: "52 per cent votes *to aa hi gayin hain* - we have got 52 per cent of the votes already:.. And the 10 per cent Muslims by that stroke of genius - the holiday... And Dr Ambedkar's portrait .... We just have to hold on .... This is just *jhaag*, just froth. They can't keep it up for a week ...."

And there is no shortage of analysts: "A master-stroke .... In one stroke he has cemented a base... In just one stroke he has made Rajiv Gandhi, Devi Lal, Chandrashekhar irrelevant... In just one stroke he has finished public discussion of price rise, Punjab, J&K, Assam .... In one stroke he has finished all that nonsense about his being indecisive..."

Not one substantive argument in favour of that has been done. Plot one point made by the critics refuted. Nor even the attempt to refute it.

Instead, "Hit the streets and give a fitting reply."

Posters: "V.P. Singh: *Janta ki or se haardhik dhanyavad*", "V.P. Singh: the people's heartfelt gratitude." You just have to change the name and you are back to Rajiv's months. In the other poster you don't even have to change the name, "Arun Shourie *hosh mein aao...*", "Arun Shourie come to your senses..."

And the same howl outside as I write: "It is all a conspiracy of the *Indian Express*."

And notice the casualness with which, the cynicism with which such an enormous step has been taken.

No minister seems to have studied the report. Quite the contrary - several of them have telephoned to say that it is only when the details were published by this paper that they realised what they had acquiesced in.

Nor has one to go by what they acknowledge in private.

Notice yesterday's announcement: in addition to the 27 per cent, another 5 to 10 per cent for the poor. Does that sudden enlargement not itself show up the casualness, the utter lack of application with which the original decision was taken? Lack of application that is to the legal and administrative aspects of the matter. There was of course application of mind of another sort, there was of course much cynical calculation. But that only proves the point further: a lot of calculation about what would accrue to the leader, the party, none about what would be visited upon the country.

Gone is all that talk of consulting the allies.

Gone too all that talk of inner-party democracy. Three ministers of V.P. Singh's cabinet and two sagacious MPs have told me personally - and that of their own accord - that their efforts to get the matter discussed have been well and truly "discouraged."

"But' his Commitment"

That is why it is such a decisive moment. The ruler has shown his perspective: that he thinks of us not as Indians but as Muslims, and OBCs and SCs and STs, as segments who can be bribed by loaves.

And he has shown more: that he would rend society, that he

would saddle the entire State with an onerous millstone for electoral gains.

More still: that having taken the step - without a whiff of that consultation of allies of which he was making such a fetish till the other day, without a whiff of that consultation with the party to which he so strenuously pledged himself just the other day - that having taken the step he will persist in it, "come what may," Mrs Gandhi's phrase and that of her executor in regard to the Assam "elections".

"But what could he do? He had made a commitment."

- What about his pledge, "I shall not join any political party"?
- What about his pledge, "I shall not contest for elections"?
- What about his repeated pledge, "I shall not stand for the Prime Minister's office .... Even if I am offered the post I will not accept it"?

What was each of those?

A commitment or a ruse?

And what about that other statement, "I shall be a disaster as Prime Minister"? What was that? A forecast he has to live up to? Or another commitment he has to fulfil?

Not commitment, but cold, cynical calculation.

A Decisive Moment

That is why if V.P. Singh prevails, if his cynical calculation prevails, a new law will become the norm - the notion that for gaining votes it is legitimate to divide society, to saddle the entire State.

A low whose effects will be as disastrous as the effects would have been if Mrs Gandhi, having clamped the country in an Emergency just to save her *gaddi*, had won in 1977.

As disastrous as they would have been if Charan Singh, having broken the party people had put in power to fulfil his personal ambition, had been confirmed as Prime Minister by the 1980 elections.

As disastrous as they would have been if Rajiv, having gamboled with the State as if it were his farm house, had been returned to office in 1989.

In each instance that particular perversion would have been legitimised, it would have become the norm for what succeeding rulers might do to further their personal interests.

The people stepped in. And the conduct, instead becoming the norm for future rulers, became the warning.

That is why it is so decisive a moment.

That is why it is so necessary for all to join the students in the struggle they have commenced.

It is not a struggle to save their jobs.

It is a struggle to determine what kind of a nation we will be, to determine what we will be - members of this caste or that sub-caste, Hindus or Muslims... Or Indians.

S.S. Gill: Mandal Myth of Merit and Equity

(Times of India, dated 4th September, 1990)

In today's atmosphere surcharged with anger and emotion, it is difficult to examine sensitive issues like the Mandal report with cool detachment. And yet certain unpleasant facts must be faced.

At what state in our history was caste-based reservation not practised? Our caste system was the most effective, water-tight and self-regulating system of reservation by birth ever created by man. Only Brahmins had access to Vedic Knowledge, only Kshatriyas could take up arms. When Shambuck, the *Shudra* went into deep meditation in the forests of Uttarkhand, Ram, the great up-holder of the moral law, chopped off his head for transgressing on an area reserved for upper castes.

Passport to Status

As Secretary, Mandal Commission, I met hundreds of caste associations during our countrywide tours, and one had to see it to believe the extent to which caste is still the passport to social status and advancement. The manner in which members of upper castes still molest women, extract forced labour, refuse to recognise tenancy rights and heap indignities on the lower castes cannot be visualised by the urban intelligentsia. Even today few Brahmins or Thakurs are prepared to dine with the backward castes, let alone intermarry. Mr. B.P. Mandal, the Chairman of the Commission and a Yadav (Gwala) by caste, used to narrate with great emotion how his teacher did not allow him to sit with the higher caste students when he first went to school. And this despite the fact that Mr. Mandal's father was the biggest land-owner of the area!

It is not my case that OBCs should now hit back to settle the wrongs of history. But those who fly into a holy rage at the mention of caste-based reservations must realise that this is not such an outlandish proposition, and its rationale is rooted in a society which has practiced it very effectively for over three thousand years. And it did so by subtly internalising a deep inferiority complex in lower castes through the moral tyranny of religious indoctrination, thus crippling the psyche of the lower castes for hundreds of generations.

Does reservation really offend the basic norms of merit and equity? The competitive mechanism supposed to reward merit is really a race between un-equals.

Merit in a competition depends on two main considerations: native endowments and environmental factors. A child born to city-bread, well-educated, affluent parents has crucial advantages wholly denied to an infant born to uneducated peasants in a remote village. The former has excellent role-models to copy and the information fall-out from his environment is colossal. But a peasant boy with the highest native endowments would probably aspire to be at most a clerk or junior revenue official. The two are not equipped to run the same race.

It is usually argued that the correct remedy to the above situation lies in giving all possible educational facilities to the children of Scheduled and backward classes. However, cultural upgradation is generational process. One full generation after the introduction of reservations for scheduled castes and tribes, only 10 such candidates got into IAS on merit in the ten years from 1969-78 less than one per cent of the total. Out of nearly 50 secretaries to the Government of India, there is, perhaps, not even one from the Scheduled Castes and Tribes.

Equality has three facets—equality of opportunity, equality of treatment, and equality of results. "Equality of opportunity... is actually a libertarian and not an egalitarian principle as it allows the same freedom to everybody in this (unequal) race of life," says the Mandal report. Equality of treatment, suffers from the same drawback, as it treats the disadvantaged on par with the advantaged.

Equality of results is the only truly equalitarian principle, as a tree must be judged by its fruits. No amount of learned hairsplitting is of any use to the vulnerable sections of society if this does not rectify centuries of deprivation.

True, the benefits of reservation are generally hogged by better-off families, and the really deprived sections are left high and dry. But is this not a universal phenomenon? Even among the higher castes the top 10-15 per cent corner the bulk of the state subsidies, export incentives, industrial licences and tax holidays. The real significance of 27 per cent job reservations for the OBCs is than the community's morale and self image will get a much needed boost.

Anti-reservationists say that the general level of administration will slump if we have OBC reservations. This is a wholly specious argument. A student from a backward family is not a dud just because he gets a few marks less in a competition. Once given the authority of office, he comes up very fast. On the other hand, his intimate experience of social deprivation is a valuable asset in dealing with grass-root problems, beside you do not need a genius to do administrative chores.

Merit-List Candidates

However, there is no reason to exclude merit-list backward class candidates from the reserved quota. Suppose there are 100 vacancies and 50 reserved quota candidates obtain the top 50 positions in an open competition. In that event the quotawallahs will get all the posts, which is indefensible.

Secondly, when the backward classes have made enough progress to secure a fair proportion of merit-based posts, reservations should be scrapped.

Thirdly, a means test (income ceiling) should be applied within the backward classes.

Large sections of our population feel they are being cheated of legitimate access to top posts by OBC reservations. We have a clash of interests between the rights of the individual and that of society. Such a conflict is inherent in all legislation aiming at the correction of structural imbalances. In the words of justice K. Subba Rao,"The right of social justice may be defined as the right of the weak to the protection of the state against the ruthless competition of life.... It is the balancing wheel between the haves and the havenots." (*Times of India*, 4th September, 1990)

Anikendra Nath Sen and Kuldeep Kumar: The Mandalising of India

(Times of India, dated 12th August, 1990)

The V.P. Singh government's decision to implement the Mandal Commission's recommendations on reservations was motivated purely by tactical and political considerations. But, warn the measure will have repercussions not only on the country's politics but also on its social equations and education and administrative systems.

It was hanging fire for the better part of 10 years, one of the many voluminous reports gathering dust in the home ministry. Very few had actually bothered to read it, barring those bureaucrats who had no choice. It surfaced periodically as an emotive issue with some politicians, most of whom had barely glanced through it, seeking mileage out of demands for its "implementation" and a few others equally vehement in their opposition to its principles.

A riot or two here and there between those in favour and those against served to keep the pot simmering and it looked as if it would become yet another mystical document like the Anandpur Sahib resolution. That is until the Janata Dal included its implementation in its election manifesto last year. But even here there was a sneaky feeling that it would not see the light of day, like so many other election promises. Consequently most people were taken by surprise when the Prime Minister, Mr. Vishwanath Pratap Singh, in a suo moto statement in Parliament, announced the government's decision to implement the Mandal Commission recommendations reserving 27 per cent of central government and public sector jobs for "socially and educationally backward classes".

This is the first time that central government and public sector jobs have been reserved for backward classes (castes) since independence and takes the total percentage of reserved jobs in these sectors up to 49.5 per cent, just 0.5 per cent short of the maximum limit set by the Supreme Court. Predictably enough the decision to enforce the Mandal Commission's recommendations has aroused contradictory reactions throughout the country. While all the mainstream political parties have no choice but to raise two qualified cheers in favour of the step, the reaction on the street has been somewhat different — spontaneous agitations by upper caste students in places as far apart as Delhi and Bihar.

Questions have been raised in political circles about the timing of the measure. The Janata Dal leader, Mr. Chandra Shekhar publicly echoed the private feelings of many in his party when he said: "The matter was hanging fire for quite some time but this decision was taken only 48 hours before the Kisan Rally (organised by supporters of the former Deputy Prime Minister Mr. Devi Lal). So, it gives an impression that the people responsible for it were apprehensive about the rally and took this decision in haste. But the decision is welcome and it should be praised."

Leaders of the BJP and the CPM, the two parties whose support is crucial for the survival of the National Front government, were not even consulted before the decision was taken. According to Mr. Prakash Karat, member of the central committee of the CPM: We were informed a day before the decision was announced." The BJP general secretary, Mr. Krishan Lal Sharma, said, "The fact that they (National Front) were thinking along those lines was conveyed to us, so we knew that the government was going ahead with it." Both declined to elaborate further but leaders of both parties have made their displeasure at not being consulted known to the Prime Minister. They have also pointed out that the decision was hasty and should have been taken after seriously considering the possible consequences that might flow from it.

While the Kisan Rally at New Delhi's Boat Club loomed

large when the decision was made public and was naturally touted as the main reason for the step, there are some other possible motives behind the timing of the measure which have not been publicly articulated. A major consideration, according to some is the threat to the Mulayam Singh Yadav ministry in Uttar Pradesh, both from within and without the Janata Dal. The decision can only strengthen Mr. Yadav's hands, putting the entire weight of the backward castes in his state behind him.

It should also serve to counter the Vishwa Hindu Parishad's plan to begin building the Ram Janmabhoomi Temple in Ayodhya from October 30. Mr. Yadav has made it clear that he will take administrative steps to prevent the construction from going through. Various political parties including the Janata Dal and the CPM-CPI combine, have said they will organise public rallies and meetings against the temple plan. The battle lines are drawn with the BJP threatening to mount the "biggest ever" public agitation in the country in support of the VHP if the construction is stopped. Implementing the Mandal Commission recommendations, it is being calculated, will rally a large chunk of people, including those who would have otherwise swung over to the VHP-BJP cause, to the side of the secular parties.

Leaders of most parties privately admit that "Mandalisation" could become a powerful counter to the growing menace of communalism, mainly Hindu communalism, in the country. They however, refuse to state this publicly. According to Mr. Chandra Shekhar, "The two things should not be mixed up. Our fight against communalism is altogether different. "The CPM's Prakash Karat says: "I have heard of this theory but I would not like think that these are the only two alternatives." CPM leaders however privately admit that the measure will do much to shore up the position of Mr. Mulayam Singh Yadav whose continued existence as chief minister they have strongly endorsed. Indeed the party has taken the unusual step of warming all those within.the Janata Dal interested in toppling Mr. Yadav to desist from doing so.

Electoral compulsions are probably the major motive force behind the decision, with possibilities of a winter election being taken increasingly seriously. This is, however, yet to be articulated in public by any political figure of worth. If it is indeed motivated by electoral compulsions, the decision to implement the Mandal Commission recommendations will need be followed up by other populist measures catering to those who have been left out of the reservation scheme of things. And therein lies the crunch.

Despite the fact that the Mandal Commission took economic considerations into account before listing the various classes it considered to be "backward," the overwhelming tenor of its report is based on caste considerations. As a result the populist measure will have to be extended to more and more people on the basis of caste. At the same time parties like the BJP and CPM are all in favour of economic criteria being applied to reservations.

According to the BJP's Krishan Lal Sharma: "We are in favour of the recommendations made by the Mandal Commission with the proviso that economic criteria should also be taken into account while extending reservations to some more castes. We feel that reservations for scheduled castes and tribes should continue as it is but economic criteria should also be applied while expanding the list of reservations to others."

This two directional pull could well result in both demands being conceded. The government is itself the fastest growing employment sector in the country. It is also the least productive. The consequences of conceding ground on reservations based on both caste and economic considerations could have a disastrous impact on the economy. As one bureaucrat pointed out: "The idea behind Mandal may have been to check communal forces. But we could end up with both communalism and Mandalisation. It could drive the upper castes towards the VHP and the rest towards government jobs."

The number of jobs will eventually have to be increased to accommodate more and more people on the reserved quota while keeping the ratio between reserved and merit jobs intact at 50:50.

"Sooner or later we will be asked to Mandalise education and the private sector. Both areas are within the sphere of the report.

Imagine the cost of having to invest increasingly on non-producive government jobs and think of the impact it will have on the private sector," he warns.

The new reservations have already set off a spate of protest movements in different parts of the country. The spectre of violence-torn anti-reservation movements in Gujarat in 1985-86 has already begun to raise its ugly head in the minds of many. The new policy could well institutionalise the fragmentations present in the traditional caste-based Indian society, indeed it could lead to further fragmentation. Mr. Chandra Shekhar, however, feels that this need not be so: "I certainly do not think that these reservations will lead to the further fragmentation of our society. The chances of fragmentation are greater if people who have been exploited and deprived for long are not given any hope for the future."

According to the CPM's Prakash Karat: "Our concern is it (reservations) should not lead to the creation of barriers between workers, employers, poor peasants, we will try and avoid that.

That is why while in principle we support reservation, economic criteria would have helped in selling this idea to the other castes. But unfortunately this has not been done."

In sum, therefore, the new reservation policy is bound to be the source of considerable controversy. While no political party can hope to actively oppose it and survive in the electoral arena, individuals within these parties are likely to strike out in different directions according to their own support bases. Parties such as the BJP and the CPM are likely to demand the inclusion of economic yardsticks to determine who should benefit and who should not. This could only lead to an expansion in the share of reserved seats since no government has been known to deprive those who already enjoy the benefits of such measures for the sake of others. This would, of course, require a constitutional amendment since the law at present allows for reservations of only fifty per cent of the jobs at stake.

The possibilities of further anti-reservation agitations, even violent ones, in states such as Gujarat cannot be entirely ruled out.

This could, of course, suit the electoral ambitions of many since such a sharp polarisation of forces can lead on to an equally sharp polarisation of votes. The losers in this game must be precisely those forces which have been banking heavily on the Hindu card so far since it will sharply polarise Hindu society. It would also upset calculations based on the AJGAR formula since the Jats are missing from the list of beneficiaries. There are some who believes that the policy merely reflects reality in so far as those who were earlier deprived of political power and who have now achieved some measure of it are now demanding a share of the economic cake. But this would seem like putting the cart before the horse since movements worldwide indicate that political power generally flows from the inside flap of a wallet.

Arindam Sen Gupta and Bishakha De Sarkar: Elusive: A Consensus on Mandal

(Sunday Observer, dated 2nd September, 1990)

The move had a touch of the clandestine. The initiative came from the Congress. It deputed two of its senior leaders, Dinesh Singh and H.K.L. Bhagat, to contact the BJP and the Left parties. Their mission was to find out whether the two groups would agree to jointly move a resolution in Parliament seeking to make economic criteria the basis for job reservation. If such a resolution was passed, the agitation against the Mandal Commission would die down, ran the Congress argument.

Bhagat and Dinesh Singh contacted the BJP first. It is believed they got in touch with L.K. Advani. Advani, a man not given to rash decisions, told them that his party would consider the proposal, but would the Congress discuss the matter with the CPI(M) first? Gandhi was sent to the Marxist chief minister of West Bengal, Jyoti Basu. On Tuesday, Basu called on Rajiv to discuss the resolution.

But that is as far as things went. After talking to Rajiv, Basu is understood to have met the Prime Minister, V.P. Singh. Perhaps the resolution on economic criteria for reservation could be passed unanimously? According to CPI(M) sources, V.P. Singh did not approve of the suggestion. In fact, he threatened to dissolve Parliament in case such a resolution was moved.

"This amounts to a no-confidence move against the government," V.P. Singh is reported to have said. The Prime Minister was, however, keen on an all-party meet to thrash out the issue. The CPI(M) leaders conveyed V.P. Singh's stand to the

Congress. And the latter appears to have lost interest, for BJP sources say that the Congress never got back. Instead, it incorporated its views in what is now known as the "Rajiv formula". The upshot of this four cornered, hush-hush discussion was that the move to bring a resolution was dropped, but it gave birth to the idea of an all-party meeting.

The backroom political exercise made another thing quite obvious. The ghost of Mandal was now haunting every political party. The initial welcome to the reservation move had given way to palpable disquiet. There were sections in every party who were angry and who cited the spreading against Mandal as proof of the decision to implement his recommendations being unpopular. The leaders were being urged to articulate the popular resentment, even if it were confined to the upper castes and the urban middle class.

If Jagannath Mishra of Congress declared was against Mandal, Atal Bihari Vajpayee of the BJP called for a review of the decision. The CPI(M), which was most unreserved in its welcome of the decision, also raised an argument. Its politburo took note of agitation and its organ, Peoples' Democracy, wrote: "In Parliament no political party opposed (V.P. Singh's) announcement. But the way it was announced, specially the suddenness and unilateralness of it surprised even well-meaning people and the parties who support the government. In the will-of-the-wisp politics today's India, the announcement might have been a clever tactical move. But we cannot afford cleverness at the cost of (political) consideration in the present state of the country."

The Marxist argument was, in fact, becoming the main objection to Mandal among the parties. Since they had all approved of his recommendations earlier, objections were now being raised about the manner of implementing them. Leave aside the Congress and the supporting parties, Janata Dal leaders, too, were objecting to what was being generally perceived as V.P. Singh's cross political opportunism in implementing Mandal at this juncture. His move was being seen as one to create a vote bank among the backward castes while marginalising Devi Lal; not one to serve the downtrodden.

The Janata Dal Chief Minister of Orissa, Biju Patnaik, wrote to the Prime Minister asking for two modifications. First, there should be an income level ceiling to qualify for reservation, and second, there should be no reservation in promotions. These modifications would "help defuse the situation created all over the country". Another Dal leader, Chandra Shekhar said that while V.P. Singh's decision to hold an all-party meet was welcome, his refusal to negotiate the government order on Mandal was strange. "Such preconditions do not make for a meaningful meeting," he said.

Yet another Dal leader, Yashwant Sinha, described it as a "hasty step". It should have been taken after consulting party M.P.s and the supporting parties. One party M.P. Vishwendra Singh, went as far as to resign from the Lok Sabha in protest against the government decision. All in all, opposition to Mandal was crystallising within the ruling party, just as it has in the other parties. There was a growing consensus, cutting across party lines, that certain modifications were necessary be they additional reservation for the upper caste poor or the introduction of economic criteria.

In this context, an important political change appears to have taken place over the last one week. What was once seen as VP's "Masterstroke"—his winning a vote bank while silencing all others political opinion had become for him a bit of a problem. The very breaking of the uneasy silence by various political leaders, as well as the clandestine moves to modify Mandal's report which forced V.P. Singh to threaten dissolution of Parliament, indicated that.

The groundswell can be seen by the number of anti-Mandal statements on Sunday last. That day, Vajpayee called for a "roundtable discussion" on the issue; M.J. Akbar accused V.P. Singh of trying to "garner sordid political gains"; Jagannath Mishra described the Mandal report as being "sketchy and trash"; Shahabuddin asked for reservation for all groups; and Vyjanthimala Bali and Subramaniam Swamy, too, came out against the decision.

That evening, V.P. Singh called a meeting of the cabinet committee on political affairs (CCPA). Sources in the CCPA said that the Prime Minister looked somewhat disturbed when it was pointed out to him that his decision was being seen as move born out of political expediency. His image would suffer as a result, as also his goodwill among the benefited sections. The CCPA eventually decided to propose in the Parliament a 5-10 per cent reservation on the basis of economic criteria. The decision was obviously meant to blunt the growing resentment among students and political parties.

Later, in the evening Jaipal Reddy betrayed the fact that the government was, indeed, on the defensive. He told journalists: "There could be two opinions about the wisdom of the decision (to implement Mandal) but not about the honesty of purpose behind the decision." But in reality, it was the latter which was being doubted by most and Reddy's vehement assertion about VP's "honesty of purpose" betrayed that the government was only too aware of this. The government's apologetic explanation of Sharad Yadav and Ram Vilas Paswan's call for a counter movement to the anti-Mandal stir also indicated the same defensive attitude.

The new somewhat conciliatory tone was apparent when the Janata Dal ideologue, Surendra Mohan, told The *Sunday Observer*.

"I agree with the general thrust of the recommendations, but not every word of the report is sacrosanct." He denied that political opportunism had dictated the move. "The NF government had promised social equality and is working in that direction," he said, but indicated that the decision was perhaps hasty. "We need to patiently explain the main purpose and objectives of the Mandal report to the younger generation," he said.

Ashok Guha: Mandal Mania and Social Justice

(Indian Express, dated 5th September, 1990)

It is trite but true that controversies generate more heat than light. The tumult over Mandalism to take the latest instance has tended to obscure one cardinal point in the debate. The advocates of reservations have argued that reservations benefit the traditionally underprivileged and correct the immemorial injustice of centuries. The critics while conceding this point generally claim that it is out-weighed by the devastating impact of reservations on efficiency and their divisive effect on political and social life. The issue has therefore been posed in terms of a choice between egalitarianism on the one hand and quality and national unity on the other.

Is this in fact a valid dichotomy? Do reservations in government employment or university admission really benefit the underprivileged Other Backward Castes (OBCs)? The obvious answer seems to be "yes" until one begins to examine the question closely... A job in Government requires as a basis minimum qualification a Bachelor's Degree or at the very least a Higher Secondary Certificate. So does university admission. Yet only 1.5 per cent of our general population graduate from college and only three per cent complete high school. Among the educationally backward castes, the figures must by definition be lower; perhaps only 2 per cent of these possess Higher Secondary certificates. Every member of an OBC who works for Government or studies in a university comes from this microscopic minority. Everyone who is eligible to apply for government employment or university admission belongs to it. Reservations are designed for the exclusive benefit of this tiny elite. They cannot by their very nature reach down to the lower 98 per cent of the OBCs.

OBC Criterion

Further, since the OBCs are "educationally backward" the handful of them who have completed high school must be drawn from groups affluent enough to offset the 'educational backwardness' of their community. On an average, they are likely in fact to be richer than the typical high school graduate from a caste which is not 'educationally backward'.

The rhetoric of reservations is addressed to the mass of the underprivileged, but their rewards are 'reserved' for the water-thin affluent upper crust of OBC society. They do exactly nothing for the submerged 98 per cent. The egalitarianism that reservationists flaunt is pure fiction.

The problem of the OBCs are indeed genuine. The criteria used by Mr. B.P. Mandal in identifying the OBCs — the absence of a supply of drinking water on OBC dominated villages, the abysmal literacy levels, the phenomenal school drop-out rates, the pathetic state of female education — reflect these problems. It is all the more curious therefore that the Government should propose to attack these problems by a policy that is totally irrelevant to them. The Government does not intend to supply drinking water to OBC villages, or to improve their literacy levels or the educational status of their women. Instead, it offers a job to the *mukhia's* son. Such a policy can only create an overwhelming incentive among the OBC elite to do everything possible to perpetuate the backwardness of their respective communities — so that the favoured OBC status of which they are the sole beneficiaries — is not lost.

Political Imperatives

The political imperatives behind reservations are now transparent. Their primary effect is to mobilise the support of the OBC elite. The latter, it is believed, will be able because of it unique status in OBC society, its wealth, its relatively high educational level and its control over caste councils to persuade or coerce the general impoverished OBC masses to vote as it desires. The OBC upper crust is viewed as the most significant group of power brokers in the country. A policy designed exclusively for its benefit therefore makes excellent political sense.

The Mandal myth that reservations really do something for the cause of social justice has therefore been readily adopted and propagated by interested politicians. But Mandal was not just a myth-maker; he was a magician as well. He demonstrated how an individual or a party could acquire a reputation for egalitarianism at no cost whatsoever. During something real for the backward masses improving their schools, educating their women or supplying them drinking water is an expensive and laborious business. Reservations, on the other hand, cost nothing. One simply gives the leader of the more numerous community a job by taking it away from somebody more qualified but commanding less political clout congratulating oneself all the while on one's social consciousness. This is a politician's dream. It also represents cut-rate bargain basement egalitarianism and like many bargain-basement wars, it is not the genuine article... .

Could a semblance of authentic egalitarianism be restored by a supplementary or substitutive scheme of reservations based on economic criteria? Could the Prime Minister's 5-10 per cent or perhaps a larger dose of 15, 20 or 25 per cent help?

Quite the contrary reservations on any ground whatsoever would simply not touch the 97 per cent of the general population who never complete school. They would among at best to redistribution within the elite.

Further, reservations on economic grounds must be based on verifiable and verified income certificates. Anyone who appreciates how fully extended the Income Tax Department is in checking the reported income of a miniscule segment of the population must marvel at the cavalier manner in which it is implied that an infinitely larger number of income certificates could be reliably verified. In fact, no credible verification system is possible. Income based reservations therefore will inevitably generate a flourishing market in income certificates, large-scale bribery of, and undue influence on the certifying authorities, preferences for the undeserving rich (who can pay the necessary bribes) at the expense of the deserving poor (who cannot) and a vast increase in the scope of political patronage. So utterly predictable are these consequences that one is hound to suspect the bonafides of parties or politicians who propose or accept such schemes.

Disguised Discrimination

Yes another reason why reservations while pretending to be egalitarian end up by being highly inequitable is their disguised discrimination against unrecognised classes of deprivation. Since the OBCs are particularly backward in the matter of sending their women to school, reservations for them will further depress the already low share of women in government jobs and higher education. Yet women constitute perhaps the most intensely deprived section of our people, systematically discriminated against across all castes and classes in nutrition, in education, in economic status. What is more, they are numerous as the OBCs and can be identified without certificates.

We have not yet mentioned the question of quality at all but that unfortunately is an issue that simply cannot be evaded in the context of reservations. It cannot be argued that since reservations affect only three per cent of the population, their impact on quality can only be peripheral; for quality is always the contribution of the select few; it is drastically affect by a lowering of standards among this handful.

The effect of reservations on quality is particularly devastating in an intensely competitive world in which India is locked in a grim struggle for her economic survival. It is too expensive now for us to continue in splendid isolation with our inefficiency fashioned by trade barriers; and in the open competition of the world market, the inefficiency induced by reservations would spell economic disaster.

Boosting Inefficiency

It may be argued that since reservations have so far been confined to the public sector, our prophecies of doom are exaggerated. Not so, however, in a country like ours, dominated by the Government, where the public sector controls the commanding heights, supplies all the essential infrastructural inputs and manipulates all the levers of policy, increased inefficiency in the public sector is bound to reverberate economy wide, ravaging the performance of the private sector as well.

Once the genie of reservations is out of the bottle, it is bound to expand to monstrous proportions. Even if the Government restricts reservations initially to public sector education and research will inevitably follow. This would accelerate the brain drain, doom the prospects of an Indian breakthrough in the high technology areas which are the focus of world economy growth, and destroy the competitiveness of Indian industry. In a world of rapid technological progress, where our highly trained and competent manpower could have been our one major asset, reservations would amount to economic suicide.

Reservations mortgage the future of India not in the interests of social justice, not even for the uplift by the backward castes, but solely and simply for the benefit of the OBC elite. The situation cries out for a leader with some vision of, and feeling for the India of tomorrow and the courage to try to break the hold of the OBC elite over the OBC masses. Without this kind of leadership, the second largest nation on earth will be doomed through the indefinite future to pay the price of one man's folly.

K.V. Ramanathan: Lessons from Experience

(Indian Express, dated 7th September, 1990)

The fact that the South is totally free of the kind of violent outbursts against the decision as the Mandal Commission report seen in Uttar Pradesh, Bihar, Delhi and other places in the North is, it has been pointed out due to the fact that the South is used to reservation for backward classes and has learnt to live with it. There are differences of opinion on the reservation issue but they are thankfully confined to academic debate. But the important point is that the South, especially Tamil Nadu, has considerable experience of working affirmative action of this kind from which lessons can be drawn.

It is undeniable that more than forty years after independence there is a large and unacceptable amount of social and educational backwardness in the country. Apart from the Scheduled Castes and Scheduled Tribes whose plight is universally acknowledged, there are large groups of people, particularly in rural areas, who are backward by any standard. There certainly has been considerable improvement after independence and the percentage of such people has indeed fallen but the absolute numbers are still large. While a wide distribution of educational facilities and creation of more employment are the basic steps needed to tackle this problem, affirmative action is called for if the balance is to be redressed; and, a country where caste is the basic determinate of many things, where social life is influenced by caste, and where caste determines to a large extent, even today, the occupations of a number of groups which in turn directly relate to their status and poverty, it is not possible to ignore caste altogether in determining backwardness. It is in this light that the courts have upheld the use, by a number of State Governments, of castes to list backward groups. It is easy enough to identify as traditionally backward, socially and educationally, occupational groups like dhobies, barbers, carpenters, potters, weavers and fishermen and non-Scheduled Castes groups that do work that is considered dirty or that are non-land owning agricultural labour. But it is in identifying other groups of castes that are predominantly backward that many commission, including the Mandal Commission, have found. And then there is the danger of using caste as the touchstone of backwardness leading to the better off and stronger among the castes and the better off and stronger in each caste shutting out the others. The basic justification of reservation is that it is necessary to eliminate backwardness. Its success should therefore be judged by how effectively and quickly it eliminates backwardness and renders reservation unnecessary. If, on the other hand, it becomes a vested interest and tends to perpetuate itself as has happened now-correctives are indeed called for.

The old Madras Presidency and Mysore State have a long history of affirmative action in favour of Scheduled Castes, Scheduled Tribes and other backward classes both by grant of educational concessions and in appointments to state services. Lists of these communities described on the basis of caste were prepared from time to time but always on an ad hoc basis, enlargements being in response to representations and pressures. In 1957, when Mr. Kamraj was the Chief Minister of Madras, it was recognised that a number of communities in the backward classes list were particularly badly off and had not gained much. They were grouped in a separate list of Most Backward Classes and given the same educational concessions as SCs and STs. The appointment of two commissions by the State Government, one in 1969 and another in 1982, to go into the question of backwardness did not result in determination of any rational criteria of backwardness. Ad hocism in the listing of backward classes has continued to be the policy. The number has gone up from 153 in 1953 to 222 in 1988 with the description of some of the later inclusions as backward being open to question. There has been no specific targeting of benefits, all those belonging to the designated class being eligible for the special concessions. The first Backward Classes Commission of Tamil Nadu chaired by Mr. A.N. Sattanathan, recommended the imposition of an income ceiling for eligibility. When Mr. M.G. Ramachandran accordingly ordered a ceiling of Rs. 9,000 per annum, there was an outcry and he promptly withdrew it.

Skewed Distribution

There is no doubt that the concessions have improved the educational status of backward classes in Tamil Nadu as a whole and that their representation, again as a whole, in the services has gone up considerably. In fact, thanks to consistent application of the policy of reservation in appointments at a number of levels, Tamil Nadu may be approaching a stage where the constitutional description in Article 16(4) of 'inadequate representation in the services' may be less and less applicable. One indication is the increasing number of backward classes securing admission or appointment in the "non-reservation" quota. But this is still not true to the SCs and STs. And, it is true of the backward classes only as a whole. Data presented in the report of the Tamil Nadu Second Backward Classes Commission by Mr. J.A. Ambasankar showed on the other hand how many of them are still to benefit. In the two year period 1980-82, 34 out of 222 communities in the list accounting for 42 per cent of the total backward class population secured 77 per cent of the reserved seats in professional courses, and 64 per cent of the reserved posts to which selection was made by the State Public Service Commission. The agitation of the Vanniars is attributable to this skewed distribution of the benefits of reservation. Mr. Karunanidhi has sought to meet this by subdividing the reserving quota for BCs and allotting a separate 20 per cent to an updated list of the category of Most Backward classes.

To go back now to Mandal, the Commission's listing of socially and educationally backward classes is a botched job. Such surveys as it conducted were very limited. The Data relating to them are not available. Having listed eleven broad criterion for identifying backwardness it had ultimately to fall back on State lists (themselves prepared on no uniform or scientific criteria) and, most amusing of all, "personal knowledge". The result is a hotchpotch, with repetitions and mistakes and a lumping together of a number of non-so-disadvantaged groups with genuinely backward, historically disadvantaged ones. There certainly was need, before accepting any of the recommendations of the commission, to have a thorough check of the lists in consultation with the States. The list has a staggering 3,743 Hindu OBCs and one is irresistibly reminded of the Government of India's statement in 1956 on the Kalelkar Commission report of the really needy being swamped by the multitude. Mr. V.P. Singh must have the lists carefully examined before finalising eligibility for the concessions he has ordered.

But this will not be enough. The concessions have to be targeted precisely to those that are most in need of them. The introduction of an economic criterion has been suggested for this purpose. There are two principal arguments advanced against this. The first is that, in the circumstances that prevail in India, it is quite possible for a rich family to be socially and educationally backward. This is true, particularly of the rural area but much less true today than say 40 years ago. Certainly in South India, there are not many well-to-do patriarchs left who sneer at formal education for their progeny. Even social disabilities affect the well to do very little. In any case reservation in appointments to the services is no answer to the backwardness of those who have it in themselves to come out of it. The second argument is that economic status may change and so eligibility should not be based on it. This is a specious argument for what is sought to be done is to determine the eligibility of a person belonging to a backward class for the benefit of reservation on the basis of his (or his parents) economic status at the time he seeks it. At that point of time, the better off BC should not deprive the less well off. Thus, an economic cut-off point for eligibility would be justified and would accelerate elimination of backwardness.

A second step that would ensure specific targeting of the benefit would be to take into account the educational and occupational status of the parents. In other words, if either parent is a graduate, and/or has employment satisfying certain present standards, the person concerned should be ineligible for the concession.

Basis for Discrimination

These two offer a clear basis for discrimination among other backward classes. In fact, they should be applied to SCs and STs also to ensure wide distribution of the benefits of reservation among them.

On the percentage of reservations, the Supreme Court would appear to have made obiter dicta to the effect that anything more than a total of 50 per cent might not be acceptable but in at least one case that came before it where it was in excess, the reservation was not struck down. In Tamil Nadu and Karnataka the total reservation for SCs, STs and OBCs is already far in excess of 50 per cent. If reservations are an exception to the principal constitutional provision of equality, even 50 per cent might be considered high. In any case, the aim should be to bring it down as more and more classes cease to require special treatment.

There should be a quinquennial review at regular intervals to assess the efficacy of the provisions for reservation and to determine which groups no longer need protection under the terms of Articles 15(4) and 16(4). The idea that reservations are intended to eliminate and not perpetuate, backwardness must be accepted and acted upon. The Mandal Commission has recommended a duration of 20 years for reservation. Time limits like this hardly ever work and tend to be routinely extended. Frequent review without a time limit would work better. But above all, sincere steps have to be taken to remove the root causes of educational backwardness by universalising primary and secondary, including vocational education, and providing generous scholarships and freeships as well as special coaching.

Meenakshi Jain: Irony of the Mandal Commission

(*Indian Express, dated 3rd September, 1990*)

It is ironic that among the prominent beneficiaries of the Mandal Commission report are Yadavs (Ahirs), Kurmis and Koiris, all of whom have been categorised as belonging to the "backward classes". Ironic because it is these very castes that have taken major strides forward in the period since independence. A number of recent studies have closely monitored the progress of these castes in the north Indian countryside. It would be instructive to look at some of the major findings.

To begin with Bihar. Yadavs are the largest single caste group in the State and comprise around 11 per cent of the total population. Together with Kurmis and Koiris they constitute 19 per cent of the population (the total backward population in Bihar is estimated to be around fifty per cent).

Yadavs in Bihar are so concentrated as to constitute over 25 per cent of the population in Bhagalpur, Hazaribagh, Gaya, Patna, Saharsa, Saran and Vaishali districts. Together with Kurmis and Koiris, they control an additional three districts (Nalanda, Giridih and Rohtas) where they comprise around thirty per cent of the population.

Bihar Scene

They have not been slow to turn this concentration to their advantage. From 1962 onwards (from when figures are available) at no point has the representation of these castes in the Bihar Vidhan Sabha been less than their percentage to the population. If anything Yadavs have been consistently over represented. As early as 1967 itself, Yadavs had emerged as the second largest caste group in the Bihar Assembly, next only to the Rajputs. By 1977 Yadavs comprised 21 per cent of the legislature, that is almost twice their strength in the population. The following years saw a further increase in the political might of the Yadavas so much so that by the 1980 assembly elections they formed the largest single caste group in the State Assembly.

Contrary to the general impression, these castes were a power to reckon with even in the Congress legislature party. In 1962, 22 per cent of the members of the CLP came from this group.

A look at their share in ministerial posts is even more revealling. As a result of an alliance between the Congress chief minister K.B. Sahay and Ram Lakhan Singh Yadav, the share of the Yadavs, Kurmis and Koiris in the 1963 state ministry increased to 20 per cent. From 1963 till the 1985 Bindeshwari Dubey government (till when information is available) their representation in Congress governments never went below 20 per cent. In governments headed by members of their own caste group their share has gone as high as 38 per cent in 1977. Moreover, in the last two decades Yadav alone have captured the chief ministership of the State no less than three times.

Political Power

The success of the top three "backward castes" in cornering political power for themselves to the exclusion of their weaker brethren can be judged from the fact that representation of the weaker backward castes (who comprise 40 per cent of the backward caste population) in the state legislature (till 1977 when figures are available) has never crossed four to five per cent. Till 1983 their share in government posts never exceeded 7 per cent even under backward caste governments. It was only in 1985 under the Congress ministry headed by Bindeshwari Dubey that they attained 12 per cent representation in the government.

It may come as a surprise that Brahmin representation in the Bihar Vidhan Sabha has been registering a downward trend. Starting with a high of 17 per cent in 1962 their representation dropped to 7 per cent in the 1977 assembly elections held soon after the lifting of national emergency. Bhumihars, Rajputs and Kayasthas have, however, held on to their positions.

Apart from their success at the Vidhan Sabha and the ministerial level, the top three "backward castes" have also been successful in capturing power at the panchayat level in villages where they command numerical superiority. Here also the traditional Brahmin leadership has been pushed aside.

It is difficult to reconcile the reality of Yadav, Kurmi, Koiri power with their claim of being "backward". Backward in reality only means belonging to the fourth *varna* in the Hindu society. But this lack of a high ritual rank has not prevented the Yadavs from emerging at the top in the political realm. And with political power has come the search for administrative and financial clout.

The Mandal Commission report (written appropriately by a Yadav) is an expression of this search, to no advantage for the truly weak among the backward castes.

We can now turn our attention to Uttar Pradesh. The social composition of the population in the UP differs somewhat from that in the other States of the North. Almost 40 per cent of the all-India population of Brahmins is concentrated in this State. Altogether the upper castes comprise 20 per cent of the State's population with Brahmins and Rajputs heading the list at nine and seven per cent respectively. Yadavs are the largest group among the backward castes and comprise almost 9 per cent of the population. The total backward caste population in UP is estimated to be around 41 per cent.

Attempts at the political mobilisation of the backward castes had begun soon after independence. By the early, sixties the Socialist Party, under the leadership of Rammanohar Lohia, had emerged as the principal spokesman of these castes. Thereafter Chaudhari Charan Singh assumed the mantle.

Principal Vehicle

By 1967, representation of the Yadavas, Kurmis, Lodhas and Gujjars in the State Assembly was proportionate to their strength in the population. It reached a high in 1974 but fell by almost 10 per cent in 1980, the last year for which data are available. Despite the fact that the top leadership position in the Congress legislature party never fell into their hands, from 1967 to 1974 (the period for which data are available). Yadavas, Kurmis, Lodhas and Gujjars never comprised less than 17 per cent of the Congress legislature party. In fact for several decades after independence, the Congress party remained the principal vehicle through which backward castes in UP sought political mobility. Their quest for independent political power began with the formation of the Bharatiya Lok Dal in 1969. By 1989, Yadavas had succeeded in installing one from among themselves in the chief minister's *gaddi*.

The rise in the economic fortunes of the backward castes in UP has been well documented. It is by now common knowledge that these castes were among the principal beneficiaries of *zamindari* abolition. Some ideas of their success in this field can be had from the fact that Yadavas, Kurmis, Lodhas and Gujjars (all of whom figure in Mandal's list) controlled 6 per cent of the *zamindari* rights in the State in the pre-independence period. After independence, however, 20 per cent of the land came to be owned by these castes (they comprise 15 per cent of population). If we take all the backward castes together, their share increased from 8 per cent *zamindari* rights in the pre-independence period to control over 38 per cent of the land after independence.

Real Losers

Brahmins more or less held on to their earlier position. (They were never a major landlord group in the State). Thakurs suffered a major loss. They controlled 34 per cent of the *zamindari* rights before independence but their share of land fell to 19 per cent after independence. Clearly they were major victims of the forces of change unleashed in the countryside.

How can castes that have acquired such clout be labelled "socially backward"? That still leaves the issue of educational backwardness. It surely cannot be anyone's argument that groups that have done so well in other fields have been deliberately kept back in the sphere of education. It would be ridiculous to suggest that educational institutions have been concentrated in Brahmin dominated villages and that Yadav-dominated villages have had no access to these facilities. If these castes have been slow to take to Western-style modern education it is only because it did not serve their immediate needs. A look at the drop-out rate of students belonging to these castes would be revealing.

Moreover, the demand for administrative jobs cannot be attributed to the rise of unemployment among their youth, as has been the case with the Sikhs. Due to certain factors (such as the average size of holdings) mechanisation has not proceeded on the same scale as in Punjab. Agriculture in UP largely remains an enterprise that involves the entire family. Now, the Mandal Report is an attempt to supplement political power by acquiring a vice-like grip on the administrative set up. The Central Government's recent offer to reserve 5 to 10 per cent jobs for the economically poor is admission that the major beneficiaries of the Mandal Report do not fall in this category.

K.V.S. Rama Sarma: V.P.'s Politics of Expediency
(National Herald, dated 27th August, 1990)

Seldom in the past the nation was forced to arbitrate on such untenable and dangerous issues as today. Ram Janmabhumi seeks to divide the people into Hindus and Muslims by appealing to their religious sentiments. The Mandal Commission reservation is on the verge of cutting the Hindus into forward and backward communities. Even before the Ram Janmabhumi problem is solved, the Mandal controversy has been brought to the centre-stage of political activity, thanks to the brazen politics of expediency Ganges would not have dried up if the Mandal Commission report was not accepted in such a great haste. If on the other hand, Mr. V.P. Singh had initiated a nation-wide debate on it he would have earned political mileage without landing the nation into a serious mess. His unthinking acceptance of the commission report as it stood today without reviewing as suggested by the commission itself exposed a certain strong streak of ruthlessness in him. It also exposed a particular style of functioning hitherto unknown to his political allies. With each issue he has been dropping a layer of the garb of democratism he donned all these years.

When the National Front government assumed office, the Congress mighty was not happy because it was once again a conglomerate that came to power. But the Congress was genuinely pleased that a popular alternative was being developed and viewed the emergence of the National Front as a healthy input to strengthen democracy. The Congress was aware that it could not stay in power all the time and that emergence of a two-party system even in the form of an integrated party-vs-coalition of parties was necessary in the interests of everyone. But the Congress was conscious that in the present form the coalition would not work and would not be able to deliver the goods. The Congress viewpoint was predictably not shared by other parties which rushed into the National Front.

That much delayed wisdom which had missed the allies of

the Janata Dal ten months has begun dawning on them now. The CPI-M General Secretary, Mr. E.M.S. Namboodiripad, had said in a signed article published in a recent issue of his party's official organ. *Peoples Democracy*, that "no sensible person will hold any brief for NF or Janata Dal".

A week or so later, the BJP's official organ, *Organiser*, delivered its judgment that Mr. V.P. Singh was "undoing" all that our forefathers had done for the unity and integrity of the nation. These are not formal no-confidence motions but they are mature political judgments issued after hard experience and not based on PR images of the Janata Dal and its leader.

These parties never perhaps thought that in less than a year, they would be reduced to mere spectators if not pawns in the power game by their best friend, Mr. V.P. Singh, and that he would land the country into an unprecedented crisis that is round the corner. The threat being issued by the ministers known to be close to him that if the current agitation by the students against the Mandal Commission recommendations continued, there would be a counter-agitation in support of the reservations has the potential of plunging the whole nation in a civil war on caste lines.

Would any patriotic Indian like this to happen when the situation in Punjab, Kashmir and Assam continues to be grim and worrisome and when the enemies are waiting on the border to strike? For Mr. V.P. Singh this hardly matters it looks. He must have his way, come what may. The growing suspicion among his allies that his moral stance was more tactical than real has led them to believe that he is interested in discreetly promoting the anti-reservation campaign so that he can have the cake and eat it too. Whether or not this is true the impression has already stuck. This explains the marked stridency in the criticism of the government on this score by the BJP and the CPI-M. While both are cut up that Mr. V.P. Singh was trying to corner all the credit by declaring the decision without consulting them, and placing them in a take-it-or-leave-it, the BJP appears to be particularly unhappy because the Mandal controversy has the potential of overshadowing the Ram Janmabhumi issues if mid-term elections are held.

Already the increasing violent nature of the reservation agitation and its spread all over the country and more importantly the distinct possibility of a counter-agitation have pushed the Ram Janmabhumi issue into the background. This suits Mr. V.P. Singh and the Janata Dal. The BJP has brought the Ram Janmabhumi issue to the fore after an untiring and relentless campaign. Since the issue had yielded handsome benefits by way of winning for the party as many as 88 seats in the Lok Sabha and brought it to power in Madhya Pradesh and Himachal Pradesh besides making it a coalition partner in Gujarat and Rajasthan, it is very doubtful if the party would allow the issue to be pushed into the oblivion. For Mr. V.P. Singh it is a godsent opportunity to cut the BJP to size in the Hindi belt. Besides yielding the ground to the Mandal Commission as the main issue, the Ram Janmabhumi controversy has stocked casteist chord in some of the backward communities which may result in a loss of support to the BJP. The Bahujan Samaj Party chief, Mr. Kanshi Ram, has already said that the Harijans had no stake in the Ram Janmabhumi controversy.

Thus, if the Mandal Commission agitation and the Ram Janmabhumi controversy run parallel to each other, the possibility of the BJP losing ground cannot be easily ruled out. In the days to come the BJP can be expected to grow more belligerent towards the Government at the Centre as well as in UP, become more aggressive and even assume a confrontationist stance, if necessary, so as to protect the vote bank that the Ram Janmabhumi issue had created for it in the last election. But the same logic the BJP may become more rigid in its approach to the issue and less amenable to compromise. Though Mr. V.P. Singh has his own men in the Vishwa Hindu Parishad, the new developments could mean the VHP clashing violently with the security agencies to insist on constructing the temple at Ayodhya if only to keep the issue in the forefront and vote-yielding.

This is likely to be the immediate political net result of Mr. V.P. Singh's decision to accept the Mandal Commission recommendations. All this does not mean that his decision on the Mandal Commission report has opened new vistas of power to Mr. V.P. Singh. Now that he has committed himself to the Mandal

Commission formulas, he is likely to face the demand for proportionate distribution of Janata Dal tickets in the next election. The OBCs constitute, according to the commission 52 per cent of the total population and it would be pretty difficult for Mr. V.P. Singh to reject out of hand any demand for 50 per cent of the Janata Dal tickets for the OBCs. They could also demand larger representation in the ministry, if the party wins the election, for the OBCs than now.

If, however, the Government is serious about preventing a possible bloodshed on account of the reservation agitation and the Ram Janmabhumi controversy, the way is still available. Though the Government has issued an executive order for the implementation of the commission report it would not be out of place to accept the demand of the political parties for a debate on the report in both houses of Parliament. This can be done on the basis that the commission itself had recommended a review after ten years (1990). Since the report was submitted in December, 1980, no effort was made to reassess the recommendations. This can be done now and a debate in Parliament followed by a consensus that the report be sent to a Joint Select Committee of Parliament to examine the complaints against it as also suggestions for modifications.

This is a national issue and the Government would do-well not to stand on prestige. In any case it has already committed a grave blunder by rushing to accept the report without any consultations whatsoever. For a Prime Minister who is never tired of teaching morals and principles to other political parties and leaders this is most unbecoming. As the practice has shown concessions such as reservations can easily be given but cannot be taken back or even revised. It is well-known how all efforts to revise the reservations already in force were thwarted by different pressure groups. It is because of this that before accepting a fresh dose of reservations, the nation as a whole must consider all the pros and cons. It cannot be left to the whims and fancies of one particular individual or a party.

The controversy over Mandal Commission has indeed exposed Mr. V.P. Singh. He can also retrieve his lost image by accepting the demand for a debate in Parliament. In fact, it would be gracious if he himself offers it. Here is a test for his statesmanship and the principles he repeats and nauseum. Even the ground realities demand that he reconsiders his action. The Karpoori Thakur Ministry had implemented the 27 per cent reservation formula for the OBCs in 1978 in Bihar. But that did not stop him and his party losing power two years later. In his own home state, UP the famous G.O. of August 1977 had earmarked 15 per cent reservation of government posts for OBCs by the Ram Naresh Yadav Ministry. But as the Mandal Commission report said: "The 1980 elections disproved the assumption of a critical change in the balance of power." What Mr.V.P. Singh has done will surely condemn the nation to a permanent state of inefficiency. This is not what he should give back to the nation that made him the Prime Minister in good faith. If he reads the Mandal Commission report and the observations of Kaka Saheb Kalelkar on this subject he would realise his folly.

M.V. Kamath: V.P.'s Mandal Folly

(Current, dated 6th-12th October, 1990)

How many students does Vishwanath Pratap Singh want to see killed and how many schools and colleges does he wish to see remain closed in order to save his face? There is no question but that he has erred grievously in proclaiming that his government has accepted the Mandal Commission Report in toto. Obviously he did not consult his colleagues. And if he did, like him, they, too, could not foresee the reaction to the report. It is quite clear that in this regard both Singh and his party are out of touch with Indian society today.

His argument that he is merely fulfilling a promise made in the Janata Dal manifesto just does not hold water. The Janata Dal came into power with about 18 per cent of the national vote. It is in power because it has the support of other parties like the BJP and the leftists (CPM, etc). The supporting parties have second thoughts on the Mandal report. But Vishwanath Pratap insists on his folly. True he has been slightly back-tracking and saying that States are free to follow their own path, but that is not the same thing as admitting to a mistake and promising to do something better. One suspects that his pride has got the better of him.

Keeping

If it is a matter of keeping to an election promise, one would like to ask what he is doing in the matter of Bofors. The Janata Dal was voted in largely on account of the peoples' hope that those involved in Bofors would be exposed. Bofors has now gone into the background. Very little of it is being heard these days. It is as if the government is most reluctant to push the investigation through. And the voter is not likely to forget it.

Even before the agitation over the Mandal report began, the Janata Dal was losing popular support. An *India Today*-MARG opinion poll taken showed that the Dal would lose heavily if elections were called soon. This has set even some members of the BJP executive worrying. One of them, Dr. Jay Dubashi, has been asking the BJP to withdraw its support to the National Front. The *India Today* MARG poll showed that if an election is held the strength of the National Front would be reduced from 144 to 127 if the non-Congress vote is united, and from 144 to 90 if it is divided. More importantly, the poll shows that the Congress might get in on its own into power even with a narrow majority.

Remember this poll was taken before the Mandal agitation. Since that was started the popularity of the Janata Dal has taken a nose dive. If Vishwanath Pratap Singh thinks that he can do without the vote of the middle class he is grossly mistaken. He probably rests on the belief that with the vote of the Scheduled Castes and Other Backward Castes and now of the Muslim as well (hasn't he declared the Prophet's birthday as a national holiday?) he can cruise along beautifully. He may come to grief. But it is not his personal success or the success of his party that should concern us. What is of concern is the battle lines drawn throughout the country between castes and castes. Vishwanath Pratap has done a distinct disservice to the country.

Protesting

Why are students so agitated that they are prepared to go into the streets and face police bullets? Does Vishwanath Pratap

Singh realise that not even during the Quit India Movement have students been so agitated as they are now? Vishwanath Pratap Singh may give his excuses; perhaps there may not be a caste war. But he has needlessly caused a rift between castes that may taken a long time to heal.

Whatever be his excuses it is clear to the average citizen that Vishwanath Pratap Singh took his step not out of love for the backward classes or the Scheduled Castes but out of a desire to beat Devi Lal at his own game. Devi Lal was trying to pitch the rural folk against the urban, not caste against caste. Devi Lal was wrong in doing so. Now Vishwanath Pratap Singh has compounded the original crime. The nation will not forget it.

Pretending to do justice to one class at the cost of doing injustice to another class is not only foolish and wrong, it is anti-national Vishwanath Pratap Singh is not going to fool anybody. What he has done is to keep himself in power, nothing more nothing less. It is the same technique that Rajiv Gandhi used in doling out money to the so-called poor farmers. Rajiv Gandhi did not succeed. Vishwanath Pratap Singh will not succeed either. He will go down in history as the man who divided the people.

Agitated

Why are the students angry? Even the wives of senior bureaucrats in Delhi have come out in the streets protesting against the Mandal report. They must have a reason. In the first place, the so-called forward castes do not have any sense of guilt about oppressing the Scheduled Castes after 40 years of independence. An earlier generation might have felt guilty. That, indeed, was the basis on which reservations were voted in. If after 40 years hundreds of seats all over the country have not been filled by those for whom they were reserved, it is unlikely that they will be filled in the forseeable future. The only result is to deny the deserving a place under the sun.

Dissatisfied

The young are just as, if not more idealistic than the prime minister. It is not that they are against Backward Classes. But there must be a sense of proportion even in trying to do justice by them. Instead of attempting a fait accompli, the prime minister should have had the good sense to publish a white paper portraying the situation as prevalent today in the country. There are over three thousand castes and sub-castes in the country. They are not equally or uniformly educated. No matter how hard one tries, in the end some castes among the backward castes will corner all the vacancies available leaving many others among the backward castes dissatisfied and angry at being left out. Backward Castes are not a monolithic community. In the end Vishwanath Pratap Singh will find to his surprise that he has made as many enemies among the backward.

The intelligentsia is up in arms and very rightly so. If Vishwanath Pratap Singh thinks that he is initiating a social revolution, he is totally wrong. What he has initiated is not a revolution but caste hatred. The two are different. Revolutions involve all people irrespective of caste. Caste war-call it caste conflict involves, segments of people. By his deliberate effort to keep himself in power, Vishwanath Pratap has shown himself not as a friend of the nation, but as its enemy.

Rajinder Puri: Politics of Pell Mell

(*The Hindustan Times, dated 2nd September, 1990*)

The Prime Minister's decision to implement the Mandal Commission Report on reservations for the backward castes has provoked widespread resentment among students. Spontaneous agitations have erupted all over the country.

One can appreciate the feelings of the students. The cost of living has ever been higher. Most families endure hardship and sacrifice to educate their children. The prospects of gainful employment remain bleak. Most students are haunted by the nightmare of unemployment or of unsuitable employment. In this situation, the Government has decided to reserve jobs, promotions and educational facilities on the basis of caste for an additional 27 per cent to the existing quota of reservations.

One can appreciate also the sentiments of the Prime Minister. He has pointed out that those who for thousands of years have suffered under the burden of discrimination and poverty deserve a share in the power and the wealth of the country. He wants the rich and the privileged to alone for their past.

But good sentiments do not necessarily indicate good reasoning. Nor need the expression of fine sentiments indicate honest motives. There is a suspicion that the Prime Minister was motivated primarily by electoral considerations when he made the announcement.

The students, therefore, are very angry that their future is being jeopardised by politicians who like to play games. But it is not enough to be angry. To succeed in their mission the students must also be wise. While fighting to obtain justice for themselves, they must ensure that there is justice for all. For this, they will have to appraise the problem with cool and dispassionate minds.

The first thing that they must understand is that the crisis they face is not the disease. The reservation policy is not the real problem. India's ruling class is the real problem. It is soft, corrupt and exploitative class which has always taken the easiest, most expedient and unprincipled option to defuse a problem.

The students will have to fight not this class only. They will have to fight the attitude which this class reflects. It is an attitude that has ruled the country since Independence, corrupted the thinking of all our society, and brought the country to its present critical condition.

In short, if the students wish to succeed in their fight against the reservation policy, it will not be enough for them to fight the Mandal Commission Report. They will have to fight the entire political system. They will have to fight the present obscurantist notions of the ruling class with the rational and scientific approach required by India to survive and thrive in the modern world.

It is India's elite that has let down the nation. The students are the future elite of the nation. If they want to protect their future, they will have to protect the country's future. They can do this successfully only by widening their perspective to encompass the basic problems of our society, of which the new reservation policy is but one manifestation. Otherwise their protest will fizzle out after causing temporary disruption and violence.

To formulate an appropriate strategy for their struggle, therefore, the students will have to understand the full implications of the Mandal Commission Report, the nature of the ruling class which wants to impose it, the agenda of alternative reforms that the students must offer to obtain justice for all sections of society and, finally, the political strategy they must adopt to ensure victory for the cause. Let us consider them in that order.

Since the Mandal Commission Report was submitted over ten years ago, certain changes have occurred in the political and economic status of castes. Some castes for instance like the Yadavs and Kurmis in Uttar Pradesh and Bihar, may no longer be considered backward.

And if the Mandal Commission Report is implemented without amendment, even among the few dominant backward castes that will hog the advantages of reservations earmarked for the entire lists of backward castes, a few families will prosper at the cost of their more unfortunate brethren. This is the experience from the reservation policy implemented among the Scheduled Castes and Scheduled Tribes. There is no limit in the Mandal Commission Report on the number of members from one family who might benefit from reservation. Nor is there any economic criteria to prevent even the most affluent member of the concerned caste from availing of the reservation quota.

Thus, the effects of such reservation are simply that a new section emerges which can merge with the existing elite, displaying the same ugly, exploitative qualities that characterise it now. This has been euphemistically described as the weaker sections "joining the mainstream". On almost all issues other than the reservation policy, the protagonists and opponents of the Mandal Commission Report are of one mind.

Let us examine further some implications of this policy. Consider the weavers of Eastern Uttar Pradesh, for example. They have been the perpetual victims of neglect and discrimination. The Government through a calculated policy has favoured the big textile firms, allowing the firms of exploit the small weaver through unfair competition. The big firms are subsidised and allowed to hog the required raw material, while the small weaver is offered neither protection nor raw material at a competitive price. This is being allowed to happen to a class of craftsmen who have centuries of fine tradition behind them, in an age when handspun cloth is all the range in the fashion markets of Japan and the western world.

Even assuming that a few of the literate and educated weavers do succeed in taking advantage of the reservation policy to get Government jobs, will this, in the prevailing circumstances, at all mitigate the real hardship and exploitation being faced by this talented and unjustly treated caste? Let us understand clearly that the weaver in India belongs not only to a class, but also to a caste. To allow the destruction and the withering away of an entire caste of talented and potentially prosperous weavers through continued neglect, while a few of their members become class four, class three of even class one government employees is this our idea of giving justice to the backward castes?

The short answer is: yes!

This, precisely, has been our traditional idea of dispensing justice. Because this is the nature of our ruling class. Being unable or unwilling to remove or face up to genuine causes of grievance and discrimination, the ruling class has invariably resorted to the expediency of allowing agitating leaders to share in the exploitation, rather than change the system that perpetuates such exploitation. This attitude has characterised our ruling class since Independence.

Many in the ruling class who now oppose the reservation policy have in the past supported this attitude. They took care to do this on issue which did not hurt their own interests. The fulminations against the reservation policy by the ruling class today carry no conviction. The ruling class has destroyed its credibility by the general attitude it has adopted on other issues in the past. Innumerable examples of this general attitude can be summoned from recent history.

The first, and most glaring, example that comes to mind is of course the partition of the sub-continent in 1947 when India became free. Leaders of the Congress and Muslim League, belonging to Uttar Pradesh and Gujarat, could not resolve their differences. They agreed instead to share the spoils by dividing Bengal and

Punjab, throwing to the wolves the people of the North-West Frontier Province who were totally against the formation of Pakistan!

Current examples are more vivid. Consider the present crises in Kashmir and Punjab. All the established national political parties are divided in their support between Farooq Abdullah and Jagmohan. But both Farooq and Jagmohan, who were cooperating with each other earlier, have confirmed in separate statements what all political observers have known for a long time: that the last assembly polls in Kashmir, which the Muslims United Front would have swept, were totally rigged. And the question troubling the mind of the Indian establishment today is whether Jagmohan or Farooq should be allowed to share power. The people who were cheated of victory figure in nobody's calculations. Is it any wonder that the youth of the erstwhile Muslim United Front has taken the violence and succession.

Consider also Punjab. In the last general election the Congress-I was almost wiped out in Punjab. The voting in Punjab was higher than in the rest of the country. The poll was entirely peaceful. Not a single election petition was filed in Punjab either by Congress-I, Janata Dal, CPI-M or BJP. Thirty-seven lakh votes went against the Akali Sikh candidates, 34 lakh votes went in their favour. This confirmed to the traditional voting pattern of Punjab. In Simranjit Singh Mann's own constituency, 55 per cent voted for him, 45 per cent voted against him. Candidates belonging to Janata Dal, Congress-I and BSP also won in some constituencies. In the interregnum between the general election and the assembly polls which followed in the rest of the country, and when the elections in Punjab were also due, there was a spectacular drop in terrorist activity. And yet, the assembly polls were postponed in Punjab on the plea of terrorism. It was actually made out that the results of the Lok Sabha polls had been distorted!

All the national parties which participated in the Kashmir chicanery also participated in the lies regarding the Punjab poll. This, despite the fact that our External Affairs Minister was elected from Punjab in that allegedly distorted poll, held under the shadow of imagined terror and continues to hold office. Why did the parties lie in this manner? Because the victors in the Lok Sabha poll were supported by the All India Sikh Students' Federation and not the Akali Dal led by the traditional Akali leaders. The Indian establishment refused to face the likelihood of an assembly poll victory by AISSF backed candidates. Therefore the lies and the poll postponement.

After repeated postponement, the Government is now making efforts to revive the previously dissolved assembly, in order to fulfil constitutional requirements. Thus, the party rejected by the voters in the parliamentary election held in Punjab, and the assembly dissolved by the Government for having failed to provide good administration to Punjab, are now sought to be foisted on the people, of Punjab. Just as the previously dismissed Farooq government is sought to be foisted on the people of Kashmir.

So, what are the people of Punjab and Kashmir being offered by all the national political parties of the country: representation or reservation? It is these same national political parties which cannot oppose the reservation policy. A few of them are merely fretting and fuming about the manner in which it was announced, being conscious that they will not be able to derive electoral advantage from this policy to the same extent as their rivals.

It is in this overall context that the anti-reservation agitation has to be viewed. However honest the motives of those who oppose the reservation policy might be, they must appreciate that if they oppose the Mandal Commission Report and remain silent about the system which has created it, they would be participating in a forward castes versus backward castes confrontation.

What, then, are the options before the students? First there is the prudent and worldy-wise option. They can propose certain amendments in the Mandal Commission Report to ensure that while implementing it the largest member of deserving people belonging to the backward castes derive advantage from it. On the basis of these proposed amendments they can initiate a dialogue with the Government and call off their agitation.

Alternatively, there is the risky and revolutionary option. The students can reject the reservation policy outright and take on the entire political establishment. This implies a long struggle with an uncertain result. And for such a struggle to be succeeded, there are several preconditions that the students will have to consider.

First, their struggle must be patient and peaceful and confined only to the students themselves. They should have no truck with any political party or group. Secondly, they must persevere till they have consolidated and unified the entire student community of India, regardless of whether it is backward or forward, urban or rural. The politicians will try their best to convert their struggle into one between the forward castes and the backward castes. The students will have to ensure that it remains a struggle between the young generation and the older entrenched generation. Thirdly, after such consolidation, the students will have to prepare an alternative agenda of national reforms which ensures justice and equal opportunity for all the oppressed and exploited sections of our society. And fourthly, the students will have to create a new political platform and take their agenda of change to the people. The reservation policy is a political challenge. The ministers in the Government are openly, tauntingly, proclaiming this. This challenge therefore can be met effectively only at the political level. It would be a challenge that involves management, organisation and communication. Can the students of India dare take up this challenge? If not, they should end their agitation and prevent damage to their academic careers.

Before they decide, they may care to reflect on an aspect of history. During the past two thousand years, perhaps the most successful ruling class was provided by the British who conquered India and then ruled it for 150 years to make Britain the world's mightiest power. The British conquest and consolidation of India was accomplished mainly by boys who came to India at the ages of 14 to 16 years as apprentices in the East India Company, and who as young officers in their early twenties conquered and ruled our country.

Can our own youth conquer India? Can it actually liberate India from the inheritors of the British attitude, those who continue to divide and rule us?"

Nikhil Chakravarty: Ghastly Outcome of Confrontation
(Current, dated 6th-12th October, 1990)

The immolation attempts by students as a mark of protest against the reservation policy for the backward classes have sent a shock wave through the political spectrum. This mark a qualitatively new and grim stage in the controversy over the government's announcement to reserve 27 per cent central government jobs for backward classes apart from the 22.5 reserved for scheduled castes and tribes.

Nobody, neither the government nor the Opposition, was prepared for such a fearsome turn in the controversy. Prime Minister V.P. Singh was blamed by the Opposition for having made the announcement about reservation on August 7 without prior consultation. This was also the burden of criticism from both National Front allies, the BJP and the Left. But nobody anticipated feelings over it would reach such frenzied heights as one could discern in outbursts of the last few weeks. It is obvious political leaders are out of touch with the temper of the people at the ground level. And many of us, ringside observers of the sordid drama on the political stage, are no less unfamiliar with the mood of the public at large.

Now has come this ghastly outcome of confrontation. The cascade of invectives and denunciations against Singh is now taking its inevitable toll. Particularly among the youth a vitriolic campaign has been on, to discredit Singh and antagonise him in a determined manner. The cumulative impact on the sensitive minds is not difficult to gauge.

No doubt the bleak prospect of shrinking job market makes life look grim for any college student. It will, however, be simplistic to trace from this economic angle alone the tragic development of attempted immolation on the part of students so deeply involved in the anti-reservation campaign.

Danger

What one has to keep in mind is the danger of equally insensate attempts at counter-immolation on the part of thousands of others who are equally determined to support the government's decision in favour of reservations for the backward classes. Nobody need have any illusion about the intensity of the likely backlash to the anti-reservation campaign among the rural youth from the backward classes. It needs to be underlined that there is practically no party which can reject Mandal. Many would make a fuss about it or find fault with one or the other point in the report, but none can afford to denounce it, for the simple reason, that every party is divided over it, as the Congress in which the leaders and workers from the backward classes want the early implementation of Mandal and many of them have already welcomed Singh's decision on this count.

Given the Billingsgate level of politics today, there is no doubt that Singh will be the sure target of attack from critics. They have already accused him of dividing the country among caste lines as it the divide has ever been absent from society. It can be argued as some well-meaning critics of the government do, that the prime minister need not have introduced this controversial measure at this stage and that too abruptly, and thereby could have avoided this controversy. It can be argued with equal weight that the anti-reservationists, by taking to the streets and going in for violent demonstrations, to the point of quarantining in the campus the students from the backward classes are no less responsible for touching off this demonstration of bitter animosity between the entrenched upper set and the rest in our traditional society.

What is more serious is the mental state to which a section of our angry youth have been pushed into by this emotionally surcharged outburst against reservation. It is actually a reflection of the divided state of society. The fury against reservation is in effect a measure to the acute antipathy between the upper and backward classes and also between them and the Harijans, still cast away as untouchables, relegated to the bottom of our social ladder. The casteist mindset comes out whenever there arises a critical social development, as now.

Passions

In this welter of bitter passions, there has to be an outcry for sanity, a stern voice of reason. This is no time for the government to stand on prestige nor for the Opposition to indulge in scoring petty points. When social antagonism threatens to break out and bring about anarchy in our body politic and social fabric, there is no moment to lose. Dialogue must start now. Let the pro and anti-reservationists get together. Let the government not stand on prestige, nor the Opposition pour fuel into the fire. Since we have to live in this great land of ours, let us work out in dispassion how the question of reservation has to be decided upon to the satisfaction of contending parties.

Jug Suraiya: Frictional Co-efficient of Mandal

(Times of India, 7th September, 1990)

At the forefront of the current anti-reservation agitation are many of those convinced that caste is a matter of consenting adults in the private parameters of matrimonial columns, and as such any attempt to bring the issue into the public domain is by definition pernicious and retrogressive, energetically to be opposed by all liberals and other right-thinking people. The lurking mofussil is seen to be cracking through the fragile veneer of the metropolitan facade; grotesque Hyde erupting out of the suave features of Dr. Jekyll in the midst of an elegant soiree.

Modern Dilemma

The unacceptable other face of our modern masquerade poses a dilemma: if he who is without caste were to hurt the first stone, the anti-caste crusade would find itself sorely lacking in ammunition. A more meritorious causa bellum has been found for the good fight, and what better was cry than merit itself, beleaguered citadel surrounded by a hostile sea of growing inefficiency. Efficiency, which is another world for progress, because of perfect mantra with which selectively to exercise the spectre of reservations; a sort of moral neutron bomb which while de-materialising troublesome inhabitants leaves intact the structures that enclose them and which can be put to future use.

Thus, commentators who otherwise are more than accommodative when it comes to the Hindu rate of inertia now discover a new virtue in efficiency, selfless handmaiden to democracy and secularism. The ruinous cost of the reservation policy is totted up on the abacus of arithmetical rhetoric: If fifty per cent of government and public sector jobs add up to caste plus lack of merit (efficiency), of which sum only forty per cent is available in the first year, by the second year the projected co-inefficient rises to sixty per cent, then to seventy, and after that to eighty! A dire reckoning indeed.

Anyone who has tried to get a file through a government department, cash a cheque in a nationalised bank or witnessed a member of a Scheduled Caste or Tribe walk past the signboard of an SC/ST medical practitioner to find another doctor knows the price we have paid already for inefficiency, a traditional commodity of which there is no dearth of export surplus. Can we afford to add to our overwhelming stocks of this truly gross national product? Certainly not. But precisely because we can't perhaps we must.

The problem with efficiency of course is efficiency of whom, by whom and for whom, "The trains ran on time", has proved the epitaph of many experiments in efficiency, from II Duce's risorgimento to Indira Gandhi's Emergency. Behavioural scientists define intelligence the efficient utilisation of mental resources, as "problem-solving capacity". An Eskimo, whose vocabulary includes 17 words for different varieties of snow, can negotiate an icy slope with as much efficiency as a Wall Street financier negotiating the slippery precipice of an arbitrage transaction. But what if Eskimo and financier were to compete on common ground? Relative efficiency would be determined by who set the context within which the problem was to be solved.

For many years, American blacks would score consistently lower than white candidates in IQ tests. This was assumed to indicate that blacks were, through nurture or nature, inferior to whites in terms of cognition. Some researchers, however, noted that the questions invariably were set by whites, and the tests were conducted in what was perceived by the examinees to be a white environment. When questions were set by blacks, in a black environment, the black candidates did significantly better. Such findings challenged traditional theories of intelligence and education, and suggested that the aptitude to solve problems did not exist in a cultural or social vacuum. In fact, very often the social environment was the problem.

Efficient Invention

Efficiency is as efficiency does, often at the expense of others. To Dr. Joseph Ignace Guillotin, his invention was the most efficient and humane was to terminte human life so as to provide a salutary example of punitive measure and public deterrent. To the other party concerned, the person about to have his or her head chopped off, the guillotine was a most inefficient way of ensuring that punitive measures and deterrents would not be needed in future. Triple bypass surgery is an efficient way of prolonging the life of a Dallas-or Delhi-magnate suffering the karmic coronary consequence of his efficiency; to a child dying of diarrhoea because of lack of safe drinking water, a bypass operation is a most inefficient way of extending the frontiers of science and medical technology to prolong his life.

The benefic calculus of efficiency is value biased. If the scientist is the atoms' way of findings out about their own limitless potential, this open-ended enterprise is short-circuited by the technocrat who would define human well-being in terms of so many pounds of hardware per head of population. God may or may not play dice with the universe, but homo efficacious does, and the dice he uses are loaded. All too often, efficiency means the most efficient way of distributing deprivation.

Norman Mailer said the American tragedy was that they got to the moon and did not know what they were doing there. Our plight is not that we haven't got to our own moon, but that we don't know what we are doing not being there. Leave us to God or to anarchy, cried out Gandhi to the British. They went one better and sought to leave us to both. But the "appalling strangeness" of God's mercy is increasingly at odds with our avowed secularism, and the anarchy that might have proved to be the turbulence of inchoate hope has long lapsed into what Amartya Sen calls a "quiet hunger" overlooked in the distraction of more clamorous crises.

Accepted Order

This "quiet hunger" which provides the forgotten underpinning of both the accepted order and the equally accepted disorder of thing, is the real "inefficiency" in which all of us above the "efficiency" line have a stake. The prosperous farmer's efficiently subsidised fertiliser owes its efficacy at least in part to the undoubted inefficiency of the marginalised cultivator and the landless peasant. The organised sector's efficiency in organising itself, if nothing else, is aided and abetted by the patent inefficiency of the unorganised sector to do likewise. The efficiency of high rise buildings is maintained by the adjacent inefficiency of shanty towns that supply the necessary menial and other services.

It is the efficient the inefficient's way of findings out its own potential? Social Darwinism might suggest so. The great white shark, which can detect a single drop of blood in a hundred gallons of water at a range of half a mile, is efficiency incarnate. But the tappering snout of the percect predator symbolises its evolutionary dead end; it has remained unchanged for twenty million years. The dinosaurs weren't so lucky; they proved so efficient at maximising dominance that their environment could no longer support them and they were swallowed up in their own efficiency.

Indian society is sometimes compared to a dinosaur. But it is really more like an amoeba; protein, adaptable, capable of sustaining itself on virtually nothing, an organism that has nowhere to go but up the evolutionay ladder by incorporating as many disparate and perhaps desperate strands as possible.

Mandal might turn out to be the amoeba's attempt to realise its full potential, however efficiency or otherwise remains to be seen.

Anti-Mandal Stir Akin to US Black Struggle Mast

A Bombay PTI release, reported in the Independent of 3 October, 1990 as follows:

"Both India and the United States the two largest democracies in the world had stood for liberty, freedom of speech and human values, noted the new US Consul General, Charles A. Mast.

Speaking at a reception in his honour hosted by the Indo-American Society here on Monday, Mast made a passing remark to the countrywide agitation against the Mandal Commission recommendations on job reservations, which he said reminded him of the 'Black struggle in America in the sixties'. Both the countries had passed through many upheavals, he added.

Mast, who was the deputy chief mission in Dhaka before his present posting, referred to the great contribution made by the one million Indians in the US to the educational and industrial spheres.

Iqbal Masud: Media vs. Mandal

(Independent, dated 30th September, 1990)

The historian Barbara Tuchman in her book on the First World War The Guns of August describes one of the biggest cannonades of the war in terms of a musical composition. Beginning on a light lyrical note the barrage increases in fury till it reaches the crescendo of total bombardment.

Some such metaphor will have to be used for the media campaign against Mandal. Beginning in August with the comparatively light abuse of the "infamous" Mandal report and barely concealed jibes at the installation of the Ambedkar portrait in the parliament, it gradually built up a fury which has not yet reached its finale. But one of its highpoints is the *India Today* dramatic photo (one of the most riveting cover photos this year) showing a bare-to-the-waist youth defiantly daring a tear gas canister. The caption is "In his bid to carve out a caste-based vote bank, V.P. Singh has unlenshed retrogressive forces."

At the time of writing (September 24) the media barrage has gone beyond this point. As a former minister, Yogendra Makvana, pointed out at a distinguished pro-Mandal forum at Delhi on September 22, the agitation is now against not merely against Mandal but against reservation itself.

It has been a well-orchestrated campaign in the media. It first roused the youth and now that they are on the rampage the cheerleaders have become the doomsayers and the martyrs the lamenters. The anti-Mandal campaign is basically a media created event and the media "creation" is worthy of serious academic study. The present piece is a concerned layman's effort.

The first point which strikes me is that in its stridency and near-unanimity the Mandal-media-war closely resembles the media attack on Muslim Personal Law following the Shah Bano case. There too a relatively disadvantaged minority was pilloried. Secular civil law was the catch-word then as merit is the catch-word today. Another point was "rationality and 21st Century" as opposed to "irrationality and backwardness". Similarly, national interest was identified with the view of the majority of the press. Finally, each campaign created its stars. It was Shah Bano then and younger women built up as 80's Joan of Arcs. Today it is the tragic martyrs.

Each media event exacted its toll, left the nation more divided than before. Strangely, many media persons figure as crusaders in both campaigns. One feature of the Shah Bano campaign was that it united progressives and fundamentalists. The Mandal campaign is doing the same — both BJP and the Communists talk implicitly or explicitly of class, not caste.

There are, of course, differences. One, no holds were barred in the Shah Bano Case because a minority, backward community was involved. In the present case there's a little more discretion involved since the numbers on each side are substantial. There's a gentlemen's agreement to pay lip service to Mandal while subverting him in effect. This politeness is the hypocritical tribute paid to the strength of numbers.

During the Shah Bano debate the supporters of the Shah Bano decision in the media divided its opponents into (1) Progressives (2) Reactionaries and (3) Fencesitters. I shall broadly divide the media critics of Mandal into (1) Storm Troopers (2) Sociological Analysts (3) Cultural Doomsayers. The examples will be illustrative: Authors' name will be avoided since the aim is to abstract media trends.

Storm Troopers

These are the unqualified opponents of Mandal who use rhetoric and emotion without eschewing "logic". Take this article evocatively called the Curse of Mandal (*Times of India*, August 13). In the very first para the name of Goebbels is invoked and though the tactic of the "repeated lie" is not explicitly associated with V.P. Singh and other votaries of backward castes and those who keep silent, it is certainly kept in their air like a polluting cloud. Now if you start an article that way there's only way you can go down. The article ignores the elaborate reasons given by Mandal for associating caste with class and the experience of many observers (See V.S. Naipaul in the recent *India: A Million Mutinies Now*) about the real damage of caste stigma despite class elevation. A sideway kick is taken against Islam and Christianity for being responsible for the rigidity of the caste system. Finally, Sanskritization is hailed as a relief from cultural attributes of backwardness and "misguided critics of Brahminism" lambasted.

What is significant in this article (typical of scores of others) is its tone. It's that of a crusader who will not make any concession. There's a continium from this kind of vanguardism to *India Today's* cover photo and the recent headlines of "self-immolation".

An editorial in the *Sunday Observer* (August 12) sums up most of the arguments in the anti-Mandal debate, so an analysis will be illuminating. Like the earlier piece Curse of Mandal the title says it all: Butchers of India.

The beginning is apocalyptic: "For India the age of enlightenment, the age of Mahatma and Jawaharlal is over. The dark ages have dawned: I think it's important to stress this rather seemingly simplistic statement. The nuances here are being echoed in almost all national papers almost everyday. India charging into the 21st Century — the example usually given is Agni. The struggle of the Orissa coastal village people against a firing range never make it to the major papers. Development is identified with Space Age, industrial and military development and that in turn is connected to "merit"—a positive term for elite domination. The development-through-domination theme is the backdrop to almost all media discussions. But it is a well-concealed theme.

Another feature of the media was is that this anti-Mandal section is fully conscious — has been fully conscious from the beginning — of its role. The same editorial goes on to say: "Criticism will be misinterpreted. It will be said that the Brahmin-Bania press has predictably rallied round its own class interests. So the press must be silenced".

Now this self-perception of the media is important. No body so far has trotted out a caste-based conspiracy theory in the media. Nor has the government indicated any intention of silencing the media. This cloak of intended persecution is both an armour and an offensive weapon.

Further in the same editorial, all the elements of the current debate are summed up. "This is how all progressive critique has been smoothered by narrow minded chauvinists through the ages. This is how the proponents of the chador in Iran and elsewhere disdainfully rejected the voices of temperance. Modernisation necessarily brings in an obscuranist backlash in its wake."

So the link between Shah's Iran-development-fundamentalism-reservations is finally established. Stay on the side of the White Revolution and space missiles based on "merit". Or go out into the outer darkness of humble helots who can never be released from the burden of the past.

Sociological Analysis

The Storm Troopers are accompanied by legions who confer legitimacy on their charge by the might of their objectivity and academicism. The sociologists' agreements are more sophisticated. Look at the ravages wrought by caste reservations in the South, they say. They distinguish between reservations for equality and reservations for power.

Unfortunately, as they develop their arguments, the sociologists come down to the level of Storm Troopers-Reservations have brought the evil of corruption, our young are fleeing to the West, universities and public institutions will be reduced to the level of caste-based panchayats.

I am summarising the argument of two eminent sociologists which have appeared in most national dailies. It is surprising that the professors have not cared to spell out the connection between reservation and corruption. It's alright for a politician like V.P. Singh to condemn "non-reserved administration" as corrupt.

But when a sociologist says the reverse we expect logic and substantiation and not a passing reference to tehsildars selling bogus OBC certificates. And the distinction between reservations for equality and power rings hollow. How do you achieve equality without power?

Ghalib wrote: Is aashiqi mein izzat-i-saadat bhi gayi. (In this passion even the honour of nobles is lost). How true of our sociologists turned politician.

Cultural Doomsayers

Not the least important are our cultural anthropologists. Reservations, they say, will disband the OBC's creative practice of our traditional designs. The only fantasy of OBC's should not be to become clerks or peons. There are two fallacies in this attractive argument. The traditional craftsmen of OBC communities have been dismantled long ago by our old friend, the modernisation process. Go to Salem in the South and find out what happened to the weavers. Secondly, the attitude displayed towards clerks and peons is neo-colonial, a reflection of the British contempt towards babus.

An occupational blindness of the groves of the academe or of the modern computerised media is that the "9 to 5 life" of administration means nothing to them. And yet that's where power lies. The hurt lied in the fact that SCs, STs, OBCs, minorities want a piece of that cake. Like Oliver, they are daring to ask for more.

Come to think of it that's one metaphor the anti-Mandal media crusaders have missed out; Tell you lot about the crusade.

Palkhivala: Government Move Violates Basic Structure

(The Hindustan Times, dated 28th August, 1990)

He held the Government's decision to implement the Mandal Commission report "without any dilution" as a Himalayan blunder.

Hindustan Times further work that the "implementation of the report would create two nations, neatly balanced numerically and never the twin shall meet, he said. Casteism would ignite an unprecedented national conflagration.

He warned that the implementation of the Mandal report

would go against the basic spirit of the Constitution and any constitutional amendment to avoid judicial scrutiny would itself be unconstitutional and void. Describing the report and Government decision to implement it as "thoughtless action", he said the Mandal report could prevail only by scrapping the noble Constitution and bringing in a backward constitution for a backward nation.

Referring to the Government decision to implement the report, Mr. Palkhivala said that perhaps there is no other country which has such a genius for inflicting torture and tribulations on itself as modern India the inheritor of the age-old practice of self-flagellation.

He said that since people were convinced that the Government understood only the language of violent agitation, there has already been an explosion of violent mass revolt in various States. He expected that this would gather momentum in the days to come, with unforeseen consequences for the integrity and unity of India.

In a sharp examination, couched in pungent language, Mr. Palkhivala said the Mandal report suffered from five major flaws:

1. It contemplates rich and rigid reservations for employment under the State in its infinite variety, and in business undertakings and educational institutions, where merit would be unable to find a berth. The sub-standard has to replace the standard, and the reins of power are to pass from meritocracy to mediocrity.
2. It enjoins reservations based exclusively on caste, as if a poor Brahmin or a rich Dalit is a contradiction in terms. It firmly ignores the stark reality that there are no backward castes but only backward individuals. Economic backwardness or the opposite is treated as wholly irrelevant.
3. Not only employment but even promotions are to be reserved for the privileged (euphemistically called "backward") castes, that would be disastrous enough for the civil administration, but far worse for the military.

Our armed forces are the pride of the nation, the only institution which we have not devalued and degraded. What kind of an Army, Navy and Air Force shall we have, when Field Marshals and Generals, Admirals and Air-Commdores, have secured their promotions on caste considerations? This raises the most momentous of all issues—the security of the State.

4. The only known solvent of casteism is change in the national consciousness; harmony among, and social intermingling of the anachronistic castes. Petrified and ossified for centuries, casteism should be the dust on the shelf of Indian history. Instead, the Mandal report emphatically ensures a fresh lease of life to the canker of casteism for a long indefinite future.
5. The progress of India has been from casteism to egalitarianism. It has been from feudalism to freedom: and equality is the very heart of a free republic. There never was, and never will be, a free democracy without equality of citizens. The foundation of a true public, the source of its inspiration, the criterion for its citizenship, the hope for its welfare—all lie in the incandescent ideal of equality.

It is the exact opposite of what is prevalent in totalitarian States where you enjoy privileges as card-holding members of the ruling party. The Bedrock of the Mandal report is discrimination in reverse: It is discrimination against merit and calibre.

Mr. Palkhivala observed that like the expanding of universe, the list of backward castes is ever expanding. The Mandal report has listed 3,743 (from 2,399 in an earlier report) backward castes. Many other are already waiting in the wings to receive recognition.

Trade and Industry

FICCI and ASSOCHAM oppose job quota

In a New Delhi PTI release dated 30 August, the FICCI and Associated Chambers of Commerce and Industry has opposed job quota. Leading chambers of trade and industry have been critical Government's reservation policy in its present form and said when the country was already with law and order and economic problems, further tensions and differences should be avoided.

The Federation of Indian Chambers of Commerce and Industry (FICCI) and the Associated Chambers of Commerce and Industry of India (Assocham) on Thursday said in a joint statement that the founders of the Constitution never thought that reservation would go on for ever or that it would be extended to other classes. This would divide society on caste lines, keep the backward classes backward and would never motivate them to make efforts to be equal to others, they said.

The statement read "the business community strongly supports assistance measures extended to backward classes. At the same time it said that eventually the country has to be classless and casteless, as equality of opportunity like equality before law was the fundamental premise on which our constitution was based."

The Chambers hailed the Prime Minister Narasimha Rao's announcement to relate assistance measures to economic criterion, as it would promote an egalitarian society without denying opportunities to those with aptitude.

At the same time the Chambers advocated that education for backward classes at schools and colleges be made free, number of seats at graduate and post-graduate levels be raised substantially, vocational training facilities expanded on a large scale while giving a reasonable preference to students from backward classes for selection of jobs.

The Chambers expressed great concern over the disturbances that have erupted in various parts of the country on the issue of reservations. Undoubtedly, the backward classes which missed opportunities to join the mainstream of national life need greater attention and assistance.

They however added that the progress of the country depended on the quality of persons who managed the affairs of the nation or of the business enterprises. For this it was required that the best persons came to the top through competition and merit, the statement said.

Commenting on the situation, the Chambers said that at a

time when the country was faced with law and order problem in Kashmir. Punjab and Assam, when the economy was threatened by oil crisis and when inflation was once again raising its ugly head to "it is essential that further differences and tensions are totally avoided and forces of cohesion and harmony are strengthened."

The joint statement said that everyone in the country shared without hesitation the final goal of largest participation by largest number in the mainstream of development. There are acceptable means of achieving this objective which should be explored and adopted through consensus and consent, the statement added.

H.M. Seervai: Judiciary threatened on job reservation: Is an efficient public service irrelevant in India?

Indian Express, 18.8.1990

A PTI message dated New Delhi, August 10, and the Doordarshan news bulletin that night stated that the Prime Minister, Mr. V.P. Singh, "today assured the Rajya Sabha that the judiciary would not stand in the way of filling of the vacancies in Government jobs by Scheduled Castes and Scheduled Tribes candidates, (and) 'that if the judiciary stood in the way, we will with your co-operation (the Opposition's) remove that-hindrance". The Prime Minister was also reported to have said that the Government would accept the verdict of the courts in the Ram Janmabhoomi-Babri Masjid dispute, whatever that decision may be.

Judiciary Threatened

The extreme gravity and the dangerous nature of the Prime Minister's observations about the judiciary have not attracted attention, since they come from a Prime Minister who is never tired of saying that in a great democracy like ours, there must be open discussion, debate and full scope for dissent. The statement that the Government would accept the decision of the courts in respect of the Ram Janmabhoomi-Babri Masjid dispute—a decision on a difficult, complicated matter—shows that when Government wants to get out of a difficult situation, full confidence is, reposed in the courts. Surely, the same confidence must be shown in the courts in their decision, whatever it may be, in filling up vacancies in Government jobs.

Besides, how could the Prime Minister assure the House that the judiciary would not stand in the way of reserving jobs? For he would be the first to admit that it would be most improper for any member of the Government to obtain an assurance from the courts that they would decide in a particular way. It is essential that the Prime Minister should withdraw the assurance he gave to Parliament, and his threat to the judiciary. History shows that dictators professing to act for the "good of the people" begin or end by destroying an independent judiciary which is a bastion of the people's safety and freedom. The "Emergency" declared by Prime Minister Indira Gandhi on 25 June 1975 is a classic example of this truth in our country, although, fortunately, her dictatorship lasted for less than two years.

A minister's oath provides, *inter alia*, "I, A.B., do swear that .... I will faithfully and conscientiously discharge the duties of my office and I will do right to all manner of people in accordance with the Constitution and the law without fear or favour, affection or ill-will". The oath of a chief justice or a judge of the Supreme Court or a High Court, provides, *inter alia*, that "I, A.B., ...:. will duly and faithfully and to the best of my ability, knowledge and judgment perform the duties of my office without fear or favour, affection or ill-will and that I will uphold the Constitution and the laws" (emphasis supplied). The minister's oath requires him to act in accordance with the Constitution and the law whereas the judicial oath requires the judge to uphold and defend the Constitution and the law.

This is as it should be, for ministers give effect to the Constitution and the law, when they take executive action and the judges defend and protect the Constitution and the laws by bringing their ability, knowledge of the law and judgment to bear on every issue, by deciding it without fear or favour, affection or ill-will. The threat held out against the judges would require the judicial oath to be altered so as to run: "I, A.B., ... having been appointed the chief justice (or a judge) of ... court will bear true faith and allegiance to the Constitution of India as by law established and I will uphold the sovereignty and integrity of India and against the best of my ability, knowledge of the law and judgment, I will perform the duties of my office by upholding the policies of the Government of the day and by rejecting everything that stands in the way of implementing those policies"!

Constitutional Provisions

The origin of reservations is well-known. For hundreds of years, "untouchables" eked out a miserable existence, because their touch and, in certain provinces, even their shadow, polluted the higher caste Hindus. Article 17 of our Constitution removed this great blot on the Hindu community by abolishing "untouchability" and by making it a crime for anyone to enforce disabilities arising from "untouchability". And Article (2)(b) threw open to "untouchables" Hindu religious temples of a public character.

These measures were taken to bring Scheduled Castes (SCs) and Scheduled Tribes (STs) into the mainstream of national life. To attain that goal, reservations in legislatures were made for a period of 10 years, in the belief that within 10 years the necessity for reservation would disappear. Further it is not generally known that for a person to belong to SCs he must profess the Hindu or the Sikh religion as required by the Presidential (SCs) Order, 1950. So the classification made between persons belonging to SCs and other persons is based on caste and religion.

Article 15(1) provides that no citizen shall be discriminated against on grounds only of religion, race, caste, sex, place of birth or any of them. To this provision, Article 15(4) provides an important exception. For it gives the State discretionary power to make any provision for the advancement of any socially and educationally backward class of citizens or for the SCs and the STs. Article 16 provides that every citizen shall have equality of opportunity in matters of public employment, for appointment to any office under the State, which opportunity cannot be denied on the ground only of caste, religion, race, sex, descent, place of birth, residence or any of them. However, Article 16(4) makes an exception, namely, that it conferred a discretion, on the State to make reservation for appointment to an office or post in favour of any backward class of citizens which in the opinion of the State is not adequately represented in the service.

Consigned to Backwardness?

Since our Prime Minister repeatedly says that secularism is the only solution in a democratic country like ours, where there are a number of languages, religions, races, castes and creeds, it would follow that any action taken or law passed which would perpetuate and divide the people on the basis of caste and religion must be rejected, except as a temporary expedient for a short period as was provided for by the framers of our Constitution. The emotional attachment of Mr. Justice Krishna Iyer to SCs and STs is strongly reflected in his judgments in the Supreme Court. Even so, he realised that the cause of socially and economically backward classes and of the SCs and STs would be gravely injured if their disabilities were treated as permanent. In his judgment in the *Karmachari Sangh Case*, he said:

"If freedom, Justice and equal opportunity to unfold one's own personality belong alike to bhangi and brahmin, prince and pauper, if (they are) to feel the social transformation which Art. 16(4) promises the State must apply equalising techniques which will enlarge their opportunities and thereby progressively diminish the need for props. The success of State action under Art. 16(4) consists in the speed with which result-oriented reservation withers away as no longer a need, not in the ever-widening and everlasting operation of an exception [Art 16(4)] as if it were a super-fundamental right to continue backward all the time, (emphasis supplied). To lend immortality to the reservation policy is to defeat its raison d'etre: To politicise this provision for communal support and party ends is to subvert the solemn undertaking of Art. 16(1), to casteify "reservations" even beyond the dismal groups of backward-most people, euphemistically described as SCs and STs, is to run a gravy constitutional risk. Caste, *ipso facto*, is not class in a secular State": (A.I.R., 1981 S.C. at p. 306).

I wish to make it clear that I wholeheartedly approve of the goal of bringing socially and educationally backward classes and SCs and STs into the mainstream of nation life. And I would approve effective measures which would make them stand on their own feet. In a public lecture which I delivered about 10 years ago, I outlined a scheme which would provide such effective measures. I incorporated that scheme in the 3rd edition of my *Constitutional Law of India*, Vol. 1(1983), and I will give that outline later in this article.

Espirit de Corps

The power to make reservations for socially and educationally backward classes of persons and for SCs and STs is conferred on the State, first, by way of a discretionary power, and secondly, by way of an exception to the principle against discrimination on the ground of religion, race, caste, sex, or descent. That principle lies at the heart of our Constitution, for to discriminate in favour of one class is to discriminate against all other classes. Confining myself to reservation to appointments and posts in public service, we must remember Article 335 which provides : "The claim of the members of the SCs and STs shall be taken into consideration, consistently with the maintenance of efficiency of administration, in the making of appointments to services and posts in connection with the affairs of the Union or of a State" (emphasis supplied). In a great democratic country like ours, an efficient public service is essential for the welfare and happiness of its people. Recent exhortations to public sector undertakings to improve their performance emphasizes this obvious truth.

Further, in considering reservations in public employment, courts have to deal with 5 parties : (i) the State, to whose services persons are recruited by open competition in examinations held by independent public service commissions; (ii) the public as the very phrase "public servant" shows; (iii) the persons who are discriminated against, by reservations in favour of members of SCs and STs; (iv) members of SCs and STs in whose favour discrimination is made by fixing reservation quotas; and (v) the service, that is, each service considered as a whole. A service which lack esprit de corps, that is, consciousness of and pride in belonging to a particular service, lacks an element essential to an efficient and harmonious administration. To balance the claim of the 5 parties requires a critical analysis and examination and it cannot be determined by anger at a great social wrong or to secure electoral support. Leaving out a large number of Government servants in service who used to be described as "menial" but are now described as "Class IV employees", reservations for SCs and STs have been tried out for nearly 40 years with the gradual erosion of standards to be reached by the SC and ST candidates in order to be eligible for employment in service. The erosion will be found described at great length in the *Karmachari Sangh Case*. But one thing is clear. A reservation quota for socially and educationally backward class of persons and for SCs and STs necessarily implies that those who enter public service as a result of a reservation quota are, meritwise, substantially inferior to those who enter the public service by selection in order of merit by open competition in examinations designed to select the best candidates. There could be no *Esprit de corps* in a service in which, in matters of promotion, people with superior qualifications are subordinated to people with admittedly inferior qualifications. If nearly 40 years of applying the remedy of reservations has failed to produce the desired result, it is obvious that an attempt must be made to find another remedy which will produce the desired result.

A Scheme

I share the general view that, by and large, intellectual capacity and general ability are more or less evenly divided among the people. A successful attempt to remove the handicap of SC and ST children must therefore begin with the school, since it is not practicable to begin with the family except very indirectly, the central idea of my scheme is to adopt measures which would put SC and ST children as near as circumstances permit, to children more favourably placed. One of the most serious handicaps of SC and ST children is that their parents find it necessary to increase the family income by making even small children earn a small income by part-time work, e.g., by selling newspapers. The time so taken up is withdrawn from studies and other activities of the school - a handicap from which children more fortunately placed are free. The compensatory measures to remove this handicap are: free education, free supply of text books, and other school requisites, free meals, free uniforms where prescribed. To remove the need for SC and ST children to earn by part-time work, it is necessary to provide a daily stipend or grant in respect of each SC and ST child.

We must begin with the primary school, for the object of the scheme is not only to put SC and ST children on a level with other children, but also to give SC and ST children an opportunity of showing their talents and general ability. Before the SC and ST child's primary education is completed, some students in each class will have shown promise as students. Special attention should be paid to them in secondary schools, and in addition to the daily stipend, merit scholarships reserved for SC and ST students should be given on their examination results in recognition of their work and also to encourage them to further effort in their studies. And these proposals must be applied to high school education and to education in colleges, with the difference that the daily stipend and merit scholarships reserved for SC and ST students would have to be increased. If this scheme is followed, then by the time that the ablest among SC and ST students come to compete for public service, they will be able to do so on equal terms with other candidates. This would transform public service by making it efficient and restoring its esprit de corps, because every one member of it will have been selected on his own merit and not by accident of caste, religion and descent.

Our courts are oppressed by the feeling that unless reservations are made for socially and educationally backward classes and for SCs and STs, in public services and also in graduate and post-graduate colleges, they cannot be brought into the mainstream of national life. And yet, oddly enough, the courts say that they are not concerned with other measures, which would bring those classes into the mainstream of national life. But this overlooks the fact that Article 15(4) does not expressly, mention "reservation". This Article uses the general expression, "The State may make any special provision for the advancement of socially and educationally backward class of citizens and for SCs and STs".

The scheme I have outlined above makes a special provision for educational advancement. But special provisions include every kind of assistance which the State can give for the advancement of backward classes and SCs and STs into the mainstream of national life. Illustratively, those measures will include grant of land either free or on nominal rent, the grant being non-transferable (i.e., to money-lenders, etc.) and by declaring such transfers to be void. Further, the State can supply seeds and agricultural implements, supply expert advice as to how to improve the yield of land provide for marketing the produce and the like. Such special provisions would also include schemes for training backward classes to pursue trade or small business which would bring in a reasonable income. No doubt the details of my scheme will have to be worked out. I need hardly add that if there is a better scheme than mine, it should be adopted.

No doubt the scheme which I have outlined will require substantial expenditure and, even more. Governmental effort to make it a success. But Union and State governments which can afford to write off debts said to be about Rs. 16,000 crore, ought not to grudge the expenditure of relatively small sums of money in order to bring backward classes and SCs and STs into the mainstream of national life, to increase their well-being and happiness and to secure an efficient public service and administration.

Sinning for the Future

It was said that those actively opposing reservations in jobs and in colleges were hooligans or mischief makers. This is patently untrue. In his Independence Day broadcast, our Prime Minister qualified this by appealing to the youth to disregard their selfish interests and work for the good of the country. This is adding insult to injury. Parents belonging to Hindu and non-Hindu advanced classes found that their children of high ability, capable of giving a good account of themselves and enriching the life of our country, deprived of educational facilities and employment in public service by classes of people who, admittedly were lacking in such capacity and ability. After our Constitution came into force in 1950 many parents were constrained to tell their gifted children that they must put up with this injustice for a limited period, because of the grave injustice done to SCs and STs. Such boys and girls have endured that injustice not for 10 years, not for 20 years, not for 30 years, and now for 40 years. If we condemn injustice of the past in strong and unmistakable language, the future will condemn the injustice perpetrated by our own governments for a period of 40 years. If reason and persuasion and the claims of justice are to be ignored by whoever is in power, and where there is no means of a legal redress, extra-legal means, violent or non-violent will he employed to secure it. Non-violence is attached to the revered name of Mahatma Gandhi as a powerful weapon to secure a just and desired goal. But his own experience showed that non-violence frequently turned into violence to achieve such goal. If these evils are to be, avoided reservations must be phased out in a period of 10 to 15 years by reducing the reservation by 20 per cent every two or three years and not by continuing job reservations as the Government proposed to do.

Quota for those Below Poverty Line

(Press Release, dated 1st October, 1990 from Madras)

In a press release dated 1 October, from Madras, the Sankaracharya of the Kanchi Kamakoti Peetham, Sri Jayendra Saraswathi, has said that reservation in government jobs should be extended only to those people who are below the poverty line among the backward classes and not to all the groups *per se* as listed under that category in the Mandal Commission report, says PTI.

This step will make sure that the economically better off sections among the backward classes did not lord over and suppress their poor counterparts, the Acharya said in his Gandhi Jayanti message today.

Justice Ensured: The Acharya said caste differences would then cease to be "big" and such concessions could be offered to all those below the poverty line in every community. But only till such a time as their economic status was bettered. This would ensure that people below the poverty line continuously benefited, affording them a chance to come up in life, he said.

He said while Gandhiji all his life struggled for the cause of national unity and brotherhood unmindful to religious and caste differences, it was unfortunate that the Mahatma's birthday came under "violence filled" circumstances.

Sri Jayendra Saraswathi said his suggestion on the reservation issue would help arrest any "anger or hatred" against the society by those groups not mentioned in the Mandal Commission report. There would also then be no plea from other communities to be included for reservation benefits, he said.

Gandhi Jayanti should not be celebrated by just garlanding the Mahatma's statue, but should also be an occasion to cherish some of the important principles like prohibition and non-violence he had stood for, the acharya added.

Dipankar Gupta: Question of Quotas: Reservation versus Affirmative Action

Times of India, 26.9.1998

The reservation policy initiated by Ambedkar in India has many lookalikes all over the world. Some kind of preferential policy exists in countries as far flung from one another as America, Canada, Ireland and Malaysia Reservations in India an affirmative action in America perhaps resemble each other the most. In both these cases, the effort is to uplift a historically disprivileged community. Just as the scheduled caste and tribes in India have suffered on account of sustained injustices against them, so also have blacks in the United States. It is not just that there exists prejudice among them but actual acts of injustices over a long period of time have prevented these communities from acquiring skills and expertise that are socially valued and coveted. Moreover these disadvantaged peoples both in America and India were also in a minority in their respective countries. But this is where the similarities end.

Rags to Riches

The major differences between reservation, in India and affirmative action in America crystallise around the question of quotas. All other divergences between these two forms of preferential policies flow from this basic distinction. In India, from the start, reservations have been operationalised on the principle of quotas. Thus, in proportion to their population, approximately 23 per cent of jobs and educational opportunities are reserved for the scheduled castes and tribes. In America, on the other hand, Title VII, which is the main weapon of the affirmative action programme, makes explicit that the quota principle will not be entertained at any cost. Title VII went on to assert that affirmative action will not, in any case, mean the lowering of qualifications and the undermining of merit. It is interesting that on this issue there has been a near unanimity in American politics. In fact a 1988 survey found that about 50 per cent of black respondents said that they were against affirmative action and would not like to benefit from it.

This in no way should suggest that racist attitudes have died in America. Though white males in America constitute only 43 per cent of the population, they hold 95 per cent of the top executive jobs in the country. Black adult males have an unemployment rate that is five times higher than the national average. Even the judicial system is weighted against blacks. Possession of crack invites much higher punishment than the possession of cocaine. In spite of medical evidence that shows that the two are equally harmful, this law is still in force. This is because black drug users are addicted to crack whereas the white addicts consume cocaine. Though about 13 per cent of drug addicts in America are blacks, which is roughly equal to their proportion of the American population, yet 74 per cent of those serving jail sentences for drug possession are blacks.

In spite of all this, many blacks still feel reluctant to take advantage of the affirmative action programme. American democracy from the very beginning has been strongly individualistic in character. The Horatio Alger story of rising from rags to riches, the tales of how the West was won by sheer individual persistence and determination, and accounts of how the early settlers refused to allow status considerations of the old world to nestle in the colonies, are all parts of the popular lore that most Americans hold very dearly.

Contrast this individualistic spirit of the Americans with the Indian case. During the Constituent Assembly debates over the making of the Constitution, the subcommittee on fundamental rights held that "it is difficult to expect that in a country like India where most persons are communally minded, those in authority will give equal treatment to those who do not belong to their community." In fact, the Constituent Assembly proceedings are littered with instances of community considerations over riding those of the individuals.

Ambedkar's Vision

Even so, it must be mentioned to the credit of Ambedkar that he saw reservations as a time bound policy, open to periodic upraisals. Often the time-bound feature in the original formulation of the reservation policy is picked up by opponents of reservations without enquiring as to whether or not the aims of the policy have actually been met. If onslaughts of this kind had continued, there is no doubt that the quota system in India would have met with an early end. That it survives today and shows no sign of diminishing is because it was picked up by the superior castes to further their community ends.

It first began with the DMK in Tamil Nadu, and then quickly spread in the early 1970s, with Indira Gandhi's encouragement, to Karnataka and on the other parts of India. The dominant peasant castes in India, from the Vokkaligas in the South to the Yadavs, and Kurmis in the North began to apply the quota system to advance their own ambitions. This tendency climaxed with the Mandal recommendations. From this point onwards, the reservation programme in India departed from Ambedkar's vision. Reservations now were no longer for the downtrodden but to help powerful agrarian castes to consolidate themselves in cities. The politically superior communities are now the beneficiaries.

Hollow Ring

Once reservations and quota were adopted by these superior communities to realise their community ends, the earlier emphasis on raising the downtrodden by enlarging socially valuable skills was given up. The quota system was now, charged with the express purpose of capturing jobs and educational opportunities for the materially and politically better off. Naturally this led to wilful abandonment of qualifications, merit and institutional standards. The scheduled castes and tribes could not have accomplished this by themselves, and they are not the ones who are principally responsible in this regard.

It is because powerful agrarian castes in India saw the quota system as a way of adding to their economic viability that the reservations for the scheduled castes and tribes have survived. If these superior castes were not allowed to play the quota system then the general animosity against scheduled castes and tribes in this society would have long seen to the demise of the reservation system. Of course, while dismantling it arguments about merit and individualism would have been forwarded, but these would have a hollow ring about them as individualism is far from being a generalised credo in India.

The author is professor, Centre for the Study of Social Systems,

Dharma Vira (Former Cabinet Secretary) tells Vinod Sharma: **Reservation will Politicise the Civil Services**

(Hindustan Times, Sunday Magazine, dated 2nd September, 1990)

He spoke on the Mandal report on reservations for Other Backward Classes (OBCs) and its likely impact on the civil services.

Q. What are your views on the National Front government's reservation policy and the manner in which it has been implemented?

A. In India, over 50 per cent population lives below the poverty line and 70 per cent are illiterate. When there is so much illiteracy and starvation, do we really have to divide the population artificially? We accepted reservations in the case of Scheduled Castes and Tribes because of the very special conditions in which these two existed. But that too was for a period of 15 years. Forty-three years have now passed and the reservations are still there. The fact is that all these reservations tend to become permanent; producing vested interests and separatism.

Instead of integrating India, we are steadily dividing it. Lately, we have had so much communal trouble. And now we are starting a caste war. Sometime back, it was ordered that caste will not be mentioned in application (for jobs). But now the applicants will have to mention their caste. Unless they do so, how will they be (known to be) Other Backward Classes (OBCs) or Scheduled Castes or Tribes? So, we are trying to fragment the entire society, atleast the Hindu society, into pieces. I do not know what is going to be the future of this country?

Are we preparing ground for another East India Company to assume control; are we thinking about the future of this country or are we only bothered about the vote bank? I really don't know... It is not only the present government (which is running after votes). It has been done in the past. It will continue to be done in the future. There is no use asking what the present government is doing? This government is also pursuing policies which will bring votes. For them the vote bank is more important than the future of the country.

Q. The Mandal Commission report is about 10-year-old.The previous government could also have implemented it. But it didn't.

A. They did for good reasons. They probably thought that it would create a lot of trouble. So they sat on it. I think that was a wiser thing to do than to have hurriedly come to a decision.

Q. What exactly were the reasons for which the authors of the Indian Constitution provided for reservations?

A. They provided for reservations only for the Scheduled Castes and Tribes. The provision didn't apply to anybody else. The Mandal Commission is a new development. It came much after the Constitution was framed. The Constitution makers, I think, had at the back of their mind that even SCs and STs, after 15 years, will be able to stand on their own and thereafter the reservations could be on economic basis. (There was no provision) on caste or communal basis (for reservation). If we are making reservation in this easy manner, I don't see any reason why the Muslims, Sikhs or Christians should not demand it now? I think some Muslims have already started saying : "aren't we not as badly off as the Other Backward Classes (OBCs)."

Q. Has the reservation policy really helped the Scheduled

Castes and Tribes? It is believed that special interest groups within these sections have been the major beneficiaries while the majority remains where it was?

A. The Kaka Kalelkar report, which was on this very subject, says that even in the Scheduled Castes and Tribes, vested interests have sprung up. Only those who initially got the benefit of reservations are the real gainers. Now what reason can there be to apply these reservations to Jagjivan Ram's children and grandchildren? He was a multi-millionaire. Similarly, how can one justify the children of IAS, IPS and IFS officers belonging to Scheduled Caste and Tribes getting the same benefit as their fathers got? The whole thing is topsy-turvy. You have to come to an economic basis at some stage. These people should be out; new people should get the chance. Only then there would be some justification. But to have to vested interests sitting there and not allowing anybody to come in is all wrong.

Q. What has been the impact of the reservation policy on the administrative set-up in our country?

A. When I was a civil servant, the reservation business was in its infancy. Some people (from the Scheduled Castes and Tribes) were coming in. But we never got enough people—even on the basis of minimum marks—who could occupy the percentage of reservation that was provided for. At that time, nobody ever thought that even promotions would be on the basis of reservation; that superiors would be passed over by their subordinates belonging to the Scheduled Castes and Tribes. You see, one thing leads to another. It was never the case in the beginning as there would be reservations in promotions also. I think Jagjivan Ram started it when he was the Railway Minister.

What are we trying to do for making the government more efficient? Not only will the reservations affect the efficiency of the administration but they are likely to politicise the civil services. They would be working on the basis of caste and creed. We are coming to a situation experienced in 1946 when the Muslim members of the services were working for Pakistan and the non-Muslims for India. In the process, there was no work done! There was total (administrative) chaos. We are steadily bringing ourselves to the same position in this country. And believe me, if it goes on, in another 10-15 years, there would the total disruption.

Already, ministers are challenging those agitating against the Mandal Commission Report that they would ask the OBCs to come out on the streets. (Such statements) are an open invitation to caste war. Are these ministers responsible ministers? Have they ever realised the consequences of it at all? We have had people agitating against many things. But never before did any minister or any sensible person take this sort of stand. This is a new development; this is war, declared and encouraged.

Q. What procedures does the government follow while considering an old report? Moreover, what is the role of the cabinet secretary in such matters?

A. I don't know whether they took the cabinet secretary's advice at all. It is easy to blame the cabinet secretary. But in many cases the cabinet secretary is not even consulted. When Indira Gandhi became Prime Minister and there was devaluation of rupee, the first time I came to know of it was in the cabinet meeting, where it was announced. And then Mrs. Gandhi said: "How could I know? Did you ever ask me" So, the cabinet secretary is not always consulted.

Sometimes things are done for various reasons, the explanation given for the decision on the Mandal Commission Report is that it was an electoral promise and it had to be acted upon. But there are various ways of taking action. If not the Congress-I also, at least the parties supporting the government should have been consulted. It was something of great national interest. Why were efforts not made to arrive at a consensus? After all, 10 years have already passed (since the Commission submitted its report) and at best another year would have got spent in consultations. One year's delay would not have damaged the country. This sort of sudden decision by a party which is not even in majority is something that is totally uncalled for. They should have worked for a consensus if they were very keen to implement the report.

Personally, I see no reason why reservations should not be on an economic basis? There are poor and illiterate, even among the Brahmins, Kshatriyas and Vaish. At the same time, we have chief ministers belonging to OBCs. They are not so backward. Quite a few of them may be illiterate but most of the OBCs are as affluent as other classes in this country. So why should we not have job reservations on an economic basis to help the poor and illiterate of all classes?

Q. You haven't answered my question regarding the procedure the government follows while taking up an old report for implementation. Don't you think some sort of reappraisal is required in such cases?

A. Normally, all reports that have been lying in the limbo for an unconscionable period are looked at the examined, upon being dug out, to ascertain whether they need to be updated. For example, my Police Commission report has been in limbo for the past six years. If they decide to take it out, they will have to update it because quite a few recommendations are now out of date; out of context. Therefore, in case of such reports, the first thing is to examine and see whether they have to be brought uptodate, or whether there are any lacunas to be gone over. Then, a sub-committee or somebody sits and examines it to determine how far the recommendations are workable and what is going to be the total effect of acceptance; whether it is going to be only of temporary benefit against long-term difficulties? All this is done within a given time-frame.

You just can't pull the damn thing out and say here it does' we accept it. That is not the way to deal with government or national work.

A.M. Khusro: Job Reservations: Pro-side, Con-side and Inside

Times of India, 3.9.1992

Poverty is a secular phenomenon; it prevails in all categories of the Indian population; but it is astonishing that nearly all anti-poverty benefits are given to members of only certain communities. Besides the Scheduled Castes and Scheduled Tribes (SC/ST) who have been given 22.5 per cent reservation, there are millions of other down-trodden and low-income people in this country, clustered in different groups and areas. A large proportion of them are as poor and with as little access to literacy, education and health facilities as the SC/STs. They have to be supported with State assistance and other means to uplift them from the zone of poverty and social backwardness to a reasonable standard of living with social dignity. India cannot afford to neglect these masses of downtrodden and cannot leave them to their fate. Governments which neglect them will not themselves survive.

Once, at a meeting of the Central Board of the Reserve Bank of India with Mrs Gandhi attending as Union Finance Minister, someone suggested that if policy harped only on welfare and neglected efficiency and growth, it would neither beget welfare nor efficiency nor growth. To this Mrs Gandhi replied that if policy in India harped only on efficiency and growth to the neglect of welfare, it would cause so much unrest that the country would get, neither efficiency nor growth nor indeed welfare. It is clear that economic and social policy in this country necessarily has to take care of growth and efficiency as well as welfare.

The privation of millions, other than SC/STs, would seem to suggest that reservations should be given to backward castes as well as SC/STs and in that case the addition of a certain percentage say 27 per cent to the existing SC/ST quota of 12.5 per cent may seem to have a justification. While it is undeniable that the backward castes have to be uplifted through social and economic policy, two serious observations are in order. First, after all the effort for four decades to reduce and obliterate caste sentiments, isn't it a tragedy that caste should be consolidated through this backdoor of reservations? Unfortunately, caste remains an important element in the politics of the ballot, but fortunately social policy until this day is geared to the elimination of caste. Here, clearly, there is a head-long collision between long-term social policy and short-term expediency. In other words, reservations by caste - backward or forward - are unacceptable unless by some wooliness of argument or some mixed-up logic we perpetrate the error of diluting our social policy. A consolidation of the caste factor in whatever garb will be preposterous and will have vastly damaging consequences for the country.

Secondly, why should there be a reservation by caste? Because the backward castes are backward and poor, that is to say economically weak. In that case, the real issue is of economic weakness and not its outward expression, the caste. So, why don't we break the outer shell of caste and come to the brass-tacks of economic backwardness and provide suitable reservations in education and jobs for a sensible length of time until the economically weak manage to uplift themselves? Why beat about the bush and talk of caste rather than come to the reality of economic privation? From whatever angle we look at this matter we reach the conclusion that the real issue is the protection of the weak and not of particular castes.

Economic Criterion

This assertion, strengthens itself when it is realised that in every caste, however backward and downtrodden, there are always some people who have reached the towering heights of prosperity. The Quraish (dealers in meat) and the Ansar (weavers and spinners) among the Muslims, have a large number of very poor people but also a number of millionaires and it would be quite objectionable to reserve jobs, etc., for them as a whole. Only the poorer elements amongst them need attention and indeed that is true of all castes. Here again, the point emerges that reservation should be by the economic criterion and not by the caste denomination.

One of the most sensible things that this country did in recent years was to run the Integrated Rural Development Programme (IRDP), the National Rural Employment Programme (NREP) and the Nehru Rozgar Yojana. Whatever the shortcomings of these programmes in terms of their mal-administration, misuse of subsidy, etc., the merit of these programmes is that they are not based on religious, caste, linguistic or regional considerations. In these programmes, you attempt to identify the poor and the poor are not designated by any of the above categories. 'Wherever the poor exist and whoever they are, they are sought to be identified for economic assistance. In fact, Indian social policy had graduated into a caste-free as well as religion-free and region-free effort with these programmes. That is how things should be. For historical reasons, the SC/ST reservations may continue for a while, so as not to raise a hornets' nest. But to this quota of 22.5 per cent could be tagged on any reasonable percentage of reservation based on economic criterion. Clearly, the Government must come off the caste argument, and adopt the economic argument which is infinitely superior. And the problem of identifying people by their poverty is no more intractable than the problem of identification by caste. Moreover, caste is full of social as well as arithmetical hazards.

One could not disagree more with the recent announcement that the 27 per cent reservations for Other Backward Classes (OBCs) will not apply to admissions to schools and colleges. This is most intriguing. If we don't admit the backward or economically poor to schools and colleges and do not create massive opportunities for them at this stage and if we do not make special arrangements for extra coaching to the economically backward, we would be recruiting at the job stage very inefficient people. In that case, the disparity between them and others would be more glaring than if we concentrated on early education of the backward and uplifted them substantially. In fact, the first priority for reservation is the educational stage without which admission of the backward to jobs would be a cause of great friction in society as well as harmful to the backward. It would thus be best to have reservations for well identified economically backward people at the school and college stage and perhaps at the stage of first employment and, thereafter, let them compete for promotions.

Yet another point which the policy must bear in mind is the need to graduate people away from reservations. Once, through the benefits of educational and first-job reservation, people make the grade and come to grips with competitive market forces, they should be graduated out of reservation category and made to stand on their own feet. Policy must help' build self-reliance as much internally in the economy as externally and it cannot be that we have a crutch-oriented, subsidised, non-self-reliant structure at home and talk of self-reliance abroad.

Weighty Considerations

There are considerations sufficiently weighty that must ultimately prevail and modify substantially the "Mandalisation" of policy. One is that the regime of reservation - even if it did not have the holes which the present one has - should not be pushed to such an extreme that efficiency of the economy is seriously compromised. In the present situation, when an increasingly efficient and technologically advancing world is closing upon us, nothing should be allowed to compromise efficiency. The other compelling consideration is that reservation should not be pushed so far that, some of the unreserved categories begin to entertain fears of becoming down-trodden and seek reservation for themselves.

Thus, a sensible system of reservation is one which (a) takes care of the downtrodden and the poor through creation of opportunities at the educational and the first-job stage; (b) identifies the poor by the level of poverty and not by caste; (c) graduates the economically weak as they become stronger; (d) provides additional assistance to the weak through coaching, hostel facilities and scholarships and stipends at the scholastic stage: (e) arranges training programmes for the weak preparatory to admissions to jobs in the public and private sectors and generally promotes self-reliance rather than doles and crutches.

What Charan Singh, the Guru of Paswan, Sharad, Mulayam, Laloo, had said: 'Reservation on Caste Basis Vicious'

Indian Express News Service, Lucknow, Sept. 14, 1990

It was not only the first Prime Minister Jawaharlal Nehru and the father of the nation, Mahatma Gandhi, who considered reservation in Services as "disastrous" and "fatal", but even Charan Singh, founder of the Lok Dal, which dominates the Janata Dal today, was opposed to it and considered it a "vicious principle."

Charan Singh was a skilled administrator with a long experience and had emerged as a charismatic leader of backward castes and classes, which formed a formidable electoral base of his political outfit of which Mr. Sharad Yadav, Mr. Ram Vilas Paswan, Mr. Mulayam Singh Yadav, Mr. Laloo Prasad Yadav, and many others are the products. His son, Mr Ajit Singh, today is the Union Industry Minister in the Central Cabinet and dares not open his mouth on the raging reservation controversy.

Charan Singh was greatly upset when the reservation for the backward castes, apart from in recruitment, was extended to promotions in Uttar Pradesh on January 19, 1978, by the Ram Naresh Yadav ministry.

The former Prime Minister and ex-Chief Minister of Uttar Pradesh wrote a long letter on February 12, 1982, to the then Janata Party Chief Minister, Mr Banarasi Das, referring to "an outflow of agitation in the neighbouring state of Rajasthan" and to "students and teachers in some western districts of Uttar Pradesh carrying on an agitation against reservation of seats for members of the scheduled castes in recruitment to Government services."

Charan Singh wrote "it must be conceded that reservation on the basis of caste is a vicious principle and creates many problems."

Referring to "another side of the picture", Charan Singh, by whose name all the backward class leaders swear even today, wrote "boys belonging to poor families, particularly those whom large sections of our people have considered socially inferior for centuries past, are entitled to consideration rather than concessions at the hands of Governments of independent India."

Quota not Beyond 10 years

Charan Singh was even against extending reservation to scheduled castes beyond ten years and wrote "if my memory does not fail me, Dr Ambedkar, who had done so much for the uplift of the poor, had himself declared in a speech some time before his death, that the provision of reservation in service should not extend beyond 1960 or 1961. All that was required to be done, was to provide educational facilities to students belonging to the weaker sections of our society. The Union Government however, has for political reasons, been extending the period of reservation decade after decade."

The Lok Dal founder, after having stated his views on reservation, referred to the crux of the problem, which made him write this letter to the then Chief Minister of his party. "My immediate purpose in writing this letter to you is that more than reservation in recruitment, it is reservation in promotions that had led to great heart-burning and great inefficiency in our Services. Such reservation whether in favour of scheduled or backward castes, was, in my opinion, beyond intentions of the founding fathers."

While accepting the fait accompli of reservations in recruitment, Charan Singh suggested for withdrawal of reservation in promotions (which was done) and then added "nor should there be any reservation in admissions to the institutions of technical education particularly of medicine and engineering. Of course, reservation in Services to graduates from such institutions may continue as in other 'services."

The former Prime Minister also strongly pleaded for bars on children of those who have benefited reservation and those who were income tax payees, even if they belong to scheduled castes or backward castes, and wrote "children of all those who have already been benefited by reservation, and have, thus, been brought up in a cultural environment higher than the average, should not be entitled to this concession. Nor should be children of those who are assessed to income tax, so that the children of those who are less fortunate than those covered in the previous two categories may also be helped."

Charan Singh concluded his letter with the hope "acceptance of my suggestions will ensure public good. May be, there will be some noise raise by vested interests, but a far larger number of people will welcome it."

Charan Singh had the highest regard for Mahatma Gandhi and had been extolling and advocating Gandhian philosophy and principles. Mahatma Gandhi in his book *The India of My Dreams* on Page 62, wrote, "so far as the employment in government departments is concerned, I think it will be fatal to a good government, if we introduce there the communal spirit for administration to be efficient. It must always be in the hands of the fittest. There should be certainly no favouritism.

Passing of Test Must

During those days, the pressure was for reservation on the basis of communities and the Mahatma wrote "if we want five engineers we must not take one from each community but we must take the fittest five even if they were all Musalmans or all Parsis. The lowest post must, if need be, be filled by examination an impartial board consisting of men belonging to different communities. But distribution of posts should never be according to the proportion of the numbers of each community."

Saying that passing of the required test should be a must, Mahatma Gandhi wrote "the educationally backward communities will have a right to receive favoured treatment in the matter of education at the hands of the national Government. This can be secured in an effective manner. But those who aspire to occupy responsible posts in the Government of the country can only do so if they pass the required test."

Madhu Limaye: Reservation: For a New Social Order

(The Hindustan Times, dated 19th September, 1990)

The developments of the past several weeks have made it clear that the entire establishment-major political leaders from Mr. Rajiv Gandhi to Mr. Jyoti Basu, the bureaucracy, the universities and the media are up in arms against the decision of the V.P. Singh Government on reservation in Central services. A terrific one-sided propaganda has been unleashed to perpetuate the dominance of the privileged minority over the Central power structure. Coercion, violence, arson and destruction of State property are the other favoured means of the dominant minority.

A miasma of confusion is being deliberately spread over the expression "backward classes" employed in Articles 15, 16 and 340. The claptrap about economic criteria and poverty would make one feel as if the Constitution makers were unaware of the meaning of this expression. Backward class reservation was in existence even before the adoption and implementation of the Constitution. The speakers from the southern province of Madras which then comprised Tamil Nadu, large parts of the present Andhra Pradesh and the northern parts of today's Kerala pointed out that the concept was not unknown in the South.

Definition

Dr. B.R. Ambedkar, who was inducted into the Constituent Assembly and the Government largely on the initiative of Sardar Patel, had made it clear that the term backward class had been left to be defined by the Government. K.M. Munshi talked of the need for a 'generic term' and had said that the Backward Classes Commission under Article 340 would investigate the conditions of the socially and educationally backward classes. Munshi also said that a definition of Backward Classes had been in existence for several years in his own province, namely Bombay. Mohamed Ismail Sahib of Madras asserted that in his province the expression had got a definite and technical meaning. He warned that the expression should not be so construed as to exclude the backward classes from among Muslims and Christians.

When the First Constitution Amendment was adopted Jawaharlal Nehru rejected the suggestion that the term "economically" backward classes should instead be adopted. The Law Minister bluntly told the Provisional Parliament that the expression backward classes meant "nothing else but a collection of certain castes."

Reality of Caste

The first Backward Classes Commission came to the conclusion that in considering social and educational bckwardness among Hindus the reality of caste could not be ignored. It said: "The Commission is justified in interpreting the terms of reference as mainly relating to social hierarchy based on caste. Caste generally depends upon birth; it may also depend upon habit and it may create further cleavage due to conversion and denominational differences."

Much is made of what Marc Galanter has called the "last minute desertion" of Chairman Kakasaheb Kalelkar which "foreshadowed the negative reception" of the Commission's report. I learnt from knowledgeable persons in the Fifties that Kakasaheb changed his views after he received a severe dressing down from Jawaharlal Nehru who was then at the height of his power and prestige. This was a turning point in Nehru's political career. The spiritual hold of Mahatma Gandhi had begun to wane and the parochial brahminical outlook had begun to dominate his thinking till the rude shock of the humilating defeat at the hands of China brought him back to his old moorings and led him to describe himself as the relic of the Gandhian age.

Adult Franchise

It is worthwhile recalling that Mahatma Gandhi was a strong advocate of adult franchise. He thought it would enable Harijans, Muslims and the backward classes to influence the working of the government. He thought that property and literary qualifications would deprive vast sections of the aforesaid castes and communities of the right to vote. About the significance of vote Gandhiji said on December 3, 1931: "I would not be satisfied without adult suffrage. At a stroke I arm the untouchables with tremendous power." Gandhiji was familiar with the expression backward classes. He had used it way back in 1933 to distinguish these classes — which also suffered from social disabilities — from the untouchables or the Scheduled Castes.

It should be remembered that in the beginning Gandhiji was opposed to both separate electorates and reservation of seats for the Scheduled Castes. But during the Yervada Pact negotiations he accepted reservation on the basis of a joint electorate. The generosity of the pact evoked a strong reaction in Bengal and the dominant Bhadralok leadership revolted against it. They fought elections to the Central Assembly on the Malaviya Aney platform and inflicted a defeat on the Congress. The Marxist Jyoti Basu is only emulating the example of the 1934 Bhadraloks. It is a pity that the Hindu upper castes are not even now prepared to overcome their intolerance and selfishness which drove vast sections of the population of Bengal and elsewhere to seek comfort in the egalitarian ethos of Islam and Christianity. But as Dr. Ambedkar has so ably shown in his extensive writings the all-pervading influence of caste has contaminated even the Muslim and Christian communities.

Peasant Proprietors

The impulse of the freedom movement was strong enough to push the programme of abolishing landlordism within the first two decades after Independence. Coupled with the new agricultural technology and increased irrigation facilities a new class of peasant proprietors is emerging in some parts of the country. This class is still socially backward. Some of the castes such as Jats for instance were torn between their links with the more backward sections and their desire to upgrade themselves in terms of the social hierarchy. Then there are the dryland farmers who cannot make out even a precarious existence. All these classes want a share in political power at the Centre, both in the Council of Ministers as well as in different classes of services. This is but natural.

Just Share

It is a pity that Nehru who played a major role in liberating this class from the shackles of landlordism should have grudged them their just share in the Central administration. The cooption of the backward classes of both types, the landholding backwards and non-landholding backwards, into the power structure will strengthen the state and the nation. However, the upper castes are afraid that the OBCs would come up very fast and swamp them. But if any caste gets representation more than its proportion in the population, economic criteria can be applied to it. This is the only way to build a mobile and dynamic social order.

Time is running out. We must do the kind of justice to the backward classes that Mahatma Gandhi did to the "untouchables" nearly 60 years ago. The directive of the Constitution embodied in the Articles 15, 16, 46 and 340 has remained unimplemented at the Centre. The preamble spoke of justice social, economic and political. It wanted to assure the dignity of the individual.

The non-implementation of the reservation policy in the North has not raised administrative efficiency. The southern States are, in fact, better administered than UP and Bihar. The V.P. Singh notification is only the first step. A many faceted offensive is needed to establish social equality, fair shares and rapid economic development.

C.P. Bhambhri: The Muslim Question: On the Problem of Minorities

Hindustan Times, 4.12.1993

The dominant sections of the Indian political class have always believed that diverse cultural groups deserve not only Constitutional; and legal protection for their specific cultural, linguistic and religious needs, they alsc require a concrete policy and programmatic interventions to take care of their perceived feelings of "psychological vulnerabilities". In spite of the various efforts made by the Government of India and political parties during the last fifty years, the question of the Muslim minority in democratic India continues to be complex, critical and in many ways unresolved.

A few facts may be stated here to highlight the problematic of the Indian Muslims. First, secular parties and important opinion makers of the Muslim community sharply reacted against the decision of the Shiv Sena-BJP Government to abolish the Maharashtra Minority Commission. Its implication is clear that the Muslim minority felt a great need for a special Minority Commission to safeguard their special interests. Second, B.S. Ramoowalia, the Welfare Minister of the Government of India and many other important political leaders have demanded the induction of Muslims in the police forces to ensure physical security to the Muslim community. The genesis of a demand like this lies in real or imaginary perceptions of the Muslim minority about the "biased approach" of the Indian police and many other functionaries of the Indian State.

Third, every communal riot has contributed to the creation of a siege mentality and a feeling of "social outsider" among the Muslims and M.J. Akbar's moving account in his book on "Riot after Riot" (1988) makes us to conclude that he problem of physical insecurity really haunts them. Fourth, every assertion of the forces of Hindutva and retreat of secular political formations have strengthened the feelings of insecurity among the Muslims.

The upshort of this is that the Muslim question in India occupies a special position and the political discourse of the 1990s around the temple-mosque controversy has brought into focus the problematic of "social insiders and outsiders" and of political Hinduism and the `others'. Political responses to such complicated political and social questions need to be based on a proper understanding of the real felt needs of the Muslim community.

It is essential to demystify the concept of the Muslim community because, like all other religious and cultural communities, the Indian Muslims are internally highly differentiates and socially stratified. Not only this. The Indian Muslims like all other communities have distinct region-based differences and also problems. India does not have any monolith religious community and the Muslims of India are an artificial political construct like the so-called Hindus of India.

The problems faced by the Muslims of north and western India are not very relevant to the Muslims of south and north-east India. Historically, the partition has left a great impact on tne memory of the inhabitants of Uttar Pradesh, Bihar and the Punjabi Hindus. Further, the contemporary politics of Pakistan attracts a lot of attention and multiple interpretations in India but, even in this, the intensity of feelings against Pakistan among the Hindus of India has great regional variations. Tamil Nadu attaches much more importance to the problem of Tamilians in Sri Lanka and the Government of Assam expresses greater concern for the happenings in Bangladesh than the involvement of Pakistan in the international affairs of Punjab or Jammu and Kashmir.

The regional diversities prevalent among the attitudes and beliefs of various communities facilitate or aggravate the problems of Indian Muslims. Social and cultural distancing among various communities which lies at the root of social stereotypes has also regional variations. Further, Muslims living in a village, or a small town or a big city or a metropolitan capital, have very different kind of inter-community relationships than a homogenized view about the Muslims which is reflected by the political class and policy makers. The emphasis on regional variations of the Muslim question has been made to suggest that some special policy responses for the Muslim community in the south of India will not have the emotive resistance as it will have in the north. Hence any all-India Muslim policy of the Government of India has to based on great caution because different regions have different social milieu and instead of resolving a minority question, an all-India uniform policy may complicate the problem.

It is essential to grapple with some basic demands of the Indian Muslim leadership for analysis and policy making while keeping in mind that any all-India Muslim policy will not have a smooth sailing given the history and politics of India. The demand for the induction of Muslims in police and para-military organisations for providing a feeling of physical security to the Muslims should be completely rejected. The implication of the Muslim quota in the services of the Government will completely communalise the Indian State apparatus as militant supporters of caste reservations have completely casteised the public services.

Further, quota-based reservations will not help the majority of Muslims who need special public promotional policies for their uplift. It may be clearly stated that communal biases play a role in the performance of public duties by a section of public services. The remedial action for effectively curbing the disease of communalism lies in the creation of a powerful quasi-judicial body and also public citizens' committees on the pattern of the Race Relations Committees in the UK. The National Commission for Women, the National Commission for SC/ST and the National Human Rights Commissions have some investigatory powers to look after the rights and interests of women, SC/ST and other citizens.

Similarly, the National Commission for Minorities should be accorded a quasi-judicial role to deal with the complaints of communal bias in public services. It deserves to be mentioned that communal bias in the services should be investigated case by case and functionaries with such bias should be severely punished, but the evil of communalism in the Government cannot be eradicated by according a communal representation to the Muslim minority.

While the demand for reservations in public services has been always voiced by the upwardly mobile Muslim or caste elite, the Indian State should respond to the real needs of the struggling Muslim artisans, unskilled workers, small shopkeepers and traders. Muslims deserve positive support by the public institutions in the form of new skills for work, loans and credits for launching trade or small industrial enterprises. Since Muslims are a highly differentiated community, the effective approach to their specific problems will also have to be highly decentralised. The Panchayati Raj institutions, the urban local governments, the State Governments under the effective leadership of the Central Government should involve themselves to promote specific programmes for the uplift of the vulnerable and socially dependent Muslim poor and lower middle classes.

The secular political class of India should unitedly campaign for widening the base of education for Muslims. Muslims like Hindus have to be gradually brought out from the influences of mullahs, imams and mosque and temple-supported educational institutions. Secular educational institutions provide a proper ethos for inter-cultural integration than the majority or minority-based educational institutions. Hindu-Muslim social stereotypical attitudes are a road block in the way of a healthy development of inter-community relationship and this distance can be shortened by secular educational institutions and not by the so-called madrasas or waqf property supported programmes.

The Indian State has to rescue the Muslims from the madrasa and also provide in a positive manner opportunities to the various deprived sections of the community for their real development. Political tokenism like reservations in public services or some restructuring of institutions for governance will not provide either physical security or a developmental future to the Muslims. A democratic system in every multicultural society is challenged by different minority groups with demands for the new space and rights in public life and every Western democracy and all liberal thinkers from John Locke to John Rawls have been struggling with the inadequacy of representational and participational institutions of democracy because groups are unequal in every society. Hence, John Stuart Mill proved to be a prophet of an empty liberty and an abstract individual, and every thinker on democracy is grappling with the problems of political accommodation of unequal social groups in political systems.

The Indian political class is also seized with the challenging task of dealing with the Muslim question which is quite complicated because of our history, but we are not alone because American democracy is also struggling to cope with the historically given race problem. If on the one hand, secular forces have to challenge the religion based political formations, on the other, specific programmes for the uplift of various categories of Muslims should be evolved by the Central and the State Governments. Politically populist responses to win over Muslim votes will prove counter-productive and in the present political milieu highly dangerous.

D.L. Sheth: Muslim Reservation: No Provision for Communal Quotas

Times of India, 20.9.1997

For sometime now, a section of the Muslim leadership has been demanding a separate ten per cent quota in reservations, for Muslims. This is despite the fact that the majority of Muslims is already covered under the existing provision of reservations for the Other Backward Classes.

The new demand, is not only for allocating a separate quota for OBC Muslims, but to extend the provision to all Indians Muslims. After Independence, the argument goes, the Muslim community as a whole in India has become backward and should be declared as such. The demand concedes that the sub-communities/biradaris of Muslims notified as 'backward', should get the first priority within the proposed separate category of 'Muslims'. The rest of the Muslims should get the benefits of reservations "only if and to the extent that Muslim quotas remain unfulfilled". A caveat is, however, added that the quotas unused by the 'backward' Muslim communities should go to other Muslims.

This demand is part of the leadership's efforts to recover lost ground in the post-Babri Muslim politics. It is, however, riot succeeding in mustering popular Muslim support for the demand and making it an issue in mobilisational politics. This is because the poor and traditionally backward Muslim communities fear that if all Muslims become entitled to reservations, their opportunities for upward social mobility will be severely curtailed, as the benefits will then go increasingly to the upper strata of Muslims. This situation may not continue for long. What can probably convert the demand into a symbolic issue of "injustice-done-to-Muslims" is the frustration among poor and backward Muslim communities who deserve to be included in backward-class lists, but have been kept waiting.

Long-term Results

The demand for a separate reservations quota for all Muslims, however, raises an altogether different set of issues. Is the demand consistent with the rationale of the established policy of OBC reservations? What implications does it have for India's existence as a plural, secular democracy? It has become necessary to study the implications of this demand and prevent it from snowballing into the dangerous symbolic politics of mobilisation and counter-mobilisation around ethno-religious nationalism. First, it will re-activate the pernicious pre-Partition discourse that essentialised religious communities as sociopolitical monoliths, disregarding vital internal social, economic and cultural differences within them-a discourse now adopted by the Hindutva movement.

Social Justice

It is sociologically established fact that within every religious community there exists a vertical hierarchy of social groups marked by economic, social and educational differences. These differences do not undermine the religious identity of a community as such, but that, by itself, does not place different groups following one religion within one single, horizontal, social, economic and cultural space. Cultural plurality in India is not just about the existence of different marco-communities of faith. Plurality is more substantively manifested through the various micro-communities and cultures that have grown historically within and across religious boundaries. The claim that a community of faith constitutes a unitary socio-economic and cultural entity, whether made by a majority or a minority, in fact, represents a political strategy of a small elite to elicit majority support from its coreligionists. In effect, such elite politics thwarts aspirations for upward social mobility of a majority within a religious community and denies it the economic and social rights which state policy extends to the poor and the 'backward' populations cutting across religions.

Second, by demanding reservations for all Muslims, the Muslim social elite has adopted a strategy of deliberate obfuscation of the terms of discourse on the issue of social justice: Again, their strategy mirrors that of the Hindu upper-caste elite which also refuses to recognise the social disadvantages and discrimination suffered by communities at the lower rungs of the Hindu social hierarchy. Just as the later seeks to project the unity of all Hindus by inducing the lower- caste Hindus to get on the Hindutva bandwagon, the former wants to project the communal solidarity of the Muslims by taking over the reins of the backward bandwagon.

Third, such a demand seeks to subvert the very rationale of the reservations policy. The policy of OBC reservations is premised on the secular principle of social and educational backwardness of any class. It recognises specific communities, cutting across religion, as backward or non-backward on the basis of what the Supreme Court has described as a 'time-tested' criteria of backwardness evolved by different states. Thus, any religious community almost invariably comprises backward and non-backward classes. Just as there are castes and classes among the Hindu majority, there are classes and caste-like formations among the Muslims, Christians and Sikhs.

Backwardness is thus a congealed social reality of an occupational or a low traditional status group within a larger, macro-community of faith. This condition of backwardness among sub-communities of a faith may or may not be theologically sanctioned, but in reality it operates at the level of relatively closed, hereditary, cross-generational status groups which prevents the occupational and social mobility of its members. This is true, for example, of the Julahas or Halakhors among the UP Muslims, the Majhabis or Ramgharias among the Christians, and so on. Similarly, some groups within each community of faith are traditionally "forward", for example, the Sayids, Shekhs and other Asharaf communities of the UP Muslims, the Thangals, Arbis, Arakkals, Koyas and Keyis among the Kerala Muslims, the Khatris and Jats among the Sikhs, the Syrians among Kerala Christians, and so on. The claim that an entire community of faith is socially and educationally backward is a travesty of sociological truth and makes nonsense of the principle of social justice.

New Demand

We must, therefore, distinguish between the political principle of minority, relevant for protecting cultural identities and rights, and the social principle of backwardness meant to settle issues of equity and justice. Today, these two separate logics are being deliberately tangled by the demand that the, whole Muslim community be allotted a separate quota of reservations as a 'backward class'. The proponents of reservation for all Muslims should, in the interest of intellectual honesty and political candour, make their demand as a "religious minority", but not as a 'backward class'.

Even this would mean a major amendment to the Constitution; one which would violate the secular spirit of the Constitution. India's Constitution recognises the cultural rights of minorities as fundamental rights and forbids discrimination on grounds of religious affiliation, but it is foundationally opposed to any idea of 'communal quotas'. The new demand of Muslim reservations is simply a stratagem to introduce through the backdoor the principle of communal quotas into the Constitution.

Iqbal A Ansari: Muslims in Need of Affirmative Action
Times of India, 16.10.1997

The Muslims' demand for reservation can be justified in terms of the historical backwardness of the community and the neutralisation of biases against them. To regard this demand as indicative of a "dangerous symbolic politics of mobilisation around ethno-religious nationalism" as Mr D L Sheth does (September 20) is to misread the post-1947 Muslim situation in the subcontinent.

The idea of exclusivist religion-based nationalism as improvised by Jinnah stands discredited in the eyes of most Indian Muslims and influential sections of Pakistani intellectuals. Moreover, the low economic status of Muslims and their thin geographical spread within India rules out in their case any separatist political ambitions. Contrary to the general assumption, Muslims have not voted en masse for any party in any of the elections. The demands that sections of Muslims are now raising for their security, identity, and economic development should, therefore, be seen as the gradual regaining of their self-confidence, so battered in the decades after partition. It is a kind of psycho-political settling down and seeking of a place in the sun.

Mr. Sheth does recognise the right of minorities to protect their cultural identities. But the measures taken by a community or a state for realisation of a distinct identity invariably arouses the suspicion of the power-wielding majority which tries to undermine the equal rights of minorities. It is this universal feature of the majority-minority situation that led the United Nations, for instance, to establish as early as 1947 the sub-commission for prevention of discrimination and protection of minorities.

Major Aspect

Yet, the phenomenon of discrimination against minorities in India is hardly ever made a subject of study. Prima facie a case of discrimination against Muslims can be easily established by considering the share of Muslims in the state's patronage system, and in discretionary appointments during the last five decades. Recognising this phenomenon and taking measures to neutralise its effects will better promote the cause of secularism. Educational schemes and political processes directed towards removing inter-group prejudices must be supplemented by legal-institutional measures, such as a quota for minorities and a commission for equal opportunities and non-discrimination.

The other major aspect of the Muslim situation in India is the community's social and educational backwardness. This has historical roots, including the development of caste-like features in the Indian Muslim society. The Mandal Commission, unfortunately, did not determine on an empirical basis the nature and extent of backwardness among minorities. It was honest enough to admit that the criteria evolved by it to determine backwardness was only "rough and ready". But no attempt has since been made to refine it.

Meaning of Class

In view of these realities the Muslims deserve an institutional set-up which addresses their particular problems. This cannot be dismissed on the assumption that it will be violative of the secular principle of the Constitution. The word 'class' used in Article 16(4) includes communities, as pointed out by K.M. Munshi during the discussion on the clause in the advisory committee. He explained that "classes have been interpreted as minorities or religious communities also."

The prenatal history of Article 16(4) shows that it was initially conceived of at the instance of a Sikh member as a special measure "to meet the claims of minorities to special representation in the services." Dr Ambedkar explained on behalf of the drafting committee that `classes' had been used instead of just `minorities' to make the provision cover similar sections of citizens from among the majority community also. When doubts were expressed whether `classes' would include minorities, Sardar Patel, the chairman of the committee, said, "This is simple English. Classes include minorities ... The whole basis of the provision is minorities."

The Supreme Court in its judgement on the Mandal Commission case has also noted that "in his speech in the Constituent Assembly Dr Ambedkar was using the word `communities' (and not castes) which expression include not only the castes among the Hindus but several other groups." The judgment illustratively and appreciatively referred to the categorisation of Muslims as a whole as a backward community in the princely state of Travancore.

Survey, Impression or Imagination?: Mandal's Expert Disowns Report (B.K. Roy Burman)

Express News Service, New Delhi. Aug. 30, 1990

Mr Mandal's technical expert has disowned his report.

Prof B.K. Roy-Burman, who headed the technical committee and chaired the research planning panel for the Mandal Commission, says that the report is totally without scientific basis. It exaggerates the number of 'other backward classes'. It ignores every suggestion that the experts associated with it made.

"We were used," says the professor, whose name figures in the preface to the report, along with Dr M.N. Srinivas and Dr Yoginder Singh. "They associated our names with the report without listening to us or even consulting us on the basis for their ultimate findings."

Mr Roy Burman, who has been the Deputy Registrar-General, Census Operations, says that Mandal's men sabotaged the experts' suggestions at every stage. To start with, the experts did not want caste to be the basis for identifying backward classes. And finally, they were not even shown the processed data on which the findings hinged.

"We don't know whether the findings were based on the survey, or personal impression or plain imagination," said Mr. Roy-Burman. Even the Home Minister of the day was unable to show him the data, he says.

When the Mandal Commission first started its proceedings, the experts were asked to determine the criteria that would decide backwardness. They were asked to design the survey. To process the data.

"Caste was not a satisfactory measure of backwardness. We were more inclined to consider occupations as a measure. Or perhaps, a mix of the two," he says.

A pilot survey was conducted in Birbhum district of West Bengal, taking this mixed approach. The result was startling. Only two occupations were truly backward-blacksmiths and potters. They also coincided, roughly, with particular castes.

After this, the tampering began. The experts had come up with a system of 'weightages' for various criteria of backwardness. The commission dumped all these and came up with its own weightages. The experts were not even told, about this.

"We had suggested a spectrum of weightages for literacy. Obviously, you can't equate a person who can barely sign his name with a post-graduate and club them both as literate. This is precisely what the commission did.

"If you go just by the literacy rate, many castes become backward. The literacy level among Jats, this way, is not very different from dhobis. But Jats have many snore post-graduates.

The system that the panel adopted is unscientific. It multiplies the number of the backward castes."

Experts given the go-by

After that, says Mr. Roy-Burman, the experts were completely given the go-by. The occupation-caste mix concept was shelved. Mr Mandal wanted caste to be the sole criterion.

The experts did not know whether their survey design was being used. They were not consulted.

The experts wanted 151 tables to be made for purposes of calculation and illustration. Arbitrarily, Mr Mandal reduced this number to just 31.

"The commission was in a hurry to wind tip its proceedings. The Government had changed and it was, perhaps, not feeling very secure about its future," says Mr Roy-Burman.

The commission wanted him to approve its own format. It said there was a time constraint. He refused.

The commission got its own back by refusing to show the social scientists the processed data. "I wrote to the commission to tell them that we had been used. The data had to be shown to us. The commission had to hear our suggestions, though it could overrule them."

At this stage, the commission finally told the experts where they stood. "We have been very cooperative with you. You are being unnecessarily strident," the commission wrote back.

The report was published. The experts were acknowledged for their contributions in the preface itself.

But they were never shown the processed data.

The Elusive Data

"I went and met Mr P.C. Sethi, who was the Home Minister then and asked him for the data. I told him that if it had been processed, it should be made available to experts. It hasn't been processed, it should be."

Even the Home Minister was not able to show Mr Roy-Barman the data on which the fate of the nation is now being decided. "I still have not seen that data. After all, I want to know how much of the report is based on data, how much, on impressions and how much on imagination," he says.

He finds Mr Mandal's projection on the 1931 data unscientific. "There has been so much social mobility since then." But there is another, more serious objection.

Mr. Roy-Burman says, that many of the castes specified to the 1931 census are just "synonyms." In other words, the same caste has been mentioned separately, according to its name, the name of the community, the name of the occupation, etc. "There is a lot of duplication. It will just multiply the number of castes that are now called other backward classes."

But none of these views were heard by the man whose report is now law.

Another Howler from Mandal!

Bhubaneswar. Aug 30 (PTI)

The Mandal Commission has blundered by including 20 scheduled tribes and scheduled castes of Orissa in the list of backward classes, according to official sources here.

The sources claimed the Mandal Commission report was based on the 1931 caste census report. On the basis of the said report, the Mandal Commission had listed 224 backward castes in Orissa to be entitled to the benefits of its recommendations. But Orissa was carved into a separate state in 1936 and in 1931 the Oriya speaking tracts were parts of different neighbouring states.

In fact, many of the 224 backward castes of Orissa listed in the Mandal Commission report were non-existent in the state, they said.

The following are the scheduled tribes and scheduled castes of Orissa added to the list of backward castes: Battada (ST), Birghia (ST), Chakliyan (SC), Dom (SC), Gonda (ST), Jaintra Pans (SC), Talwar (ST), Koda Kuda (ST), Kond (ST). Kond-Dessy Kondh (ST), Kota (ST), Koyi (ST), Laher (SC), Omeyita (ST), Porja-Boda Bonda (ST), Rajwar (ST), Sahabar (ST), Savara (ST), Tiyar (SC) and Tonla Gadu (SC).

Dr. Srinivas says he was not consulted: Another Expert Disclaims Responsibility

Express News Service, New Delhi: Aug. 31, 1990

Mr. Mandal tried to give his report a veneer of respectability by acknowledging the contribution of Dr. M.N. Srinivas one of India's foremost sociologists, to the survey. Dr Srinivas clarified on Friday that he hail almost nothing to do with the report.

"We also acknowledge with gratitude the valuable assistance given by Prof. M.N. Srinivas, Prof Jogendra Singh and Prof B.K. Roy-Burman in this connection," the Commission noted in its preface.

In chapter XI, the Commission went on to note: "Subsequently a Panel of Experts led by Prof M.N. Srinivas, met in Delhi from July 16th to 20th, 1979 and after detailed deliberations, prepared a complete design of the survey along with a set of schedules, dummy tables, instructions, etc."

Prof Srinivas, on Friday, disclaimed all this. He said:

"The Mandal Commission mentions me as one of the experts consulted. 1 wish to make it clear in this context that all I did was to attend a one-day workshop conducted by the Commission in New Delhi when they were about to start their inquiries. That was the only occasion I met them on a professional basis.

"Subsequently, some members of the Commission paid a courtesy visit to me in Bangalore. I gave them a cup of coffee.

"In view of the above, it would not be correct to describe me as one who advised the Commission in the formulation, of the report or, its recommendations."

Earlier, in a recent interview to a weekly, Prof Srinivas had hit out at the system of reservations and at the Mandal report.

"The policy of reservations has extracted a big price—the level of corruption and inefficiency is very high. Another pointer is the level of attention at the work place, because incompetent people have acquired jobs on the basis of caste," he had said.

"The biggest crime is, of course, the reservation of jobs, on the basis of caste, in schools and universities. Setting aside a professor's post and then filling the vacancy in an arbitrary fashion because the right applicants of a particular caste are not available is not in the interest of the students, the education system and the country. Is it fair for the first generation school-goers from the poor and backward classes to be taught by an unqualified, unsuitable teacher, merely because the latter belongs to a caste which is eligible for reservation? While seeking to do justice by one individual, one is condemning the students to perdition.".

Prof Srinivas had concluded: "With the reservation system, we are fast moving away from the egalitarian society which our Constitution had enshrined."

The views of another of Mr Mandal's experts according to Prof Singh was confined to the secretarial staff provided by the Government to assist it.

Expressing his opinion about the report, Prof Singh said it failed to take into account the different levels of economic, social and educational status between the groups clubbed together as backward.

Prof Singh asserted that "there is no adequate data base to say that caste is the basis for determining class. It was this fact that had led to such strong resentment against the report, he felt.

Talking about reservation policy, he said reservation should not be a fixed status. He pointed out that in the old Indian society, it was caste that perpetuated status and now the reservation for the Other Backward Castes will reinforce the same status.

"Taking such a step after over 40 years of independence is not desirable," Prof Singh said.

He opined that even if the really deprived sections are given reservation, there should be some mechanism, some corrective for them to come out of it.

The Missing Data

B.K. Roy Burman's letter to the Editor, Indian Express, 23.8.1990

Sir: I have been associated with the study of castes and communities for more than three decades. As part of the 1961 Census, apart from the rapid study of all the Scheduled Castes and Tribes a rapid survey of about 500 villages was conducted under my guidance. The socio-economic and educational status of all castes and communities in these villages was documented and published in separate monographs. I found that there were many castes and communities in different parts of the country whose condition of life was no better than those of the Scheduled Castes and Tribes. I felt that reservation in educational institutions and in jobs in favour of them was necessary. I, therefore, gladly joined the Technical Committee of the Backward Classes Commission (Mandal .Commission) in an honorary capacity. At that time I was Professor of Anthropology at Viswabharati, Santiniketan. While the format for a socio-economic survey was designed by an expert committee the criteria for identification of the Backward Classes were formulated by me and were adopted by the Technical Committee. A pilot survey was also conducted in Birbhum district of West Bengal under my guidance and I made the processed data available to the Commission.

A massive survey based on the same format was conducted by the Commission all over the country with the assistance of State Statistical Organisations. As I did not attend the last meeting of the Technical Committee, I am not sure that the data for the whole of India were processed. But when the report was published, I was surprised to see the long list. I wrote to the Home Ministry requesting it to make public the data, if these had actually been processed. I had a discussion with the then Home Minister in this regard: Mr B.G. Deshmukh, who was then Additional Secretary in the Ministry, and Dr J.N. Barthakur, Joint Secretary dealing with the Mandal Commission Report, were present.

I suggest that the data if processed (or after processing if not processed) should be made public. It will then be possible for the people to look into the whole issue in an objective manner. It has been claimed that the list has bean prepared on a scientific basis. The people must be in a position to judge.

Arun Shourie: The Mandal Report: The Stench of Casteism
Indian Express, 23.8.1990

"The Commission," wrote Mandal in his letter forwarding the report to the President, "consisted of members from Other Backward Classes and one Shri L.R. Naik from the Scheduled Castes."

And the Commission according to its report operated on the following rule:

- "During the visits of the Commission of any sub-committee appointed by them to any State and during any sittings held by the Commission or the sub-committee in any State, the Commission may co-opt two persons, who belong to the State and who are members of backward classes, to be additional members of the Commission or the sub-committee, as the case may be."

A Commission to determine benefits to the "Other Backward Classes" all of whose members save one are from the "Other Backward Classes," all of whose additional members are from the "Other Backward Classes".

A packed bench, if you ask me.

And that "one Shri L.R. Naik" much to Mandal's chagrin as we shall see submitted a note of dissent to the report!

Worse, the methodology the Commission follows rests on caste. Worst, its approach to everything — from the way as we have seen it enumerates its members to the way it counts chief ministers - reeks of casteism.

This is not "caste as a factor of analysis". It is not even caste as the basis of a policy". It is casteism. Blatant, rampant casteism.

Backward "Castes"?

Mandal talks of "Other Backward Classes" of course.

But as I said that is just a euphemism, one employed to bring his casteist recommendations in line with the Constitution. For the relevant Articles of the Constitution - Articles 15(4), 16(4), 46, 335 - do not recognise anything called "Backward Castes".

As an exception to the requirement that it must not discriminate against anyone on grounds of religion, race, caste, place of birth. Article 15(4) allows the State to make "special provisions for the advancement" of "any socially or educationally backward classes of citizens or for the Scheduled Castes and Tribes."

The framers could well have said "socially and educationally backward castes." They used the word "caste" for the Scheduled

Castes after all. By using "classes" they made a distinction as glaring as the sun at noon.

Article 16(4) is the one that allows reservations in posts. It should be read to believe the contrast between what the Constitution permits and what Mandal advocated and what the government has perpetrated. The sub-Article and the principal one to which it is an exception read as follows:

- Article 16(1): There shall be equality of opportunity for all citizens in matters relating to employment or appointment to any office under the State.
- Article 16(4): Nothing in this Article shall prevent the State from making any provision for the reservation of appointments or posts in favour of any- backward class of citizens which, in the opinion of the State, is not adequately represented in the services under the State.

The Article deliberately refrains from using the word "caste" - unlike Article 15(4), this one does not refer even to castes in the Schedule as such. It talks of "any backward class of citizens".

Article 46, a Directive Principle, urges the State to "promote with special care the educational and economic interests of the weaker sections of the people, of the Scheduled Castes and Tribes" and to protect them from social injustice and all, forms of exploitation.

Again "Other Backward Castes" do not figure, and conspicuously so.

And then comes the critical Article 335 which again deals with appointments to offices of State. It reads:

- Article 335: The claims of the members of the Scheduled Castes and Scheduled Tribes shall be taken into consideration, consistently with the maintenance of efficiency of administration, in the making of appointments to services and posts in connection with the affairs of the Union or of a State.

Whose claims? Only of the Scheduled Castes and Scheduled Tribes. Not even of Article 15(4)'s "socially or educationally backward class of citizens". Nor of Article 16(4)'s "backward class of citizens". Nor again of Article 46's "weaker sections". Only of castes and tribes in the Schedule. And their interests too only to the extent that this can be done "consistently with the maintenance of efficiency of administration". –

And now Mandal

By contrast Mandal starts and ends with castes. Recall his starting point. How does he determine that what he calls "Other Backward Classes" are 52 per cent of India's population?

He begins and ends by tabulating the castes in the 1931 census.

He does absolutely nothing else. That is in paragraph 12.19 on page 56 of the report.

Paragraph 12.20 also talks of castes. By the next paragraph on the same page these castes become "Other Backward Classes". And the constitutional requirement is satisfied! Again, when it comes to identifying individual entities which should qualify for reservations, he looks for castes. The survey is organised around castes. The "intimate personal knowledge" he deploys is about castes.

And the list in use in the states which he adopts is a list of castes. The list of 3743 things he furnishes as the result of his labours is a list of castes, castes, nothing but castes.

True, he says he adopts some social, educational and economic criteria. But we have also seen what he says about how he uses them!

Progressive Perversion

How very low we have descended. Mandal cites what the reaction of the central government was to the use by the First Backward Classes Commission, of caste for assessing "backwardness":

- "It cannot be denied", Pandit Nehru's government informed Parliament in its Memorandum of Action Taken on that Commission's report, "that the caste system is the greatest hindrance in the way of our progress towards an egalitarian society, and the recognition of specified castes as backward may serve to maintain and even perpetuate the existing distinctions on the basis of caste".

His report contains too the Home Ministry's 1961 circular to state governments on the matter:

- "While the state governments have the discretion to choose their own criteria for defining backwardness, in view of the Government of India it would be better to apply the economic tests than to go by caste".

And today? V.P. Singh's government parades its embracing Mandal's crass casteism as its progressive credential!

The scheme of the Constitution is clear as can be. The object is to help those who are backward. Accordingly it is backwardness which is to be identified. When governments yielding to casteist pressures sought to inveigle reservations etc. centred on castes; when they tried to pretend that these were in fact in consonance with the Constitution's injunction that schemes be formulated for backward classes, the Courts struck them down decisively, declaring them to be, as in the basic case on the subject, *M.R. Balaji* v. *State of Mysore*, "a fraud on the Constitution".

Caste "may be a relevant factor to consider in determining social backwardness (but) it cannot be made the sole or the dominant test," the Supreme Court declared in Balaji. Caste is not class, the Supreme Court reiterated in *R. Chitralekha* v. *State of Mysore*; it may be a relevant factor in assessing backwardness but it is backwardness which must be identified and it is not obligatory to even employ caste as an indicator to locate it, the Court declared.

From this straightforward position progressive perversion set in. From "Identify backwardness, using caste as one of the factors to identify it if in the particular circumstance caste seems relevant," it became "Caste is an important indicator of backwardness"; and that has become, the camouflage apart, "Caste is the sole and sufficient determinant of this".

To get over the Constitution's deliberate use of the word "class" instead of "caste", it came to be held that in any case a "caste" is also a "class" - a proposition that means no more than our saying, "The chairs in this room are a class" in that they too are a collection of entities. That "A caste is also a class" became "Caste has always been recognised as a class". And that has now been taken to mean "Rooting things in 'castes' is to fulfil the requirement of the Constitution to formulate schemes for 'classes'."

This progressive perversion is what V. P. Singh and Co. are now set to push farther.

Secular Casteism!

Nor is that all. Emulating Mandal they are dressing up their casteism as secularism!

The benefits of reservation shall be extended to Muslims and Christians also, they have proudly announced. Thereby once again striking at a tenet of the Constitution.

The object then was, as ours must be, to wipe out the cancer of caste even from Hindu society. It was with the greatest reluctance that reservations, etc. were allowed for the Scheduled Castes and Scheduled Tribes for it was felt that doing even this much would perpetuate caste distinctions.

The reservations, etc. were therefore to be exceptions to the general rule.

Moreover, Articles 15(4), 16(4), 335 were to confer no more than a discretionary power on the State. They were not to confer a right on any one.

And the whole scheme was to be a temporary affair, a scheme made necessary by the circumstances of the moment.

Proposals were made during the debates that there be reservations for Muslims, etc. also. After reflection the representatives of these communities themselves decided that such reservations on communal lines would be harmful to the country, and to the communities themselves.

When reservations in government jobs for Scheduled Castes were discussed accordingly no one demanded that these be extended to non-Hindus in general. Two Sikh members however said that these should be applicable to the Sikhs also. "And so when these proposals were brought to us," Sardar Patel informed the Constituent Assembly, "I urged upon them (the Sikh members) strongly not to lower their religion to such a pitch as to really fall to such a level where for a mess of pottage you really give up the substance of religion".

"But they did not agree", he lamented. "These people have now agreed to be lumped into the Scheduled Castes; not a very good thing for the Sikh community, but yet they want it..."

The Scheduled Caste representatives protested vehemently against this inclusion. And that approach remained the beacon.

Mandal himself records the poignant realisation which led Kaka Saheb Kalelkar at the very eve of submitting his report to virtually disown it. As Mandal records "The 30-page forwarding letter of Shri Kaka Kalelkar to the President....demolished the very basis of the report". Mandal quotes Kalelkar but without learning a whit from it:

- Being convinced that the upper castes among the Hindus have to atone for the neglect of which they were guilty towards the 'lower' classes". Kalelkar told the President, "I was prepared to recommend to Government that all special help should be given only to the backward classes and even the poor and the deserving among the upper classes may be safely kept out from the benefit of this special help. My eyes were however opened to the dangers of suggesting remedies on the caste basis when I discovered that it is going to have a most unhealthy effect on the Muslim and Christian sections of the nation ....

"This was a rude shock and it drove me to the conclusion that the remedies we suggested were worse than the evil we were out to combat.

"This painful realisation came to me almost ' towards the end of our labours. I could not stem the current of opinion within the Commission itself and ultimately decided, though reluctantly, to side with the majority with whom I had cooperated throughout in formulating remedies on caste basis. It is only when the Report was being finalised that I started thinking anew and found that backwardness could be tackled on a basis or a number of bases other than that of caste. I only succeeded in raising the suspicion of the majority of my colleagues that I was trying to torpedo the recommendations of the Commission ...."

The Sardar .... Kaka Saheb Kalelkar.....

That was integrity.

That was secularism.

And our government's secularism? To perpetuate, nay to make more virulent, the cancer in all religions equally!

Backward

But it isn't just that in Mandal "class" is a euphemism.

"Backward" is a euphemism too. Several of the castes to which reservations, etc. are now to be extended are not backward at all. They are not even merely well to do. They are the dominant castes of the regions and the states.

The progressive expansion of the number of castes in the "Other Backward Classes" itself bears testimony to this. Castes have gone on being added to these lists not because successive surveys have chanced upon castes whose backwardness was hitherto unknown. New castes have had to be included because they have acquired power and clout.

Mandal's own report talks of the power their growing prosperity, their growing organisation is giving them. The report itself alludes to how they sit over and exploit the poor Harijans, how they are better able to take advantage of the new facilities which become available.

Mandal lists 168 castes as "backward" in Bihar. Among these are Kurmi, Koeri and Yadava. That is on pages 178 and 179 of Volume VI of his report. But on page 34 of Volume I of that very report he says of those very castes:

- "The abolition of all intermediaries has definitely helped the hard working peasant castes like Kurmis, Koeris and Yadavas. These small peasant proprietors `work very hard on their lands and also drive their labourers hard' and any resistance by the agricultural labourers gives rise to mutual conflicts and atrocities on Harijans ...."

"The Kurmi, Koeri and Yadava peasant proprietors have been in a better position to take advantage of these factors (like new agricultural inputs, rising agricultural prices, etc.)", says the study commissioned by Mandal and included by him in Volume

IV of his report. And, it adds, "If the agricultural labourers show restiveness or political resistance, they do not hesitate to commit atrocities on them. This factor is at the root of the reprisals on the Harijans at Belchi, Pathada, Gopalpur, Bishrampur, Parasbigha, etc. " As a consequence, it says, "...there is no love lost between the peasant backward castes, on the one hand and the Scheduled Castes and Scheduled Tribes, on the other."

On pages 211-212 of Volume VI of his report Mandal anoints 116 castes as "backward" in Uttar Pradesh. Among these are Gujar, Koeri, Kurmi, Lodh and Yadava. But on page 35 of Volume I of the same report Mandal himself has this to say about these very castes:

- "Land reforms produced similar changes in the political economy of Uttar Pradesh as in Bihar. `The tenant and share-cropping castes of Yadavas, Kurmi, Lodhs, Gujars, Koeris became owner cultivators, and industrious as they are, they are better qualified to take advantage of the modern agricultural inputs'.

The study he reproduces in Volume IV of his report adds, "Unlike the `umbrella farmers' of the forward castes, they are autonomous in their agricultural operations. Like their counterparts in Bihar they drive their agricultural labourers very hard. While striving to socially catch up with the forwards, they resent the rising political consciousness among the agricultural labourers."

But anointed "backward" by Mandal, these very castes are now to get reservations, separate financial Institutions, exclusive and centrally funded development programmes.

The Dissent

Now these are exactly the points that the Central Government has itself been emphasising hitherto. Namely, that things have been changing rapidly in the countryside, that therefore several castes which were "backward" once are dominant today; that it would be unjust therefore to give them these special benefits; that indeed to afford them access to the general pool of special benefits will be to put the benefits out of the reach of the really needy.

As usual Mandal himself provides the apt quotation!

Recalling the Memorandum of Action Taken on the First Backward Classes Commission tabled by the Central Government in Parliament he writes:

- "Regarding the recognition of a large number of castes and communities as backward, it was pointed out, "If the entire community, barring a few exceptions has thus to be regarded as backward, the really needy would be swamped by the multitude and hardly receive any special attention or adequate assistance, nor would such dispensation fulfil the conditions laid down in Article 340 of the Constitution".

And this is precisely the point which the member whom Mandal refers to as "one Shri L.R. Naik from the Scheduled Caste" makes in his note of dissent. He records plaintively:

- "I held very sincerely that castes/classes mentioned in the common list, each having homogeneous and cohesive characteristics, are not at the same degree or level of social and educational backwardness and I fear that the safeguards recommended for their advancement will not percolate to less unfortunate (sic !) sections among them and the constitutional objectives proclaiming an establishment of an egalitarian society will remain a myth.".

He therefore partitions Mandal's list of "Backward Classes" into one of "Intermediate Backward Classes" and one of "Depressed Backward Classes".

He says:

- "During the course of my extensive tours throughout the length and breadth of India, I observed that a tendency is fast developing among `Intermediate Backward Classes" to repeat the treatments or rather ill-treatments, they themselves have received from times immemorial at the hands of the upper castes, against their brethren. I mean, `the Depressed Backward Classes'. In an unequal society like ours, it is necessary that the Commission take all precautions so that the more helpless and needy segments are not deprived of the benefits of the various safeguards by avoiding cut-throat competition among unequals. The casteism is still very much in our midst and this is assuming new forms without showing much loss of its original vitality. In fact, several observers feel that the logic of democratic politics and mass mobilisation has brought casteism to the centre of the stage. It is with regret, I affirm that political leaders belonging to 'Intermediate Backward Classes' are not immune from such aberration nor they are imaginative enough to bring about the advancement of the people who are at the bottom of our society, such as these `Depressed Backward Classes'. All that they seem to be doing is to emulate some disgruntled upper castes in usurping economic and political power in the name of backward classes. This is a mental aberration which deserves outright condemnation from whatever quarters it may emanate - whether from Upper Castes or Intermediate Backward Classes."

A Blind, but Also, Foolish Casteist

But Mandal, who was himself a zamindar of very substantial means, has no time for any of this.

He is not just a reeking casteist. He is precisely for that kind of dominant caste politics. Citing authority he laments:

- "Like Karpoori Thakur, Ram Naresh Yadav too tried to telescope the backward classes mobilisation into a span of less than one decade. Unlike Devraj Urs, they did not try to divide the forward castes with the help of any well conceived strategy..."

But he is also a foolish one. His entire castes that the 3743 castes he is listing are terribly off, that they are unorganised, that they do not have political power, that they are today as they have been for millennia oppressed and exploited by Brahmins, etc. He reproduces what Manu said as if it applies today. He cites what Manu says about Shudras as if that applies undifferentiated to each of his 3743 castes!

The picture thus not just of an exploitative, oppressive society. The picture is of an unchanging society.

But here is a typical passage from Mandal himself:

- "One interesting question (No. 9) (in his questionnaire that is) pertained to the 'Varna' of the Chief Ministers of various States since Independence. It will be revealing to know that whereas immediately after Independence the Chief Ministers of all except a couple of States an the country were Brahmins, after the 1977 and 1980 assembly elections only a couple of States had Brahmins as their Chief Ministers. This is a telling evidence of the inexorable logic of electoral politics and a very significant pointer to the direction in which the events are moving."

The boast explodes the case!

Govind Narain (A former ICS officer): **Caste cannot be the sole criterion**

(Times of India, dated 4th October, 1990)

He writes:

"The Mandal Commission report is not sacrosanct. There are grave misgivings about its methodology, its indicators, the narrowness of its field survey, its faulty deductions from the 1931 census and its unscientific and outmoded approach and inferences. Nevertheless, it touches upon some important and basic elements of our national ethos and makes very controversial recommendations on sensitive issues. If so, why could there not have been a dispassionate and scientific analysis and detailed discussion before this arbitrary attempt to implement the report?"

Blatant Untruth

To suggest that those who oppose the report do not care for the backward classes and are against social justice would be a blatant untruth. The intelligentsia, the media and social organisations have repeatedly focussed attention on urban slums, landless and bonded labourers, small marginal farmers and village artisans. But the focus has been on class, not caste.

The Constitution was adopted on the basis of an egalitarian, secular and casteless society. It took into account the injustice done to the Scheduled Castes and Scheduled Tribes by the social order for centuries. A deliberate step was, therefore, taken to provide certain safeguards for them. However, the safeguards were for a limited period and no one grudged the time-bound extensions of these safeguards. But we swear by equality and we are determined to take all possible measures to enforce this and eliminate casteism.

We cannot say that caste considerations do not influence attitudes but we condemn them openly in the knowledge that the forces of equality today are stronger than caste constraints. If the government revives caste consciousness by implementing the Mandal report, it will certainly be a regressive step. It is one thing if caste considerations exist in isolated sections of society, but it is an entirely different matter of caste is given official recognition at the government level. Caste then becomes a prime concern in all departments of government and the public sector. All our efforts at national integration will then go waste.

Some of the protagonists of the report have already started a campaign dubbing the contributions of some of our intellectuals as caste-biased and attributing the failure of some poverty relief schemes to the faulty caste-based structure of the civil administration.

Surely this is not the best way to ensure that backward people get to participate in decision-making. The cause of this backwardness is not due to discrimination by the upper castes as it was in the case of the scheduled castes. Certain social scientists are of the views that some of the so-called OBCs have practiced greater cruelties and discrimination against the scheduled castes than have any of the upper castes. What happens to our sense of social justice then? Economic backwardness is the root-cause of the social and educational backwardness of OBCs. Therefore, economic backwardness deserves the maximum attention.

Again, backwardness is not a uniform feature in any caste. There is no justification in saying that a particular caste is backward. Backwardness is peculiar to the individual and his family and it is this individual to whom we should address ourselves with regard to social justice. Backwardness by this yardstick will be found among certain classes and not caste alone. This would be a much better of ensuring social justice. Any concession to the backwards should be in progressive manner and not linked with the antediluvian considerations of caste.

It is argued that the Mandal report has also taken economic criteria into account in determining backwardness. Even disregarding the quality of these economic criteria, the fact remains that Mandal Commission uses them only to determine the backwardness of a caste and not of the people in general.

The fact that social justice cannot be secured by reservations is evident from the example of the scheduled castes and scheduled tribes. Despite the extensions of the reservation system, there have been no tangible results. Only a few among the scheduled castes have benefited but the benefits have not percolated down to the bulk of the scheduled castes and tribes.

The government is trying the same experiment again while it should be concentrating on the educational and economic fronts. Free education, books, uniform, hostel facilities and special coaching institutions will go a long way towards ensuring that the youth from backward categories get jobs. There is no need for too much rigidity in respect of merit for a certain period but there certainly should be insistence on competence.

Social Justice

Besides jobs, real social justice will be ensured by vigorous economic programme for all the backward classes. There have been vigorous schemes and programmes but there again the benefits have been cornered largely by a dominant few. Even in the agricultural sector, big farmers and the owners of large holdings have improved their position utilising the policies and programmes of the government. Increased prices for agricultural produce have so far helped only those who have surplus to sell, not those who can hardly support their families. These inequities have to be tackled.

"The current agitation against the report by the youth who will be adversely affected by its implementation should be taken seriously. The offer of a dialogue to the students is meaningless when the government has declared its intention to implement the controversial report at all cost. Nothing can be achieved by unleashing the police on the students. They should be tackled with wisdom, tact and patience. They should not be dubbed urban elitists or casteists. India will go down if this generation gets suffocated."

P.P Rao: Caste and the Constitution
Hindustan Times, 9.8.1998

Once again caste is at the centre of a controversy in the context of the census operations. In the S. R. Bommai case, (1994), the Supreme Court declared that secularism was part of the basic structure of the Constitution. The Constitution aims at a classless and casteless society. Dr. Ambedkar declared in the Constitutional Assembly that castes were anti-national. The Chief Justice, Gajendragadkar, warned that caste posed a serious challenge to secularism. Strictly-speaking, caste should have no place or relevance in a secular polity.

However, the fact remains that caste is a powerful factor influencing democratic decisions. Unfortunately, it acquired legitimacy when the Supreme Court declared that caste was a relevant factor in determining the backwardness of a person and identification of backward classes could be made through castes.

In the *Indra Sawhney* vs. *the Union of India* case (1992), popularly known as the Mandal Commission case, there was a vigorous debate before a nine-judge Bench of the Supreme Court on the relevance of caste in the context of reservation of appointments or posts under the state for the backward classes. The Bench was divided on the issue.

The majority rejected the contention of N.A. Palkhivala that Implementation of the Mandal Commission report would revitalise casteism, cleave the nation into two - forward and backward - and open up new vistas of internecine conflicts and fissiparous forces and make backwardness a vested interest. His submission that the report gave a new lease of life to the canker of casteism for a long and Indefinite future violating the basic structure of the Constitution - which envisaged a cohesive, unified, casteless society in which casteism, petrified and ossified for centuries, should become the dust on the shelf of Indian history - made no impact.

So long as this decision holds the field, caste cannot be wished away in secular India notwithstanding the express prohibition of discrimination on the ground of caste by Articles 15(1) and 16(2) of the Constitution. The influence of caste in elections despite Section 123(3) of the Representation of the People Act, 1951, which declares an appeal to vote on the ground of caste a corrupt practice is a blot on our democracy.

The origin of the caste system is traced to the Bhagavad Gita. In Chapter IV - Jnana Yoga, Lord Krishna declares:

"*Chaturvarnyam maya srstam/gunakar mavibhagasah/ tasya kartaram api mam/ viddhy akartaram avyayam*" (The four-fold order was created by Me according to the divisions of quality and work. Though I am its Creator, know Me to be incapable of action or change). Dr. S. Radhakrishnan attempted to remove the misunderstanding of the "sloka' by pointing out that in the four-fold order, the emphasis is on 'guna' (aptitude) and 'karma' (function) and not on 'jati' (birth). In his commentary, he says that a class determined by temperament and vocation is not a caste dominated by birth and heredity. He points out: "The present morbid condition of India broken into castes and sub-castes is opposed to the unity taught by Gita which stands for an organic as against atomistic conception of society."

Functional groupings are bound to be there. For example, the civil servants are divided into four classes depending upon the nature of work, the qualifications required, the level of responsibilities attached to a post and the remuneration payable. Hierarchical order exists. In every segment of society. In the teaching profession, there are professors, readers, lecturers and assistant lecturers.

Scientists are classified according to grades. Such classification based on the nature and quality of work or occupation is understandable. It is the rigidity imparted to the classification of occupations solely on the ground of birth that makes the caste system totally out of place in a republic.

Dr. Ambedkar fought against the caste system; throughout his life. He asserted that caste was not based on division of labour but that it brought about a division of labourers. He pleaded for the annihilation of caste and advocated Inter-caste marriages as a possible solution. Article 17 of the Constitution is the culmination of Gandhiji's crusade against untouchability.

As Mr. Justice V.R. Krishna Iyer points out, "The most alarming virus inducing communal malignancy in the national system is casteism. The British regime benefited by this cancer and, did nothing to transform society into a casteless polity... The national movement frowned on these non-secular factors, but the promise has largely proved illusory. Castes and denominations, instead of, showing signs of vanishing, are coiling up their strength, organising for electoral bargaining and showdowns. And *de facto* castes exist among Christians and, to a lesser extent, among Muslims and Jews. There are a score of non-intermarrying Harijan castes, a hundred such non-Brahmin castes and several among Brahmins themselves, even among Muslims and Christians. In short, India was and still is a social jungle of communities, castes and sects."

The Constitution provided for reservation in favour of the backward classes as a transitory arrangement until the goal of socio-economic uplift of the weaker sections is achieved. Although the Constitution has been in operation for almost five decades, no worthwhile effort has been made to achieve the goal of speedy uplift of the weaker sections as a whole. Reservation is more rewarding in terms of votes to our political leaders.

The saving grace in the Mandal case is that the Supreme Court did not go to the extent of holding that any identification of backward classes made without any reference to caste would not be valid. Identification through caste is permissible, but not compulsory. Therefore, it is open to the state to identify the backward classes without reference to caste. In Gujarat, the Justice C.V. Rane Commission succeeded in listing backward classes without any reference to caste.

Yet another redeeming feature of the Mandal Judgment is the finding that the creamy layer of every backward class shall be excluded as members constituting, it have ceased to be backward. This finding necessarily requires examining individual cases within a backward class in order to weed out those constituting the creamy layer. In this changed scenario, collecting caste-wise data for census will not be necessary, as no caste can be regarded as backward in its entirety. Instead, data may be collected with reference to income, nature of occupation, level of literacy of the family, locality of residence and the like. Such information would help revise the existing lists of the backward classes in various States and Union Territories on a more rational basis.

The endeavour should be to go behind caste and try to identify the backward classes with reference to the traditional occupations involving manual labour carried on by persons in the traditional manner, even now. For example, a village barber, whose family is carrying on the occupation in the traditional manner, will undoubtedly be a member of a backward class irrespective of his caste, but not a person who has shifted to a big town or a city and is running a hair-dressing saloon employing a number of workers.

Similarly, a village washerman who carries on the occupation today in the same manner in which washermen did for generations will fall within a backward class whatever his caste, but not one who has established dry-cleaning business in a town or city and is earning good income though belonging to the caste.

Simply because the Supreme Court has permitted the identification of backward classes through caste, it is not imperative to re-introduce caste into the census now, having given up the practice for good reasons after the 1931 census. It is time that the Central Government and Parliament took up positive measures including electoral reforms to eliminate the influence of caste in any sphere of state activity, remembering the words of Mr. Justice D.A. Desai that "a society fragmented on caste and communal lines would be a danger to the secular character of the state" and "caste considerations, caste and communal consciousness are the antithesis of secularism."

A.M. Shah: Double Talk on Castes

(The Hindustan Times, dated 7th September, 1990)

In the discussions on reservations for Other Backward Classes there is a great deal of confusion and often mischievous play on the world 'class'. Frequently people first show high idealism by talking about the uplift of the backward classes in the sense of the poor, weak, underprivileged, deprived, downtrodden sections of society, and then switch over to advocating reservations for them as castes, revealing narrow political ends. One should beware of such double talk. The Government plans to introduce 27 per cent reservation for castes, not classes.

It is true that caste is a powerful force in Indian society, that caste based reservations have existed in many States for many years, and that reservations for Scheduled Castes and Scheduled Tribes have existed in the Central sector also for many years. However, the fundamental question is: Should the scope of caste-based reservations be enlarged and that too by the Central Government? Should the Central Government provide statutory recognition to caste throughout the country.

Casteless Society

The Central Government has the special responsibility to lead the nation towards the constitutional goal of creating a casteless society. The constitutional provisions for Scheduled Castes, Scheduled Tribes, and Other Backward Classes is a secondary provision and it should not be allowed to gain precedence over the primary provision to create a casteless society. If the Central Government introduces reservations for Other Backward Castes in the Central Sector, then the States which do not have these reservations will be forced to have them, and the States which already have them will never withdraw them. Similarly, it will become impossible to withdraw the reservations for SCs and STs. Any hope that a caste which is granted special benefits by the Government will agree to withdraw them is mistaken. In fact it will always try to use the special benefits to deepen its entrenchment. All in all, if the Central Government introduces reservations for OBCs, all hopes of moving towards a casteless society will have to be given up, and the foundation for a caste-based polity will be firmly laid. If the Central Government does not come to its senses, one hopes the Supreme Court will bring some sense into it.

The judiciary in the country has so far exercised its mind on the issue of reservations for OBCs mainly in the context of the States. It should now apply its mind to the same issue in the new context. The Central Government controls the commanding heights in every sector of national life. Jobs in the Central Government and public sector undertakings cover a very vide spectrum. The governance of this huge and complex country as well as the management of public sector undertakings require experts of the highest order at the top as well as competent supporting staff at the lower levels. It should be realised that appointment of substandard supporting staff in a scientific laboratory, a modern factory, or a government office can seriously affect the functioning of the entire unit. Therefore, compromise with merit involved in making caste based appointments is sure to lead to inefficiency and mediocrity all along the line. The long-term effect of caste based appointments will thus be the weakening up of the Central Government. One hopes this dimension of the problem of reservations enters the parameters of political as well as judicial thinking on it.

After the recent statements by Professors M.N. Srinivas, B.K. Roy-Burman and Yogendra Singh that the Mandal Commission had little concern for their expert advice, one need not even discuss the many technical flaws in the methodology used by the commission to make its recommendations. Apparently, it had made up its mind about its basic recommendations before it started its deliberations. It used the names of distinguished social scientists only to gain respectability. In reality it produced a highly biased report.

Horizontal Unit

Every caste is what sociologists call a horizontal unit with members spread over villages and towns in a certain area. At one end there are small castes and at the other huge castes, rather conglomerations of many castes, spread over a very wide area, sometimes covering even more than one State. The large scale migrations during the last four or five decades have widened the spread of every caste. While every caste is heterogeneous, the larger castes have extreme heterogeneity to an extent that the entire caste cannot be considered as occupying the same economic, social and educational status. One large OBC I know in Gujarat included princely families at one end and landless labourers at the other.

The boundaries of every caste are fuzzy to verying extent. There are always claims and counterclaims to inclusion of not only individuals and families but also large groups of people in a particular caste, so much so that almost every census report till 1931 included a chapter on caste claims. Consequently, any exercise to identify backward castes is bound to be fuzzy, and the implementation of the policy of caste-based reservations is sure to lead to conflicts as well as corruption in obtaining the label of backward caste. Since backwardness confers vital benefits, there are vested interests in being backward. The very effort to identify backward castes therefore encourages many castes rather their privileged leaders not only to claim being backward but also to try many stratagems before committees and commissions to get themselves declared as backward.

Many Problems

There are many problems with the indices used by the Mandal Commission for identifying backward castes. Even if these indices are accepted as valid, the commission overplayed the backward and underplayed the forward elements in identifying most of the backward castes. Basically, it used the cover of the 1931 census to ignore the upward mobility that had taken place in many castes from 1931 to 1980. It turned a blind eye to this mobility mainly to inflate the number of backward castes and their population. I also suspect it allowed itself to succumb to pressures from the leaders of these castes. During the 10 years after the commission made its recommendations, the forward elements in the so-called backward castes have grown, and so has the clout of the leadership in these castes, due to green revolution, land reforms, commercialisation, industrialisation, urbanisation, bureaucratisation, and the growth of local level political institutions. The present government is ignoring not only the changes that have taken place in these castes since 1980 but also the distortions that had crept into the recommendations of the Mandal Commission, again mainly to oblige the leaders of these castes.

The country is still fumbling with the implementation of 22.5 per cent reservations for Scheduled Castes and Scheduled Tribes. The hefty addition of 27 per cent reservations for OBCs is sure to place an enormous strain on the social system. In fact, it is already time to make an objective assessment of the gains of reservations for SCs and STs and draw lessons from it. The main lesson to learn is that in a regime of caste-based reservations the maximum benefit is cornered by the more powerful castes and by the more powerful families within a caste.

To blunt the strong opposition to the Mandal Commission's recommendations several suggestions are now made: (1) reservations for only the economically backward class within every recognised backward caste; (2) a separate quota for all economically backward classes side by side the 27 per cent quota for Other Backward Castes; (3) to add a provision for de-reservation for the children of those who receive benefits of reservation under the present plan; and (4) to exclude educational institutions from the reservation plan and to restrict it to jobs in government and public sector undertakings.

All these suggestions, however, do not alter the basic plan to introduce 27 per cent reservations for the Other Backward Castes. These are stratagems to allow the politicians of these castes to consolidate their position and promote their political interests. What is really required is the realisation of the folly of introducing the caste-based reservations.

Curiously many Leftists and progressives advocate the class-within-caste approach to reservations. Since caste is the first principle in this approach, one wonders how these Leftists and progressives reconcile their declared concern for secularism with the caste principle. Or, do they continue to hang on their long held illusion that caste is only another form of class?

Knowing the dynamics of caste based reservations, one can be sure that the OBCs will force the Government to extend reservations to educational institutions in the course of time. These reservations will then have disastrous consequences on these institutions. Human resource development and scientific and technological progress are so crucial for the future of the country, including its defence and security, that we cannot afford to compromise with standards in these institutions. Since caste-based reservations will lead to their deterioration, the very purpose of encouraging children of backwad classes to go to these institutions will be defeated. We will be starting a terrible vicious circle from which we will not be able to come out.

Judicious Choices

Public policy requires making judicious choices between alternatives. Surely, we have not yet exhausted all alternatives for bringing about social equality and justice. In fact we have not seriously worked for them. For example, we have not worked seriously for universal primary education—good primary education — as the foundation for good higher education, without which reservations in jobs are meaningless.

By and large the country has worked against the caste badge during the independence movement and for more than 40 years after independence. The caste badge was removed from the census after 1931. The column on caste was deleted from application forms and other documents. Do we want every Indian to wear that badge again? Do we want the nation to rise to a higher level of caste consciousness.

M.N. Srinivas: Divide and Rule: Counting on Caste in Census

Times of India, 7.5.1998

The enumeration of castes and tribes in the decennial census is not a mere numerical exercise for it affects the nature and functioning of the enumerated groups.

British administrators learnt this truth the hard way after conducting the first three or four censuses. They also learnt to use the census, along with other measures, to keep Indians divided. For instance, the Scheduled Castes were listed separately from the other Hindu castes, while the existence of caste distinctions among Muslims and Christians did not find mention. As the nationalist movement gained strength, its leaders opposed the census enumeration of castes on the ground that it was divisive.

First Census

In the first census conducted in independent India, Sardar Patel took a policy decision to drop the enumeration of castes except for the SCs and STs as data regarding their numbers was essential for ensuring their representation in legislatures and Parliament.

But caste had also been omitted in the wartime census of 1941 for reasons of economy; and because the British census commissioner was confronted with innumerable petitions requesting changes in caste name and rank.

As far back as 1867-1871, when the first census operations were conducted in India, two peasant castes of Madras Presidency wanted to be classified as high castes, one as Kshatriya and the other as Vaishya. The tendency to claim Kshatriya or Vaishya status by low status groups increased significantly in 1881 and 1891 censuses. Sir Herbert Risley, author of the well known book, *The People of India* and commissioner of the 1901 census, took a decision to determine, through the census operations, the precise rank of each *jati* in the local hierarchy, and its correct *varna* affiliation. His idea was the result of a colossal misunderstanding of the nature of caste, of confusing *varna* with *jati*, and ignorance of the dynamism inherent in the *jati* system. *Jati* ranking, unlike *varna*, is a fuzzy, affair, especially in the middle ranges where disputation regarding mutual rank is the rule and not the exception. Such ambiguity is the essence of the system, for it favours mobility. And historically speaking, the ranks of Kshatriyas, Vaishyas, and more rarely, even Brahmins, have been occupied by upwardly mobile low status groups. It was British rule and the imposition of Pax Britannica that froze that kind of ability.

One gets an idea of the widespread discontent which Risley's efforts caused in the following extract from the report of LSS O'Malley, census commissioner of Bengal and Orissa in 1911: ... "Hundreds of petitions were received from different castes requesting that they ought to be known by a new name, be placed higher up in the order, of precedence, be registered as Kshatriya and Vaishya, etc. Many castes were aggrieved at the positions assigned to them, and complained that it lowered them in public estimation." Risley's efforts also encouraged, over a period of time, the formation of caste sabhas which, in turn, became extremely active in petitioning census authorities for assigning their castes a higher status, than that conceived by local opinion. Caste sabhas also became agencies for reform, of caste custom and ritual which occasionally led to clashes with higher and dominant castes. The point which I wish to stress is that Risley's efforts to determine the rank of each *jati* had exactly the opposite effect, and led to considerable unrest among the people.

Strident Demands

Since the reservation of seats in educational institutions and jobs in the government started in the 1920s in parts of South India, cognate sub-castes found it advantageous to form alliances if not mergers, in order to increase their political clout, and secure a greater share of such scarce resources as education and employment. The size and scope of "reservation" has risen substantially since 1901. The Scheduled Castes and Scheduled Tribes, constituting 18 and five per cent respectively of the population, are entitled to not only reservation in education and employment, but reservation in all legislatures, state assemblies and Parliament. Reservation for the backward classes is restricted to education and employment, though it is as high as 70 per cent in Karnataka and 69 per cent in Tamil Nadu.

Since August 1990, the OBCs are entitled to reservation of 27 per cent jobs in the Central and State governments, following the implementation of the Mandal Commission's recommendations. The Commission listed 3,743 jobs as backward among Hindus, and referred to the existence of backward castes among Muslims. And as everyone knows, in recent years, Dalits Christians have been demanding that they be treated on par with SCs among Hindus, Sikhs and Buddhists. Once the census commission starts its activities in earnest, all demands for classification as OBC, SC and ST, are going to become strident.

Other Complication

Groups which are today an integral part of a single backward caste may claim to be distinct in the hope, that its claims might get better attention. For there is a widespread feeling among backward classes that the more influential and powerful sections and families are siphoning off the benefits at the cost of the poorer and weaker groups. Not many people are aware that there exists a division of castes into right-hand and left-hand — a division that runs through the hierarchy - in large parts of South India and many groups belonging to the left hand division think that they are not getting their share of the benefits. A fresh census enumeration might result in their demanding a separate listing which will have political repercussions.

Another complication is that there are many groups all over the country which think that they have been unjustly denied OBC, SC or ST status. They will seize the census as an opportunity for redressal and will exert tremendous pressure on political parties to push their demands through. Counting heads in each caste will also pose problems to the hapless enumerators. There are likely to be complaints that the census figures have underestimated the numerical strength of the caste or other groups, a situation which may lead to litigation. Last but not the least are the middle classes. Not only have their numbers increased significantly during the last two decades, but they are also far more vocal and demanding. They will have visceral objections to the enumeration of castes in the census.

Even more important, educated youth all over the country, hailing largely from the middle classes, will stage protests, burn effigies and even immolate themselves. What happened in the months following August 1990, might seem utterly insignificant compared to the scale of the disturbances which are likely to materialise.

Ghanshyam Shah: Caste-based Census will Compound Past Blunders

Times of India, 22.5.1998

Caste in India cannot be wished away. At the same time, the dream of a casteless social order cannot be given up. Efforts should be made to weaken the caste structure based on pollution and purity, and the oppression experience by those who have been at the bottom of the caste hierarchy. There is no grand path to attain the objective. This calls for understanding of caste - its changing nature - without justifying the system.

The proposed census of caste and collation of information under the categories created by experts, as done by colonial rulers in the past, would hardly enhance our understanding of caste. Nor will it facilitate in weakening the caste system. Nor again will it help the oppressed castes to expand their material and political base. However, I am not arguing that by not enumerating caste, it will get weakened.

Enumeration of *jati*, i.e., caste has been discontinued in post-independent India. Nonetheless, the census does enumerate scheduled castes and tribes (SCs and STs) since 1951. The list of SCs and STs has been promulgated by the President of India on the basis of representations, reports and studies. Earlier censuses and the consequent socio-political processes that went along with them, have certainly contributed in identification of SCs/STs.

There is ambiguity as to why the government now wants to introduce a caste category in the forth-coming census of 2001. Has the demand for caste enumeration come from census users, namely, administrators, social scientists, political leaders, or other cross-sections of society?

We may assume five principal reasons behind the move. One, the Backward Classes Commission has asked for the caste enumeration to identify the OBCs. Two, the ministry of welfare favours the proposal to facilitate and monitor implementation of welfare programmes for the OBCs.

Three, it is suggested that since reservation for women is on the agenda, a caste census would help towards this end. Four, political parties have demanded such enumeration. Five, argue that since the next census would be in 2001, scholars interested in ethnographic data feel that it is good to have a caste census, which is an important social category, once in a millennium.

Each objective requires different methods of collection and classification of information. The present census, notwithstanding technological advancements, is not equipped to meet these diverse objectives.

Though the literature on *jati* is large, so far there is no precise definition of caste which can help a quantitative study. A definition encompassing different marks and boundaries of the numerous *jatis* among Hindus and non-Hindus in different parts of the country is a *sine qua non* for census enumeration.

Caste is not an "objective" measurable category like occupation, age, sex, education, etc. It is to some extent a "subjective" category related with identity and perceptions which change from time to time. That is the reason different censuses during the pre-independence period did not provide uniform data on caste.

Today, the definition of caste for an individual varies from context to context.

For instance, in south Gujarat one is a Matiya when one meets acquaintances within the village. The same person calls himself a Koli at the taluka level. And he identifies himself as a Kshatriya at the state level. Even at the village level one identifies with these categories interchangeably depending upon the purpose.

It is also possible for two brothers to report different caste labels for themselves. One may call himself a Matiya and another report himself as a Kshatriya. As a result the former gets classified in the backward category and the latter in the upper caste category.

Today, caste carries at least four simultaneous identities. First, it plays a role in day-to-day social relationships for the purpose of *roti-beti vayavahar*. Second, caste signifies one's status in relation to purity and pollution. Third, identity of caste is for the purpose of demanding reservation benefits. Fourth, there is the political definition of caste. Which version of caste would the census propose to enumerate?

Some years back the Anthropological Survey of India (ASI) under the "People of India" project carried out several "anthropological" studies of castes. Though its reports provide a broad picture, the overall information and analysis of caste is far from satisfactory. Anthropologists involved in the study faced innumerable difficulties relating to definitions of castes, differences between caste and sub-caste, caste organisations, etc. The ASI tried to quantify the data not because it was valuable, but because it was there. A census of the castes will have the same fate.

Assuming that the census does manage to formulate a working definition of caste, then one would end up enumerating several thousand castes in most of the states. The census would not publish a listing of the castes.

Such a list would be meaningless for policy and administrative purposes. Would the census officials who are not trained sociologists be in a position to collate the data? In the past, they would end up putting different castes under a single rubric. The state will thus create categories which have not existed so far.

Once such categories are created, they will in course of time emerge as "facts". Such generation of "facts" has dangerous implications for the future as shown in the past. Do we learn from history or repeat the blunders of the colonial state?

Further, there is no uniform definition of the Other Backward Classes across the states. The Constitution under Articles 15(4), 16(4), 46 and 340 refers to "socially and educationally backward classes" or "backward class citizens".

Though in practice "class" has been used by the State as well as the judiciary to be synonymous with "caste", there is no agreed criteria, however, as to whether a social group as a whole ought to be considered socially, economically and educationally backward, or only a part of its population be categorised as backward. And if the latter, in what proportion?

A homogeneity test has not yet been agreed upon by the various OBC commissions. Moreover, it is difficult to define social backwardness without eliciting information on customs and rituals and social status in caste hierarchy.

The Baxi Commission in Gujarat, under the guidance of an eminent sociologist, carried out an extensive survey to find out the "socially and educationally" backward castes in the mid-seventies.

In their findings, the sociologists found that the data collected was not helpful in identifying OBCs. If the government aims at using the census data on the basis of the social and economic backwardness for identifying the OBCs, then-it will meet the same fate as that of earlier exercises.

Nonetheless, the problems faced by the ministry of welfare are genuine. The State on the one hand has accepted reservation for the OBCs who have been identified by various commissions. Such identifications usually have a political flavour.

After all, reservation has become a political issue. Therefore, survey data is needed to monitor welfare programmes for these castes. The census is not equipped to collect meaningful data for all castes for inclusion and exclusion from the OBCs list.

For that, other mechanisms will have to be evolved as in the case of SCs/STs. However, if the caste census along with the introduction of caste on identity cards is after all carried out, it would not only be waste of resources but will not prove useful to administrators in formulating policies.

It will also have a disastrous impact on the dalit and the Bahujan movement as it will further intensify the internal conflicts within them.

Three

Agitations

How could so-called national leaders like Devi Lal and V.P. Singh arrogate to themselves the credit for "discovering" rural India or the deprivation of the so-called "Other Backward Classes"? Rather it was Jawaharlal Nehru, B.G. Kher, Dr. V. Kurien and Tribhuvandas Patel in Anand and Norman Borlaug who did the most to revolutionise life in rural India, through land reforms, social planning and the white and green revolutions.

The posturings and pretensions of both Devi Lal and V.P. Singh had brought them success in the 1989 elections. However, the fact that the so-called masses were with them did not translate itself into giving these leaders a political majority. Their hold over the government was tenuous, hence they had to resort to all types of gimmicks, rifts, stances and compromises in order to retain power. Devi Lal, V.P. Singh and Mulayam Singh Yadav, as well as Laloo Yadav and Biju Patnaik felt that their survival was best ensured by creating cleavages and controversies in office, either by attacking the urbanites and the press, espousing the cause of the Backward Classes, fighting corruption, eliminating English, misbehaving with the bureaucrats and ostentatiously using public transport and doing away with security. As a contrast to the supposedly arrogant and imperial standards of the previous government, these attempts could attract the people for just a limited period of time, beyond which they would demand performance and action. With prices soaring and the "Jhagdas" within the Janata Dal becoming a daily feature, mere gimmickry would not keep public criticism at bay forever.

It was against this backdrop that the Mandal Commission recommendations were decided to be implemented and with it the government of Vishwanath Pratap Singh expected accolades and enthusiastic support from the nation. The violence and spontaneous fury of the anti-reservation stir took even seasoned politicians and their careful calculations completely by surprise. They had not anticipated that a populist step of this dimension would not receive wholehearted support from a majority of the people. So much so, that even the backward sections for whom it was meant did not unite for any enthusiastic counter-movement of support. Apart from caste-based calculations, there were many fresh factors which the narrow, mofussil minds of key politicians did not take into consideration. More than fifty years had passed since Independence and as India inched towards the 21st century, caste-based reservations seemed to be an anachronism and an affront to people's sensibilities. Not only had India made great strides in all fields, right from sending a man into space, to launching missiles, exporting passenger cars and establishing an observation station on Antartica but there was a growing segment of middle class people within the country as well as a significant number of technically qualified personnel in all fields, who were striving to usher in modernity in society.

Simultaneously there was a feeling that politicians, in search of vote banks were pampering the so-called weaker sections as it was politically wise to do so. Moreover, they were ever ready to fish in troubled waters, to stir communal passions and play on caste loyalties in order to create divisions in society. The worst atrocities on Dalits were perpetrated by the new class of Kulaks in the rural areas of Bihar and Uttar Pradesh, while politicians and political parties were devoid of any ideology except acquiring and clutching on to power.

In view of the phenomenal rise in the population, the employment figures of the educated unemployed youth ran into millions. Educational standards have reached unrealistic levels with a student securing 90 per cent marks often failing to gain admission into engineering or medical colleges. In view of this frightening competition where careers are made or marred by half a mark, the idea that more than 50 per cent of all jobs, seats in educational institutions and promotions were going to be "reserved" on the basis of birth and caste came to be seen as a galling prospect. Many in the younger generation, especially those growing up in urban and semi-urban areas, were not consciously aware of caste and there were others who wanted to forget this age-old tradition which had saved and yet destroyed so much in our culture and society.

Whereas caste and its divisions had been a vivid reality in 1947, by the 90s there were many who wanted to relegate caste to their subconscious, perhaps to be considered only at the time of an arranged marriage. At the time of Independence, our founding fathers rightly felt that centuries of victimisation and discrimination heaped on the lower castes had to be eliminated. Hence they had formulated the policy of protective discrimination for a decade. Now more than two generations of Indians had tried to provide psychological, social and economic confidence and support to the Scheduled Castes and Scheduled Tribes and other weaker sections for over forty years.

V.P. Singh

In re-opening the caste question and infesting an entire generation with the caste virus, a single man thrust to the forefront of politics by a peculiar set of events can be held responsible—Vishwanath Pratap Singh, the ninth Prime Minister of India. Time and history alone will judge his role in the fragmenting India and introducing social engineering that would rival the British proficiency of dividing and ruling the country. The unseemly haste in recommending the dust covered Mandal Report for implementation aroused suspicions because of the timing of the announcement just before Devi Lal's rally. His sanctimonious brand of value-based politics was combined with blatant hypocrisy and opportunism in playing the reservation card and inciting caste passions with the help of his two lieutenants, Sharad Yadav and Ram Vilas Paswan. V.P. Singh polarised the nation, revived sectional animosity and raised political and social temperatures for political gains. In fragmenting the "Mandalising" India V.P. Singh unleashed dormant feelings and prejudices resulting in bloodshed and violence in all states.

Since 1986, V.P. Singh had become proficient in setting the national agenda on non-issues. During his "raid raj" and subsequently, it was the issue of corruption and Bofors. Later, it was the concept of value-based politics and his constant shunning of public office. But by 1990, when he was in office and facing threats and competition from Devi Lal, V.P. Singh once again turned to a non-issue like caste-based reservation to embroil the nation in violence and turmoil even as the crucial problems regarding Kashmir, Assam, the Gulf and most importantly, the economy and galloping inflation, were overlooked or glossed over with stale cliches. Just as in 1986 when the issue of corruption, unproved even in 1991, could not but be taken up by all political parties so too in 1990 the question of caste could not be overlooked by politicians. Unless bent on certain political "harakiri" no Indian politician or political leader could openly oppose the principle of extending reservations to the Backward Classes, as the policy already existed in principle for the Scheduled Castes and Scheduled Tribes. No one could risk alienating either the Scheduled Castes, the Scheduled Tribes or the Backward Classes since they constituted a sizeable segment of the electorate. Having freed the genie from the bottle, V.P. Singh watched in glee as all leaders were reduced to quibbling over the manner of implementing the Mandal Report, the necessity of having an economic slant and their inability to initiate a debate on whether reservations were still a relevant and effective tool ensuring social justice.

In a forthright analysis of V.P. Singh's modus operandi, Vir Sanghvi, editor of *Sunday*[1] came to the following conclusions about the Prime Minister's style and the key to his success.

> "Invent an essentially hollow and fraudulent vision. Ensure that it has little to do with India's real problems and frame your position so that nobody dares oppose you.
>
> Today, we are appalled by the cynicism. But last year, we were convinced enough to make him Prime Minister.
>
> "The Raja is far from other-worldly. Over the last year, he has shown himself to be devious and manipulative. He craves desperately for public office—he just doesn't like saying so. And as for cleanliness in public life, we have not heard much about that ever since V.P. Singh decided that Mandal was the way ahead and that the corruption issue had run its course.

As V.P. Singh bartered the future of a whole generation gifting reservation to the Backward Classes, the poor, the handicapped and women in the quest of satisfying vote banks, his manipulations were at a premium as hundreds of young men and women lost their lives in the violence that rocked the nation in anti-Mandal riots that swept State after State, leaving a heap of dead bodies, burnt buses, damaged trains and renewed caste tensions.

The Violence in the Aftermath

The announcement of the unilateral decision of the V.P. Singh government to implement the Mandal Commission Report was made in the Lok Sabha on August 7, 1990 ostensibly as part of keeping the comments made in the National Front election manifesto. In truth, the implementation of the long-forgotten Mandal Report which had been kept in cold storage by the previous governments came only on page 27 of the 36-page English version of its election manifesto. However, in view of V.P. Singh's ability for double speak and duplicity and his ability to set the agenda for all political action, the elevation of the Report for such hasty implementation was only to be expected. He had become adopted at stealing the thunder from his opponents and therefore he did not hesitate to openly play the hitherto taboo caste card. In a career full of compromises, V.P. Singh had made the greatest gamble in an effort to woo the cow belt and it remained to be seen to what extent his caste calculations would succeed. On such emotionally charged issued it was easy to sway the public in favour of either pro- or anti-reservation without any attention to the success achieved by the reservation policy for the protected till date.

Time and again, the Indian politician had let down the people, espousing policies which have created cleavages and conflicts in society for their own partisan ends. In any act of violence and during riots, the common man in whose name and for whose benefit these decisions are apparently taken, becomes its first victim. Unprotected by security guards, often without shelter, it is their bodies which litter the streets during any kind of confrontation between opposing factions. But ultimately, the millions of student and an untapped resource which could unite and bring down governments anywhere in the world—stepped in, in India too. It was amazing that such a blatant politically motivated move should result in such spontaneous, apolitical, uncoordinated action by students all over the country.

Even before the Central Government notification implementing the recommendation of the Mandal Report and providing 27 per cent reservation in government jobs for the socially and educationally Backward Classes with retrospective effect from August 7, 1990, the violence in the States had already started. The Labour and Welfare Minister Ram Vilas Paswan also announced that similar instructions in respect of public sector undertakings and financial institutions and banks were being issued by the Department of Public Enterprises and Ministry of Finance. There was no decision on fixing the duration of the reservation period although the Mandal Commission had recommended twenty years for it. At the same time, he announced the government's "open mind" in extending job reservation in Central government services to economically backward sections of the upper castes and minorities. Similarly, he declared that "we have not shut our eyes" on the demand for reservation in educational institutions for OBCs.

Politics being a game of chance even the most carefully laid out calculations can come a cropper. V.P. Singh and his cohorts had expected to become the champions of the so-called downtrodden OBCs even if it meant unleashing a caste war on the streets of India. However, he had not anticipated the violence or the bitter criticism in the print media, which had hitherto portrayed him as a messiah.

Violence and protests started in Delhi, Bihar and most surprisingly in peaceful Orissa and Himachal Pradesh as early as August 10, 1990.

By August 14, 1990 a writ petition challenging the decision of the Union Government on the fresh 27 per cent reservation was filed by Mr. Ujjal Singh, President of the All-India Anti-Reservation Morcha before the Supreme Court in Delhi. The petition stated: "The decision of the Central Government to implement the report by reserving 27 per cent of seats to Backward Classes is only a political decision meant as a vote catching exercise."

Pointing out that for the past 43 years the reservations in favour of Scheduled Castes and Scheduled Tribes had not brought about a general amelioration in their condition, except to a chosen few, the petitioner sought a stay order on the Report and its implementation as well as on the reservations. A similar petition was filed in the Allahabad High Court.

Orissa

By August 10th itself the students' agitation against the Centre's decision to implement the Mandal Report had commenced. This was despite the fact that it was an overwhelmingly Janata Dal stronghold, with the Congress and BJP having been virtually decimated by Biju Patnaik in the 1989 elections.

Right from the time that an Orissa State Road Transport Corporation bus was hijacked and taken into Vani Vihar University[2] campus and burnt, seriously injuring the driver, to the violent lathi charge on students by the police during a peaceful protest at the BJB College, Bhubaneshwar, till the firing and curfew in Cuttack on August 31, 1990, Orissa was rocked by unprecedented violence. Hitherto, Orissa had always been noted for the peace loving if not apathetic views of its people on most issues. The new trend of violence resulting in the death of innocent students barely out of school stunned the State as caste and communal tensions are against and tradition of Oriyas, who rarely vote according to caste. The Mandal muddle had turned the State into a Kurukshetra as students and police indulged in pitched battles in the narrow alleys of the thousand-year-old Cuttack city. In view of the peaceful temperament of the people in the State—the last that people could remember of student violence had occurred in 1964 bringing down the government of the then Chief Minister Biren Mitra—the police and the politicians displayed their incompetence in handling the much violence. In the political game, despite striding Orissa politics like a colossus, Biju Patnaik also had to guard his flanks against such detractors as Srikanta Jena and Bhagey Gowardhan who were waiting to snipe at him at the earliest opportunity. Although Biju Patnaik became the first Chief Minister and national leader of eminence to openly criticise the Mandal Report and its implementation to V.P. Singh, the caste virus had already been injected even in Orissa.

The erstwhile Congress government under the helm of J.B. Patnaik had rejected the recommendations of the Mandal Commission as early as 1982 as being irrelevant for the State. He had pointed out that "it was imperative to bring about social cohesion and emotional integration. Classification and isolation of communities on the basis of caste may run counter to these objectives." Moreover, it was said that in Orissa there was no scope for any special reservation for the 224 Backward Classes identified by the Mandal Commission in the State. 111 Backward Classes were identified in 1950, comprising 41.73 per cent of the population for the purpose of receiving financial assistance and concessions but not job reservations. In 1964, the State government discontinued this list, withdrawing these concessions when Biju Patnaik and Biren Mitra were at the helm of affairs. Since 66 per cent of the people were below the poverty line what was needed was not job reservations but various anti-poverty programmes. J.B. Patnaik favoured educational and economic programmes such as Economic Rehabilitation of the Rural Poor (ERRP) rather than increasing the quantum of reservation which already included 38 per cent for SCs/STs, 3 per cent for the handicapped and 7 per cent for Ex-Servicemen. With barely three per cent left if one were not to violate the 50 per cent stipulation of the Supreme Court, the 224 classes categorised by the Mandal Commission and their population would be about fifty per cent of the State. The whole thing was therefore not a workable proposition in Orissa.

The Mandal Commission's survey in Orissa was not comprehensive and only two persons had tendered evidence before the Commission. The flaws in the Report as regards Orissa are glaring since it is based on the caste-based census of 1931 when the State had not been formed. 14 castes who belong to the Scheduled Tribes and 6 from the Scheduled Castes, to whom the benefits of reservation had already accrued were included in the list prepared by the Mandal Commission Report.

As the violent anti-reservation stir continued, causing great damage to government property, and delaying trains, and disrupting life, the credibility of the six month old Biju Patnaik government suffered a loss of prestige. The open factionalism in the police because of the appointment of D.N. Singh as DG Police for political reasons, the whimsical call of the Chief Minister preventing the police from opening fire on crowds without clearance from the Home Department, all contributed to the police's inept handling of the situation. Along with people's simmering discontent over the price rise and the hefty hike of the daily wages of unskilled workers from Rs. 11.25 the anti-reservation riots brought to the fore the Chief Minister's frequent absence from the State to solve the perennial problems of discord among the stalwarts of the Janata Dal in Delhi.

For three weeks, Biju Patnaik, like a true politician, waited to see which way the wind was blowing as the agitation mounted and students were killed. The gamble of blaming the opposition Congress(I) did not cut much ice as in a later enquiry, the DG Police himself deposed that the Congress stalwarts were not involved. The initial firm action of the government in which the students were mercilessly beaten only intensified the stir, with the agitators protesting against police brutality as well. Rather than allowing his opponents to get the upper hand, Biju Patnaik did a volte-face and wrote a letter to V.P. Singh on August 28 protesting that there should be an income ceiling and that no reservation in promotion should be made. At a Press Conference on August 29, he denounced the Mandal Report and said it would not be implemented in Orissa. When violence and curfew continued well past the first week of September it seemed that his concessions had come just a little too late.

Himachal Pradesh

Like Orissa, Himachal Pradesh had also been a zone of peace traditionally. However, all this changed with the introduction of the Mandal Report.[3] Simla, Nahan, Dharamshala and the beautiful Kangra valley were engulfed in flames and the army had to stage flag marches and assist the civil administration in the confrontation between anti and pro-reservationists. Finally, after a Cabinet meeting on September 6, 1990, the BJP Chief Minister, Mr. Shanta Kumar, announced that the state would seek to impress upon the union government the need to scrap the Mandal Report and adopt the state's Antyodaya scheme based on economic criterion. Asserting that the Prime Minister himself had clarified that the Report was not binding upon the States, he said that the Mandal Report would not be implemented in Himachal Pradesh. Reiterating his government's commitment to providing assistance to the downtrodden, the poor and the Backward Classes, his administration had implemented the Antyodaya scheme under which 100,000 needy families, two-third of whom belonged to Scheduled Castes, Scheduled Tribes and Other Backward Classes (OBCs) had been selected. The scheme covered only needy families of all castes, even while excluding the rich among the backward castes. Mr. Shanta Kumar pointed out that the "stark reality" was that in India if any caste or class was given any facility, only the prosperous and influential people within these segments cornered the benefits. Under the Antyodaya scheme, which covered all needy families, the socially, economically and educationally backward would be able to rid themselves of all disabilities. Mr. Shanta Kumar claimed that it was the only surefire method of raising the poorest of the poor above the poverty line. He felt that even with regard to Scheduled Castes and Scheduled Tribes, it would be best to apply economic criterion in the future.

In fact, the agitation in Nahan took a dramatic turn when anti-reservations demanded that even the existing 22.5 per cent reservation for Scheduled Castes and Scheduled Tribes be scrapped!

Till September 9, 1990 the situation in the State was tense as normal life remained paralysed on account of the indefinite strike by government officials and public sector employees protesting against the Report. The strike ended only on the twelfth day by September 15, but deaths due to anti-quota stirs went right into October.

West Bengal

West Bengal, despite its other drawbacks, had always eschewed the politics of casteism and communalism. Chief Minister Jyoti Basu declared that there were no Other Backward Classes (OBCs) in W. Bengal and that people in the State would be deprived under the new dispensation.[4]

Criticising V.P. Singh for not having consulted either the Left Front or any other parties over the Mandal Report which had already become outdated due to the fact that many changes had occurred in the intervening decade, Mr. Basu said that the State government had suggested that the Centre earmark two per cent of those jobs which are to be brought under quotas for West Bengal, in accordance with only certain economic and not caste criteria.

The two per cent figure had been suggested because that would be the loss to the State on account of not having any OBCs. In order that the economically backward were not left out in the all-India and Central recruitment examinations or jobs these suggestions were made by the Chief Minister.

Jyoti Basu however defended the system of quotas as he felt that even the constitutional safeguards for Scheduled Castes and Scheduled Tribes had failed to erase their backwardness. The only way to bring them on par with the rest of the population was by improving their lot through land reforms, irrigation, provision for educational and medical facilities and the creation of more jobs.

Lamenting the loss of life of young boys and girls in the anti-reservation stir, he exhorted them to read the complete report so that they would know exactly against what they were railing. In Barasaat in West Bengal there was an immolation bid and throughout the State rail and road traffic had been disrupted. In Calcutta, students came out onto the streets against the Mandal Report, boycotting classes and staging protests.

The CPI(M) students wing, the Students Federation of India, had not anticipated the violent reaction to the Mandal Report in the State and their initial reaction was to dismiss the protests as "insignificant". However, within a few days, students of Jadavpur University, Presidency College, Scottish Church, St. Xavier's and many others also boycotted classes and the agitations continued. The students formed an "Equality Forum" to protest against caste-based reservation.

Initially, Jyoti Basu had lent his support to the reservation policy of the National Front government even as late as August 1990. Later he had to change his views and by September he came down heavily on the V.P. Singh government and said that it should take a "realistic view of the situation, instead of a hasty step for political gains. In the meanwhile the Gorkha National Students Front in Darjeeling opposed the Mandal Commission recommendations to reserve seats on the basis of caste. The student leader Mr. Ashoke Chettry[5] accused the Centre of trying to "gain the votes of the Backward Classes by dividing the nation on caste lines. He asserted that rather than play casteist politics the government should provide financial assistance to the poor for better education."

Sikkim

Chief Minister Mr. Nar Bahadur Bhandari[6] rejected the Mandal Report as "discriminating" and decided not to implement it in the state. He wanted the Nepalese of Sikkimese origin to be included in the list of backward communities.

Maharashtra

Maharashtra was one of the few States where violence was not widespread although 42 persons were arrested for staging a *rasta roko* in various parts of the State amidst chants of "Down with Mandal".

The Shiv Sena Chief Bal Thackeray was one of the few prominent politicians to attack the Report saying, "What is this mandal-bandal? It is an election stunt. If the Mandal Report is capable of providing more employment opportunities to the backward cases, I will support it. But this is not going to be the case. It is only an eyewash; an advance notice for the elections."[7]

Kashmir

Here too there was an anti-reservation stir but in view of other overwhelming problems faced by the State the violence was limited in Jammu and Udhampur, where a 17-year old boy set himself aflame.

As Nero fiddled while Rome burnt, so too V.P. Singh neither opted to reconsider the decision on Mandal nor would he respond to the increasing call to base reservations on the economic criterion. Even as the nation, especially the northern states were up in flames, V.P. Singh held on to his "carefully considered" views on the Mandal Report, his eyes blinded by the lure of a captive vote bank which would give him a legitimate majority.

Uttar Pradesh

Uttar Pradesh where as Chief Minister in 1982, V.P. Singh himself had not opted to implement the Mandal Report, witnessed agitations in over 26 districts and particularly in Allahabad, Lucknow and Meerut.

With Mulayam Singh Yadav,[8] the strongman Chief Minister of U.P. at the helm of affairs, the Mandal Report received his unstinting support as he was not only an important member of the National Front but also an emerging backward class leader who tried to portray himself as the messiah of the backward castes. With his accession to power, the undercurrents of a caste war had already been felt by upper caste officers who had been transferred in favour of bureaucrats from the backward segments. He also sought to actively woo the Muslims and statements were made that Muslims too should come within the ambit of reservation. Traditionally, the most educationally and economically backward, they stood to lose.

The stir in Uttar Pradesh was completely spontaneous with police firing, mob violence, the burning of buses and trains and looting of public property. The railways were singled out for attack in Lucknow and sadly the computerised reservation office at the Badshahnagar station and its computers were destroyed. In Jhansi, agitating students attacked the houses of railway officials, ransacked the station and set the parcel godown ablaze, resulting in a loss of property worth Rs. 50 lakhs.[9]

Mahendra Singh Tikhait, the maverick BKU leader, was vehemently anti-Mandal and after tangling with him over the farmers' agitation in July, the U.P. Chief Minister was cautious as no reservations had been made for Jats. The percentage of reservation in U.P. was already 49 per cent including an existing 15 per cent for the Backward Classes, but Mulayam Singh Yadav was not daunted by the prospect of exceeding the 50 per cent. Supreme Court limit citing the example of some southern States where reservation was over this stipulated limit.

Being a member of the Backward Classes himself, Mulayam Singh adopted an aggressive attitude towards reservation and was indifferent to the protests of students, doctors and others. Instead he said, "There should be more reservation than what is suggested in the Report. Only a handful of people are feeling had and our government is not bothered about them." Moreover, he egged on the backwards saying "Come out and fight these anti-reservationists on the streets."

Such were the leaders of the National Front government who had become so accustomed to being irresponsible members of the Opposition that they carried their rashness even into their newly acquired offices.

The Times of India correspondent in Lucknow, Purnima S. Tripathy[10] reported that the reservation was being viewed in Lucknow as a totally political move triggered by vote considerations and detrimental to the healthy growth of society by bureaucrats, housewives, students and educationists. Most felt that it would raise caste tensions as the general category would rise against those who had been covered by reservation. The repeated assertions were that despite reservations the Scheduled Castes and Scheduled Tribes had not really benefitted and that the benefits had been cornered by a small section of society for generation after generation, while others amongst them had received nothing.

Bihar

Within hours of the Mandal Commission announcement, anti-reservation agitations were quick to begin in caste-ridden, violence-prone Bihar. The reaction to the latest reservation announcement was instant and volcanic, as frenzied youths and students went on the rampage, damaging and setting on fire railway stations and trains, police and public vehicles, government offices, post offices, telephone exchanges and completely disrupting rail and road traffic. Life came to a grinding halt with bandhs and the closure of all educational institutions and the eviction of students from hostels.[11] The State Government's directive to district officials to ruthlessly deal with agitators only made matter worse as there was a total breakdown of law and order and thousands of passengers were left stranded when the railways cancelled all trains.

Even as telecommunication installations were damaged and Laloo Prasad Yadav took exception to the allegedly "arbitrary" cancellation of trains, a red alert, shoot at sight and curfew were ordered throughout the State. The toll of people killed or injured in police action rose everyday and Independence Day was marked by clashes, explosions and destruction of government and railway property.

In a virtual repetition of history the agitation of Jayaprakash Narayan repeated itself but this time round, the crowds were agitating not against corruption, but against the decision of a government which apparently swore by his ideals. Even rains failed to soothe the anger of the agitators at a rally at Patna on September 24. The police had asked the crowds to disperse as they were violating prohibitory orders but the students virtually broke the police cordon, throwing stones and brickbats. As the agitators became violent, the police too went berserk and in the two-hour pitched battle, which ensued for no less than thirty rounds were fired and as many as 125 teargas shells were used.

While four students reportedly died, the students claimed that more than eleven had been killed but their bodies had been removed to keep the death toll figures down. Although there were attempts to form bands of pro-reservationists, as in Sasaram district and elsewhere, in clashes between pro- and anti-reservationists, the former refrained from major confrontation.

Even girls took part in the reservation stir in the state and burnt effigies of V.P. Singh. Initially all political parties in Bihar had reacted cautiously to the reservation announcement but feeling the intensity and magnitude of the anti-reservation stir they began to change their stance, with some of their leaders indulging in double-speak and showing their dread of facing the electorate.

Even though senior BJP leader Kailashpati Mishra vaguely applauded the decision, his forthright party colleague and MP Janardhan Tiwari charged the Prime Minister with arousing caste tensions saying, "the last parliamentary elections were fought on economic issues without any considerations of caste and creed and the people gave a massive mandate in favour of the issue-based policies of the Janata Dal and its allies. But the Prime Minister took this sudden decision to safeguard his personal interests and tide over the internal dissensions plaguing the Janata Dal."

Another ally of the ruling Janata Dal, the CPI(M) too

expressed opposition to caste-based reservation of jobs which it saw as a "dangerous concept." The State Council of the CPI also warned that vested sections of the backward castes who are influential and economically well-off, will derive most of the benefit from the job reservations recommended by the Mandal Commission unless an income ceiling for prospective beneficiaries is imposed. The ultra-Leftist Indian People's Front (IPF) said the National Front Government had accentuated social tensions and the anti-reservation stir was an expression of the frustration of the youth resulting from bleak career prospects, which was being exploited by vested interests for their personal ends.

Jagannath Misra, the former chief minister also vented his concern at the sudden implementation of the report, in a telegram to V.P. Singh stating, "your sudden decision to implement the Mandal Report has sent shock waves in the country and in Bihar particularly. The reaction has been sharp and violent. This decision, whether you agree or not, requires a thorough reappraisal." He suggested that a national consensus should have been reached and a seven per cent reservation for women and 10 per cent each for socially and economically backward classes with an annual income ceiling of Rs. 10,000 be made. He charged the Prime Minister's haste as aimed more at securing political mileage over Devi Lal rather than ensuring social justice, social change and economic uplift of the downtrodden.

On the other hand, Sita Ram Kesari, the AICC Treasurer and Congress MLA Ramlakhan Singh Yadav[12] (both themselves belonging to backward castes) welcomed the implementation of the Report with Kesari's strongly worded statement that any anti-reservation stir was unjustified. The vitiated atmosphere was further aggravated by such statements as by Laloo Yadav as "this government is not going to reverse its decision even if people opposed to it break their heads and social changes invariably trigger reaction, but this is certainly no agitation, much less a mass movement.

Even in mid-October the situation continued to be tense with pro-reservationists getting massive support from V.P. Singh's rally at Gandhi Maidan on October 8, 1990. Ram Vilas Paswan's inflammatory speech encouraged the backwards to fight against the Bhumihar-Brahmin combine resulting in a fresh round of violence with emboldened Yadavs assaulting the S.P. in Madhepura district.

Rajasthan

Rajasthan was affected by the anti-Mandal agitation by mid-August with school and college students in Jaipur, Jodhpur, Bikaner and Udaipur taking part in antireservationists.[13] The long tradition of communal amity was broken by communal violence and the Pink City turned red with bloodshed during the Rath Yatra undertaken by the BJP later on.

The Mandal agitation caused damaged to the century-old Albert Hall Museum and Sharad Yadav, the Union Textile Minister's visit in September prompted the anti-reservationists to clamp a "Janata curfew" in which the walled city was left in total disarray after residents took to the streets, causing immense destruction to public and private property.

Student leaders and educated unemployed youth already faced shrinking job avenues and the new reservation policy was perceived as a mere vote gaining stunt by opportunistic politicians which would add to their frustration. The then BJP Chief Minister Mr. Bhairon Singh Shekhawat said his government supported the reservation policy and warned agitators against indulging in violence. He also asked the State MPs and MLAs to visit their constituencies and make sure that there was no caste or class struggle. However, the stir did not abate and agitations spread to Kota, Alwar, Bharatpur, Sanganer and several other places. The alleged threat of firm action by the police did not deter the anti-reservationists who warned the government against its divide and rule policy. Even till mid-October self immolation bids and violence went on until it was overtaken by the Rath Yatra-communal uprisings.

Gujarat

There is a good article on "Agitation in Gujarat by Ghanshyam Shsh (Seminar, Novemebr, 1990, No. 375).[14] He listed three anti-reservation agitations in Gujarat, first in 1981, second in 1985, and third in 1990. The first agitation was against Scheduled Castes and

Scheduled Tribes and the last two agitations were against other Backward Classes. The agitation of 1990 began in Gujarat after it took of in Delhi, U.P., and Bihar. It spreaded to many parts of the State such as Baroda, Surat and Ahmedabad. He found reasons of such luke warm response to the agitation activists. One against reservation per se and the other against the Mandal commission. Also, a sizeable section of students and social workers were trying to pressure the pro-agitation student leaders into conditioning the anti-reservations agitation alongwith their studies for that education is not disturbed. In the agitation movement the those who have procongress leanings are ideological supporters of reservations for the OBCs. These leaders were GPCC President Natwar Lal Shah, Jinabhai Darjee, Yogendra Mokwana and Harobhai Mehta. They openly supported V.P. Singh's decision on the Mandal Commission.

If the situation in Gujarat did not degenerate into a repetition of the orgy of violence when the State Chief Minister Madhav Singh Solanki had to be replaced by Amar Singh Chaudhury as Chief Minister in 1985 when the State Government enhanced the reservation from 10 to 28 per cent, it was due to the shrewed handling of the situation by the State's canny Chief Minister Chimanbhai Patel. He announced that the State would not implement the report as even the existing 31 per cent reservation quota, of which 10 per cent were for OBCs, had not been filled.[15]

However, well past the second week of October seven incidents of self-immolation were reported from Gujarat and the Chief Minister said that the government should not remain passive in the face of such acts. He not only told the Prime Minister to meet agitating students but along with Orissa's Biju Patnaik was said to be instrumental in issuing of the clarification by V.P. Singh that the Mandal Report would not be imposed on the States.

To gain more time, the Chief Minister extended the term of the Justice Mankad Commission, appointed to review the reservation policy in which 82 backward communities benefitted job reservation of 10 per cent in the State government. Mr. Patel, perceived as the representative of the landed Patel community, and his BJP supporters did not want to upset their caste constituencies by further raising job quotas for the backward communities.

On the other hand, the Congress(I) leaders, especially Madhav Singh Solanki, who had earlier been committed to increasing the quotas maintained a baffling silence. Members of the backward communities believed that the current rulers, including the BJP and Chimanbhai Patel, were the main forces behind the anti-reservation stir in 1985 with the agitation leader at that time Mr. Shankarbhai Patel openly acknowledging their support. It was now felt that the Chief Minister, with the aid of Shankarbhai Patel was encouraging the anti-reservation stir help so that the reservation quota would not be raised! Moreover the support base of the Janata Dal in Gujarat was more pronounced in the upper castes and landed gentry. Gujarat therefore afforded an interesting example of political management and social engineering. With the installation of Chimanbhai Patel as Chief Minister many Patels focussed their guns against their lower caste rivals. Despite the hue and cry in the press and the alertness of the law and order machinery, this attitude was a reflection of their strength and sense of security under the new authority. Despite the threat of Mr. Mandal, the spectre of Madhav Singh Solanki no longer haunted the upper castes in Gujarat, who now felt that their reactions between 1981 and 1985 were exaggerated and that neither the Scheduled Castes and Tribes nor the OBCs constituted a threat to their well-entrenched positions in the bureaucracy, in education or in industry and trade. With the debacle of the Congress (I) in the election of 1989, the backward classes were left without effective representatives. As Surendra Makwana a youth leader of the backward community, observed "The stark reality is that Gujarat is under upper caste rule" and their leaders were in the defeated. Congress (I) while the present ruling alliance of the BJP and Janata Dal did not take up their cause vociferously.

However, by October 3, 1990, there were division in the Gujarat Cabinet on the issue of Chimanbhai's decision of not implementing the recommendations of the Mandal Report in the State.[16] Pro-reservationists pointed out that the Chief Minister was engaged in a balancing act whereby he wanted the anti-reservation stir to go on without disrupting law and order. Two Gujarat

Ministers Pravinsingh Jadega and Karamsingh Makwana made efforts to disturb the Chief Minister's carefully laid out plans by encouraging pro-reservationists at the Palanpur convention held in the State in October and tried to play down the numerous self-immolation and suicide attempts throughout the State as an "ugly tactic" on the part of the upper castes to make sure that the backward communities did not rise above their station.

Delhi

Delhi, despite being the nation's capital has rarely been a politically volatile centre. However, the Mandal Commission recommendations changed all that. Life in Delhi was paralysed by bandhs, rallies, student and police confrontations and a spate of self-immolations.[17] It was evident that the student reaction was completely spontaneous and there was little coordination either between student groups or political parties. As students took to the streets to protest against what they considered as reverse discrimination, schools and colleges in the capital were closed and traffic thrown out of gear by them at the city's busiest intersections. Initially the police remained mute, even sympathetic spectators. But as the stir went on and interrupted life in West and East Delhi as well as South Delhi, the law and order machinery swung into action and pitched battles ensued.

These battles between the spontaneous, leaderless and apolitical students and the police were recorded for posterity in the October *Newstrack*[18] filmed between September 18 and 25 when the anti-reservation stir was renewed. Rajeev Goswami's self-immolation bid, the heckling by students of L.K. Advani when he attempted to enter Safdarjung Hospital to visit the critically burnt youth and give a speech, and the police firing on September 25, 1990 subsequent to the death of S.S. Chauhan who succumbed to burn injuries after immolating himself, all went on record. Pawan Sahani, President of the Pragatisheel Yuva Manch and a school student Aditya Narain, succumbed to bullet injuries at the police firing at INA Market and Sarojini Nagar Market in South Delhi. DTC buses were burnt and damaged and their tyres deflated. Doctors at the AIIMS and Safdarjung Hospital also went on strike. The anti-Mandal riots in Delhi spearheaded by the Anti-Mandal

Forum was fuelled by spontaneous outrage of the students over what they thought was a cynical political move on the part of the government: "We are not against the beneficiaries of reservations. We are only against its political implementation and the adoption of the policy of the Britishers again to divide society in the name of caste and religion.

At their headquarters in *Kranti Chowk*, at Maurice Nagar near Delhi University an activist pointed out, "What is remarkable about the movement is its spontaneity. Support has been forthcoming from the most unexpected quarters. University sanitary staff, many belonging to the Backward Classes are supporting the stir." The agitation was very peaceful to begin with, with students adopting novel methods of protest such as cleaning shoes and cars and making bonfires of their degrees and begging for money of their movement. The violence brokeout on August 24, when 10,000 students including school children tried to form a human chain around Parliament House and this continued till September end.

The move by the two stalwarts of the Reservation Policy, Ram Vilas Paswan and Sharad Yadav, to have a pro-reservation rally on August 26, 1990 was a rent-a-crowd affair with people from Delhi's unauthorised resettlement and *jhuggi-jhompri* colonies in which the two ministers exhorted the backwards to take out the streets and fight those 12 per cent who were exploiting them.

Madhya Pradesh

Madhya Pradesh was also witness to self-immolation bids and there was curfew in Gwalior when a youth Akhilesh Pandey suffered 50 per cent burns after setting himself ablaze. Violence, agitations, self-immolations and other protest continued and the rigid stance of the Prime Minister and the inflammatory speeches by his reservation duo of Paswan and Yadav. Punjab and Haryana were also embroiled in the anti-reservation stir with violent incidents occurring all over Haryana, particularly Sirsa. Bandhs, firings, road and rail blockades and self-immolation bids were widespread while the Chautala protege Chief Minister Hukam Singh at first welcomed the decision to implement the Mandal Report but later appointed a Backward Classes Commission. His justification was that delegations of Jats, Jat-Sikhs, Ahirs, Gujjars, Sainics, Rodes and Meos had complained that they had not been included in the list of beneficiaries despite being socially and economically backward. Once again the forceful hand of the father-son duo of Devi Lal and Chautala was in action as they sought to declare the entire agricultural community in Haryana as backward.

The South

The South had traditionally been more advanced than the North in adopting reservation for the Backward Classes with Tamil Nadu (Madras) being a pioneer right from the 1920s. Despite this, there were token anti-reservation protests in both Kerala and Karnataka while Andhra Pradesh which had just extended reservation for the Backward Classes for one more decade had its share of rail and *rasta rokos*, protest rallies and bandhs. The fact that there was no loss of life proved that it was a spontaneous student reaction without any engineering by politicians. Tamil Nadu offered a salve to V.P. Singh after the violent reaction to his decision to implement the Mandal Commission Report in the North.[19]

The DMK and its leader M. Karunanidhi had arranged an extravaganza with a massive procession consisting of 500 floats and a public meeting at the Marina from a dias modelled after the massive temple car of Tiruvarur. The DMK's three-day tribute to V.P. Singh's "bold decision to implement the Mandal Report" and the glorification of V.P. Singh as the saviour of the Backward Classes costed approximately 50 lakhs. The ostentatious celebration of the birth centenary of Dr. B.R. Ambedkar and Tamil poet Bharatidasan appeared incongruous at a time when Tamils were facing bullets in Sri Lanka and when V.P. Singh's solemn advice to the nation was to save petrol and diesel. In order to make the show a success, thousands of buses, lorries, vans, and cars were being commandeered to bring in DMK workers from throughout the State.

There lay some cold calculations and strategy beyond the ostensible purpose. Firstly, it capped a number of felicitations extended to Karunanidhi on getting the Mandal Commission report implemented for the State's Backward Classes who formed seventy per cent of the population. Moreover, in the power struggle between V.P. Singh and Devi Lal, the DMK and Karunanidhi in particular had inadvertently backed the latter by organising many farmers rallies in the state prior to the Deputy Prime Minister's dismissal from the government. This move had not gone unnoticed by either V.P. Singh or his supporters who wanted Karunanidhi's nephew Murasoli Maran to be dropped in the next Cabinet reshuffle. When the uncle and nephew duo became aware of this plot, they immediately took to making amends which came in the shape of the ostentatious gala in Madras on September 16 at which V.P. Singh was the main attraction.

It may therefore be concluded that whereas the anti-reservation was a spontaneous student outburst in all the States, the response of the State Chief Ministers was directed by purely political considerations based on the prevailing power alignments within the states. Moreover, it was only after they noted the determined stand of the students that they felt impelled to speak out as was the case of Biju Patnaik, Shanta Kumar, Chimanbhai Patel and Jyoti Basu. On the other hand, Chief Ministers who were themselves from the Backward Classes such as Laloo Prasad Yadav and Mulayam Singh Yadav were carried away by caste feelings and attempted to encourage a confrontation between backward and forward classes castes.

Agitation: Psycho-analysis

From the time that V.P. Singh announced the National Front government's decision to implement the Mandal Report, there had been a series of protests, some of them ending in violence. However, the Prime Minister and his two pro-reservation stalwarts Ram Vilas Paswan and Sharad Yadav were adamant about the implementation of the Report. Pleas for economic criteria were not given due weightage and even as late as September 23rd when self-immolation bids were at their highest point, V.P. Singh declared that there would be no dilution of the Report. Earlier he had asserted at Madras, "It is a decision impelled by our conscience, it is a fulfilment of our commitment to our people." However, these fullsome phrases and apparently determined rhetoric appeared to the students involved in the anti-reservation stir to be a glaring example of cynical political calculation which would forever finish their chances for educational and employment opportunities. Hitherto, when State after State pondered to the requirement of political expediency and reserved jobs on the basis of caste, sex, for the handicapped and ex-servicemen, students were able to bank on the chance of gaining employment with the Central Government.

The high percentage of reservation in Tamil Nadu, 42 per cent for non-Brahmin Hindus, have forced those affected to seek employment elsewhere. Hence there is a large percentage of Tamilians in all echelons of the Central Government, whether in clerical or executive posts as the reservation policy in Tamil Nadu has shut the doors on their getting jobs there. Those with professional expertise either as doctors or engineers make a beeline for job outside the State and the country. Brilliant doctors and scientists from Tamil Nadu are manning American hospitals and their space programmes. While politicians congratulate themselves for their vote banks, the best brains migrate from the State and the country to escape reverse discrimination. By infesting the Central Government with the same virus a whole generation of students saw the slim chances which they had of acquiring employment also disappearing so that vested interest could be accommodated.

The self-immolation bids in which more than two hundred young people between the ages of 16 and 25, sometimes even younger, lost their lives. It proved the frenzy aroused by the implementation of the Mandal Report—a feeling of shock and outrage that even after Independence of the country allegedly responsible national leaders would use caste and caste-based reservation to retain power and usher in progress.

Psychiatrists attributed the increasing number of attempted self-immolations to mass hysteria and opined that the suicidal trend would continue and increase in the absence of any dialogue between the government and the students. Ramesh Chandra, a practising psychiatrist in Delhi said that a rare phenomenon had occurred in which a social issue was driving young people to suicide. Experts however have observed that genuine self-immolators could not be absolutely normal people and that they may have had some actual or imagined personal shortcoming or some real or imagined resentment against either parents or teachers. The anger is transformed into action in the form of suicide or self-immolation.[20]

Shalini Dave, another psychologist said, "Mass hysteria can just build up in crowds. If a person is already severely depressed, you can't say what will trigger off the (suicide) attempt." Doctors also felt that a concept termed "group think" had emerged regarding the reservation issue. In this, member of a group reinforce each other's thinking and in the prevailing situation, group thinking was dominating both sides.

Ramesh Chandra pointed out "The lack of a dialogue has led to anger and frustration being turned inwards. Both sides are now displaying what in game theory is called a competitive approach, an unwillingness to relent. This sort of thing cannot persist for long, something has to change." Doctors at the All India Institute of Medical Sciences observed that suicide bid in India are lower than those of the West and are less frequent than attempts made by adults.

The Times of India in an editorial entitled "Victims of Mandal,"[21] criticised the attempted self-immolation of Rajeev Goswami, a third year student of Deshbandhu College, for being beyond the "bounds of legitimate protest, and was, to say the least, a grossly irresponsible act" as such an act of self-destruction was calculated to arouse emotions to a hysterical pitch. It is imperative that students and some other anti-reservationists realise that such gruesome protests can only inflame passions and aggravate the polarisation of society along caste lines."

However, the editorial further says "despite serious misgivings over the novel forms of protest to highlight the inequity of the new reservations policy, there can be no denying that the self-immolation is indicative of the depth of feeling against a cynical government that is unable to look beyond narrow electoral expediency."

Convinced that the government's concern was exclusively electoral and that the political establishment was not reacting to rational arguments and smug in its electoral arithmetic, V.P. Singh's exemption of promotions and strategic departments from the purview of reservations, only strengthened the students' resolve that the Mandal Report was unjust and that V.P. Singh was playing with their future for electoral gains. "Suicide fever" struck every town in North India. There were also some isolated incidents in the South as in the case of Susarla Vamsee Mohan, 20, who said, "There is no other reason but the Mandal Commission Report which made me take such a step" in order to dispel V.P. Singh's notion that the agitation had not spread South of the Vindyas.[22]

It was fallout of the deaths that gave a fillip to the agitation which would otherwise have petered out for want of organisation and finances. Alongwith the concept of personal sacrifice for a national cause the media attention that every such act received also spurred the self-immolation bids for as the Head of the Psychiatry Departament at the All India Institute of Medical Sciences pointed out, "the otherwise lost souls started finding mention in newspapers." D. Mohan was not wrong for while 19 year old Monica Chadha battled with her 90 per cent burns she still questioned. "Has my photograph appeared in the newspapers?"

Nevertheless, the immolation epidemic could not be attributed only to a desire for media attention but as Mohan pointed out, because "more and more people identified with what they believed was a cause". The list of martyrs earned praise from peers and parents, sometime even social and parental deification as was evidenced when S.S. Chauhan's father touched his dead son's feet and said, "He has sacrificed his life for the sake of the country." Sarita Verma whose son suffered 62 per cent burns in Indore after an immolation bid echoed similar sentiments when she said, "He should not have done it, but he did it for the country."

A survey of the socio-economic background of the immolators showed them to be the products primarily of governments schools in lower middle class colonies and of the "lower ring of colleges" such as Deshbandhu and Dayal Singh College, such as Rajeev Goswami and S.S. Chauhan. Ashish Nandy observed, "It is students from this category—middle class—who feel the psychological impact of such a movement. They are the street fighters while the others are theoreticians..."

Veena Das "There is a tremendous sense of betrayal by the

State, even though the students have probably not calculated how many jobs and promotions the Mandal Commission would mean. This kind of a desperate action will, therefore, not take place amongst the really poor or the elite... Every movements looks for its martyrs and some people — in this case, middle class students — are forced to become martyrs."

While the elite of the top colleges could afford to go off abroad or set up their own business and the poor already had enough of their own problems or the option of working with their hands, it was the middle class who felt trapped into the concept of jobs for upward socio-economic mobility. They were neither rich enough to go abroad or establish their own business nor were they able to think in terms of manual labour or a traditional craft. Hence their dependence on government jobs and their deep sense of anguish at this closing option. Said a 13-year-old Chetan Gautam who had several years to go before being affected by the Mandal crunch on employment, "I won't get a job even if I happen to get 70 per cent marks. Somebody with just 30 per cent will get what is my due."

Clearly, those who immolated themselves were imprinted by the events and their actions went beyond the demands of narrow self-interest.[23] Shama Gupta, 16, of Chandigarh burnt herself to death after hearing about another girl's suicide on television and the talk of good students who failed to secure jobs despite good marks due to the reservation policy. Her firm belief in equal rights for women led her to write a suicide note in which she said, "V.P. Singh, you can see it is not just the boys but also the girls who are making sacrifices." As in many other cases, her parents appreciated her idealism.

The question of the jobs at stake made no difference to the students for whom despair was the *leitmotif* fuelled by the atmosphere and motivated by reasons which were greater than themselves, the main target for the students anger was V.P. Singh and his recalcitrant attitude. The students equated the Prime Minister with the father or head of the family, who, in this case and in their opinion was being unjust with his reservation policy favouring some and thus creating inequality. Even when inflamed, many of them shouted, "V.P. Singh hai,

hai" and "V.P. Singh murdabad." As an evening student of Deshbandhu College Surinder Singh Chauhan had little reason to end his life, as he was already working as a clerk in the Defence Ministry, no monetary problem and was of a cheerful disposition. However, when he torched himself on September 24 he left a note which said, "The responsibility for my death lies with those people who consider reservation a vote bank, people like V.P. Paswan, Yadav...."

V.P. Singh was clearly regarded as the villain of the piece and all his confused statements, vague clarifications, shifty interviews and lachrymose appearance on television could not convince the students.

Social Cleavages

V.P. Singh's decision to implement the Mandal Report a decade after it had been presented to the government revealed that once again the caste system had proved its influential presence and politicians used it as a weapon to divide society. In view of the self-immolations, the riots, the politicians, inflammatory speeches, it was evident that political arithmetic was being combined with rhetoric to create further division in society into rigid segments. Although protest and violence against the implementation of the Report was widespread what was clearly remarkable was its spontaneity and the lack of involvement either by political parties or their politically affiliated student unions. And despite every attempt by politicians, especially those belonging to the Backward Classes like Ram Vilas Paswan, Sharad Yadav and the two Yadav Chief Ministers of Bihar and Uttar Pradesh the pro-reservationists exercised considerable discretion and did not unflash a caste war in the country on the scale as expected by the politicians.

The Delhi-based Anti-Mandal Commission Forum (AMCF) at its meetings not only demanded the withdrawal of the Mandal Report but also put forward a plea to review the existing reservation for SCs/STs so that the existing elite among them could be deserved. With tempers soring high the six rounds of talks between Janata Dal President S.R. Bommai and Telecommunications Minister Janeshwar Mishra failed because the minister believed that the agitation was caste-based and that the "agitators were unable to rise above their emotions. Our offer of dialogue is basically aimed at convincing them about reservations." However, how could the minister claim that the agitation was caste-based when the reservations itself were caste based. In the attempt to brand 3,743 castes under the nomenclature of Other Backward Classes, the Mandal Commission had equated caste and class and hence the ensuing turmoil. The students spurned political support and were successful, in many cases breaking through the caste barrier as in the case of Sevacutt Dongre, an OBC student from Madhya Pradesh who said, "I do not want to have the prop of my caste to achieve something in my life. V.P. Singh has announced Mandal for his vote bank. But he will not get our votes."

Urban Scene

The Mandal Report had the unique distinction of stirring up caste awardness in the post-1970 boys and girls who were at the forefront of the anti-reservation stir. "Reservation was bad enough. But what Mandal has done is sharpened the caste divide. It's only now that we have begun scrutinising the surnames of our fellow students to check whether they belong to the backward castes." Although the elite professed a disregard for the concept as the question of colour prejudice in America, when pricked prejudices did gush forth.[24]

In Delhi V.P. Singh was the target of much anger and many slogans one chant heard was, "V.P. Singh mein hoon chamar, pehnao jooten ke haar" (I am a chamar, so let me wear a garland of shoes). Although the casteist connotation was evident the students maintained that they harboured no prejudice against the castes the order sought to uplift. Journalists writing in favour of reservations as also backward caste students in hostels were often subjected to harassment although many among them, as pointed out earlier, also spoke out against the Mandal Report and its implications.

Historian K.N. Panicker attributed the prevailing anarchy to the fact that the Mandal Report agitation was "much more than a struggle against reservation. Mandal merely provided a peg for the students to articulate the sense of deprivation which has been snowballing over the years." Claiming that the present stir was not casteist in nature he cautioned, "It could be that in future, but as of now, the attack is directed at the government. A caste war has not yet broken out."

Both V.P. Singh and the OBCs were the students' targets as they pointed out, "These are the castes which are perpetrating atrocities on Harijans. Why should they be given concessions?" The students were quick to point out that they were not against reservations, only against Mandal and that "reservations should be restricted to the poorer classes, and should not be extended to the backward castes. After all, what justification can there be to give concessions to children of IAS officers? They are better off than many of us from the upper castes. In such cases, caste should not be the criterion.

Although many students held that they would be unaffected by the reservations they nevertheless were demonstrating against it, "I plan to go abroad for higher studies after I take my degree. And this is the case with 30 per cent of the students here. They will either go West or join private organisations."

Two volunteers engaged in adult literacy work in Jaipur thought it wrong and "demeaning" to go on propping up the weaker sections and further alienating them in joining the mainstream. Rather than reservation, it would be more effective to spend money on mass education, literacy and vocational and training programmes. Such steps would boost the economy, lead to greater employment opportunities. A 30-year old officer in the Defence Ministry pointed out that if OBC quotas are included along with the existing SC/ST one he would get his next promotion at the age of 53. Another officers says, "Most of the Mandal Commission beneficiaries are just like any of us. Extending reservations to the OBCs would mean that a good number of well-educated and well-off employees would get quicker promotions. I ask you, is this fair?"

In fact in a town in north India, a crude graffiti could be noticed on the walls as early as December '89 January 1990 when an anti-reservation stir was on against the government's decision to extend reservations in legislatures also. Written on walls was one word—"aa-ra-ksh-an (reservation) and two diagonal slashes across the word with the unambiguous message-down with reservations for the Scheduled Castes and Scheduled Tribes." The anti-reservationists had neither any cohesive leadership nor any support from political parties but evolved their own ways of showing resentment and a foretaste of what would happen in the National Front government went ahead in its decision of implementing the Mandal Report "expeditiously". Malku Ram, a Harijan Inspector-General of Police in Bihar did not think that his children should not get the benefit of reservation despite his being an officer of the IPS saying that although "they studied in the best of schools yet, they still developed an inferiority complex. I remember my son returning from school and asking me the meaning of chamar."

On the other hand, there is 28-year-old Naresh Saxena of Uttar Pradesh who is a typical educated unemployed anti-reservationist. Despite two post-graduate degrees and a course in electrical engineering and a total of six years' of temporary service with the State Electricity Department he finds himself out of a job because when the reserved quota was filled, temporary posts were scrapped. His views: "If the government wants to uplift the backward castes' status, give them free houses, free education. Why free jobs?"

While Jagbir Kataria, 15, could complete his schooling in the Navodaya Vidyalaya under the reservation scheme for scheduled castes, Siddalingaiah, 36, a well-known dalit poet in Kannada and a nominated member of the Karnataka Legislative Council feels: "There is no escape from reservation as long as we continue to be prejudiced, in human society".

Rajiv Sharma, an intern at the King George Medical College, Lucknow, said, "Ever since the Mandal Commission Report was announced and our agitation started, our Yadav and Gujjar friends stopped talking to us."

A police officer in the Delhi Police said that he would like to be "de-scheduled" so that he would not face the prejudices that are directed toward "quotawallahs."

Rural Scene

If the Mandal Report caused spontaneous anti-reservation, anti-V.P. Singh and other negative feelings amongst the educated youth in the urban areas, then these feelings were even more pronounced in the rural areas, shorn of intellectual educated rhetoric and the genuine outrage that caste-based reservations would tear India's fragile social fabric.

Harijans in Khamanoo Khurd[25] in Ludhiana district were vague about the Mandal Report and the implications of its acceptance by V.P. Singh. A Harijan village elder said, "We have heard that the government wants to give more reservations to the Dalits and the other Backward Classes. We welcome the move but wonder how reservations alone will help in improving our economic and social status when a majority of our children are still illiterate. After all, there have been reservations for the Dalits since Independence but only a small majority of our community have been benefited. The rest still suffer the cause of backwardness. Reservations for the Dalits and backwards are necessary for their social and economic uplift but these alone won't do. If Mr. V.P. Singh is really sincere in improving our lot then he has to focus his thrust on issues like the basic and compulsory education of our children."

When interviewed, Mr. Mohinder Singh, a Jat retired school teacher and a social activist from the village, echoed similar sentiments when asked about his opinions on the Mandal Report and reservation. He said, "Reservations should only be for the poor and illiterates living below the poverty line" and that there should be an effort to have a casteless society. Although he has no political affiliation, he thought that the Prime Minister had accepted the Mandal Report purely on a political basis "with an eye to the new vote bank". The Prime Minister is following the typical Congress (I) politics of creating vote banks. I firmly believe that reservations is a method to help the Dalits and the backwards has not really succeeded and the benefits of reservations have gone to only a small number of people who have now become upper castes among the Dalits but continue to enjoy the benefits of reservations. This has to be done away with if V.P. Singh sincerely wants to improve the lot of the backwards." He felt that the government should provide thrust to compulsory job-oriented training and economic assistance, "Let the government adopt the children of the Harijans and the backwards and give them free job-oriented education, free food and economic assistance. This will be the right approach to the long-standing problem. Giving more reservations is not the remedy but can only be described as yet another political study by the powers that be."

Sumata Sen reporting for *The Times of India*[26] in the Bihar countryside found that the situation looked like as if it was a scene from the middle ages when just a few kilometres from Patna people accousted those on the highway and wanted to know their caste affiliations! If unsatisfied by the reply, a solid beating could befall the hapless victims. Hence drivers of tankers and lorries were unwilling to move out and as a result Patna had been hit by a shortage of essential commodities and petroleum products.

While the Bhumihars were initially the most active in the anti-reservation stir, the pro-reservationists took advantage of Laloo Yadav's interia in tackling the caste war. Hence the pro-reservationists devised to hit back from smaller district towns and villages so that in the absence of instant communication systems, the mayhem unleashed by them would not attract much attention and the resources of the police force would also be stretched in the remote areas.

While caste considerations have always had undue significance in public and private life in Bihar, especially in the feudal Bihar countryside where a man lives by his caste, the Mandal Report had further divided society, a process encouraged by so-called leaders, shamelessly trying to take advantage of this division.

Kapildeo Singh, 80, a Bhumihar in a village in Patna district says,[27] "A kind of political poison has suddenly paralysed village society. People have started hating each other." Said Bindeshwari Rai, 50, "All we understand of the Mandal Commission Report is that there will be reservation of jobs for the backward castes. I think that only those who will qualify for the examinations will get jobs. So why is there so much hatred?"

Umesh Prasad Singh observes, "People are yet to realise that the Mandal Report, instead of benefiting either the backwards or the forwards, is aimed at splitting and destroying traditional village society."

As insane violence spreads, turning neighbours against one another as happens during communal riots, a police officer in

Patna said, "Illiterate and semi-literate people have turned against each other without any inkling of the suggestions in the Mandal report."

What was most shocking in Bihar was the extent to which Chief Minister Laloo Prasad Yadav encouraged the Yadavs to cross swords with the anti-reservation Bhumihars with matters coming to a head at the pro-reservation Sadbhavana rally in Patna on October 8, 1990.

Falsification

The spectre of unemployment looms large over millions of highly educated men and women graduating every year. Many find it worthwhile to obtain false caste certificates in order to secure a job. Even a top-ranking IAS officer was found to have submited such false certificates. The scope for manipulation and the desperation for employment is exemplified in the case of Sanjay Bhatia who had appeared and failed to clear the Civil Services Examination in 1979 and 1980. In 1982 he got former Delhi MP Sajjan Kumar and an obliging magistrate to get a certificate as a Scheduled Caste Adi Dharmi. While undergoing training at the Academy in Mussoorie the CBI registered a case against him for forgery as his father was a member of a Rajput organisation in the city. The case is pending in the court while Bhatia continues to serve in the Haryana Police Cadre.

Artisans in the rural areas form the second largest group after those engaged in agriculture. The rural craftsman, weaver, potter, musician who were made the prime exhibits abroad at the festivals of India or during Apna Utsavs within the country, require special patronage to keep them away from clerkdom. Although their ideal is to be a bada admi—a person who wears a safari suit and sits in an office—it would be a gross miscalculation to heard them under the blanket label of OBC and try to "improve their self-image and raise their social status". These innovative and creative master craftsmen must be trained to sharpen their traditional expertise along with some basic education. As Veena Das and Ayeste Kagal point out,[28] "What such creative communities need is not a few token seats in dingy central officers to work as peons, clerks, and even IAS officers, but opportunities to develop their crafts; institutions in which their pedagogic practices would provide models for teaching and policies that would not destroy them in the name of modernisation." Alka Raghuvanshi explains the plight of semi-educated children of crafts persons who neither find satisfaction in employment as peons nor are their skills enough profession. The miserable plight of educated, half-trained craftsmen will affect the quality of traditional arts, crafts and performing arts, which constitute a significant portion of India's handicraft exports and cultural diplomacy. The divide between education and the lack of it vis-a-vis vocation must be resolved quickly so that artisans may not exploited by middlemen or driven into jobs as peons.

Every type of assistance—educational, financial and vocational—must be extended to these communities so that they flourish or otherwise as one artisan said, "When my own livelihood is not assured, why should I push my children into this mess? Your art can only live if you live. If you die of starvation, then what's the point of your art?"

By extending reservation to such communities their situation is hardly improved. In fact reservation is just a way of glossing over the real needs of the people which have not been attended to even five decades after Independence. While politicians and intellectuals can split hairs of caste versus economic criteria for reservation, the crying need to fulfil the basic requirements of the people regarding shelter, medicine, water and education are swept under the carpet and politicians flex their muscles trying to project themselves as saviours of the downtrodden.

Politics

In 1973 when a few Buddhist *bhikshus* in Saigon immolated themselves as a protest against the presence of US troops in South Vietnam, there was a massive response amongst the American people to pressurise the unresponsive US administration to withdraw. When constitutional obligation and his personal obsession for Hindi combined in changing the official link language from English to Hindi in 1965, Lal Bahadur Shastri came across seven self-immolations in Tamil Nadu. The Prime Minister and the nation were shocked and even the Hindi chauvinists gave reacting positively to the highly emotional reaction of a section of their countrymen, their rigid stand on volatile language, the social and emotional integrity of the nation.

But in 1990, it took the Prime Minister several weeks before he made his single, half-hearted appeal on television on September 26, 1990 to the youth to desist from this drastic step. The Prime Minister and his Cabinet Ministers sincerely could be correctly in their actions which spoke louder than words, exemplified by their blatantly casteist and inflammatory rhetoric at the Patna Rally on October 8, 1990 which was ostensibly a "*sadbhavana* (harmony) meeting."

While the Bihar Chief Minister Laloo Prasad Yadav bellowed that even a heaven and hell clash would not stop the implementation of the Mandal Report, Union Home Minister of State Subodh Kant Sahay said, "Whoever opposes one chakra of social justice will be crushed and wiped out." An IIT graduate from the US like Ajit Singh shouted, "Only the newspapers and some political leaders are opposing the Mandal Commission, as well as English-educated people who say Mandal will finish merit. You should prepare to even die for the Mandal Recommendations."

Despite Patna being turned into an armed camp with SPG securitymen and paramilitary troops, a crowd which was incited to such levels by responsible political leadership inevitably turned violent as an after-effects of such rhetoric.

While Sharad Yadav and Ram Vilas Paswan convinced V.P. Singh that the decision to implement the Mandal Report had made his position unassailable dissidence within the party and the Cabinet started increasing. Even while V.P. Singh reiterated that the Mandal Report would be implemented without dilution, reservation in key sectors such as Defence and Science, Technology and Space were omitted. Initially the decision to implement the Mandal Report was notified with retrospective effect from August 7, 1990 but later it was declared that the Report would not be implemented even by October. At first, the Supreme Court did not stay the operation of the Mandal Report but on October 1, 1990 the Court had no option but to respond to the large of petitions which it received challenging the validity and the legality of the Report. Moving the Court for a stay order after the orgy of violence and self-immolations K.K. Venugopal said, "I argued not only on the issue on unconstitutionality, but also on the issue of the youngsters' death and meanings."

Since no political leader or political party could unequivocally come out against the Mandal Report or against reservations *per se*, they quibbled over minor details such as the caste versus class, the caste versus economic criteria and how many more categories of people could be included to come within the purview of the privileges extended by the Report.

While Rajiv Gandhi had initially responded that job reservations without reservation in educational institutions was meaningless, he later gave an extensive interview to Dileep Padgaonkar in which he said that the equation of caste with class had become an unfortunate reality of Indian socio-political life and that he was disturbed at the trend of promoting social equality on the basis of caste which was harmful to the national objective of forming a casteless and classless society.

The Left Parties who were supporters of the National Front government were also constrained to call for modifications in the implementation of the Mandal Report. The CPI member Mr. Bhogendra Jha said in Parliament that in the absence of economic criteria the affluent among the Backward Classes would get all the advantages, the poor continued to remain poor as the reservation notification had been issued legislation on the right to work. Mr. Somnath Chatterjee (CPM) noted with concern that such a significant decision had been taken with due political consultations even with friendly parties.

Later on, seeing the inflamed passions of the students, Jyoti Basu shed his initial indifference and wrote to V.P. Singh to bring in economic criteria and to ensure that students from West Bengal were not deprived as there were no OBCs in the state. The bizarre repercussions of this vexed issue were brought out in the contradiction between the CPM's opinions on reservation as contained in its central committee's resolution on August 30, 1990 and the policy it had been pursuing in Kerala. The Mandal virus let loose by V.P. Singh led to dividing of the Left Parties, with the CPI, more in defence of reservation and the CPI(M) divided with West Bengal anti-Mandal and Kerala in favour.

The Bharatiya Janata Party was the hardest hit by the Mandal missile as it sought to defeat their ploy of uniting all Hindus under their saffron emblem. At the all-party meeting convened on September 3 to discuss the issue of job reservation, L.K. Advani said that it would have been best if the government had held such a meeting prior to taking the reservation decision while Atal Behari Vajpayee noted that since all parties were thinking in terms of elections of the BJP would be forced to do the same and since caste-based reservations would create a "sharp divide" in society he felt that an economic criteria should be added.

As the student agitation and self-immolations swept State after State and when politicians evinced that the backwards had not really been provoked into any significant backlash, they became more and more vocal against the Prime Minister and his Mandal "Salhakars", Sharad Yadav and Ram Vilas Paswan.

During its 11 month tenure the National Front government had solved no problems but instead had brought up some new and imagined ones, such as urban vs rural, English vs. Hindi, forward vs. backward and majority vs. minority. The Janata experiment of '77 had ended with embittered old men fighting with each other while the nation and national problems took a back seat. A decade latter, the predictions of the I-told-you-so's was coming true once again as internal dissensions and power politics within the party gave rise to populist gimmicks and populist rhetoric, while the real problems faced by the nation remained unattended. The repeated crisis within the Janata Dal and the intensity of the anti-reservation stir led one senior official to remark "Work has practically come to a standstill since the anti-reservation stir began. Most people are reacting as though V.P. Singh has snatched away their rights." A minister confessed, "The image of a crisis ridden government has an effect on the officials. It is becoming more difficult to get a positive response to new ideas from the bureaucracy now."

Dissident activity within the Janata Dal was simmering even as the Prime Minister, aided and abetted by his two ministerial demagogues, was convinced that the caste card would work and that it would lead him to victory the next election simply because he had dared to break the final taboo of Indian politics. He was convinced that despite the indignation of Rajiv Gandhi, Jyoti Basu and L.K. Advani at the caste-based formulas, none could risk dunking the concept of reservation. In the past, Indira Gandhi and Rajiv often blamed the mysterious foreign hand either of the CIA or Pakistan whenever there was an outbreak of violence in the country. This time, there was no mention of a foreign hand as once again, as has happened several times before in Indian history, the leaders for their own selfish and sectarian unleashed both caste and communal passions in an autumn of uncertainty and violence.

As L.K. Advani set off on his Rath Yatra determined that on October 30th Kar Seva would take place on the disputed Ram Janmabhoomi-Babri Masjid complex, it became clear that time was running out for V.P. Singh. With Advani making his way through Bihar and into UP it became a race between the two Yadav Chief Ministers as to who would arrest Advani. Ultimately, it was Laloo Yadav who did so, on October 23 in Samastipur. Atal Behari Vajpayee came back to Delhi from Calcutta and at 10.30 a.m. he called on the President and formally withdrew support to the V.P. Singh government.

It was then at last that V.P. Singh and his hollow pretensions stood exposed as he defied both logic and arithmetic and told President R. Venkataraman that he would prove his majority in the House on the floor of the Lok Sabha. For someone who had shown great reluctance in becoming Prime Minister and who always sought the image of being disintegrated and indifferent towards holding office, he now clung on in a ridiculous bid to stop Chandra Shekhar from becoming Prime Minister. November 7 was fixed as the date for the vote of confidence in Parliament. In the meanwhile, despite the best efforts of Mulayam Singh Yadav, Hindu fundamentalists did manage to enter the disputed Ram Temple at Ayodhya and at least 35 persons were reported to have died.

It was a foregone conclusion that V.P. Singh would lose the vote of confidence in the Lok Sabha. Some streak of masochism or mistaken martydom made V.P. Singh to sit through the harsh speeches of his detractors in Parliament.

It was only when Chandra Shekhar of the breakaway Janata Dal (Samajwadi Janata Dal) was sworn in as Prime Minister on

November 21, 1990 that it appeared that a semblance of order had been restored. Prime Minister addressed the nation after winning a vote-of-confidence in the Lok Sabha, supported by his allies the Congress (I) it appeared that he was genuinely interested in assuaging hurt feelings and providing a healing touch after the bitter confrontation and violence of the last eleven months. Appealing to all to desist from violence the Prime Minister broached the requirement for dialogue and discussion in tackling the awful manmade problems of the recent past. The *padayatri* had finally arrived at his destination eager to make his contribution to the country in his first stint in office.

References

1. *Sunday*, 21-27 Oct. 1990.
2. *The Sun Times*, Bhubaneshwar, August 12-Sept. 6th, 1990.
3. *The Times of India*, Sept.7, 1990 - Sept. 16th, 1990.
4. *The Statesman*, Oct. 6, 1990.
5. *The Telegraph*, Sept. 16, 1990.
6. *The Statesman*, Sept. 8, 1990.
7. *The Telegraph*, Oct. 2, 1990.
8. *Frontline*, Sept.. 1-14, 1990.
9. *Sunday*, 16-22 Sept. 1990.
10. *The Times of India*, Aug. 10, 1990.
11. *Frontline*, Sept. 1-14, 1990.
12. *The Telegraph*, Aug. 14, 1990.
13. *The Times of India*, Jan. 3, 1991.
14. Shah, Ghanshyam. "Agitations in Gujarat", in Seminar (375), Nov., 1990, pp. 54-57.
15. *The Statesman*, Sept. 4, 1990.
16. *The Times of India*, Oct. 3, 1990.
17. *India Today*, Sept. 30, 1990.
18. *The Times of India*, Sept. 26, 1990.
19. *The Telegraph*, Sept. 16, 1990.
20. *Sunday*, Oct. 14-20, 1990.
21. *The Times of India*, Sept. 21, 1990.
22. *India Today*, Oct. 31, 1990.
23. *Sunday*, Nov. 4-10, 1990.
24. *The Times of India*, Sept. 30, 1990.
25. *The Statesman*, Sept. 18, 1990.
26. *The Times of India*, Oct. 17, 1990.
27. *India Today*, Nov. 15, 1990.
28. *The Times of India*, Sept. 16, 1990.

Index